Personnel Economics

PETER KUHN
University of California, Santa Barbara

New York Oxford
OXFORD UNIVERSITY PRESS

Oxford University Press is a department of the University of Oxford.
It furthers the University's objective of excellence in research, scholarship,
and education by publishing worldwide. Oxford is a registered trade mark of
Oxford University Press in the UK and certain other countries.

Published in the United States of America by Oxford University Press
198 Madison Avenue, New York, NY 10016, United States of America.

For titles covered by Section 112 of the US Higher Education
Opportunity Act, please visit www.oup.com/us/he for the
latest information about pricing and alternate formats.

Library of Congress Cataloging-in-Publication Data

Names: Kuhn, Peter, 1955- author.
Title: Personnel economics / Peter Kuhn, University of California, Santa
Barbara.
Description: New York : Oxford University Press, [2017] | Includes index.
Identifiers: LCCN 2017041292 (print) | LCCN 2017021686 (ebook) |
ISBN 9780199378012 (hardcover) | ISBN 9780190262181 (ebook)
Subjects: LCSH: Personnel management. | Employee motivation. | Teams in the
workplace.
Classification: LCC HF5549.K7744 2017 (ebook) | LCC HF5549 (print) |
DDC 658.3—dc23
LC record available at https://lccn.loc.gov/2017041292

9 8 7 6 5 4
Printed by Sheridan Books, Inc., United States of America

This book is dedicated to Barbara, my wife of 33 years, and my two wonderful sons, Mike and Jon. The three of you are the warm and intellectually stimulating center of my life.

About the Author

Peter Kuhn is a labor economist at the University of California, Santa Barbara. He grew up in Kitchener, Ontario, Canada, the son of immigrant parents who worked in factories making shirts and fire hydrants. He received his bachelor's degree from Carleton University and his PhD from Harvard University. Over his career, he has published over 50 peer-reviewed articles on topics including personnel economics, the effects of information technology on labor markets, wage and employment discrimination, China's labor markets, trade unions, immigration, and displaced workers. His research has been funded by the National Science Foundation, the National Institutes of Health, and the Ford Foundation, among others. Kuhn is a Research Associate of the National Bureau of Economic Research (NBER), the Institute for the Study of Labor (IZA), and the Center for Economic Studies (CES). He currently serves on the editorial board of *AEJ: Applied Economics* and *Labour Economics* and serves as associate editor of the *Journal of Labor Economics* and the *Industrial and Labor Relations Review.*

Contents

Preface

For Students: What Is Personnel Economics?

Two years after quitting her first career job to start the business she has always dreamed of, Shelly's new enterprise has grown to the point where she needs to hire her first employee. As she enters into this new phase of her career, Shelly realizes that a vast majority of the challenges she'll face in becoming an employer can be reduced to two simple words: **selection** and **motivation**. Selection, Shelly realizes, in the broadest sense means inducing the "right" people to work for her. Motivation means inducing those people to internalize the goals of her enterprise, in a way that ultimately benefits not only Shelly but all the members of her new team. This book is about Shelly's two main challenges. Put a different way, personnel economics studies employment relationships between workers and firms; it studies what makes them work well from the perspectives of all the parties involved, and how even the most well-intentioned ideas for how to structure employment relationships can sometimes go sadly, and embarrassingly, wrong.

We start the book in Parts 1 and 2 by studying Shelly's *motivation* problem in relative isolation. Part 1 imagines that she has picked a particular worker to hire (call him Adam), and thinks theoretically about what is the "best" way to structure that worker's *monetary* incentives. This question is a classic one in economics, called the *principal–agent problem.* Studying it suggests answers to questions that include "How strongly should workers be incentivized?"; "How should financial incentives vary across different types of jobs?"; and even "What do we mean by 'best'?" In other words, is the employment relationship a zero-sum game in which every gain for the employer is a loss for workers, or are there policies that make both parties better off?

Part 2 takes a broader and more empirical look at the question of employee motivation. Not only do we look at a wide array of examples and case studies of which motivational systems "work" and don't in real firms, we'll go beyond financial incentives to consider a broader set of motivating factors, including the intrinsic satisfaction of a job well done and perceptions that one is treated fairly. We'll ask whether these "psychological" incentives sometimes make financial ones unnecessary. Or is the reverse true? More generally, how do financial and other sources of motivation interact?

Next, we'll turn our attention in Part 3 to the *employee selection* problem. Of course, one important aspect of employee selection is choosing which persons to hire from the pool of candidates who have applied to a firm. But the problem of employee selection goes far beyond this, for at least two important reasons. First, picking the best candidate won't get Shelly very far if the applicant pool doesn't contain the types of workers she needs! Importantly, the types of workers who *apply* to a firm depend on a whole host of human resource policies, including not only how *much* it pays but how strongly its workers are incentivized. So, the selection and motivation problems are, in fact, closely linked. Second, workers don't just join firms, they also leave. Thus, *managing turnover* is also a key part of employee selection—it helps little to attract the best people if they all quit within 6 months. Accordingly, in Part 3 we'll ask questions like "When is it most important to search broadly for the best available candidate, versus restricting your search to an applicant pool that has performed well in the past?"; "Should you always avoid hiring workers whose future performance is hard to predict?"; "How generous should the overall compensation package be?"; and "Are there effective ways to attract (and keep) better employees, without necessarily spending more money?"

Although Parts 1 through 3 develop the core concepts of motivation and selection, they do so in a context that focuses mostly on the interaction between an employer and each of her workers. Parts 4 and 5 go beyond this by applying these core concepts to *interactions between workers*. In Part 4, we consider models of *competition between workers*. Whenever workers are evaluated on the basis of their relative performance, or whenever they compete for bonuses or promotions, there is an element of competition in the workplace—in a sense, workers are engaged in a *tournament* against each other. Questions addressed here include "When should firms use relative performance evaluation?" and "What is the optimal design of promotion ladders in a company?" Finally, in Part 5, we study the economics of *teams*; in other words we study models of *cooperation* between workers. Here, we'll answer questions like "When should workers be organized into teams?" and "How can a principal motivate a team of workers when that person only observes the performance of the entire team (not of its individual members)?"

As you might have guessed by now, personnel economics studies many of the same issues as human resource management (HRM) and operations management, both of which are key fields of research and teaching in most business schools. Personnel economics also studies issues covered in industrial engineering, where researchers who study physical aspects of the production process find that they can't do so in isolation from the issues of incentives, personnel selection, and motivation at the heart of this book. Increasingly, personnel economics is also being taught in undergraduate economics programs, and that is one of the key purposes of this book: to be the first widely used text to approach personnel economics *as an economics course*. Just like courses in public economics, environmental economics, financial economics, and many others, we'll use the tools of introductory and intermediate-level microeconomics to study all the questions outlined previously and many more. As a teacher of personnel economics in an economics department (not a business school), I've felt the need for this type of book for many years. I hope that you find it useful, not only as a student but in your future career as an employee or manager.

If you're an economics student, you may also be interested in how personnel economics relates to other branches of economics. In fact, it's closely related to a number of areas in which you may have, or will soon, take a course or two. First, you'll see and use the indifference curves and budget constraints you may have used in an intermediate microeconomics course, but you'll apply these tools to problems that are directly relevant to most peoples' daily lives. The leading example in this book is on workers' *effort allocation* decisions: how hard, in total, to work and (equally importantly) how to allocate one's scarce time, attention, and mental and physical resources to the many competing demands of a job. This focus on effort allocation links personnel economics closely to labor economics, especially the analysis of the income–leisure tradeoff and labor supply decision. In fact, personnel economics can be thought of as a branch of labor economics: it is sometimes (half-jokingly) referred to as "what labor economists teach when they work in business schools." That said, although both labor and personnel study workers, their focus is quite different. Labor economics focuses on overall markets for (different types of) workers: for example, why do college-educated workers earn so much more than high-school educated workers, what are the effects of immigration policies on migrant and U.S.-born workers, and are minimum wage laws "job killers"? Personnel economics focuses more on what happens *inside* firms: how do (or should) firms set up their internal HRM policies, and which policies work best where?

Another field you'll encounter is econometrics: Whereas much of the empirical evidence summarized in this book uses no more statistics than doing *t* tests to see if two means are significantly different, some important studies use *regression analysis* to help tease apart which of several competing explanations for, say, a difference in workplace productivity really matter. In fact, there's a whole subfield within personnel economics called "insider econometrics" that applies regression analysis to large internal company data sets to figure out exactly "what works" when it comes to different types of work organization, communications systems, and pay policies. You won't need an econometrics course to understand my summaries of these studies, but having had such a course will deepen your appreciation of what these fascinating studies do.

In this book, you'll also run into a little game theory. Game theory is a formal way to think about strategic interactions between people whose interests aren't perfectly aligned (i.e., just about everybody—though here our focus will be on interactions between workers, as well as between workers and employers). And again, although you won't need a game theory course to understand the simple models in this book, your understanding will be enriched if you've heard the terms "Nash equilibrium" or "perfect equilibrium." In fact, game theory buffs might be interested to note that much of personnel economics is an applied version of a part of game theory called "mechanism design." Mechanism design studies the optimal design of contracts—in other words, it asks what is the best way to structure the "rules of the game" that will govern the future interactions between two parties (e.g., a worker and a firm) who have decided to enter an economic relationship. When we talk in this book about "optimal" human resource management policies, the definition of optimality will be precisely the one that is used in standard microeconomics and in formal mechanism design theory: Pareto optimality. The "best" employment contract is not the one that makes profits as high as possible, nor the one that makes workers as well off as possible. The best contract maximizes *total social surplus* by making the pie shared by workers and firms as large as possible; and as we'll argue, this is also the package that genuinely competitive labor markets will force firms to supply.

Finally, unlike other personnel economics texts, this book will draw heavily on the burgeoning fields of experimental and behavioral economics. Many of the empirical results we'll study come from experiments, ranging from laboratory studies of basic human interactions to large-scale field experiments where an economist has worked closely with a company to test the effects of different HRM policies on employee performance. An interesting result from many (but certainly not all) of these experiments is that real peoples' behaviors often violate the most basic predictions of "classical" economic theory, which assumes that people care only about their own well-being. As we shall see, as a species, humans (and therefore workers) are considerably more generous and cooperative, but also more jealous and vindictive than "standard" economic theory predicts. This human element—which is emphasized in the study of behavioral economics—has a crucial bearing on which types of personnel management practices work best and where.

Aside from pure intellectual curiosity, why is it important to study personnel economics? First of all, with the exception of a few people who can't, or don't need to work, paid work is how most people earn the vast majority of our income and how we spend most of our waking hours. Surely, this fundamental bargain at the heart of our lives—where we exchange our effort, commitment, and creativity for pay—is worthy of close and rigorous study because it plays a huge role in every worker's financial and emotional well-being. Second, the choice of HRM policies matters a lot for firms; indeed, it is often said that a company's most important assets are the ones that go home every night. If firms use these resources inefficiently, by wasting workers' knowledge, time, and motivation, even companies with the best technologies and coolest concepts can fail.

In fact, although engineering improvements and technological innovations such as computers, fiber optics, social media, and DNA sequencing have played obvious and critical roles in raising firms' productivity, you might be surprised to learn that innovations in HRM have been shown to yield productivity improvements that dwarf those of many engineering innovations. We'll consider cases where the introduction of a simple incentive pay plan raised productivity by 36%—an improvement production engineers in that industry could only dream of—or where the use of paid company time for team-based problem-solving was instrumental in allowing U.S. steel mini-mills to survive competition from low-priced imports. In another example, we'll argue that both the near demise of the U.S. auto industry in the 1980s *and* its subsequent resurgence are best explained not by cheap foreign labor, too-powerful unions, or by new developments in the *physical* technology of auto manufacturing such as robots. Instead, it was an innovation in HRM practices that first allowed Japanese companies to outcompete their U.S. rivals, and the subsequent adoption of those practices that helped U.S. companies ultimately survive this challenge.

Finally, I offer a heads-up: In the interests of full disclosure, one thing you should know (that I've learned from personal experience) is that some students can find this course frustrating until they get used to it. That's not because it's technically demanding—it isn't, especially if you've taken an intermediate micro course. It's because *I'm never going to tell you "the" right way* to organize pay, incentives, and job structure in a company. The reason is not that I'm a devious person, but because (a) there *is* no single right way to do things—the optimal policy can vary dramatically across workplaces, technologies, and job and worker types; and (b) even when faced with a very specific situation, our knowledge about what works best remains spotty.

So, instead of giving you well-established formulas for optimal policies, my goal in this book is to build insight and intuition for *which kinds of policies are likely to work under which conditions.* You'll also learn, I hope, to anticipate some of the unintended consequences of the many "brilliant ideas" that often promise to improve workplace performance, then end up disappointing their advocates. We'll build this intuition from a dialogue between simple **models** (or if you prefer, theories or hypotheses) about how things *might* work and **evidence**, which comes from lab experiments, field experiments, company case studies, and insider-econometrics studies from real firms. In fact, I'll sometimes propose a simple theoretical model—which might take you a little effort to understand—then test that model against some data that shows the model is "wrong." Some students (especially at first) find this quite frustrating: "Why did you make me work so hard to understand your stupid model if it isn't even true?"

But—as I hope you'll come to appreciate as we work our way through the book—that's really not the point. We test some models because they are compelling ideas in their own right (isn't it obvious that the more you tax something, the less of it you get?); so it's really important to learn that sometimes—for very good and intuitive reasons that we learn in the process—these simple ideas aren't always correct. The point, instead, is to learn *which* models shed useful light on *which* circumstances we're likely to confront in our real, working lives. This learning results from what is essentially a dance between models (things we think *might* be true) and situation-specific evidence. It's a dance that I've loved (both as dancer and audience) during my whole life as a scholar, and I hope that you'll enjoy it too.

For Instructors: What's Different about This Book?

This book applies a simple but formal microeconomic approach to the study of workplace organization and incentives in a way that incorporates the exploding experimental and behavioral literature in personnel economics and related fields. Together, these two features distinguish this book from the very small stable of existing personnel economics textbooks. On the one hand, my somewhat more formal microeconomics-based approach contrasts with textbooks aimed primarily at students in U.S.-style MBA courses, where—with the obvious exception of finance students—there is perhaps less patience with abstraction and mathematics than among economics students. At the same time, to my knowledge this is the first personnel economics textbook that incorporates many new experimental and behavioral insights directly into the fabric of the book. For both these reasons, I believe the book fills an important and growing need: for an accessible personnel *economics* text—not a business book—that makes interesting, fun use of the simple tools available to all students with basic training in microeconomics. At the same time, the book aims to be up to date in its incorporation of the many new insights from behavioral economics, and to be interesting and relevant to anyone with an interest in how the world of work is organized.

Although this book grew out of an upper-division undergraduate course I teach at the University of California, Santa Barbara, it is designed to work well for any student who has had some basic training in microeconomics and who has an interest in the real world of work, compensation, training, incentives, and employee selection in modern workplaces. In addition to upper-division U.S. undergraduates, this group includes students in master's level courses (including economics, business economics, and some styles of MBA programs), and even as background material for PhD students. All that's needed is an acquaintance and willingness to work with core tools of microeconomics, such as budget constraints and indifference curves, and an interest in the topic. Because this is an economics book, I take some care to highlight the material's many synergies with other economics courses the reader may have taken, or plan to take. Key synergies are those with applied econometrics, game theory, experimental economics, behavioral economics, and especially labor economics. Indeed, the book covers many core topics in labor economics, including labor supply, labor demand, training, wage-setting, discrimination, and compensating differentials; labor instructors who enjoy this book's approach might consider it as a main or supplementary text.

Although this book *uses* some simple economics tools, it's worth emphasizing that the tools are not the goal here. Instead, I've endeavored throughout to keep the technical aspects to the minimum level that is required for a full understanding of the main ideas. Aside from thinking graphically about maximizing utility or profits in the presence of a budget set (the how-tos of which are all introduced in the book), all the math a student needs to do is find the maximum of a quadratic function of a single variable. Although calculus is an option here (and is mentioned), there are other, easy ways to solve this same problem. Also, all of the mathematics are administered with plenty of hand-holding. Optional problem sets are available; these make extensive use of Microsoft Excel (or any simple spreadsheet program). In my experience, these problem sets allow students to discover the optimal contract and really see *why* it is optimal in intuitive ways. *Truly* understanding what it means for an arrangement to be Pareto-optimal (as opposed to reciting the definition), and understanding why one might expect competitive markets (or experienced bargainers) to attain such an outcome remains, in my experience, one of the subtlest challenges in teaching economics; but I think these exercises make some good progress in that direction. A nice byproduct of these problem sets is that every student who solves them finishes the course with a good working knowledge of one of the most basic business tools: the spreadsheet.

A final feature distinguishes this book from many of the economics texts I grew up with, some of which remain influential today. These books focused on developing a set of theoretical models that were then illustrated by carefully selected facts and evidence. My approach here is conceived, instead, as an ongoing *dialogue* between simple theoretical models and empirical evidence. Thus, at a number of points in the book, I'll spend some time working out the consequences of an idea and then present a clean empirical test that soundly rejects that idea. Some students can find this frustrating at first, but I find that after a while they come to enjoy the back and forth between hypotheses and evidence in a way that I hope will make them more critical, sophisticated, and dispassionate thinkers when they leave the classroom (and the campus).

Somewhat related, compared to a more typical text, I probably spend more time discussing *individual* experiments and econometric studies in detail rather than summarizing the results from a larger number of studies. The goal (at least I'd like to believe) is not to make my own job a little easier. Instead, my intent is to give students a real *sense for how good empirical analysis is done* via a collection of what I judge to be top-notch examples. So I end up going some distance into the details of the empirical studies in what I hope is a clear but nontechnical way. As it turns out, this approach lends itself naturally to the many experimental studies covered in the book. It is harder with the econometric studies, but I've tried my best, and I hope the result works for you and your students. If not, please email me at peter.kuhn@ucsb.edu. All comments and suggestions for improvement are most welcome.

Using the Book

Part 1 develops some basic tools that are used throughout the book. Instructors who prefer to move on to applications more quickly can cover the essentials by skipping Section 3.1, Chapter 4, Section 5.2, and Chapter 6.

Chapter 7 reviews regression and experimental methods and can be skipped by students who already have this background. Aside from that, the rest of **Parts 2 and 3** consist of various applications that can be used in any order.

Chapters 20 and 24 provide the fundamentals of tournaments and teams, respectively. With that exception, the rest of **Parts 4 and 5** can also be used in any order. That said, a treatment of teams that didn't include Chapter 25 would be much less interesting and would probably exaggerate the importance of free riding in typical workplace teams.

The Oxford University Press Ancillary Resource Center (ARC) for *Personnel Economics* (found at www.oup.com/us/kuhn) includes a number of useful materials to help you teach with this text. Among them are the author's lecture slides, slides of figures and other exhibits from the book, and answers to the chapter discussion questions. Also included are sample questions (both traditional and spreadsheet-based) that can be used for practice or examination purposes.

Acknowledgments

I'd like to acknowledge the contributions of the many people who helped in the preparation of this text. First, great thanks are due to my colleague Ted Frech, who read the entire manuscript. I would also like to thank the Oxford University Press reviewers who read chapters at various stages of the book's development. These include: Nick Adnett, *Staffordshire Business School*; Julian Betts, *University of California, San Diego*; Richard Boylan, *Rice University*; Jeffrey Carpenter, *Middlebury College*; Wei Chen, *Lewis University*; Susan Davies, *University of*

Wisconsin—Milwaukee; Jed DeVaro, *California State University, East Bay*; Tor Eriksson, *Aarhus University*; Mark Frascatore, *Clarkson University*; Jaoquin Gomez-Minambres, *Bucknell University*; Darren Grant, *Sam Houston State University*; Maija Halonen-Akatwijuka, *University of Bristol*; Santhi Hejeebu, *Cornell College*; Kevin Lang, *Boston University*; Ron Laschever, *Purdue University*; Stephanie Lluis, *University of Waterloo*; Brian G. M. Main, *University of Edinburgh*; Robert L. Moore, *Occidental College*; Georgios A. Panos, *University of Stirling*; Kerry Papps, *University of Bath*; and Madelyn V. Young, *Converse College*.

Last but not least, I want to thank Michael Cooper and Charles de los Reyes, who provided indispensable editorial assistance at many stages of the book's production and my Oxford University Press editor, Ann West, for her patience, support, and encouragement.

Part 1
Principal–Agent Models

In Part 1 of this book, we introduce a simple but profound way to think about economic relationships between two or more people: the principal–agent model. Although this model has many applications, in this book we'll use it to understand the relationship between employers and workers. In the way it studies employer-worker interactions, Part 1 differs from other parts of this book in three important ways.

First, our analysis in Part 1 is mostly theoretical; that is, we start with some simple assumptions about the structure of interactions between two parties, and some simple assumptions about their motivations. Based on those assumptions, we then work out exactly how we'd *expect* our two parties to act: If a firm wants to maximize its profits and a worker his utility, exactly what kind of compensation agreement do we expect they'll agree on? Part 2 of the book will confront most of these theoretical predictions with evidence on how workers and firms actually behave, so if you find Part 1 a bit tedious, I hope you'll hang on till Part 2, when the payoff to all that work is received.

Second, although this book is about motivating and selecting employees, Part 1's main focus is on *motivation* alone. This is partly because we have to start somewhere, and it's better to start with simple models and add complications later. It's also because the simplest possible principal–agent problem has one principal and one agent, so the decision on *which* agent to hire doesn't really come up. We'll turn our attention to selection in Part 3, then look at selection and motivation together as we work our way through the rest of the book.

Third, again because we want to start simple, our assumptions about the agent's and principal's motivations in Part 1 are both the most traditional in economics and the most restrictive: We assume that both parties are rational economic actors, caring only about maximizing their own, absolute self-interest. Understanding how these types of principals and agents should behave will provide us with useful guideposts for our study of what actually happens in real-world employment relationships, as we do starting in Part 2.

1 Structure of the Principal–Agent Problem

Suppose you've just been injured in a freak accident in a department store: A hundred cases of Neck n' Torso shampoo have fallen off a shelf and dislocated your back. The injury will cost you $50,000 in lost earnings and medical bills, and you sincerely believe that the store's negligence in maintaining its property caused your accident. So you need to hire a lawyer.

Imagine also that you've never hired a lawyer before, and you don't know anyone who has hired one. To make the example even more improbable, let's say you have an unemployed friend of a friend who just passed the bar; and because you have very little money, you are considering engaging this person to represent you in a civil suit. So now at least two questions come up: (a) How much should you pay this person?, and (b)—probably more important—exactly *how* should you pay her? For example, one option might be a flat fee of, say $10,000, paid up front. Another might be to split the fee over time, for example $5,000 on signing and $5,000 after your acquaintance has done all the work and the case has been heard.

Yet another option would be to make the lawyer's fee contingent on the *outcome* of your case; for example, she could get the second $5,000 payment only if she wins you a settlement of an agreed-on minimum amount. For that matter, why does the lawyer's "bonus" have to be all-or-nothing? To really align her incentives with yours (so she works hard and learns all she needs to know to win), you could give her, say, 20 cents out of every dollar she wins on your behalf—or more. An even more extreme approach would be to ask the lawyer to pay *you* up front: For example, the lawyer could pay you $5,000 up front for your case; in return, you might let her keep not 20 cents but 50 or 80 cents of every dollar she wins on your behalf. Clearly, there are many (in fact an infinite number) of options.

In Chapter 1, we will show you how to think about this problem like an economist. We will impose mathematical structure to describe the incentives that you and your lawyer are facing, and work through the solutions to find out what a rational self-interested actor would do. Understanding this simple model will provide you with the intuition you need to approach all sorts of fascinating questions in personnel economics.

1.1 What Is a Principal–Agent Problem?

The question of how you should pay your newly minted lawyer in the preceding story is a simple example of a type of problem that people confront and solve every minute of every day in our modern economy. Whenever a consumer engages a service provider, such as a lawyer, contractor, doctor, or even a hairdresser; whenever a company contracts with a supplier or engages a franchisee; and whenever a firm hires a worker, the former party (whom we'll call the principal) pays the second (whom we'll call an agent) to take some action on the principal's behalf. The question of how best to structure the agreed-on "arrangement" (or "contract") between these two parties is a canonical problem in economic theory called the "principal–agent problem."

Of course, because people in our economy solve these types of problems over and over again, some pretty standard practices have emerged over the years. For example, a common arrangement in the case of lawyers in civil cases is called a contingency fee. Here, the client (you) pays nothing up front, and the settlement (if any) is divided between you and the agent according to a fixed fraction that is set in advance. The reason I asked you to imagine that neither you nor the person you were thinking of hiring knew anything about how lawyers are usually hired was to encourage you to think about the problem from the point of view of its underlying principles, as if you were trying to solve it for the first time. This "first principles" approach is useful in two distinct ways.

First, thinking without preconceptions about what might be the best way to structure an economic relationship, then comparing your answer to how that type of relationship is typically managed, often gives us useful insights into *why things are the way they are*. After all, in competitive markets, efficient arrangements are more likely to survive than inefficient ones. At the same time, however, an old Chinese proverb says that "If a thousand men do a foolish thing, it is still a foolish thing." Sometimes taking a fresh look at a problem yields new solutions that are better than the accepted way of doing things. In fact, some of the most productive innovations in human resource management (and in other aspects of business) arise from rethinking everyday problems, including different variants of the principal–agent problem, from first principles.

In Chapters 1–4, we'll formally study the simplest possible version of the principal–agent problem. We'll show that in this very simple case (which is close but not identical to our imaginary hiring-a-lawyer problem), the problem has a simple, "best" solution. (Of course, to do this, we'll first have to define what "best" means in a rigorous way.) The solution is both surprising and extreme, and this fact will force us to think hard about what aspects of this simplest case explain why the solution is so extreme. Once that is done, in the following chapters we'll use the simplest case as a jumping-off point to explore a rich set of theories and facts about different types of employment contracts and how they do or do not make sense in different economic environments.

1.2 Timeline of the Principal–Agent Problem

Consider a single *principal* who is contemplating hiring a single *agent* to do some work on the principal's behalf, and imagine (as seems reasonable) that the process happens in the following order. First, the principal offers the agent an *employment contract*, laying out the proposed terms of their business relationship. This tells the agent exactly how he will be paid (whether an hourly wage, a commission, or some combination thereof).[1] Second, the agent then chooses whether or not to accept this offer. Next, if the agent has accepted the offer, he chooses how much *effort* (E) to devote to the task, which affects how much *output* (Q) he produces on the principal's behalf.[2] Finally, the agent gets paid according to the formula that was stipulated in the contract. This formula is a function $Y(Q)$ that relates the agent's *compensation* (Y) to his *performance* (Q).[3]

Putting this all together, Figure 1.1 shows the timeline of interaction between the principal and agent.

In this chapter, we'll assume that both the principal and agent are purely self-interested actors, each of whom tries to maximize their own well-being. ("Behavioral" considerations are introduced in Part 2.) Thus, the principal tries to structure the contract in such a way that (a) it will be acceptable to the agent (because otherwise the principal won't earn *any* profit), and (b) the agent's effort choice under the contract maximizes the *principal's* profit. The agent, in turn, will only accept the offered contract if the expected value of doing so is better than the agent's best alternative activity; and once he has accepted the contract, he'll pick an effort level that maximizes his utility taking the terms of the contract as given.

---

[1] Frequently in this book, we'll adopt the convention, pretty standard in principal–agent theory, that the principal is a "she" and the agent a "he." Because we will be discussing these two parties a lot, this makes it easier to keep track of which one we're talking about. Also, because most of this book uses principal–agent theory to understand *employment* contracts, we'll often refer to the principal as a *firm* and the agent as a *worker* who is hired by that firm.

[2] Throughout this book, we'll measure the agent's output—whatever task is performed—in terms of *dollars of net revenue* he produces for the principal. Accordingly, we'll refer to Q as "output," "revenues," and the agent's "performance" synonymously. "Net" revenue, in turn, means "net of all variable costs except the agent's compensation." We'll be more specific about what's included in net revenue in Section 3.3.

[3] Throughout this book, we'll assume that the principal can't pay the agent directly on the basis of his effort, E. Although this could be very helpful if it were possible, it's not clear how effort could be measured directly. In practice, most employment contracts either stipulate a fixed level of compensation that is independent of both effort and performance, or tie pay to some explicit measure of performance, Q.

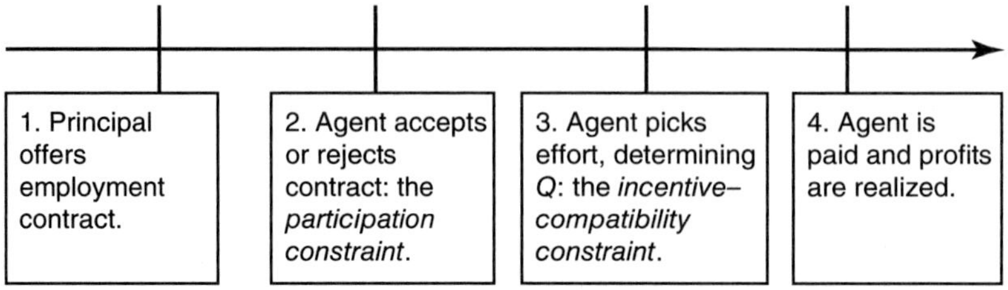

FIGURE 1.1. Timeline of Actions in the Principal–Agent Problem

In the next few Sections (1.3–1.6), we'll flesh out the details of the preceding problem in enough detail that we'll be able to solve for the optimal contract mathematically.

1.3 Profits

As noted, we assume throughout Part 1 of this book that both the principal and agent are purely self-interested; each cares only about maximizing his or her well-being, subject to the constraints imposed by markets and limited resources. The principal's well-being is thus measured by her *profit*, given by the difference between her revenues, Q (think of this as the size of the settlement earned by the lawyer on your behalf), and her costs. In this simple example, the principal's only costs are what she pays the agent, so we have

$$\textit{Profit} = \textit{Revenue} - \textit{Costs}. \tag{1.1}$$

Or using our notation,

$$\Pi = Q - Y. \tag{1.2}$$

1.4 Utility

If the principal's well-being is given by Equation 1.2, what about the agent's? To keep our model as simple as possible, we'll assume the agent's utility is given by the equation

$$\textit{Utility} = \textit{Compensation} - (\textit{Cost of effort}) \tag{1.3}$$

or

$$U = Y - V(E). \tag{1.4}$$

Throughout this book, we'll assume that the agent's cost-of-effort function, $V(E)$, looks like the curve in Figure 1.2. Another name for $V(E)$ is the *disutility-of-effort* function.

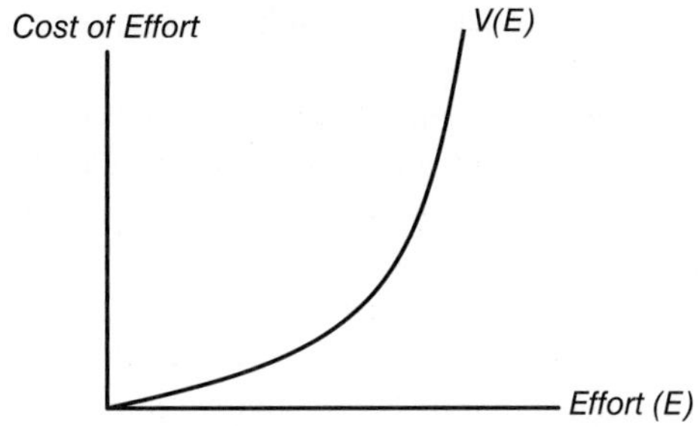

FIGURE 1.2. The Cost-of-Effort Function, *V(E)*

In words, we assume that effort is costly [$V(E) \geq 0$]; that no effort costs are incurred when no effort is supplied [$V(0) = 0$]; that working harder costs the agent more [$V'(E) > 0$; i.e., the slope of the function is positive]; and that there are increasing *marginal* costs of effort [$V''(E) > 0$; i.e., the slope of the function is increasing].[4] The reason why we assume increasing marginal effort costs is simple realism: Even the most dedicated workaholic eventually gets to a point where putting in one more hour or concentrating even harder on a task becomes extremely painful. Thus, the last unit of effort supplied in any given period of time is more painful than the earlier ones.

At a number of points throughout the book, we'll use a specific cost-of-effort function that satisfies all the preceding properties. This example will help us solve a number of problems much more easily, without affecting any of the main results. This illustrative, or *baseline cost-of-effort function* has the following formula:

$$V(E) = E^2/2. \tag{1.5}$$

In other words, the cost of effort just equals the amount of effort squared, divided by two. (You'll see why we divide by two later.)

At a number of other points in this book, it will be helpful to illustrate the agent's utility function in Equation 1.4 graphically. To do this, we'll use a familiar tool of microeconomics: indifference curves. Thinking back to your last microeconomics course, you may remember using indifference curves to depict a consumer's preferences between two goods he or she might consume. For example, in the case of choosing between apples (A) and bananas (B), a consumer's utility function, $U(A, B)$ can be represented in two dimensions by a set of downward-sloping curves in a diagram, with B on the vertical axis and A on the horizontal. Utility is fixed along any curve, and the slope of the curve gives the consumer's willingness to trade off apples for bananas, that is, the *marginal rate of substitution* between the goods.[5]

---

[4] Throughout this book, primes denote derivatives, that is, $V'(E) = dV/dE$ and $V''(E) = d^2V/dE^2$. It will help if you know enough calculus to maximize a function of a single variable, but calculus is not essential to understanding any of the main ideas in the book.

[5] Please see any intermediate microeconomics textbook for a review.

What do the indifference curves look like for our agent's utility function, $U = Y - V(E)$, in Equation 1.4? Just as in the apples–bananas case, our agent's utility depends on two things; now the two things the agent cares about are the amount of income (Y) he earns and the amount of effort he expends (E). A key difference, though, is that whereas apples and bananas are both things that our consumer enjoys (i.e., they are economic "goods"), higher levels of effort (holding income constant) make our agent worse off. In other words, whereas income (Y) is an economic good to the agent, effort is an economic *bad*. As a result, the agent's indifference map comes out looking like Figure 1.3:

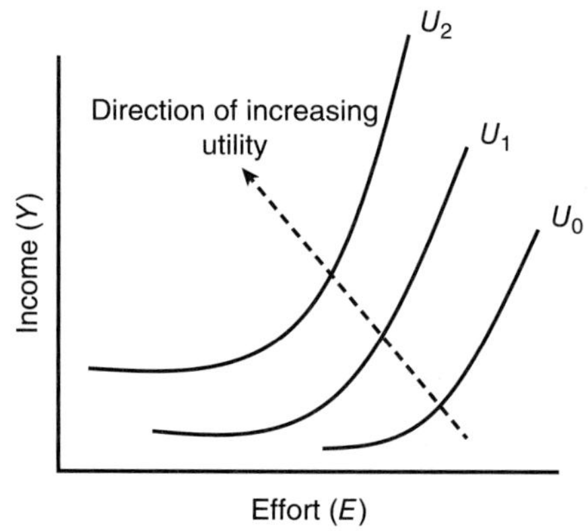

FIGURE 1.3. Indifference Curves between Effort and Income

Because effort is costly to the agent, the agent's indifference curves will now be *upward sloping*, and the agent becomes better off as we move north*west* in the picture, not northeast. To find the equation of an indifference curve, simply rearrange Equation 1.4 as

$$Y = U + V(E). \tag{1.6}$$

For any given level of utility, U, Equation 1.6 gives the amount of income the agent needs to attain that level of utility when he is supplying E units of effort. The slope of an indifference curve is given by the following:

$$\textit{Slope of indifference curve} = V'(E) = \textit{marginal cost of effort} > 0. \tag{1.7}$$

Indifference curves between income and effort are upward sloping, and get *steeper* as we move from left to right, because the agent has *increasing marginal costs of effort* [$V''(E) > 0$]. The more he is already working, the more cash we need to give him to keep utility constant as we ask him to provide even more units of effort. As in the case of a consumer choosing between apples and bananas, to maximize utility, the agent should still try to get himself onto the highest indifference curve possible in Figure 1.3 (i.e., the indifference curve that is as far to the northwest as possible), subject to whatever budget constraint(s) he faces.

1.5 The Contract

As we noted, the agent's pay, Y, depends on his performance according to the contract that is agreed on, $Y(Q)$. Because our main question is to figure out the *best* function, $Y(Q)$, it's not clear what we should assume, if anything, about $Y(Q)$. To keep things simple, however, we will assume for now that $Y(Q)$ is *some* linear function:

$$Y = a + bQ. \tag{1.8}$$

Although the formula in Equation 1.8 rules out lots of possibilities, it still includes many options for how the agent could be paid. As we already noted, the agent could be paid a fixed wage, regardless of his job performance ($a > 0, b = 0$). Or the agent could get, say, 20 cents out of every dollar he produces for the principal ($a = 0, b = 0.2$). Or, the agent could get some combination of base pay and incentive pay ($a \neq 0, b \neq 0$) where it is even conceivable (though perhaps not optimal) that one of these parameters is negative.[6]

In sum, in Part 1 of this book, we assume that the contract between the principal and agent is just a linear function that can be completely described by two numbers: the function's intercept (a) and its slope (b). The intercept, a, stipulates the agent's *base pay* (the minimum amount he gets paid, even if he produces absolutely no results for the principal); and the slope, b, represents a *piece rate* or *commission rate*.[7] High values of b mean the worker is highly incentivized: Even small improvements in performance will raise the worker's pay a lot. And of course, one of the key questions we're trying to answer in this chapter is "Just *how* incentivized should workers be?"

1.6 The Production Function

We need one more piece of information to complete our description of the principal–agent problem: so far we have said that higher effort (E) by the agent tends to result in a higher level of output (Q), but we haven't been specific about this relationship. If we think of our principal as a firm that is hiring a worker, this relationship is essentially the firm's *production function*, $Q(E)$. In reality, of course, $Q(E)$ can take many forms; and in most realistic cases, it will include some element of uncertainty: sometimes the worker produces a bad outcome even when he works hard, and at other times even lazy workers get lucky. We'll incorporate uncertainty and other additional features of the production function

---

[6] We'll discuss the advantages and disadvantages of nonlinear contracts starting in Chapter 5, Sections 5.5 and 5.6.

[7] In addition to *base pay*, we'll sometimes refer to a as the agent's *fixed pay*, or *show-up pay*, as he receives a just for showing up for work, and a is the component of the agent's compensation that does not depend on his job performance. *Piece rates* refer to the practice of paying production workers according to the number of units—"pieces"—they produce, while commission rates link salespeoples' pay to the dollar value of their sales. The product bQ is called the agent's *variable pay* because it is the component of the agent's total pay that *does* depend on his performance.

later, but for now we'll ignore uncertainty and assume the simplest possible production function, namely,

$$Q(E) = dE. \tag{1.9}$$

In words, output is proportional to effort, with the parameter d measuring just how productive effort is. One reason why d can take different values in Equation 1.9 is because different agents might have different abilities to do this task: One unit of effort by worker A might yield more output than the same amount of effort from a different worker. A second reason relates to the firm's technology: A technical innovation such as a new software program might make the *same* worker more productive by raising the level of d. Both of these interpretations of the productivity parameter—ability and technology—will play important roles in our book.

Just as it is sometimes helpful to have a baseline cost-of-effort function, it will also be helpful to have a *baseline production function.* In this book, our baseline production function is

$$Q(E) = E, \tag{1.10}$$

which just sets $d = 1$. A useful way of thinking about this is that when we use our baseline production function, we have simply decided to *measure effort* (which in most cases doesn't have any natural units anyway) *in terms of the number of units of output it yields.* In our lawyer example, $E = 1$ would then just mean that the lawyer *worked hard enough to generate* (a settlement of) *one (thousand) dollars.* This convention works well (and simplifies our notation) as long as we don't have to think about there being two alternative, differently skilled lawyers, or about technological improvements that change an agent's productivity (per unit of effort). When we consider questions like that, we'll bring our handy d parameter back into the picture.

1.7 Backwards Induction

Now that we've laid out the *timeline* of interactions between our principal and agent, their respective *payoffs* (profits and utility), and the underlying *economic relationships* (the production function and the contract), we are ready to start solving the question of "What is the optimal contract?" Notice that because of the way we have simplified the problem, this boils down to just finding the optimal values of two parameters: a and b. So how should we proceed?

Looking back at the timeline in Figure 1.1, one might think the easiest way to solve the problem will be to start the analysis at the beginning, that is, at Point 1 where the principal offers the agent a contract. This seems sensible—after all, shouldn't the solution begin where the problem begins? Doing so, however, soon gets us into trouble: The principal wants to maximize her profit, but how does she have any clue as to what contract to offer the agent? Ideally, the principal would first like to have some idea as to how the agent will respond so as to not make a mistake. To do this, it actually makes more sense to work backwards: hence the term *backwards induction.*

Backwards induction will be a familiar concept to anyone who has studied game theory or intermediate microeconomic theory. For example, a well-known micro problem that needs to be solved by backwards induction is the Stackelberg leader–follower model of duopoly: If there are two firms in an industry who have to decide on their output levels in turn, the first mover (i.e., the Stackelberg leader) needs to forecast how the follower will respond to *every possible output level* the leader might consider producing. So to maximize her own profits effectively, the leader needs to put herself into the mind of the follower and work out how the follower is likely to respond to each one of the leader's possible choices. Although this way of thinking might seem unrealistically complex, notice that it's actually something all of us do, quite automatically, in everyday life. Suppose, for example, that you are considering asking a classmate out on a date. Before asking a classmate (agent) on a date, the proposer (principal) tries to forecast how the classmate will respond to not be embarrassed.

Following this useful principle, we start our analysis of the principal–agent problem by solving the agent's (i.e. the second mover's) problem first. Specifically, Chapter 2 studies the decision that is made at Point 3 in our timeline (Figure 1.1): Taking the employment contract (a, b) as given, *and* assuming that the agent has already accepted the contract, how hard do we expect the agent to work? We'll solve this problem for *every conceivable* contract the principal might offer the agent. Having done that, we'll work backwards in Chapter 3 to figure out (a) which contracts the agent will find acceptable (Point 2 of the timeline) and (b) what is the best contract to offer in the first place (Point 1).

Chapter Summary

- ☐ In the simplest possible principal–agent model, a principal who wants to maximize her profits hires an agent to work for her.

- ☐ The principal's profits are given by $\Pi = Q - Y$, where Q is the agent's output and Y is what the principal pays him.

- ☐ The agent's utility is given by $U = Y - V(E)$, where V is his disutility of effort. In general, we assume $V(E)$ exhibits increasing marginal costs of effort; an example (baseline) $V(E)$ function we'll often use is $V(E) = E^2/2$.

- ☐ Another way to illustrate the agent's utility function $U(Y, E)$ is as a set of indifference curves. In a graph with Y on the vertical axis and E on the horizontal axis, these curves have a positive slope, and curves further to the northwest correspond to higher levels of utility.

- ☐ Throughout Part 1 of the book, we'll assume that the principal and agent agree on a linear contract, which stipulates that the agent will receive a dollars in base pay, plus b dollars for every dollar of output the agent produces. In other words, the contract stipulates that $Y = a + bQ$.

- ☐ Throughout most of Part 1, we'll assume that the production function linking the agent's effort to his output takes the form $Y = dQ$. In our baseline example, we'll simplify this even further and just assume that $Y = Q$. Note that this doesn't allow for any uncertainty in the production process.

- ☐ Because we assume the agent chooses his effort level after both parties agree on the contract, we have to solve the principal–agent problem by *backwards induction*. In other words, we first have to figure out how the agent will react to *every possible contract* (a, b). Only once we've done that can the principal figure out which contract will yield the highest profits for her while still remaining acceptable to the agent.

Discussion Questions

1. Aside from firms hiring workers, what are some other examples of a principal–agent relationship?

2. Suppose the agent described in this chapter receives a generous employment offer from another firm while he's deciding whether to accept this principal's contract. Mathematically, how would that enter into the principal–agent problem outlined here?

3. True or false: In the model described in this chapter, we assume that effort, E, is an *inferior good* to the agent because it is something he dislikes. Hint: you might want to consult a basic microeconomics textbook (or Wikipedia) for the definition of an inferior good.

4. True or false: The contract $(a, b) = (-5, 0.6)$ is one of an infinite number of possible contracts the principal could possibly offer the agent. Under this contract, the agent must *pay the principal* 5 dollars to get the job. Once he has the job, the agent will earn 60 cents for every dollar of output he generates for the principal.

2 Solving the Agent's Problem

Before the principal decides on the best contract to offer the agent, she must correctly anticipate how hard the agent will work under any given contract. In Chapter 2, we will approach the principal–agent problem solely from the agent's perspective. The core of our agent's problem (and maybe a good metaphor for life!) is that the agent likes income, but generating income requires effort, and effort is costly. So, what's the right level of effort to choose? In our example, if we can work out how much income and utility are generated from any given effort level, we should be able to characterize this trade-off exactly and find the optimal balance between these two objectives, given the contract the agent faces.

2.1 A Mathematical Solution

Under any contract (a, b) and with the production function $Q = dE$, the income generated by E units of effort is given by

$$Y = a + bdE \tag{2.1}$$

(to get this, just substitute the production function $Q = dE$ into the contract in Equation 1.8).

The agent's utility under any contract (a, b) can then be written as

$$U = Y - V(E) = (a + bdE) - V(E). \tag{2.2}$$

The agent's choice of how hard to work under any given contract therefore boils down to finding the level of effort (E) that maximizes Equation 2.2.

One way to solve this maximization problem uses (a tiny amount of) calculus: Just take the derivative of Equation 2.2 with respect to E and set it equal to zero, yielding $bd - V'(E) = 0$; or

$$V'(E) = bd. \tag{2.3}$$

The left-hand side of Equation 2.3 is the marginal cost of an extra unit of effort to the agent; we have assumed that this is increasing in E. The right-hand side is the marginal benefit of effort; in our model, this does not depend on E but does depend on the levels of b and d. Thus, if the contract gives the worker a bigger share of what he or she produces (b is higher), effort is more worthwhile. The same is true if the worker is abler, or if that person's working with a better technology (i.e., if d is higher).

Figure 2.1 illustrates Equation 2.3 graphically. It also shows how the agent's optimal effort decision responds to changes in his economic environment.

Part (a) of Figure 2.1 shows the agent's total income line, $Y = a + bdE$, which increases by bd dollars for each unit of effort he provides. It also shows the agent's total cost-of-effort curve, $V(E)$, which rises at an increasing rate with effort. Recall that the agent's utility is simply income minus cost of effort, so utility is shown in the graph by the vertical gap between the income line and the cost-of-effort curve. Therefore, the agent's utility-maximizing choice of effort occurs where this gap is largest, at E^*.

To understand why E^* is the best the agent can do, consider an agent thinking through whether he should provide more or less effort. To the left of E^*, the agent's income is rising faster with E than the costs of effort, so it pays to work a

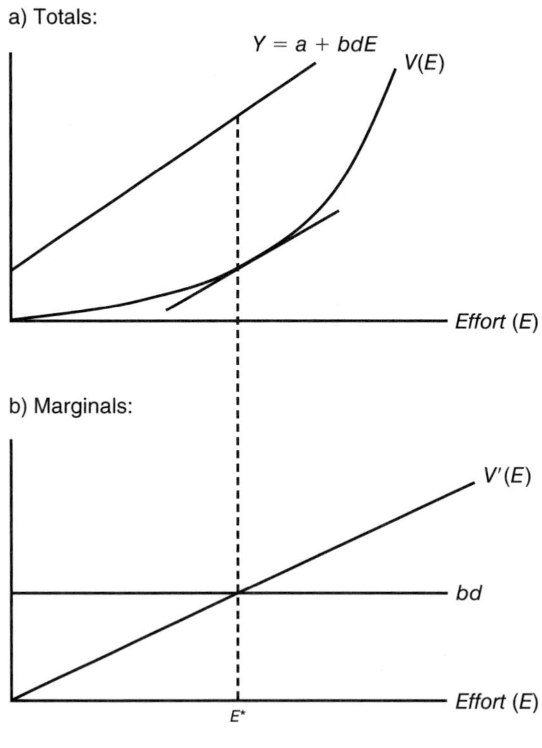

FIGURE 2.1. The Agent's Optimal Effort Decision

little more. To the right of E^*, the opposite is true, so it pays to work a little less. Together, this means that the agent can always make himself better off by adjusting his effort toward E^* from any other level.

Another way to frame this intuition is by thinking about the marginal benefits and marginal costs of providing additional effort, shown in Part (b) of Figure 2.1. Graphically, the two lines you see are the slopes (derivatives) of the income line and cost-of-effort curve from Part (a). The *marginal benefit* of effort is the extra income earned (bd), which is the same for every unit of effort supplied (and therefore a horizontal line). The *marginal cost* of effort, $V'(E)$, rises with effort (so it is an upward-sloping line).[1] The optimal effort (E^*) is where marginal cost equals marginal benefit at the intersection of the two lines in Part (b), in other words where $V'(E) = bd$. This same concept is illustrated in Part (a) where the tangent line to the $V(E)$ curve has the same slope as the income line at E^*. The simple idea underneath this math is that the agent will provide additional effort whenever it gives the agent greater benefit than cost. He will stop providing additional effort once the marginal benefit exactly equals marginal cost, so that he has extracted the maximum utility possible under his contract.[2]

2.2 Comparative Statics

How does the agent's optimal effort change when he faces different types of contracts (a, b), or when a new technology is invented that makes him more productive (d)? To see this, Figure 2.2 shows the agent's marginal costs and benefits of working for different levels of these parameters.

If we raise b from some initial level (b_0) to a higher level (b_1), the agent's optimal effort level, E^*, moves to the right, at a higher level of effort. The same would be true if technological change or an increase in ability or training made the agent more productive (higher d). None of the lines in Figure 2.2 depend on the level of the worker's base pay, a. Together, this gives us the following (Result 2.1):

☑ RESULT 2.1

Agents' Reactions to Changes in the Employment Contract (*a*, *b*) and Productivity (*d*):

1. For any given contract, more productive agents (with higher *d*) will work harder than less productive agents.
2. Raising the slope parameter (*b*) of the employment contract will make the agent work harder.
3. Changing the intercept parameter (*a*) of the employment contract will have no effect on the agent's optimal effort level.

---

[1] The marginal-disutility-of-effort function, $V'(E)$, shown in Figure 2.1(b), is a straight line through the origin. This is what $V'(E)$ must look like for our baseline cost-of-effort function, $V(E) = E^2/2$. For other $V(E)$ functions, the curve will have a different appearance.

[2] This intuition closely mirrors that taught in many introductory microeconomics courses, where firms will keep producing additional units of output until the marginal revenue equals marginal cost.

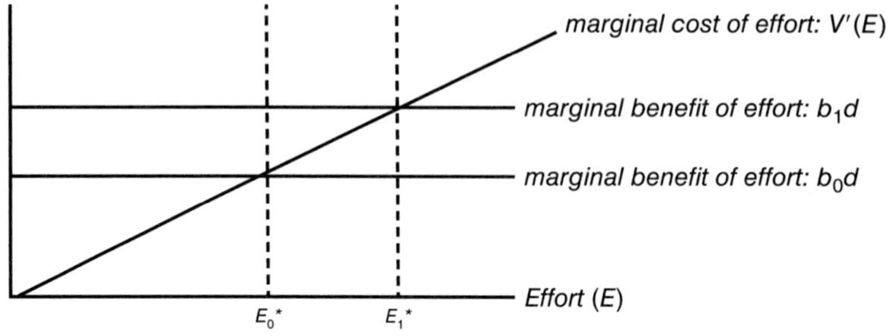

FIGURE 2.2. Effects of Increases in *b* on the Agent's Effort Choice

Taken together, the three parts of Result 2.1 make a lot of sense. Although the overall principal–agent problem is far from completely solved, we are now in a position to predict how our agent's effort choice will respond to any possible employment contract (a, b) the principal might propose. Most readers probably won't find it surprising that according to our model, strengthening the agent's incentives (raising b) induces this agent to work harder. And making the agent more productive (raising d) also raises the agent's effort for exactly the same reason. What may be a little more surprising, though, is "the dog that didn't bark": Raising the agent's compensation in a different way (via a higher level of base pay, a), is predicted to have no effect on the agent's effort at all. After all, the agent gets his base pay *no matter how well he performs*, so why would he change his effort when a rises?[3]

Result 2.1 is true for any level of worker productivity, d, and for *any* cost-of-effort function $V(E)$ that exhibits increasing marginal costs of effort. If we use our *baseline* effort cost and production functions—$V(E) = E^2/2$ and $d = 1$, respectively—however, we can be even more specific about the agent's preferred effort levels. Under these assumptions, because $V'(E) = E$, Equation 2.3 becomes

$$E = b. \tag{2.4}$$

(Now you see why we divided by two in Equation 1.5: It makes our equation for optimal effort super simple and eliminates the need to divide by two throughout much of the book.) Result 2.2 summarizes:

[3] A highly observant (and well-trained) reader will notice that the result that effort is unaffected by a results from our assumption in Equation 1.3 that utility is linear in income. By writing utility this way, we are thus assuming away any *income effects* on labor supply. We study how income effects influence effort decisions in Chapter 11.

> ☑ **RESULT 2.2**
>
> **Agents' Reactions to Changes in the Employment Contract (*a*, *b*) with the Baseline Production and Cost-of-Effort Functions:**
>
> 1. The agent's optimal effort, *E*, now equals *b* exactly ($E = b$).
> 2. Raising the slope parameter (*b*) of the employment contract will still make the agent work harder.
> 3. Changing the intercept parameter (*a*) of the employment contract will still have no effect on the agent's optimal effort level.

2.3 The Solution with Indifference Curves

Yet another way to illustrate the agent's optimal effort choice—which will turn out to be useful throughout the book—is using indifference curves.

Figure 2.3 shows three of the agent's indifference curves between income and effort. If we also include the relationship $Y = a + bdE$ in the diagram, we can think of this line—just as in standard consumer theory—as the agent's *budget constraint*. It shows us all the bundles of *E* and *Y* that the agent can afford. Just as in regular consumer theory, the highest indifference curve the agent can reach is the one that is just tangent to the budget constraint, in this case the curve labeled U_1. At the optimal effort level, E^*, the slope of the indifference curve must equal the slope of the budget constraint (bd). Because (from Equation 1.7) the slope of the indifference curve at any point just equals $V'(E)$, this just gives us back the same conditions for optimal effort we already have: $V'(E) = bd$ in general, and $E = b$ in our simple baseline example.

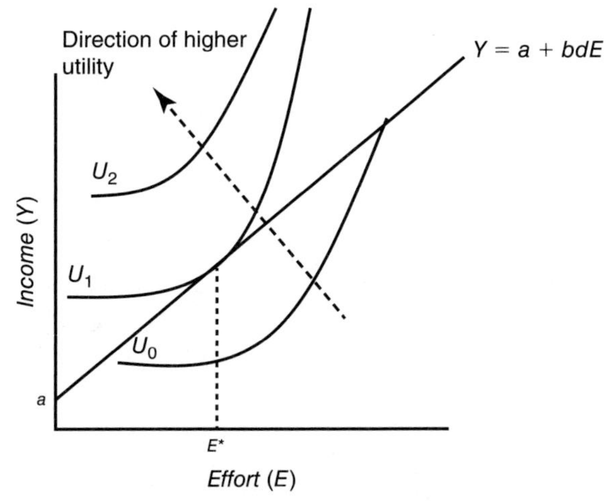

FIGURE 2.3. Illustrating the Agent's Optimal Effort Using Indifference Curves

Chapter Summary

- ☐ In the basic principal–agent problem, the agent chooses effort (E) to maximize his utility, taking the terms of the contract (a, b) as given.
- ☐ For any agent utility function of the form $U = Y - V(E)$, where $V(E)$ exhibits increasing marginal costs, the agent's preferred effort increases with the commission rate (b) and with his productivity level (d). The agent's effort will be unaffected by the level of his base pay, a, because he receives this regardless of how much he produces.
- ☐ For the special cases of our baseline effort cost and production functions [$V(E) = E^2/2$ and $d = 1$], the agent's (privately) optimal effort choice is given by the simple equation $E = b$.
- ☐ The agent's optimal effort choice can be illustrated as the tangency point between his highest attainable indifference curve and the budget constraint defined by the contract: $Y = a + bQ$.

Discussion Questions

1. Suppose $V(E) = E^2$ instead of $E^2/2$. What is the agent's optimal effort when $d = 1$?
2. Suppose $V(E) = E^3/3$ instead of $E^2/2$. What is the agent's optimal effort when $d = 1$? Hint: you'll need to use a tiny bit of calculus, that is, the derivative of E^3.
3. Suppose that instead of increasing marginal costs of effort, the marginal costs of effort were constant; for example, suppose that $V(E) = mE$, where $m > 0$. What is the agent's optimal effort when $m < bd$ or when $m > bd$?

3 Solving the Principal's Problem

Now that we know how the agent will respond to any contract the principal might offer him, we are in a position to find the optimal contract from the principal's point of view. What should this contract look like? Since we have just shown that rational agents will increase their effort in response to a higher commission rate (b) but not to a higher base pay (a), it seems reasonable to suppose that the profit-maximizing level of base pay should simply be zero: Why, after all, would the principal choose to give away money for nothing? In Section 3.1, we will follow this intuition by doing a simple warm-up exercise: we find the profit-maximizing commission rate (b) when $a = 0$.[1] As we'll see, the profit-maximizing commission rate when $a = 0$ will be some number strictly between zero and 100%—a number that balances out the competing goals of incentivizing the agent (with a higher b) and keeping more output in the principal's hands (a lower b).

But is this really the best the principal can do? In Section 3.2 we show, perhaps surprisingly, that it is *not*. When we derive the full solution to the principal–agent problem by letting the principal choose any level of a or b that she wishes, we'll show that this contract takes a very special and perhaps surprising form known as the *franchise solution*. Although this solution may seem counterintuitive at first, in Section 3.3 we will show that this contractual arrangement is actually used in many sectors of our economy.

3.1 Warm-Up Exercise: The Principal's Problem when $a = 0$

To keep things as simple as possible, we start by assuming our baseline $V(E)$ and $Q(E)$ functions, so the principal can easily compute how hard the agent will work

[1] A second way we simplify the principal–agent problem in this section is to ignore Point 2 of the problem's timeline (Figure 1.1): For now, we'll assume that our agent accepts any contract the principal offers him. (Imagine, for example, that our agent has been unemployed for a long time and is willing to take any job that is offered.)

for any b the principal might post: $E^* = b$. To maximize the principal's profits (Equation 1.2), we substitute the production function ($Q = E$) and the employment contract into that equation to get the following:

$$\Pi = E - (a + bE). \tag{3.1}$$

Setting $a = 0$ and substituting the agent's optimal effort choice ($E = b$) into Equation 3.1 yields

$$\Pi = b - b^2. \tag{3.2}$$

Finding the commission rate (b) that maximizes the principal's profit using calculus is straightforward. Taking the derivative and setting it equal to zero,

$$1 - 2b = 0, \tag{3.3}$$

or

$$b = 0.5. \tag{3.4}$$

Another way to find the profit-maximizing commission rate is just to graph Equation 3.2, which gives profits as a function of b. This graph is shown in Figure 3.1.

Thus for our baseline cost-of-effort and production functions, the piece rate (b) that maximizes profits when $a = 0$ is precisely 50%: The principal should allow the agent to keep 50 cents out of every dollar the agent produces. Whereas this exact solution (50%) is a special feature of our baseline example, it is easy to see why the optimal level of b is always strictly greater than zero, and strictly less than one, regardless of the production function or the cost-of-effort function: A commission

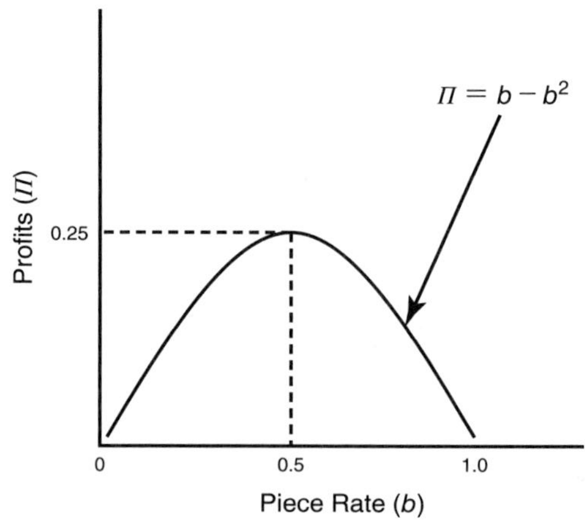

FIGURE 3.1. Profits as a Function of the Piece Rate (b) when a Is Fixed at Zero

rate of zero never yields any profit because it gives the agent no incentives—he'll do nothing ($E = 0$). At the other extreme, a commission rate of 100% is highly motivating to the agent, and the agent will supply lots of effort. But profits are once again zero because a 100% commission rate lets the agent keep *everything* he produces. Thus, it stands to reason that the profit-maximizing commission rate is one that balances two objectives: *efficiency* versus *distribution*. On the one hand, stronger incentives (b) motivate the agent to work harder and produce more output (efficiency), which the principal likes. On the other hand, strengthening the agent's incentives means letting the agent keep more of what he makes (distribution), which the principal dislikes. The profit-maximizing contract trades off these two objectives, which in our baseline example involves exactly equal sharing of the agent's output between the agent and principal ($b = 0.5$).
Result 3.1 summarizes:

RESULT 3.1

The Profit-Maximizing Contract when $a = 0$:

1. Suppose the agent's base pay (a) is fixed at zero. Then the profit-maximizing commission rate (b) is positive but strictly less than one ($0 < b < 1$).
2. Using our baseline production and cost-of-effort functions, the profit-maximizing commission rate is exactly 50% ($b = 0.5$).

Before leaving this simplified version of the principal–agent problem, it will be useful to characterize not only how the principal feels about different commission rates as we did in the previous figure, but how the *agent* feels about them. To see this, substitute the employment contract and the baseline cost-of-effort function into the definition of the agent's utility, Equation 1.4, to get

$$U = a + bY - E^2/2. \tag{3.5}$$

Incentivizing Agents and the Laffer Curve

Some readers might notice a parallel between Figure 3.1 and the well-known Laffer curve for a government's tax revenues. In fact, it is exactly the same curve, just in a different setting. To see this, think of the principal as the government and the agent as the workers and businesses in the economy. Think of the principal's profits as the government's tax revenues and of $t = 1 - b$ as the government's tax rate: t is the share of what the private sector produces that the government takes in taxes (so, e.g., when $b = 1$, the agent keeps everything he makes and the tax rate is zero). It follows immediately that the government collects zero revenues when the tax rate is zero and when the tax rate is 100%. Further, there is a tax rate between zero and 100% that maximizes tax revenues, and raising the tax rate beyond this level reduces the total tax revenues the government collects.

Setting $a = 0$ and substituting in the equation for how the agent responds to the contract ($E = b$),

$$U = b^2 - b^2/2 = b^2/2. \tag{3.6}$$

Equation 3.6 makes it clear that utility increases without limit as b rises. In fact, utility rises at an increasing rate with b. This is because the agent benefits in two ways from a higher b. One is the direct gains from keeping a bigger share of what he makes; this effect alone would make utility rise linearly with b. But there's an additional gain: When b rises, the agent can adjust his effort in whatever way best takes advantage of the new level of b (which in this case is upward). This option gives an extra little "kick" to the positive effects of higher b's, giving rise to the convexity in the curve. The relationship in Equation 3.6 is shown in Figure 3.2.

To conclude this section, let's compare Figures 3.1 and 3.2 and think specifically about what happens at the point $b = 0.5$. If we raised b just a little above 0.5, how would the principal and agent feel about this? Clearly, the agent will like it. And at least for small changes in b, the principal won't really mind: Because profits are maximized at $b = 0.5$, the profit function is flat at that point (a tangent line will have a zero slope). So, at least for small changes in b, *the agent benefits more from an increase in b (beyond 0.5) than the principal loses.* This suggests an intriguing possibility: Maybe the principal can do *better* than offering the agent a 50% commission rate. To exploit this opportunity, she'd need to make a deal with the agent that went something like this: I'll agree to raise your commission rate from 50% to, say, 60% in return for a small, lump sum cash payment *from* the agent. As long as this cash payment isn't so large as to wipe out all the agent's gains from the higher commission rate, both the principal and agent will be better off than when

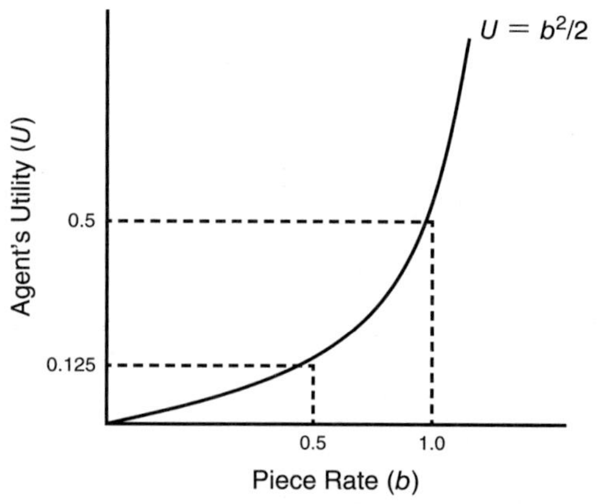

FIGURE 3.2. The Agent's Utility as a Function of b

$b = 0.5$ and $a = 0$. The next section of this chapter works out the best way for the principal to take advantage of this idea by (finally) solving the full version of the principal–agent problem.

3.2 The Full Solution to the Principal–Agent Problem

Now we can finally solve the complete principal–agent problem as set out in Figure 1.1. We'll work out not only the principal's profit-maximizing commission rate (b) but also the profit-maximizing level of base pay (a). And we'll incorporate not only the *incentive-compatibility constraint* facing the principal (Point 3 of the timeline in Figure 1.1 where the agent chooses effort given the structure of the contract) but the *participation constraint* imposed by Point 2 of the timeline: Whatever contract is offered has to be attractive enough to ensure that the agent actually accepts it rather than engaging in his next-best activity (e.g., working for a different principal).

Mathematically, the agent's participation constraint requires that

$$U \geq U^{alt}, \tag{3.7}$$

where U^{alt} ("alternative utility") is the value to the agent of his next-best option, whether this be watching infomercials at home, going to grad school, caring for his kids, or simply taking another job. The participation constraint of Equation 3.7 incorporates the extremely important fact that *firms operate in labor markets*: If they ask too much of their workers, or pay them too little, those workers will go to work elsewhere. As we'll see, these labor markets not only force firms to treat their workers with a certain minimum level of generosity, they also guarantee that the employment contracts offered by firms are not only profit maximizing but also—in a limited but well-defined sense—best for society as a whole.

Continuing to stick with our baseline cost-of-effort and production functions, we start by posing the following question: How can a smart, forward-looking principal anticipate which contracts will be acceptable to the agent and which will not? To see this, recall from Figure 3.2 that the agent likes higher levels of b; in consequence, the higher a level of b the principal offers the agent, the less base pay (a) the principal will need to offer to make the contract acceptable to the agent. Substituting the definition of utility (Equation 1.4) and the baseline cost-of-effort function (Equation 1.5) into Equation 3.7, a contract is acceptable to the agent if

$$a + bE - E^2/2 \geq U^{alt}. \tag{3.8}$$

Substituting in the incentive-compatibility constraint $E = b$,

$$a + b^2/2 \geq U^{alt}. \tag{3.9}$$

Finally, rearranging Equation 3.9 gives us the following very useful way to write the agent's participation constraint in the baseline problem:

$$a_{min} = U^{alt} - b^2/2. \tag{3.10}$$

Essentially, Equation 3.10 tells us *the minimum level of base pay the principal needs to offer the agent to ensure that the agent will accept the job.* It does this for every possible commission rate the principal might contemplate offering the agent and takes into account the fact that whatever b the principal imposes, the agent will react to it by choosing how hard to work. We'll use it (and equations like it) many times in this book. Notice that it shows a negative relationship between a and b: The more generous the principal is on any one dimension of the compensation package (a or b), the less generous she needs to be on the other to get the agent to accept the contract she's offering.

Now we can choose *both* a and b to maximize the principal's profits, subject to *both* the incentive-compatibility and participation constraints. As always, profits are given by

$$\Pi = Q - (a + bQ). \tag{3.11}$$

Substituting in the baseline production function ($Q = E$) yields

$$\Pi = E - (a + bE). \tag{3.12}$$

Substituting in the incentive-compatibility constraint ($E = b$) and simplifying gives

$$\Pi = b - b^2 - a. \tag{3.13}$$

Finally, substituting in the participation constraint $a = U^{alt} - b^2/2$ lets us express profits purely as a function of the commission rate, b, as we did in Equation 3.2 of our warm-up exercise:

$$\Pi = b - b^2 - (U^{alt} - b^2/2) = b - b^2/2 - U^{alt}. \tag{3.14}$$

Taking the derivative with respect to b and setting that equal to zero yields

$$1 - b = 0. \tag{3.15}$$

So, the *profit-maximizing commission rate is 100%*. This is a surprising and almost paradoxical result. The theory dictates that to maximize profits, the principal should (in a very important, marginal sense) *give all those profits away to the agent!*

If you prefer to see the previous solution graphically (or not to use calculus at all), Figure 3.3 graphs the parabola in Equation 3.14 directly. Consistent with our solution in Equation 3.15, profits reach their highest point at $b = 1$.

An important insight from Figure 3.3 is that although the principal is worse off when the agent has better outside options (higher levels of U^{alt} reduce the y-intercept of the profit function), improving the agent's outside options doesn't change the fact that the optimal commission rate, b, is 100%. Not only does this simplify the principal's decision, it has an important implication for the types of contracts that are *socially* optimal, which we'll explore in the following section.

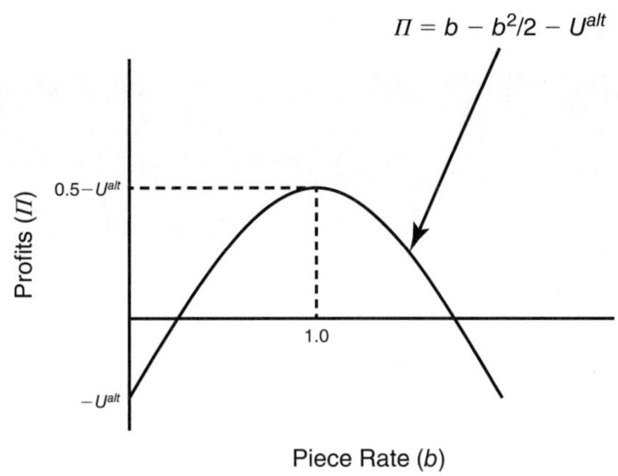

FIGURE 3.3. Profits as a Function of b in the Full Principal–Agent Problem

To conclude this section, Table 3.1 lists the agent's effort, income, utility, and the firm's profits at two different commission rates (50% and 100%), with a set in both cases to guarantee the worker a utility level (U^{alt}) of 0.25. If you weren't convinced that "giving it all away" (at the margin) is the principal's profit-maximizing strategy, this should help explain why that is the case.

According to Table 3.1, when the principal offers the agent a 50% commission rate, the agent will supply 0.5 units of effort (and produce 0.5 units of output because $Q = E$). This yields a total commission ("variable") income of $bQ = 0.5 \times 0.5 = 0.25$.[2] Using the participation constraint in Equation 3.8, with $U^{alt} = 0.25$, this means that the principal has to offer the agent 0.125 units of base pay (a) to get him to take the job. Column 5 (in Table 3.1) uses the formula for the agent's utility to verify that this combination of a and b, together with the agent's optimal response to b, gives the agent just enough utility to make the job acceptable. Finally, the highest profit the principal can earn if she offers a piece rate of 50% is calculated in column 6 as 0.125. (As a convenience, the square brackets in the table break down the numerical calculations.)

What happens, in contrast, if the principal decides to offer a 100% commission rate? Now the agent will supply 1 unit of effort (and produce 1 unit of output, because $Q = E$). This yields a total commission income of $bQ = 1 \times 1 = 1$. Using the participation constraint in Equation 3.8 with $U^{alt} = 0.25$, this means that the most the principal has to offer the agent to take the job is *minus* 0.25. In other words, at a 100% commission rate, *this job is so attractive the principal can ask the agent to pay her for access to the job!* Column 5 again verifies that this combination of a and b, together with the agent's optimal response to b, gives the agent just enough utility to make the job acceptable to the agent. Finally, the highest profit the principal can earn if she offers a piece rate of 100% is double what it was at 50%, at 0.25.

[2] "Variable" income refers to the fact that this component of pay depends on the agent's performance.

TABLE 3.1 COMPARING OUTCOMES AT A 50% AND A 100% COMMISSION RATE

(1)	(2)	(3)	(4)	(5)	(6)
Piece Rate (b)	Effort (E) [using $E^* = b$]	Agent's Variable Income (bE)	Agent's Fixed Income (a)	Agent's Utility (U^A) [using $U^A = a + bE - E^2/2$]	Principal's Profits (Π) [using $\Pi = E - a - bE$]
0.5	0.5	0.25 [0.5 × 0.5]	0.125	0.25 [0.125 + 0.25 − 0.125]	0.125 [0.5 − 0.125 − 0.25]
1	1	1 [1 × 1]	−0.25	0.25 [−0.25 + 1 − 0.5]	0.25 [1 + 0.25 − 1]

RESULT 3.2

The Full Solution to the Principal–Agent Problem (when *a* Can Take Any Value):

1. Suppose the principal can pick any level of *a* or *b* as long as she offers the agent a contract that is attractive enough induce the agent to accept it. Then the profit-maximizing commission rate (b) equals 100% ($b = 1$), both in general and for our baseline production and cost-of-effort functions.
2. Because $b = 1$, *all* the profits earned by the principal come from "selling" the job to the worker ($a \leq 0$, and $\Pi = -a$). Because the agent pays up front for access to the job, then keeps everything he produces on the job, this contract is known as **the franchise solution** to the principal–agent problem.

Why can the principal do so much better now than before? In the previous case (with *a* fixed at zero), the principal had only one tool (*b*) with which to pursue two objectives: *motivating* the agent ("efficiency") and *dividing the pie* between the agent and the principal ("distribution"). This created a trade-off for the principal: incentivizing the agent with a higher *b* generates more output, but the higher *b* means that the principal has to give the agent a larger share of the pie. Now, the principal has two tools. This allows her to use the commission rate (*b*) to motivate the agent (the efficiency goal), while using the show-up fee (*a*) to divide the pie (the distribution goal). The principal no longer needs to keep *b* low for distributional reasons.

An important lesson from this exercise for the optimal design of contracts is that it makes sense to *put rewards where the decisions are made.* A key feature of our basic principal–agent model is that the only party who takes an action after the contract is signed is the *agent.* (We'll relax this assumption later.) When $b < 1$, however, the agent's actions affect not only himself but the principal as well, and a rational, selfish agent will not take those "external" benefits into account when deciding how hard to work. As the mathematics in this chapter have shown, a simple solution to the problem is to give the agent 100% of the marginal returns from his own effort.

3.3 Is It Crazy to Sell the Job to the Worker?

Although the results of Section 3.2 follow inevitably from the assumptions of the basic principal–agent model, on first glance they seem divorced from reality: Aside from a few highly publicized cases of corruption and bribery, who has ever heard of workers having to pay for a job? And isn't it even illegal to charge workers an upfront fee for access to a job?

Whereas "selling the job to the worker" might seem crazy, there are in fact three different senses in which this occurs every day in our economy. The first sense, and probably most common, is that in many cases it is optimal for firms to buy a product from a supplier rather than hire a worker to make that product in-house. (In fact, the *buy-versus-make* decision is one that receives lots of attention in business schools and receives a lot of thought in most firms.) Imagine, for example, that the University of California, Santa Barbara (UCSB) wants students to have options to buy tasty lunches on campus. It is sunny and pleasant most of the time, so having a bunch of food carts outdoors works well. One way to provide those lunches would be for the university to hire some agents to work in them, paying them either a fixed hourly salary ($a > 0$, $b = 0$) or some positive level of base pay plus a share of the proceeds from selling burritos or hot dogs ($a > 0$, $0 < b < 1$). Another is simply to sell the equipment (or simply the right to operate their cart on campus!) to the individual vendors, and let them keep *everything* they earn ($b = 1$). So whenever a firm chooses to "buy" (or if you prefer, outsource) a task rather than pay a worker to do it in-house, there is an important sense in which it has chosen to "sell the job to the worker." A critical lesson from solving our principal–agent problem is therefore the following:

RESULT 3.2 (restated)

The Franchise Solution to the Principal–Agent Problem

If the principal–agent problem is simple enough (as it is in this chapter), the profit-maximizing way to hire a worker may not be to hire him at all. Instead, *buy* the product the worker produces from him. If only you (the principal) have the knowledge, capital, or rights to produce that product, sell those rights to the worker at the best price you can get.

In the second sense, some workers really do pay for the right to work at their job. In addition to the 795,932 franchise owners in the United States (Rogers, 2016), taxi and Uber drivers (who must supply a vehicle) also have to pay up front for their jobs. Hairdressers at "booth rental salons" rent a chair from a shop owner, then keep all their proceeds, as our model predicts (Gentile, 2016). FedEx Ground workers in the United States have to purchase their delivery route from FedEx and buy their own vans (for a total cost of \$22,000 in a recently litigated case), plus purchase their own uniforms, decals, mapping software, and scanner before they can even start work (Rooney, 2014). Manicurists in New York City also pay for jobs, then work for tips until their

The Buy-versus-Make Decision

Whether a firm should produce a product or service in-house or purchase it on the market is one of the most common and important business decisions. Perhaps surprisingly, it is also one of the most profound questions in economics. To see this, notice that—despite all the praise given to free markets by most members of the business community—most resource allocation decisions within firms are not made using markets. When a manager needs more people on project X than project Y, the manager doesn't usually raise wages in division X and cut them in Y hoping that workers will move in response to this price signal. Instead the manager just assigns (orders) some workers to move from X to Y. So, in an important sense, firms are islands of authority in a sea of competition. It's almost as if our economy consisted of a large number of mini-Soviet Unions (within which resources are allocated by fiat), with the important proviso that unlike the Soviet Union, workers are free to leave any firm if they find a better deal elsewhere. Thus, the "buy versus make" decision is really about the boundaries of the firm—should a given activity be conducted inside or outside the boundary—and hence also about whether the firm should use markets or internal authority to produce it.

As you might guess, both markets and authority have their advantages. One advantage of authority is that it can be faster and more reliable: When something very specific needs to happen quickly, it may be best just to order it done. One advantage of markets is that they require less centralized knowledge to operate effectively. The rapid rise of internet-mediated transactions via business-to-business platforms has probably reduced the cost of using markets and increased the extent to which businesses now outsource everything but their core competencies.

boss decides they are skilled enough to earn a wage (Maslin Nir, 2015). As a final example, most strip clubs charge their strippers a flat "house fee" to work. These typically work out to between 10% and 20% of a stripper's nightly earnings (Wu, 2000).

A third group of workers who effectively "buy" their jobs, and who may in fact be earning 100% piece rates are many workers, including salespeople, who are paid by piece rates or commission. To see this, recall first that our measure of the agent's output (Q) is the *total net revenues produced* (for the firm) by the agent. "Net" here means net of all costs that are tied directly to the agent's performance other than the amount paid to the agent himself. For example, if a Sears salesperson sells a $1,000 fridge to a customer that Sears paid $850 for, the salesperson's output or net revenues (Q) is not $1,000, but $150. In this example, a 15% commission on *gross* sales *is* in fact the 100% commission on net revenue predicted by our model.

Whereas the distinction between gross and net revenues explains why the commission rates we see in real sales jobs could plausibly correspond to the 100% rate predicted by our model, what about paying for the job? As it turns out, even workers who don't explicitly pay up front for their sales jobs may do so implicitly. Essentially, this is because the company's pay scheme *builds the job fee into the first few units the salesperson sells.* To see how this works, consider Figure 3.4.

In Figure 3.4, the 45-degree line starting at point a on the vertical axis is the linear reward schedule $Y = a + bQ$ predicted by Result 3.2, with $a < 0$ and $b = 1$. Using the agent's indifference curves, we can depict the agent's optimal effort choice as the tangency point labeled e, with effort level E^*. Because the firm earns all its profits from the job entry fee $(-a)$, its profits $(Q - Y)$ can be shown in the diagram as the vertical distance between the reward schedule and a 45-degree line through the origin. (Notice that because we are using our baseline production function $Q = E$, the horizontal axis measures both the agent's effort and his output, which conveniently lets us plot both the pay schedules and the indifference curves in the picture at the same time.)

The darkly shaded lines in the diagram depict an *equivalent* reward schedule in the sense that it induces the worker to select the same effort level and yields the same output, profits, *and* worker utility as the original one. This reward schedule works as follows: Salespeople who regularly produce less than Q_0 in net revenue (say, per month) eventually lose their jobs; in this sense, Q_0 is the minimum, long-term, average performance needed to keep the job. To keep things simple, we'll just say these workers (at least eventually) are paid nothing. Of the salespeople who stay as relatively permanent employees, those who produce between Q_0 and Q_1 in a given month are paid a constant "base" amount,

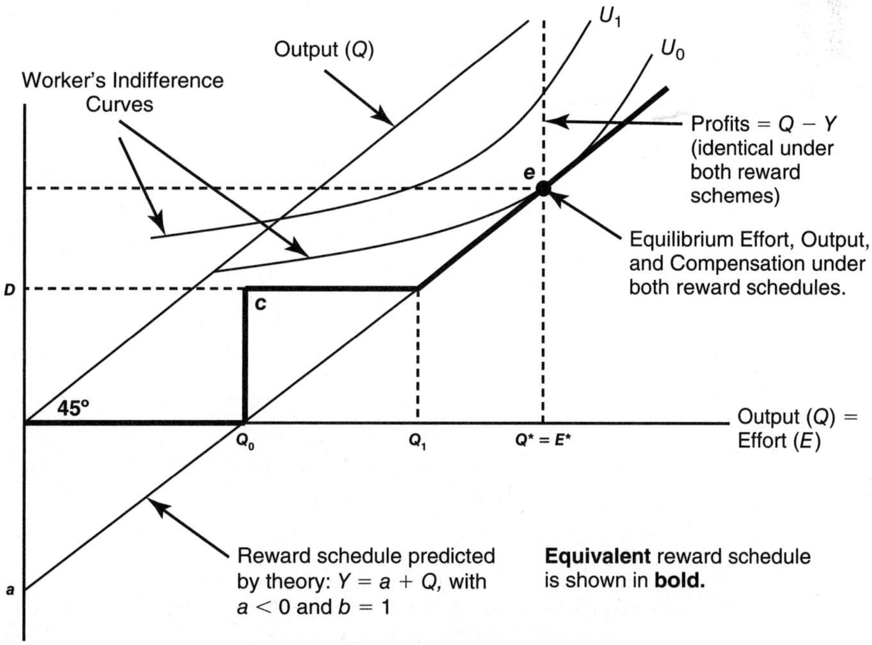

FIGURE 3.4. Charging the Agent for the Job

D, regardless of how much they sell. In some workplaces, *D* is referred to as the salesperson's "draw." Finally, for all sales in the month beyond Q_1, the salesperson keeps 100% of net revenues produced; in this section of the diagram, the new compensation schedule coincides with the original one. Because Q_1 is the level of sales the agent has to reach to qualify for receiving a commission (or to qualify for receiving incentive pay), we'll refer to Q_1 as the agent's sales (or performance) *target*.

Looking at Figure 3.4, it is clear that any agent who picked E^* under the original reward schedule (where he is forced to explicitly pay for his job) will choose to do exactly the same thing under the alternative reward schedule. Everything else (profits, utility, output) will also be exactly the same.[3] But under the new scheme, nobody is explicitly paying for their job. Instead they are doing so implicitly: One way to think about the new arrangement is that in effect, *the salesperson has agreed, every month, to sell the first Q_0 units for free* (or equivalently if you prefer, the salesperson sells the first Q_1 units for a total pay of *D*, which is less than those units are worth to the principal). After that, the agent gets to keep all he makes.

RESULT 3.3 **Equivalent Pay Schemes**

Pay schemes in which a salesperson (worker) has to attain a minimum sales (performance) level in a given period to qualify for a commission (incentive pay) are one way in which workers effectively pay for jobs ($a < 0$).

Chapter Summary

- If we arbitrarily force the fixed component of the agent's pay (*a*) to equal zero, the principal's optimal commission rate (*b*) must trade off two objectives: inducing the agent to supply effort ("efficiency"—which requires a higher *b*) and keeping as much of the agent's output as possible ("distribution"—which requires a lower *b*).

- In general, the tension between these two objectives means the principal's optimal commission rate when $a = 0$ is strictly between zero and one. In the special case of our baseline cost-of-effort function, $V(E) = E^2/2$, this number is exactly 50%, that is, $b^* = 0.5$.

---

[3] The key to making this work, of course, is to make sure the "draw" is not too attractive, and that the sales target (Q_0) is high enough. For example, if *D* was too much higher, the indifference curve through the original optimum (labeled U_0) would pass below the "corner" of the budget constraint at point *c* (which will be vertically above where it is now). If that were the case, salespeople will choose to produce Q_0 instead of Q^* under the new compensation scheme, shattering the equivalence of the two schemes.

- ☐ When the principal and agent are free to agree on any level of a, the profit-maximizing contract that satisfies any given worker participation constraint has workers paying firms for jobs, and a 100% commission rate, that is, $a <= 0$ and $b = 1$.

- ☐ Although it seems unrealistic to think of workers "paying" for jobs, there are at least three important senses in which this happens regularly in the real world. One is that "selling the job to the worker" is effectively what firms do when they buy a service on the market rather than producing it in-house. Second, some workers (including franchisees) explicitly pay for jobs; and a third group do so implicitly by being required to produce a minimum level of output to qualify for an incentive-pay plan.

Discussion Questions

1. In Section 3.1, we argued that there was a parallel between the principal–agent problem when $a = 0$ and the well-known Laffer curve for a government's tax revenues. What does the full solution to the principal–agent problem in Section 3.2 suggest about optimal tax policy? How practical is this suggestion?
2. "Incentive pay exploits workers by forcing them to work hard just to make a living. Therefore we can make workers better off by banning incentive pay." Comment, in light of this chapter's results.
3. "It is unethical to ask workers to pay for the right to work at any job." Comment, in light of this chapter's results.
4. Can you think of any other jobs (besides those listed in Section 3.3) where workers pay firms up front for the right to work there? What features distinguish these jobs from jobs without entry fees? Can these features help explain why upfront fees are used there?

Suggestions for Further Reading

For readers interested in the buy-versus-make decision and the boundaries of the firm, Coase (1937), Simon (1951), Alchian and Demsetz (1972), Weitzman (1974), and Williamson (1975) are all classic papers.

References

Alchian, A., & Demsetz, H. (1972). Production, information costs, and economic organization. *American Economic Review, 62,* 777–795.

Coase, R. (1937). The nature of the firm. *Economica, 4,* 386–405.

Gentile, M. (2016). How does commission work at a hair salon? *Chron.com*. Retrieved from http://work.chron.com/commission-work-hair-salon-21357.html

Maslin Nir, S. (2015, May 7). The price of nice nails. *New York Times*. Retrieved from https://www.nytimes.com/2015/05/10/nyregion/at-nail-salons-in-nyc-manicurists-are-underpaid-and-unprotected.html?_r=1

Rogers, K. (2016, March 15). The franchise industry has gotten more good news. *CNBC*. Retrieved from http://www.cnbc.com/2016/01/20/us-franchises-set-to-grow-in-2016-report.html

Rooney, B. (2014, November 21). The FedEx driver who sued and won. *CNN Money*. Retrieved from http://money.cnn.com/2014/11/20/news/companies/fedex-driver-lawsuit/

Simon, H. A. (1951). Formal theory of employment. *Econometrica, 19,* 293–305.

Weitzman, M. L. (1974). Prices vs. quantities. *Review of Economic Studies, 41*(4), 477–491.

Williamson, O., Wachter, M., & Harris, J. (1975). Understanding the employment relation. *Bell Journal of Economics, 6*(1), 250–278.

Wu, K. (2000). Stripper-faq. Retrieved from http://www.stripper-faq.org/faq.htm

Best for Whom? Efficiency and Distribution

4

So far, we've characterized the contract that maximizes the principal's profits, subject to the constraint that the contract needs to be (at least minimally) acceptable to the agent. This seems like a realistic way to think of the situation facing a principal who is hiring an agent to do a job. But is the best contract for the principal also the best one for the agent, or for the two of them as a group? In Chapter 4 we'll show, perhaps surprisingly, that in a well-defined sense it is. Specifically, we'll first define an *economically efficient* contract as the contract that maximizes the *sum* of the principal's profits and the agent's utility, and we'll show that all economically efficient contracts have the same optimal structure ($a \leq 0$, $b = 1$) as the profit-maximizing contract we just studied.

Further, because lump sum payments between firms and workers (a) can be used to redistribute resources between workers and firms, contracts with $a \leq 0$ and $b = 1$ are the best ones to choose, *regardless of how much we care about helping workers versus firms*. Indeed, these contracts are the best arrangement *even if we care only about workers*, that is, if our goal is to make workers as well off as possible subject only to the constraint that the principal earns enough profits (zero) to agree to employ them.

4.1 Economically Efficient Contracts

Instead of caring only about the principal, suppose now that we care about *both* the principal and the agent in designing our optimal contract. Specifically, suppose that our "ideal" contract (a, b) is one that maximizes the *sum* of the principal's profits and the agent's utility, or *social welfare* (W), as defined by Equation 4.1.

$$W = \Pi + U. \tag{4.1}$$

Another way of saying this is that we care only about the total size of the "pie," W, that emerges from the interaction of the principal and agent, not about who gets what share. Another phrase we'll use for W (in addition to social welfare and the "pie") is *total social surplus*.[1]

DEFINITION 4.1 **Economically efficient** contracts maximize the sum of the principal's profits plus the agent's utility, $W = \Pi + U$. Words that are frequently used to refer to W include *social welfare, social surplus*, and the "size of the pie" to be divided between workers and firms; all these terms mean the same thing in this book.

To find the economically efficient contract in our model of principal–agent interactions, we start by noticing that Equation 4.1 can be written as follows:

$$W = (Q - Y) + [Y - V(E)], \tag{4.2}$$

or just

$$W = Q - V(E). \tag{4.3}$$

The algebraic step from Equation 4.2 to Equation 4.3 actually contains an important insight: Whereas payments from the firm to the agent (Y) make the firm worse off and the agent better off, *the total amount the firm pays the worker subtracts out of our definition of social welfare* because raising or lowering Y just "moves money (or utility) around" without affecting the total amount of utility that is produced. Equation 4.3 provides a very simple expression for the social surplus that is generated by any contract: It just equals the total amount produced, Q, minus the cost of producing it, $V(E)$. Exchanges of money between the principal and agent are irrelevant unless those exchanges affect the amount of output that is produced.

Having figured out which function we need to maximize (Equation 4.3), we can now follow the same steps we used in Chapter 3 to find the economically efficient levels of a and b, assuming that agents will optimize against any contract that is written. Substituting the baseline production and cost-of-effort functions and the agent's optimal behavior ($E = b$) into Equation 4.3 now yields

$$W = b - b^2/2. \tag{4.4}$$

Aside from a constant term, this is identical to the expression we maximized to solve the original principal–agent problem (Equation 3.14). Thus the social-welfare-maximizing contract and the profit-maximizing one *have the same solution for b*: $b = 1$. Further, notice that the maximized value of W (i.e., the biggest pie that can be produced with our baseline production and utility functions) is $W^* = 1 - 1^2/2 = 0.5$.

[1] Notice that our definition of social surplus in this book includes only the principal and the agent; thus, it ignores other parties such as consumers as well as *other* firms and workers. For most purposes, this does not matter; in cases where there could be important effects of contractual arrangements between workers and firms on third parties, we'll indicate that in the text.

> ☑ **RESULT 4.1**
>
> **The Economically Efficient Contract**
>
> Just like the principal's most preferred contract, the economically efficient contract (which maximizes the sum of the principal's profits plus the agent's utility) has a 100% commission rate ($b = 1$).

4.2 Dividing the Pie: What's Feasible?

Once we've made the pie as large as possible (at $W = 0.5$ in our baseline example) how much utility and profits can we allocate to the principal and the agent? Because $b = 1$, as we've already noted, $\Pi = -a$. The agent's utility is given by $U = a + Q - V(E) = a + W = a + 0.5$. Thus, by choosing a level of a between 0 and -0.5, we can divide W between the agent and principal in any way we like. Figure 4.1 illustrates the situation. The pie (W) in this figure is given by the horizontal distance of 0.5 between the two thick vertical lines. When $a = 0$ (at the rightmost line), profits are zero (because the worker pays nothing for the job) and the agent's utility is $a + W = 0.5$. Because zero (economic) profits is the lowest level any principal would accept, the highest agent utility we can attain is also 0.5. When $a = -0.5$, profits are 0.5, and utility equals zero.[2] Intermediate levels of a split the surplus between the agent and principal; for example, when $a = -0.2$, profits are 0.2 and utility is 0.3. Thus, in general, the worker's share of the pie is the distance between a and the leftmost line (at -0.5); and the firm's share is the distance between a and the rightmost line (at zero).

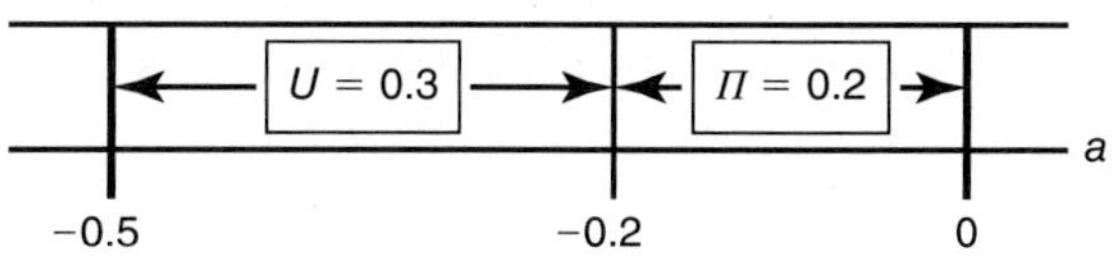

FIGURE 4.1. Feasible Levels of Profits and Utility with an Economically Efficient Contract (Base-Case Example)

The main point of Figure 4.1 is that once a "pie" (in this case a social surplus of $W = 0.5$) is produced, workers and firms can agree to split that pie in any way they like. Thus, regardless of whether we personally care more about the well-being of workers or firms, we (as personnel economists) feel confident in advising contracting parties to make economically efficient arrangements. In the basic principal–agent problem, this means setting $b = 1$ to make the distance between the two bold vertical lines in Figure 4.1 as large as possible.

[2] Of course, if the worker has an outside option, U^{alt}, that is strictly greater than zero, the worker would not accept this contract. For example, if $U^{alt} = 0.25$, as it was in Table 3.1's example, workers will only accept contracts to the right of a = -0.25 in Figure 4.1.

RESULT 4.2

Economically Efficient Contracts Are the Best Ones Regardless of One's Distributional Preferences

Contracts that maximize the *total social surplus* produced by the interaction of the agent and principal are the best ones to choose, regardless of which party's well-being you want to maximize.

To sum up this short chapter, we have found that the optimal contract between a principal and an agent has a 100% commission rate ($b = 1$) regardless of whose welfare (the agent's, the firm's, or both) we want to maximize. This is because *it makes sense to maximize the size of the pie regardless of how we ultimately decide to divide that pie.* Essentially, because we can allocate the surplus that is produced any way we want by adjusting the size of the fixed payment between the parties (a), we can devote each of our two parameters, a and b, to two separate objectives: Choose b to maximize the size of the pie, which requires $b = 1$ (this is the efficiency objective), then choose a to divide the pie however you want (the distribution objective).[3]

Thus, the contract that maximizes social surplus ($W = \Pi + U$) is the "best" contract in a very general sense: It's best *regardless of your distributional preferences.* For this reason, throughout the rest of this book we'll focus our attention on identifying such *surplus-maximizing* contracts. As we do so, please remember that the contracts we thus identify as optimal are the best ones regardless of whether you are a "loony leftist" (who cares only about workers' utilities), or a "raving rightist" (who cares only about firms' profits), or something in-between. This book is about identifying social arrangements (contracts) that make sense *regardless* of your distributional preferences.

Chapter Summary

- ☐ When a principal–agent contract can stipulate both a fixed payment (a) and a contingent payment (b), there is no conflict between efficiency and distribution: Both principals *and* agents will prefer a contract that sets $b = 1$ over contracts with other levels of b.

[3] A well-trained reader will recognize that this convenient separation between efficiency and distributional goals results from our (implicit) assumption of *transferable utility.* We'll maintain this assumption throughout the book because it seems reasonable that financial transfers between firms and workers can be arranged to attain any desired goal that is consistent with both parties' participation constraints.

- ☐ In part, this is because setting $b = 1$ maximizes social welfare, which is defined in this book as the sum of profits and utility. This makes the pie that is shared between the firm and worker as large as possible.

- ☐ The combinations of the principal's profits and agent's utility that are attainable in a principal–agent relationship are, in general, illustrated by the length of a line segment in a diagram such as Figure 4.1. Setting $b = 1$ makes this segment as long as it can possibly be, allowing us to achieve the largest possible range of utilities or profits. It is therefore the best policy, regardless of one's distributional preferences between workers and firms.

Discussion Questions

1. Making workers pay for their jobs, then strongly linking their pay to their performance, sounds pretty draconian. Yet in the simple model we have studied so far, this is exactly what workers want. What aspects of reality might our model have omitted, which might explain our model's counterintuitive result?

2. One way to think about this chapter's lesson is that the principal and agent should think about their relationship as follows: "First let's figure out how to make the pie we can produce together as big as possible. Then let's figure out how to divide it." This seems like good advice for other economic interactions too. What would be some examples?

5 Extensions: Uncertainty, Risk Aversion, and Multiple Tasks

In the analysis we've done so far, we've made a lot of assumptions, and we've reached two strong conclusions: Specifically, the optimal b is 100%, and the optimal a is less than or equal to zero. Some of these assumptions were made just for convenience—to simplify the math—whereas others really matter. Changing those assumptions could dramatically change the nature of the optimal contract. In Chapter 5, we'll start by going over all the assumptions we've made so far and work out which ones matter for our two key results ($a \leq 0$ and $b = 1$) and which ones don't. We'll then spend some time studying how the model's predictions change when some of its key assumptions are relaxed. Finally, we'll look at some real-life examples of what happens when those assumptions don't apply.

5.1 Which Assumptions Matter? Which Ones Don't?

Let's start with a list of assumptions we've made just for convenience. They simplify the math without changing the main result that $b = 1$ and $a \leq 0$.

1. *The production function is linear:* $Q = E$ in the baseline case, and $Q = dE$ in our more general case.

Notice that this production function assumes there are no diminishing returns to the agent's effort, which may not be realistic. But adding diminishing returns would just add a little algebra and not change the result. As a matter of fact, we could change this production function to almost any increasing function, $Q(E)$, and still get both our main results: $b = 1$ and $a \leq 0$.

2. *The cost-of-effort function is quadratic*: $V(E) = E^2/2$ in our baseline case.

We used this quadratic function to derive all the results in Chapters 3 and 4. Relaxing this assumption doesn't change our results: All we need is for $V(E)$ to be increasing, eventually at an increasing rate.

3. *The contract is linear,* $Y = a + bQ$.

As it turns out, even if we allow the firm to pick any $Y(Q)$ function, if agents are fully rational, the firm can't do any better than with the optimal linear $Y(Q)$.[1] That said, firms sometimes use nonlinear incentive schemes, like lump sum bonuses for attaining a certain target, for reasons we discuss in elsewhere in the book (e.g., they may provide useful focal points for agents [Section 10.4] or help to coordinate a team [Section 24.4]). We'll discuss some complications raised by these nonlinear incentives in Section 5.6.

4. *There is no uncertainty in the production process.*

We have assumed, without discussing it much, that if the agent picks a given effort level E, both the agent and the firm know exactly how well he is going to perform his task, Q. In reality, of course, luck matters: Sometimes a bad outcome occurs even when the agent works hard (e.g., the rare event of bad weather on the UCSB campus could occur, so very few burritos are sold); sometimes even lazy workers get lucky and do well.

So it might be more realistic to write the production function as $Q = dE + \varepsilon$, where ε is a *random variable* whose realization isn't known when the contract is being agreed on. Perhaps surprisingly, making this change doesn't alter our main results ($b = 1$ and $a \leq 0$) either, *under one very important condition*: The agent needs to be risk neutral. If that is the case, whenever Q appears in our algebra, we can simply replace it with its expected value, and all the same results continue to go through.

5. *The agent produces a single type of output.*

Again without any discussion, we have created a caricature of a "job" by imagining that our principal cares only about one summary measure of what the agent does: How much "Q" does he produce? But it's hard to think of very many jobs that are even close to that simple: Even a *McDonald's* server needs not only to serve customers quickly but also to get the order right, smile, flip the burgers at the right time, prevent grease fires, and make change correctly (just for starters). As it turns out, this isn't a problem at all for our model *if* the principal is able to separately observe the agent's performance on every one of the tasks he is asked to perform *and* to base the agent's reward on his performance in every one of the tasks. Thus, for example, a comprehensive, multidimensional performance review could be a way of implementing the optimal incentive plan derived in this chapter. Essentially, this review could let the principal set $b = 1$ on every task the agent performs.

---

[1] For a demonstration of this result in a much more general context, see Holmstrom and Milgrom (1987).

6. *There's only one agent.*

If agents don't interact with each other in the production process, then nothing is really lost by thinking about a principal's interactions with each of several agents in isolation from one another. A consumer hiring a lawyer to sue a store for negligence and a contractor to renovate her kitchen can probably write separate contracts with each of these people along the lines we have discussed already without thinking about how they relate to each other. The same may be true of FedEx Ground, which writes individual incentive contracts with each of its drivers linking their pay to their performance.

And now here are five *assumptions that really do matter.* We'll explore the first two later in this chapter. The third and fourth assumptions are studied in Parts 4 and 5 of this book, which study tournaments and teams, respectively. We encounter the fifth at many points in the book because *repeated interactions* are an important feature of virtually all principal–agent interactions.

1. *Adding uncertainty and risk aversion together.*

If there is uncertainty in the production process *and* the agent is risk averse, the optimal contract may no longer have a 100% piece rate. It is also possible that the optimal level of a is positive. The reason, as we'll show in the following, is that a 100% piece rate could expose the agent to a great deal of risk. For example, a residential solar energy salesperson paid on a pure 100% commission basis could see his income go from many thousands of dollars in one quarter to a negative amount (if they pay for the job and/or cover their own costs) in another. If principals are less risk averse than agents, they might be wise to absorb some of this risk themselves rather than pass it on to workers. As we'll show, bundling a little insurance into the employment contract might actually *raise* the firm's profits by allowing it to pay workers a lower (but more predictable) level of total compensation.

2. *Adding multiple tasks and partial observability together.*

Although (as noted) multiple tasks per se do not change the main results from this section, things can get very different if the principal cares about multiple things the agent does, but the principal cannot measure (and hence reward) the agent's performance on some of the tasks he does. An oft-discussed example is the case of teachers: Although it may be easy to reward some aspects of teachers' performance by tying teacher pay to students' test scores, there may be other, less tangible aspects of "what teachers do" that parents and schools care about but can't measure reliably. Such activities might include teaching "soft skills," such as communication and leadership that are harder to measure, and mentoring students more generally. Cases like these are referred to as *multitask principal–agent problems*, and we will study them in Section 5.5. There, we'll show that weak incentives, or even *no* incentives ($b = 0$), might be the best policy.

3. *Involving the principal in the production process.*

A crucial feature of the way we have set up our problem so far is that *the only party that takes an action after the contract is signed is the agent*, who picks effort at that time. But what if some things the *principal* does after the contract is signed also affect the amount of output (Q) that is produced? For example, in the hiring-a-lawyer example, the agent (lawyer) probably needs the principal's continued cooperation to mount an effective case. In this instance, the principal probably needs to provide important information, documentation, and testimony to help win the case. Similarly, the car salesman's performance might depend on the amount of advertising done by the owner of the dealership, or on how the dealer maintains the premises. In both of these cases, it might be quite unwise for the principal to "wash her hands" of responsibility for getting the job done by effectively selling the job to the agent. Situations like these, where production depends on the actions of more than one party after the contract is signed, are called *team production* problems. As noted, we'll study them in Part 5 of this book.

4. *Multiple agents who interact in the production process.*

Although having multiple agents per se doesn't affect our analysis, that is not the case when agents interact with each other in the production process. We'll first encounter such interactions in Section 10.7 when we examine workers' concerns with how they're treated by the principal, compared to their coworkers. We'll then devote two entire parts of the book to study competitive interactions among workers (Part 4 on tournaments) and cooperative interactions (Part 5 on teams).

5. *Repeated interactions between principals and agents.*

Although we have focused so far on a one-shot interaction between a principal and agent, most principal–agent interactions take place repeatedly and over time, sometimes lasting for a worker's entire career. Repeated interaction introduces possibilities for workers and firms to react to each other in ways we haven't considered yet, such as *punishing or rewarding* each other for past actions and acquiring *reputations* (e.g., for being a hard worker or a tough boss). Because repeated interactions are so pervasive, we'll study them at many points throughout the rest of the book. The first time is later in this chapter when we discuss the problem of *timing gaming* in Section 5.6. In the study of procrastination in Section 9.7, we'll look at how workers allocate effort over time. In Chapter 10, we study employment relationships as repeated "gift exchanges" (of effort and pay) between workers and firms. Investments that firms make in workers (that pay off later) come up in our study of hiring risky workers (Chapter 13), recruiting and screening workers (Chapters 14 and 15, respectively), and training (Chapter 19). Selection and incentive effects of how workers' pay levels change over time are treated in Sections 15.4 and 18.3 respectively, and workers' advancement through multistage promotion ladders in Section 22.4. Finally, we look at how workers discipline their teammates for their past actions in Section 25.1.

5.2 Uncertainty and Risk Aversion: State-Contingent Contracts

Suppose that instead of $Q = dE$, our production function takes the form

$$Q = dE + \varepsilon, \tag{5.1}$$

where ε is a random variable with a mean of zero. The idea of ε is to capture a wide array of possible unpredictable events in the production process that are outside both the agent's and principal's control. For example, the profitability of a wide array of activities (including farming, retail, ski resorts, construction, and golf clubs) is affected by the weather. Indeed, weather plays such a large role in many economic outcomes that it's common to refer to the realization of ε as the "state of nature."[2] Fluctuations in the local, national, or international economies can have an even more widespread effect on an individual worker's capacity to generate revenues for his or her employer. And of course there's just plain luck: one hundred medical researchers searching for a new antibiotic might all work equally hard trying out different formulations more or less at random, but only one researcher might find a formula that works.

Because piece rates tie a worker's pay to performance, using a 100% piece rate when there's a lot of uncertainty in the production process could expose the agent to a lot of income risk.[3] Of course, if the agent is risk neutral, this is not a problem: $a \leq 0$ and $b = 1$ is still the optimal contract. But if workers are risk averse *and* firms are risk neutral (or at least less risk averse than workers), the best contract from both the firm's and the worker's point of view may be for the firm to build some insurance into the employment contract. The way this works, and whether it requires the firm to reduce the commission rate below 100%, depends on whether it's possible to measure the state of nature with sufficient objectivity that it can be written into the employment contract.

In the rest of this section, we'll consider what happens when the answer to this question is "yes"; this is the case of state-contingent contracts. We'll consider non-contingent contracts in Section 5.3. In both cases, we'll abstain from deriving the optimal contracts mathematically (by now you should have a pretty good idea of how this might go); I'll just tell you what they look like.[4]

Imagine a car dealership with a loyal, experienced sales force. And imagine also that there's an objective, reliable indicator of whether the current month is an easy or a hard month in which to sell cars. More specifically, imagine (just to simplify the exposition) that the state of nature, ε, can take only two possible values—ε_g and ε_b—with $\varepsilon_g > \varepsilon_b$, and g and b denoting good and bad times, respectively. So, in good times, a salesperson's performance is $Q = dE + \varepsilon_g$; and

---

[2] Air pollution can also have unpredictable effects on workers' productivity. For recent evidence, see Graff Zivin and Neidell (2012).

[3] Because $Y = a + bQ$, Equation 5.1 implies that $Y = a + b(dE + \varepsilon)$. Thus, if ε is highly variable and b is high, a worker's pay could fluctuate dramatically due to factors like weather or business conditions that are outside the worker's control.

[4] Readers interested in more detail should look at Harris and Raviv (1978).

in bad times, $Q = dE + \varepsilon_b$: An agent working equally hard sells more in good times than in bad. The dealership's salespeople are risk averse, but (at least to a first approximation) the owner is risk neutral. This may be because the dealership (due to its size) has better access to capital and insurance markets than an individual worker or simply because the dealer has more wealth with which to cushion month-to-month economic fluctuations.

Now suppose it is possible to write and enforce employment contracts between firms and workers that explicitly depend on the state of nature. Instead of stipulating a single ordered pair (a, b), such *state-contingent contracts* can stipulate, if desired, a different a and b for each possible state of nature. In our current example, this means that the contract now consists of two ordered pairs: (a_b, b_b) and (a_g, b_g). In other words, the contract can have a different intercept, and a different slope, in good times versus bad times.

As it turns out, the best state-contingent contract when firms are risk neutral and workers are risk averse has a 100% commission rate in both good and bad times ($b_b = b_g = 1$), but a higher (i.e., less negative) intercept in bad times than good, that is, $a_b > a_g$. It is even possible to have $a_b > 0$ if bad times are particularly bad, but the expected level of a must still be negative if the dealership is to earn any profits. The optimal pay schedules in the two different states of nature are illustrated in Figure 5.1.

The optimal state-contingent contract gives agents some stability in their take-home pay by giving workers a higher pay intercept in bad times. Because this insurance is provided purely through the intercept of the reward schedule, it is possible to preserve the agents' 100% marginal incentives by keeping the slope of the pay schedule at 100% in both good and bad times. Finally, recall from Figure 3.4 that, instead of explicitly paying for the right to sell cars each month (the way taxi drivers pay up front each week to drive a cab), salespeople may *implicitly* pay for this right by needing to sell a minimum "target" number of cars to qualify for the (100%) incentive pay system. If this is the way the dealership

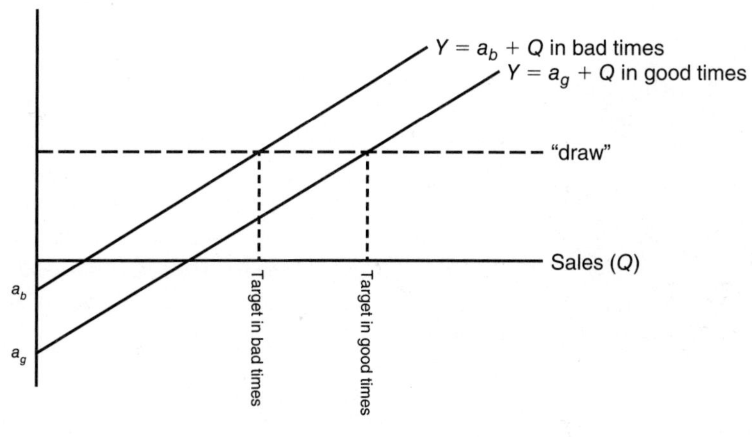

FIGURE 5.1. The Optimal State-Contingent Contract for Risk-Averse Workers

works, the scheme in Figure 5.1 (with $a_b > a_g$) can also be implemented by keeping the salesperson's "draw" the same in good and bad times but raising his sales target in good times (relative to bad times), as shown. Thus, by raising the standards workers need to meet to qualify for incentive pay in good times, firms can insure workers without compromising incentives.

☑ RESULT 5.1

The Profit-Maximizing, State-Contingent Contract for Risk-Averse Workers

If firms are risk neutral, workers are risk averse, and the employment contract can be explicitly indexed to the state of nature, the profit-maximizing contract sets $b = 1$ in all states, but insures workers by offering a higher intercept (a) in worse states of nature. Now, the optimal a could be positive in some states.

5.3 Optimal Non-Contingent Contracts

If we can't write the state of nature into the employment contract (or, more likely, we *choose* not to because we can't measure the effects of nature very accurately), it is no longer possible to offer agents a payment (a) that depends explicitly on whether times are good or bad. All we can do is to design a single "one-size-fits-all" (or *non-contingent*) compensation schedule $a + bQ$ that applies to all possible states of nature. We won't solve this problem explicitly here, but the solution is pretty intuitive.[5] Specifically, it has four key features, described in Result 5.2.

☑ RESULT 5.2

The Profit-Maximizing, Non-Contingent Contract for Risk-Averse Workers

If firms are risk neutral, workers are risk averse, and the employment contract cannot be indexed to the state of nature, the profit-maximizing contract has the following features:

1. The optimal commission rate, b, is now less than 1.
2. The optimal commission rate declines as the amount of uncertainty in the production process (i.e., as the variance of ε, or simply the difference between ε_g and ε_b) rises.
3. The optimal commission rate declines as the worker's level of risk aversion rises.
4. For sufficiently high levels of uncertainty or risk aversion, the optimal a can be positive.

[5] Interested readers should again consult Harris and Raviv (1978).

Intuitively, because firms are (by assumption) less risk averse than workers, there are still potential gains from trade if the firm insures workers against fluctuations in their income between states. But now the only way to do this is by blunting the incentives in the contract (i.e., reducing b). The optimal b, instead of only incentivizing workers, now has to trade off two objectives: incentives *versus* insurance. The more uncertain the world is, and the more workers value predictability in their earnings stream, the lower the optimal b will be. Thus, medical researchers searching for a new drug are typically paid a very stable salary, even though their output is highly uncertain. The same is true of development officers, who might bring in only a few thousand dollars in donations in some years and many millions in the next.[6]

The Principal–Agent Problem and the Economics of Insurance

If you have studied the economics of insurance (or if you recall the debate during the Great Recession about whether the government should bail out insolvent banks), you have probably heard the term "moral hazard." Moral hazard refers to the fact that insuring someone changes that person's incentives to avoid the loss they are insured against. For example, having generous car insurance might induce drivers to take more chances on the road, to be less consistent about locking their parked car, or to be less consistent with their car maintenance.

You might be surprised to learn, though, that the mathematics behind Result 5.2 are in fact identical to the mathematics of moral hazard in insurance. To see this, return to our example of car insurance, where the insurance company and the driver take the roles of the principal and agent, respectively, in this book. Just like our principal, the insurance company is hoping to make money by protecting its customers from fluctuations in their wealth (in this case the value of their car). And just like our agent, the insurance customer chooses an action (care) that has a direct effect on the amount of wealth that is available.

Although it might be desirable to offer both the worker and the car driver complete protection against possible losses, this is impractical in the worker's case because it destroys work incentives, and in the car insurance case because it reduces the incentives to take care (i.e., it creates moral hazard). Thus, in both cases, the optimal non-contingent contract has to trade off insurance versus incentives. In the worker's case, generous insurance (low b) blunts work incentives. In the car insurance case, generous insurance (in the form low of deductibles and low levels of coinsurance) blunts the customer's incentives to avoid having a loss. The optimal contract, in both cases, provides *some* insurance ($b < 1$), but less than full insurance ($b > 0$).

[6] There may be other more important reasons (than employee risk aversion) for the lack of incentive pay for development officers. Indeed, the Council for Advancement and Support of Education (2016) strongly recommends against incentive pay, in part to avoid encouraging "inappropriate conduct by fundraisers anxious to secure gifts at any cost." Major gifts, which often require long-term cultivation, could be jeopardized by fundraisers seeking a swift donor response to benefit their own personal compensation goals. We discuss these types of reasons for avoiding incentive pay in Section 5.5, where we study multitask principal–agent problems.

Importantly, note that offering insurance to risk-averse workers *doesn't lower the firm's profits*. In fact, if the contract offered to workers gives them their alternative utility level, U^{alt}, firms who are smart enough to offer insurance to their workers will make more profits than firms who don't because they can attract workers at a lower wage than the firms whose pay is more unpredictable. This benefit to firms occurs while keeping the workers at least as happy as they were before, so providing insurance to risk averse workers yields a net welfare gain to society.

5.4 Evidence on the Insurance-Incentives Trade-off: Sharecropping in the South

Is there any empirical support for Result 5.2's prediction that optimal agency contracts should provide more insurance when the production process is subject to greater uncertainty? One source of evidence comes from a study of agricultural contracts in the postbellum South (Higgs, 1973). To see this, think of a principal (landowner) hiring an agent (worker) to farm land owned by the principal. The main contract types the principal might consider are the following:

1. **Pure wage labor ($b = 0$):** Pay the worker a fixed amount per hour (or week, or season) worked, regardless of the amount of corn or cotton that is harvested. Although it gives the worker no cash incentives to increase farm output, this contract exposes the worker to very little risk from factors, such as the weather, which influence crop yields.

2. **Share contracts ($0 < b < 1$):** Here, the agent's pay is a share, b, of the crops he grows in a season. Just as in our model, the principal gets whatever is not paid to the agent ($1 - b$). There is of course an infinite number of possible share contracts depending on the value of b, although in practice most contracts used very simple fractions such as a half or a third. Higher levels of b give the agent stronger incentives but expose him to more risk.

3. **Rental contract ($b = 1$):** Here, the landowner simply rents the land to the agent for a fixed dollar amount for the season ($a \leq 0$, just like the taxi driver rents the car for the week). The agent keeps the entire crop. Here, both risk and incentives are high. For ex-slaves with little or no assets to fall back on, being exposed to this much income risk may have been highly unattractive and could even expose them to the threat of starvation if the weather is bad.

Prior to conducting his study, Higgs (1973) collected data on the year-to-year variation in corn and cotton yields in hundreds of Southern counties. He found that due to differences in weather patterns, agricultural production was much more uncertain in some counties than others, and these patterns in "unpredictability" were different for corn and cotton. Higgs then went on to ask which types of contracts were used for *which* crops in *which* locations, finding two key results. First, as the uncertainty in production went up, fewer pure rental contracts ($b = 1$) were used, and more pure wage-labor contracts ($b = 0$) were used. Thus, the overall mix of contract types shifted in the direction of contracts that insure workers more and incentivize them less. Second, looking only within the share contracts, as the uncertainty in production went up, the farmer's share of the output went down.

Did these patterns emerge because landowners in counties with unpredictable weather were worried about their workers' well-being? This seems unlikely given the tense race relations between white landowners and the many former slaves who worked the land under the preceding contractual systems. Instead, as our theory suggests, it is likely that landowners in unpredictable areas took advantage of their greater wealth to bundle some insurance into the contracts they offered, as the theory predicts. If the theory is correct, then landowners who offered more insurance (e.g., a wage labor contract or a low share) should have been able to extract a lower expected wage from their workers in return for this predictability. Indeed, desperate former slaves may have been willing to make big sacrifices in their expected level of compensation in return for greater predictability of their income.

5.5 Multitask Principal–Agent Problems

Another important extension to our basic model is to ask how things change when the principal has more than one task she'd like the agent to do at the same time. Although workers in some jobs perform a single activity whose output can be easily measured, most jobs are multidimensional. A professor, for example, not only teaches but is also expected to conduct original research and to perform administrative tasks like admissions and faculty recruiting. Computer programmers and home renovators have to balance the goal of completing a project on time with the goal of keeping quality high. Even salespeople, whose output (sales) would seem to be one-dimensional, need to balance the gain from making a quick sale against treating customers fairly and honestly to maintain the reputation of the company. Indeed, simply *behaving honestly* could be viewed as an important second aspect of almost any job and an aspect that principals may care a lot about.

How do multiple tasks change the results from our basic principal–agent model? If the principal can observe and reward the agent's performance on all aspects of the job, very little changes. In fact, you could just think of the agent as holding multiple "mini" jobs simultaneously and being rewarded optimally for each task. At the end of each year, for example, a professor might receive separate bonuses for her research, teaching, and administrative performance. And according to the basic model, her incentives should be high powered ($b = 1$) on *every* aspect of the job unless employee risk aversion plays a major role. Indeed, a central component of employee *performance management systems*, like the *Balanced Scorecard* system or *360 Degree Feedback*, is to evaluate employees' performance in highly multidimensional jobs.

Problems arise, however, when some aspects of a job that matter a lot to the employer cannot be measured well, or at all. In these cases, the optimal incentive scheme can change dramatically because incentivizing the tasks you *can* measure leads rational agents to emphasize those tasks, while neglecting the non-incentivized tasks. The consequences of incentivizing some but not all of a worker's tasks range from the amusing to the disastrous.

Incentive Problems in Multitask Environments: Some Examples

On the amusing end of the spectrum, consider the case of Ken O'Brien, an NFL quarterback in the 1980s. O'Brien had a reputation for throwing too many interceptions. To correct this problem, one of his contracts included a financial penalty for every interception thrown. The result ended up being even worse for the team because he simply stopped throwing the ball! And have you ever wondered why Charles Dickens's books sometimes seem to wander, going off on tangents unrelated to the main story line? The reason may lie in the structure of his contracts with his publishers, which had a very specific format. Dickens was paid one shilling for every installment (which was published monthly). Each installment contained 32 pages of text, two illustrations, and various advertisements. Thus Dickens was paid to produce a certain number of pages of text each month, which incentivized him to "fill up" every installment with sufficient text, whether it contributed to the overall quality of the novel or not.[7]

In the "important, but not quite disastrous" category, Griffith and Neely's (2009) study of a leading UK distributor of heating and plumbing products found that (inadvertently) incentivizing only part of a job led to inefficient behavior. At this company, individual pay depended (in part) on profits at each local branch office. How did workers respond? In addition to trying harder to serve the needs of their existing customers, salespeople also worked hard to "steal" business from other branches of their own company. In addition, branch managers emphasized short-term profits at expense of longer term customer loyalty and satisfaction, for example, by encouraging workers to "upsell" customers into items they didn't really need.

In five factories in China's Fujian province (producing GPS devices, alarm devices, and clocks), Hong, Hossain, List, and Tanaka (2013) studied the effects of introducing strong cash incentives, worth about 40% of a worker's base pay, for extra units of output produced. For workers who previously faced no cash incentives, these led to a huge (50%) increase in the number of units produced. Output quality, however, which was not explicitly incentivized, fell dramatically: The defect rate on items that were (randomly) inspected increased by 97%!

Finally, in this category, Jacob and Levitt (2003) looked at how Chicago teachers responded to the introduction of high-powered incentives. Specifically, a standardized test of student achievement (the Iowa Test of Basic Skills), which was previously used only for informational purposes, became the basis for putting

[7] For more details, see University of California, Santa Cruz, *The Dickens Project*, Was Dickens Really Paid by the Word? Retrieved from https://dickens.ucsc.edu/resources/faq/by-the-word.html.

schools "on probation." Schools were automatically put on probation if less than 15% of their students scored at or above national norms on the test. Probation schools that didn't exhibit sufficient improvement could be closed, with their staff being dismissed or reassigned.

As other studies have shown (e.g., Jacob, 2003; Figlio & Getzler, 2006), high-stakes testing might have several undesirable side effects, such as neglecting nontested areas ("teaching to the test") or shifting low-performing students out of the classroom into special education. Jacob and Levitt (2003), however, focus on another side effect: *cheating by teachers*. Perhaps shockingly, in at least 4%–5% of classrooms subject to high-stakes testing, answer patterns on tests revealed that some form of cheating by teachers or administrators must have occurred. Possible mechanisms include changing student responses on answer sheets, providing correct answers to students, or illegitimately obtaining copies of an exam prior to the test date. Clearly, these responses by teachers did not serve the incentives' goal of raising student achievement.

Finally, on the disastrous side, between 2011 and 2015, Wells Fargo Bank (one of the largest in the United States) relentlessly pursued an internal goal of selling at least eight financial products to each customer, an initiative the company called the "Gr-eight initiative." Reportedly, managers and workers were under tremendous pressure (in terms of job security, raises, and advancement) to sell additional products (internally referred to as "solutions") to their existing customers, a practice also known as *cross-selling*. According to a lawsuit filed by Los Angeles against Wells Fargo in May 2015, some Wells Fargo district managers pushed these goals by discussing daily sales for each branch and employee "four times a day, at 11 am, 1 pm, 3 pm and 5 pm" (Egan, 2016, September 9).

To meet these stringent goals, as you might expect, employees (sometimes at the behest of their managers) engaged in practices that neglected another important dimension of the job: honesty and the company's long-run reputation. According to a consulting firm hired by Wells Fargo, these practices included opening over 1.5 million deposit accounts without a customer's permission and submitting applications for 565,443 credit card accounts without the customer's knowledge or consent (Egan, 2016, September 8). Another practice was internally called "pinning," in which an employee issued ATM cards and assigned PIN numbers to customers without their authorization. According to the Los Angeles lawsuit, employees would impersonate their customers and "input false generic email addresses such as 1234@wellsfargo.com, noname@wellsfargo.com, or none@wellsfargo.com to ensure the transaction is completed" (Egan, 2016, September 9).

What were the consequences for the company? During the month of September 2016, when this news became public, Wells Fargo's stock lost 12.8% of its value. Wells Fargo agreed to pay penalties of $185 million; and its longtime CEO, John Stumpf, was forced to retire. Wells Fargo scrapped its controversial "Gr-eight" sales goals on October 1, 2016. All in all, 5,300 workers were eventually fired for dishonest behavior, and morale at the company since the scandal has been described as "toxic." According to a Wells Fargo mortgage consultant, customers now assume "Wells is scamming them." The consultant was taking Xanax to control his panic attacks and said, "It's beyond embarrassing to admit

I am a current employee these days. My family and friends think I'm a fraud for working at Wells" (Egan, 2016, November 3).

Did Excessive Incentives Cause the Great Recession? The Countrywide Case

In October 2008, the U.S. and international financial systems almost collapsed when major financial institutions were forced to acknowledge that a large share of their assets—specifically, mortgage-backed securities—were worthless. The ensuing collapse of the real economy is now known as the Great Recession and is widely acknowledged to be the worst downturn in the U.S. economy since the Great Depression of the 1930s.

The story of how the world's major financial institutions acquired so many worthless assets is a long one and is well told in several easy-to-watch documentaries, such as *The Big Short* and *Inside Job.* Interestingly, from the point of view of Personnel Economics, high levels of employee incentive pay at various points in the system may have played a contributing role. To see this, we consider the case of Countrywide Financial Corporation. Countrywide was a mortgage *originator,* that is, a company that markets mortgages to the general public. Although a relatively small player in this market in the 1990s, Countrywide grew rapidly to have the largest share of the market in the United States (15.5%) by 2007. During this period of rapid expansion, Countrywide relied heavily on incentive pay for its originators, with incentive pay amounting to about 40% of base pay during the 1990s, then rising sharply to a peak of 100% in 2004 (and remaining over 60% till the company's demise).[8]

Importantly, however, incentive pay at Countrywide depended only on the type and *dollar value* of loans originated; the performance metric did *not* depend on whether the borrower eventually defaulted. This practice of ignoring the loan's long-term performance was frowned on by many lenders at the time and incentivized Countrywide's originators to lend the largest amounts possible to borrowers, regardless of their ability to pay. Thus, Countrywide became known as specializing in low-quality or "sub-prime" loans—including loans with low teaser rates that reset to double-digit levels, loans with prohibitive prepayment penalties, and the now-notorious *ninja loans* (mortgages given to individuals with "no income, no job, and no assets").

What were the consequences of these practices for Countrywide, especially as interest rates rose and the supply of qualified new borrowers began to dry up? By June 30, 2007, almost one in four sub-prime loans serviced by Countrywide was delinquent. In October 2008, Countrywide settled a civil suit with eleven state attorneys general over alleged predatory lending practices. In the settlement, Countrywide agreed to $8.4 billion in direct loan relief for some 400,000 mortgagers—the largest predatory lending settlement in history. The failing Countrywide Corporation was acquired by Bank of America in July 2008, which spent years litigating its responsibility for bad loans originated by Countrywide.

[8] See Eastburn (2011) for these statistics.

In August 2014, Bank of America agreed to a near $17-billion settlement relating to the sale of toxic mortgage-linked securities, a large percentage of which had been sold by Countrywide (Eastburn, 2011).

Countrywide's chairman and CEO, Angelo Mozilo, retired when the company was sold to Bank of America. A year later (in June 2009), the Securities and Exchange Commission (SEC) indicted him for fraudulent misrepresentation of credit and market risk inherent in the Countrywide mortgage portfolio. In the film *Inside Job*, Mozilo is cited as one of the persons responsible for the economic meltdown of 2008. He was named by *Time Magazine* as one of the "25 People to Blame for the Financial Crisis." And *Condé Nast Portfolio* ranked Mozilo second on their list of "Worst American CEOs of All Time."[9]

The case of Countrywide contrasts somewhat with Wells Fargo's in that Countrywide's incentive plan appears to have been *deliberately designed* to ignore loan quality. Indeed, because Countrywide sold the mortgages they originated to others (who then packaged them into financial instruments called Collateralized Debt Obligations—CDOs—which they in turn sold to third parties), Countrywide had no financial interest in the mortgages' long-term performance. Thus, rather than being a by-product of a perhaps overzealous incentive scheme, the emphasis on quantity over quality was a *feature* of the company's business strategy.[10] Because the collapse in the value of low-quality CDOs was what precipitated 2008's financial collapse, employee incentive plans in companies like Countrywide appear to have played a role in creating the Great Recession. Thus, and most important for our purposes, *getting employees' incentives right matters*. Designing incentive pay is not just a minor concern of HR departments: It is a central component of business strategy with implications for the long-term success of companies, and indeed for the entire economy.

We summarize all the previous examples of "incentives gone wrong" in a multitask context with the following definition and result:

DEFINITION 5.1 In a multitask, principal–agent context, **incomplete incentives** refer to financial incentives that apply only to a strict subset (i.e., to some but not all) of the tasks performed by an agent that a principal cares about.

☑ RESULT 5.3

Effects of Incomplete Incentives in a Multitask Context

When a principal employs an agent to perform multiple tasks she cares about, but the principal uses incomplete incentives to motivate the agent, we expect agents to re-allocate their effort toward the incentivized tasks and away from the non-incentivized tasks. The results can be highly undesirable for the principal.

[9] These facts are from Wikipedia's article on Angelo Mozilo.

[10] See Morgenson (2007) for a detailed analysis of Countrywide's performance pay plan.

When Are Effort-Allocation Problems Most Likely in a Multitask Context?

Under what conditions are agents' effort-shifting responses to incomplete incentives likely to be *most* problematic for the principal and for economic efficiency? To state these conditions, a few definitions are helpful first.

DEFINITION 5.2 In a multitask, principal–agent context, two tasks are **complements to the principal** if the principal strongly prefers the agent to do *some of each* task versus doing only one or the other. Tasks are **substitutes to the principal** if the principal (although benefiting from both tasks) is roughly indifferent as to how the agent allocates his effort across the tasks.

In a multitask, principal–agent context, two tasks are **complements to the agent** if the agent strongly prefers to perform *some of each* task to doing only one or the other. Tasks are **substitutes to the agent** if the agent doesn't care too much which one he performs (as long as he's at work anyway).

Although task complementarity and substitutability can be defined and studied mathematically, in this section, we'll stick with the preceding intuitive definitions. Essentially, two tasks are complements to a principal if it's really important to her that both be done. For example, the principal may care both that a sale is made *and* that it be done legally and ethically. Tasks are substitutes when principals don't care very much how the agent allocates his effort between then. The head of a research lab, for example, may not care much which of several projects a scientist pursues as long as the outcome yields a patentable invention. From the agent's point of view, tasks are complements if the agent prefers doing a mix of them. For example, if the agent prefers splitting her day between time working at her desk and in-person meetings versus spending the entire day doing one of these activities, these two activities are complements. If the agent doesn't care about the mix of her activities during the day, the tasks are substitutes.

RESULT 5.4 Task Substitutability and Agents' Responses to Partial Incentives

The mix of tasks chosen by the agent will be most sensitive to task-specific financial incentives when tasks are *substitutes to the agent*.

This makes sense: When agents don't care too much how they allocate their effort across tasks, attaching a financial incentive to one task but not another will lead to a large re-allocation of the agent's time and effort. The consequences of this re-allocation for the principal (and for economic efficiency), however, depend on how the principal views them.

RESULT 5.5

Effects of Task-Specific Financial Incentives on Economic Efficiency

The efficiency costs of partial financial incentives will be greatest when the tasks are *complements to the principal and substitutes to the agent*. Efficiency costs will be lower when the tasks are substitutes to the principal, or when they are complements to the agent.

This also makes sense. If the principal really needs both tasks to be done, but the agent doesn't care which one he performs, incentivizing the agent in only one of the tasks will lead to a large reallocation of the agent's effort: an outcome the principal really doesn't like. On the other hand, if the principal doesn't care which job is done, she isn't harmed by changes in the agent's effort allocation. Or, if the agent strongly prefers a mix of tasks, he won't reallocate his effort much when just one task is incentivized.

Efficient Contracts in Multitask, Principal–Agent Problems

Having described the effort-misallocation problems that can arise in multitask, principal–agent interactions, and the conditions under which those problems are likely to be most severe, we now ask how these problems can be *remedied*.

One obvious way to mitigate the effects of partial incentives is to try to **design more complete performance measures** that "leave nothing out." As already mentioned, employee performance management systems, such as the *Balanced Scorecard* system or *360 Degree Feedback*, aim to do just this. Although they appear to have achieved some success, certain hard-to-measure aspects of employee performance—in particular, various types of dishonest behavior that people have a strong incentive to hide—may always remain beyond the reach of these management systems.

Given that 100%-complete performance measures will probably never be feasible, a second approach is the same as the optimal response to agent risk aversion: **reduce the strength of incentives** (i.e., pick a level of b that is substantially below 100%). Although this may reduce the agent's performance on the incentivized task (e.g., selling more furniture), it may have the beneficial effect of increasing his attention to the hard-to-observe, non-incentivized tasks such as cultivating long-term customer relationships. In fact, under some conditions, economists have argued that a policy of **zero explicit financial incentives** ($b = 0$) might be the economically efficient contract between the agent and principal in a multitask context.[11] The situations in which low, or zero, incentives are likely to be optimal are summarized in Result 5.6.

[11] Probably the earliest formal argument that zero incentives might be the optimal policy in a multitask environment was Farrell and Shapiro's (1989) *principle of negative protection*. For more formal derivations of the results in this section, see Holmstrom and Milgrom's (1991) seminal article. Lundesgaard (2001) provides a more accessible mathematical derivation of their arguments; and Dewatripont, Jewitt, and Tirole (2000) provide a nice, short summary of the main results.

RESULT 5.6 **Weak or Zero Financial Incentives ($b \approx 0$) May Be Economically Efficient in Multitask, Principal–Agent Contracts, Especially when:**

(a) only partial incentives are possible;
(b) effort-misallocation effects of partial incentives are likely to be severe (i.e., tasks are complements for principals and substitutes for agents);
(c) agents have high levels of *intrinsic motivation*; and
(d) *input-based employment contracts* are a good substitute for performance-based contracts.

Intrinsic motivation, that is, *positive* utility derived from doing a job well (as opposed to the *dis*utility of effort we've been assuming so far in the book) will assure that agents continue to supply reasonable effort levels even in the absence of explicit performance incentives. We'll study intrinsic motivation further in, Section 9.2. *Input-based employment contracts* differ from the performance- (or output-) based contracts we've studied so far in this book because they base workers' pay on various indicators of their inputs to the production process that are correlated with effort. Definition 5.3 explains this in more detail.

DEFINITION 5.3 So far, all the employment contracts we have studied in this book are **output-based**, in the sense that they link workers' pay, *Y*, to some measure of their output or "performance," *Q*, via a function *Y(Q)*. In part, this is because we have ruled out contracts that link pay directly to worker effort, *E*, as being infeasible.

Although perfect measures of effort are probably never available, some aspects of workers' *inputs* to the production process are imperfect indicators of how much effort was exerted. Examples include the total number of hours spent at the workplace or logged onto the company server, the number of personal phone calls and emails that are sent, and visits to non-work-related websites. Employment contracts that link pay and other sanctions to these sorts of measures are called **input-based contracts**. For example, an input-based contract might enforce strict business hours, prohibit working from home, and place limits on the types of Internet use and personal phone calls made during the work day.

Job Design in Multitask Environments

So far in this section, we've assumed that jobs consist of a fixed set of tasks, some of which may have easily measurable performance and some of which may not. But in many cases, especially when firms have a large number of tasks to do, those tasks can be bundled into jobs in many different ways. Finding the best way to do this is an important aspect of HR research and Personnel Economics and is called the problem of optimal *job design*. As it turns out, a final way to mitigate effort-misallocation problems associated with multitask problems involves improvements to job design.

To see how this works, imagine a sales and marketing division that has two employees and four tasks that need to be performed: domestic sales, domestic market research, international sales, and international market research. For the sake of argument, let's say that sales performance is easy to measure, but the performance of market researchers is not. If the company assigns one of the two employees to domestic issues, and the other to international ones, and gives both employees high sales commissions, they will both neglect their market research duties, and the company's long-term growth might suffer due to a failure to identify new market segments.

One way to address the problem would be to organize jobs by function rather than by region. In the new, redesigned jobs, one person would do both domestic and international sales. If she gets a 100% commission on her sales (regardless of destination), there is no aspect of her job she'll neglect. Thus, the tasks with easy-to-measure outputs are grouped together into a job where incentive pay is high. Notice that it probably makes sense to give the employee a considerable amount of discretion in this job: that employee has every incentive to use time wisely because his or her financial incentives are closely aligned with the company's. Also, the company may not need to recruit very carefully for this job: Because pay is strictly by performance, relatively little is lost by letting people "try their hand" at the job and quit if they're not successful. The second employee in the new job categorization handles all the market research. Here, output is hard to measure, so cash incentives are unlikely to be effective. Instead, the market researcher may have a much more *input-based* contract with less discretion. The researcher's job might have strict business hours, prohibit working from home, and so forth. The company might also be well advised to recruit more carefully for this job, to identify someone who truly enjoys market research for its own sake. Summarizing the general principles behind our example is Result 5.7:

☑ RESULT 5.7

Using Job Design to Mitigate Effort Misallocation in Multitask, Principal–Agent Problems

To minimize the reallocation of agents' effort from hard-to-observe toward easy-to-observe tasks, employers may consider grouping easy-to-observe tasks into the same jobs and the hard-to-observe tasks into other jobs.

In the easy-to-observe jobs, financial incentives should be strong ($b \approx 1$). Employee discretion can be high, and careful screening to identify new employees with high intrinsic motivation and low desires to shirk is less important.

In the hard-to-observe jobs, financial incentives should be weak ($b \approx 0$). Employees should be given less discretion about work hours and other input-related measures. Careful screening to identify new employees with high intrinsic motivation and low desires to shirk is more important here.

To be sure, many important considerations other than effort substitution affect optimal job design. For example, information flows also matter; and if it's important for the domestic market researcher to have personal contact with domestic customers, this consideration could outweigh the moral-hazard-related considerations underlying Result 5.7. The main takeaway from Result 5.7 is that job design is an important tool that should be considered when dealing with *any* HR policy problem, including multitask agency situations.

5.6 Nonlinear Incentives and the Timing Gaming Problem

Gaming Nonlinear Incentives

We've already noted that in our basic principal–agent model, there's no point in making the agent's reward schedule $Y(Q)$ any more complicated than a linear function, $Y = a + bQ$. Sometimes, however, firms do use nonlinear reward schemes, such as lump sum bonuses if an agent reaches a performance target, or "accelerating" piece rates that increase with the amount produced. We'll discuss reasons why firms might want to use such policies later in the book. In this section, our goal is to describe an important consequence of nonlinear incentives known as *timing gaming*. This pitfall applies to *all* situations in which an agent faces a nonlinear reward schedule on a repeated basis.

To illustrate the timing gaming problem, imagine an automobile sales agent (we call him Rodrigo) who is paid on a monthly basis according to the $Y = R(Q)$ schedule in Figure 5.2. Under this nonlinear $R(Q)$ schedule, the agent's commission rate (i.e., the slope of the curve) starts out high but decreases as he sells more and more units, that is, it has a *decelerating* piece rate. Economists and mathematicians refer to functions of this type (whose slope diminishes as we move from left to right) as *concave* functions.[12]

DEFINITION 5.4 Concave and convex functions of one variable: A function, $R(Q)$, is concave if its slope diminishes as Q increases. It is convex if its slope increases as Q increases. Equivalently, using calculus, concavity means that $R''(Q) < 0$ and convexity means that $R''(Q) > 0$, where the double primes denote second derivatives.

Imagine that Rodrigo sells $Q_1 = 12$ cars in one month (Month 1) and $Q_2 = 4$ cars the next (Month 2). If he is paid according to the concave reward schedule $R(Q)$, his average monthly sales over those 2 months, $\bar{Q}$, is 8 cars, and his average monthly pay over those 2 months, $\bar{Y}$, is given by $[R(Q_1) + R(Q_2)]/2$.

[12] A note to the mathematically inclined: To simplify the presentation, we use the terms convex and concave to imply *strict* concavity or convexity here. Thus, a linear function is neither concave nor convex.

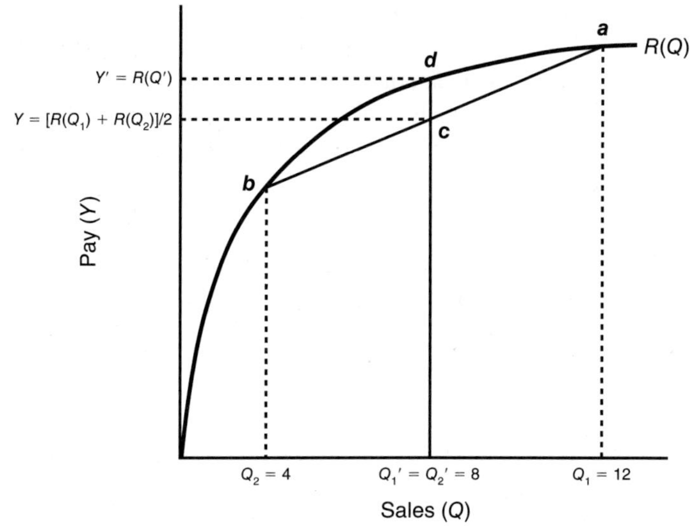

FIGURE 5.2. Timing Gaming with a Concave Reward Schedule

Diagrammatically, this is given by the height of a ray drawn between points *a* and *b* on the $R(Q)$ curve, at $\bar{Q} = 8$ units of sales, that is, by the height of point *c*.[13]

Now imagine that near the end of Month 1, Rodrigo (who is on track to sell 12 cars that month) already knows that Month 2 is going to be much slower. Anticipating this uneven sales pattern, Rodrigo finds a way to "move" some of his Month 1 sales into Month 2. This could be done a number of ways, such as slowing down some paperwork, offering a customer a free upgrade if the customer signs on the first of the next month instead of the last of the current month, or simply logging the sale later than he should. To make the math and the picture simpler, imagine that Rodrigo is able to do this with four of the 12 vehicles he initially expected to sell in Month 1. Thus his *recorded* sales are $Q_1' = Q_2' = 8$ cars in both months, and he'll earn $R(Q') = R(8)$ dollars in each of those months, which is given by the height of point *d* in Figure 5.2. Because $R(Q)$ is concave, this exceeds his average monthly pay when Rodrigo doesn't "game" the pay system. Thus, by strategically shifting his recorded output so as to *even it out* between periods, Rodrigo can "game" a concave pay schedule in a way that may not be in his employer's or his customers' best interests.

Now, let's consider a *convex* reward schedule, with an accelerating commission rate, as shown in Figure 5.3. Now imagine Rodrigo is on track to sell eight

[13] To see this, note that the slope of the line between points *a* and *b* equals $[R(Q_1) - R(Q_2)]/(Q_1 - Q_2)$. Denoting this slope by *s*, the height of point *c* is then given by $R(Q_2) + s(Q_1 - Q_2)$, which yields the stated result.

cars in Month 1 and expects to sell eight in Month 2 as well. Thus, $Q_1 = Q_2 = 8$, a very constant pattern of sales over time, which would yield a pay of $R(Q)$ per month, at point *d* in Figure 5.3. To improve on this by "timing gaming," Rodrigo now needs to *widen* the difference in sales between the 2 months, in this case from zero to a positive number. One way to do this, as before, is to delay the (recorded) sale of four cars into Month 2, making Rodrigo's sales now look very *uneven* across the months: four in Month 1, and 12 in Month 2. Rodrigo's average monthly income with these recorded sales is $Y' = [R(Q_1') + R(Q_2')]/2$, which is given by the height of point *c* in Figure 5.3. Because his reward schedule is convex, this is higher: The extra income from his really "big" (recorded) month exceeds the lost income from his "bad" month. Thus, Rodrigo is again incentivized to distort the timing of his reported output. Finally, note that Rodrigo could have achieved the same result if instead of *delaying* four sales into Month 2, he induced or pressured four customers to buy *earlier*—in Month 1 instead of Month 2. The key point is that concave pay schedules reward constant sales patterns, and convex pay schedules reward variable sales patterns, thus inducing agents to generate recorded sales patterns that fit those patterns, regardless of whether this is in the firm's or the customers' interests.

Finally, before summarizing all these results, consider a linear incentive scheme. If you imagine a version of Figure 5.2 or 5.3 with *any* linear $R(Q)$, you'll see immediately that all these incentives for "timing gaming" are gone: Nothing can be gained by moving sales across periods or misreporting sales dates. This *immunity to timing gaming* is an important advantage of linear incentives. Result 5.8 sums it up.

RESULT 5.8 **Only Linear Reward Schedules Are Immune to Timing Gaming**

Concave reward schedules, *R*(Q), incentivize agents to change the timing of recorded output to be as *constant* as possible over time.

Convex reward schedules, *R*(Q), incentivize agents to change the timing of recorded output to be as *variable* as possible over time.

Linear reward schedules are the *only* type that does not incentivize agents to manipulate the timing of their actual or reported output.

Whereas Figures 5.2 and 5.3 show the cases of "smoothly" increasing and decreasing piece rates, respectively, many other forms of nonlinear compensation schemes are of course possible. These include piecewise-linear schemes where different piece rates apply to different ranges of output, schedules that are concave at some output levels and convex at others, and bonus schemes where pay "jumps" up discontinuously when a performance target has been attained. Similar arguments to those in Figures 5.2 and 5.3 can be used to show that *any* nonlinear scheme creates opportunities for agents to profit by timing gaming. In this chapter's Discussion Questions, there's a simple example of how to "game" a bonus pay scheme for you to work out.

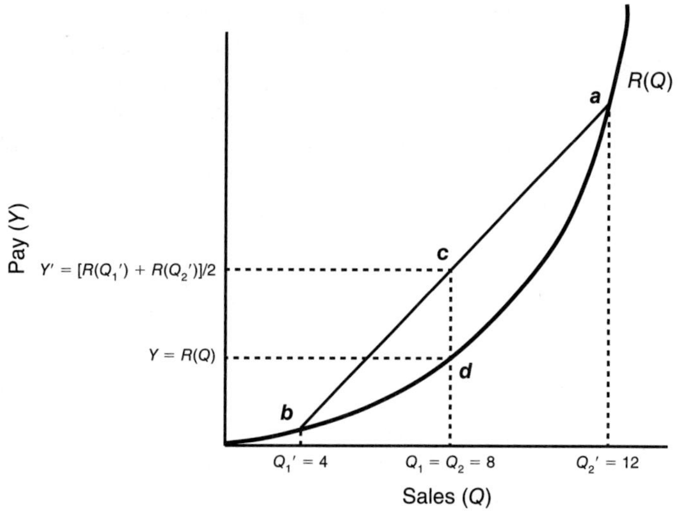

FIGURE 5.3. Timing Gaming with a Convex Reward Schedule

Is timing gaming a significant problem in real organizations? In a careful study that followed 981 U.S. **manufacturing firms** over 32 quarters, Oyer (1998) shows that sales in these companies exhibit strong *fiscal-year effects*, tending to increase as the end of a company's fiscal year approaches. Because firms' fiscal years differ substantially—over a third of companies' fiscal years end between January and November—Oyer can rule out simple seasonality as a source of these effects and instead links fiscal-year effects to incentive contracts for managers and salespeople. These contracts generally take the form of a bonus for reaching a sales or profit target (for salespeople and managers, respectively) in a fiscal year. Oyer argues that these fiscal-year effects (which are not necessarily in shareholders' interests) result, at least in part, from the ability of some salespeople (such as those who work closely with customers over a long buying cycle) to influence the timing of customer purchases. Supporting Oyer's explanation, the fiscal-year seasonality he detects is more pronounced in companies where salespeople and executives can affect the date of customer purchases.

Whereas Oyer does his best to infer timing gaming of sales from *company-level* data, Larkin (2014) uses detailed data on performance of **individual salespeople of enterprise software** (such as the systems produced by Oracle, IBM, and SAP). As in many business-to-business technology companies, these salespeople faced a convex reward schedule, that is, they had an *accelerating* commission scale. This meant that a salesperson's commission for the same deal could vary dramatically depending on the quarter in which the deal closes. Importantly, Larkin was able to show not only that these salespeople gamed the system by manipulating the timing of sales, but that this behavior was quite costly to their employer. In particular, Larkin found that salespeople agreed to significantly lower pricing in quarters where they had a financial incentive to close a deal; the resulting mispricing cost their employer about 6%–8% of revenue.

Closely related to our theoretical car-sales example, Owan, Tsuru, and Uehara (2013) conduct a detailed study of individual salespeople at **two car dealerships** in Canada. These salespeople faced a highly nonlinear and accelerating reward schedule that "jumped up" at certain points. For example, the marginal reward to selling a 12th, 14th, and 16th car in a month were $1,400, $1,200, and $1,400, respectively, compared to only $200 for the first through the 11th cars, creating tremendous incentives to change the timing of sales in certain situations. Owan et al. provide strong evidence of such behavior, including the fact that 23% of all sales were made on the last day of the month. Also, it was clear that salespeople discounted prices to game the system: The cars the agents had the strongest incentives to sell (e.g., their 12th in a month) were priced much lower than other units.

Nonlinear compensation schemes can also distort firms' **accounting decisions**. For example, Healy's (1985) much-cited analysis notes that bonus schemes create incentives for managers to time accruals to maximize the value of their bonus awards.[14] Using information on the structure of managers' bonus contracts at 94 companies, Healy found a strong association between accruals and managers' income-reporting incentives: Managers were more likely to choose income-decreasing accruals when they were at a maximum or minimum

Did Fiat Chrysler Automobiles (FCA) Pay Auto Dealers to Mis-Date Sales?

In another example relating to car sales, Valdes-Dapena (2016) reports on a federal lawsuit filed by two car dealers accusing Fiat Chrysler of paying dealers to falsely report sales of dozens of vehicles on the last day of the month, and then to "back-out," or undo the sales on the first day of the next month. FCA's purported motive for doing so was to allow them to inflate the company's reported year-over-year sales figures. According to the suit, the payments from Fiat Chrysler for faking sales were to be counted as an "advertising credit" to avoid triggering an audit. FCA was also accused of rewarding dealers who mis-dated sales by giving them more hot-selling cars in later months in return for falsely reporting sales of those vehicles in earlier months. Of course, accelerating the timing of sales can only benefit a company for a limited period of time; so why would Fiat Chrysler engage in this behavior? Apparently it had been on a "winning streak" with 69 consecutive months of year-over-year sales increases and didn't want to break the pattern!

[14] In accounting, an expense can be *accrued* (and thus deducted from accounting profits) at a different time from when the money is actually paid out. Although firms are expected to use a consistent method to define their accruals, in practice there can be considerable flexibility in when an expense or revenue item is recognized. In Healy's (1985) case, this flexibility allowed managers to opportunistically change the timing of revenues and expenses to maximize their personal bonuses.

income in their bonus plan (so their pay was not sensitive to profits) and to choose income-increasing accruals otherwise (when their pay was affected by accounting profits).

Finally, Benson (2015) provides an interesting analysis of timing gaming by 7,492 **sales managers** who were the immediate supervisors of 61,092 salespeople, mostly doing business-to-business sales. Benson's data come from 244 firms that subscribed to a cloud-based service for processing sales compensation. In Benson's case, both the sales managers and their subordinates had sales quotas. (Managers' quotas applied to the total amount sold by their subordinates.) Managers had some discretion to hire and fire their subordinates and in some circumstances were allowed to adjust their subordinates' quotas.

As we have seen in other contexts, sales managers who were just below their own fiscal year quota in Benson's data had a strong incentive to "pull sales into" the current fiscal year from the next year, to "make their quota." How could they do this, given that they weren't actually engaged in sales themselves? First, Benson shows that managers who were just under quota near the end of the year were much less likely to dismiss underperforming salespeople than at other times. This is because replacement salespeople take quite a while to train; thus, even an underperforming incumbent performs better than a new hire *in the short run*. Second, managers who were just under quota were much more likely to adjust their underperforming subordinates' quotas downward near the end of the fiscal year. Although companies normally frown on downward quota adjustments, sometimes these are the best way to motivate salespeople who have had a bad year for reasons outside their control. Still, downward quota adjustments should be used sparingly, and there is no obvious reason for *salespeoples*' quota adjustments to depend on whether *managers* are just below their quota. In sum, by being "easier" than they should normally be on their subordinates when managers are just shy of their own quotas, the managers "bumped up" their subordinates' sales at the end of a fiscal year in ways that do not reflect their company's long-term interests.

☑ **RESULT 5.9**

Evidence of Timing Gaming

Studies of fiscal year revenues of U.S. manufacturing firms, of salespeople selling enterprise software and cars, of managers' accounting decisions for accruals of costs and revenues, and of sales managers' personnel decisions all show significant timing gaming effects for two types of nonlinear incentive schemes: lump sum bonuses and accelerating commission rates. In some of these cases, the gaming resulted in significantly higher costs or lower profits for the firm.

Importantly, Result 5.9 *does not mean* that firms should avoid nonlinear incentives, which are in fact quite popular forms of variable pay. Instead, Result 5.9 summarizes an important *cost* of nonlinear reward systems. In any actual workplace, these costs must be weighed against the possible benefits of nonlinear reward schemes, some of which we'll study later in this book.

Chapter Summary

- Many of the assumptions in our simple principal–agent model are not essential to our main result (Result 3.2), that $a \leq 0$ and $b = 1$ in the optimal contract. These noncritical assumptions include the linear production function, the quadratic disutility-of-effort function, the linear contract, and the absence of uncertainty in production (as long as the agent is risk neutral).

- Other changes to our assumptions that can dramatically alter our main result are (a) adding both production uncertainty *and* agent risk aversion; (b) involving the principal in the production process; and (c) giving the agent multiple tasks, some of which are hard to incentivize directly.

- In situation (a), the optimal contract depends on whether the contract can depend directly on the state of nature. If it can—the case of state-contingent contracts—the optimal contract still has $b = 1$ in all states of the world because the contract insures the agent by making the fixed payment (a) more generous to the agent in bad times.

- If contracts cannot be state contingent, then the optimal contract needs to trade off a desire to incentivize agents (via a high b) against a desire to insure them (via a low b). This is the same trade-off faced by insurance companies worried about inducing moral hazard when they reduce their customers' exposure to risk.

- When contracts have to trade off insurance and incentives, we'd expect optimal contracts to offer more insurance (lower b) when the production process is inherently riskier. Higgs's evidence on postbellum agricultural contracts in the Southern United States is consistent with this prediction.

- The multitask, principal–agent problem redirects our attention from inducing agents to work *hard* to inducing them to work *smart*. In many cases and in many ways, the most important aspect of motivating agents is not getting them to devote more effort, concentration, and hours to their jobs but inducing them to use their time at work wisely—allocating their time and energies to all the tasks that matter for the principal, not just some of them.

- Incomplete incentives in a multitask environment can cause agents to neglect the non-incentivized aspects of their job. The results can be highly undesirable for principals, especially when the neglected aspects include honesty and affect the long-term interests of the firm. In these cases, the optimal incentive scheme can involve zero performance incentives ($b = 0$), relying instead on input-based rules and intrinsic utility to motivate workers.

- Job design (the way tasks are bundled into jobs) can also be used to mitigate effort-misallocation problems in a multitask setting and is a useful tool to consider when addressing other HR challenges as well.

- ☐ Timing gaming is an important potential cost of nonlinear incentive schemes whenever agents and principals interact over several periods of time. In these situations, nonlinear incentives encourage agents to re-allocate actual *or* reported output between periods in ways that may not be in the principal's (or society's) interests.

Discussion Questions

1. Equation 5.1 introduced uncertainty into the production process as follows: $Q = dE + \varepsilon$. One consequence of this assumption is that the marginal productivity of additional effort, d, is the same regardless of the state of nature, ε. Is this realistic?
2. How would you write the production function if, instead, effort was more productive in good times? (For example, it might be easier to sell an extra car when the local economy is good than when it is bad.) How do you think that might change the results in this chapter?
3. Other than agricultural contracting, what are some additional situations where contracts have to trade off incentivizing agents against a desire to avoid exposing agents to excessive risk?
4. Have you ever been in a job where "incentives went wrong," in the sense that attempts to encourage some forms of profit-enhancing behavior "backfired" by encouraging employees to neglect other, potentially more important activities? If so, describe the situation, and the task switching that employees engaged in. In your opinion, were these tasks substitutes or complements to your employer? Propose a change to the company's HR policy to address this misalignment of incentives.
5. Imagine you are a car salesperson with a bonus contract that pays you $3,000 in a month if you sell less than 10 cars, and $4,500 if you sell 10 or more. If you expect to sell eight cars each of the next 2 months, discuss how you can game this system to raise your average monthly pay from $3,000 to $3,750. Illustrate using a diagram like Figure 5.2 or 5.3.
6. Now imagine you are expecting sales of eight cars this month and 12 next month. Show, verbally and diagrammatically, how you can raise your average monthly pay from $3,750 to $4,500 by "timing gaming."

Suggestions for Further Reading

For a skeptical assessment of the importance of risk-incentives trade-offs like those studied by Higgs (1973), see Prendergast (2000).

For recent laboratory evidence of the risk-incentives trade-off, and an extension of the model to incorporate loss aversion (as distinct from risk aversion), see Corgnet and Hernán-González (2015).

For additional empirical examples of multitask agency problems, see Brickley and Zimmerman's (2001) study of a business school; Fehr and Schmidt's (2004) and Oosterbeek, Sloof, and Sonnemans's (2011) lab experiments; and Bartel, Cardiff-Hicks, and Shaw's (2013) study of a law firm.

Multitask agency models also have useful applications to the key issue of project selection among innovators. For example, see Hellman and Thiele (2011) and Onishi, Owan, and Nagaoka (2016).

Effects of nonlinear reward schemes on the timing of actual and reported performance have also been documented for Navy recruiters (Asch, 1990), and for students in introductory economics courses (Oettinger, 2002).

References

Asch, B. J. (1990). Do incentives matter? The case of navy recruiters. *Industrial and Labor Relations Review, 43*(3), 89S–106S.

Bartel, A., Cardiff-Hicks, B., & Shaw, K. (2016). Incentives for Lawyers: Moving Away from "Eat What You Kill". *Industrial Labor Relations Review, 70*(2), 336–358.

Benson, A. (2015). Do agents game their agents' behavior? Evidence from sales managers. *Journal of Labor Economics, 33,* 863–890.

Brickley, J. A., & Zimmerman, J. L. (2001). Changing incentives in a multitask environment: Evidence from a top-tier business school. *Journal of Corporate Finance, 7,* 367–396.

Corgnet, B., & Hernán-González, R. (2015). Revisiting the tradeoff between risk and incentives: The shocking effect of random shocks. *Management Science.*

CASE: Council for Advancement and Support of Education. (2016). CASE statements on compensation for fundraising performance. Retrieved from http://www.case.org/Samples_Research_and_Tools/Principles_of_Practice/CASE_Statements_on_Compensation_for_Fundraising_Performance.html

Dewatripont, M., Jewitt, I., & Tirole, J. (2000). Multitask agency problems: Focus and task clustering. *European Economic Review, 44*(4–6), 869–877.

Eastburn, R. W. (2011). Countrywide Financial Corporation and the subprime mortgage debacle. Gamble–Thompson: *Essentials of strategic management: The quest for competitive advantage,* 2nd ed. II. Cases in Crafting and Executing Strategy, Case 15. New York: McGraw–Hill Companies. Retrieved from http://w3.salemstate.edu/~edesmarais/courses/470general/semesters/Archived%20semesters/Fall%202010/Countrywide%20Financial%20Corporation%20and%20the%20Subprime%20Mortgage%20Debacle.pdf

Egan, M. (2016, September 8). 5,300 Wells Fargo employees fired over 2 million phony accounts. *CNN Money.* Retrieved from http://money.cnn.com/2016/09/08/investing/wells-fargo-created-phony-accounts-bank-fees/index.html

Egan, M. (2016, September 9). Workers tell Wells Fargo horror stories. *CNN Money.* Retrieved from http://money.cnn.com/2016/09/09/investing/wells-fargo-phony-accounts-culture/index.html

Egan, M. (2016, November 3). Inside Wells Fargo, workers say the mood is grim. *CNN Money.* Retrieved from http://money.cnn.com/2016/11/03/investing/wells-fargo-morale-problem/index.html

Farrell, J., & Shapiro, C. (1989). Optimal contracts with lock-in. *American Economic Review, 79*(1), 51–68.

Fehr, E., & Schmidt, K. M. (2004). Fairness and incentives in a multi-task principal–agent model. *Scandinavian Journal of Economics, 106*(3), 453–474.

Figlio, D. N., & Getzler, L. S. (2006). Accountability, Ability and Disability: Gaming the System? In *Improving School Accountability Chec-Ups or Choice* (Vol. 14, pp. 35-49). (Advances in Applied Microeconomics; Vol. 14.) doi: 10.1016/S0278-0984(06)14002-X

Graff Zivin, J., & Neidell, M. (2012). The impact of pollution on worker productivity. *American Economic Review, 102*(7), 3652–3673.

Griffith, R., & Neely, A. (2009). Performance pay and managerial experience in multitask teams: Evidence from within a firm. *Journal of Labor Economics, 27*(1), 49–82.

Harris, M., & Raviv, A. (1978). Some results on incentive contracts with applications to education and employment, health insurance, and law enforcement. *American Economic Review, 68,* 20–30.

Healy, P. M. (1985). The effect of bonus schemes on accounting decisions. *Journal of Accounting and Economics, 7*(1–3), 85–107.

Hellmann, T., & Thiele, V. (2011). Incentives and innovation: A multitasking approach. *American Economic Journal: Microeconomics, 3,* 78–128.

Higgs, R. (1973). Race, tenure, and resource allocation in southern agriculture, 1910. *Journal of Economic History, 33,* 149–169.

Holmstrom, B., & Milgrom, P. (1987). Aggregation and linearity in the provision of intertemporal incentives. *Econometrica, 55*(2), 303–328.

Holmstrom, B., & Milgrom, P. (1991). Multi-task principal–agent problems: Incentive contracts, asset ownership, and job design. *Journal of Law, Economics and Organization, 7,* 24–52.

Hong, F., Hossain, T., List, J. A., & Tanaka, M. (2013, November). *Testing the theory of multitasking: Evidence from a natural field experiment in Chinese factories* (NBER Working Paper No. 19660). Cambridge, MA: National Bureau of Economic Research.

Jacob, B. (2003). "A Closer Look at Achievement Gains under High-Stakes Testing in Chicago." In Paul E. Peterson and Martin R. West, eds., *No Child Left*

Behind? The Politics and Practice of School Accountability (pp. 269–291). Washington, D.C.: *The Brookings Institution.*

Jacob, B. A., & Levitt, S. (2003). Rotten apples: An investigation of the prevalence and predictors of teacher cheating. *Quarterly Journal of Economics, 118,* 843–877.

Larkin, I. (2014). The cost of high-powered incentives: Employee gaming in enterprise software sales. *Journal of Labor Economics, 32*(2), 199–227.

Lundesgaard, J. (2001). The Holmström–Milgrom model: a simplified and illustrated version. *Scandinavian Journal of Management, 17*(3), 287–303.

Morgenson, G. (2007, August 26). Inside the countrywide lending spree. *The New York Times.* Retrieved from http://www.nytimes.com/2007/08/26/business/yourmoney/26country.html?mwrsm=Email

Oettinger, G. (2002). The effect of nonlinear incentives on performance: Evidence from "Econ 101." *Review of Economics and Statistics, 84,* 509–517.

Onishi, K., Owan, H., & Nagaoka, S. (2016, March). Monetary incentives for corporate inventors: Intrinsic motivation, project selection and inventive performance. Unpublished manuscript, Osaka Institute of Technology, Osaka, Japan.

Oosterbeek, H., Sloof, R., & Sonnemans, J. (2011). Rent-seeking versus productive activities in a multi-task experiment. *European Economic Review, 55,* 630–643.

Owan, H., Tsuru, T., & Uehara, K. (2013). Incentives and gaming in a nonlinear compensation scheme: Evidence from North American auto dealership transaction data. *Evidence-based HRM: A Global Forum for Empirical Scholarship, 3,* 222–243.

Oyer, P. (1998). Fiscal year ends and nonlinear incentive contracts: The effect on business seasonality. *Quarterly Journal of Economics, 113*(1), 149–185.

Prendergast, C. (2000). What trade-off of risk and incentives? *American Economic Review, 90,* 421–425. doi: http://dx.doi.org/10.1257/aer.90.2.421

Valdes-Dapena, P. (2016, January 15). Dealer to Fiat Chrysler: Stop making us report fake sales. *CNN Money.* Retrieved from http://money.cnn.com/2016/01/14/autos/fiat-chrysler-lawsuit-fake-sales/index.html?iid=Lead

6 Noisy Performance Measures and Optimal Monitoring

So far in this book we have assumed that the agent's level of job performance (Q) is costlessly observed by the firm. But in many cases this is not so. For example, the results of an electrician's carelessness might never be observed (if the electrician and homeowner are lucky) or might only be apparent in a tragic fire decades after their employment relationship has ended. Or a manufacturing firm might know, based on high product failure or rejection rates, that *someone* in the plant isn't adhering to protocol, but the firm may not have an easy way to determine where the fault lies. In many situations like these, firms will need to spend some resources if they want to get an accurate measure of their workers' performance. If both workers and firms are rational, self-interested maximizers, what can economic theory tell us about how intensely firms should monitor their workers' performance?

Perhaps surprisingly, under quite general conditions (though certainly not in all cases), economic theory delivers a simple and stark solution to this question. The original insight comes from Nobelist Gary Becker's early research on the economics of crime. According to University of Chicago lore, Becker was running late for a PhD oral exam one day and needed to park his car. Given the importance of the occasion, he weighed the chances of being ticketed and the likely price of the ticket, and decided to park illegally. Then, as a true economist, he began to think about the problem from the university's point of view: Given the two ways to deter illegal parking—raising fines, versus hiring more officers to catch violators—which is economically most efficient? In this chapter, we derive Becker's (1974) famous theoretical solution to this "monitoring puzzle" in the context of worker effort decisions. We conclude by discussing the limitations of his "extreme" recommendation for how to deal with poorly performing employees.

6.1 A Simple Model of Shirking with Monitoring and Fines

We consider a principal–agent model with a general production function $Q(E)$, where the agent's utility is given by

$$U = Y - V(E), \tag{6.1}$$

which is identical to Equation 1.4. To allow us to focus on a new aspect of the agency relationship, however, we'll now make a simplifying assumption about the effort choices available to the agent. Specifically, instead of picking any effort level he wants, we'll imagine the worker can choose between just two possible effort levels. One of these is the socially optimal effort level, E^*, that maximizes the sum of profits and utility. If the agent and firm could make binding agreements about what will happen after the employment relationship has begun, this is what both of them would want the agent to do. The other choice the worker can make after the contract is in place is to exert no effort at all, $E = 0$. It will be convenient to refer to these two choices as "working" and "shirking," respectively. Compared to working, shirking saves the worker E^* units of effort, which (assuming he is not caught or punished) raises his utility by an amount, B:

$$B \equiv V(E^*) - V(0). \tag{6.2}$$

We'll refer to B as the benefits (to the worker) of shirking. In a parallel fashion, we define

$$G \equiv Q(E^*) - Q(0) \tag{6.3}$$

as the cost to the firm (in reduced output) if the agent shirks.

Now, to incorporate the possibility that shirking isn't perfectly detectable, we define p as the probability that a worker *who has decided to shirk* is detected:

$$p = Prob(\text{detect shirking} \mid \text{worker shirks}). \tag{6.4}$$

Whenever $p < 1$, Equation 6.4 represents the idea that in the real world, shirking workers can often "pass" (for a time, at least) as having worked hard, either through skill or luck.[1]

Assuming that it is socially optimal to deter shirking, what tools can the firm use to achieve this goal? One possible tool is to penalize those who are caught shirking. In this chapter, we'll imagine this penalty takes the form of a fine, F, paid by the worker *to the firm*. You can think of fines as either explicit (e.g., reimbursing the firm for the cost of damages done) or implicit, such as docking the worker's pay for a period or denying the worker a raise. In any free labor market, however,

[1] In the language of probability, the vertical line in Equation 6.4 means "given that." Thus Equation 6.4 says that if a worker chooses to shirk, the probability he'll be caught equals p. Put a different way, the firm's detection technology delivers some *false negatives*: Some workers who shirk aren't detected. Notice that our simple model in this chapter does not allow for any false positives: We assume that the firm's detection technology never mistakenly labels an honest worker as a shirker. As it turns out, this does not change the main results, at least if workers are risk neutral.

there's a maximum penalty any firm can plausibly inflict on a worker, which in most cases will amount to firing that person. We denote the maximum feasible fine by $\bar{F}$. The other tool at the firm's disposal is to invest in better monitoring. If the firm monitors workers more closely, the detection rate can be greater. Let the cost to the firm of maintaining a detection rate of p be the increasing function $C(p)$.

6.2 Solving the Agent's Problem

Proceeding via backwards induction, we begin to solve our new principal–agent problem by characterizing how the agent will behave under any given contract. In this chapter, the contract is described by the ordered pair (p, F).[2] Given such a contract, a rational, risk-neutral worker will shirk if and only if the benefits to shirking (B) exceed its expected cost (pF). In other words, the agent's optimal effort decision is described by Equation 6.5:

$$\text{Refrain from shirking if and only if: } B \leq pF. \tag{6.5}$$

We'll refer to Equation 6.5 as the *no-shirking condition*. The no-shirking condition *is* the agent's *incentive-compatibility constraint* in this version of the principal–agent problem.[3]

6.3 Efficiency: The Pie-Maximizing Solution

Now that we've characterized the agent's incentive compatibility condition, we are in a position to characterize the socially optimal contract, (p, B), which maximizes the sum of the firm's profits and the worker's utility. To focus on the interesting case, we'll start by assuming that it's socially efficient to deter shirking. In other words, we'll assume that

$$G - B > C(p^*). \tag{6.6}$$

In words, the social gains from preventing shirking—which consist of the gains to the firm from preventing shirking, G, minus the loss to the worker from preventing shirking, B—exceed the monitoring costs the firm needs to spend to prevent shirking, $C(p^*)$.[4] Note that this is not a trivial assumption: Some forms

---

[2] As we'll see throughout the book, because they are just agreements between principals and agents, contracts can take many forms besides the combination of base and incentive pay (a, b) we've studied so far. In the current example, the agent and principal agree on a different two-dimensional bundle—how closely the agent will be monitored (p) and how severely the agent will be punished if he's caught shirking (F), then try to find the socially optimal levels of p and F. More generally, contracts can have any number of components (not just two), and are sometimes much less formal than the precise mathematical formulas we use here.

[3] The weak inequality in Equation 6.5 means that the agent does not shirk if the costs and benefits of shirking are exactly equal. This presumption in favor of honesty is a common assumption in agency and in mechanism design theory, although it is not without consequences or pitfalls.

[4] Note that the monitoring costs are evaluated at p^*, the optimal detection probability. We haven't worked out what p^* is yet, so in any actual example of the problem we need to check that Equation 6.6 is indeed satisfied at the optimal level of p^*.

of "shirking," such as reading personal emails on company time or stealing pencils—which aren't very harmful but are hard to prevent—should probably be tolerated by a rational, profit-maximizing firm. This is because they are worth more to employees (B) than the firm would benefit from preventing them $[G - C(p^*)]$.

Given Equation 6.6, there will be no shirking in any socially efficient arrangement. Workers will never get B, never pay F, will always receive their wage Y, and always supply effort E^* (never zero). It follows that the total social welfare (profits plus utility) generated by the employment relationship will just be

$$W = Q(E^*) - V(E^*) - C(p). \quad \textbf{(6.7)}$$

Choosing the socially efficient contract then amounts to maximizing Equation 6.7 subject to the no-shirking constraint (Equation 6.5). Because effort will equal E^* in all socially efficient contracts, this in turn reduces to

$$\text{Min}_{p,\,F}\, C(p), \text{ subject to } pF \geq B \text{ and } F \leq \bar{F}. \quad \textbf{(6.8)}$$

Assuming the first constraint (incentive compatibility) is satisfied with equality at the optimum (it will be), we can substitute $p = B/F$ into Equation 6.8, and the problem reduces to

$$\text{Min}_{F}\, C(B/F), \text{ subject to } F \leq \bar{F}. \quad \textbf{(6.9)}$$

Because $C(\cdot)$ is an increasing function, C is decreasing with F. The optimal fine, F^*, is therefore the highest possible value of F, that is, $F^* = \bar{F}$. To see this graphically, plot the required expenditures on monitoring against every possible level of the fine (see Figure 6.1).

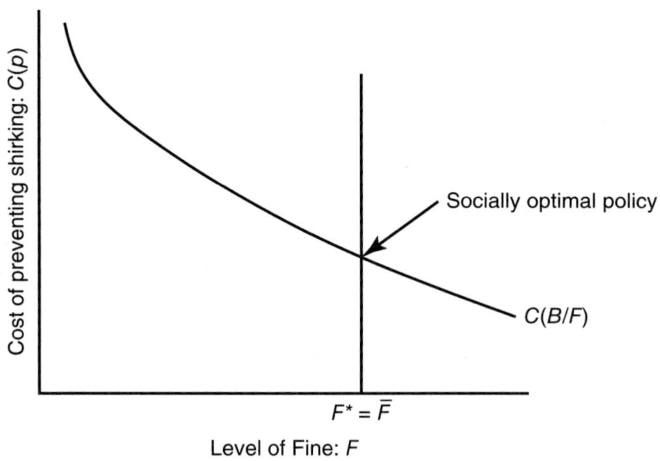

FIGURE 6.1. The Socially Optimal Fine in Becker's Model

Picking the highest possible fine allows one to spend the least on monitoring, which is socially costly. In fact, if one could set F even higher somehow, that would be *socially* even more efficient.

RESULT 6.1

The Socially Efficient Monitoring Policy in Becker's Model of Shirking Combines the Strictest Possible Penalties (F) with Lax Enforcement (low p).

In this contract, workers who choose to shirk will only rarely be caught, although the penalty for being caught is severe.

In sum, even though the firm has two tools to prevent shirking in Becker's model (monitoring and fines), it optimally decides to "put all its eggs in one basket"—by placing as much emphasis as possible on fines, thus minimizing the need to monitor. Why is the optimal policy so lopsided? There are actually two important reasons.

One reason stems from our assumption that the fine is a payment from the worker to the firm. Thus, the fines are just a transfer from one party to another. But as we already saw in Chapter 4, any transfer of this type just nets out of our measure of social welfare, which is the sum of profits plus utility. Thus, from the point of view of social welfare, monitoring wastes valuable resources, whereas increasing the level of the fine does not (all it does is discourage workers from shirking).

The second reason high fines are optimal in our example is that *they are never paid!* Indeed, if we only restrict our attention to contracts that satisfy the incentive-compatibility constraint (Equation 6.5), penalties will always be severe enough to ensure that no worker ever chooses to shirk. Thus, severe penalties combined with lax enforcement (low p) would be the optimal policy *even if* the penalty, F, was not a fine that simply transferred resources from one party to another. In the context of employment relations, an example of such a resource-using penalty would be forcing the worker to take an unpaid leave; unlike a fine, this type of penalty results in foregone worker output.

In the context of crime—where Becker originally developed the preceding model—the classic example of a socially costly penalty is putting criminals in jail, which can cost tens of thousands of dollars per inmate, per year. In this context, Becker's model says that the optimal deterrence policy is to *make jails so unpleasant that they will always be empty.* This extreme result—of severe penalties combined with lax enforcement—is an old and well-known one in the economics of crime. It has led many observers to wonder why it conflicts with most peoples' visions of their ideal systems of crime and punishment. One possibility, suggested by a behavioral theory of choice among risky options known as *prospect theory* (see Section 9.5) is that humans don't perceive small probabilities very accurately and so might not respond to low apprehension probabilities the way Becker's model predicts. Another might be a concern for fairness, though it is unclear exactly what's unfair about Becker's proposed solution. Perhaps the notion that "the punishment should fit the crime" doesn't mesh well with the idea of massive penalties for parking illegally.

Chapter Summary

- ☐ To study a principal's decisions on how many resources to spend on employee monitoring, this chapter introduces a simplified version of the principal–agent model where the agent chooses between just two effort levels: "working" ($E = E^* > 0$) and "shirking" ($E = 0$).

- ☐ Assuming it is socially optimal to prevent worker shirking, any optimal contract must therefore satisfy a no-shirking condition. This condition guarantees that the product of the fine for shirking (F) and the probability of getting caught (p) is high enough to deter all shirking.

- ☐ Under the previous assumptions, the socially optimal monitoring policy is an extreme one: the highest possible penalties combined with low levels of monitoring.

- ☐ One reason for this extreme result is that any penalty that takes the form of a fine paid by the worker to the firm (or by the criminal to society) is not a *social* cost. It is just a transfer from one person to another.

- ☐ Another reason is that, at least in our model, fines are never actually paid when the no-shirking condition is satisfied. Thus, it still makes sense to post the highest possible fines *even when* F is a social cost (such as unpaid leave, or putting a criminal into jail).

Discussion Questions

1. If you've ever taken public transportation in Europe, you are probably familiar with their policy of letting anyone walk on a train or streetcar, with inspectors only occasionally coming aboard to check tickets. If you are caught without a ticket, you face a stiff fine. According to the logic in this chapter, European cities should go even farther and raise fines to astronomical levels. That way they could hire even fewer inspectors and still achieve the same reduction in shirking. Why do you think they don't do this?

2. By the same logic, we could save money on highway patrollers in the United States by instituting the death penalty for speeding. What aspect of reality does the model in this chapter miss by arguing that this extreme policy makes sense?

3. How do you think Result 6.1 would change if the firm's measurement technology sometimes delivered some false positives (i.e., it sometimes labels non-shirkers as shirkers). Does the answer depend on whether workers are risk averse?

4. How do you think Result 6.1 would change if workers have imperfect control of their own actions (i.e., even though you always want to choose E^*, sometimes "nature" intervenes and makes you do the wrong thing). Does the answer depend on whether workers are risk averse?

Suggestions for Further Reading

Wikipedia's article on Becker's "crime and punishment" model provides useful, additional context and a less technical discussion than the original: http://en.wikipedia.org/wiki/Gary_Becker#Crime_and_punishment.

Reference

Becker, G. S. (1974). Crime and punishment: An economic approach. In G. S. Becker & W. M. Landes (Eds.), *Essays in the economics of crime and punishment*. Cambridge, MA: National Bureau of Economic Research. Retrieved from http://www.nber.org/chapters/c3625.pdf

Part 2
Evidence on Employee Motivation

Part 2 of the book differs in two key ways from Part 1. First, our focus, which was theoretical in Part 1, becomes unabashedly empirical: Instead of thinking through what we might *expect* to happen given some simple assumptions, we look at how people *actually* behave in real firms, using our model as a guide. Second, Part 2 focuses most of its attention on one specific aspect of the principal–agent problem we sketched out way back in Figure 1.1: Point 3, which is about how agents' work behavior responds to changes in the (formal and informal) rules affecting their jobs. Some of the main questions addressed are the following: "How do workers' effort levels and job performance actually respond to financial incentives?"; "How important are financial incentives compared to other motivators such as intrinsic and social motivators?"; and "Can financial incentives sometimes get in the way of the intrinsic satisfaction of a job well done?"

Throughout the chapters, we'll compare the evidence from these empirical studies to the main theoretical predictions of Part 1's principal–agent model. Specifically, recall Result 2.1, which is that a rational agent facing a linear pay schedule with intercept a and slope b should not change his behavior when a is changed and should work harder when b is raised. To what extent is this prediction supported by the evidence? And *when* is it supported? From time to time, we'll also focus on a different prediction from Part 1; specifically Result 3.2, which says that (under certain conditions) the profit-maximizing *and* socially efficient contract is a highly incentivized one in which the agent receives 100% of the fruits of his labors at the margin. Are strong incentives always profit maximizing in reality?

As we go, we'll find that financial incentives are sometimes highly effective motivators. We'll also discover that they can sometimes backfire and have unexpected effects, and that nonfinancial incentives can have powerful effects too. In the end, we'll argue that even in the simplest of employment relationships, great care is required in designing both financial and nonfinancial incentives. As we expand our attention to more complex employment relationships (teams, tournaments, and multitask and multiperiod interactions) later in the book, we'll find that this basic message is strengthened even further.

Because the focus of this part is empirical, we'll begin with a brief introduction to the main empirical research tools of personnel economics: experiments and regression analysis.

7 Empirical Methods in Personnel Economics

Consider a company that has introduced a new HRM policy—say, a new incentive pay scheme—in all its operations. Imagine that this change was motivated by dissatisfaction with the company's results and a belief that the new system will raise worker productivity. Happily, employee productivity in the year after the new policy is introduced turns out to be higher than the year before. Claiming that their new policy was responsible for this increase in performance, the managers receive sizable bonuses and promotions, and the business press celebrates their remarkable vision in turning around an ailing company.

Did these managers deserve their bonuses? Can we, in fact, conclude from the facts presented here that the managers' HRM innovation actually *caused* worker productivity to increase? I hope you will agree that any such claims should be treated with considerable skepticism. After all, there are many factors other than the HRM innovation that could also cause productivity to increase between any 2 years at any company. These factors include ongoing technical and IT improvements, changes in personnel that are unrelated to the new HRM scheme, and changes in business conditions.

Given the aforementioned problems, how can we ever know whether a change in company policy has been effective? In this chapter, we'll describe the two main methods used by personnel economists to isolate the causal effect of policy changes: experimental methods and regression analysis.

7.1 Inferring Causality: The Advantages of Randomized Controlled Trials (RCTs)

We begin with experiments, and specifically with a particular type of experiment called a *randomized controlled trial* (RCT). RCTs are generally considered the "gold standard" in many contexts where inferring causation is critical but challenging, including medical research. For a company introducing an HRM innovation, an RCT would work as follows. First, rather than applying the HRM innovation at the same time to all its workers at all its locations, a company takes a pool of workers or locations and randomly divides them into two groups: a *treated* group that receives the treatment (in our example, the new incentive plan) and a non-treated, or *control* group, which does not.[1] Randomization into these groups has to be explicit (e.g., using a computer-generated random number, or even a bingo machine, or a deck of cards) rather than subjective; and data should be collected on both the treatment and control groups, before *and* after the treatment is imposed. If the randomization has been correctly done, we should observe no statistically significant difference in the outcome of interest (productivity) between the treatment and control groups before the treatment is imposed.[2] Finally, assuming randomization has been successful, we can compare the outcomes of the treated and control groups *after* the treatment has been imposed to see whether the treatment has had any effect. The reason this procedure works, even though many factors other than the treatment might affect the outcome, is that randomization ensures that in a large enough sample, the *net effect of all the possible confounding factors is the same on average for the treatment and control groups.* In other words, if workers were randomly assigned to the treatment and control groups, confounding factors such as weather, business conditions, workers' individual personalities and family situations, and changing technology cannot explain the difference in outcomes between the two groups. Throughout this book, we'll study a number of RCT-based evaluations of personnel policy changes. Although even RCT research designs can have problems, in personnel economics, just as in medical research, they have become the gold standard test for whether an innovation is effective.

To make the idea of an RCT more concrete, consider a recent study of a particular personnel policy change—allowing workers to telecommute—on worker productivity at a company called CTrip (Bloom et al., 2014). At the time the study was conducted, CTrip was China's largest travel agency, with 16,000 employees and a market capitalization of about U.S. $5 billion. Beginning in December 2010, CTrip conducted a randomized experiment that compared the productivity of employees working from home (WFH) versus those working in one of its call centers.

---

[1] Whether the treatment should be randomized at the worker level or the location level depends in part on the nature of the treatment and the workplace. For example, if workers interact a lot within locations, then it's possible that the behavior of treated workers in one location could affect the non-treated workers they interact with. Because this makes the non-treated workers an inaccurate control group for the treated workers, in those cases, randomization at the location level probably makes more sense. However, randomization at the location level may not be feasible if a company has only a small number of locations.

[2] This is an important test—you'd be surprised how often investigators fail to conduct it and how often experiments don't pass! In the case of drug trials, a common reason is that fewer subjects drop out of the treatment group than the control group both before and after the treatment begins. That would be the case, for example, if the subjects expected the treatment to cure them. Often this particular problem can be avoided by a "blind" procedure in which subjects don't know which group they're in (e.g., the non-treated subjects could be given a placebo—i.e., a sugar pill—that looks like the real one). Unfortunately, that is not possible in most personnel economics experiments where the treatment of interest is an HRM or pay policy that workers would need to be aware of to react to it.

One of the study's authors was James Liang, CTrip's co-founder and a former PhD student at Stanford University's Graduate School of Business. Liang decided to do the experiment because the company was considering allowing its workers to telecommute but was genuinely unsure about whether that was a good idea. Although there were important potential benefits—such as reduced commuting time for employees and reduced expenses for office space—there was also a concern that persons working from home would be easily distracted and might be hard to monitor.

CTrip conducted their experiment in the airfare and hotel booking departments at their Shanghai call center, where they invited all of the 994 employees to participate. A condition of participation was that—if the employee qualified for the experiment—the employee *agreed to be randomly assigned* to either a treatment group, who agreed to work from home during the experiment, or a control group, who continued to come into the office as before. To qualify for the experiment, a worker had to meet a number of conditions, including having worked at CTrip for at least 6 months, being willing to work from home for 9 months, and having access to broadband Internet and an independent workspace at home during their shift. Of the 994 employees, 503 volunteered for the experiment, and 249 of these satisfied all the conditions.

Next, the qualifying workers were randomly assigned to two groups: From December 2010 to August 2011, applicants with even-numbered birthdates worked from home as part of the 131-member treatment group. The 118 workers with odd-numbered birthdates continued working in the call center as the control group. The home workers worked from home 4 days per week, returning to the call center for one shift on one day. This was for training, supervision, and other activities that were best done in person. To give you a feel for these two working environments, Figure 7.1 shows photos of the call center and a typical home work location. As you can see, home workers were supplied with all the necessary equipment and were not allowed to participate in the experiment unless they had a quiet place to work.

So, did WFH raise or lower job performance at CTrip? The employee performance measure CTrip cared most about was the number of phone calls an employee successfully handled per week; average weekly performance of the

FIGURE 7.1. CTrip's Call Center and a Typical Home Worker
From "Does Working From Home Work? Evidence from a Chinese Experiment", by Nicholas Bloom, James Liang, John Roberts and Zhichun Jenny Yang, Quarterly Journal of Economics, Volume 130, Issue 1, 2015; by permission of Oxford University Press.

treatment and control groups both before and after the treatment was introduced are shown in Figure 7.2.

Figure 7.2 shows four main things. First, in both the control and treatment groups, there is a lot of week-to-week "noise" in job performance. An important reason for this is that call volume and type varies over time—one can't serve customers who haven't called, and the average complexity of customers' requests varies too. So it would be a mistake to assess the treatment's effects on just a few weeks of data, for example, using just the 3 or 4 weeks after the treatment was introduced. Second, notice that the performances of the treatment and control groups track each other (both in their overall level and in their week-to-week variation) very closely during the pre-treatment period. This is critical evidence that CTrip's randomization of qualified workers into treatments and controls was successful and means that we can interpret that the gap between their performances after the treatment was introduced as a *causal* effect of WFH on productivity. A nonrandomized pilot program (which the firm had been considering) would not have had this property.

Third, notice that the performance of the treatment group actually *fell* around the time the treatment was introduced; in fact, it was clearly lower during the month after the treatment was introduced than during most of the pre-treatment period. Importantly, *if CTrip had not created a control group, they could easily have misinterpreted this decline in performance as a negative effect of WFH on employee productivity.* As it happens, however, the period of the experiment (December 2010 to August 2011) coincided with the end of Shanghai

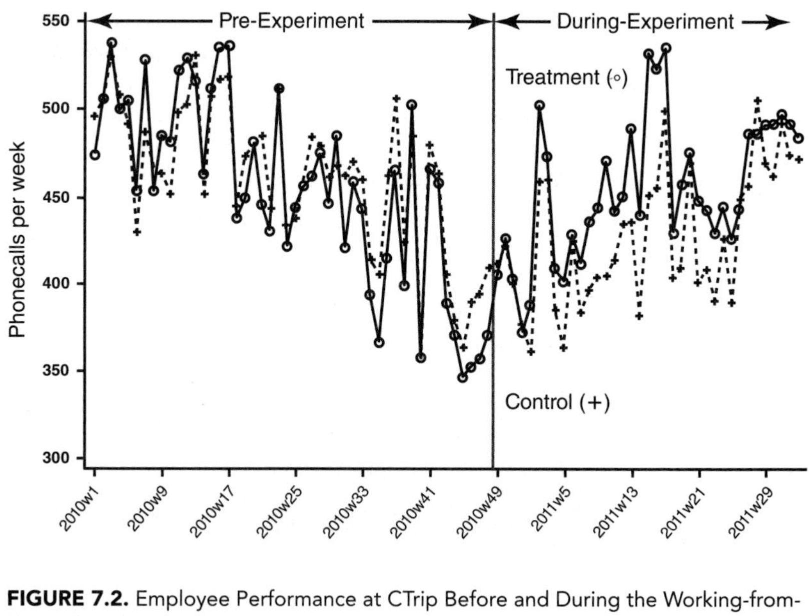

FIGURE 7.2. Employee Performance at CTrip Before and During the Working-from-Home Experiment
From "Does Working From Home Work? Evidence from a Chinese Experiment", by Nicholas Bloom, James Liang, John Roberts and Zhichun Jenny Yang, The Quarterly Journal of Economics, Volume 130, Issue 1, 2015; by permission of Oxford University Press

Expo 2010 and an increase in competition from other travel agencies, both of which reduced CTrip's business. Fortunately, because this decline in business affected both the treatment and control groups, CTrip did not mistakenly identify it as a consequence of WFH. Finally, the treatment group clearly performed better than the control group after the treatment was introduced. Overall, during the 9-month trial period, the home workers were 13% more productive than the control group, with no measurable difference in the quality of calls. It is this piece of evidence that proves that *working from home "worked"* at CTrip. Without a randomized control group with which to compare the treatment group's performance, CTrip might have wrongly concluded that WFH was ineffective.

Why did working from home raise productivity at CTrip? Fortunately the authors collected data on many aspects of worker performance and also interviewed the workers to shed light on this question. They found that because home workers took fewer breaks, they worked, on average, 9.2% more hours per shift. They also took fewer sick days: With an average commute of 80 min per day, the employees reported that on some days, they felt well enough to work at home but not well enough to commute. In addition to this additional work time, the home workers also handled 3.3% more calls per minute *while* they were working. The workers attributed this to the quieter home environment. Home workers were also more satisfied with their jobs, and their quit rate was half that of the control group working in the call centers.

Did WFH raise CTrip's profits? According to the company's estimates, the improvement in performance was worth about $375 per employee per year. WFH reduced CTrip's office costs by $1,250 per employee per year. The reduction in quits associated with WFH reduced hiring and training costs by about $400 per employee per year. The only negative consequence of WFH was that home workers' promotion rates were only about half those of the control group, perhaps because they were not as visible to managers. Indeed, because CTrip's WFH experiment was so successful that at the end of the experiment, the company extended the WFH option to all its call center employees. Had they not done a controlled experiment, CTrip may have missed out on this opportunity to raise both their own profits *and* their workers' job satisfaction at the same time.

7.2 Inferring Causality in Non-Experimental Settings: Regression Analysis

Now imagine you are a business consultant who has just received data from a small pizzeria chain (let's call it Pizza Hat) that is in the process of introducing a new, standardized system for handling its online takeout orders. The decision on when to introduce the new system is, in part, under the control of Pizza Hat's individual store managers. Specifically, although all managers are required to adopt the new technology by a certain deadline, within this period, the timing is up to the local managers. And although the company headquarters offers support services to assist with the transition, access to these services is limited by a first come, first served rule for the stores that request it.

TABLE 7.1 RAW DATA ON LOCATION PERFORMANCE AND TREATMENT STATUS, PIZZA HAT EXAMPLE

	NUMBER OF STORES	
Order Processing Speed	Non-Treated Stores	Treated Stores
1	1	0
2	4	2
3	1	0
4	0	0
5	0	0
6	0	0
7	0	1
8	2	4
9	0	1
Total number of stores	8	8
Mean processing speed	3.5	6.5

The raw data you have received from Pizza Hat is presented in Table 7.1. The data refer to a single point in time (say, 1 month), in the middle of the rollout process, at which time some stores have adopted and others have not. For each of Pizza Hat's 16 stores, Table 7.1 shows the store's mean takeout order processing speed and its treatment status (i.e., whether it has already adopted the new technology). Thus, for example, in the month you have data from, precisely half (eight) of Pizza Hat's 16 locations had already adopted it. Of these "treated" stores, two had a processing speed of 2, one had a processing speed of 7, four had a processing speed of 8, and one had a processing speed of 9. You can read the statistics of the non-treated stores the same way. Taking the means of these numbers reveals that on average, the treated stores processed orders much faster (6.5) than the non-treated stores (3.5), suggesting that the new ordering system increased processing speed by 6.5 – 3.5 = 3.0 units.[3]

Graphically, the data in Table 7.1 can be represented in a scatter plot, as in Figure 7.3. On the horizontal axis, Figure 7.3 measures the location's treatment status, which can be either 0 (non-treated) or 1 (treated), while the vertical axis shows the location's order processing speed. Each "X" in the diagram represents one store; so, for example, four non-treated stores, and two treated stores, had a processing speed of 2. Figure 7.3 also shows the mean speed of the treated and non-treated stores (6.5 and 3.5, again). Drawing a straight line between these two

[3] Remember that you need to weight by the number of stores to compute these averages. So, for example, the mean for the non-treated stores is calculated as [1(1) + 4(2) + 1(3) + 2(8)]/8 = 3.5.

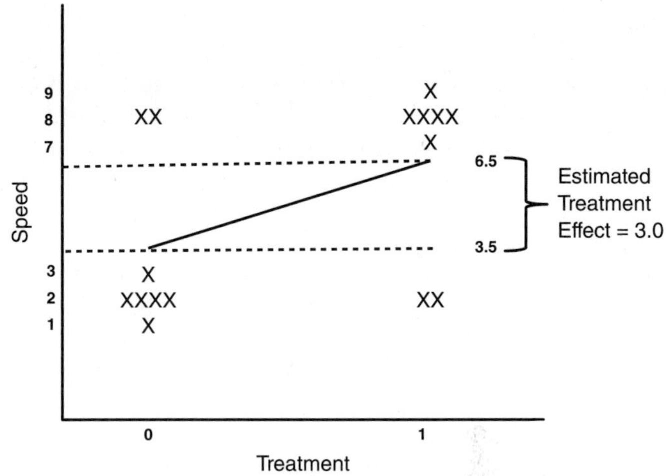

FIGURE 7.3. Scatter Plot and Simple Regression Line, Pizza Hat Example

means, as shown in Figure 7.3, is another way of illustrating the estimated effect of the new order-processing treatment (3.0).

As it turns out, the bold line in Figure 7.3 is also the *ordinary least squares (OLS) regression line* through the data. Specifically, suppose that you (as Pizza Hat's efficiency consultant) estimated the following simple linear regression model on the data in Figure 7.3:[4]

$$S_i = \alpha + \beta T_i + \varepsilon_i. \tag{7.1}$$

In other words, you propose that a store's speed, S_i, is a linear function of its treatment status, T_i, and a random component (which is zero on average but varies across individual stores in ways that we can't account for), ε_i. When you ask your statistical software package to estimate the model (Equation 7.1) by OLS, it will find the line that best fits the scatter of points in Figure 7.3.[5] The answer you'll get (try it yourself!) is *exactly*

$$\hat{\alpha} = 3.5; \hat{\beta} = 3.0, \tag{7.2}$$

where the "hats" denote the estimated values. The estimated intercept of the line, $\hat{\alpha}$, gives the mean speed of a non-treated store, that is, the mean speed when $T_i = 0$. The estimated slope of the regression line, $\hat{\beta}$, gives the difference between the mean speed of treated and non-treated stores, or our estimated "treatment effect" of $6.5 - 3.5 = 3.0$.

---

[4] In this book, *simple linear regression* refers to an OLS regression with one outcome variable and one explanatory variable. *Multiple regression* refers to OLS with one outcome variable and more than one explanatory variable.

[5] OLS defines "best fit" as the line that minimizes the sum of squared vertical distances between the 16 data points in Figure 7.2 and the line.

Is it reasonable to interpret the preceding simple regression estimate as the *causal* effect of the new ordering system on order processing speed? Unfortunately, in contrast to our CTrip example, now the answer is "no." This is because—in contrast to CTrip—*the "treatment" of Pizza Hat's ordering system was not randomly assigned.* Instead, it was determined by some other process—in this case, the interaction of store managers' timing decisions and the availability of support services from the head office. As a result, it is likely that—rather than being statistically identical in large-enough samples—the treated and non-treated stores differ in many other ways that could also affect their processing speed. For example, the treated stores could be on average larger, newer, have more experienced managers, or have more motivated managers (e.g., the real "go-getters" who wanted to be the first to adopt the new system). Unfortunately, *any* difference of this kind could invalidate our estimate that the new system almost doubled the stores' order-processing speed, from 3.5 to 6.5.

To illustrate how uncontrolled differences between treatment and control groups can seriously bias estimates of treatment effects when treatment is not randomly assigned, Figure 7.4 illustrates the effects of just one possible source of contamination. Specifically, imagine that Pizza Hat has two types of stores, regular restaurants (that serve both takeout and eat-in diners) and Pizza Hat Express locations, which cater exclusively to takeout customers.[6] Importantly, the data illustrated in Figure 7.4 are *exactly the same data* shown in Figure 7.3, with an average speed of 3.5 in the non-treated stores and 6.5 in the treated stores. The only difference between the figures is that Figure 7.4 indicates (with an "E") which of the stores are Express locations, and which are regular ("R") locations.

Among the non-treated stores, Figure 7.4 shows that the six regular locations (with an average speed of 2) serve their takeout customers much more slowly than the two Express locations (which have an average speed of 8). This is, of course, not surprising because the Express locations specialize in takeout orders. Interestingly, exactly the same is true for the treated stores, where the two regular restaurants have an average speed of 2 and the six Express restaurants also have a speed of 8. In fact, Figure 7.4 shows that if we compare treated versus non-treated stores of the same type (R or E), *the treated stores process orders no faster than the non-treated stores.* Put another way, the *within-group effect* of the new technology equals zero, as illustrated by the two horizontal lines in Figure 7.4. As it turns out, these two lines show the estimated effects of treatment from a *multiple* regression on our data, which estimates the effects of both treatment status and store type on speed at the same time.

Specifically, suppose you now estimated the following multiple regression model on the data in Figure 7.3:

$$S_i = \alpha + \beta T_i + \gamma E_i + \varepsilon_i, \qquad \textbf{(7.3)}$$

---

[6] Remember that our (made-up) data refer only to the *takeout* customers at both types of Pizza Hat stores; the slow speeds at the regular stores have nothing to do with the sit-down diners at those restaurants.

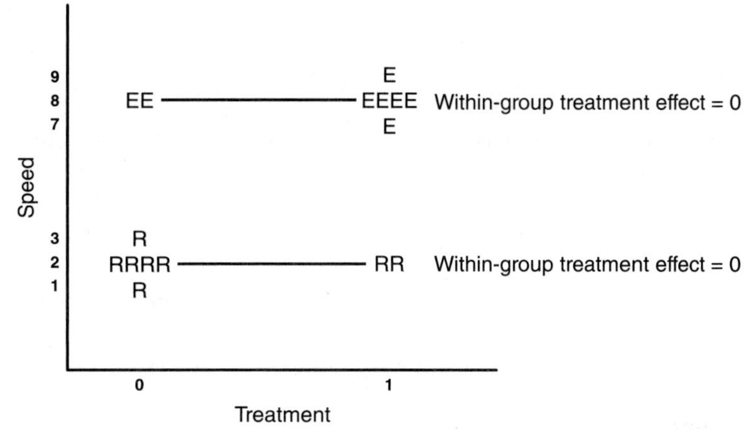

FIGURE 7.4. Scatter Plot and Within-Group Regression Lines, Pizza Hat Example

where $E_i = 1$ for the Express stores and 0 for the regular stores. Now your statistical package will give you the following estimates:

$$\hat{\alpha} = 2.0; \hat{\beta} = 0.0; \hat{\gamma} = 6.0. \quad \textbf{(7.4)}$$

Now, $\hat{\alpha}$, the estimated intercept of the line, gives the mean speed of a non-treated, *regular* store, that is, the mean speed when $T_i = 0$ and $E_i = 0$. The value $\hat{\beta}$, which is the estimated effect of the treatment on speed *when store type is held constant,* gives the *within-group treatment effect* of 0.0. Finally, $\hat{\gamma}$ gives the effect of being an Express store when treatment status, T_i, is held constant, which equals 6.0. Therefore (at least if store type is the *only* confounding factor in our comparison), it appears that the true effect of the treatment is not 3.5, but 0. The new order processing system is actually completely ineffective!

Why is a simple comparison of means (or, equivalently, a simple OLS regression) so misleading in this context? The answer, once again, is precisely *because the treatment was not randomly assigned*, which means that potential confounding factors (such as, but not limited to, store type) are not guaranteed to be *balanced* between the treatment and control stores. Instead, as Figure 7.4 shows, a large majority of our treated stores (six out of eight, or 75%) just happen to be Express outlets, whereas a large majority of our non-treated stores just happen to be regular outlets. Indeed, this is not at all surprising because—given that takeout is their only business—one might expect the Express stores to be more eager to adopt the new technology.[7]

[7] Of course, the unexpectedly low productivity of the treated stores in our example could result from glitches related to the startup of any new software system. One way to expand our simple statistical analysis of treatment effects to allow for time-varying treatment effects of this type would be to introduce an additional variable to our regression, equal to the time since the treatment was introduced into each treated store.

In reality, of course, there are many other store characteristics (and worker characteristics) that might not be perfectly balanced between our treatment and control group whenever treatment is not randomly assigned. Importantly, a useful and powerful feature of multiple regression is that *as long as we can measure these confounding factors,* controlling for them in a multiple regression (as we did for store type in Figure 7.4) *allows us to remove their influence and uncover the true treatment effect.* With modern information technology, this can be done in a split second, even with thousands of possible confounding variables (provided, of course, that one has enough data). That is the beauty and power of multiple regression analysis. Its chief limitation, however, is that *we can never be sure we have measured all the possible confounding factors.* For example, the personalities and abilities of the managers may differ systematically between the early and late adopters in ways that can't be precisely quantified. Thus, despite their power, multiple regression studies can never give as definite an estimate of the true effectiveness of a treatment as a well-designed RCT.

Unfortunately, in many cases, RCTs are not possible, for both practical and ethical reasons. For example, randomly assigning a more generous retirement package to a subset of one's employees might generate concerns about fairness and be difficult to administer. Even more problematic, it could take decades to estimate this policy's most important effects. Indeed, modern business moves extremely fast and often has neither the time nor resources to conduct RCTs of possible policy changes. In those cases, we are stuck with only observational data of the type in our Pizza Hat example, yet we still have to make the best decision we can. Therefore, in many situations, simple regression-based studies or even cruder intuitive judgments of "what seems to be working" are all we can do. Accordingly, we shall present many forms of evidence (from anecdotal, to regression-based, to RCT-based) throughout this book. Hopefully, by learning how to critically assess all types of evidence against the gold standard of an RCT, you'll develop a sharp eye for the common pitfalls in inferring causal relationships from evidence and make better decisions as a result.

Chapter Summary

- ☐ Randomized Controlled Trials (RCTs) are the gold standard for estimating the causal effects of HRM innovations on organizational productivity, profits, workers' job satisfaction, turnover, and other outcomes.
- ☐ RCTs require random assignment of workers (or organizational units) to a treatment and a control group and should collect data from both groups before as well as after the treatment is introduced.
- ☐ Before using the data from an RCT, it is important to check whether the treatment and control groups are in fact statistically identical before the treatment is imposed. This confirms that random assignment has been successful.
- ☐ If an RCT has been designed and executed correctly, a simple comparison of mean outcomes between the treated and control groups after the treatment is imposed will measure the causal effect of the treatment.

- ☐ Multiple regression analysis is a statistical technique for removing the confounding effects of *observable* factors in situations where a treatment of interest has been assigned by a non-random process.

- ☐ Multiple regression analysis can easily control for a very large number of confounding factors, but only those factors that can be measured and entered into your analysis.

Discussion Questions

1. Why did CTrip need an RCT to measure whether WFH raises or lowers productivity? Couldn't it just introduce the policy and see whether productivity goes up or down?
2. Alternatively, couldn't CTrip just let workers pick whether to work at home or not, then compare the productivity of the workers who picked home to those who chose to keep coming into the office?
3. Recall that in the CTrip experiment, volunteers were first screened to see whether they had a quiet home work location, *then* randomly assigned to work at home or not. Because the control group didn't need to work from home, wouldn't it have made more sense to screen only the treatment group for adequate home space? (That would have saved on screening costs, and given the authors a bigger control group.) Please discuss.
4. Aside from store type (regular vs. Express), what other features of Pizza Hat stores might confound simple comparisons of order processing speed between locations that adopted the new system and locations that didn't?

Suggestions for Further Reading

For a more complete and formal discussion of regression analysis, consult any introductory econometrics textbook.

For many more applications of experimental and regression analysis to issues in personnel economics, keep reading this book.

Reference

Bloom, N., Liang, J., Roberts, J., & Ying, Z. J. (2014). Does working from home work? Evidence from a Chinese experiment. *Quarterly Journal of Economics, 130*(1), 165-218.

8 Performance Pay at Safelite Glass: Higher Productivity, Pay, and Profits

The very first theoretical prediction derived in this book, Result 2.1, says that strengthening the financial incentives a worker faces (i.e., raising the slope parameter, b, in a principal–agent relationship) should increase the agent's work effort E and thereby improve his job performance Q. Although this seems intuitive, is there any hard evidence to support it? By "hard" evidence, of course, we mean carefully designed experimental and regression-based studies like those we just discussed, which make serious efforts to isolate the true causal effects of changes in compensation policy on worker performance. A classic study of this question was published in 2000 by Edward Lazear, a professor at Stanford University's Graduate School of Business. Professor Lazear is widely considered to be the "father of personnel economics." You'll see his name and research frequently in this book.

Years ago when I asked Professor Lazear how this famous study got started, he mentioned a meeting in the early 1990s with Garen Staglin and John Barlow, CEO and president, respectively, of Safelite Glass. Based in Columbus, Ohio, Safelite is the largest installer of auto glass in the United States. If you have ever had a crack in your windshield, chances are that you have called a local Safelite shop to have it fixed. Repairs can be handled either in the shop or elsewhere (e.g., the company can dispatch a truck with the replacement glass to your driveway). When the aforementioned meeting took place, Safelite's installers were paid on an hourly basis, regardless of the number of windshields they replaced in each hour, day, or week. Because Safelite already had accurate data collection systems in place that measured the number of repairs each employee performed on an ongoing basis, Lazear wondered if it might make sense to link workers' pay to this measure of their performance. In terms of Part 1's model, he was suggesting that the firm raise its piece rate (b) from zero to some positive number. The leaders of the company, who had recently taken over as a new management team, were receptive to the idea.

In a number of ways, the work environment at Safelite was an ideal one in which to introduce a simple incentive plan based on each individual worker's performance. For example, Safelite installers work independently, with one installer doing the entire job of fixing one customer's car. In contrast to workplaces where employees work in teams to produce a joint product, this makes it possible to measure each individual's productivity independently.[1] Also, Safelite's environment largely avoids a common problem with piece rate pay schemes, namely, the quality issue: If workers are paid, say, for the number of windshields repaired, this incentivizes them to work fast, perhaps sacrificing quality in the process. In Safelite's case, quality was measured relatively easily by customer complaints; and because workers had to fix any defective repairs on their own time, the quality issue was easily resolved. Essentially, workers were paid only per *successful* windshield replacement.

8.1 Safelite's Performance Pay Plan (PPP) and Its Predicted Effects

Precisely what was the new incentive pay plan that was introduced by the Safelite Corporation in the mid-1990s? To see how this plan worked, consider a Safelite installer who puts in an 8-hr day. Under the old system, that worker was paid \$20 per hour, regardless of how many units he repaired in a day, for a total of \$160.[2] The only exception to this rule, as you might expect, was that if the worker consistently produced less than some minimum threshold output, Q_0 (say, three units per day), he wouldn't keep his job. Thus, Safelite's old incentive scheme can be represented by the bold, solid line in Figure 8.1, which "jumps" upward from zero to \$160 per day at Q_0 units of output. The new scheme, called the Performance Pay Plan (PPP), paid workers a piece rate of \$32 per unit repaired and is illustrated by the bold dashed line in Figure 8.1. (Presumably, these workers would also be fired if they consistently produced less than $Q_0 = 3$ units per day.)

An important feature of Safelite's new policy, however, was that the workers could still choose to be paid according to the old hourly rate if their daily PPP earnings would fall below what they'd earn at their old hourly rate, that is, below \$160. Thus, the workers' *overall* compensation scheme after the PPP was introduced was identical to the old, hourly one, except that workers earned \$32 for every unit they installed *beyond* 160/32 = 5 units in a given day, that is, beyond the breakeven point between the two pay schemes. PPP thus added a new segment to the budget constraint, to the right of 5 windshields per day. The slope

[1] Even when "teams" aren't explicitly defined in a workplace, interactions between workers that affect each other's measured performance (such as sharing information, helping each other, or even undermining another's work to win a promotion) are commonplace. Designing incentives in these situations can be considerably trickier than in places like Safelite; we consider these situations in Parts 4 and 5 of the book

[2] Exact pay rates varied by location according to local labor market conditions; \$20 is a typical example. Safelite measures its workers' productivity by counting the number of "units" successfully repaired, where units can be pieces of auto glass other than windshields. That noted, we'll sometimes refer to the number of units repaired as the number of windshields replaced in our discussion.

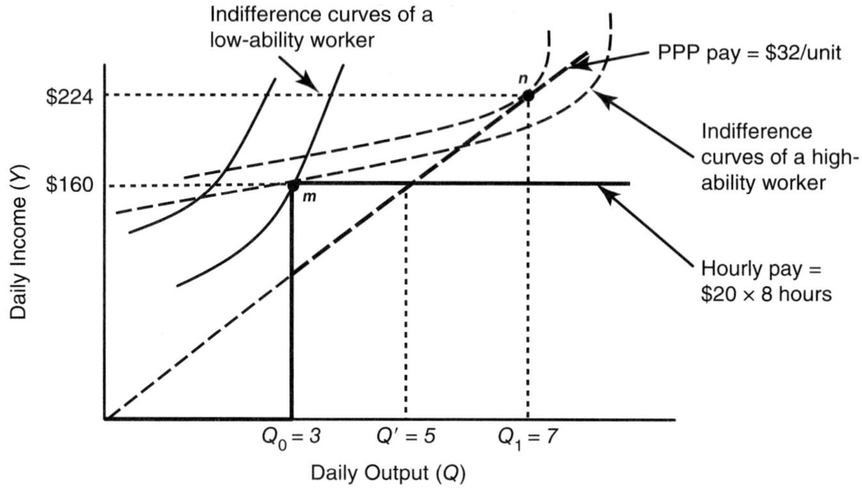

FIGURE 8.1. Predicted Effects of Safelite's Incentive Pay Plan

of this new segment equals 32 because that is the amount by which the worker's daily income will rise if he installs one additional windshield.

To see how we might expect workers to respond to the PPP, Figure 8.1 shows two sets of indifference curves. One set of indifference curves—the thin, solid curves with the steeper slopes—represent the indifference map of a "low-ability" worker. Remembering (from Section 1.4) that workers are by definition indifferent among all bundles on the same indifference curve, a steep indifference curve means that if we asked this worker to provide a little extra effort (thereby producing a higher Q) and then asked how much additional money he'd need to be just as well off as before, the answer would be *a lot of money* (dY/dQ along an indifference curve is a large, positive number). The reason we refer to these steep indifference curves as belonging to a less-able worker is that by definition, such a worker would have to work harder to produce the same amount of additional output as an abler worker. As a result, if the two workers have the same tastes for income and leisure, the less-able worker needs to receive more additional income than the high-ability worker to keep his utility constant when we require him to produce more output.[3] Remembering that any given worker's indifference curves can't cross and that indifference curves to the northwest represent higher levels of

[3] To see this a little more formally, suppose that high-ability workers have a higher d parameter (representing productivity), as defined in the worker's production function $Q(E) = dE$ (Equation 1.9). Suppose also that both high- and low-ability workers have the same utility function (i.e., their indifference maps, as shown in Figure 1.3, where the axes are E and Y, are identical). Then when we draw the two workers' indifference maps in (Q, Y) space as in Figure 8.1, the horizontal scale is more *compressed* for a low-ability worker (because producing one more unit of output, Q, consumes more units of effort, E). This makes the low-ability worker's indifference curves steeper in (Q, Y) space even if the two worker types have the same utility functions. Of course, it is also possible that differences in workers' indifference curves, like those in Figure 8.1, are driven simply by differences in tastes, not ability. In that case, the steep curves would belong to a "lazy" worker (one that valued leisure highly, relative to income) and the flatter ones to "ambitious" workers.

utility, this worker maximizes utility at point *m* with output level Q_0 under both the old and new compensation schemes.[4]

Now consider a "high-ability" worker who can produce lots of windshields with little effort; following the same reasoning, this worker's indifference curves are shown by the flatter, dashed curves in Figure 8.1. Under Safelite's old (hourly) pay scheme, this worker's optimal point is at *m*, the same as the low-ability worker's: Because the dashed incentive pay scheme is not available, there is no point in producing more than Q_0. Once the new plan is made available, however, we'd expect the high-ability worker to change his behavior, shifting to the new optimum at point *n*. At point *n*, the high-ability worker works harder ($E_1 > E_0$), produces more ($Q_1 > Q_0$), earns more money ($Y_1 > Y_0$), and—despite working harder—is better off ($U_1 > U_0$) than before. In other words, the increase in income between points *m* and *n* in Figure 8.1 is more than enough to compensate a high-ability worker (but not a low-ability worker) for the fact that he's working harder at point *n*.

All in all, our theoretical analysis of Safelite's incentive pay plan yields three results. The first, which is not particularly surprising, is that average worker output should rise when the PPP is introduced: Even if low-ability workers don't change their behavior, high-ability workers should choose to produce more, so the average should rise. Second, because the PPP should raise high-ability workers' utility while leaving low-ability workers' utility unchanged, the new work environment should make it easier for Safelite to attract and retain abler workers. Third, consider the *variance* in output across Safelite's workers, before and after the change. Before the change, both our worker types (high- and low-ability) behaved the same, producing the minimum output needed to keep their jobs. After the change, they behave differently, so the variance of output across workers is predicted to rise. Of course, this makes total sense as soon as you think about it, but we may not have thought about it if we hadn't worked out the simple model in Figure 8.1. These predictions are summarized in Result 8.1.

RESULT 8.1

The Principal–Agent Model in Part 1, Applied to Safelite's PPP, Predicts That Introducing PPP Will:

(a) increase average job performance;
(b) make it easier for Safelite to attract and retain good workers; and
(c) increase the variance of job performance across workers.

A final, critical feature of Safelite's PPP is that unlike CTrip's WFH experiment, the PPP was *not* implemented as an RCT. Instead, the company gradually rolled out the PPP scheme across its U.S. locations, beginning with locations

[4] Point *m* is the low-ability worker's most preferred point under the new incentive scheme because the indifference curve through point *m* passes everywhere above the thick, dashed line representing the additional options associated with the new payment scheme: Using these additional options would not help the less-able worker attain a higher indifference curve than he attained before.

close to its Ohio home office, then expanding outward based on a variety of factors including the readiness of the local managers. Thus, as in our fictitious Pizza Hat example, Lazear had to rely on regression analysis to control for as many confounding factors as possible, including seasonality, changes in management, and changes in car technology. Using this approach, Lazear was able to develop estimates of the effect of performance pay at Safelite that cannot be easily explained away as the coincidental effects of seasonality or long-term changes in car technology. We describe Lazear's approach to these issues in the next section.

8.2 How Did the PPP Affect Employee Performance at Safelite?

We'll start our empirical analysis of Safelite's PPP with a look at the raw data, simply comparing the output of all Safelite workers before and after the change, bearing in mind that these comparisons aren't conclusive for reasons we've already discussed. These numbers are shown in Table 8.1.

The data in Table 8.1 were collected from the individual performance records of 2,755 workers over a period of 19 months in 1994 and 1995, the period during which the PPP scheme was rolled out. For each month in that period, Lazear knew the average daily number of windshields produced by each worker and whether that worker was working under the original hourly pay scheme or the new PPP scheme in that month. Altogether, Lazear had data on 28,352 person-months of output. A little less than half of these (13,106) were from months in which the worker in question was paid strictly by the hour; the remaining 15,246 were under the PPP scheme.[5]

According to Table 8.1, in 1994 and 1995, Safelite workers produced an average of 2.70 windshields per working day when they were paid by the hour, compared to 3.24 windshields per day when the PPP was in place. This amounts to a 20% higher output level under the piece rate plan. Also, consistent with Result 8.1(c), the standard deviation of worker output was higher under the PPP. But does this difference actually represent a causal effect of the PPP? Maybe productivity was trending upward during this time period anyway, so the higher numbers under the PPP are just because they are from a later time period. Or maybe the PPP periods in Lazear's data were disproportionately from high-demand months, such as summer? After all, windshield repair is a highly seasonal business, and the PPP scheme was introduced in different seasons in different locations.

To address these questions, Lazear estimated some multiple regression equations that control for the effects of seasonal factors and a time trend on Safelite worker output, just like the multiple regressions in our Pizza Hat example

[5] Of course, if Safelite had no turnover or absenteeism, Lazear would have had 2,755 × 19 = 52,345 person-months of data on worker output. But of course some workers quit, others are hired, and data are sometimes incomplete for other reasons (e.g., absenteeism or vacations). Lazear also excluded person-months during which the switch to PPP occurred from his sample because these observations can't be neatly classified as either PPP or non-PPP.

TABLE 8.1 MEAN OUTPUT UNDER HOURLY PAY VERSUS THE PIECE RATE PLAN, SAFELITE GLASS

	HOURLY PAY		PIECE RATE PAY	
Number of Observations (Person-Months)	13,106		15,246	
	M	*SD*	*M*	*SD*
Windshields per Worker, per Day	2.70	1.42	3.24	1.59

controlled for the effects of store type. Specifically, Lazear proposed that the output of Safelite worker *i* in month *j* of his data could be expressed as

$$ln(Q_{ij}) = \alpha + \beta \times PPP_{ij} + M_j + Y_j + \varepsilon_{ij}. \quad \textbf{(8.1)}$$

The left-hand side of Equation 8.1 is the natural logarithm of worker *i*'s mean output in month *j*.[6] This is proposed to depend not only on whether the PPP scheme is in place but also on which month of the year it is, and on which year (1994 or 1995) the data are from. And of course, because even together these factors can't predict worker output perfectly, an error term, ε_{ij}, also has to enter the equation. The variable PPP_{ij} equals zero in months where the individual is under hourly pay and one in months when he's under the PPP. The "month effect," M_j, is actually 12 separate variables, which allow the equation to have a different intercept in each of the 12 months of the year. This accounts in a flexible way for seasonal demand patterns. The year effect lets observations (from the same calendar month) drawn from 1995 have different outputs from 1994 observations. This is to capture long-term changes in car technology, among other factors that change slowly over time. Because these statistical controls are included in the regression, the estimated coefficient β in Equation 8.1 tells us how much higher log productivity is in months when the PPP is in place for that worker, *holding constant the remaining variables in the regression equation*, that is, the month and year the observation was taken from. Put a different way, estimating regression Equation 8.1 generates an estimate (β) of the productivity impact of the PPP that is purged of the possible confounding effects of seasonality and any technological improvement that raised 1995 productivity relative to 1994 levels.

The estimated value of β in Equation 8.1 is 0.368, indicating that controlling for seasonal factors and differences between 1994 and 1995, output was 0.368 log units higher under the PPP. This effect is highly statistically significant and corresponds to a *44%* higher level of productivity under the PPP, much higher

[6] Economists often express variables in logarithmic terms when estimating regression models. There are at least two good reasons for doing this. One is that the estimated coefficients can then be interpreted, roughly speaking, as percentage effects. So, for example, if β was estimated to equal 0.05, that would mean that the PPP is associated with about a 5% higher level of productivity. (This approximation becomes less exact when the estimated effect is larger, as we'll note in the text.) A more technical reason is that expressing the dependent variable in log terms means the homoskedasticity assumption is more likely to be satisfied (see any introductory econometrics textbook for a discussion of homoskedasticity and its role in regression analysis).

than the 20% gap in Table 8.1.[7] Apparently, Table 8.1's raw data *underestimate* the productivity impact of the PPP, possibly because the PPP was first introduced in months where output is usually low for seasonal reasons.[8]

RESULT 8.2

Controlling for Seasonal Factors and a Time Trend

The introduction of individual performance pay (specifically Safelite's PPP) appears to have raised installer productivity at Safelite by 44%.

Having confirmed the prediction of Result 8.1(a), we now empirically test Result 8.1(b), which predicted that the PPP scheme should make the workplace more attractive to high-ability workers but not to low-ability workers. Thus, over time, we might expect Safelite's mix of workers to change, as it becomes easier both to hire and retain abler workers relative to others. In fact, because turnover at Safelite tends to be relatively high, some of the productivity gains estimated in Equation 8.1 could have resulted not from a tendency for Safelite's existing workers to work harder but from the possibility that, on average, less-able workers were replaced by abler ones. To see whether changes in employee mix explain some (or all) of the productivity increase associated with the PPP, Lazear estimated a second regression model, given by

$$ln(Q_{ij}) = \alpha + \beta \times PPP_{ij} + M_{ij} + Y_{ij} + W_i + \varepsilon_{ij}. \quad \textbf{(8.2)}$$

The only difference between Equations 8.2 and 8.1 is a new set of terms, W_i, called *worker fixed effects*. These effects allow the productivity equation to have a different intercept for each Safelite worker. Thus, whereas Equation 8.1 estimates β by comparing all Safelite workers under the PPP in a given month and year to all Safelite workers under hourly pay in the same month and year, Equation 8.2 makes a more narrow comparison. Specifically, after allowing for the same seasonal effects and time trends as Equation 8.1, Equation 8.2 estimates β by comparing the output of *the same worker before and after the change* to the PPP. Any effects of the PPP on productivity that operate through a change in the mix of workers are now absorbed into the person effects (W_i) and are thus removed from our estimate of β. Put a different way, Equation 8.2's estimate of β is a *within-worker* estimate, in the same sense that Equation 7.3's estimate was a within-restaurant-type (Express vs. regular) estimate in the Pizza Hat example.

The estimated value of β in Equation 8.2 was 0.197, indicating that controlling for seasonal factors and an annual time trend, a typical worker *who worked*

---

[7] To convert the estimated β from a logarithmic regression like Equation 8.1 to an exact percentage difference, simply compute e^{β} - 1, where e is the base of the natural logarithms. Thus, for example, $e^{.368}$ - 1 = 0.44.

[8] Notice that this contrasts to the Pizza Hat example in which the raw data overestimated the treatment effect. It is important to remember that the bias from not controlling for confounding factors can go in either direction!

at Safelite both before and after the PPP was introduced produced 0.197 more log units of output under the PPP. This effect is highly statistically significant and corresponds to a 22% higher level of productivity under the PPP, exactly half of the 44% effect estimated in Equation 8.1. Thus, only *half* of the PPP's effect was because it induced Safelite's existing workers to produce more output. The remaining half was a pure employee *selection effect*: incentive pay made Safelite a more attractive workplace for abler workers.

In addition to comparing β in Equations 8.1 and 8.2, Lazear also collected some more direct evidence on the hypothesis that abler workers became more likely to remain at Safelite after the move to piece rates. Because Safelite collected worker performance information both before and after the change, it was not hard to identify who were Safelite's most productive installers even before the PPP was introduced. If we then ask *which* workers were more likely to leave Safelite within the first 2 months of the PPP, we find that less-able workers were more likely to do so than abler workers.[9] More significantly, Lazear was able to compare the productivity (under the PPP) of workers who were hired after Safelite's switch to the PPP was essentially complete (i.e., under its "new regime") to those who were hired before the PPP was in place. He found that they were .243 log points, or 27.5%, more productive. Summing up Lazear's results on employee selection yields Result 8.3:

☑ RESULT 8.3

Half of the 44% Productivity Increase Associated With Performance Pay at Safelite Is an Employee Selection Effect

Low-performing workers appear to have been replaced by higher-performing workers as a result of introducing the PPP.

The final prediction of Lazear's simple theoretical model is the hypothesis that the variance of job performance across workers should be higher under the PPP [Result 8.1(c)]. As it turns out, this hypothesis wasn't confirmed in Lazear's study. Although the workforce was more able, on average, after the PPP was introduced, the variance in worker performance remained the same. A possible explanation for this is related to the selection effect described previously: If the less-able workers disproportionately left Safelite, the new workforce may have become more homogeneous, with only abler workers remaining.[10]

[9] Some of this effect could be because abler workers are in general less likely to quit, regardless of the compensation scheme in place.

[10] Notably, despite favoring abler workers, there is an important sense in which Safelite's PPP scheme was perceived as an *equalizer*: A feature of the old pay system (which continued after PPP was introduced) was that Safelite's hourly wage rates increased with a worker's seniority. Because the PPP bonus for extra units was available to all workers, it enabled young, motivated workers to earn as much as their senior colleagues for the first time. In that sense, at least, the PPP was more meritocratic than the old system.

Was Workers' Response to Safelite's PPP Just a Hawthorne Effect?

Some of the earliest experimental studies of the effects of the work environment on worker performance were conducted in a large factory complex built by Western Electric called the Hawthorne Works in Cicero, Illinois, between 1924 and 1932. The most famous of these experiments involved a group of six female factory workers who assembled telephone relays in a dedicated room over a period of 5 years (1927–1932). During this period, the researchers changed a variety of working conditions and measured their effects on the workers' productivity, measured by the number of finished relays. The working conditions included the number and length of break times, food during the breaks, a shorter work day, and even the lighting in the room. A surprising result that is often attributed to these studies is that *changing almost any one of these variables, regardless of the direction of the change, gave rise to short-term increases in productivity.*

Many researchers have speculated on the possible causes of the previous findings; a common explanation is that the workers either felt they were appreciated, or worried that they were being monitored as a consequence of these interventions, and responded with higher effort as a result. Since then, the term "Hawthorne effect" has been widely used to refer to situations where experimental subjects (especially workers) change their behavior not because of the experimental treatment they are receiving but *simply as a consequence of knowing they are being studied.* As it turns out, some recent re-analyses of the original Hawthorne data by economists Stephen Jones (1992), and Steven Levitt and John List (2011), suggest that the original statistical analysis of the data may have been flawed. (See References and Suggestions for Further Reading at the end of this chapter.)

To check whether Safelite workers' positive response to the PPP was a Hawthorne effect, Lazear asked whether the productivity increases associated with the plan were permanent. Specifically, he added another variable to regression equation (9.2), measuring the number of months that had elapsed since the worker's shop was first subject to the PPP scheme. If the improvements in productivity were only temporary, this variable would have a negative coefficient, implying that productivity eventually returns toward its original level after an initial "bump." As it turned out, the variable had a positive coefficient, suggesting that workers' responses to the PPP actually became *more* positive as time passes, perhaps because workers figured out new ways to raise their productivity in response to the new incentives. Thus, the productivity increases at Safelite do not appear to have been a Hawthorne effect.

8.3 Did the PPP Raise Safelite's Profits?

Of course, just because piece rate pay raised the number of windshields repaired each week per Safelite worker, it does not follow that the PPP scheme raised Safelite's profits. After all, the workers were *paid* for each additional unit replaced beyond 22 per week, which resulted in an increase in Safelite's labor and materials costs. As it turns out, however, the increase in labor costs associated with PPP was only 7%, which compares very favorably with the 44% increase in productivity. Assuming that the additional materials costs did not eat up the remaining difference, it appears very likely that the PPP raised Safelite's profits.[11] In fact, the firm's earnings did increase after PPP was introduced, and although this increase could be due to a variety of other factors, the evidence strongly suggests PPP was actually the reason.

8.4 Lessons from Safelite

The successful HRM innovation implemented at Safelite yields at least two main lessons. The first lesson is about *possibilities*: Safelite's success story demonstrates that, in the right conditions and when properly implemented, *HRM innovations can have large positive effects on productivity.* Engineers, employed in many companies to constantly improve and fine-tune the production process, often struggle (especially when working with mature processes) to eke out tiny productivity improvements to raise a company's bottom-line performance. Viewed in this light, Safelite's 44% increase in output—resulting not from any technological change but simply from changes in compensation policy—is an eye-opener. So, although it can certainly be more difficult to identify *which* HRM change will raise productivity than it is to make an engineering improvement, Safelite's case dramatically illustrates the potential rewards from doing so.

As we move through this course, we'll see a number of other examples of successful HRM innovations: giving workers the option of working from home at China's largest travel agency (CTrip), introducing *kanban*-based team production system at a Northern California garment factory, and even an innovation as simple as raising pay (Henry Ford's five-dollar day). In all of these cases, large productivity improvements were achieved with essentially no change in the physical production process at all. In sum, HRM improvements are an important, but often overlooked, way to improve not only a company's bottom line but in many cases workers' financial well-being as well.

The second key lesson from the Safelite case is about *mechanisms.* Turning back to Section 8.1's theoretical model, the obvious reason why we might expect piece rates to increase productivity is by incentivizing Safelite's existing workers to improve their performance. But as things turned out, this effect was only half of the story behind why the PPP "worked" at Safelite; the other half is that *changing the structure of pay changed the type of workers who were attracted to Safelite jobs.* This finding highlights the key role of employee *selection* in the design of HRM policies, one of the two main themes of this book. As we argued in the book's preface, designing a personnel system that selects the right workers can be just as important (or even more important) than designing one that ensures existing employees perform optimally. More practically, Safelite's experience suggests that any HRM practitioner would be wise to remember that a change in

[11] It is unlikely that additional variable costs could wipe out the productivity gains at Safelite because any firm with positive fixed costs (such as rent and utilities for the shop) would need to earn a positive markup on materials and other variable costs per unit of output sold to break even overall.

HRM policy may not only change the behavior of a firm's existing employees but will also change the mix of workers who will be attracted to the firm.

We conclude our study of the Safelite case with a caution. Indeed, because productivity, profits, and wages all appear to have increased at Safelite, it may be tempting to conclude that this "win-win" effect of introducing incentive pay can be duplicated at many more workplaces. Although Safelite is undoubtedly an interesting model for some other firms with similar characteristics, it's important to remind ourselves of some special features of Safelite that make it an especially promising place to institute individual piece rate pay. These include the fact that it is easy to measure an *individual* worker's contribution to the firm's revenues and that potential product quality problems can be readily addressed. Another special feature of Safelite is that it already had a sophisticated information system in place that generated timely information about workers' performance. In companies where such a system in not already in place, the cost of installing it just to implement piece rate pay could easily outweigh any additional output generated by the new pay scheme. That said, as more and more companies implement Enterprise Resource Planning software systems such as Oracle, SAP, and many open-source alternatives, individual output data will be more readily available as an input into incentive pay plans.

Putting the previous considerations together, you might even wonder whether piece rate pay is suitable for very many firms at all. In fact, if your impression is that a PPP-type scheme probably wouldn't be appropriate in most modern workplaces, you'd be right. As it turns out, only 3.3% of young U.S. workers reported being paid on a piece rate basis in 1990.[12] Although the share of workers receiving some form of *variable pay* is considerably higher and has been increasing over the past few decades, even this broader notion of incentive pay affects only a minority of U.S. workers.[13] Thus, whereas Part 1's study of explicit piece rate schemes yields valuable insights about the optimal design of compensation schemes, it's important to bear in mind that this analysis does not *directly* apply to the vast majority of U.S. workers. The majority of U.S. workers receive either a straight hourly rate of pay, or a fixed monthly salary, independent of their current job performance.

The preceding observation, of course, raises the interesting and important question of "What motivates workers who are not explicitly incentivized by variable pay to do their jobs well?" As we'll see in much of the rest of the book, a number of factors play a role, both economic and noneconomic. Economic factors include the desire not to be fired, the hopes of winning a promotion, and the desire to demonstrate you are a good employee to others, including future potential employers. Fortunately, many of the theoretical and empirical tools we have developed in our study of the simplest of all incentive schemes—piece rates—will prove useful in studying these more complex, and common, situations as well. Non-economic motivators are studied in detail in our next chapter.

---

[12] See Table 7 in Lazear's (2000) article.

[13] Variable pay is any type of pay that is linked to recent employee performance in some way, including commissions and bonuses, for example.

Incentive Pay in Developing Countries: Getting Teachers to Come to School and other Successful HRM Interventions

Some of the most dramatic evidence that incentivizing workers can improve their job performance comes from recent randomized experiments conducted in developing countries. For example, Esther Duflo, Rema Hanna, and Stephen P. Ryan (2012) designed an HRM intervention intended to reduce rampant absenteeism among public elementary school teachers in India. In part because teachers have secure government jobs, nationally representative evidence shows that 24% of teachers in India were absent during school hours. Not surprisingly, students in these schools exhibit very low levels of achievement. In a randomized experiment, Duflo et al. monitored teachers' daily attendance using cameras and linked teachers' salaries to their own attendance. Teacher absenteeism in the treatment group fell by 21 percentage points relative to the control group. More important, their students' test scores increased dramatically. Incentivizing teachers also yielded substantial test score gains in a field experiment across 400 schools in India's Andhra Pradesh state, conducted by Karthik Muralidharan and Venkatesh Sundararaman (2011). The "incentive" treatment in this experiment rewarded teachers for improvements in their students' test scores. The authors also found that incentivizing teachers yielded much bigger gains in test scores than simply giving schools more resources, that is, than providing schools with equivalent amounts of money to spend as they thought most appropriate. In the arena of medical care, Paul Gertler and Christel Vermeersch (2013) generated large improvements in child health by introducing performance pay for Rwandan medical care providers. Although all these success stories are highly encouraging, they share a common feature of introducing incentives for the first time into a system that had previously tolerated very low levels of employee performance. As we'll see later in this chapter, generating similar improvements just by raising incentives in other contexts—including American schools—can be much more challenging.

8.5 Safelite 20 Years Later: An Epilogue

After teaching Lazear's Safelite paper in class recently, I began to wonder what had happened in the company in the two decades that have elapsed since the PPP was introduced. Fortunately, I was able to have an extended telephone conversation with Clayton Frech, Safelite's Regional Vice President for the greater Los Angeles area, in January of 2014.

Interestingly, Mr. Frech informed me that the PPP system was still in existence but barely "hanging on." Whereas some workers in high-volume locations (like the one near Los Angeles's international airport—LAX) were able to produce enough to qualify for the per-unit pay, in many locations, the qualifying standard (Q' in Figure 8.1) was so high that few or no workers could benefit from the plan. Mr. Frech attributed Safelite's recent neglect of the PPP system to three main factors.

Two of these factors are perhaps best described as nonfatal "headaches" associated with the system from the beginning. The first was that it frequently put Safelite's management *and* workers into conflict with California's overtime laws, which mandate overtime pay after 8 hours each day. Because the PPP paid per job completed *during their regular working day*, it incentivized workers to put in extra hours but not report them. This led to conflicts with California regulators concerning time clocking compliance issues. The second is a common problem with incentive pay in many environments, specifically any situation where work flow is highly variable. Workers who are paid according to *what they do* will suffer income losses when there is no work available for them *to* do. This can lead to frustration and turnover, compared to companies that promise a steady stream of both work and income. Although Safelite implemented various policies to mitigate this issue, some frustration remained.[14]

Most important, however, PPP appears to be on its way out because Safelite has been acquired by Belron, which claims to be "the world's largest dedicated vehicle glass repair and replacement company." Historically, Safelite emphasized *productivity*, and treated its workers as much as independent tradesmen as employees. These workers owned their own tools, paid relatively little attention to their personal safety, and worked independently. Under Belron, the emphasis has shifted from productivity to *quality, safety, and customer satisfaction*. To promote these goals, Belron introduced a standardized set of tools that raise safety and quality but tend to slow things down, making it harder to qualify for the PPP bonus. In 2013, Belron also introduced (on top of the PPP) a new incentive plan that explicitly rewards quality and customer satisfaction. Essentially, individual workers now get a bonus that depends on a quality indicator, plus a customer satisfaction score, computed from customer feedback surveys.[15]

In a sense, Belron has moved Safelite's HRM system in the direction of "make" on the *buy-versus-make* spectrum of contractual arrangements that is available in the principal–agent relationship. One reason is that—whereas it might seem simple to measure the output (Q) of a Safelite worker as the number of complaint-free windshield replacements per week—the "output" of a Safelite worker is actually something much more complex than this. It includes, for example, keeping the worker safe, making the customer happy, and maintaining the parent company's reputations for quality and service. In other words, even in a work environment as simple as Safelite's, workers' "output" has many dimensions. In such cases, it can be very challenging to design explicit incentives that encourage workers to care adequately about *all* the important aspects of their jobs.

---

[14] These policies included encouraging workers to take vacation in their slowest period (November–December in Southern California) and encouraging a 10-2 (10 months on, two off) work year, like teachers.

[15] Specifically, they use the Net Promoter Score, a proprietary system marketed by Fred Reichheld, Bain & Company, and Satmetrix. More information is available at http://en.wikipedia.org/wiki/Net_Promoter.

Chapter Summary

- ☐ In the mid-1990s, Safelite Auto Glass introduced an incentive scheme called the Performance Pay Plan (PPP) that gave its installers a cash bonus for each unit installed above a weekly target.

- ☐ Section 8.1's simple model of agents' responses to PPP predicts that this scheme should increase workers' output and make it easier for Safelite to attract and retain the most talented installers.

- ☐ Multiple regression analysis suggests that the PPP system raised overall installer productivity by 44%.

- ☐ Only half of this increase occurred because Safelite's existing installers increased their output; the other half was a *selection effect*: The PPP raised the average ability of the workers Safelite was able to attract and retain.

- ☐ This increase in productivity almost certainly raised Safelite's profits. Workers' pay also increased.

- ☐ Although introducing incentives has also yielded positive results in a number of other contexts (including developing-country schools), Safelite has now largely abandoned its PPP scheme in favor of an incentive scheme based more on quality and customer satisfaction.

Discussion Questions

1. Think about a job you have recently held or currently hold. What sort of incentive plan, if any, is there? Do you think that introducing a scheme like the PPP would be likely to improve worker performance there? Why or why not?
2. In his regression analysis, Lazear controlled for seasonal effects and a time trend related to changes in management and technology. Can you think of any other possible confounding factors he perhaps should have controlled for, if possible?
3. Explain how adding a complete set of worker fixed effects, W_i, tell us the extent to which the 44% productivity improvement at a Safelite location was due to employee selection versus changes in the performance of the existing workers.
4. Are you convinced that Lazear has ruled out Hawthorne effects as responsible for the success of the PPP? Why or why not?

Suggestions for Further Reading

Duflo, Hanna, and Ryan (2012) present dramatic evidence of just how effective performance incentives can be when designed well and when introduced into a context where they are really needed. If you check it out, you'll probably want to focus your attention on the "reduced-form" results, not the structural labor supply model estimates, which are more technical in nature.

References

Duflo, E., Hanna, R., & Ryan, S. P. (2012). Incentives work: Getting teachers to come to school. *American Economic Review, 102,* 1241–1278.

Gertler, P., & Vermeersch. C. (2013, May). *Using performance incentives to improve medical care productivity and health outcomes* (NBER Working Paper No. 19046). Cambridge, MA: National Bureau of Economic Research.

Jones, S. R. G. (1992). Was there a Hawthorne effect? *American Journal of Sociology, 98*(3), 451–468.

Lazear, E. P. (2000). Performance pay and productivity. *American Economic Review, 90*(3), 1346–1361.

Levitt, S. D., & List, J. A. (2011). Was there really a Hawthorne effect at the Hawthorne plant? An analysis of the original illumination experiments. *American Economic Journal: Applied Economics, 3,* 224–238.

Muralidharan, K., & Sundararaman, V. (2011). Teacher performance pay: Experimental evidence from India. *Journal of Political Economy, 119,* 39–77.

9 Some Non-Classical Motivators

This chapter introduces a number of factors that have been found to affect employee motivation and performance, which go beyond the "classical" motivators (the agent's absolute levels of income and leisure) we considered in Part 1. In contrast to the analysis so far, which started with a simple economic model and then turned to some relevant evidence, in this and the next few chapters we'll take the opposite approach. Specifically, we'll start by describing some key pieces of evidence, many of which were actually experiments designed to test simple "classical" models of motivation. Many of those experiments provide powerful evidence that non-classical factors also affect job performance.

9.1 Pay Enough or Don't Pay at All

In an article published in 2000 (the same year Lazear's Safelite article was published), economists Uri Gneezy and Aldo Rustichini conducted an influential pair of experiments that were in many ways similar to Lazear's. Indeed, just like the Safelite study, both of Gneezy and Rustichini's experiments looked at what happened to workers' job performance when marginal financial incentives are increased. In fact, Gneezy and Rustichini's experiments correspond almost exactly to the situation faced by the agent in Chapter 2's theoretical model: The workers all received the same, fixed amount of base pay (a) for participating in the experiment, then were randomly assigned to groups that received different piece rates (b) per unit of output they produced. Of course, if Chapter 2's model of agent behavior is correct, workers' job performance should increase as we increase their marginal financial rewards, b. Did it?

The subjects in Gneezy and Rustichini's (2000) first experiment were 160 undergraduate students at the University of Haifa who were randomly assigned to one of four different groups of 40 students each. Students in all groups were paid to answer 50 questions taken from a test used in the university's admissions process, which is similar to the GMAT exam. Importantly, although the authors refer it as an "IQ test," the questions were chosen to rely more on the students' effort (in computation and reasoning) than on general knowledge. All the students were paid 60 New Israeli Shekels (NIS) for participating in the experiment.[1] The only difference between the groups was that in addition, students in one group were promised 0.1 NIS per question they answered correctly; whereas in two other groups, students were promised 1 NIS per question and 3 NIS per question, respectively. [Notice that this last situation is quite a nice deal: a student who answered 30 questions correctly—which was around the average—would earn a total of $0.3(60 + 3 \times 30) = \$45$ U.S. for participating in a 1-hr-long experiment.] The fourth group just received the 60 NIS show-up fee and wasn't paid anything per question correctly answered. None of the groups knew that there were other groups being paid different amounts for doing the same "job."

Table 9.1 shows the average number of questions answered correctly by the four groups of students.

TABLE 9.1 MEAN STUDENT PERFORMANCE IN GNEEZY AND RUSTICHINI'S (2000) IQ EXPERIMENT

	PAYMENT PER CORRECT ANSWER (NIS)			
	0	0.1	1.0	3.0
Mean Performance	28.4	23.1	34.7	34.1

NIS = New Israeli Shekels

Consistent with the results of Lazear's (2000) Safelite study, students in Gneezy and Rustichini's (2000) experiment improved their performance substantially when their pay per correct answer was increased from 0.1 to 1 NIS. (The improvement from 23.1 to 34.7 correct answers constitutes a 50% increase—even higher than the improvement at Safelite.) Raising incentives beyond that, to 3 NIS per question, didn't generate any better performance, probably because students were already performing at capacity. The most surprising result of Gneezy and Rustichini's experiment, though, is what happened when the experimenters cut their "workers'" piece rate from 0.1 NIS to 0: instead of falling even further, performance *improved* by a statistically significant $(28.4 - 23.1)/23.1 = 23\%$.[2]

To ensure that the results from the preceding lab experiment weren't specific to one particular task or to university students, Gneezy and Rustichini (2000) performed a second experiment, which involved "real" work and took place in a field setting. Here, the subjects were 180 high school students. The students' jobs were to go door to door soliciting contributions to a well-known charity over the course of 5 days. Because these 5 "donation days" were widely advertised, a student's performance depended, again, mostly on effort (in this case, just the

[1] At the time of the experiment, 60 NIS was worth \$18 U.S. (1 NIS was about 30 cents).

[2] All the differences between the columns of Table 9.1, except those between the 1.0 and 3.0 payments, are statistically significant.

number of homes they decided to visit during the 5-day period). The students were randomly divided into three groups, one of which was paid a commission equal to 1% of the amount of donations they solicited, and one of which was paid 10%.[3] The third group wasn't paid at all. Table 9.2 shows the average performance (in total NIS collected per student) of these three groups.

TABLE 9.2 MEAN STUDENT PERFORMANCE IN GNEEZY AND RUSTICHINI'S (2000) DONATION EXPERIMENT

	COMMISSION RATE PER NIS COLLECTED		
	0%	1%	10%
Mean Performance (NIS Collected)	238.6	153.6	219.3

NIS = New Israeli Shekels

Once again (just as in the IQ experiment and in the Safelite study), these workers' performance improved markedly when their piece rate was raised from 1% to 10% of receipts. But as in the IQ experiment, performance was higher under zero marginal incentives than under low-level, positive incentives. In fact, in this experiment, *the best performance was attained when the subjects weren't paid at all.*[4] Putting these two experiments together, we can say the following:

RESULT 9.1

Gneezy and Rustichini (2000)

These IQ and donations experiments demonstrate that introducing small marginal incentives (i.e., setting $b > 0$ but small) can *reduce* agents' performance relative to an identical situation with zero marginal incentives ($b = 0$). So, as the title of their article says, when designing incentive pay systems, the best policy may be either to "pay enough or don't pay at all."

What explains this puzzling feature of Gneezy and Rustichini's (2000) two experiments? Before describing one theory in the next section, it's interesting to note that whatever explained the students' behavior in Gneezy and Rustichini's experiments is an aspect of their behavior *that the students themselves did not expect.* We know this because of two clever companion experiments the authors conducted. After the IQ experiment, Gneezy and Rustichini recruited 53 undergraduate students from the same university in the same way. But now the students were put into the role of a principal in the IQ experiment. Each of these 53 students had an agent working for him or her (whom they did not meet) doing exactly the same task as in the IQ experiment. Each principal was informed that they'd be

[3] Importantly, the students were paid by the experimenters (Gneezy and Rustichini), not by the charity. Thus, if they cared about the charity, they didn't need to worry that a higher pay rate for them took money out of the charity's hands.

[4] All the differences between columns of Table 9.2 are statistically significant except for the difference between 0% and 10%.

paid 1 NIS for every question their *agent* answered correctly. The principal's only decision was whether their agent would be paid zero NIS per correct answer or 0.1 NIS per correct answer. (These payments came from the experimenter's funds, not the principals'.) Of course, if these principals knew the results of Gneezy and Rustichini's experiment in Table 9.1, they would have selected the zero piece rate option, because that would maximize their agent's performance and therefore their own payoff. But 46 of the 53 subjects (87%) instead chose the positive pay rate!

A similar companion experiment was done with 25 high school students who were put into the role of principals in the donation experiment: 19 of them choose to pay "their" agent 1% of collections rather than 0%. In sum, the high school and university students in Gneezy and Rustichini's (2000) study seem to have expected their classmates to behave exactly the way a simple economic model predicts: working more under a small positive piece rate than a zero piece rate. But in both cases, they were wrong, just like the simple economic model. (Perhaps they had taken too many economics courses!)

☑ RESULT 9.2 **Incentives and Profits**

Students who took the role of principals in Gneezy and Rustichini's (2000) IQ and donations experiments overwhelmingly behaved as though they expected small positive incentives to improve their agents' performance, rather than reduce it. Student principals who chose to offer their agent small positive incentives earned less profits than those who offered no incentives at all.

9.2 Non-Monetary Incentives: Intrinsic, Symbolic, and Image Motivation

Motivated by Gneezy and Rustichini's (2000) experiments, which suggest that agents may have derived some non-monetary satisfaction from their work, this section explores three different sources of non-monetary motivation in greater detail. We begin with the idea of intrinsic motivation—utility derived from enjoyable aspects of the task itself.

What's Meaningful Work Worth? The Economics of Intrinsic Motivation

To measure the effects of intrinsic motivation, Dan Ariely, Emir Kamenica, and Drazen Prelec (AKP; 2008) paid two groups of male Harvard undergraduates to assemble Legos (Bionicles). Each Bionicle consisted of 40 pieces and took about 10 min to build (instructions were provided). The subjects were paid \$2.00 for the first Bionicle they assembled, \$1.89 for the next, and 11 cents less for each subsequent Bionicle they assembled. If they got up to 20 Bionicles, they got only 2 cents for each additional one. The subjects could stay in the experiment as long as they liked; their only decision was when to stop making Bionicles. The subjects were divided into two groups; importantly, *both* groups were told their Bionicles would be disassembled after the experiment so they could be used in other experiments. All subjects worked alone.

An Assembled Bionicle

One group of 20 students worked in what was called the *meaningful* condition, where the Bionicles a student built were lined up in a row in front of him as he completed the work. For the second, called the *Sisyphus* condition, each Bionicle the student assembled was disassembled by the experimenter *while the student was working on the next one*. The experiment's main result was that subjects built a lot more Bionicles under the meaningful condition: They built an average of 10.6 Bionicles, earning \$14.40, compared to 7.2 Bionicles and \$11.52 in the Sisyphus condition. Put a different way, the median student stopped working at a price per Bionicle of \$1.40 in the Sisyphus condition, compared to \$1.01 in the meaningful condition. So, even in as trivial a case as building Legos, adding *meaning* to an employee's work can have sizable effects on how much work that person is willing to do for the same wage.

To quantify the value of "meaningful" work to AKP's subjects, Figure 9.1 interprets their choices using a diagram just like the bottom panel of Figure 2.1

Sisyphus

In Greek mythology, Sisyphus was a king of Ephyra (now known as Corinth) punished for chronic deceitfulness by being compelled to roll an immense boulder up a hill, only to watch it roll back down, and to repeat this action forever (source: Wikipedia).

Titian, 1490-1576 Sisyphus Prado Museum

or Figure 2.2, which shows agents working up to the point where the marginal disutility of effort just equals its marginal cash reward. Two (minor) differences between Figures 9.1 and 2.2 are (a) that the horizontal axis measures the amount of output (Bionicles) produced rather than effort, and (b) that in the Bionicles experiment, instead of being paid a flat amount per unit of output produced, the subjects were paid a declining amount, starting with $2.00 for the first Bionicle produced and declining at a rate of 11 cents for each successive Bionicle.[5]

[5] Because the subjects were allowed to build Bionicles as long as they wanted, this declining marginal piece rate served a very practical purpose: to guarantee that the experiments didn't go on all day long. More important, as we'll see following, this declining marginal price per Bionicle also allows the authors to compute the cash value of meaningful work to their experimental subjects.

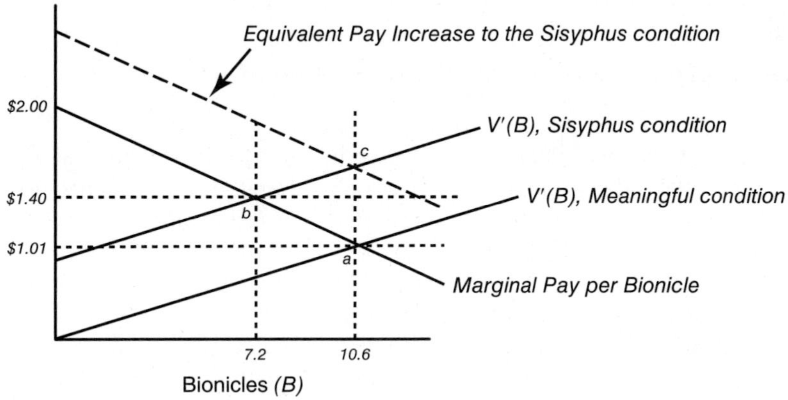

FIGURE 9.1. Implications of the Bionicles Experiment for the Disutility of Effort Function

Given this pay schedule (shown by the solid downward-sloping line), the subjects' marginal-disutility-of-effort curve in the meaningful condition must have looked something like the solid upward-sloping line labeled meaningful condition. Presumably the marginal disutility is rising, and it must intersect the marginal pay schedule at point *a* for a typical subject because this is what a typical subject chose: to produce 10.6 Bionicles, at which point the marginal reward to producing Bionicles had fallen to $1.01 per piece. By the same reasoning, the disutility-of-effort-curve under the Sisyphus condition must look something like the higher *V'(B)* line because in this condition, a typical subject stopped working after making only 7.2 Bionicles, when the pay per Bionicle was $1.40.

With this information, we can now place a hard monetary value on how much AKP's undergraduate subjects were willing to pay for "meaningful" work. One way to do this is to ask how much we would need to raise the workers' pay rate in the meaningless condition to get them to do just as much work as they did in the meaningful condition. A pay schedule with this feature is the dashed downward-sloping line in Figure 9.1. Although we can't say exactly how much higher this pay schedule needs to be in general (that depends, in part, on the slope of the marginal-disutility-of-effort curve, which we don't observe), a quick glance at Figure 9.1 reveals that at output levels near the desired equilibrium level (10.6), the new pay schedule must be *at least* 39 cents per Bionicle ($1.40–$1.01) higher.[6] Put a different way, you'd have raise workers' pay by almost 40% to get them to be just as productive doing meaningless work as meaningful. This suggests *it might be really good for firms' bottom lines to make workers' jobs meaningful.*

[6] To see why this is true, consider the two polar cases for what the marginal-disutility-of-effort curve, *V'(B)*, could look like. If the curve was perfectly horizontal (i.e., infinitely elastic), then the vertical distance between points *c* and *d* would be exactly 39 cents. If the curve was any steeper, this distance will be greater than 39 cents. In the limit (vertical, infinitely inelastic curves), no amount of money could adequately compensate workers for giving up the pleasure of building more Bionicles.

More on Intrinsic Motivation: How Much Does the Mission Matter?

One important source of intrinsic motivation is whether a worker believes in the organization's mission. To assess the relative importance of "mission" and financial incentives, Jeffrey Carpenter and Eric Gong (2016) conducted an experiment at a U.S. college during the 2012 U.S. presidential election. Several weeks after surveying the students about their political preferences, they randomly assigned individuals to work for either the Obama or Romney presidential campaigns, thus creating both mission "matches" and "mismatches." Their jobs were to stuff and address letters to independent voters, a job that campaign volunteers frequently perform and where output is easily measured. Compared to people who did not care intensely about the candidates, Carpenter and Gong found that matched Democrats or Republicans assigned to work for their preferred candidate had 27% higher productivity. Mismatched workers assigned to work for the other candidate worked 43% less than "neutral" workers. Thus, perhaps not surprisingly, believing in an organization's mission has large effects on workers' effort. The authors also found, however, that workers who were assigned to work for their opposition could be "bought": Although financial incentives had little effect on workers who believed in their organization's mission, performance-based incentives for mismatched workers dramatically increased their job performance. Thus, financial incentives matter too, especially for "non-believers."

Symbolic Awards as Motivators

Another type of nonfinancial reward that has been argued to motivate workers is a *symbolic award*, such as an "employee of the month" certificate that has no cash value but may involve some public recognition. One reason symbolic rewards may be effective is that they "look good on a resume," that is, they provide important information to one's future bosses and employers that one is a conscientious, or public-spirited employee. Personnel economists refer to this source of motivation as *career concerns*, and we'll study it in detail in Section 18.3. Another possibility is that employees simply get utility from winning a competition of any kind—we'll return to this possibility when we study competition among workers in Part 4. Some recent evidence on the causal effects of purely symbolic awards on employee performance, however, is available from a clever recent study of Zambian health care trainees by Ashraf, Bandiera, and Lee (2014).

A key insight of Ashraf et al.'s (2014) article is that most symbolic award programs (i.e., policies of publicly recognizing top performers) actually have two distinct components. One is to give *workers themselves* information on their performance relative to their peers. For example, when a worker learns he did not win an award, he learns that he was not one of the best-performing employees in the current period. The authors call this the *social comparisons* effect of an award program. The other effect is to give *public recognition to* the winners; this is the effect of the award itself, which could be different from the information it provides on relative performance. In their experiment, Ashraf et al. are able to "unbundle" these two effects by sometimes giving the trainees their relative performance information *without* making a public announcement of the award.

Importantly, Ashraf et al. (2014) found that these two distinct aspects of award programs had *opposite* effects on trainee performance. On the one hand, Ashraf et al. found that public recognition of the top performers—that is, knowing, before you start working, that good performance could win you a public recognition—was highly motivating, raising average trainee performance by 0.4 standard deviations. This is strong evidence of the power of purely symbolic incentives, with no cash value or financial cost to the employer. On the other hand, knowing (again, before you start working) that you will be informed of your relative performance when the job is done was highly demotivating, especially to the least able trainees. The authors argue that these workers deliberately tried less hard *to preserve their beliefs that they had high relative ability*: by slacking off, they could attribute their failure to win to a lack of effort rather than low ability. (This type of behavior has been documented in other settings as well. For example, Oster, Shoulson, and Dorsey [2013] show that many individuals at high risk of Huntington's disease refuse tests because they prefer to continue holding optimistic beliefs about their health status.)

Because of these opposing effects, the total effect of having an award program in Ashraf et al.'s (2014) experiment was zero: Average performance was no better with the program than without. However, because the strongest de-motivating effects of the program were among the least-able trainees, Ashraf et al.'s results suggest that awards can increase the *dispersion* of performance by *weakening the weakest*. In their developing-country health care setting, this could have life-and-death consequences. In sum, Ashraf et al.'s findings are an important cautionary tale about the use of symbolic rewards such as "employee of the month" certificates that facilitate interpersonal comparisons, especially in contexts where worsening performance at the bottom of the distribution is problematic for the employer.

Image Motivation: Working to Influence What Others Think of You

A third and final type of non-monetary motivation we'll consider here is *image motivation*. As we've already discussed, intrinsic motivation is working because you enjoy the job or believe in it, and symbolic rewards may motivate workers because they provide information to oneself or others about the worker's relative job performance. *Image motivation*, on the other hand, applies especially to work that is seen as *socially desirable* by people you care about. This can include volunteering for a charity or even doing extra work at one's workplace. The key distinguishing feature of image motivation is *visibility*: What matters is not doing good per se but *being seen to be* doing good. A person who is motivated by image cares about others' opinions of him or her.

To measure the importance of image motivation, Dan Ariely, Anat Bracha, and Stephan Meier (ABM; 2009) conducted a lab experiment where 161 Princeton undergraduates "worked" by sequentially pressing the "X" and "Z" keys on the keyboard for up to 5 min. For every completed pair of key presses, the experimenters donated a fraction of a cent to a charity that was viewed positively by a large majority (92%) of Princeton undergraduates: the American Red Cross. Some of the students received no money per click themselves (the *no incentives* condition); others were paid an amount exactly equal to what they earned for the Red Cross (the *incentives* condition). At the end of the task, students in the *public* condition had to tell the other lab participants whether they had been incentivized and how much money they had earned for themselves and the charity. Students in the *private* condition weren't asked to disclose anything to the other participants. Altogether, the authors studied the behavior of students under four different sets of circumstances: no incentives, public; no incentives, private; incentives, public; and incentives, private.

ABM (2009) find that image motivation is, indeed, quite important for their subjects: In the absence of incentives, students pressed the keys an average of 900 times when others could see their actions, compared with 517 times in the "private" condition. In both cases, the students were earning money only for the Red

Will There Be Blood? Financial Rewards Don't Always Crowd Out Pro-Social Behavior

One activity where you might think intrinsic motivation matters a lot, and where introducing financial incentives might really "crowd out" those incentives, is donating blood. Indeed, ever since R. M. Titmuss (1971) famously claimed that offering material rewards for blood donations might backfire and either reduce total donations or reduce the quality of donated blood, organizations like the Red Cross have been highly skeptical of introducing financial incentives for their donors. Interestingly, however, recent evidence from a study of nearly 14,000 American Red Cross blood drives by Lacetera, Macis, and Slonim (2012) shows that economic incentives have a positive effect on blood donations without increasing the fraction of donors who are ineligible to donate (the most important indicator of quality). Thus, adding financial incentives doesn't always crowd out other motives to "do the right thing." Perhaps financial incentives didn't crowd out blood donations because *image* is not an important element of giving blood: there are many valid medical reasons for not giving blood, and whether one has donated may not be visible to most of one's friends, coworkers, and neighbors. This would reduce the signaling value of giving blood, which we might expect to be most fragile to the introduction of cash incentives.

Unfortunately, however, the main effect of economic incentives in Lacetera et al.'s (2012) study was not to raise the total amount of blood supplied in a region but to shift donors from blood drives without incentives to neighboring drives with incentives. This highlights the fact that—in introducing any kind of incentives—it's important to look at not only at how agents substitute *toward* the newly incentivized activity but also whether they substitute *away* from other, non-incentivized activities. We discussed these issues with multitask principal–agent problems in Section 5.5.

Cross (not for themselves); the only difference was whether other students knew how much they earned. The authors' second main result is that adding monetary incentives appears to crowd out image motivation. Specifically, adding monetary incentives in the private condition raised the students' mean key press output from 517 to 737. But in the public condition, adding monetary incentives actually *reduced* click output from 900 to 814.

Thus, the idea of image motivation—which received its first rigorous theoretical statement in a seminal article by Benabou and Tirole (2006)—provides one possible explanation for why adding a small amount of monetary incentives can reduce job performance in some settings, such as Gneezy and Rustichini's (2000) donations experiment: If you are doing something *for money*, doing it is no longer an effective signal to others that you are a good or generous person.

9.3 Large Stakes and Big Mistakes

So far in Chapter 9 we've seen experimental evidence of two apparent "anomalies" in agents' effort supply behavior. These anomalies are aspects of worker or agent behavior that are at odds with the simple model in Chapter 2, where agents trade off the disutility of performing the task against the financial reward associated with it. Specifically, Gneezy and Rustichini (2000) found that subjects work harder when not paid at all than when paid a small amount; and AKP (2008) found that the extent to which workers were willing to perform exactly the same task for pay was strongly affected simply by whether workers were able to *see* the products of their labor. Letting workers see the results of their work generated the same increase in performance as would a 40% increase in the piece rate.

One critique that's sometimes applied to the previous studies (and indeed to many personnel economics experiments that use students as subjects) is that the stakes are too small: Noneconomic considerations such as intrinsic meaning might trump economic ones when the financial stakes are small. But if serious money was at stake, subjects would pay more attention to the strict economics involved and behave more closely in line with the purely self-interested, rational agent from Chapter 2. Motivated in part by this critique, Dan Ariely, Uri Gneezy, George Loewenstein, and Nina Mazar (AGLM; 2009) conducted a series of experiments on how financial incentives affect performance. As in the previous studies described in this chapter, the tasks were simple ones, but the stakes were much higher. In part, this is because the experiments were performed in a rural village in India. Because the village's residents were very poor, the authors were able to offer them very high incentives for task performance at a reasonable cost.

Three of the tasks in AGLM's (2009) "high stakes" experiment mostly required motor skills: "Dart Ball" is a lot like darts, except with tennis balls and Velcro; "Roll-up" involves using two rods to drop a ball into the highest possible slot on a board; and "Labyrinth" is a maze game with a steel ball on a tilted wooden surface with holes. Two other tasks used mostly memory skills: In "Recall Last Three Digits," the experimenter reads a sequence of digits and stops

FIGURE 9.2. Some of the Tasks in AGL's "High-Stakes" Experiments

at a random time. At that time, the subject is asked to repeat the last three digits the experimenter read. "Simon" is an electronic game that was popular in the 1980s. Here, the game flashes a series of colored buttons (with sounds), and the subject's job is to imitate ever-longer sequences played by the machine. (Current versions are called "Bop-It.") The "packing" task mostly requires creativity: the subject has to fit the largest possible number of wooden pieces of a given shape into rectangular wooden frame. The "Labyrinth," "Simon," and "packing" tasks are shown in Figure 9.2.[7]

For each of these six tasks, AGLM (2009) defined two performance targets: "good" and "very good." Subjects who performed at the "very good" level or better for that game received full payment. Subjects who attained "good" but not "very good" received half payment; and subjects who attained neither target received nothing. The level of the full payment depended on the stakes, which were either low (4 rupees), medium (40 rupees), or high (400 rupees). To get a sense for how these stakes compare to the subjects' economic circumstances, note that the average per-person monthly expenditure in rural India at the time of the experiment was 495 rupees, or about $10 U.S., and the average wage was about 3 rupees per hour. So, the highest possible payment in the low-stakes treatment was small but not trivial: subjects who performed at the "very good" level in all six of their tasks would earn 24 rupees, or about 8 hr worth of income. In the high-stakes treatment, however, attaining "very good" performance in all six games would yield about six months' worth of income for less than a day's work!

In setting up their experiment this way, the authors had three main hypotheses they hoped to test. First, in line with standard economic reasoning, they expected that going from low to medium incentives would probably raise the subjects' performance levels. Based on some previous literature in psychology, however, they thought that raising incentives from medium to high levels might

[7] Figure 9.2 shows a "packing circles" task. AGLM's packing task actually used quarter-circles but the principle is exactly the same.

have detrimental results: psychologists have shown that many subjects exhibit a "choke" response when performing in high-stakes situations.[8] Finally, based on the same literature, AGLM expected choking to be more of a problem for the motor skills and creativity tasks than the memory tasks. Essentially, the idea was that higher stakes would lead subjects to focus their attention more intently on the task at hand. Unfortunately, consciously thinking hard about the task can actually be detrimental to physical tasks (indeed, athletes often strive to make their actions completely automatic and *un*conscious) and to creativity (thinking "sideways" or "out of the box" tends to work best when you're not 100% focused on a task). But paying really close attention might help on memory tasks.

The results of AGLM's (2009) experiment are shown in Figure 9.3. Somewhat to their surprise, when the stakes were raised from low to medium, performance improved on only two tasks: packing quarters (creativity) and dart ball

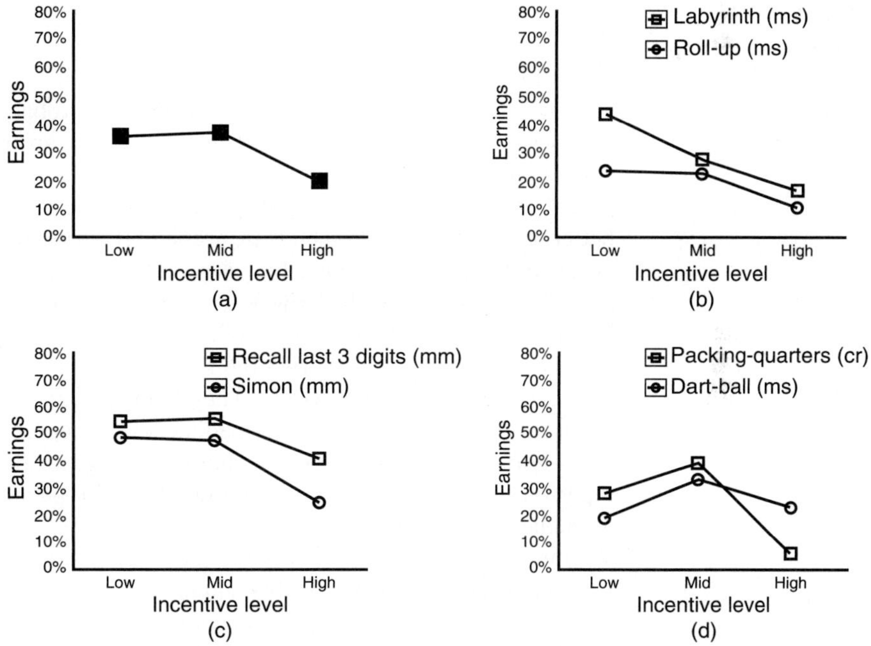

FIGURE 9.3. Performance in AGLM's High-Stakes Experiments

Figure 1 in AGLM (2009) figures show means of the share of earnings relative to the maximum possible earnings for the three payment levels for all six games combined (a), and plotted separately by game (b–d). Games are indicated by their category: motor skills (ms), memory(mm), and creativity (cr).

[8] For the most part, however, psychologists didn't study the effects of high *monetary* stakes. Indeed, stakes were raised by making people do the task in front of an audience, or in competition with other agents, or in a way that the outcome might threaten the subject's self-image.

(one of the motor skills tasks). In all the other cases, performance either remained flat or deteriorated. More in line with the authors' expectations, performance deteriorated *in all nine tasks* when the stakes went from the medium to the high level. Finally, contrary to the authors' expectations about where "choking" would be more severe, there was no consistent difference across the three types of tasks in the amount of choking that occurred.

RESULT 9.3 **AGLM (2009)**

Their "high-stakes" experiment in rural India found that raising the piece rate (*b*) from a low to a medium level had mixed effects on task performance, whereas raising *b* from a medium to a high level reduced performance on all nine tasks studied. This deterioration in performance did not differ markedly between tasks requiring mostly motor skills, memory, or creativity.

What explains the detrimental effect of incentives on task performance in AGLM's (2009) experiment? Put most simply, it probably arises from a distinction between *motivation* and *performance,* which are not distinguished in the simple model of the agent in Section 2.1. According to the standard economic model, trying harder (exerting more effort) automatically results in performing better, at least on average, because we simply write the production function as $Q(E)$.[9] But psychologists have long argued that the two need to be distinguished; indeed, this idea goes all the way back to a phenomenon known as the Yerkes-Dodson law, first published in 1908. Yerkes and Dodson were training rats to perform a task, and they varied the size of the punishment (electric shock) the rats received if they got it wrong. They found that the rats learned most quickly when the punishment was at intermediate levels, not too high or too low.

More generally, psychologists have long argued that raising an animal's or a person's *motivation* to complete a task (e.g., by paying more or by providing an audience or a competitor) doesn't necessarily mean they'll perform better. We might really *want* to do a better job when we're playing that instrument or giving that speech in front of a big audience, or when lots of money's at stake, but the extra focus *we can't help but devote* to the task in those situations can actually reduce our performance. Put a different way, in the simple economic model, *there's no such thing as trying too hard*—higher effort always yields better outcomes, at least on average. In a more psychological model, there are cases where it would actually be helpful to try less hard, but our minds and bodies won't allow us to. Higher stakes lead, involuntarily, to a higher state of *arousal* that can inhibit the performance of some tasks.

[9] Of course, it is common for economists to recognize that trying harder doesn't *always* result in better results because random chance can affect work outcomes as well. Indeed, we've already examined some important consequences of this fact in Chapter 5. But even the many economic models that incorporate the effects of luck all assume that, on average, agents who try harder will attain better results.

RESULT 9.4

"Motivation, Effort, and Performance"

The deterioration in performance at higher stakes in AGLM's (2009) experiment may be explained by a distinction between motivation and effort on the one hand, and performance on the other. Higher stakes raise the motivation to do well and lead people to "try harder." But in many cases, this extra effort (or involuntary arousal, as some psychologists conceptualize it) can actually be detrimental to performance.

9.4 Are High Stakes Really a Problem? The Role of Self-Selection

On the surface, AGLM's (2009) results seem to suggest that the high financial stakes faced by employees in certain jobs, such as currency or options traders or CEOs, might in fact be detrimental to those employees' performance (and perhaps for the economy as a whole). But jumping to that conclusion would ignore one of the main lessons of another classic study in personnel economics: Lazear's Safelite study. In particular, Result 8.3 told us that *incentive schemes tend to attract people who perform well under those incentives.* So, even if most people choke when placed in high-stakes situations, perhaps those people who are attracted to (and survive in!) high-stakes situations are precisely those people who *thrive* under pressure. If that's true, then the small minority of U.S. workers who work in high-stakes jobs may in fact be facing exactly the right incentives *for them.* Lazear's self-selection idea is an important, powerful, and highly plausible one, but it's a hard one to test directly.

That said, here are a few pieces of evidence that are relevant to the self-selection idea as it applies to high-stakes jobs. First, one might think that really intelligent people might be less likely to choke in high-stakes situations. To check this, AGLM (2009) did another high-stakes-and-performance experiment involving undergraduate students at the Massachusetts Institute of Technology. (This one cost the experimenters a little more money.) Here they also found significant choking on a task that involved *basic* cognitive activity (adding three-digit numbers) for these highly selected students. So, whatever it is that helps people perform under pressure, it's probably not pure intelligence. Second, AGLM asked the subjects in some of their experiments to predict which level of incentives would produce the best results. (Subjects received a moderate reward if they got the answer right.) Like the principals in Gneezy and Rustichini's (2000) experiments, most subjects *incorrectly* predicted that higher stakes would improve performance. If these inaccurate perceptions are widespread, it's possible people might systematically select into environments where they *think* they'll perform best, when in reality it is not the best environment for them.

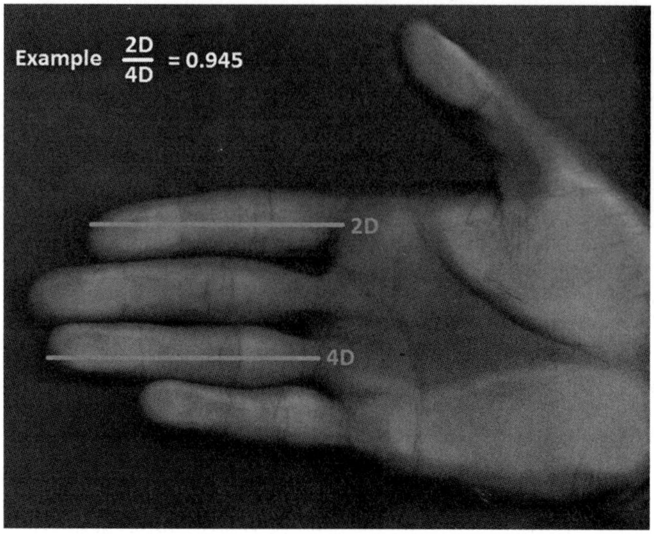

FIGURE 9.4. A Low 2D:4D Ratio
A low 2D:4D ratio is associated with success in noise trading and with high prenatal androgen exposure. Wikimedia Commons. 2011.

Hand_zur_Abmessung

Is your index finger much shorter than your ring finger? This physical trait is called the second to fourth digit (2D:4D) ratio, and low values mean your index finger is much shorter than your ring finger (see Figure 9.4). If you have a low 2D:4D ratio, and you're male, you're more likely to be better at competitive sports, to be more aggressive, and to be a good musician than other men. And, according to a recent study conducted in London's financial district, you would likely be a better "noise" trader in financial markets. According to Coates, Gurnell, and Rustichini's (2009) study, men with unusually short index fingers earned higher long-term profits and lasted longer in this highly competitive, high-stress business than other male traders.[10] What explains this effect? According to the authors, a number of other studies have linked a low 2D:4D ratio to higher prenatal androgen exposure. According to Coates et al., prenatal androgens increase men's risk preferences in adulthood and promote more rapid visuomotor scanning and physical reflexes—exactly what's needed to do well in this high-stakes business. Coates et al.'s study is a fascinating example of a case where precisely those people who don't choke under pressure self-select into high-stakes jobs and outperform others in those jobs.

[10] Almost no London noise traders were female when Coates et al. (2009) did their study. Garbarino, Slonim, and Sydnor (2011) provide direct laboratory evidence that 2D:4D ratios are higher among men than women, that they are correlated with risk preferences within either gender, and can account for part of the gender gap in risk-taking.

Do Professionals Choke? Evidence from Sports

Just because people who do relatively well under pressure self-select into high-pressure environments doesn't mean they are completely immune from choking. In fact, a number of authors have studied the effects of high stakes on the performance of the world's top athletes. If even these people perform worse when the stakes are high, employers of "regular" people might indeed want to use caution when applying high-powered incentives.

Although there is some dispute in the empirical literature, overall it seems to suggest that top sports professionals do, on average, perform worse when the stakes are high. For example, Cao, Price, and Stone (2011) study performance on a simple, standardized task—free throws—in the National Basketball Association and find strong evidence that players choke under pressure: they shoot 5%–10% worse than normal in the final seconds of very close games. In a similar vein, Dohmen (2008) studies penalty kicks in soccer and finds that performance declines when there are more spectators and when the point matters more. Apesteguia and Palacios-Huerta (2010) study shoot-outs in major soccer tournaments, where the team that shoots first is decided by a coin toss. They argue that pressure is, on average, higher if you shoot second because there's a higher chance you'll need to make a "do or die" shot. They find that being randomly selected to shoot second dramatically reduces a team's odds of winning the game. Working with a larger sample of shoot-outs, however, Kocher, Lenz, and Sutter (2012) find no significant difference.

9.5 Reference Points: Theory and Laboratory Evidence

Some undergraduate students at my institution, UCSB, participate as subjects in economics experiments. Many find it interesting, and because experimental subjects earn typically about \$15 or \$20 per 1-hr session (depending of course on the decisions they make in the experiment), it can be a nice source of extra income. Imagine for a moment that you are one of these students. For the past 10 weeks, you've participated in one experiment per week and earned at least \$20 each time. You've come to rely on this extra income and have begun to build it into your weekly entertainment budget; it seems, in fact, like a reasonable goal to strive for every time you participate in an experiment.

Now, imagine that this week's experiment is a simple labor supply experiment (like, e.g., Gneezy and Rustichini's [2000] "IQ" experiment or AKP's [2008] Bionicles experiment) where your only job is to do some task. Your payoff depends only on how well, or how often, you perform that task. Given that earning at least \$20 is in some way meaningful to you, how could we represent that fact in Chapter 2's simple model of your behavior as an agent?

Introducing Prospect Theory

As it turns out, ever since psychologists Daniel Kahneman and Amos Tversky introduced economists to the idea of *prospect theory* in a seminal 1979 article, personnel economists have had a natural way to think about this idea.[11] Fundamentally, Kahneman and Tversky proposed that in many important situations, human beings evaluate their well-being not on some absolute scale (such as their total wealth or consumption) but against some *reference point*. Although the theory itself is silent on how that reference point is established—it could, for example, depend on social context, recent experience, and/or goals—Kahneman and Tversky propose that once a reference point has been established, human beings exhibit *loss aversion* with respect to that point. Specifically, Kahneman and Tversky argue that a \$1 loss of income *below* the reference point hurts people *more* than a \$1 gain *above* the reference point benefits them.

A little more formally, recall the agent's utility function we proposed way back in Equation 1.4:

$$U = Y - V(E). \quad \textbf{(1.4, repeated)}$$

Kahneman and Tversky (1979) argue that when an agent's reference point matters, Equation 1.4 should be replaced by

$$U = H(Y) - V(E), \quad \textbf{(9.1)}$$

where the function $H(Y)$ (which gives the agent's utility from income) is depicted in Figure 9.5; there, R shows the reference level of income. Figure 9.5 shows

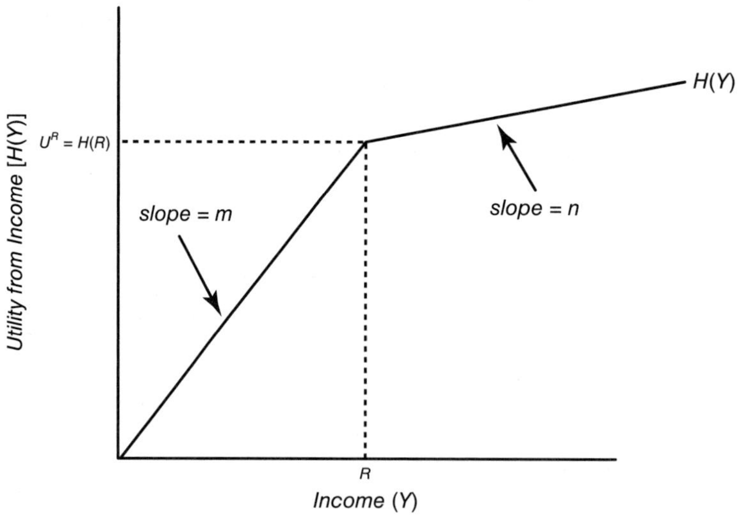

FIGURE 9.5. Utility from Income in Prospect Theory

[11] Kahneman was awarded the 2002 Nobel prize in Economics, in part for his work with Tversky on prospect theory. Unfortunately, Tversky was no longer alive at the time, and Nobel prizes are not awarded posthumously.

that there is a *kink* in the utility function at the reference point, where its slope (i.e., the agent's *marginal* utility) jumps downward, from m to n, when his actual income rises above the reference level.[12]

Mathematically, $H(Y)$ in Figure 9.5 can be written

$$H(Y) = U^R - m(R - Y) \text{ if } Y \leq R$$
$$H(Y) = U^R + n(Y - R) \text{ if } Y \geq R, \quad \textbf{(9.2)}$$

where U^R is the utility of being at the reference point, R.[13]

How does Chapter 2's analysis of the agent's optimal effort choice change when agents are loss averse with respect to a reference income level, R? Perhaps the best way to see this is in Figure 9.6, which shows the agent's *marginal* benefits and costs from effort as a function of the amount of effort supplied. Figure 9.6 is identical to the bottom panel of Figure 2.1 (which shows marginal benefits and costs in the absence of loss aversion), with two main differences. The first is that, due to loss aversion, the agent's marginal benefit of effort jumps downward, from *mbd* to *nbd*, at the point E^R, where

$$E^R = \frac{R-a}{bd}. \quad \textbf{(9.3)}$$

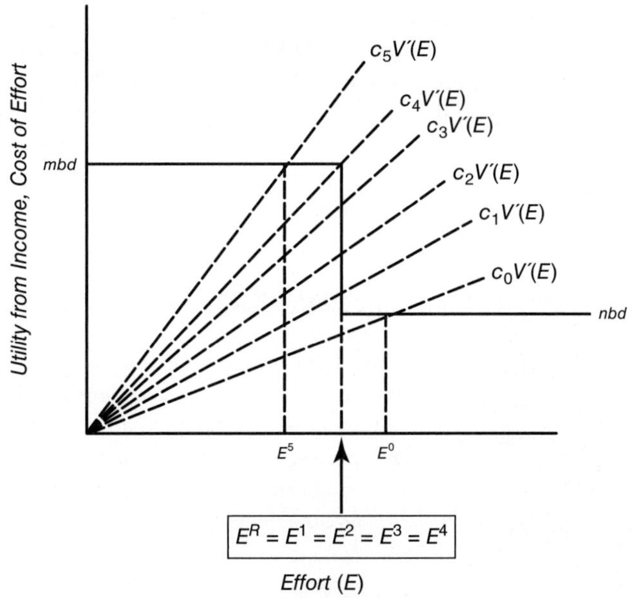

FIGURE 9.6. Optimal Effort Choices with a Reference Point

[12] The $H(Y)$ function in Figure 9.5 presents the simplest (piecewise-linear) version of prospect theory and loss aversion. Other versions, where utility can be nonlinear on both sides of the kink, are also used in a variety of contexts, including Kahneman and Tversky's original (1979) article.

[13] In some applications of prospect theory, U^R is referred to as a person's "set point," or the baseline level of utility that person tends to revert to after adapting to a new environment. See Section 10.5.

E^R is the amount of effort the agent has to expend to just attain his target level of income, R.[14] The *marginal utility* of effort drops down at point E^R because even though an extra unit of effort raises the agent's income by bd dollars on either side of E^R, the utility value of that dollar is m to the left of E^R and n to the right of it.

The second new feature of Figure 9.6 is that it shows not one marginal-cost-of-effort curve but six different ones. You can think of these different curves as applying to the same person on different days or weeks (e.g., depending on how much partying or Iron-Man training he did the day before) or as representing different people with different tastes. The main idea is that marginal effort costs can range from the very low, $c_0V'(E)$, to the very high, $c_5V'(E)$. Despite this wide variation in effort costs, the main message of Figure 9.6 is that most of the time—regardless of how tired or rested he is—the agent in Figure 9.6 picks exactly the same effort level. This level equals E^R, which is the minimum effort required to achieve the agent's reference income, R. Specifically, E^R is the optimal effort when c (the effort cost parameter) equals c_1, c_2, c_3, or c_4; it is only in the extreme cases of c_0 or c_5 that the agent does anything different.

Put another way, imagine again that you are the UCSB student who has a target income of \$20 per experiment. If we were to collect a year's worth of data on your experimental earnings, which will include weeks when you're tired and weeks when you're pumped, we'd expect to see a lot of *bunching*: Compared to any other possible level of earnings, we'd expect to see a lot of weeks in which you earned *exactly* \$20 (or a little more).[15] And we'd expect to see very few weeks where you earned just a little less. This is because, with a \$20 reference point, you'll work very hard to get your earnings per session at least up to that point. As it turns out, looking for bunching of this type is one of the ways personnel economists try to test for whether reference points and loss aversion actually exist in the real world.

☑ **RESULT 9.5**

Bunching as Evidence of Reference Points

Suppose we have reason to expect a certain level of income, *R*, to be a reference point for a group of individuals with heterogeneous abilities and preferences. A simple test for whether people are truly treating this as a reference point is to see whether people "bunch" at this assumed kink in their utility-of-income function, *H*(*Y*). In other words, we should observe many more people earning *exactly* *R* dollars than other incomes in the neighborhood of *R* dollars.

[14] To see this, recall that the agent's income is given by $Y = a + bdE$ (Equation 2.1), then just substitute R for Y and rearrange.

[15] Although the model in Figure 9.6 predicts bunching at exactly the reference point, this model assumes that there's no uncertainty in the production function. If experimental earnings are not perfectly determined by agents' effort or working time decisions, we'd expect agents with earnings targets to systematically err on the positive side of their targets.

Evidence that Reference Points Matter: Bunching of Performance Levels

A recent example of this "bunching" approach is a lab experiment on effort supply by Abeler, Falk, Goette, and Huffman (2011). Participants in Abeler et al.'s experiment were paid to count the number of zeros in tables that consisted of 150 randomly ordered zeros and ones.[16] They could work as long as they wanted up to 1 hr, and they were paid as follows: When the agent announced that he or she was done working, the experimenter flipped a coin. If the coin came up heads, the agent was paid 20 cents for each table he'd correctly solved. If the coin came up tails, the agent received a fixed payment for the entire session, regardless of how many tables he'd solved. In some sessions, this fixed payment was 3 euros; in others it was 7 euros.[17] The subjects knew all of this (including the level of the fixed payment they'd get if the coin turned up tails) before they started working. The idea of Abeler et al.'s experiment was that because the subjects had a 50% chance of earning exactly their fixed payment, this *anticipated* payment might be a natural reference point to their subjects.

Now suppose you are a rational agent who cares only about income and leisure just like the agent in Chapter 2 of this book. It's pretty obvious that (a) there's no particular reason to pick your effort in such a way to ensure you earn exactly 3 or 7 euros if you end up being paid according to the piece rate; and (b) there's no reason to change your effort based on what you'd be paid *when your pay doesn't depend on performance*. But as Figure 9.7 shows, both of these things happened in Abeler et al.'s (2011) experiment: When the fixed payment for the session was 3 euros, more subjects worked just enough to earn exactly 3 euros under the piece rate *than any other level of earnings* (including even 5 and 10 euros, which are popular digits). And when the fixed payment for the session was 7 euros, 7 euros was by far the most common variable earnings amount the subjects picked; in fact almost one-third (17 of 60) subjects decided to earn exactly 7 euros in these sessions.[18]

In sum, Abeler et al.'s (2011) experiment shows that a reference point that is easily manipulated by an employer (who in this case is the experimenter) can have large effects on employees' work effort. Of course, in Abeler et al.'s experiment,

---

[16] The experimenters chose this task for two reasons. First, performance at this task depends mostly on effort, not ability, and the experimenters were most interested in the supply of effort. Second, because the task is boring and pointless, it was unlikely that subjects had any intrinsic motivation to do it.

[17] The experimenters picked 3 and 7 euros to avoid conflating reference points they could manipulate—by changing the subject's fixed payment—from the well-documented phenomenon called *digit preferences*. This is a preference for numbers ending in "0" or "5," which is frequently observed among people making all kinds of decisions, including just reporting a statistic or making a bargaining offer.

[18] It's reasonable to wonder if simple risk aversion among experimental subjects might explain the behavior of Abeler et al.'s (2011) subjects. After all, many of the subjects seem to be taking actions that guarantee their payment for the session won't depend on the experimenter's coin flip, sometimes working much longer just to achieve this goal. In one sense, you'd be completely right, but notice that a specific *type* of risk aversion is required to explain Abeler et al.'s result: Subjects need to be averse not just to income risk in general but to income risk relative to a reference point (in this case 3 or 7 euros, an amount that is easily manipulated by the experimenter). *Risk aversion relative to a reference point is in fact the central idea of prospect theory*, and that is what distinguishes prospect theory from more traditional models of economic behavior.

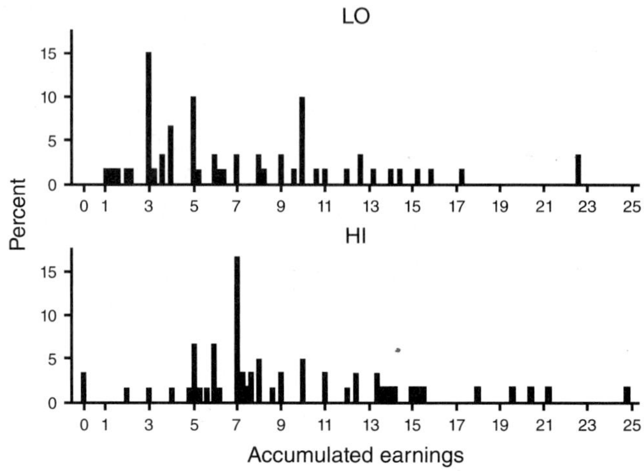

FIGURE 9.7. Accumulated Earnings (in Euros) in Abeler, Falk, Goette, and Huffman's (2011) Experiment

The top panel (LO) is a histogram of the subjects' accumulated earnings when the fixed payment was 3 euros; the bottom panel (HI) is when the fixed payment was 7 euros.
Abeler, J., Falk, A., Goette, L., & Huffman, D. (2011). "Reference points and effort provision. American Economic Review, 101(2), 470–492. (Figure 1). Reprinted with permission.

manipulating the subjects' reference points is actually quite costly for the principal: To get many of the 50% of subjects receiving variable pay to raise their effort levels enough to earn 7 euros, the experimenters had to raise the other half of the subjects' *fixed* pay to 7 euros! But as we'll see in the next section, sometimes reference points can be manipulated—resulting in substantial increases in agents' performance—at essentially no cost to the principal.

RESULT 9.6 **Laboratory Evidence on Reference Points (Abeler et al., 2011)**

Abeler et al. (2011) asked a group of laboratory subjects to perform a task for pay. But the subjects were paid according to their task performance only if a coin, flipped after the work was done, came up "heads." By manipulating the fixed dollar amount the subjects would earn if the coin came up "tails," Abeler et al. created a natural "focal point" that subjects might treat as a reference income level when deciding how hard to work. Evidence that subjects tailored their work decisions to "bunch" at exactly these income levels supports the idea that workers' reference points can be manipulated by changing the decision environment in which effort decisions are made.

9.6 Reference Points: Evidence from the Workplace

Compared to many other high- and middle-income countries, American children perform quite poorly on comparable standardized tests. Recently, much attention has been devoted to identifying effective ways to improve U.S. students' outcomes, including a variety of plans designed to incentivize teachers based on their students' test scores. In fact, in some ways America's schools have recently become a laboratory for ideas proposed by personnel economists and others to improve the job performance of one of the most important groups of workers in any country—teachers.

As part of this trend, by July 2012, at least 10 states and numerous school districts in the United States had adopted programs that reward teachers with extra pay after students achieve certain goals on tests or report cards. Unfortunately, in contrast to Safelite's PPP plan, most of these new incentive schemes failed: Incentivizing teachers, even with substantial rewards, has not generated large, lasting improvements in their students' performance.[19] This unfortunate record of teacher incentives makes a recent success story—based on an experiment by Roland Fryer, Steven Levitt, John List, and Sally Sadoff (2012)—especially noteworthy. Interestingly, the new "twist" that seems to make Fryer et al.'s incentive scheme work is the fact that it takes advantage of teachers' loss aversion combined with a method of manipulating teachers' reference points. In Fryer et al.'s scheme, these two factors work together to strengthen the effectiveness of financial incentives *without increasing their cost* to the school district.

Fryer and his coauthors (2012) worked with schools in Chicago Heights, Illinois, a low-income school district with 3,200 mostly minority students, located 30 miles south of Chicago, during the 2010–2011 school year. Before the experiment, test scores in the district were low, and the schools were struggling to find ways to improve the students' learning outcomes. In cooperation with school administrators and the teachers' union, Fryer et al. randomly selected 150 volunteer teachers and divided them into three categories. The *control* group didn't qualify for any new incentives. Teachers in the *gain* group could earn a bonus of up to $8,000 if their students scored well on a standardized test at the end of the school year. This treatment was similar to teacher incentive plans that had been implemented in other states and cities.

Finally, the *loss* group received a payment of $4,000 at the start of the school year. These teachers could earn an additional $4,000 if their students scored well in the same standardized test at the end of the school year. But if their students scored below average at the end of the year, they were informed they'd have to *pay back* the difference between the upfront payment and their final reward to the school district. Thus, aside from the negligible amount of interest a teacher might earn on keeping $4,000 in the bank during the school year, the two bonus schemes were financially *identical*. The idea behind the *loss* treatment was to manipulate the teachers' reference point (so that the upfront payment of $4,000 was something they *already had*), then rely on the teachers' loss aversion to motivate them to keep their upfront bonus.[20]

---

[19] That said, Lavy (2009, 2015) finds recent evidence that incentivizing teachers can have substantial long-run effects on students' achievement in Israel.

[20] The authors also subdivided the "gain" and "loss" groups into teachers who received individual-based versus team-based incentives, but they didn't find any difference between team and individual incentives.

Consistent with other U.S. studies, Fryer et al. (2012) found that—when compared to the control group with no incentives—the *gain* students performed no better, despite the extra \$8,000 in bonuses their teachers could earn if the students' scores improved. But when the exact same incentive plan was framed as a loss (by giving some of the money to the teachers up front), students showed large and statistically significant gains in math scores. Specifically, the increase in students' scores was equivalent to being assigned a teacher who is one standard deviation better than before.

Why did Fryer et al.'s (2012) *loss* treatment work so much better than their equally generous *gain* treatment? Importantly, because high stakes increase the teachers' incentives to cheat, the authors were careful to limit opportunities for doing so. Also, they found that the *loss* students exhibited similar gains on a separate, *no-stakes* test where there was no incentive to cheat. So, changes in teacher or student cheating are not a likely explanation. Did the *loss* group do better because low-performing students were more likely to drop out of their classrooms? (In fact, one could even imagine some teachers encouraging their worst-performing students to drop out to qualify for a large bonus!) Again, the answer is "no" because low-performing students were no more likely to leave *loss* than *gain* classrooms. Did the *loss* teachers put in more hours preparing lesson plans? Apparently not, according to the authors' survey of the teachers. Overall, although the authors found it hard to pinpoint the exact changes the "loss" teachers made to achieve these gains in student achievement, it appears that (a) these gains were real (not due to cheating or changes in dropout behavior), and (b) the teachers were responding to the fear of losing money they'd already received. One possibility is that they devoted more attention to classroom management, which is reportedly both effortful for teachers and beneficial to students.

RESULT 9.7 **Loss Aversion among Teachers (Fryer et al., 2012)**

In a field experiment on Chicago Heights schoolteachers, Fryer et al. were able to reframe essentially the same financial incentives as a possible "loss" rather than a gain by giving teachers some of their performance pay at the start of the school year. Thus, underperforming teachers would have to pay some money back to the school at the end of the year. Consistent with the theory of loss aversion, this simple change in framing had substantial effects on the teachers' job performance, at zero additional cost to the school district.

In addition to teachers and undergraduate students, evidence that reference points and loss aversion affect workers' effort and labor supply decisions in real workplaces is also available from a number of other workplace settings. For example, a series of studies of New York City taxi drivers seems to suggest that—rather than working long hours on "good" days as Chapter 2's model of agent behavior predicts—some of these drivers use daily *earnings targets* in deciding how many hours to put in each day. Earnings reference points also seem to matter for the labor supply decisions of bicycle messengers—another group of workers who can decide how many hours to put in each day or week.[21] Alexandre Mas (2006) found that New Jersey police appear to withhold effort—by letting arrest rates and average sentence length decline, and crime reports rise—when they receive a lower wage than a natural reference point: the police union's own wage proposal in a final-offer arbitration context.[22]

As noted, although loss aversion and prospect theory seem to help us understand some types of human behavior that would be very hard to understand otherwise, an important limitation of the theory is that it provides little guidance regarding how people get their reference points. Possible reference points include a person's own (nominal) income in the recent past (people may dislike nominal wage cuts much more than they enjoy increases); the *expected* gain from an endeavor as in Abeler et al. (2011); the amount of payment one has *already received* (as in Fryer et al., 2012); and the incomes of people in the person's peer group at work, in the neighborhood, family, church, or children's school. As it stands, the theory merely suggests that people might behave in a loss-averse way with respect to these types of reference points; it is then up to empirical researchers, such as Abeler et al. and Fryer et al., to demonstrate that a particular reference point matters in a given work situation.

Paradoxically, however, this apparent weakness of prospect theory might also constitute an important *opportunity* for managers. Indeed, as Fryer et al.'s (2012) teacher incentive plan suggests, managers who can successfully influence their workers' reference points can have powerful effects on how the *same* incentives are valued, and thereby on behavior. For example, reframing a proposed pay raise—by noting that although it may seem small in some ways, it actually compares favorably with what others in the firm or industry have received—can make it seem bigger and more acceptable. And depending on how a new job duty is framed, it can seem either intrinsically rewarding or burdensome. Indeed, anyone with practical leadership experience knows the immense importance of framing: Whether your team members are happy or sad, or motivated or not, can depend critically on *the standard against which they assess* their current and possible future situations.[23]

---

[21] See, for example, Camerer, Babcock, Loewenstein, and Thaler (1997); Farber (2005, 2015); and Crawford and Meng (2008) on taxi drivers; and Fehr and Goette (2007) on bicycle messengers.

[22] New Jersey police are subject to final offer arbitration—where an impartial arbitrator must pick either the union's *or* their employer's wage proposal (numbers in between are not permitted). So, as in Abeler et al.'s (2011) experiment, the union's offer is *what the workers would be paid* if an exogenous "coin flip" (in this case the arbitrator's decision) turns up heads.

[23] For example, it is not unknown for chairs of academic departments to receive visits from faculty members who are unhappy with their current salary. In one of these meetings, a faculty member might say "I've published much more than Professor X at University Y, yet I'm paid less. That's not fair and you should do something about it." A common response by the chair (especially in times of budget restraint) is precisely to try to reframe the professor's salary and change his or her reference point. For example, the chair might respond, "Yes, that's true, but all of us in our department have had to experience lower-than-normal salary growth in recent years because of the state's budget. And compared to your colleagues in our *own* department, you're actually paid very well." Of course, reframings like this don't work every time, but it's surprising how powerful they can be. Good leaders, to some extent, are good "framers."

Goals as Motivators

In a randomized field experiment, Sebastian J. Goerg and Sebastian Kube (2012) investigate the connection between work goals, monetary incentives, and work performance. Employees are observed in a natural work environment where they have to do a simple but effortful task. Output is perfectly observable and workers are paid for performance. Whereas a regular piece-rate contract serves as a benchmark, in some treatments, workers are paid a bonus conditional on reaching a prespecified goal. Goerg and Kube show that the use of personal work goals leads to a significant output increase. The positive effect of goals prevails not only if they are self-chosen by the workers but also if goals are set exogenously by the principal—although in the latter case, the exact size of the goal plays a crucial role. Strikingly, the positive effect of self-chosen goals persists even if the goal is not backed up by monetary incentives. Thus it appears that *merely setting a goal creates an important reference point* for workers and that such goals can be effective motivators.

9.7 Present Bias and Procrastination

Have you ever planned to spend the evening studying, then ended up at a sports bar instead? Did you plan to work out tomorrow morning, only to end up lazing on the couch? These problems of *self-control* lead to what economists call *time inconsistency* in choices, in the sense that the things we want our future selves to do are not always the ones that end up getting done. In this section, we explore how self-control problems in exerting effort affect workers, firms, and the types of employment contracts they might agree to.

DEFINITION 9.1 **Self-control problems,** or **time inconsistency** in choices, refer to situations where the choices an agent makes in the future are different from the ones he wanted his future self to make, even when nothing unexpected has happened or been learned in the interim.

The qualification that nothing unexpected has happened or been learned in Definition 9.1 is an important one because human beings frequently end up doing things they didn't expect to do for reasons that have nothing to do with self-control. For example, the student who ends up at the sports bar may have learned that his team unexpectedly qualified for the playoffs or that tomorrow morning's calculus test has been cancelled. The athlete who ends up on the couch may have unexpectedly sprained her ankle while getting out of bed. Humans frequently change their plans because their environment changes in unexpected ways; doing this is rational and is not a symptom of self-control problems. Self-control problems occur when people deviate from their plans for tomorrow not because something new has happened or been learned, but simply because *tomorrow has arrived.*

Although economists have several ways of modeling self-control problems (including models of "conflicting selves" in which, for example, a hard-working and a lazy self play games against each other), in this book, we'll consider only one way to model self-control problems—the *present bias* approach.[24] In this approach, we model an agent's utility as depending on outcomes that occur at different times, both today and in the future. But before we can introduce self control and the present bias approach, we first need to describe the simpler and much better-known model of *exponential utility discounting*, to which it is closely related.

The Exponential Discounting Approach to Intertemporal Choice

If you've ever studied economic decisions that involve making tradeoffs over time, such as how much to save for retirement or conducting cost-benefit analyses of long-term investments, you have almost certainly done so using exponential discounting. Exponential discounting is the standard approach to studying choice over time in economics.

DEFINITION 9.2

Suppose we denote U_t as the utility experienced by an agent on date t. For example, if the agent receives an income Y_t and exerts an effort of E_t on date t, $U_t = Y_t - V(E_t)$, where (as always) $V(E_t)$ is the disutility of effort.

Suppose also that this agent is planning a series of decisions that affect utility in each of the $T + 1$ periods, $t = 0, 1, 2, \ldots, T$, where $t = 0$ denotes the present.

Such an agent exhibits **exponential utility discounting** if the agent's preferred choices for today ($t = 0$) and the future maximize the function

$$M = U_0 + \delta U_1 + \delta^2 U_2 + \ldots + \delta^T U_T,$$

where $0 \leq \delta \leq 1$ is the agent's **utility discount factor.**

Exponential utility discounting is the standard assumption that is used by economists more than any other approach to model how people make decisions over multiple periods of time.

Thus, for example, if $\delta = 0.9$, a unit of utility that you expect to receive tomorrow (at $t = 1$) is worth only 90% as much to you as a unit of utility received

[24] For theoretical investigations of the conflicting-selves approach, see Shefrin and Thaler (1988), Bernheim and Rangel (2004), and Fudenberg and Levine (2006).

today (at $t = 0$). A utility unit that you expect to receive at $t = 2$ is only worth $0.9^2 = 81\%$ of a unit received today, and so on. Mathematically, exponential utility discounting is analogous to taking the present value of a stream of monetary payments at a given interest rate, r; the only difference is that—instead of reflecting objective market interest rates—the discount factor, δ, is a *subjective* utility parameter summarizing how much an agent *cares* about utility received at different points in time.[25]

To illustrate exponential utility discounting and its consequences, we imagine a worker named Ramesh who has a 3-day workweek, consisting of days $t = 0$, 1, and 2. On each of these days, Ramesh faces our baseline production function, $Q = E$, and has our baseline disutility-of-effort function $V(E) = E^2/2$, both of which were introduced in Chapter 1. Like most workers, Ramesh does not get a paycheck every day he goes to work. Instead, he's paid at the end of the week for his entire week's work. In our simple example, we'll assume that Ramesh is paid the full value of his output, which means he is paid an income of $Y = Q_0 + Q_1 + Q_2$ on Day 2. He is not paid on any other days.

Assuming that Ramesh has exponential utility discounting, let's now derive the optimal time path of his effort decisions over his entire workweek, as seen from the perspective of each day of the week. His optimal plan for the entire week, viewed **from the perspective of Day 0**, solves

$$\text{Max}(E_0, E_1, E_2): \quad U_0 + \delta U_1 + \delta^2 U_2, \tag{9.4}$$

where "Max(E_0, E_1, E_2):" means to choose values of E_0, E_1, and E_2 so as to maximize the expression that follows.

Substituting in Ramesh's utility, production, and compensation functions, this becomes

$$\text{Max}(E_0, E_1, E_2): \quad \delta^2 (E_0 + E_1 + E_2) - V(E_0) - \delta V(E_1) - \delta^2 V(E_2). \tag{9.5}$$

Notice that Equation 9.5 reflects the fact that he is only paid on the last day of the week. This is because the first term in the equation, which represents his full payment (equal to the sum of his efforts, or equivalently production), is discounted for being received two days in the future.

Setting the derivatives of this expression with respect to E_0, E_1, and E_2 equal to zero and rearranging, Ramesh's optimal effort levels on the 3 days are $E_0 = \delta^2$, $E_1 = \delta$, and $E_2 = 1$.[26] Thus, if Ramesh discounts the future (i.e., if $\delta < 1$), his planned effort will increase gradually as his payday approaches. For example, if $\delta = 0.9$, his effort path will be $E_0 = 0.81$, $E_1 = 0.90$, and $E_2 = 1.00$.[27]

---

[25] The present value of a stream of monetary payments, Y_t, is given by $Y_0 + \theta Y_1 + \theta^2 Y_2 + \ldots + \theta^T Y_T$, where $\theta = 1/(1 + r)$, and r is the market rate of interest. (For example, $r = 0.05$ denotes a 5% interest rate.) Thus, Definition 9.2's criterion function for intertemporal decisions, M, just takes the "present value" of a stream of utilities using a subjective discount *factor*, $\delta = 1/(1 + \rho)$, where ρ is a subjective discount *rate* analogous to an interest rate.

[26] For example, differentiating Equation 9.5 with respect to E_0 yields $\delta^2 - V'(E_0) = 0$. Because $V'(E_0) = E_0$ in our baseline disutility-of-effort function, it follows that $E_0 = \delta^2$.

[27] Note that $\delta = 0.9$ implies a very high utility discount rate, specifically, $\rho = 1/0.9 - 1 = 11\%$ per day, which works out to about one million percent on an annual basis. We use 0.9 purely for easy computation.

Now suppose that Day 1 has arrived. **From the perspective of Day 1**, Ramesh now only has to decide on how much to work on Day 1 (which is now "today" for him) and Day 2. Thus, his desired choices for these two periods will satisfy the following:

$$\text{Max}(E_1, E_2): \quad \delta(E_1 + E_2) - V(E_1) - \delta V(E_2). \qquad \textbf{(9.6)}$$

Setting the derivatives with respect to the E's equal to zero and rearranging, the optimal effort levels are $E_1 = \delta$ and $E_2 = 1$. By the same logic, **from the perspective of Day 2**, Ramesh's optimal plan for Day 2 (the only day that is left) is $E_2 = 1$.

Overall, Ramesh's optimal behavior under exponential utility discounting exhibits two main features. The first is that Ramesh's effort levels increase gradually over time, from 0.81 to 0.90 to 1.00, as his payday approaches.[28] This pattern results from the important fact that *exponential utility discounting does not imply that you value the future as much as the present.* Indeed, there are several rational reasons—including the fact that you might not be alive tomorrow!—why people might place less subjective value on consuming something (like a nice meal or leisure) in the future than today. Second, under exponential discounting, Ramesh's optimal plans are *time consistent.* Specifically, the work plan that Ramesh envisioned as optimal on Day 0 ($E_0 = 0.81$, $E_1 = 0.90$, and $E_2 = 1.00$) is exactly the one he decides to stick to when Days 1 and 2 actually arrive. In fact, intertemporal choices are time consistent in this way *only* when utility discounting is exponential.

☑ RESULT 9.8

Intertemporal Effort Choices of Agents Under Exponential Utility Discounting

Consider an agent who discounts future utility exponentially. Imagine that he is choosing effort levels in $T + 1$ periods given by $E_0, E_1, \ldots E_T$ to generate a payoff given by $Q = E_0 + E_1 + \ldots + E_T$. The agent receives this entire payoff in period T. If the agent discounts the future (i.e., if $\delta < 1$), the agent's effort levels will *increase smoothly* over time as his payday approaches. Further, the agent's effort choices will be *time consistent* in the sense that (absent any new information) the agent's actual choices when a period arrives are exactly what he previously planned to choose in that period.

Exponential discounting is the *only* form of utility discounting that leads to time-consistent agent behavior.

Intertemporal Choice with a Present-Biased Utility Function

Having studied exponential utility discounting, we are now in a position to introduce present bias and to show how it can generate time-inconsistent choices. The idea of present bias refers to utility functions in which agents place special

[28] When the periods in question are literally 1 day apart, this predicted increase in effort is actually infinitesimal for any realistic utility discount factor. As noted earlier, we use unrealistically low values of δ in these examples to simplify the arithmetic.

and disproportionate emphasis on "today"—that is, the current period—relative to all future periods.

DEFINITION 9.3 Consider the same sequence of decisions we studied in Definition 9.2.

An agent exhibits **present bias** if her preferred choices for the current and all future periods from the point of view of date zero maximize the function

$$M = U_0 + \beta\delta U_1 + \beta\delta^2 U_2 + \ldots + \beta\delta^T U_T,$$

where $0 \le \delta \le 1$ is the agent's utility discount factor, and $0 \le \beta < 1$ is the agent's **present bias parameter**. The present bias parameter distinguishes utility received today from utility received in *any* future period.

Intertemporal utility functions with present bias were introduced by Laibson (1997) and O'Donoghue and Rabin (1999); they capture the fact that utility comparisons between today and any future period may be different from utility comparisons between any pair of future periods. For example, if $\beta = 0.6$ and $\delta = 0.9$, we'd only have to give the agent 0.54 units of utility today to compensate him for a 1-unit loss of utility tomorrow. On the other hand, we'd have to give the same agent 0.90 units of utility on Day 1 to compensate him for a 1-unit utility loss on Day 2. Yet in both these situations, the dates are only one day apart. In essence, because the present is especially valuable to him, *a present-biased individual is less patient regarding choices between today and* k *periods in the future than he is between two future dates that are* k *periods apart.*

Now let's assume that Ramesh is present biased and once again derive his optimal effort decisions over the entire workweek, as seen from the perspective of each day. His optimal plan for the entire week, viewed **from the perspective of Day 0**, solves

$$\text{Max}(E_0, E_1, E_2): \quad U_0 + \beta\delta U_1 + \beta\delta^2 U_2. \tag{9.7}$$

Substituting in Ramesh's utility, production, and compensation functions, this becomes

$$\text{Max}(E_0, E_1, E_2): \quad \beta\delta^2(E_0 + E_1 + E_2) - V(E_0) - \beta\delta V(E_1) - \beta\delta^2 V(E_2). \tag{9.8}$$

Setting the derivatives equal to zero and rearranging, the optimal effort levels satisfy $E_0 = \beta\delta^2$, $E_1 = \delta$, and $E_2 = 1$. Thus, a present-biased Ramesh *wants* to work just as hard in the future (Periods 1 and 2) as a non-present-biased Ramesh, but he wants to take it easier "just this once" today. For example, if $\delta = 0.9$, and $\beta = 0.6$, his preferred effort path from the point of view of Period 0 will be $E_0 = 0.49$, $E_1 = 0.90$, and $E_2 = 1.00$.

Now suppose that Day 1 has arrived. **From the perspective of Day 1**, Ramesh now only has to decide on how much to work on Day 1 (which is now "today" for him) and Day 2. Thus his desired choices for these two periods will satisfy

$$\text{Max}(E_1, E_2)\text{: } \delta\beta(E_1 + E_2) - V(E_1) - \beta\delta V(E_2). \tag{9.9}$$

Setting the derivatives equal to zero and rearranging, the optimal effort levels satisfy $E_1 = \beta\delta$, which equals 0.54 in our example, and $E_2 = 1$. By the same logic, **from the perspective of Day 2**, Ramesh's optimal plan on Day 2 is just $E_2 = 1$.

In contrast to the case of exponential discounting, Ramesh's preferred choices are *time inconsistent*. Instead of the $E_1 = 0.90$ effort level he'd initially planned for Day 1, when Day 1 actually arrives, Ramesh reneges on that plan and ends up only supplying 0.54 units of effort. Because each day Ramesh can only implement his decision plan for that day, Ramesh's *actual* effort path will be $E_0 = 0.49$, $E_1 = 0.54$, and $E_2 = 1.00$. In other words, Ramesh will *procrastinate*, choosing low effort levels until the last day, when his effort "jumps" up to a much higher level. Put another way, Ramesh's work behavior exhibits a *payday effect*, jumping upward on the final day of every pay cycle.[29]

RESULT 9.9 **Intertemporal Effort Choices of Present-Biased Agents**

Consider an agent who is present biased, as in Definition 9.3. Facing the same choice problem as in Result 9.8, this agent's effort levels will increase smoothly over time until the day before his payday. Between the second-last and last day, however, his effort will jump up discontinuously, thus exhibiting a *payday effect*. On all days except the payday, this agent's choices will be time-inconsistent, in the sense that the agent ends up working less on each day than he had planned in the past.

A second implication of present bias for intertemporal effort choices is that agents who *anticipate* their own present bias (i.e., *sophisticated* agents) might voluntarily demand restrictions on their own, future behavior, that is, they might try to take actions that "tie their hands" and limit their future ability to renege on their plans to work hard. Economists refer to such actions as *commitment devices*. For example, if Ramesh could somehow force his future (Period 1) self to supply 0.9 instead of 0.54 units of effort—perhaps by leaving his cell phone at home so he can't check social media—he might do so, even though the absence of a phone might restrict him in other important ways.

DEFINITION 9.4 In general, **sophisticated** agents are those who have a behavioral bias (e.g., loss aversion) but are aware of that bias. **Naïve** agents are not aware of their own behavioral biases.

Present-biased agents are sophisticated if they understand *today* that they will want to renege on their plans to work hard tomorrow when tomorrow arrives.

[29] Payday effects have been observed for salespeople in large U.S. firms, where sales frequencies tend to increase over the fiscal year, with a spike in the last quarter when bonuses are computed and paid (Oyer, 1998, Figure 1).

Ulysses and the Sirens: The Oldest Recorded Commitment Device?

In Greek mythology, the Sirens were beautiful and dangerous creatures (combining features of women and birds) who lived on the rugged coast of their Mediterranean island. By singing an irresistible song, the Sirens lured passing sailors to shipwreck and death on the rocks. The legendary Greek king Odysseus (Ulysses to the Romans and the hero of Homer's Odyssey) was curious to hear the Sirens' song, but knew he wouldn't be able to resist their charms. Because Ulysses was *sophisticated*, he ordered his sailors to tie him to the mast of his ship and to plug all their own ears with beeswax. He further ordered his men to leave him tied to the mast no matter how much he begged to be set free, and to disobey his pleas to steer closer to the rocks as they passed. This way Ulysses became the only person to hear the Siren's song and survive.

Whereas Ulysses' request may be the oldest recorded example of a sophisticated, present-biased person requesting a commitment device, such devices are frequently observed today. In addition to certain features of self-help programs such as Weight Watchers and Alcoholics Anonymous, a more recent implementation is the website StickK.com. Designed by two Yale University professors, Dean Karlan and Ian Ayres, the site allows users to set up a "commitment contract" where they agree to achieve a certain goal, such as losing weight, exercising more, quitting smoking, or spending less time on social media. Users sign a legally binding contract that will send their money to third parties if they fail to achieve their goal (whether the goal has been met is determined by a third-party referee). In medicine, a *Ulysses pact* or *Ulysses contract* is a freely made decision that is intended to bind a patient in the future, such an *advance directive* or a *living will* that specifies what types of treatment the patient wishes or does not want to receive if that patient is too ill or incapacitated to make those decisions.

Present Bias and Time-Inconsistency in the Workplace

Are present bias and time inconsistency significant problems in workplaces? If so, how might they affect the types of employment contracts that firms offer to workers, and that workers accept? A recent field experiment in an Indian data-entry firm, conducted by Kaur, Kremer, and Mullainathan (2015) sheds some interesting light on these questions. Following standard industry practice, workers in Kaur et al.'s experiment were paid piece rates based on the number of accurate fields they entered. (Accuracy was measured using dual entry of data, with manual checks of discrepancy by separate quality control staff.) The baseline piece rate was 0.03 rupees for each accurate field entered. In addition, all the workers received a flat daily show-up fee of 15 rupees; this amounted to about 8% of their compensation. In all the treatments, just as in our theoretical model of Ramesh's behavior, workers were paid their total earnings for the workweek at the end of the week. In Kaur et al.'s experiment, the work week lasted 7 days (not 3); paydays were randomly assigned to workers (for the duration of the experiment) as on Tuesdays, Thursdays, or Saturdays. All in all, the authors observed the daily output levels of 102 workers over an 8-month period.

Is there any reason to think that self-control problems might be an important issue for the workers in this firm? One piece of evidence on this point is subjective: In a questionnaire, 76% of firm's workers agreed or strongly agreed with the statement, "Some days I don't work as hard as I would like to." More quantitatively, Kaur et al. (2015) found that under the baseline, piece-rate contract, workers' output patterns exhibited significant payday effects, increasing rapidly as their personal payday approached. According to Result 9.9, this is a pattern we should expect to see if workers are present biased but not if they are exponential discounters.

The main goals of Kaur et al.'s experiment, however, were to assess workers' *demand for commitment devices* and the *effects* of those devices in this workplace. To do this, the authors randomly gave workers the option of selecting a different contract from the baseline, piece-rate scheme. This alternative contract penalized the workers for not attaining an output goal that was chosen by each worker him- or herself.[30] In more detail, the structure of this alternative, "bonus" contract is illustrated in Figure 9.8. As a reference, the solid line illustrates the baseline contract, where subjects received a base pay of $a = 15$ rupees per day and were paid a piece rate of $b = 0.03$ rupees for every correct data field they entered. The bonus contract was identical to this baseline contract, except that it *withheld half of the workers' piece rate income* unless they attained their own, chosen target of at least Q' fields that day. If that goal was reached, all the withheld piece-rate income was restored to workers in the form of lump-sum bonuses,

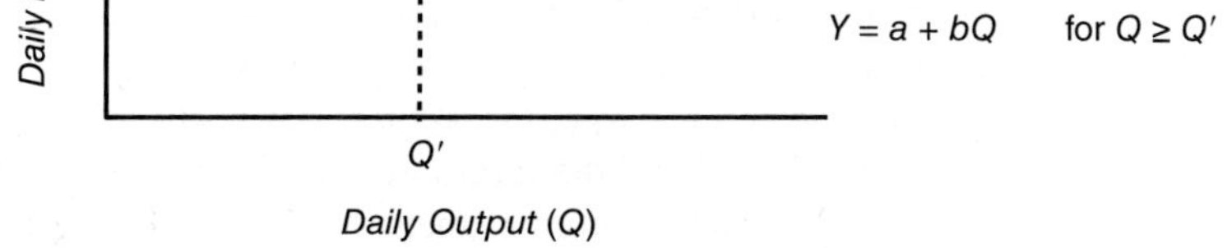

FIGURE 9.8. The Dominated Contracts Used in Kaur, Kremer, and Mullainathan (2015) Data Entry Experiment

In Kaur et al.'s experiment, a was 15 rupees and b was 0.03 rupees per completed field.

---

[30] Kaur et al. (2015) also experimented with contracts where the target was set by the employer and changed the timing of when the worker selected his or her own output goal. Here we only describe the results of the worker-selected goals, regardless of whether the goal was set the night before or the morning of the workday.

so total pay jumped upward at that point. Thus, the bonus contracts had the same intercept (*a*) but half the slope (*b*) of the baseline contract up to Q' units of output. At all output levels of Q' or higher, the bonus contracts paid exactly the same as the baseline contract.

DEFINITION 9.5 Consider two contracts, A and B, that an employer might offer a worker, described by the functions $Y = F^A(Q)$ and $Y = F^B(Q)$, where Y^i is the worker's pay under contract *I*, and Q is the worker's output, or performance.

Contract A **strictly dominates** contract B if $F^A(Q) > F^B(Q)$ for at least one value of Q, and $F^A(Q) \geq F^B(Q)$ for all possible values of Q. Informally, contract A dominates contract B if it pays the worker more than B does under some circumstances, and never pays the worker less.

As Figure 9.8 makes clear, an important feature of the bonus contracts used in Kaur et al.'s (2015) experiment is that they were less generous in a well-defined sense than the baseline contract. Specifically, all bonus contracts were *strictly dominated* by the baseline contract. This was a deliberate choice by the experimenters because their goal was to assess workers' demand for commitment contracts. By ensuring that these bonus contracts were no more generous than the baseline contract under *all possible circumstances*, it would seem that workers had no reasons *other than self-control problems* to pick a bonus contract.

What did Kaur et al. find? First, they found that when workers had the option to choose a dominated contract, 36% of workers chose one. Thus, the workers' demand for commitment devices was substantial. Furthermore, it was not just *any* workers who picked these contracts: The demand for commitment contracts was highest among the workers whose effort choices exhibited the strongest payday effects under the baseline piece rate, that is, specifically among the workers whose behavior suggested they had self-control problems. Second, Kaur et al. estimated that choosing these commitment contracts raised the output of the workers who picked them by 6%. For workers with above-average payday effects in the baseline treatment, this number was 9%. Although these numbers may not seem large, the authors also estimated that eliciting a 6% output increase by raising the level of the linear piece rate would require an 18% higher rate! In contrast, commitment contracts cost the employer nothing (and in fact could *save* money because these contracts are less generous than the baseline piece rate contract).

Finally, Kaur et al. (2015) found that workers' *sophistication* (i.e., their awareness of their own self-control problems) was not fixed over time. Instead, the workers appeared to learn about their self-control problems as the field experiment progressed. Specifically, as they gained experience with the experiment, the workers with large payday effects chose the dominated contracts more often, while workers with small payday effects—who don't need commitment devices—chose them less. Thus, workers appeared to *acquire self-knowledge* during the course of the experiment.

RESULT 9.10

Self-Control in the Workplace: Evidence from Kaur et al.'s Data Entry Experiment

In their study of an Indian data entry office, Kaur, Kremer, and Mullainathan (2015) observed substantial *payday effects* on effort, suggesting that some workers had self-control problems.

Consistent with this, 36% of workers demanded a commitment device, in the form of a dominated contract that withheld half of the worker's piece-rate income if he didn't attain a self-selected target output. These contracts proved effective in raising workers' outputs and earnings.

Workers' demand for commitment contracts suggests that they were *sophisticated*, in the sense of being aware of their own self-control problems. As the experiment proceeded, sophistication seemed to increase, with the high-payday-effect workers selecting commitment contracts more often, and the low-payday-effect workers—who didn't need these devices—selecting them less often.

Kaur et al.'s (2015) article convincingly shows that self-control problems among workers were a significant issue in a real workplace, and that a particular type of commitment contract—specifically, a *voluntary, performance-based* commitment contract—can mitigate these problems. The introduction of this contract raised output and workers' earnings, despite paying workers no more at any given amount of output than a pure, piece-rate contract would.

Disadvantages of Commitment Contracts

Although Kaur et al.'s experiment demonstrated the potential value of commitment contracts, it's important to note that these contracts have some disadvantages as well, which can limit their applicability in many situations. One such disadvantage is a *loss of flexibility*: By tying the worker to a particular output goal, they limit the worker's ability to efficiently adjust to new information and developments. For example, on days when the company's computer network is slow (or when the worker is feeling unwell), it may not make sense to set a high output goal. Indeed, when unexpected developments make a high goal infeasible, the only effect of the commitment contract is to cut the worker's piece rate in half, which is probably not efficient. More generally, making any sort of binding commitments in advance may have benefits but prevents the contracting parties from optimally responding to new information that comes to light after the commitment is made. Although these costs can be mitigated by letting workers choose their own quotas shortly before starting work, this could increase workers' temptation to set low targets (because the time to work has almost arrived).[31]

[31] Letting workers choose their quotas has two additional benefits. First, it guarantees that the commitment contract can't make workers worse off, at least in terms of their *expected* utility when they select their quota. Second, it takes advantage of information workers may have—such as their own ability and effort costs, or conditions in the workplace—that employers may not have access to. This allows workers to choose an output goal, Q', in the performance range that is most relevant and motivating to them, personally, on a particular day.

A closely related disadvantage is the fact the quota-based commitment contracts of the form used in Kaur et al. (2015) expose workers to *more risk* than pure, piece-rate contracts. If something unexpected—like a network slowdown—happens in the production process that prevents a worker from achieving a goal, the worker has unnecessarily thrown away half of the piece-rate income for that day. Although the principle is a general one, this might be especially concerning to the low-income workers in Kaur et al.'s study. Indeed, the high levels of risk borne by workers in performance-based commitment contracts suggests that employers might want to consider using a different type of commitment contract altogether, which was not studied by Kaur et al.: *input-based commitment contracts*. Input-based employment contracts, which reward measurable behaviors that are *associated* with effort (such as hours and the types of activities engaged in during the workday) were introduced in Section 5.5. Because they don't link pay to random elements of the production process, they could limit shirking without exposing workers to high levels of compensation risk.

Finally, Kaur et al.'s (2015) study of commitment contracts has interesting implications for the optimality of the franchise solution to the principal–agent problem derived in Chapter 3. Specifically, if workers have self-control problems, "selling the job to the worker" (effectively making them self-employed) may *not* be the most efficient solution to the principal–agent problem. Left to their own devices, some self-employed workers might end up procrastinating *more than they themselves would like to do* in the longer run. Given that a sophisticated, present-biased worker might prefer to remain employed in a firm that *helps workers* solve their own self-control problems via a combination of output- and input-based commitment devices! In this view of the employment relationship, an employer is in a sense an *ally* of the worker's longer term self in imposing discipline on the worker's temptation to shirk in the present; workers essentially *delegate* the problem of managing their own self-discipline problems to an employer.[32]

How important is this aspect of the employment relationship in today's labor markets? Although it is impossible to provide even a rough estimate, it seems plausible that whereas many people are highly suited to self-employment, others with higher levels of present bias might rationally prefer the external discipline offered by a more traditional employment relationship with rigid hours and rules. Indeed, at least one influential economic historian has argued that the *contractual* innovation of "factory discipline," as much as newly invented machines and sources of power, gave rise to England's Industrial Revolution (Clark, 1994).

[32] The employer's role as ally of the worker's "better" self contrasts with the incentives of companies selling goods that appeal to consumers' present-biased selves (like gambling, cigarettes, and unhealthy food). Here, consumers are "on their own" when trying to combat short-term impulses. The difference, of course, is that effort is an immediate cost with a long-term benefit, whereas smoking is an immediate benefit with a long-term cost. For a fascinating theoretical analysis of both these cases, see DellaVigna and Malmendier (2004).

Chapter Summary

- ☐ In two experiments that studied the effects of the piece rate (*b*) on worker performance, Gneezy and Rustichini (2000) found that average performance was lower at small, positive levels of *b* than when *b* was equal to zero.

- ☐ One possible explanation is that adding even a small economic incentive destroys agents' intrinsic motivation to do the job. This may be especially relevant in Gneezy and Rustichini's "donation" experiment where the work—soliciting charitable donations—may have been seen as socially desirable.

- ☐ In an experiment designed to measure the intrinsic value of a simple job, Ariely, Kamenica, and Prelec (AKP; 2008) show that simply letting workers see the immediate results of their labor (building Legos) increases worker output by the same amount as a 40% pay increase. This suggests that providing meaningful work might be highly profitable for employers.

- ☐ Ariely, Bracha, and Meier (ABM; 2009) demonstrate the importance of *image* motivation in a "Click for Charity" experiment that manipulates whether others can see how hard one is working for a charitable cause. Visibility increased effort a great deal. There was also evidence that financial incentives *crowded out* image motivation because incentives increased agents' performance when their charitable efforts were private but reduced agents' performance when their efforts were known to others.

- ☐ In a series of experiments in rural India designed to measure the effects of very strong incentives (*b*) on performance, Ariely, Gneezy, Loewenstein, and Mazar (AGLM; 2009) found that performance declined when incentives were raised to the highest levels in all six tasks they studied.

- ☐ AGLM's (2009) results highlight the difference between economists' concept of effort—which is completely under the agent's control—and psychologists' concept of arousal, which is *involuntary* and physiologically measurable. People who are highly aroused by high financial stakes may wish they could relax and try less hard but be incapable of doing so.

- ☐ Just because many people "choke" in the presence of high stakes does not mean that high stakes are counterproductive in all jobs. Indeed, Coates et al.'s (2009) study of noise traders suggests that this job attracts workers with physiological traits that are correlated with better performance under pressure.

- ☐ According to *prospect theory* (Kahneman & Tversky, 1979), human beings often behave as if they assess their well-being with respect to their current *reference point*. Specifically, a $1 loss of income hurts people significantly more when their income is below the reference point than when their income is above the reference point. This phenomenon is known as *loss aversion*.

- ☐ Abeler et al. (2011) demonstrate the importance of reference points in a lab experiment, where subjects exerted significant additional effort to attain a financially irrelevant reference income level that was manipulated by the experimenter. Their experiment relied, in part, on prospect theory's prediction that the choices of people with different tastes will "bunch" at common reference points.

- ☐ Fryer et al. (2012) demonstrate the power of loss aversion in a field experiment on Chicago schoolteachers. The teachers' performance was considerably higher when the same financial incentive plan was framed as a loss rather than a gain by giving the workers some of their expected bonus "up front."

- ☐ Because working hard involves short-term pain for long-term gain, present-biased workers may not supply the effort levels they would *themselves* prefer to supply in the longer run. In these situations, *sophisticated* present-biased workers might demand both output- and input-based *commitment contracts* that improve their own self-discipline. Firms who offer such contracts are, in a sense, the allies of workers' longer term interests by providing a source of discipline that is not available to self-employed workers.

Discussion Questions

1. This chapter gives a number of examples where introducing financial incentives improves agents' performance and others where it reduces performance. Based on all the examples in this chapter, can you summarize what types of situations are most conducive to financial incentives being effective? When are they most likely to backfire?
2. What is the difference between *intrinsic* motivation and *image* motivation? Give some examples of each.
3. In AKP's (2008) Bionicles experiment, we concluded that the *minimum* dollar value the subjects placed on "meaningful" work was 39 cents per Bionicle, which is also equivalent to a 39% wage increase. Is it possible to put an *upper* bound on how much they value meaningful work?
4. One possible way to study whether symbolic awards improve worker performance might be to compare the job performance of award winners with non-winners after the award is received. What are some potential problems with this approach?
5. Can "doing well" (financially) eliminate the perception that one is "doing good'? Explain why this might occur and provide an example.
6. Contrast economists' concept of *effort* with psychologists' concept of *arousal*.

7. Suppose it was true that higher attendance at soccer games, like losing the coin toss, reduced a team's win rate. In contrast to the coin toss, why would this *not* be good evidence that soccer players are negatively affected by psychological pressure?

8. "Prospect theory is useless because it tells us that people care about 'reference points' without ever saying what those reference points are." Discuss.

9. Suppose you were a teacher in the *loss* treatment of Fryer et al.'s (2012) experiment. It is now March and your students are not doing well; in fact, it looks like unless they improve dramatically, you might have to pay back most of your $4,000 advance. As it turns out, this would be very difficult and painful for you because you have already spent all the money. What actions might you take to try to get your students' test scores up before the end of the school year? Which of these actions would actually be good for the students? Which would not?

10. In Kaur et al.'s (2015) Indian data-entry experiment, they randomly assigned paydays to workers, with some being paid on Tuesdays, others on Thursdays, and yet others on Saturdays. Why do you think they did this? Why do you think they picked these days?

Suggestions for Further Reading

If you're interested in whether New York City taxi drivers have reference points based on daily income targets—a practice that, at least on the surface, is highly suboptimal—you might enjoy the series of articles by Camerer, Babcock, Loewenstein, and Thaler (1997); Farber (2005, 2008, 2015); and Crawford and Meng (2011). Fehr and Goette (2007) conduct a similar study of bicycle messengers in Vancouver and Zurich.

Ariely, Kamenica, and Prelec's (2008) article on intrinsic motivation for subjects building Legos is short, interesting, and easy to read.

To see the scientific process of replication in action, it is interesting to read Apesteguia and Palacios-Huerta's (2010) article on soccer kickoffs; and the follow-up article by Kocher, Lenz, and Sutter (2012), which challenges their main finding. It is this kind of careful review of each other's work that moves science forward.

Ashraf, Bandiera, and Lee's (2014) study of Zambian health care trainees and Oster et al.'s (2013) study of Huntington's disease patients provide fascinating evidence of cases where humans seem to deliberately *avoid* acquiring useful information to preserve beliefs that are more pleasant to hold than the truth.

For more on present bias, sophistication, and time inconsistency in effort choices, see Augenblick, Niederle, and Sprenger (2015).

For recent evidence on whether people are sophisticated with respect to their own loss aversion (as opposed to their present bias), see Imas, Sadoff, and Samek (2016).

Kosfeld and Neckermann (2011) provide additional evidence on the effects of symbolic rewards.

Doerrenberg, Duncan, and Löffler (2016), and Horton and Chen (2015) provide additional evidence on the effect of wage cuts on effort. Falk, Kosse, Menrath, Verde, and Siegrist (2016) document physiological responses to wages that are seen as unfair.

For an excellent recent article on reciprocity and gift exchange at work, see DellaVigna, List, Malmendier, and Rao (2016).

References

Abeler, J., Falk, A., Goette, L., & Huffman, D. (2011). Reference points and effort provision. *American Economic Review, 101,* 470–492.

Apesteguia, J., & Palacios-Huerta, I. (2010). Psychological pressure in competitive environments: Evidence from a randomized natural experiment. *American Economic Review, 100,* 2548–2564.

Ariely, D., Bracha, A., & Meier, S. (2009). Doing good or doing well? Image motivation and monetary incentives in behaving prosocially. *American Economic Review, 99,* 544–555.

Ariely, D., Gneezy, U., Loewenstein, G., & Mazar, N. (2009). Large stakes and big mistakes. *Review of Economic Studies, 76,* 451–469.

Ariely, D., Kamenica, E., & Prelec, D. (2008). Man's search for meaning: The case of Legos. *Journal of Economic Behavior and Organization, 67*(3–4), 671–677.

Ashraf, N., Bandiera, O., & Lee, S. S. (2014). Awards unbundled: Evidence from a natural field experiment. *Journal of Economic Behavior and Organization, 100,* 44–63.

Augenblick, N., Niederle, M., & Sprenger, C. (2015). Working over time: Dynamic inconsistency in real effort tasks. *Quarterly Journal of Economics, 130,* 1067–1115. doi:10.1093/qje/qjv020

Benabou, R., & Tirole, J. (2006). Incentives and prosocial behavior. *American Economic Review, 96,* 1652–1678.

Bernheim, B. D., & Rangel, A. (2004). Addiction and cue-triggered decision processes. *American Economic Review, 94*(5), 1558–1590.

Camerer, C., Babcock, L., Loewenstein, G., & Thaler, R. (1997). Labor supply of New York City cabdrivers: One day at a time. *Quarterly Journal of Economics, 112,* 407–441.

Cao, Z., Price, J., & Stone, D. F. (2011, June). Performance under pressure in the NBA (2011). *Journal of Sports Economics* 12(3), 231–252.

Carpenter, J. P., & Gong, E. (2016). Motivating agents: How much does the mission matter? *Journal of Labor Economics,* 34(1), 211–236.

Clark, G. (1994). Factory discipline. *Journal of Economic History, 54,* 128–163.

Crawford, V., & Meng, J. (2011). New York City cab drivers labor supply revisited: Reference-dependent preferences with rational-expectations targets for hours and income. *American Economic Review, 101,* 1912–1932.

Coates, J. M., Gurnell, M., & Rustichini, A. (2009, January 13). Second-to-fourth digit ratio predicts success among high-frequency financial traders. *Proceedings of the National Academy of Sciences, USA, 106,* 623–628.

DellaVigna, S., & Malmendier, U. (2004). Contract design and self-control: Theory and evidence. *Quarterly Journal of Economics, 119*(2), 353–402.

DellaVigna, S., List, J. A., Malmendier, U., & Rao, G. (2016). *Estimating social preferences and gift exchange at work* (NBER Working Paper No. 22043). Cambridge, MA: National Bureau of Economic Research.

Doerrenberg, P., Duncan, D., & Löffler, M. (2016). *Asymmetric labor-supply responses to wage-rate changes: Evidence from a field experiment* (IZA Working Paper No. 9683). Bonn, Germany: Institute of Labor Economics.

Dohmen, T. J. (2008). Do professionals choke under pressure? *Journal of Economic Behavior and Organization, 65,* 636–653.

Falk, A., Kosse, F., Menrath, I., Verde, P. E., & Siegrist, J. (2016, June). *Unfair pay and health* (HCEO Working Paper No. 2016-015). Chicago, IL: Human Capital and Economic Opportunity Global Working Group.

Farber, H. S. (2005). Is tomorrow another day? The labor supply of New York City cabdrivers. *Journal of Political Economy, 113,* 46–82.

Farber, H. S. (2008). Reference-dependent preferences and labor supply: The case of New York City taxi drivers. *American Economic Review, 98,* 1069–1082.

Farber, H. S. (2015). Why you Can't Find a Taxi in the Rain and Other Labor Supply Lessons from Cab Drivers. *The Quarterly Journal of Economics, 130*(4), 1975–2026.

Fehr, E., & Goette, L. (2007). Do workers work more if wages are high? Evidence from a randomized field experiment. *American Economic Review, 97,* 298–317.

Fryer, R., Jr., Levitt, S., List, J., & Sadoff, S. (2012, July). *Enhancing the efficacy of teacher incentives through loss aversion: A field experiment* (NBER Working Paper No. 18237). Cambridge, MA: National Bureau of Economic Research.

Fudenberg, D., & Levine, D. K. (2006). Superstition and rational learning. *American Economic Review*, *96*(3), 630–651.

Garbarino, E., Slonim, R., & Sydnor, J. (2011). Digit ratios (2D:4D) predict risk taking for men and women. *Journal of Risk and Uncertainty, 42,* 1–26.

Gneezy, U., & Rustichini, A. (2000). Pay enough or don't pay at all. *Quarterly Journal of Economics, 115,* 791–810.

Goerg, S. J., & Kube, S. (2012, October). *Goals (th)at work—Goals, monetary incentives, and workers' performance.* Unpublished manuscript, Department of Economics, Florida State University, Tallahassee, FL.

Horton, J. J., & Chen, D. L. (2015). *Are online labor markets spot markets for tasks? A field experiment on the behavioral response to wage cuts.* Unpublished manuscript, Stern School of Business, New York University, New York, NY.

Imas, A., Sadoff, S., & Samek, A. (2016). Do people anticipate loss aversion? *Management Science, 63*(5), 1271–1284.

Kahneman, D., & Tversky, A. (1979). Prospect theory: An analysis of decision under risk. *Econometrica, 47,* 263–291.

Kaur, S., Kremer, M., & Mullainathan, S. (2015). Self-control at work. *Journal of Political Economy, 123,* 1227–1277.

Kocher, M. G., Lenz, M. V., & Sutter, M. (2012). Psychological pressure in competitive environments: New evidence from randomized natural experiments. *Management Science, 58,* 1585–1591.

Kosfeld, M., & Neckermann, S. (2011). Getting more work for nothing? Symbolic awards and worker performance. *American Economic Journal: Microeconomics, 3,* 86–99.

Lacetera, N., Macis M., & Slonim, R. (2012). Will there be blood? Incentives and displacement effects in pro-social behavior. *American Economic Journal: Economic Policy, 4,* 186–223.

David Laibson. (1997). Golden eggs and hyperbolic discounting. *Quarterly Journal of Economics* 112(2): 443–477.

Lavy, V. (2009). Performance pay and teachers' effort, productivity and grading ethics. *American Economic Review, 99,* 1979–2011.

Lavy, V. (2015). *Teachers' pay for performance in the long-run: Effects on students' educational and labor market outcomes in adulthood* (NBER Working Paper No. 20983). Cambridge, MA: National Bureau of Economic Research.

Lazear, E. P. (2000). Performance pay and productivity. *American Economic Review, 90*(3), 1346–1361.

Mas, A. (2006). Pay, reference points, and police performance. *Quarterly Journal of Economics, 121,* 783–821.

O'Donoghue, Ted, and Matthew Rabin. (1999). "Doing It Now or Later." *American Economic Review*, 89(1): 103-124.

Oster, E., Shoulson, I., & Dorsey, E. R. (2013). Optimal expectations and limited medical testing: Evidence from Huntington disease. *American Economic Review, 103,* 804–830.

Oyer, P. (1998). Fiscal year ends and nonlinear incentive contracts: The effect on business seasonality. *Quarterly Journal of Economics*, *113*(1), 149–185.

Shefrin, H. M., & Thaler, R. H. (1988). The behavioral life-cycle hypothesis. *Economic inquiry*, *26*(4), 609–643.

Titmuss, R. M. (1971). *The gift relationship.* London: Allen and Unwin.

Yerkes, R. M., & Dodson, J. D. (1908). The relationship of strength of stimulus to rapidity of habit-formation. *Journal of Comparative Neurology of Psychology, 18,* 459–482.

10 Reciprocity at Work: Gift Exchange, Implicit Contracts, and Trust

Imagine you have agreed to participate in an online economics experiment. The experiment involves playing an extremely simple game involving a chance to earn some money. In the experiment, you are randomly paired with another person somewhere else in the world. No information about this person is given to you, and there is no way for you to *ever* learn their identity, or for them to learn yours. The game goes like this: First, the experimenter gives your partner \$12 to use in the experiment. Your partner then decide how much, if any, of her \$12 to give to you; if you like, you can imagine that the money is instantly transferred into your bank account.[1] Next, after you find out how much money you've received (which could be zero), you decide how much money to give back to your partner. You're allowed to transfer any amount (including zero) of the money you received from your partner. The only twist is that, for every dollar you give back, your partner receives *\$2*. The game we've just described is an example of a *gift-exchange game*. Personnel economists use this gift-exchange game to explore the complex social elements involved in workplace interactions that are entirely missing from the standard principal–agent model in which the economic actors are purely self-interested.

10.1 The Gift-Exchange Game (GEG)

Human behavior in gift-exchange games has been studied in dozens of experiments all over the world. Whereas the gift-exchange game has been used as a model of various kinds of human interactions, behavioral economists often use it

[1] Following our convention of having a female principal and a male agent, we refer to your partner as a "her." This simplifies the discussion, but you should think of the principal as being completely anonymous.

to think about firm–worker or principal–agent interactions.[2] Essentially, we think of the first mover as the principal, who commits to hire the agent for a period of time for a fixed amount of pay. Then the agent responds by deciding how much effort to supply during that period. Multiplying the agent's effort by two reflects the idea that there are *gains from trade* between the principal and agent. Interpreted this way, the gift-exchange game is just a special case of the principal–agent model we studied in Chapter 1; specifically, the case where $a > 0$ and $b = 0$.[3]

How do you think you'd behave as the "agent" in the online principal–agent game? Imagine, for example, that your anonymous "principal" sent you \$12 (the maximum amount allowed). If you send nothing back, she will earn nothing from participating in this experiment, and you'll end up with \$12. If you send \$4 back, you'll end up with $12 - 4 = \$8$, and she will end up with $2(4) = \$8$, for a total of \$16 between the two of you. If you send back \$6, you'll end up with \$6; but the principal will get \$12, for a total of \$18. There are other options as well, of course. And now that you've considered your own options, how do think the principal will behave? Clearly she faces an even tougher decision because she would very much like to know how you'd respond to different actions she might take. Will you "reciprocate" a generous payment with a high effort level? Or will you send her little or nothing no matter how much she sends you?

In Section 10.3, we'll work out exactly how rational, self-interested people should play this game. We'll also present empirical evidence on how real people *actually* play it. But before doing so, I'd like to explain to you why personnel economists have studied this game so much. To do that, we need to discuss a concept we introduced in Section 1.5—the *contract* between the agent and the principal—in greater detail.

10.2 Incomplete Contracts

As we discussed in Section 1.5, a contract is a set of rules that a principal and agent (or an employer and worker) agree on before the agent starts working for the principal. In Chapter 1's simple model, the contract between the agent and principal was an ordered pair (a, b) that completely describes how the principal will treat the agent for every possible action the agent might take in that fictional relationship. In the real world of employer–employee relations, of course, contracts can be much more complex, ranging from CEOs' and baseball players' written individual contracts; to written collective (union) contracts; to policies for evaluation, promotion, and benefits set out in company personnel manuals; to informal agreements like "I'll pay you minimum wage as long as I'm satisfied with your work"; and even to aspects of a company's culture that a new hire

[2] Other applications include bribery and organized crime. It's not a coincidence that these activities are illegal: The gift exchange paradigm is meant to describe economic exchanges in cases where complete contracts either can't be written (due to complexity) or can't be enforced in a court of law.

[3] Technically, the only difference is that the disutility-of-effort function is linear, rather than convex. Essentially, the gift-exchange game we've described here is Chapter 1's principal–agent model with $V(E) = E$ and $Q = dE$, where E is measured in dollars and $d = 2$.

implicitly consents to when signing up with a firm. Because there is such a wide range of actual contracts, it is helpful to have a few definitions that help us keep track of contracts' key features.

One obvious distinction among contracts, of course, is whether they are written.

DEFINITION 10.1 A labor contract (or an aspect of a labor contract) is **implicit** if it isn't specified in writing.

Even when a firm and a worker have a mutual understanding of the worker's duties and how the firm will reward him, these understandings are often not expressed in writing.[4] One advantage of such *implicit* contracts is that they convey the sense of what the parties owe each other while avoiding red tape, litigation, and maintaining flexibility. It's essentially the practice of doing business "on a handshake." One disadvantage of implicit contracts is that they are not easily enforceable in a court of law. When that is the case, the parties' only real remedy if the other egregiously violates the contract is to terminate the relationship. Another disadvantage of implicit contracts is that—even more than in explicit contracts—the parties may sometimes have conflicting understandings of what's actually in their agreement.[5]

Two related concepts that affect whether contracts are explicit are observability and contractibility.

DEFINITION 10.2 An aspect of worker or firm performance is **observable** if both the worker and firm can see, and agree on, exactly what the level of performance was.

For example, if a Safelite worker satisfactorily replaced 15 windshields last week, and if both Safelite and the worker can agree that this is what occurred, the number of windshields replaced per week is an *observable* feature of the interactions between Safelite and its workers. This contrasts, for example, to the level of *effort* the Safelite worker exerted to produce this output, which is probably not quantifiable enough to avoid disputes over what the worker actually did.

DEFINITION 10.3 An aspect of worker or firm performance is **contractible** if the parties can write and enforce an explicit contract that depends on that aspect of performance.

---

[4] Of course, the firm's contractual obligations can be implicit too. For example, a company might have a history of always making layoffs on the basis of seniority, or of always hiring new division managers from inside rather than outside. This isn't written down anywhere (even though it could be), but both workers and firms perceive that this is "how things are done," and how they expect things to be done in the future.

[5] Indeed, if I had even a millionth of a cent for every time that a lack of shared perceptions of what was in an *implicit* contract ("that wasn't the deal!") caused difficulties in economic transactions, I expect I'd be the world's wealthiest man!

Output (Q) in Part 1's principal–agent model is *contractible* by assumption, because the contract $Y = a + bQ$ specifies that the worker's pay will depend on Q. Typically, economic theorists argue that contractibility requires not only that performance be observable to both workers and firms, *but also to a disinterested third party*, such as a court system or arbitrator. So, for example, both a worker and firm might agree that a firm violated its obligations to adequately fund its pension plan. But writing a contract that imposes penalties on firms for underfunding pensions might not be possible because the cost of using the courts to enforce such a penalty would be prohibitive for workers.[6]

DEFINITION 10.4 A labor contract is **incomplete** if the agent's compensation under the contract is not explicitly linked to *every* aspect of his performance that the principal cares about.

Although the (a, b) contract in Chapter 1 is complete in the context of that model, the vast majority of real labor contracts are not. For example, in many contexts, a simple piece-rate contract based on output might ignore the *quality* of output. Safelite's PPP, as we learned from the epilogue to the Safelite story in Section 8.5, ignored customer satisfaction and worker safety. And although some management consulting companies have tried to design comprehensive measures of employee performance in a variety of contexts, their success record is mixed.[7] Essentially, because there is almost always some aspect of the job that can't be codified and explicitly linked to pay in a contract, incompleteness is the rule for labor contracts.

This is why personnel economists find the GEG so interesting. The GEG, after all, is an extreme case of an incomplete labor contract: In the GEG, the employee's pay is a lump sum that is completely unaffected by *any* aspects of job performance (that's because the employee decides how hard to work *after* being paid!). Thus, personnel economists use the GEG as a tool for understanding behavior when labor contracts are incomplete. Although one might expect a highly incomplete contract like the GEG to perform very poorly, in the rest of this chapter, we'll show that the opposite is often true. In fact, sometimes the GEG can yield better results (for both firms and workers) than the highly incentivized contracts Part 1 suggests are best. In the next few sections, we'll first demonstrate this, and then we'll try to understand why.

10.3 Laboratory Evidence on Gift-Exchange Games

Before considering the evidence on how people actually play GEG's, let's return to the imaginary online experiment we described at the beginning of this chapter. Suppose for the sake of argument that both you (as the agent) and the anonymous

[6] Company personnel manuals are an interesting case here: Even though they are written documents, they are not necessarily legally enforceable contracts. Some U.S. states recognize them as such, but not others.

[7] See, for example, Griffith and Nealy (2009), who study the *Balanced Scorecard* system, as implemented by a large, British-based supplier of heating and plumbing supplies.

principal you are matched with are rational and purely self-interested. How should you play this game?

Theory: How Should Rational Agents Play the Gift-Exchange Game?

Just as we used backwards induction to solve the principal–agent model, we need to do the same thing here. After all, the only way for the principal to make an informed decision about what wage to pay you is to first figure out how you are likely to respond to each possible wage she might offer.

So, let's start with your behavior as the agent. Clearly, no matter how much money the principal has sent you, every dollar you send back to principal makes you a dollar poorer. And because you're guaranteed never to interact with this person again, there's no way she can ever reciprocate a favor from you, or punish you for being selfish. So, if you're a purely self-interested person, you'll send no money back to your partner, *no matter how much money she has sent to you, and despite the fact that sending money benefits her more than it costs you*. This solves the agent's behavior in the game.

Now put yourself in the shoes of a rational, self-interested principal who expects her agent to also be rational and self-interested. Clearly, because you expect the agent to give you nothing back *regardless of what you give him*, there's no point in sending him any money. So the rational thing to do is to send no money. Put another way, the *subgame perfect equilibrium* of the gift-exchange game is for the agent to supply zero effort and for the principal (anticipating this) not to hire the agent (that is, to send no money to him in the first stage).[8] Neither the principal nor the agent will earn any money from participating in the experiment if they behave as rational economic agents.

Having noted these theoretical predictions, how would *you* actually play this game? And how do most people play it? If you've done a classroom GEG experiment, you probably know that many if not most principals do in fact pay their agents, and that most agents who received a positive wage supply some effort. In fact, a common feature of GEGs is that agents' effort levels depend positively on the wage they've received from principals, suggesting that they *reciprocate* generous wage offers from firms. Also, because agents' effort levels are usually at least high enough to compensate the principal for the wage that was paid, it's common for both principals and agents to do better, at least on average, than in the game's subgame perfect equilibrium. For example, if the principal in our imaginary online experiment sends the agent \$9 and the agent responds by sending \$6 back, the principal will end up with \$15 and the agent with \$3.[9] Thus both finish the game with \$3 more than in the subgame perfect equilibrium (where they earn \$12 and \$0 respectively).

---

[8] Perfect equilibrium is a formal concept in game theory. Loosely, a perfect equilibrium to a game is a strategy for each play that maximizes the players' utility each time they make a decision, anticipating that all other players will also maximize their utility when it's their turn to move.

[9] The principal's payoff would be $12 - 9 + 2(6) = 15$, and the agent's would be $9 - 6 = 3$. Essentially, by returning \$2 to the principal out of every \$3 he receives from her, the agent can ensure that he gains from participating in the game while ensuring that the principal does so too.

Notice that the anonymity of the gift-exchange experiment is absolutely essential to our claim that subjects who use the above strategies are behaving "irrationally." If there was any chance this principal and agent might knowingly interact again, it might be quite rational to behave generously in the hopes of sustaining a long-term pattern of cooperation. These *repeated game effects*, or *reputation effects*, are no doubt important in real-world interactions, especially in the workplace. The main message of the gift-exchange experiment is that *even when these reputation effects are absent*, humans seem to behave reciprocally.

Evidence: How Do Real People Play the Gift-Exchange-Game?

This surprising ability of gift-exchange contracts to produce good results for both principals and agents is explored in more depth in a series of lab experiments published in 2007 by Fehr, Klein, and Schmidt. In Fehr et al.'s experiments, the agent's effort, as in our imaginary online experiment, was not an actual work task but simply sending money to the principal in a situation where sending this money generated "gains from trade." In this context, Fehr et al. compared the performance of three types of contracts:

Trust contracts: In a *trust* contract, the principal offers a wage and simply requests that effort satisfy $e \geq e^*$.

Bonus contracts: Here, the principal announces a wage, a *desired* effort e^*, and her (unenforceable) intention to pay a bonus b if $e \geq e^*$.

Incentive contracts: An *incentive* contract consists of a wage w, a *required* effort level e^*, and a fine F (all set by the principal). If the agent accepts the contract, he is "audited" with a probability p that was set by the experimenter and is forced to pay the fine if the effort he has chosen (e) falls short of e^*. In the experiment, principals had to pay a small fixed cost to use this contract; we can think of this as the cost of operating the agent monitoring technology.

Trust contracts in Fehr et al.'s experiment are gift-exchange contracts: The principal offers a wage first, then the agent decides how much effort to supply. Although Fehr et al. allow principals to request a desired effort level in their *trust* contract, these requests are unenforceable (they are what game theorists call "cheap talk," and don't affect the perfect equilibrium of the game). *Bonus* contracts add an extra, final stage to the *trust* contract: After the principal has committed to a wage, and the worker has responded with an effort choice, principals have an option to reciprocate high effort levels with a second gift to workers (a "bonus"). This mimics the idea that if principals and agents interact repeatedly, the additional opportunities to reciprocate each other's voluntary "gifts" might lead to better outcomes than if they interact only once. Finally, *incentive* contracts represent a situation where effort is *contractible* but at a cost: As in Chapter 6's model of monitoring, by spending some money, the principal can check up on the agent from time to time and punishes the agent with a fine if his effort isn't what the principal asked for. This more "hard-nosed" approach to HRM doesn't rely on reciprocal behavior to elicit effort from agents. Notice that the subgame perfect equilibrium (which you can work out yourself via backward induction) of both the *trust* and *bonus* contracts is for wages, effort, and bonuses all to equal zero. Only the *incentive* contract is predicted to generate positive levels of effort, profits, and worker utility when principals and agents are rational, self-interested maximizers.

A final important feature of Fehr et al.'s (2007) experiment is that instead of randomly offering the previously mentioned contracts to subjects themselves, the experimenters put other experimental subjects in the role of principals and let them *choose* which of the those contracts to offer their agents. In one set of experiments, principals could choose to offer either an *incentive* or a *trust* contact. In second set of experiments, principals could choose between *incentive* and *bonus* contracts. As a result, the experiment can show us not only which contracts worked best for principals but also whether principals were ultimately able to identify and select better-performing contract types. Think of Fehr et al.'s experiment as a microcosm of a labor market, where different firms are experimenting with different types of employment contracts they could offer workers. The possible contracts range from a hard-nosed one, "Do what I ask and if I catch you doing otherwise you pay a fine"; to perhaps a naïve and overly trusting one-shot interaction, "Here's what I'll pay you for the week. Please do at least X"; to a third contract that is also based on trust but allows for more repeated interaction between the principal and agent. Which contract worked best?

Focusing first on the experiments where principals were choosing between *trust* and *incentive* contracts, Fehr et al. (2007) found that average effort levels were well above zero in *trust* contracts. Consistent with other gift-exchange experiments (and inconsistent with self-interested, rational behavior), a substantial share of principals offered positive wages, and agents reciprocated generous wages by working harder. That said, the "soft-touch" approach of the *trust* contract wasn't as profitable to principals as the harder-nosed incentive contract. In fact, whereas many principals first experimented with the trust contract, most did poorly because workers didn't respond with enough effort for principals to break even. Many of those principals then switched to *incentive* contracts, which improved both the principals' profits *and* the workers' payoffs.

☑ RESULT 10.1

Trust and Incentive Contracts

Many agents supplied positive effort levels under Fehr et al.'s (2007) *trust* contracts. The level of effort supplied rose with the wage received, suggesting that agents reciprocated generous wage offers by working harder. Still, principals who offered trust contracts earned lower profits than more hard-nosed principals who offered *incentive* contracts where workers who were caught supplying less than the contracted effort level were punished.

Things turned out differently, however, when Fehr et al. let firms choose between *incentive* and *bonus* contracts. Faced with this choice, the overwhelming majority of principals chose the *bonus* contract; generous bonuses were common. Not all the principals actually paid the bonus they promised; but on average, bonus contracts outperformed incentive contracts in all dimensions: higher wages, higher effort, higher agent utility, and higher profits. So, in these experimental sessions, a contract relying purely on gift exchange (the *bonus* contract) worked *better* than an explicit contract where effort is contractible (the *incentive* contract).

RESULT 10.2 **Principals Who Offered *Bonus* Contracts in Fehr's et al. (2007) Experiment Earned Higher Profits *and* Paid Higher Wages Than Principals Who Offered *Incentive* Contracts**

What explains Results 10.1 and 10.2? According to Fehr et al. (2007), the main reason *incentive* contracts outperformed *trust* contracts was that the reciprocity relationship (which is needed to elicit effort in the *trust* contract) was relatively weak and unreliable when principals and agents interacted only once. As a result, offering a high wage in a *trust* contract was very risky for firms, so both wages and effort ended up pretty low. The main reason why *bonus* contracts outperformed *trust* contracts, even though both rely on gift exchange, is that there's more repeated interaction with *bonus* contracts; firms have a chance to reward high effort (and punish low effort) by adjusting a bonus that is paid after the work is done. A key lesson is the following.

RESULT 10.3 **Incomplete Contracts Work Better**

Fehr et al.'s (2007) experiment suggests that incomplete contracts that don't contain explicit financial performance incentives work better in long-term employment relationships (where both parties have repeated opportunities to reward or punish bad past behavior by the other) than in one-shot interactions.

Finally, there are at least two reasons why *bonus* contracts were able to outperform *incentive* contracts in Fehr et al.'s experiment. The more obvious one is that bonus contracts economize on monitoring costs: Rather than spend money trying to catch workers cheating, firms just wait to see whether they like what the worker has achieved, then pay a bonus or not as they see fit.[10] A second possibility is that agents may have reacted negatively to the principal's *decision* to monitor them, for example, because that decision is a signal that the firm does not trust the worker. In fact, some recent experiments (and field studies) have shown that (strategically) *relinquishing control* over workers can yield surprising benefits to firms. We'll look at one of the earliest and most influential of those experiments in Section 10.5.

[10] You might ask why it costs firms to punish workers whose effort is below the threshold in the *incentive* contract, whereas in the *bonus* contract, they can do the same by withholding a bonus without incurring a monitoring cost. This is a good question! The answer refers back to the distinction between *contractibility* and *observability*: Fehr et al. (2007) assume that firms can costlessly observe workers' performance levels, but an outside observer can't. So if the firm is going to write and operate an explicit contract that is enforceable in court, some extra expenses are required. (For example, the firm may need to document the worker's shortcomings in a convincing way if it wants to enforce a fine.)

The (Pre-)History of Gift Exchange in Human Societies

A parable that's often told in introductory economics textbooks, usually when explaining the nature and origins of money, is that over the course of human (pre-) history, societies gradually moved from a system of barter, where goods were exchanged directly for one another, to systems of money where one item—currency—could be exchanged for any good whatsoever. (For a formal version of this parable, see Kiyotaki and Wright [1991].) Of course, the big disadvantage of barter was that it required a *coincidence of wants*; if I had an extra ax but needed new shoes, I had to find a shoemaker who needed an ax. Needless to say, this left many potential gains from trade unrealized; and as the parable goes, money was invented to solve the problem.

As it happens, this simple parable omits probably one of the most important features of premodern economies, one you might think of as an intermediate stage between barter and money: gift exchange. In particular, suppose I find myself a shoemaker, but he doesn't need an ax (or anything else I have today). A smart shoemaker might just decide to *give* me some extra shoes he has lying around. Explicitly or implicitly, the understanding is then that I *owe* him something in the future: The next time I have something that he needs, I'll give him something in return. Thus, the coincidence of wants problem can be substantially reduced if the act of giving a gift *creates a sense of obligation in the recipient*. This sense of obligation ensures that the gift is *reciprocated* in the future. Essentially, gift-exchange economies are based on "trading favors."

Can an economy be built on gift exchange? A large empirical literature in anthropology suggests that it can. Indeed, one of the most influential early books in that field is titled *The Gift* by French anthropologist Marcel Mauss. Based on case studies of the Pacific Northwest, Polynesia, and Melanesia, among others, he argues that gift exchange forms the basis of many premodern economies. His work has been very influential among anthropologists. More recently, an interdisciplinary team—Henrich, Boyd, Bowles, Camerer, and Fehr (2001), Heinrich et al. (2005, 2010)—has actually conducted a set of simple economic games like the gift-exchange game in 15 different premodern societies that are still in existence to see whether notions of fairness, such as the obligation to reciprocate, are universal among humans (and thus possibly "hardwired" into our brains). Interestingly, although very widespread, these notions of fairness are relatively absent in the least "modern" societies, suggesting that they are cultural, not biological, in origin. To be fair, however, this evidence is based on a small handful of surviving small-scale societies.

10.4 Intentions, Reference Points, and Positive versus Negative Reciprocity

As we've noted, a central finding in gift-exchange experiments is that agents who receive higher wages "reciprocate" by selecting higher effort levels. *Why* they do this is less clear, however; in fact, there are at least two broad types of explanations for this kind of behavior. Although both explanations assume that workers care about fairness, one focuses purely on whether the ultimate *outcomes* of the exchange (i.e., the principal's and agent's payoffs) are seen as fair. The other argues that something besides outcomes also matters—the parties' *intentions.*

Outcomes-Based Fairness and Reciprocal Behavior

To understand the *outcomes*-based explanation of reciprocal behavior, let's return to the online experiment we described at the start of this chapter and imagine that you, as the agent, have just received a wage of $9 from the principal. If you respond to this by doing nothing at all (i.e., supply zero effort), the principal will end up with a payoff of $3 and you'll end up with a payoff of $9. It's possible that this outcome doesn't feel right to you, either because you and the principal have benefited unequally from participating in the experiment, or simply because you care about the well-being of this anonymous person. If that is the case, you might very well decide to send back $2 instead of none because that way you and the principal would both end up earning $7 each. If this is how your (perhaps subconscious) thinking goes, it's easy to see that you'll behave in a *reciprocal manner*: The more money the principal sends you, the more money you'll send back.

It's possible, however, that outcomes-based explanations like the one just described miss something important about why people behave reciprocally in the gift-exchange game. To see this, let's compare two situations in the online experiment: In one, the principal has chosen to send you a wage of just $1. In the other, the principal was *forced* by the experimenter to send you a wage of $1. It's possible that you might respond more negatively to this low wage in the former than in the latter case. Even though the principal's actions are the same in both cases, in one case the principal *intentionally* chose to pay you a low wage. It's not so much that you and the principal will end up with different amounts of money; it's that the principal deliberately chose an action you perceive as hurtful, relative to some reference point. As you might expect, understanding the difference between intentions- and outcomes-based reciprocity is important if we want to apply gift-exchange theory to real firms: A world in which intentions matter is a lot more complicated than a world in which people care only about outcomes! But how can this be done?

Intentions-Based Fairness and Reciprocal Behavior

As it turns out, a classic lab experiment by Theo Offerman (2002) at the University of Amsterdam does the trick.[11] The Dutch students in his experiment were paired into first and second movers (we'll also call them principals and agents here) and played a game called the *hot response game*. Here's how it went: The principal moves first, by choosing one of two actions: the *hurtful* action subtracts 4 guilders from the agent's experimental payoff, but adds 11 guilders to

[11] Charness (2004) also distinguishes intentions-based from outcomes-based reciprocity in a lab experiment, but Offerman's results are presented here because the design is a little easier to summarize.

the principal's. The *helpful* action adds 4 guilders to the agent's payoff but only adds 8 guilders to the principal's. If you like, you can think of the hurtful action as a firm that is cutting wages relative to their current level and the helpful one as raising wages.

After seeing whether the principal chose the helpful or hurtful action, it's the agent's turn to make a decision. Agents must pick one of three actions: labeled *reward*, *cool*, and *punish*. Of these, the *cool* action is the best for the agent: it adds 10 guilders to the agent's payoff, and has no effect on the principal's payoff at all. Both the *reward* and *punish* actions add 9 guilders to the agent's payoff but have opposite effects on the principal's payoff: *reward* adds 4 guilders to the principal's payoff, whereas *punish* subtracts 4 guilders. Put another way, by sacrificing one guilder of his own money, the agent has the option of raising or lowering the principal's payoff by 4 guilders.

Clearly, if agents are purely selfish and rational, they should always pick the *cool* strategy, regardless of what the principal did first. (And rational selfish principals should always pick the hurtful action: *hurtful*, *cool* is the subgame perfect equilibrium of the hot response game.) If agents behave reciprocally, however, they may sacrifice some of their own payoff to punish principals who behave hurtfully and to reward principals who behave helpfully. But as we just argued, such behavior alone doesn't necessarily imply that agents are responding to principals' *intentions.* To tease this out, Offerman (2002) takes the clever approach of running his experiment two ways: In the *flesh and blood* condition, principals chose between the helpful and hurtful actions. In the *nature* condition, the principal's choice was determined by rolling a die: if 1, 2, or 3 came up, she was forced to pick "helpful"; if 4, 5, or 6 came up, she had to choose "hurtful." In the *nature* condition, agents knew that the principal's choice was determined this way. The genius of Offerman's (2002) experiment, of course, is that if agents' reciprocal behavior was motivated only by a concern with (both their own and the principal's) *outcomes*, their choices to reward, punish, or just "be cool" should be the same in the *nature* and *flesh and blood* conditions. On the other hand, if their behavior is affected by the principal's *intentions*, then it will matter whether a principal chose or was forced to choose (say) a hurtful action.

Table 10.1 shows the share of agents picking each of the three possible choices (punish, cool, reward) in Offerman's (2002) hot response experiment. The results are shown separately for the *nature* condition and the *flesh and blood* condition. A first pattern to note is that *in both conditions*, agents were more likely to reward the principal when they'd been helped than when they'd been hurt. (In the *flesh and blood* condition, 75% of the agents who were helped—i.e., 12 out of 16 subjects—chose to reward their principal, compared to 0% of the agents who were hurt. In the nature condition, these rates were 50% and 25%, respectively.) Second, and closely related, in both conditions agents were more likely to punish the principal when they'd been hurt than when they'd been helped. (In the *flesh and blood* condition, 83.3% of the agents who were hurt chose to punish their principal, compared to 0% of the agents who were helped. In the nature condition, these rates were 16.7% and 0%, respectively.) Taken together, these two findings indicate that *there was reciprocal behavior in both conditions.*

TABLE 10.1 SHARE OF AGENTS CHOOSING THE PUNISH, COOL, AND REWARD ACTIONS IN OFFERMAN'S HOT RESPONSE GAME

	AGENT'S ACTION					
PRINCIPAL'S ACTION	PUNISH		COOL		REWARD	
	Nature	Flesh & Blood	Nature	Flesh & Blood	Nature	Flesh & Blood
Helpful	0% (0/16)	0% (0/16)	50% (8/16)	25% (4/16)	50% (8/16)	75% (12/16)
Hurtful	16.7% (2/12)	83.3% (10/12)	58.3% (7/12)	16.7% (2/12)	25% (3/12)	0% (0/12)

Third, looking at the size of agents' responses to hurtful or helpful actions it's clear that agents' reciprocal responses were much stronger when they were hurt by the decisions of "*flesh and blood*" principals than by principals whose hand was forced by nature. For example, almost all the agents (83.3%) punish their principal when they are hurt in the flesh and blood condition, compared to only 16% in the *nature* condition. (Indeed it's easy to imagine the hurt agents in the nature condition thinking, "He didn't *mean* to hurt me: The experimenter forced him to do so!") This aspect of Offerman's (2002) experiment is clear evidence that (at least in the economics laboratory) agents care not just about *what* principals do to them, but *why*. In short, *principals' intentions matter* for agents' behavior.

RESULT 10.4 Offerman's (2002) experiment shows that reciprocal behavior in laboratory games is caused, at least in part, by a response to other peoples' *intentions*, as distinct from their actions alone. Agents respond in a helpful way to others' intentional actions that help them, and they respond hurtfully to intentional hurtful actions.

Positive versus Negative Reciprocity

The fourth and final result of Offerman's (2002) experiment is reflected in the title of his article, "Hurting Hurts More than Helping Helps." To see this, Offerman uses his agents' responses in the *nature* condition as a measure of how much reciprocal behavior is generated by purely *outcome-based* motivations. He then measures the strength of *intention-based reciprocity* by the *difference* in the rate at which hurtful actions are punished (or helpful actions are rewarded) between the *flesh and blood* and *nature* conditions. Measuring the strength of intention-based reciprocity this way, it's clear that intention-based *negative* reciprocity is much stronger than intention-based *positive* reciprocity. To see this, notice that 16.7% of unintentionally hurt agents punished their principal compared to 83.3% of intentionally hurt agents; this difference is highly statistically significant. So agents are very keen to punish principals who intentionally hurt them, but they are quite forgiving of principals who unintentionally hurt them. On the positive side,

75% of intentionally helped agents rewarded their principals compared to 50% of unintentionally helped agents. Not only is this difference smaller, it's not statistically significant at the typical thresholds used in experimental research.

> **RESULT 10.5**
>
> **Hurting Hurts More than Helping Helps, or Negative Reciprocity Is Stronger than Positive Reciprocity**
>
> Offerman's (2002) experiment shows that agents punish intentionally harmful actions much more strongly than they reward intentionally helpful actions.

If Offerman's (2002) "Hurting Hurts More than Helping Helps" result reminds you of prospect theory—where a $1 loss of income *below* an agent's reference point hurts him more than he gains from a $1 gain *above* the reference point—you are right. While Offerman's results refer to the effects of one person's intentional actions toward another, and prospect theory refers to payoffs in general, both concepts have empirical support and "feel" intuitive. Both concepts, of course, share a weakness as well: They only make sense relative to some reference point, and neither theory offers much of a guide as to how that reference point is determined.

To see the difficulties this can cause, consider a worker who has just had her annual performance review and is wondering what sort of raise she is likely to get. In each of the past 5 years, she has received a 3% raise. Would giving her a 2% raise this year be perceived as a *hurtful* action by the firm or a helpful one? The answer is unclear because it depends on the worker's reference point, or frame, relative to which we measure the proposed raise: Is the reference point the employee's current wage (in which case 2% is perceived as a helpful action), or is the reference point her *expected* wage for the current year based on recent experience (in which case she's getting a disappointing cut)? As in the case of Fryer, Levitt, List, and Sadoff's (2012) public schoolteachers, this suggests that reference points can have big effects on how compensation is perceived and that shaping reference points in a way that reduces perceptions of unfairness can be a powerful managerial tool.

Implicit Contracts and Reciprocal Behavior

As a final example of how reference points can shape peoples' perceptions of pay *and thereby their actual work behavior*, let's return one last time to Gneezy and Rustichini's (2000b) IQ and donations experiments in Section 9.1. In that section, we discussed one possible interpretation of their results: the idea that cash compensation can destroy intrinsic motivation. Interestingly, although that is a possible explanation, it is not the one the authors themselves consider the most likely. Instead, as it happens, Gneezy and Rustichini's (2000b) preferred explanation is based on their agents' understandings of their *implicit contract* with the experimenters and on how the different experimental treatments changed the subjects' understanding of those contracts by changing their *reference points*.

To see how shifting understandings of what the actual contract is might affect employee performance in Gneezy and Rustichini's (2000b) IQ experiment, put yourself in shoes of one of their experimental subjects in the zero piece-rate treatment. You've arrived at the room where the experiment is conducted and have been informed that you'll be paid 60 NIS (or if you prefer, $20) for participating in the experiment. You don't know yet what the experiment is, but you know that whatever task you're asked to perform will take about 1 hr. That's what you "owe" the experimenter in return for the $20, and it seems reasonable. So, in this scenario, the implicit contract is a *gift-exchange contract*: Essentially, you've agreed to make a good faith effort to do whatever the experimenter asks (within reason) in return for the $20 dollars that experimenter has agreed to pay you. There's no reason to be reluctant to "do your best" or to feel the experimenter is being "cheap."

Now consider a second scenario where you arrive and are informed you'll be paid 60 NIS to show up and stay for an hour. You have in fact shown up and plan to stay for the duration of the experiment, so in that sense, you've fulfilled your perceived obligation to the employer. But now the employer tells you he'll pay you a penny for every question you answer correctly. This feels incredibly cheap! So you're insulted by the low rate of pay for this additional activity you've been asked to perform and choose to exert only minimal effort.

The main difference between these two scenarios is the perception of what has been agreed to as part of the contract and what is an "extra" request that requires additional compensation. In the former case, you interpreted your "contract" with the experimenter as gift-exchange contract. In other words, you had the perception that you owed the experimenter a decent performance in return for your fixed show-up fee. In the latter case, you thought you'd already fulfilled your obligations by showing up (that was the gift-exchange part of the contract). But now you are being offered a tiny amount of pay for doing a good job. In other words, Gneezy and Rustichini's (2000b) argument is that the mere act of offering a piece rate (no matter how small) might change workers' *perception of the implicit contract* they have with the experimenter, from a reasonably generous gift-exchange contract to a reasonably generous gift-exchange contract combined with a really cheap piece-rate contract.

If you find yourself skeptical about Gneezy and Rustichini's (2000b) implicit-contract-based explanation for why workers' performance fell when a small financial incentive was introduced, you're probably not alone. It's a pretty complicated story. But the general lesson that workers' implicit understandings of the contract they have with their employer can matter a lot, and that changing, or "reframing" those understandings can have large and hard-to-reverse effects on employee performance is an important one. To illustrate this broader point, let me tell you about one more study by these same two authors (Gneezy & Rustichini, 2000a) that was published in the same year. Instead of looking at *rewards* (for task performance), this study looked at the effects of *penalties* for an undesirable action. The action—familiar to many parents of young children—is picking your kids up late from preschool.

Here, Gneezy and Rustichini (2000a) first introduced a fine of 10 NIS if parents were more than 10 min late to pick up their child. Contrary to the standard economic model (but perhaps not surprising given what happened in their other experiment!), parents became *more* likely to pick up their kids late when the fine was introduced. Gneezy and Rustichini's (2000a) explanation is, again, that introducing the fine *changed parents' perception of their "contract"* with the day care: Before the fine was introduced, it was simply considered parents' duty or responsibility not to be late. Introducing a small fine meant that being late was OK, as long as you were willing to pay the price (hence the article's famous title, "A Fine Is a Price"). Interestingly, when the day care subsequently got rid of the fine, the parents' behavior didn't improve. Parents' sense that they "owed" the center something was hard to restore after a small financial penalty changed the idea of what it meant to be late.

10.5 Positive and Negative Reciprocity in the Field

Taken together, Fehr et al.'s (2007) and Offerman's (2002) laboratory results show that when experimental subjects representing firms "do a favor" for experimental subjects representing workers by paying them a high wage, the workers tend to reciprocate by supplying more effort. In the lab, these responses are sometimes so strong that firms paying high wages earn higher profits than firms paying low wages, even when these high wage payments are not contractually linked to worker performance. Workers also respond negatively and even more strongly to wage cuts than raises. Finally, an important component of this worker response is a reaction to the *intentions* behind a firm's actions, as distinct from the *outcomes* resulting from those actions.

Although the preceding evidence is both dramatic and fascinating (at least to behavioral economists!), it's based completely on lab experiments on college students. Is there any evidence that intentions-based reciprocity plays an important role in the behavior of other types of people, and (more important) in real workplaces? As it turns out, the answer to the first of these questions is a pretty solid "yes": Gift-exchange experiments have been conducted on a diverse set of populations other than college students, with broadly similar results. One interesting and quite robust pattern in these studies is that older people generally are more reciprocal than younger people, suggesting that rewarding kind acts is, at least in part, a learned behavior.[12]

That said, the evidence that workers' reciprocal responses to management's actions play an important role in real workplaces remains very limited. On balance, the evidence seems to point to a very short-term effect of unexpected, unconditional pay raises on worker performance. For example, Bellemare and Shearer (2009) conduct a field experiment in a tree-planting firm; they find evidence that a surprise, one-day-long pay raise increases worker productivity on that day, but they don't study longer term effects. Gneezy and List (2006) hire workers to do various tasks and find similar short-term effects

[12] See, for example, Sutter and Kocher (2007), who study reciprocity in a sample ranging from eight-year-old children to people in their late 60s.

Taking a Good Turn for Granted: Hedonic Adaptation

The idea that workers' perceptions of what constitutes a kind employer action adapt quickly to wage increases is an example of a phenomenon known as *hedonic adaptation* in psychology. The idea is that even after large positive or negative shocks to their life situations (such as losing a limb or winning the lottery), most people eventually return to a constant level of happiness or life satisfaction, referred to as the individual's "set point." For a recent empirical assessment of this idea, see Oswald and Powdthavee (2008).

of unexpected pay raises. But these increases in worker performance *disappear after as little as 3 hr, even if the wage remains at its new, higher level!* So, although real workers seem to reciprocate generous wage payments by working harder, available evidence suggests that this effect wears off very quickly as workers adapt to (or perhaps "take for granted") the new, higher wage. Put a different way, the workers' *reference point* shifts relatively quickly to the new, higher wage; so the wage that was originally perceived as a generous gift becomes "the new normal." This suggests that unconditional pay increases are very unlikely to "pay for themselves" by generating additional, voluntary worker effort in real workplaces.

But what about pay cuts? If Offerman's (2002) lab results generalize to the real world, then unexpected, intentional pay cuts could still have negative, longer term effects on worker effort even if pay raises have ephemeral effects. In fact, some recent evidence suggests that this may be true. For example, Kube, Maréchal, and Puppe (2013) conduct field experiments where some subjects (being paid to do real jobs) got an unexpected hourly pay increase, and others got an unexpected cut. They found much stronger responses to the pay cut, and these responses were more long-lasting too.

Perhaps more convincingly, in a well-known study the economic theorist, Truman Bewley (1999) interviewed scores of managers in New England manufacturing firms to try to solve a decades-long puzzle in macroeconomics: Why are firms so reluctant to cut wages in recessions—when workers are easier to get and willing to work for less than in economic booms? Interestingly, many of Bewley's interviewees thought that such wage cuts would be very foolish, precisely because of the effect they would have on worker morale and performance. Although more evidence is needed on this issue, Bewley's results suggest that the current nominal wage is an important reference point for workers, and that negative reciprocity with respect to that wage level may be a powerful force in real workplaces. Firms would be well advised to be very careful when considering cost-saving wage cuts, and—because the firm's intentions may matter to workers—to pay close attention to explaining why such cuts are necessary.

10.6 Trust Can Pay: The Hidden Cost of Control

For obvious reasons, relying on incomplete labor contracts that, by necessity, don't incentivize workers on all the dimensions that matter to firms can seem risky from an employer's perspective. In these situations, it might seem reasonable for employers to wonder, "Is there some way I can force my workers to produce at least a certain minimum amount on the job?" In an ingenious laboratory experiment published in 2006, economists Armin Falk and Michael Kosfeld show that attempts to explicitly control workers in this way could backfire. Interestingly, "backfiring" is more likely when employers exert small amounts of control than larger amounts.

Here's how Falk and Kosfeld's (2006) experiment worked. Agents, who—as usual—move second, are endowed with 120 lab dollars in each round of the experiment.[13] Agents choose effort, x (which can be any number between 0 and 120). An effort level of x costs the agent x, but yields a benefit of $2x$ to that agent's principal. Principals in Falk and Kosfeld's experiment (who move first) only make one decision: *whether or not to impose a minimum effort level, x_{min}, on the agent.* This minimum effort level (which principals chose whether or not to impose) was set by the experimenters. In some experimental sessions, the minimum was 5 units of x; in other sessions x_{min} was set at 10 or 20 units of x. As in many of the lab experiments we've already discussed, Falk and Kosfeld ensured that each no principal–agent pair ever interacted more than once and that subjects' identities were strictly confidential. This eliminates the possibility that agents might choose to work hard at one time, for example, to curry favor with "their" principal in the future.[14]

Before we ask how principals and agents actually behaved in Falk and Kosfeld's (2006) experiment, let's take a moment to work out how we'd expect them to behave if they were purely rational, self-interested actors. Focusing first on agents (using the now-familiar reasoning of backwards induction), it's easy to see that because effort is costly to the agent, and the agent will never see this same principal again, an agent's rational effort level is the minimum one allowed by the principal. So, if the principal imposes a minimum effort level of 10, a rational agent should supply exactly 10 units of effort. If the principal chooses not to impose a minimum effort level, a rational agent should supply zero effort. Anticipating this, rational principals should always impose a minimum effort level, that is, they should always try to *control* the agent to the maximum extent possible.

But now, let's take a step beyond pure self-interest and ask how we might expect agents *who care about fairness* to behave. In particular, suppose each agent has in mind (either consciously or unconsciously) a "fair" level of effort to provide. For example, an agent who feels that an equal "division of the

---

[13] Lab dollars are units of currency used to keep track of earnings in experiments. They are generally worth much less than real dollars.

[14] Obviously, working hard to impress your boss (or just keep your job) can be an important motivator in real workplaces, and we'll study these incentives in detail in Chapter 18. Most of the experiments on reciprocity discussed in this section, however, deliberately abstract from those factors to better understand the pure effects of morale and reciprocity, which can also have important, but distinct, effects on worker performance.

spoils" from the experiment is a fair one would choose 40 units of effort because that leaves both the agent and the principal with a payoff of 80 lab dollars. One could easily imagine other notions of fairness, but it seems reasonable to suppose that an agent's idea of what's a fair effort level *shouldn't depend on actions taken by the principal that have no consequences for the agent.* In other words, if I thought that 30 is a fair amount of effort to provide, my decision to provide 30 units of effort shouldn't be affected by my principal's decision to require me to provide at least 10 units of effort. Put yet another way, suppose that $x_{min} = 10$. If agents choose effort levels on the basis of fairness, and if their idea of fairness is purely *outcomes based* (as opposed to intentions based), then *the fraction of agents who supply 11 or more units of effort should not depend on whether the principal forces agents to supply at least 10 units of effort.* Forcing agents to supply at least 10 units of effort should raise the effort levels of agents who think that $x < 10$ is the rational or fair thing to do while having no effect on the behavior of agents who prefer $x \geq 10$. Given this, a profit-maximizing firm's best strategy is once again always to restrict its agent's behavior.

Is this what actually happened in Falk and Kosfeld's (2006) experiment? As Table 10.2 shows, the answer to this question is a resounding "no." Consider, for example, the sessions where principals decided whether or not to force their agents to supply at least 5 units of effort, summarized in column 1 of Table 10.2. When principals decided not to control their agent, four out of five agents (80%) voluntarily decided to give their principals 6 or more units of effort. But only one in two (50%) of the agents whose principals forced them to supply at least 5 units of effort provided 6 or more units. Therefore, it must be the case that some agents who otherwise would have provided higher effort levels (say, 15 units) when the principal doesn't try to "control" them reduce their effort to the minimum level allowed (5 in this case) when control is introduced. Similar results occur in the sessions where x_{min} was set at 10 or at 20. Importantly, this is evidence not only against a purely selfish model of agent behavior; it also contradicts a purely outcomes-based model of fairness-motivated behavior. Agents respond negatively to principals' attempts to control them, even when those attempts don't actually constrain what the agent originally "wanted" to do.

TABLE 10.2 FRACTION OF AGENTS SELECTING *MORE THAN* X_{MIN} UNITS OF EFFORT LEVEL IN FALK AND KOSFELD'S (2006) EXPERIMENT, BY TREATMENT

	(1)	(2)	(3)
Treatment	$x_{min} = 5$	$x_{min} = 10$	$x_{min} = 20$
Control: Principal imposed x_{min} on the agent	50%	48%	41%
Trust: Principal did not impose x_{min} on the agent	80%	69%	59%

Source: Figures are approximated from Figure 1 in Falk and Kosfeld (2006).

RESULT 10.6 **(Falk & Kosfeld, 2006)**

The Hidden Costs of Control." Attempts to control workers behavior can backfire by inducing some workers—who otherwise would have exceeded firms' minimum performance standard—to reduce their performance levels to the minimum required level. This type of worker behavior is inconsistent with both purely selfish models as well as models of outcomes-based fairness.

Of course, just because a principal's decision to impose control "angered" some workers enough to lead them to cut their effort doesn't mean that imposing control reduces firms' profits. After all, control also has a direct positive effect on some workers' efforts by forcing those workers who would otherwise work at less than the minimum to raise their performance to the minimum standard. The *overall effect* of control on profits depends on whether the *direct effect* of control on the "slackers" outweighs its *indirect effect* on the morale of the hard workers, who might react negatively to the firm's imposition of control. Which of these factors dominated in Falk and Kosfeld's (2006) experiment?

As Table 10.3 shows, imposing small amounts of control (specifically, requiring worker effort to be at least 5 or 10 units) is, on net, counterproductive for firms—it *reduces* firms' profits.[15] For example, firms who impose $x_{min} = 5$ on their workers earn *less than half* the profits of firms who choose not to impose this requirement. Profits are also lower for firms who impose $x_{min} = 10$ or $x_{min} = 20$ than firms who don't, but the difference is smaller (and statistically insignificant when $x_{min} = 20$). Essentially, this means that the indirect, or "hidden" costs of control outweigh the direct benefits (to firms) of control for small levels of control, but this balance can change for stronger forms of control.[16] Clearly, if a principal in Falk and Kosfeld's (2006) experiment could simply force its agent to supply at least 100 units of effort, it would earn more profits than a firm that didn't restrict effort at all.

TABLE 10.3 AVERAGE PROFIT OF PRINCIPALS IN FALK AND KOSFELD'S (2006) EXPERIMENT, BY TREATMENT

	(1)	(2)	(3)
Treatment	$x_{min} = 5$	$x_{min} = 10$	$x_{min} = 20$
Control: Principal imposed x_{min} on the agent	24.4	35	50.8
Trust: Principal did not impose x_{min} on the agent	50.2	46	53.4

Falk and Kosfeld's (2006) numbers are multiplied by 2 to convert them to measures of firms' profits.
Source: Figures are taken from Table 1 in Falk and Kosfeld (2006).

[15] Recall that firms don't pay wages to workers in Falk and Kosfeld's (2006) experiment—their only decision is whether to impose control or not. So, firms' profits depend only on the worker's effort level; in fact, they just equal $2x$, where x is effort.

[16] This is subject, of course, to the proviso that firms don't push workers so hard that they leave the firm: As always, what firms can ask workers to do in any free labor market must satisfy workers' *participation (or individual-rationality) constraint.*

RESULT 10.7

(Falk & Kosfeld, 2006)

The "Don't Try to Control the Small Stuff" attempts to forcibly impose small, profit-improving behavioral changes on workers can reduce profits. This is because the direct benefits of such actions can be outweighed by control's hidden costs. Controlling larger aspects of workers' behavior can be profitable as long as it doesn't induce too many workers to quit.

By now, I hope I have convinced you that control can have hidden costs. But *why* do workers in their experiment react negatively to firms' attempts to control their actions? As it happens, Falk and Kosfeld (2006) provide some additional clues for what motivates this behavior, one of which comes from some additional experimental sessions they ran. These sessions were exactly the same as the ones we've just discussed, with one exception: Instead of letting principals choose whether or not to control their agents, the experimenters now made this decision on the principals' behalf. Agents still worked for principals on the same terms as before, with each lab dollar of agent effort generating 2 lab dollars of profits for the agent's principal. Interestingly, Falk and Kosfeld found that agents did not reduce their efforts when their principal was forced to control them, even though the objective conditions under which these agents were working were exactly the same for agents whose principals *chose* to control them. Clearly, this is additional evidence that *principals' perceived intentions matter for agents' behavior.*

A second clue regarding agents' motivations comes from a question in the exit survey Falk and Kosfeld (2006) conducted at the end of their experiment.

Extreme Trust: What Happens when Workers Can Set Their Own Wages?

In an even more dramatic laboratory illustration of the "trust can pay" idea, Charness Cobo-Reyes, Jimenez, Lacomba, and Lagos (2012) compared a standard gift-exchange labor contract (where firms set wages and workers choose effort) to one in which workers can set their own wages. Instead of picking high wages and low effort (as a neoclassical model would predict), Charness et al. (2012) found that, on average, workers set high wages, but then—perhaps out of a sense of responsibility—chose high effort levels also. In fact, these effort levels were higher than in the standard gift-exchange contract where the employer sets the wage. Although only a few real firms—Brazil's highly successful manufacturer *Semco* among them—allow workers to set their own wages, the *Semco* case and Charness et al.'s (2012) experiment illustrate how powerful trust *can* be, at least in the right circumstances.

Trust Can Pay in the Real World Too: Tools and "the HP Way"

In his influential memoir, *The HP Way*, David Packard, one of the Hewlett Packard company's founders, provides a nice illustration of the value of trust that compares his experiences as an employee of General Electric with HP's policy. Packard writes, "In the late 1930s, when I was working for General Electric . . . , the company was making a big thing of plant security. . . . GE was especially zealous about guarding its tool and parts bins to make sure employees didn't steal anything. Faced with this obvious display of distrust, many employees set out to prove it justified, walking off with tools and parts whenever they could. . . . When HP got under way, the GE memories were still strong and I determined that our parts bins and storerooms should always be open. . . . Keeping storerooms and parts bins open was advantageous to HP in two important ways. From a practical standpoint, the easy access to parts and tools helped product designers and others who wanted to work out new ideas at home or on weekends. A second reason, less tangible but important, is that the open bins and storerooms were a symbol of trust, a trust that is central to the way HP does business" (Packard, 1995, p. 135).

An interesting feature of Packard's example is that it pertains to firms controlling a relatively minor aspect of employees' choices—access to the tools and parts bin. According to Falk and Kosfeld's (2006) experimental results, it's exactly in these situations where control policies are most likely to backfire.

This open-ended question asked, "What do you feel if [the principal] forces you to transfer at least [*x*] points?" The most common response was "distrust," especially among those agents who reacted negatively to control. That's why I chose to title this section "Trust Can Pay." Finally, consider the evidence from a clever follow-up experiment conducted by Schnedler and Vadovic (2011). Here, each principal

Controls Can Work, Too: Checklists as Managerial Controls

Checklists, which can function both as memory aids and employee monitoring systems, have been found to reduce errors in medicine and aviation. In a recent field experiment in a chain of auto repair shops, C. Kirabo Jackson and Henry S. Schneider (2015) randomly provided detailed checklists to mechanics and monitored their use. Revenue was 20% higher under the experiment, which compares favorably with the revenue effects of increasing the mechanics' commission rate. The authors also find some evidence that checklists and stronger financial incentives (higher commission rates) work even better together; that is, that they are complementary. Jackson and Schneider's results are an important reminder that managerial control and explicit economic incentives can be beneficial in the right circumstances.

had two agents—one was a "real" agent in the lab working under exactly the same conditions as in Falk and Kosfeld's (2006) experiment. The other was a computerized automaton that was programmed to always behave in a rational, selfish way—supplying the minimum effort that was allowed. To mimic the idea that employers generally set HRM policies that apply to large groups of workers, in this experiment each principal had to make a control decision that applied to his or her entire "workforce": either both agents were controlled, or both were not. Perhaps not surprisingly, (real) agents in this situation seem to "understand" the principal's decision to impose control and do not reduce their effort when controls are imposed. Results like this suggest that both the exact situation (and mix of workers) in the workplace *and the way that firms explain and justify their policies to impose controls* can have significant effects on workers' job performance.

10.7 Fairness Among Workers

So far in this book, we've focused almost exclusively on the one-on-one relationship between a principal and a single agent: our theoretical models only have a single worker, and our empirical examples were carefully chosen to represent situations where employees work independently and are compensated independently of each other. We do this, of course, because it makes sense to start simple, and we will expand our theoretical and empirical analysis to multiworker firms in Parts 4 and 5. We'll conclude this chapter, however, by studying one aspect of multiworker firms that is closely related to the issues of wage fairness, reciprocity, and reference points we've just discussed. Specifically, we'll ask, "How do the wages received *by other workers* in the same firm affect workers' perceptions of wage fairness, as well as those workers' effort and job performance?"

The idea that workers use their co-workers' wages to judge the fairness of their own wages has a long history in psychology, but the first economists to formalize this idea were the distinguished couple, George Akerlof and Janet Yellen, in 1990.[17] In an influential article titled "The Fair Wage-Effort Hypothesis and Unemployment," the authors argued not only that workers' effort decisions depend on whether they feel fairly paid, but also that one of the main reference points workers use to determine whether their wages are fair is their co-workers' wages. Although this seems highly plausible, the first formal test of this idea was conducted by Gary Charness and Peter Kuhn, in 2007. In a gift-exchange experiment where firms are motivated to pay their two workers differently because the workers have different productivities, they found that workers' effort levels did *not* depend on how well their co-workers were paid. Despite this, Charness and Kuhn found that the principals in their experiment were more likely to compress wages (i.e., to reduce the gap between their two workers' wages) when those wages were public than when each worker knew only his/her own wage. Thus, it appears that experimental subjects acting as

[17] Akerlof won the 2001 Nobel Prize in economics, and Janet Yellen is the current chair of the Federal Reserve.

principals *expected* some sort of negative reaction to large wage gaps between workers when workers knew each other's wages.

More recently, the effect of co-workers' salaries on workers' *job satisfaction* has been studied by David Card, Alexandre Mas, Enrico Moretti, and Emmanuel Saez (2012), in an ingenious field experiment involving employees of the University of California. Like many public universities, information on the current salaries of UC staff and professors is available to the general public. Not only does the university itself make this available, but a newspaper based in the state's capital, the *Sacramento Bee,* posts it online in a user-friendly way. Surprisingly, though, even though any UC employee could use this website to learn what each one of their co-workers is paid, relatively few workers actually used it.

This relatively unique situation gave Card et al. (2012) the opportunity to *experimentally manipulate* (via random assignment) the amount of information a UC employee had about his or her co-workers' wages. As we discussed in Chapter 7, it is only with random assignment that we can be sure that we've measured the *causal effect* of knowing what your co-workers are paid on your job satisfaction. Here's how they did it. First, they randomly divided all the workers

Peer Effects in Worker Performance: Evidence from Envelope Stuffers, Fruit Pickers, and Supermarket Checkout Clerks

Related to the issue of how workers are affected by their co-workers' wages is how they are affected by their co-workers' *job performance.* Can the mere fact of being surrounded by low-performing workers reduce a worker's job performance? Could moving a worker into a better-performing peer group cause him or her to work harder or more carefully? Although measuring the causal effects of one worker's performance on co-workers raises some significant technical difficulties, a number of recent studies have made some progress. Among them, Falk and Ichino (2006) find that simply being in the presence of a high-output worker raises the productivity of low-output workers. This happens in an experimental context where workers are paid independently and where there is no possible connection between the worker's job performance and the worker's chances of being rehired or promoted in the future. Bandiera, Barankay, and Rasul (2010) find similar results for fruit pickers, but *only when the co-workers were friends.* They also found that workers who are more able than their friends *reduce* their output when working with those friends. Because these workers were paid on a piece-rate basis, this means that abler workers *sacrificed some of their own income* to perform more like their friends. Mas and Moretti (2009) found that supermarket cashiers work faster when being observed by abler cashiers. Ichino and Maggi (2000) found that being transferred into a bank branch where shirking was common increased the transferee's shirking rate. Horton and Zeckhauser (2016) argue that peer effects are motivated by a desire to maintain fairness between workers in effort levels; and Mas and Herbst's (2015) meta-analysis shows that peer effects are widespread across real occupations and laboratory experiments.

at three UC campuses into two groups. The treatment group got an email from the authors informing them that any UC employee's salary can be looked up on the Sacramento Bee website. The control group did not receive this email.[18] A few days after the treatment email, the authors sent a survey to *all employees* at the three campuses. The survey asks questions about knowledge and usage of the Sacramento Bee website, job satisfaction, and job search intentions. Because receiving the treatment email caused a significant number of UC workers to look up their colleagues' salaries, the authors were able to learn how this information affects job satisfaction by comparing the satisfaction levels of the control and treatment groups.

Modeling Wage Comparisons Among Workers

Theoretically, how might we expect learning your co-workers' wages to affect your job satisfaction? For the sake of argument, suppose first that workers care only about their own incomes (as we assumed in Part 1 of the book). In such an *absolute income model*, there is no clear reason to expect that learning what your co-workers are paid should affect your job satisfaction. In fact, if workers care only about their own incomes, one might even expect learning that your colleagues are paid more than you are could even make you happier. That is because it might reveal information about *possibilities:* "If some people in my unit are paid that much, that means I have a chance of earning that too." In sum, in an *absolute income model*, we'd expect Card et al.'s (2012) treatment either to have no effect on workers' job satisfaction, or to make low-paid workers happier.

Next, consider a *symmetric relative income model* in which workers care not only about their own pay but about how it compares to the average wage in their unit. In other words, suppose that the worker's utility-from-income function, $H(Y)$, takes the form

$$H(Y) = Y + n(Y - \overline{Y}), \tag{10.1}$$

where $\overline{Y}$ is the average wage in your unit and $0 < n < 1$. According to Equation 10.1, workers get utility from two aspects of their income—their absolute income Y and their relative income $(Y - \overline{Y})$. The parameter n measures how much they care about their relative income, and Equation 10.1 indicates that—holding constant your absolute level of income—being paid more than your co-workers adds to your utility and being paid less subtracts from your utility. Put a different way, Equation 10.1 says that you can make a worker happier by reducing his co-worker's income while holding his own income fixed.

[18] Some of the control group received no email at all. The rest received an email informing them about the research project, with a link to a website containing information on a few top position earnings at UC. This link could not be used to look up one's co-workers' salaries. The purpose of this "placebo" treatment was to check whether the mere fact of receiving an email on the topic of wages had any effects on workers' job satisfaction. No such effect was observed; thus, the authors were able to eliminate Hawthorne effects as explanations for their findings.

According to the relative income model, what is the likely effect of Card et al.'s (2012) treatment, which made it easier for workers to learn about their co-workers' incomes? Perhaps surprisingly, we would probably not expect much of an effect overall. That is because, when pay information is revealed, approximately half the workers are likely to find out they are paid less than the average, whereas the other half will learn they're above the average. Thus, the symmetric relative income model predicts that Card et al.'s treatment will raise the job satisfaction of highly paid workers within a unit and reduce the job satisfaction of below-average-salary workers in a unit, with little or no effect on mean job satisfaction.

Finally, consider the *relative income model with loss aversion.* Here we imagine that the utility-from-income function, $H(Y)$, takes the form indicated in Figure 9.5, with $\overline{Y}$ acting as workers' reference point. In other words, we assume that

$$H(Y) = U^F - m(\overline{Y} - Y) \text{ if } Y \leq \overline{Y}$$

$$H(Y) = U^F + n(Y - \overline{Y}) \text{ if } Y \geq \overline{Y}. \quad \textbf{(10.2)}$$

Equation 10.2 is identical to Equation 9.2, with $\overline{Y}$ replacing R. In other words, workers still care about their relative income, but *having more income than your co-worker helps less than having less income hurts.* Now, making workers' pay public makes above-average workers only a little happier and makes below-average workers much less happy. Because the latter effect outweighs the former, Card et al.'s (2012) information treatment is predicted to make workers less satisfied, on average.

To evaluate which of the previous models best describe UC employees, Card et al. (2012) first define a worker's reference group, or "unit," as follows. For a faculty member, the reference group was assumed to be the other faculty in the department. For a staff member, the reference group was the other staff in the department. Then Card et al. looked at how the workers below the median salary in their unit responded to the information treatment. These workers experienced lower job satisfaction (as measured on a 10-point scale) when treated, and treatment made them more likely to say they were looking for a new job. There was an even larger increase in the share of workers who both became less happy *and* said they were looking for a different job in the treatment group. In contrast, above-median workers experienced no change in job satisfaction when workers were alerted to the possibility of learning their co-workers' pay.[19] Thus, Card et al.'s empirical findings supported the *relative income model with loss aversion* over the other two models described previously.

---

[19] One reason why above-median workers may not have reacted to Card et al.'s (2012) treatment is that (because they were on average more senior and in higher level positions) they already knew their co-workers' salaries before the treatment. This is an important limitation of the article. Another is that their job satisfaction variable doesn't really measure utility; low reported job satisfaction and job search might just be a rational response to learning you are underpaid in your current job.

RESULT 10.8 **(Card et al., 2012)**

Increasing employees' knowledge about their co-workers' wages at three campuses of the University of California reduced the job satisfaction of workers earning less than the median salary in their unit, without raising the job satisfaction of workers earning more than the median. These results are consistent with the *relative income model of job satisfaction with loss aversion.*

While it is interesting to know that learning one is paid less than the median in one's unit reduces reported job satisfaction and raises reported intentions to quit, it might also be interesting to know whether learning this information affects *job performance*. This question was addressed by Axel Ockenfels, Dirk Sliwka, and Peter Werner (2014) using personnel and performance records for managers in a large multinational company. Importantly for their purposes, the company uses exactly the same bonus scheme for its managers in Germany and the United States, but the German managers know much more about their co-workers' wages. This is because of German labor market regulations, which require a much greater degree of transparency.

In a little more detail, managers in the same department are rated on a percentage scale, where a 100% performance score means that the manager's performance

Public or Secret? What's the Best Pay Policy?

Over the past several decades, HRM guidebooks and manuals have offered changing and sometimes conflicting advice on the question of whether firms should keep their workers' wage information confidential or whether this information should be transparent and public (at least within the organization). Proponents of making pay information public argue that doing so can illustrate how a company's rules work. It also lets workers know what they can aspire to and how they need to perform to get there. In the language of contract theory, this type of transparency illustrates that the company has a clear and even-handed set of rules—that is, a *contract*—to which it has committed itself in a verifiable way. Proponents of secrecy, however, argue that information like this can lead to emotional responses of jealousy that can be destructive to the firm. As we have shown here, empirical evidence from two workplaces—the University of California and a large multinational firm—seem to support this claim. Proponents of secrecy also point out that making wages public may restrict a firm's flexibility to reward high performance. This is illustrated by Charness and Kuhn's (2007) laboratory study where student "employers" reduced the compensation gap between high- and low-productivity workers when pay was made public. It is also illustrated by Gartenberg and Wulf (2012), who show that the greater salary transparency associated with the 1992 Securities and Exchange Commission proxy disclosure rules reduced salary differentials among U.S. division managers working for the same firm. Thus, firms considering how much co-worker pay information to disclose need to balance some important costs and benefits of doing so.

"fully meets expectations." Managers within each department are then awarded annual bonuses proportional to their score. Thus, for example, a score of 110% gives a manager a 10% larger bonus than a score of 100%. Because each department's bonus budget is fixed, any workers scoring more than 100% must be balanced by workers scoring below 100%. Taken together, this means that a 100% score/bonus is a natural reference point to managers for three reasons: (1) it is a round number (i.e., digit preference); (2) it denotes "fully adequate" performance; and (3), by construction, it is the average bonus earned by the managers in your department.

Consistent with the *relative income model with loss aversion*, and consistent with Card et al.'s (2012) findings, Ockenfels et al. (2014) found that receiving a bonus of less than 100% reduced a managers' job satisfaction, whereas bonuses above 100% had little effect on job satisfaction. Consistent with the fact that German compensation policies are more transparent than U.S. policies, this effect was much stronger in Germany than the United States. A more novel feature of Ockenfels et al.'s study, however, is that they also had data on the job performance of managers after they received these bonuses.

Interestingly, receiving a bonus of less than 100% reduced the *future* job performance of managers, and again this effect was stronger in Germany where the managers actually knew their relative evaluations. Although models of reference points and loss aversion don't have predictions about how worker effort should respond to such "reference point violations," it seems that managers in this large multinational company responded either by becoming discouraged or by reciprocating the firm's ungenerous bonus offer with a low effort level.

Designing Pay Policies That Are Seen as Fair: The Role of Job Evaluation Systems

Perhaps the strongest evidence that workers care a lot about wage fairness is the amount of resources spent by most large companies in designing internal pay scales that attempt to assign salaries to all jobs in the company on an objective basis. Most formal pay systems have three main components: a worker's base wage, merit pay, and variable pay. **Base wages** are attached—not to workers, but to *jobs*—usually based on a company-wide process of *job evaluation*. Typically, job evaluations are contracted out to an HRM consulting firm, such as Hay Associates or Mercer LLC, who begin by evaluating a set of "key" jobs on a series of factors like mental effort, physical effort, responsibility, supervisory duties, problem-solving abilities, and know-how. Once a key set of jobs is evaluated, the company then decides how much weight to assign to each of these factors in calculating each job's base wage.[20] Finally, the company compares all the remaining jobs to the original list of key jobs and uses a formula based on these weights to assign wages to them as well. Notably, this entire process is about *jobs*, not about the specific individuals currently doing them.[21]

---

[20] Studies of what other local firms are paying for similar jobs are also frequently used to set base wages.

[21] See, for instance, WorldatWork (2007), Chapter 11; or Berger and Berger (2012), Chapter 10, for further details on internal/job evaluation and salary structures.

Merit pay results from periodic (typically annual) evaluations of an *individual* worker's performance and determines where the worker stands in the pay range for the job, relative to the job's base wage. Although many companies have their own performance evaluation systems, designing and operating these systems can *also* be contracted out to compensation consulting companies who offer systems like the *Balanced Scorecard* and *360 Degree Evaluation*. Once a raise

Moving from Informal to Formal Compensation Policy: Evolution of a Growing Manufacturing and Logistics Company

Riddell (2017) describes the compensation structure of a small-to-medium-sized North American-based manufacturing and logistics company a over the 13 years from its initial public offering (IPO) to the point where it had reached maturity in its industry and had global operations. Its transition from an informal to formal pay setting illustrates a typical process as small enterprises grow and mature.

During the first 3 years after its IPO, the company had no written compensation policy. Starting base salaries for new employees, annual pay raises, and bonuses were all largely made on an ad hoc basis based on CEO discretion. No systematic procedure for evaluating employee performance was in place.

Once the company reached a certain size, they hired a consulting firm to design formal compensation programs. These programs introduced formal policies for all major HR decisions, including the three "core" components of pay: base pay, merit pay (base pay increases), and variable pay (such as annual bonuses). The pay systems used by the company are quite typical for a modern North American company, and worked as follows.

Base Pay was determined by a point-factor job evaluation system that assigned each job a score depending on its skill requirements, responsibility, and other factors. Using these scores, all jobs were placed into a formal salary structure based on a set of pay grades that included minimums, midpoints, and maximums. In addition to systematizing the salaries of existing jobs, this system provided a basis for assigning base pay levels to all future positions.

Merit Pay (annual raises in base pay) was determined by a formal system where salary increases depended only on the employees' current position within the pay grade and the employees' current performance rating. Performance ratings came from a framework designed by the pay consultants in which employees were rated for a set of competencies (e.g., "Foster Teamwork and Cooperation") on a numerical scale, and then all of these ratings were averaged. No other increases to base pay were possible. Interestingly, although raises depended positively on performance, the formula made them *smaller* in size for employers who were already higher within their pay grade. This (very typical) practice limits the amount of salary growth an employee can achieve while remaining in the same pay grade.

Annual bonuses were set by the company's Short-Term Incentive Plan ("STIP"); they depended both on the company's overall performance and the individual's performance, each of which had to pass a threshold for the bonus to be paid. Once the threshold was attained, the bonus increased with the individual's and the company's performance according to a set schedule.

has been earned via this process, that amount is typically added to the employee's salary on a fairly permanent basis. Finally, **variable pay** comprises bonuses, commissions, and other payments that are linked to the individual's or the company's performance in a given period. Unlike merit pay, variable pay applies only to the current period (usually a year): A high bonus this year, for example, does not have any effect on your pay next year.

Arguably, companies use formal pay systems like these for at least two main reasons. First, once organizations reach a certain size, informal wage-setting processes can become unmanageable. Employees who know that raises can be awarded on a discretionary basis have incentives to constantly lobby for raises, to identify wage comparisons with fellow workers that make their compensation seem too low, and to curry favor with supervisors (i.e., to waste time and energy on "influence activities") rather than doing their jobs. Second, as noted, having a formal set of rules that applies to all employees creates a sense of fairness that could improve morale and productivity. Possible drawbacks of formal pay schemes include the fact that the systems can be hard to understand, even for supervisors, and a lack of flexibility that can make it hard to change a firm's pay policies in response to rapidly changing technologies and business conditions.

Chapter Summary

- ☐ In the gift-exchange game (GEG), a principal pays a "wage" to an agent. The agent then decides how much effort to supply. Personnel economists use the gift exchange as a laboratory model of principal–agent interactions when labor contracts are incomplete.

- ☐ Labor contracts are incomplete if the agent's compensation is not explicitly linked to all aspects of the agent's performance that the principal cares about. Almost all real labor contracts are incomplete in some way.

- ☐ Fehr, Klein, and Schmidt (2007) found that "one-shot" gift exchange contracts (which they called "trust contracts") were not as effective in a lab experiment as contracts with explicit incentives. However, gift exchange contracts that allowed firms to reciprocate the worker's effort with a bonus performed much better than both trust or incentive contracts.

- ☐ Fehr et al.'s results suggest that informal, repeated exchange between principals and agents might yield better outcomes for both principals and agents than contracts with explicit incentives.

- ☐ Theo Offerman's (2002) hot response game shows two important results: Negative reciprocity is stronger than positive reciprocity, and *intentions matter* for reciprocal behavior: It is not just what you did to me, but *why*.

- ☐ Offerman's results suggest that firms should carefully consider whether to make nominal wage cuts and how to explain those cuts if they occur.

- ☐ Falk and Kosfeld (2006) show that trust can pay in principal–agent interactions: Specifically, exerting small amounts of control can destroy enough trust that profits will fall.

- ☐ In an experiment on University of California employees, Card et. al (2012) show that workers become less satisfied with their jobs and more likely to look for other jobs when they learn they are paid less than their peers. Learning they were better paid than their peers had no effect on these outcomes.

- ☐ Card et al.'s results are consistent with a relative income model of job satisfaction, with loss aversion. They suggest that making salary information publicly available within workplaces may be costly in worker morale and turnover.

- ☐ Once companies grow to a certain size, formal pay systems, often designed by consulting companies, can be useful ways to limit perceptions of wage unfairness. Most such systems contain three main elements: a base wage that is attached to jobs, merit pay that assigns permanent wage increases based on an individual's performance, and variable pay that rewards current performance only.

Discussion Questions

1. Consider a job you currently hold or have recently held. What were the main factors that motivated you to do a good job? Explicit financial incentives provided by the employer? Or an informal desire to fulfill the employer's expectations? Or a desire not to get fired or to be rehired in the future? Relate these motivations to Fehr et al.'s (2007) trust, incentive, and bonus contracts.
2. Describe how Offerman (2002) was able to measure agents' responses to principals' intentions, as distinct from principals' actions alone. Why do you think agents in laboratory experiments seem to care about their principal's intentions? After all, it's only *what* the principal does to the agent, not why, that affects the agent's material well-being.
3. Imagine your employer gave you a surprise 20% pay increase. Do you think your job performance would improve enough for this pay hike to actually "pay for itself" from the employer's point of view? For how long is your job performance likely to improve?
4. Now imagine your employer gave you a surprise 20% pay cut. For the sake of argument, assume this isn't enough of a cut to cause you to immediately quit

the job. Do you think your job performance would deteriorate enough for this pay cut to actually reduce the employer's profit? Compare your answers to the previous question. If there's a difference, discuss why.

5. "Controlling the small stuff is often counterproductive for employers. But exerting large amounts of control can actually raise worker performance and profits." Discuss in view of Falk and Kosfeld's (2006) experiment.

6. In discussions of how much information about worker pay firms should reveal, a distinction is sometimes made between making the rules for pay determination public and making peoples' actual salaries public information. In view of the various studies discussed in this chapter, would you be more concerned about making disclosing rules or results?

Suggestions for Further Reading

Bandiera, Barankay, and Rasul's article (2010) is part of an impressive series of studies the authors conducted on a British fruit farm operated by Iwan Barankay's brother-in-law. The fruit pickers on this farm were migrant workers from Eastern Europe, and Bandiera et al. collected a massive amount of data on the workers, their performance levels, the fields they worked on, and the pay they received. The authors even gathered information on all the friendship networks among the workers and were able to conduct a number of HRM experiments in the firm. Taken together, Bandiera et al.'s papers are a great example of what can be learned from careful empirical research in personnel economics.

If you're Italian (or know a little bit about Italy), you'll be familiar with the stereotype that people from Southern Italy have a more casual attitude toward work than the Northerners. Is this stereotype valid? If so, what explains it? Read Ichino and Maggi's (2000) study of a large Italian bank with branches all over the country to learn more.

For additional perspectives and results on wage fairness among workers and job performance, see Breza, Kaur, and Shamdasani (2016); Charness, Gross, and Guo (2015); and Cohn, Fehr, Herrmann, and Schneider (2014).

References

Akerlof, G., & Yellen. J. (1990). The fair wage-effort hypothesis and unemployment. *Quarterly Journal of Economics, 105,* 255–284.

Bandiera, O., Barankay, I., & Rasul, I. (2010). Social incentives in the workplace. *Review of Economic Studies, 77,* 417–458.

Bellemare, C., & Shearer, B. (2009). Gift giving and worker productivity: Evidence from a firm-level experiment. *Games and Economic Behavior, 67,* 233–244.

Berger, L., & Berger, D. (2012). *The compensation handbook, 6th edition: A state-of-the-art guide to compensation strategy and design.* New York: McGraw-Hill Education.

Bewley, T. (1999). *Why wages don't fall during a recession.* Cambridge, MA: Harvard University Press.

Breza, E., Kaur, S., & Shamdasani, Y. (in press). The morale effects of pay inequality. *Quarterly Journal of Economics.*

Card, D., Mas, A., Moretti, E., & Saez, E. (2012). Inequality at work: The effect of peer salaries on job satisfaction. *American Economic Review, 102,* 2981–3003.

Charness, G. (2004). Attribution and reciprocity in an experimental labor market. *Journal of Labor Economics, 22,* 665–688.

Charness, G., & Kuhn, P. (2007). Does pay inequality affect worker effort? Experimental evidence. *Journal of Labor Economics, 25,* 693–724.

Charness, G., Cobo-Reyes, R., Jimenez, N., Lacomba, J. A., & Lagos, F. (2012). The hidden advantage of delegation: Pareto improvements in a gift exchange game. *American Economic Review, 102,* 2358–2379.

Charness, G., Gross, T., & Guo, C. (2015). Merit pay and wage compression with productivity differences and uncertainty. *Journal of Economic Behavior and Organization, 117,* 233–247.

Cohn, A., Fehr, E., Herrmann, B., & Schneider, F. (2014). Social comparison and effort provision: Evidence from a field experiment. *Journal of the European Economic Association, 12,* 877–898.

Falk, A., & Ichino, A. (2006). Clean evidence on peer effects. *Journal of Labor Economics, 24,* 39–57.

Falk, A., & Kosfeld, M. (2006). The hidden costs of control. *American Economic Review, 96,* 1611–1630.

Fehr, E., Klein, A., & Schmidt, K. M. (2007). Fairness and contract design. *Econometrica, 75,* 121–154.

Fryer, R., Jr., Levitt, S., List, J., & Sadoff, S. (2012, July). *Enhancing the efficacy of teacher incentives through loss aversion: A field experiment* (NBER Working Paper No. 18237). Cambridge, MA: National Bureau of Economic Research.

Gartenberg, C., & Wulf, J. (2012, November 1). *Pay harmony: Peer comparison and executive compensation.* Unpublished manuscript, Stern School of Business, New York University, New York, NY.

Gneezy, U., & List, J. (2006). Putting behavioral economics to work: Testing for gift exchange in labor markets using field experiments. *Econometrica, 74,* 1365–1384.

Gneezy, U., & Rustichini, A. (2000a). A fine is a price. *Journal of Legal Studies, 21,* 1–18.

Gneezy, U., & Rustichini, A. (2000b). Pay enough or don't pay at all. *Quarterly Journal of Economics, 115,* 791–810.

Griffith, R., & Neely, A. (2009). Performance pay and managerial experience in multitask teams: Evidence from within a firm. *Journal of Labor Economics, 27,* 49–82.

Henrich, J., Boyd, R., Bowles, S., Camerer, C., & Fehr, E. (2001). *Cooperation, reciprocity and punishment in fifteen small scale societies* (Santa Fe Institute Working Paper No. 2001-01-007). Santa Fe, NM: Santa Fe Institute.

Henrich, J., Boyd, R., Bowles, S., Camerer, C., Fehr, E., Gintis, H., . . . Tracer. D. (2005). "Economic man" in cross-cultural perspective: Behavioral experiments in 15 small-scale societies. *Behavioral and Brain Sciences, 28,* 795–855.

Henrich, J., Ensminger, J., McElreath, R., Barr, A., Barrett, C., Bolyanatz, A., . . . Ziker, J. (2010). Markets, religion, community size, and the evolution of fairness and punishment. *Science, 327,* 1480–1484.

Horton, J. J., & Zeckhauser, & R. J. (2016, July). *The causes of peer effects in production: Evidence from a series of field experiments* (NBER Working Paper No. 22386). Cambridge, MA: National Bureau of Economic Research.

Ichino, A., & Maggi, G. (2000). Work environment and individual background: Explaining regional shirking differentials in a large Italian firm. *Quarterly Journal of Economics, 115,* 1057–1090.

Jackson, C. K., & Schneider, H. S. (2015). Checklists and worker behavior: A field experiment. *American Economic Journal: Applied Economics*, *7*(4), 136–168.

Kiyotaki, N., & Wright, R. (1991). A contribution to the pure theory of money. *Journal of Economic Theory, 53,* 215–235.

Kube, S., Marechal, M., & Puppe, C. (2013). Do wage cuts damage work morale? Evidence from a natural field experiment. *Journal of the European Economic Association, 11,* 853–870.

Mas, A., & Herbst, D. (2015). *Laboratory experiments generalize to the field in the estimation of productivity spillovers.* Unpublished manuscript. Department of Economics, Princeton University, Princeton, NJ.

Mas, A., & Moretti, E. (2009). Peers at work. *American Economic Review, 99,* 112–143.

Mauss, M. (1966). *The gift: forms and functions of exchange in archaic societies* (I. Cunnison, Trans.). London: Cohen and West.

Ockenfels, A., Sliwka, D., & Werner, P. (2014). Bonus payments and reference point violations. *Management Science*, *61*(7), 1496–1513.

Offerman, T. (2002). Hurting hurts more than helping helps. *European Economic Review, 46,* 1423–1437.

Oswald, A. J., & Powdthavee, N. (2008). Does happiness adapt? A longitudinal study of disability with implications for economists and judges. *Journal of Public Economics, 92*(5–6), 1061–1077.

Packard, D. (1995). *The HP way: How Bill Hewlett and I built our company.* New York: HarperCollins Publishers.

Riddell, C. (2017). *Compensation inequality within the firm: A field study of a multinational.* Unpublished manuscript, School of Industrial and Labor Relations, Cornell University, Ithica, NY.

Schnedler, W., & Vadovic, R. (2011). Legitimacy of control. *Journal of Economics and Management Strategy, 20,* 985–1009.

Sutter, M., & Kocher, M. G. (2007). Trust and trustworthiness across different age groups. *Games and Economic Behavior, 59,* 364–382.

WorldatWork. (2007). *The WorldatWork handbook of compensation, benefits & total rewards: A comprehensive guide for HR professionals***.** Hoboken, NJ: Wiley.

11 Pigeons and Pecks: Incentives and Income Effects

One of the oldest economics experiments to study the effect of incentives on work effort was an experiment on pigeons, published by Raymond Battalio, Leonard Green, and John Kagel in 1981. We study it here because Battalio et al.'s experiment sheds light on an effect of incentives that is all but impossible to demonstrate experimentally for humans. This aspect is the *income effect*, a consequence of purely rational, self-interested (or "classical") behavior that can cause stronger incentives to induce less, not more, effort.

11.1 The Backward-Bending Labor Supply Curve (BBLS)

How is it even possible to conduct labor-supply experiments on pigeons? Battalio et al. (1981) did their experiments on a group of hungry lab pigeons who had to "work" to eat. The pigeons worked by doing a familiar task—pecking on a key—and their reward for a certain number of pecks was food. Specifically, one unit of income, Y, for these lab pigeons was 3 seconds of access to a hamper of "mixed pigeon grains." The beauty of Battalio et al.'s experiment for our purposes is that it put pigeons into *exactly* the situation faced by the agent in Part 1's principal–agent model. In the experiment, each pigeon's income was set by the experimenters to be a linear function of its job performance, that is, $Y = a + bQ$, where Q is the number of pecks on the key. By changing the levels of a and b and waiting a bit (until pigeons have adapted to their new reward schedule, or "contract"), the experimenters could see (i) whether pigeons work harder when they are more incentivized (higher b), and (ii) how pigeons' work effort is affected by the amount of "free income" they receive (a).

If you are interested in the details of how Battalio et al. (1981) conducted this experiment, I strongly encourage you to read their article (see the References at the end of this chapter). But here we'll cut directly to their main results.

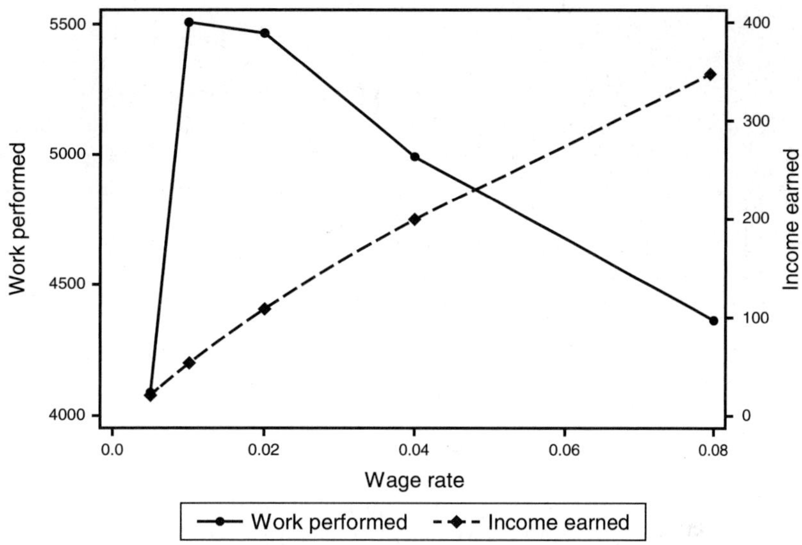

FIGURE 11.1. Pigeons' Work Effort and Income as a Function of Incentives (*b*)

The first is about how the pigeons' work effort responded when the experimenters increased the pigeons' "wage rate" (*b*) [while holding the amount of free income the pigeons received (*a*) fixed at zero]. The results are shown in Figure 11.1.

The horizontal axis in Figure 11.1 shows the pigeons' wage rate (*b*), which varied from 0.005 (indicating that a pigeon had to peck 200 times to get access to a unit of income) to 0.080 (where a pigeon only had to peck only 12.5 times per unit of income).[1] Notably, this represents a much wider range of wages than an experimenter could impose on humans; in fact, the highest wage these pigeons faced was *16 times* the lowest wage they faced. Being able to manipulate pigeons' well-being in such a drastic fashion might shed light on the effects of wage changes that have large effects on human well-being, or the sort that we cannot ethically manipulate in an experiment.

Did Battalio et al.'s (1981) pigeons work harder when the experimenters incentivized them more? The simplest way to put the answer is probably "not really." According to the solid labor supply curve in Figure 11.1, a wage increase from the lowest level (0.005) to the next-highest level (0.010) did in fact increase effort quite a bit (from 4,000 to 5,500 pecks, or about 38%). But any wage increases beyond that level actually induced the pigeons to work *less*. By the time the wage got up to its maximum level (0.080), the pigeons' work effort was essentially the same as at a wage of 0.005. Put another way, starting at a wage of 800, the experimenters could cut the pigeons' wage by a factor of 16 (or equivalently, impose a marginal tax rate of 15/16 = 94%!) without a significant negative effect on the pigeons' work effort.

[1] .005 = 1/200, and .080 = 1/12.5.

RESULT 11.1 **Backward-Bending Labor Supply**

In Battalio et al.'s (1981) pigeon labor supply experiment, the effect of incentives (b) on effort had an inverted U-shape: At low levels of incentives, effort is an increasing function of b; but at high levels of incentives, effort is a decreasing function of b. This pattern, which contradicts Result 2.1, is referred to as a *backward-bending labor supply curve*. Put another way, Battalio et al.'s results imply that *taxing* the highest-wage pigeons in their experiment (by taking away some of the food they earn) actually *increases* the amount of work the pigeons do.

11.2 Explaining the BBLS: The Role of Income Effects

At first glance, the labor supply behavior of the pigeons in Figure 11.1 seems puzzling—isn't it just obvious that when the rewards to effort rise, the pigeons should work harder? One possibility, of course, is that pigeons are just stupid, but this seems unlikely when it comes to effort supply decisions. Indeed, evolutionary considerations suggest that any animal's "work" behavior should, in fact, be finely tuned to balance the inflow of calories from food versus the calories consumed by effortful food seeking, in a way that maximizes evolutionary fitness. In fact, in the rest of this chapter, I'll try to convince you that these pigeons' puzzling behavior (a) is in fact highly rational (in the sense that it consistently maximizes something we could call either utility or fitness), and (b) can be explained by a pervasive and well-documented phenomenon that labor economists call an *income effect*. Income effects can be important for humans too, but their importance is likely to vary greatly depending on precisely *how* work incentives are increased. We'll describe those conditions, and what they mean for HRM policy, toward the end of this chapter.

What is an "income effect" in Battalio et al.'s (1981) pigeon experiment? The income effect for Battalio et al.'s pigeons is illustrated in Figure 11.2, which shows the results of a second experimental manipulation conducted by these authors. Specifically, Figure 11.2 shows what happened to the pigeons' work effort when the experimenters changed the other parameter of their "labor contract," a. Now, the experimenters held the strength of marginal work incentives (b) fixed while increasing the amount of noncontingent, or "free" income each pigeon received.

In a little more detail, the experimental manipulations behind Figure 11.2 worked as follows. Suppose, first, that a pigeon (receiving zero free income, i.e., $a = 0$) has gotten used to working at a wage rate of 0.020, pecking at a rate of (say) 5,000 times in a laboratory session, and earning $0.020 \times 5{,}000 = 100$ units of food. Next, we keep the pigeon's wage rate ($b = 0.020$) fixed but raise a from zero to 50. In other words, we just give the pigeons an amount of free food that equals half of what they previously earned, keeping everything else the same. Figure 11.2 shows that no matter what the wage rate (b) was, the pigeons always reduced their work effort when they got more free income. Although this seems intuitive

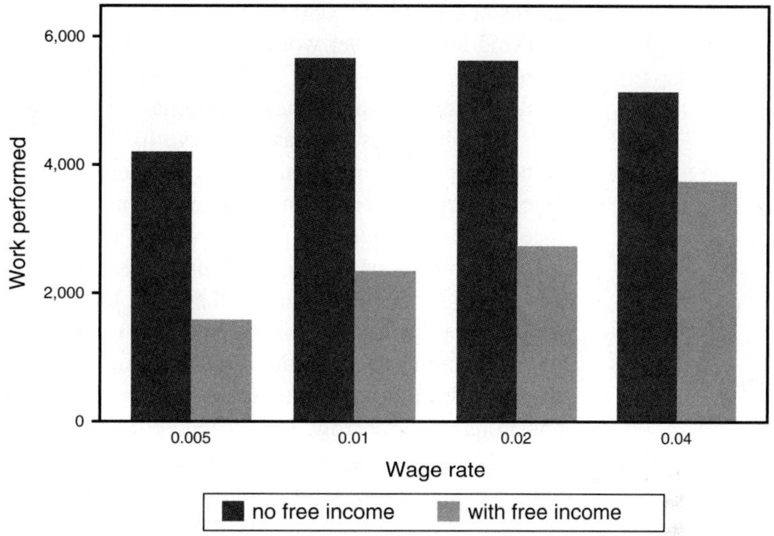

FIGURE 11.2. Pigeons' Work Effort by Wage Rate, With and Without Free Income

and corresponds with the intuition that giving people things for free reduces their work incentives, notice that—just like the pigeons' responses to *b*—this finding *also* conflicts with Result 2.1, which predicted that changes in *a* should have no effect on the agent's work effort.

> **RESULT 11.2** **Leisure Is a Normal Good**
>
> Contrary to Result 2.1, pigeons' work effort fell when Battalio et al. (1981) increased the pigeons' fixed income (*a*) while holding the level of marginal work incentives (*b*) constant. In other words, when Battalio et al. made the pigeons better off by giving them some free food, the pigeons decided to consume more leisure.

Taking Results 11.1 and 11.2 together, we have two violations of Result 2.1: effort can fall when marginal incentives (*b*) rise, and effort falls when free income (*a*) rises. As it turns out, however, the second (which seems fairly intuitive) actually helps us understand the first. To see this, take a look at the dashed curve in Figure 11.1, which we haven't yet discussed. This curve shows the total *income* earned by the pigeons, that is, $Y = a + bQ$.[2] It shows that even though effort fell when work incentives were increased, the pigeons definitely *ate better* when incentives (*b*) were increased. For example, they ate more than three times as many

[2] Notice that the pigeons' "labor contract," $Y = a + bQ$, is exactly the one we studied theoretically in Part 1 of the book, starting with Equation 1.8. Of course, because $a = 0$ throughout Figure 11.1, the pigeons' total income, Y, just equals their variable income, bQ.

grains at a wage of 0.080 than at a wage of 0.020, despite the fact that they were working less. In other words, at a higher wage, the pigeons could afford both to *work less and eat more*. Because effort is costly and income is desirable, this could actually be an eminently rational thing to do when wages rise!

But what does the dashed curve in Figure 11.1 have to do with income effects? Recall that in the pigeon experiment, income effects refer to the fact that when the experimenters made their pigeons better off without changing the work incentives they face, the pigeons decide to consume more leisure. More generally, economists use the term *income effects* to refer to the fact that when people have more financial resources, they tend to consume more of *all* the things they like.[3] If you have taken an intermediate microeconomics course, you have very likely encountered these income effects in the context of consumers' choices between different goods, like apples versus bananas, or consumption today versus consumption tomorrow. In the context of labor or effort supply, income effects refer to the notion that when a worker is better off, he or she will want to have not only more income but also more *leisure* as well. Because (just like increases in a) increases in b make workers better off, the income effects associated with higher b's can, under the right circumstances, induce *rational workers to become lazier when incentives are strengthened*. Very likely, this is exactly why Battalio et al.'s (1981) pigeons chose to work less when the experimenters incentivized them more.

Can income effects cause a "perverse" labor supply response to wage increases among humans? Certainly they can: Consider what happened to the length of the typical work week in the United States during the first half of the 20th century. At the turn of the 20th century, a typical American manufacturing worker put in 12 hr per day, 6 days per week; 72-hr work weeks were the norm. And the phenomenon we call "retirement" today did not exist: People simply worked until they died or were physically incapable of continuing. During the next 50 years, real wages rose about *eightfold*, while the typical work week fell to about 40 hr.[4] And as lifespans lengthened, an ever-longer period of leisure began to emerge late in the life cycle. Putting these factors together, the share of humans' lifetimes devoted to working for pay declined dramatically. Although factors such as unions and hours legislation may have played some role in these developments, most labor economists agree that they were not the main factor at work.[5] Put most simply, when real wages rose, just like the pigeons in Battalio et al.'s (1981) experiment, *American workers decided (quite rationally) to take it easier.* After all, by working less (but not too much less) at the higher wage, workers could enjoy both higher incomes *and* more leisure.

---

[3] The astute reader will recall that the rare exceptions to this pattern are called *inferior goods.*

[4] See Costa (2000) for a detailed description of work hours trends in the 20th century.

[5] The reason why so many labor economists are skeptical that unions and legislation played a major role in the decline in the work day is that the timing doesn't fit well. For example, much of the decline in weekly work hours took place well before the dramatic expansion of unions in the mid-1930s.

Would You Quit Your Job if You Won the Lottery? Quasi-Experimental Evidence of Income Effects Among Humans

If income effects matter for humans' work decisions, people who unexpectedly receive a large amount of "free income" (just like the pigeons' free food) should reduce the amount they work. Although it is not practical (or perhaps even ethical) to do experiments on people where we randomly give them large amounts of money, lotteries provide a *natural experiment* that, even though imperfect, come close to duplicating the random assignment of treatment status that's essential to estimating the true causal effect of receiving extra free income. Imbens, Rubin, and Sacerdote (2001) took advantage of this idea by interviewing 496 winners of the Megabucks lottery from the years 1984–1988. Some of the people in Imbens et al.'s sample won only token amounts of money (e.g., one-time prizes of as little as $100). But the median amount won was $1,104,000, and the most was $9,696,000. Large prizes like these were paid out in yearly installments over a period of 20 years. Although Imbens et al.'s results apply to a selected sample of the population—that is, only to people who choose to play the lottery—the amount of money these players win is essentially randomly assigned, at least *once the authors include statistical controls for the number of tickets they have purchased*, which they are of course careful to do.

Looking at the amount of money these winners earned in the labor market in the 6 years after their lottery win, Imbens et al. found that on average, a 10% increase in the amount won reduced their earnings by about 1.1%; in other words, the winners' marginal propensity to earn (MPE) was minus 11%. Their marginal propensity to *consume leisure* (i.e., the percent increase in time not worked) was plus 11%, with larger effects for winners between 55 and 65 years old.

Overall, although Imbens et al. show convincingly that leisure is a normal good for people, the size of the MPE in their study seems in some respects rather small: Big winners didn't reduce their labor market activity by very large amounts. One reason, though, might be that even these large prizes, when spread over 20 years (and in most cases shared with a number of family members) may not be that large relative to many winners' expected lifetime earnings. Still, Imbens et al. convincingly show that large increases in unearned income reduce work effort among people.

11.3 When Are Income Effects Likely to Be Important?

So far, we've argued that income effects can lead to a "perverse" effect of increased financial incentives (b) on work effort. And I've given you two empirical examples—one from laboratory pigeons and the other from historical changes in American workers' labor supply—of exactly this kind of behavioral response. But do income effects also come into play when, say, a modern firm strengthens its incentive pay scheme? As it turns out, in most cases they probably won't. The reason is that these two empirical examples actually share an important feature that is not usually present when an individual firm is deciding how much to incentivize its workers. To see what this feature is, I'm going to ask you, for a moment, to imagine yourself in the unenviable position of the pigeons in Battalio et al.'s (1981) experiment.

A Thought Experiment on Income Effects

Imagine, therefore, that you've been kidnapped, and your captors make you work for your food each day by doing some unpleasant task (say, breaking rocks with a sledgehammer). You are paid b ounces of runny gruel for every rock you prepare to the desired specifications. Some days b is very low; other days it is quite high, enabling you to earn more than enough to get full if you do a reasonable amount of work. Gruel goes bad very quickly; and in any case, any gruel you don't eat on a given day is quickly spirited away by your guards. Ask yourself, in this situation, if you'd always choose to break more rocks on high-wage days than low-wage days. My guess is that your behavior will be very much like Battalio et al.'s (1981) pigeons: At some very low wage (like the wage of 50 in Battalio et al.'s case), you might work very little. Even though you are very hungry, obtaining even a tiny amount of food might require superhuman effort. Calories in (from the food) wouldn't even balance calories used up by working and the logical thing to do might just be to be miserable and not work. Increases in the wage above this level might make it worth working. But eventually, as the wage rises high enough, you can eat your fill by working only three-fourths of the day, or maybe even just half the day. So, just like Battalio et al.'s pigeons, you might have a BBLS curve: Wage increases from a low level raise your effort; but as wages rise above some threshold, you may start to *consume additional wage increases in the form of increased leisure, not just increased income.*

Now, let's change our unpleasant thought experiment in just one detail: the work is still hard, and average daily pay is low, but now you're paid in biscuits, not gruel. The key feature of biscuits for our purposes is that they don't spoil. And luckily, your jailer now lets you keep any uneaten biscuits as long as you want. Now, will you still work less on high-wage days? My guess is probably not: you'll work like crazy on high-wage days, and save some biscuits for low-wage days. On the low-wage days, you'll probably work less than in the days when you were paid in gruel: Why work for close to nothing on a low-wage day when you can enjoy the fruits of your past labors instead? If this scenario seems logical to you, then I have convinced you of the following.

☑ RESULT 11.3

When Income Effects Are Unimportant

Income effects on labor supply (or work effort) are likely to be unimportant in situations where workers can save income earned in high-wage periods to finance consumption at other times, or when they can borrow income to live on during low-wage periods.

Incidentally, Result 11.3 is probably why pigeons slack off when food is plentiful, but squirrels do not: Squirrels are very busy in the fall, when the acorns are ripe. Indeed, not working hard when the "wage" is high would probably be suicidal for an organism like a squirrel that faces a highly variable wage rate and has access to (an admittedly imperfect) storage technology. Put another way, adding a storage technology turns an organism's short-term labor supply choice from a decision on *how much to work* (a problem economists call the *static labor supply problem*) to a decision of *when to work* (a problem economists call the *dynamic labor supply problem*).[6] In the dynamic case, but not the static one, the worker's utility-maximizing choice is always to "make hay when the sun shines," that is, *work hard when the wage is high*. So we expect greater effort when b rises.

Should Employers Worry about Income Effects?

Having retreated into a prison cell for a while, let's now return to personnel economics and think about a company that is considering whether to raise its workers' piece rate (b): Are its workers better described by the "biscuits" or "gruel" scenario in the prison cell? I think you'll agree that for most workers today, the "biscuits" scenario is more appropriate: If a company offers generous incentive pay, its workers have the option of taking advantage of that by working hard and putting the extra money aside for another day. This is especially true for temporary increases in b, and probably also the case for permanent increases in *b at any one company*. (Workers can save their extra income for the future when they are working elsewhere or for spending in retirement.) Therefore, from the point of view of any one company, it is usually safe to ignore income effects when designing incentive pay plans.

There are, however, four important exceptions to this rule, the first of which is *permanent wage increases for lifetime employees*, that is, for workers who expect to remain with the same firm for a long time. To see why income effects can be important in that context, recall that in response to a large real wage increase, U.S. workers dramatically cut their labor supply during the first half of the 20th century. Why did income effects matter there? Precisely because these were wage increases that workers expected to be permanent and because we are considering their effects on total lifetime labor supply. Because "you can't take it with you," a lifetime is like a single day in the prison camp under the "gruel" scenario: There is no way to take income you've earned during that period and save it for another time. So, when your wage rises, you might as well consume the extra leisure the higher wage allows you to enjoy.

A second exception pertains to *liquidity-constrained workers*, that is, workers who are currently living "hand to mouth." If workers are sufficiently poor or cash constrained that saving for the future is not currently a realistic option for them, higher wages may lead them to work less via an income effect. More to the point, and sadly, cutting those workers' wages might actually lead them to work harder because that is the only way to keep their heads above water.[7]

---

[6] For a formal analysis of the dynamic labor supply problem, see Heckman and MaCurdy (1980).

[7] Another factor that can prevent workers from saving is *insecure property rights*: If any cash on hand or in the bank can be taken by a thief, a corrupt official, or an unscrupulous family member, then saving is not a realistic option. In all these situations, one could also see a "perverse" response of work to incentives.

A third case is where workers have an option to save their earnings for a rainy day but choose not to use it. Such cases of *myopia* include persons who do not plan for the future and persons who have a reference income in each period of their lives, such as Camerer, Babcock, Loewenstein, and Thaler's (1997) taxi drivers, who we discussed in Section 9.6. Anyone who stops working whenever they have reached a fixed target income for the day, week, or month will automatically work less in periods when it is easier to make money, that is, when marginal work incentives, b, are high.

Finally, put yourself into the position of a government deciding how highly to tax its citizens. As we've already observed (see Section 3.1), you can think of the commission rate in our principal–agent problem (b) as equal to the share of income the government allows its residents to keep, that is, as 1 minus the income tax rate. For the same reason that permanent wage increases can make workers lazy via income effects, permanent tax cuts can do the same thing. To be clear, the types of tax cuts we are talking about are tax cuts that make the workers who receive them better off on a lifetime basis. Tax cuts that are connected to reductions in government spending that benefits those workers would not necessarily have an effort-reducing effect.

☑ RESULT 11.4

When to Ignore Income Effects

Because any one company's pay is usually a small share of a worker's lifetime income, it is usually safe to ignore income effects in the design of compensation policy, with the following exceptions:

- permanent wage increases for lifetime employees;
- liquidity-constrained workers;
- myopic workers; and
- permanent changes in real wages, or in income tax policy.

In sum, although we'll ignore income effects in the remainder of this book, it's important to know why. Relatedly, it's important to be aware of the cases where it's not safe to ignore income effects: Granting permanent piece-rate increases to workers with highly secure jobs may reduce, not raise, their work effort. The same is true of raising the wages of myopic, liquidity constrained workers, or of workers living in environments with insecure property rights. A wise HRM manager or public policymaker would be well advised to be aware of these exceptions.

11.4 The Shape of the Utility Function and the Mathematics of Income Effects

If you've made it this far in this chapter, there is one question that I hope is still bothering you: What was "wrong" with Part 1's simple theory (specifically, the theory that led to Result 2.1) that led to predictions that are so much at odds with

Battalio et al.'s (1981) evidence? The reason for the discrepancy is that in Part 1, we intentionally *assumed* that agents have a utility function that has no income effects: Specifically, we wrote the agent's utility function as $U = Y - V(E)$. Thus, utility was a linear function of income (Y), which means that our agent had a *constant marginal utility of income*. If, instead, we'd picked a function with diminishing marginal utility of income, we would have had some income effects.[8] Instead of being unaffected when fixed pay (a) went up, our agent would be predicted to reduce his effort. And increases in b would no longer necessarily raise the agent's effort.

Essentially, making utility linear in income is a shorthand way of describing the effects of having a storage technology: When you have a storage technology, you don't care *when* your income is earned. Earnings in any given period of your life are a perfect substitute for earnings in another period.[9] Graphically, assuming $U = Y - V(E)$ means that indifference curves in (E, Y) space, such as those drawn in Figures 2.1, 2.3, and 3.4, are "vertically parallel." By this we mean that all the indifference curves have the same slope along any vertical line in the figure, that is, at any given level of E. Vertically parallel indifference curves are illustrated in Figure 11.3. Because the tangency point to a budget constraint with

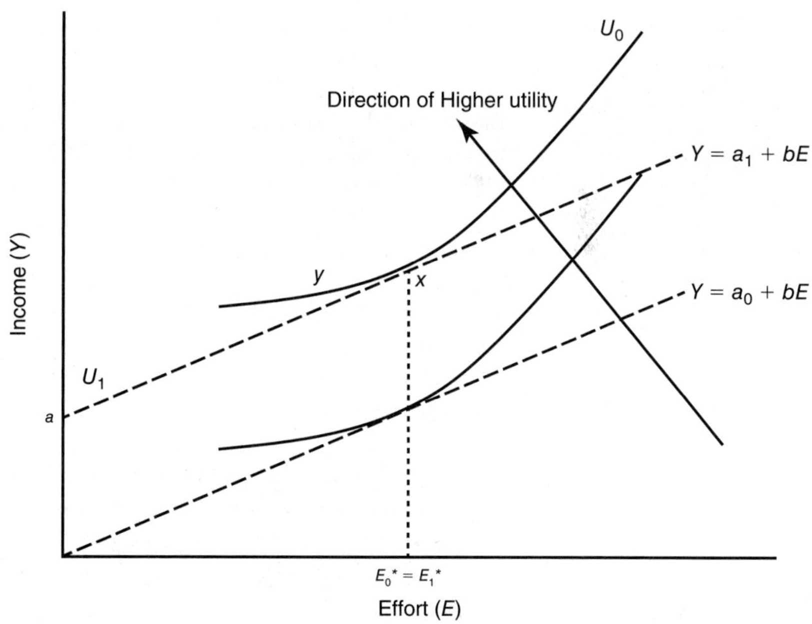

FIGURE 11.3. Vertically Parallel Indifference Curves and the Absence of Income Effects

[8] One example of a utility function with diminishing marginal utility of income is $U = H(Y) - V(E)$, where $H' > 0$ and $H'' < 0$. Another is the Cobb-Douglas function, $U = Y^{\alpha} (T - E)^{\beta}$, with $0 < \alpha < 1$, $0 < \beta < 1$, and $T > 0$.

[9] You do, of course, care about when you *consume*, but the storage technology allows you to consider that decision independently of the decision on when to work hard and when to take it easier.

a given slope b will be always at the same level of effort, no matter how much fixed income (a) the agent has, the parameter a has no effect on the agent's optimal effort. As it turns out, this also means that increases in b will always induce the agent to work harder, whether a is fixed or not.

From this point forward in the book, we'll use the utility function $U = Y - V(E)$ whenever we want to abstract from income effects (which is almost always). Bear in mind, though, that although the lack of income effects is the leading case in most personnel applications, it is nonetheless still a special case. As Battalio et al.'s (1981) laboratory experiments suggest, if a company raises the wages of its lifetime employees, or if the government permanently cuts some workers' taxes in a way that makes them much better off, income effects may lead those workers to take it easier instead of working harder. This can be the case even if the extra pay is directly linked to employee performance or to hours worked.

Chapter Summary

- Battalio et al. (1981) conducted an experiment on pigeons where they put pigeons into exactly the situation faced by the agent in Part 1 of this book. They found that increasing marginal work incentives (the parameter b in that model) had a hump-shaped effect on effort. This phenomenon is known as the backward bending labor supply curve.

- Battalio et al. also found that increases in the pigeons' fixed, or unearned, income (a) caused them to work less. Another way of saying this is that leisure is a normal good to pigeons, that is, it is something they like to consume more of when they are better off. The negative effect of a on the supply of labor or effort is also referred to as an income effect.

- The income effect also helps explain why, once we raise incentives (b) beyond a certain point, pigeons start to work less, not more. A higher b makes the pigeons better off, allowing them to have both more food *and* more leisure than when b is lower.

- Turning to humans, income effects probably help explain why people in developed countries now spend a much smaller fraction of their lives working for pay than 100 years ago. They also explain why winning the lottery tends to reduce work activity.

- Theoretically, income effects should be much less important for temporary than for permanent wage changes. Thus, they should not be a major concern to employers who hire workers for a relatively short portion of the worker's lifetime.

- Exceptions to this rule include permanent wage increases for lifetime employees, credit-constrained workers (i.e., workers living hand to mouth), myopic workers (i.e., workers who don't plan ahead), and permanent changes in real wages or in tax policy.

- ☐ The reason there weren't any income effects in Part 1's theoretical model of agent behavior was because we assumed the agent's utility was a linear function of his income, that is, $U = Y - V(E)$. This is a shorthand way of representing the idea that most workers can easily save and borrow money, which implies that income effects should not apply to their interactions with any one employer. We'll continue to assume this throughout the rest of the book.

Discussion Questions

1. Suppose I offered you a job for the next 24 hr that paid $5,000 per hr. Compared to your current plan for the next 24 hr, I expect you will probably decide to work much more. Now, suppose I offered you a job that paid you $5,000 per hr, whenever you wanted to work, for the rest of your life. Compared to your current plan for the rest of your life, I expect you will now work a lot less. What property of income effects is illustrated by this thought experiment?
2. Is it silly to think we can learn *anything* useful about peoples' work incentives by doing lab experiments on pigeons? What do you think?
3. An interesting feature of Battalio et al.'s (1981) results is that *taxing* the highest wage pigeons in their experiment (by taking away a fraction of the food they earn) actually *increases* the amount of work the pigeons do. This contrasts with some economists' claims that cutting taxes on high-earning workers will incentivize them to work harder. In your opinion, do Battalio et al.'s results have *any* relevance to human tax policy? Why or why not?
4. In their study of Massachusetts lottery winners, Imbens et al. (2001) found that the share of "big winners" (people who won $160,000 *per year* for 20 years, on average) who were employed fell from around 60% before they won to about 40% in the 6 years afterward. So, roughly speaking, only about one-third of those who were the working winners stopped working within 6 years of winning. Does this seem like a plausible response to you? Why or why not? Do you think your own responses would be different from this?

Suggestions for Further Reading

Economists have studied the effects of winning a lottery on a long list of outcomes, including consumption, savings, happiness, and physical and mental health. For a recent example that focuses on labor supply, see Cesarini, Lindqvist, Notowidigdo, and Östling (in press). To see what happens to the next-door neighbors of lottery winners, check out my own article (Kuhn, Kooreman, Soetevent, & Kapteyn, 2011).

References

Battalio, R., Green, L. & Kagel, H. (1981). Income-leisure tradeoffs of animal workers. *American Economic Review, 71,* 621–632.

Camerer, C., Babcock, L., Loewenstein, G., & Thaler, R. (1997). Labor supply of New York City cabdrivers: One day at a time. *Quarterly Journal of Economics, 112,* 407–441.

Cesarini, D., Lindqvist, E., Notowidigdo, M. J., & Östling, R. (in press). The effect of wealth on individual and household labor supply: evidence from Swedish lotteries *American Economic Review.*

Costa, D. L. (2000). The wage and the length of the work day: From the 1890s to 1991. *Journal of Labor Economics, 18,* 156–181.

Heckman, J., & MaCurdy, T. E. (1980). A life cycle model of female labour supply. *Review of Economic Studies, 47,* 47–74.

Imbens, G. W., Rubin, D. B., & Sacerdote, B. I. (2001). Estimating the effect of unearned income on labor earnings, savings, and consumption: Evidence from a survey of lottery players. *American Economic Review, 91,* 778–794.

Kuhn, P., Kooreman, P., Soetevent, A. R., & Kapteyn, A. (2011). The effects of lottery prizes on winners and their neighbors: evidence from the Dutch post-code lottery. *American Economic Review, 101,* 2226–2247.

Part 3
Employee Selection and Training

In Part 3, we shift our attention from the problem of *motivating* employees to the second main focus of personnel economics—*selecting* employees. By employee selection, however, we mean much more than choosing workers from a group of applicants because the set of workers who end up working at a firm depends on much more than this. It depends also on how a firm goes about finding applicants (e.g., formal advertising vs. referrals), on the type of workers it targets in the recruiting process, on the number and quality of applications a firm gets, and on who *leaves* the firm (not just who joins!). All of these processes, in turn, are affected by how much a firm pays relative to its competitors in the labor market, as well as by other aspects of its compensation policy and culture. In Part 3, we'll consider all these ways in which HRM policies affect the size and quality of a firm's workforce.

Chapter 12 will be most familiar to students who have already taken an intermediate microeconomics or labor economics course: It develops the traditional microeconomic theory of a firm's optimal choice between factors of production and applies it to the question of choosing between broad categories of workers when recruiting for a particular job. Workers are differentiated by many different aspects—including education, experience, location, and training—and this chapter sheds light on optimal choices between such groups in labor markets where, for example, hiring a college-educated worker can cost much more than someone with only a high school degree.

Whereas Chapter 12 asks how to pick the most cost effective labor type when the types differ in their expected productivity, Chapter 13 asks a different question: What's the best choice when two labor types (or two individual workers) have the *same* expected productivity, but one's productivity is harder to predict? A shorthand for workers whose productivity is uncertain, or hard to predict, is "risky workers," and Chapter 13 demonstrates some surprising results about the potential attractiveness of such workers to firms.

In Chapters 14–16, we study the process of recruiting new workers in detail. Issues covered include the choice of recruiting channels (such as informal networks vs. formal job boards), how narrowly or broadly to focus the search, whether or not to test job applicants (for skills, drugs, etc.), and the effects of bias in the recruiting process.

Chapters 17 and 18 study an often ignored, but critical aspect of recruiting and retention: No matter how energetically a firm recruits or how carefully it selects personnel, its ability to hire and retain workers also depends on how well it pays. Accordingly, these chapters dissect the question of optimal generosity of pay. We start with *monopsony models* of the interaction between hiring, retention, and pay; then we broaden our focus to other impacts of pay generosity, including labor quality and the job performance of a firm's existing workers. In addition to the theory, these chapters include some fascinating case studies of how dramatic changes in pay generosity have affected the firms that implemented them.

In Part 1, we introduced the critical decision of "buy versus make" as it applies to the products or services needed by a firm (such as bookkeeping services, or components of a physical product the firm assembles). In Chapter 19, we apply the same question to a firm's *employees*: When should a firm "buy" them "ready-made" with all the training, experience, and qualifications needed, and when should it "produce" them in-house by hiring less qualified candidates and training them internally? We'll show that optimal training decisions can be tricky to make for both workers and firms, especially when the skills imparted are useful only in the workplace where they are taught, that is, when the skills are *firm specific.*

Throughout Part 3 (with the exception of Chapter 18, where we make an important detour), we'll make a very strong assumption in all our theoretical models, relative to the principal–agent model we studied in Part 1. Specifically, to focus more simply on the topic of worker selection, we'll completely *ignore* the problem of motivating workers. Instead, we'll assume that firms have somehow solved the motivation problem in such a way that each worker who is hired automatically exerts a fixed amount of effort, E, for the firm. Because a worker's effort is always the same, her utility in this part of the book depends on one thing only: the total wage, w, the firm pays the worker.[1] Under these assumptions, we can focus directly on the questions of how many and what types of workers to hire, and what wages to offer them, without dealing with motivation issues at the same time.

[1] One way to think about this is that workers get no disutility from working. Another is that effort causes some disutility, but the amount of effort associated with working is the same regardless of how much the worker is paid. Thus, the only aspect of the job that matters to the worker—in deciding whether to take the job or not—is what it pays.

12 Choosing Qualifications

One question that often arises when recruiting employees is what *type* of employees to seek, or "what pool to fish in" when seeking and screening workers. Examples of this question include what types of qualifications (including education, experience, and training) to seek, which demographic groups to target, or where to locate the firm's operations. For example, some firms focus on workers willing and able to work full time, whereas others design schedules and hours that appeal more to students, retired people, or people with childcare responsibilities. Firms might even design different types of jobs with different types of workers in mind. Goods-producing firms decide where to locate their supply chains, and firms of all types may decide whether to outsource services like accounting, payroll, customer service, or tech support within the country or elsewhere.

In this chapter, we'll study the case of a theoretical firm choosing between two *types* of workers for a particular job. The worker types differ both in (average) productivity and in wage costs: For example, college-educated workers might be more productive or reliable but cost more to hire than workers with only a high school degree. We'll assume that the firm can hire as many workers of either type as it wants at a fixed wage per hour. Is there a simple rule for finding the profit-maximizing mix of workers in situations like these? We'll begin with the simplest case, where the firm's output depends linearly on the number of workers of each type it hires.

12.1 Optimal Worker Mix When Workers Work Independently

Consider the (fictitious) case of Snuggly Sales, a retailer that advertises a popular product on television and takes phone orders. Snuggly has had good experiences with hiring two types of workers: youth (Y) and seniors (S). Youth must be paid the local minimum wage of $w_Y = \$10.00$, while seniors command a wage of $w_S = \$12.00$. Seniors, on average, however, are more productive, processing $700 worth of sales per hour compared to $500 for youth.[1] One possible reason for lower youth productivity is a higher turnover rate: With changing class schedules, students might quit more often, leading to higher training costs for that group.

Thus, Snuggly faces a dilemma: Should it focus its recruiting efforts on the cheaper, less-productive group, or on the more expensive and productive group? Firms face similar choices between high- and low-wage strategies all the time, and the solution is not always obvious. Indeed, some employers profitably and deliberately choose to focus on worker types—such as ex-offenders or parolees—that are shunned by other employers, in part because those workers are cheaper to hire.[2]

Suppose that in a typical hour, Snuggly receives orders for $35,000 worth of sales. What mix of seniors and youth should the firm use to process those sales at minimum cost?[3] In this first example, we'll assume the workers in the call center work completely independently. Specifically, we'll assume that each individual worker's productivity is unaffected by the number and type of other workers *of either type* working at Snuggly, an assumption that seems at least plausible in the case of a phone sales environment.[4] Before we work out the single best mix of workers in this case, let's work out Snuggly's total costs under a few different scenarios.

Scenario 1: Hire seniors only. To process $35,000 in reservations, Snuggly needs to hire 35,000/700 = 50 seniors. In this case, its total hourly wage bill will be 50 × $12.00 = $600.

Scenario 2: Hire youth only. To process $35,000 in reservations, Snuggly needs to hire $35,000/500 = 70 youth. In this case, its total hourly wage bill will be 70 × $10.00 = $700.

Scenario 3: Hire a mix of seniors and youth. Clearly there are many different mixes of seniors and youth Snuggly could hire to process $35,000 in reservations. One such combination is to hire 25 seniors and 35 youth [because 25(700) + 35(500) = $35,000]. The total hourly wage bill for this mix is 25 × $12.00 + 35 × $10.00 = $650.

---

[1] Of course, not all seniors are equally productive, nor are all youth. And the same is true of college-educated versus non-college-educated workers. In Chapter 13, we'll focus on some consequences of this within-group variability in productivity.

[2] Jobs that employ disproportionate numbers of ex-offenders include construction, food services, retail, manufacturing, waste management, auto mechanics, hairdressers, laundry workers, and repair workers (Schnepel, 2017).

[3] In this chapter we focus only on the optimal (cost-minimizing) way for a firm to produce a given amount of output, that is on the question of optimal input *mix*. Most intermediate microeconomics texts also cover the related issue of optimal firm *scale*, that is how much output should the firm produce in the first place? We abstract from this issue here since it's not central to personnel economics, though Section 26.5 does consider the closely-related question of optimal *team* size.

[4] Note that working independently does not mean that two inputs (or worker types) are *equally productive*. It could be, for example, that one Type-1 worker can do the work of two Type-2 workers. In our case, 1 hr of a senior worker's time yields the same output as 1.4 hr of a youth's time ($700/$500 = 1.4).

Interestingly, the best of these three options is to hire only seniors, who happen to be the more expensive type of labor. These simple calculations illustrate a basic economic principle, namely, that the most cost-effective labor to use is not necessarily the one with the lowest wage. Hiring decisions should always take into account both the differential cost and productivity of different labor types. This means that sometimes the cost-minimizing policy is to hire the more expensive category of workers. In other situations, the optimal hiring strategy may be to focus on hiring a cheaper but less-productive category of workers.

Having costed out a few specific cases, we'll now work out the best overall mix of worker types for a firm like Snuggly to hire. We'll use the standard tools of microeconomics—isocost curves and isoquants—to do so. To that end, we now formally consider a firm using two types of labor, L_1 and L_2, receiving wages w_1 and w_2. The firm has a linear production function given by

$$Q = d_1L_1 + d_2L_2, \tag{12.1}$$

where Q is total output and d_1 and d_2 are the marginal products of the two labor types (in Snuggly's case, d_1 = \$700 and d_2 = \$500).

DEFINITION 12.1 Suppose that a firm can produce output using N different types of inputs, labeled $L_1, L_2, \ldots L_N$. Then in general, we can describe the amount of output it produces using a **production function**, $Q = F(L_1, L_2, \ldots L_N)$, where L_i is the amount of input i that the firm uses.

The **marginal product** of input i, MP_i, is the amount by which output increases when the firm uses one more unit of input i. (For the mathematically inclined, this is the partial derivative of output with respect to input i: $MP_i = \partial F/\partial L_i \equiv F_i$.) In general, the marginal productivity of input i depends on the amount of input i the firm is using and on the amounts of *all the other inputs* it is using as well. In other words, the marginal product of input i—like the production function itself—is a *function* of the form $MP_i = F_i(L_1, L_2, \ldots L_N)$.

The linear production function in Equation 12.1 is the simplest production function we can use and reflects a situation in which workers do not interact in production. Specifically, in a linear production function, the marginal product of every input is independent of the amount of that input that is used, and of the amounts of other inputs that are used. Thus, in Equation 12.1, every Type-1 worker produces d_1 and every Type-2 worker produces d_2, regardless of how many workers of either type have been hired. Instead of $MP_1 = F_1(L_1, L_2)$ and $MP_2 = F_2(L_1, L_2)$ in a linear production function, we can simply write $MP_1 = d_1$ and $MP_2 = d_2$.

Our firm's total labor costs can be written

$$TC = w_1L_1 + w_2L_2. \tag{12.2}$$

Thus, the problem faced by our firm is to choose levels of L_1 and L_2 that are sufficient to produce some target level of output, Q, at lowest total cost. Mathematically, we want to

$$\text{Minimize } TC = w_1L_1 + w_2L_2, \text{ subject to } Q = d_1L_1 + d_2L_2. \quad \textbf{(12.3)}$$

To solve this problem, let's start by working out what the isoquants look like.

DEFINITION 12.2 In a diagram showing two inputs used by a firm (one on each axis), an **isoquant** connects all the combinations of inputs that yield the same output. A firm's production function can be represented by an infinite number of isoquant curves, each showing a "contour line" for a different level of output. In general, isoquants are downward sloping because both inputs are productive. Thus, using more of one input means less of the other is needed to produce the same amount of output. Isoquants that are further from the origin represent higher levels of output, Q.

For the linear production function in Equation 12.1, we can derive the isoquant for Q units of output (in a diagram with L_1 on the horizontal axis and L_2 on the vertical) by rearranging Equation 12.1 to isolate L_2:

$$L_2 = Q/d_2 - (d_1/d_2)L_1. \quad \textbf{(12.4)}$$

Equation 12.4 shows that the isoquants are parallel, downward-sloping, straight lines, with a constant slope equal to $-d_1/d_2$. An example of such an isoquant is shown by the bold, solid line in Figure 12.1.[5]

RESULT 12.1

Explaining Isoquant Results

In a linear production function involving two inputs, L_1 and L_2, the firm's isoquants will be downward-sloping straight lines. In a diagram with L_1 on the horizontal axis and L_2 on the vertical, all the isoquants will have a constant slope equal to $-d_1/d_2$, where d_1 is the marginal productivity of input L_1, and d_2 is the marginal productivity of L_2. Put another way (in absolute value), the slope of the isoquant is just the ratio of the inputs' marginal productivities, MP_1/MP_2.

[5] Readers interested in microeconomic theory may wish to note that the linear production is not the only one with linear isoquants. For example, the production function $Q = (L_1 + L_2)^a$ has linear isoquants with a slope of –1. Unlike the linear production function which has constant returns to scale, functions of this form have diminishing returns to scale—a useful property when we want to model the optimal size of the firm. Since our focus in this chapter is on optimal input *mix*, we abstract from the issue of optimal firm size.

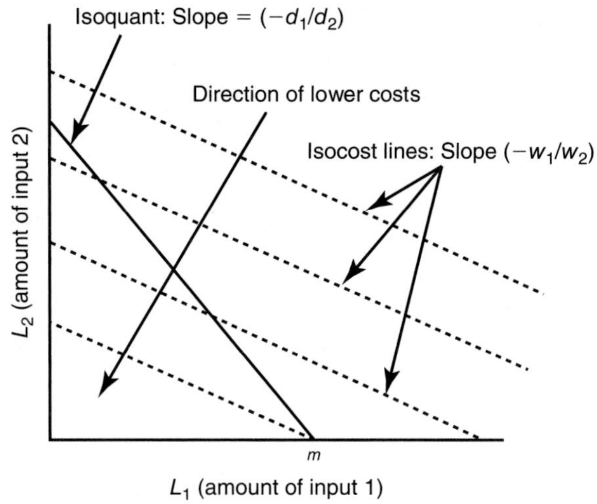

FIGURE 12.1. Optimal Input Mix with a Linear Production Function, Case 1 ($d_1/d_2 > w_1/w_2$)

Now, let's turn to the isocost curves.

DEFINITION 12.3 In a diagram showing two inputs used by a firm (one on each axis), an **isocost curve** connects all the combinations of inputs that cost the same to hire. There is a different isocost curve for every possible level of total costs (*TC*). Isocost lines closer to the origin correspond to lower levels of total costs.

We can derive the isocost curve (in a diagram with L_1 on the horizontal axis and L_2 on the vertical) simply by rearranging Equation 12.2 to isolate L_2:

$$L_2 = TC/w_2 - (w_1/w_2)L_1. \quad \textbf{(12.5)}$$

Thus, the isocost curves are negatively sloped straight lines, with slope equal (in absolute value) to the relative wage cost of the two inputs (w_1/w_2). A family of isocost curves is shown by the dashed lines in Figure 12.1.

RESULT 12.2

Regardless of the Shape of a Firm's Production Function, a Firm's Isocost Curves Are Always Downward-Sloping Straight Lines

In a diagram with L_1 on the horizontal axis and L_2 on the vertical, all the isocost lines will have a constant slope equal to $-w_1/w_2$, where w_1 is the wage cost of input L_1 and w_2 is the wage cost of input L_2.

Now that we can graph *all* the different ways a firm can produce a target amount of output (the isoquant) plus the total cost of every possible input mix

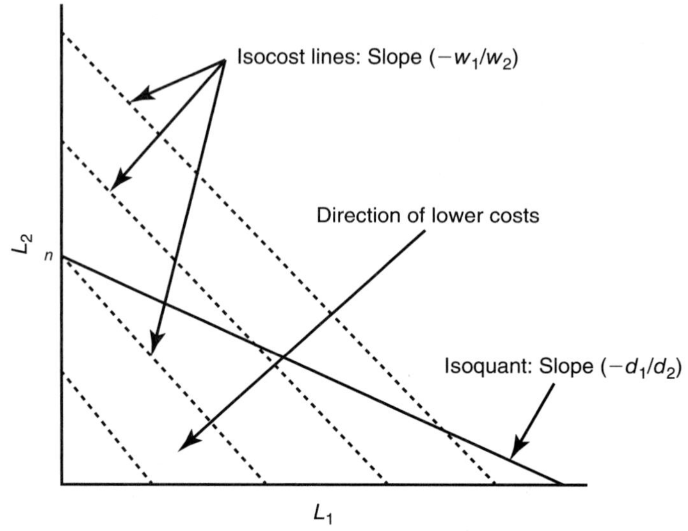

FIGURE 12.2. Optimal Input Mix with a Linear Production Function, Case 2 ($d_1/d_2 < w_1/w_2$)

(the family of isocost curves), it is straightforward and intuitive to find the firm's optimal input mix diagrammatically. There are two interesting cases, depending on the relative costs and productivities of the two worker types.

Case 1: Type-1 workers' relative productivity **exceeds** their relative cost: ($d_1/d_2 > w_1/w_2$).
This case is illustrated in Figure 12.1 where the isoquant for our target output level, Q, is steeper than the isocost lines. Recalling that isocost lines closer to the origin represent lower levels of total costs, to solve Equation 12.3, we just need to find the lowest isocost line that somehow touches the target isoquant. This occurs at point m, where the firm hires only Type–1 workers.

Case 2: Type-1 workers' relative productivity **is less than** their relative cost: ($d_1/d_2 < w_1/w_2$).
This case is illustrated in Figure 12.2, where the isoquant for our target output level, Q, is now flatter than the isocost lines. Now, the lowest isocost line that touches the target isoquant does so at point n, where the firm hires only Type–2 workers.[6]

Summarizing our insights from Cases 1 and 2 yields the following result for the cost-minimizing input mix with a linear production function:

[6] Logically, it is also possible (though highly unlikely) that Type 1 workers' relative productivity happens to *exactly* equal their relative costs ($d_1/d_2 = w_1/w_2$). In this "Case 3" scenario, the lowest attainable isocost curve coincides with the target isoquant along its entire length, so the firm should be indifferent to all combinations of workers that yield the desired output level.

RESULT 12.3

Corner Solutions and the Bang-per-Buck Rule

When a firm has a linear production function, the best hiring policy is an *extreme* policy, or "corner solution": The firm should specialize its recruitment policy by hiring only one type of worker.

Which worker type to hire in this situation depends on a simple "bang-per-buck" calculation. Simply compare the groups' relative productivities (d_1/d_2 or MP_1/MP_2) to their relative wage costs (w_1/w_2), then hire *only* the group whose relative productivity exceeds its relative cost. A different way to express this rule is to compute the "bang per buck" (MP/w) the firm gets from each labor type, then hire the group with the highest bang per buck.

Applying the bang-per-buck rule to our Snuggly example yields a bang-per-buck (MP/w) ratio of 700/12 = 58.33 for seniors and 500/10 = 50 for youth, leading immediately to the conclusion that the firm should hire only seniors. Another advantage of the bang-per-buck rule is that—even though all our calculations in this chapter look only at a choice between two alternative labor types—the bang-per-buck rule applies to *any* number of input types as long as they don't interact in production: A firm can simply compute the bang-per-buck ratio for every possible labor type it might hire, then focus only on the type with highest ratio.[7]

Because the firm's optimal labor mix is either at one "corner" or the other, its optimal hiring mix must respond in a very particular way to changes in the relative costs of the two types of labor. Specifically:

RESULT 12.4

When a Firm's Production Function Is Linear, Its Optimal Hiring Mix Responds Discontinuously to Changes in the Relative Cost of Different Types of Labor

Specifically, as the wage of the worker type it is currently using gradually rises, in most cases the firm will make no changes to its input mix. However, once that wage reaches a certain critical point, a cost-minimizing firm will suddenly abandon that worker type completely and use only a different type of labor.

Result 12.4 has some interesting implications when applied to firms' choices of where to locate their supply chains. Consider for example a U.S. firm's choices between producing a component using maquiladora workers just across the Mexican border or their American counterparts. According to Result 12.4, the profit-maximizing location decision can be very sensitive to those workers'

[7] Another application of this section's bang-per-buck rule is when a firm needs to choose *which* worker(s) of a given type to hire from a pool of applicants where the applicants can differ both in productivity and the wage each must be paid. Here, the general rule is to rank the applicants in terms of bang per buck and hire in that order.

relative wage costs (w_1/w_2) *if the production processes are independent* on both sides of the border. Specifically, as the type of worker a firm is using (say Type 1, or U.S. workers) gradually gets more expensive, a cost-minimizing firm should make no changes to its input mix until w_1/w_2 just equals d_1/d_2. But when w_1 rises even an infinitesimal amount higher, the firm should replace *all* its U.S. workers with Mexican workers.

12.2 Optimal Worker Mix When Workers Interact in the Production Process

The "extreme" nature of Results 12.3 and 12.4—that firms should always pick *corner solutions*, and "flip" from one to the other when relative wage costs cross a threshold—raises the obvious question about when less-extreme, *interior* solutions make sense. By interior solutions, we simply mean cases where firms hire some of each type of worker.

In general, there are two main reasons why "some of each" makes sense. One is the possibility that a firm may not be able to find enough of its preferred type of worker, or—perhaps more accurately—when hiring that many workers of a given type would require the firm to raise its wages enough to eliminate that type's bang-for-buck advantage. This possibility refers to the fact that individual employers might face *upward-sloping labor supply curves*, a situation labor economists refer to as *monopsony*. We'll deal with this possibility in Chapter 17.

The other reason for interior solutions is when workers interact in the production process. Firms are full of examples where the marginal productivity of one type of worker depends on the number of workers (of *either* type) that are employed. One way this can occur is if the two worker *types* do different jobs which support each other. For example, suppose in the Snuggly case that the two worker types were salespeople (L_1) and IT experts who keep the computers, billing, and phone systems running (L_2). In that case, it seems likely adding more IT people helps the salespeople make sales; and adding more salespeople actually converts the IT people's efforts into revenues for the firm. A second source of interactions occurs *within worker types*: if there is only a limited pool of customers who can be served, adding additional salespeople will reduce the amount of work available to the others.[8]

To find the cost-minimizing way to produce a given amount of output when workers' marginal productivities interact, we first need to define the marginal rate of substitution, or MRS, between any pair of inputs.

[8] Mathematically, the two interactions between workers we have just described can be written as $F_{12} > 0$ and F_{11} (or F_{22}) < 0. These two properties—positive interactions between the inputs and diminishing returns to each individual input—are the two reasons why we usually assume that isoquants get flatter as we move from left to right.

DEFINITION 12.4 In Section 12.1, we showed that the (absolute value of the) slope of an isoquant for a linear production function is given by the ratio of the two inputs' marginal productivities, that is, the |slope of the isoquant| equals $MP_1/MP_2 = d_1/d_2$. Because the inputs didn't interact in production, that slope was the same at every point on every isoquant.

When inputs interact in production, the relative marginal productivities of the inputs and thus the slope of the isoquant will typically change as we move along an isoquant from left to right, thus gradually increasing the firm's relative reliance on input L_1. We refer to the *slope of the isoquant at any point* as the **marginal rate of substitution between the inputs.**

With the MRS in hand, we can now summarize the three possible ways that inputs' relative marginal productivities can interact in the production of a fixed amount of output.[9]

DEFINITION 12.5 (a) If the marginal rate of substitution between two inputs *does not depend* on the ratio of the inputs used (i.e., on L_1/L_2), the two inputs are said to be **perfect substitutes** in the production of a fixed output. In this case, the isoquants are straight lines, as they were in Section 12.1.

(b) If the marginal rate of substitution between two inputs (MP_1/MP_2) *decreases* with the ratio of the inputs (L_1/L_2), the two inputs are said to be **imperfect substitutes** in the production of a fixed output. In this case, the isoquants become *flatter* as we move from left to right (in a diagram with L_1 on the horizontal and L_2 on the vertical axis).

(c) If the marginal rate of substitution between two inputs (MP_1/MP_2) *increases* with the ratio of the inputs (L_1/L_2), the two inputs are said to be **antagonists** in the production of a fixed output. In this case, the isoquants become *steeper* as we move from left to right (in a diagram with L_1 on the horizontal and L_2 on the vertical axis).

We have already studied the problem of optimal input mix in the perfect substitutes case in Section 12.1, where we studied the linear production function. In those situations, cost-minimizing input mixes are at corners, and firms' input

[9] Readers who go on to Part 5 of the book will notice that we use a different definition of the substitutability or complementarity between workers (or worker types) there. Here, because our interest is in the cost-minimizing way to produce any particular amount of output, our focus is on substitutability in the production of a *fixed amount of output*, that is, on the curvature of a firm's isoquants. In Part 5, because our interest is in what happens to a team's output when more and more workers are added (or when they raise their effort), the focus is on substitutability or complementarity in the production of a *variable amount of output*. These are conceptually and mathematically distinct questions. For the most part, we won't use the qualifiers "in the production of a fixed/variable output" in either part of the book, but we'll be careful to define our concepts in both places.

demands can shift abruptly when relative input prices change. Here we simply note that the linear production function is *only one example* of a production function whose inputs are perfect substitutes in the production of a fixed output. For example, the inputs in the production function $Q = (L_1 + L_2)^\alpha$ are also perfect substitutes in this sense. Now, let's turn to the two remaining cases.

Optimal Worker Mix when Types are Imperfect Substitutes

Next we turn our attention to inputs that are *imperfect substitutes*. Examples of production functions whose inputs are imperfect substitutes include the *additively separable* function: $Q = F(L_1, L_2) = L_1^\alpha + L_2^\beta$, or the widely used Cobb-Douglas production function:

$$Q = F(L_1, L_2) = L_1^\alpha L_2^\beta, \tag{12.6}$$

where $0 < \alpha < 1$ and $0 < \beta < 1$ in both cases.

What will be the firm's optimal input mix when worker types are imperfect substitutes in production? This is depicted in Figure 12.3, where the firm's isoquants now get *flatter* (i.e., the absolute value of their slope decreases) as we move from left to right (i.e., as L_1 increases and L_2 falls).

In Figure 12.3—as in Figures 12.1 and 12.2—the slope of the isoquant is still given by the ratio the two worker types' marginal products, that is, the slope equals minus MP_1/MP_2. The difference is that now, as we move from left to right along the isoquant, the relative marginal product of the two worker types changes. Specifically, as we move to the right, L_1 workers become more plentiful relative to the increasingly scarce L_2 workers. This makes the L_1 workers

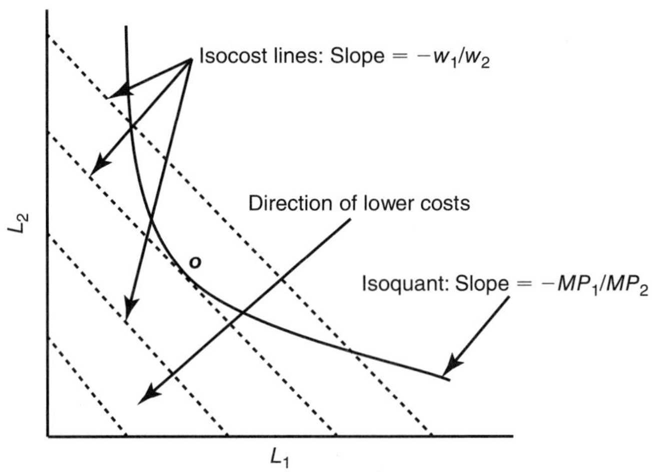

FIGURE 12.3. Optimal Input Mix When Worker Types Are Imperfect Substitutes in Production

relatively less productive. (There's not much point having another salesperson if the computers are always down!) This decline in MP_1/MP_2, in turn, flattens the isoquant as we move rightward.[10]

Because the isoquants are now curved as shown, the cost-minimizing input mix in Figure 12.3 is at an "interior" tangency point (*o*), using positive amounts of both worker types. At the tangency point, the slope of the target isoquant just equals the slope of the isocost lines; thus

$$\frac{MP_1}{MP_2} = \frac{w_1}{w_2}. \tag{12.7}$$

Just like the hiring rule in Result 12.3, the rule in Equation 12.7 also has an intuitive "bang-per-buck" interpretation that generalizes naturally to the case of more than two inputs. To see this, first note that Equation 12.7 can be rewritten in bang-for-buck form as

$$\frac{MP_1}{w_1} = \frac{MP_2}{w_2}. \tag{12.8}$$

RESULT 12.5

When Workers Are Imperfect Substitutes, the Optimal Input Mix Is an Interior, Some-of-Each-Type Policy

At the optimal input mix, the firm allocates its hiring across worker types in such a way that *the marginal "bang-per-buck" (MPi/wi) is equalized across all worker types that are hired.*

As was the case in the linear production function (Section 12.1), Result 12.5's bang-per-buck rule also generalizes easily to the choice between more than two inputs. Specifically, to minimize costs when using any number (n) of inputs, firms should choose an input mix that equates the marginal bang per buck (MP_i/w_i) from every one of those inputs.

Finally, consider what happens in Equation 12.7 when there is a change in the wages the firm has to pay for a given type of worker. Suppose, for example, that a local minimum wage ordinance has increased the wages Snuggly must pay its telephone salespeople (w_1). A rise in w_1 raises the right-hand side of Equation 12.7, making all the isocost curves in Figure 12.3 steeper. In consequence, the cost-minimizing input mix will need to be at a point further up the isoquant, where it is steeper. The process is shown in Figure 12.4, which shows that the new, optimal input mix at point *x* uses less Type-1 labor (the type that has become more expensive) and more Type-2 labor than the old optimal input mix at point *y*.

[10] In the specific case of the Cobb-Douglas production in Equation 12.6, it is not hard to work out the explicit formula for the slope of the isoquant: slope of isoquant $= -MP_1/MP_2 = -\alpha L_2/\beta L_1$. For the additively separable function, it is $-MP_1/MP_2 = -\alpha L_1^{\alpha-1}/\beta L_2^{\beta-1}$.

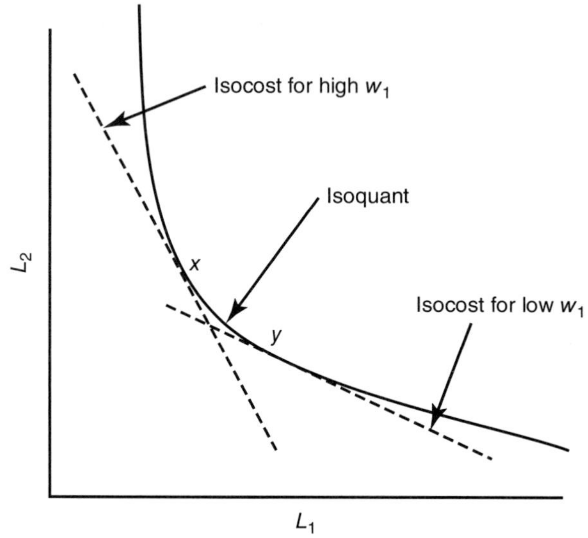

FIGURE 12.4. Effects of Wage Changes on Optimal Input Mix

RESULT 12.6

When Workers of Different Types Are Imperfect Substitutes in Production, the Optimal Hiring Mix Responds Smoothly to Changes in the Relative Cost of Different Types of Labor

Specifically, as one type of worker gets more expensive, a cost-minimizing firm should adjust its input mix away from that worker type but without abandoning the use of that worker type completely.

The smooth adjustment in Figure 12.4 and Result 12.6 contrasts with the "jumpy" adjustment we should see when production is independent as in Result 12.4. There, depending on the relative wage (w_1/w_2), the firm either used all of one type or all of the other. The input mix changes only when the relative wage crosses a threshold (where $w_1/w_2 = d_1/d_2$), at which point the firm switches abruptly between these two extremes. Returning to Section 12.1's example of the U.S. versus Mexican manufacturing workers, the optimal mix of these workers will be much less sensitive to their relative wages if the two types of workers interact positively in production (e.g., because one group makes parts for the other to assemble).

Although the "equate the marginal bang per buck" rule might seem obvious, notice that it differs from a number of common rules of thumb that people sometimes use to make the decisions described previously and that *also* seem obvious and sensible. These rules include allocating equal effort to each prospect, and equating the *average* return per unit of input across projects. Although these alternative rules can sometimes yield results that are close to the best you can do, the only way to ensure your scarce resources to all possible uses is to equate the

Equate the Marginal Bang Per Buck: A General and Useful Rule

One optimization problem you have probably faced as a student is the question of how to allocate your scarce study time (and perhaps mental resources) to different courses. Similarly, companies exploring for oil, natural gas, or other resources have to decide how to allocate a finite budget to different fields or countries to maximize expected profits. The same is true of pharmaceutical companies who are allocating research funds to different drugs and diseases. All these problems and many more share the feature that a limited budget has to be allocated to various uses, with different costs and different (expected) benefits. A firm's input mix choice has the same structure. And although each of these different problems has its own details and nuances, the solution to every one of them has the same broad feature: allocate your money (or other resources such as time) across all the possible uses in such a way that—once you've made your choice—one *additional* dollar (or hour, or unit of mental energy) allocated to each project would yield exactly the same expected return.

marginal product per dollar. Thus, the principle of equating the marginal bang per buck is worth keeping in mind as a very general rule.

Optimal Worker Mix when Types are Antagonists

For completeness, we conclude this chapter by asking what happens when worker types are *antagonists* in production, in other words, when an input's marginal productivity *increases* with a firm's relative use of that input. Intuitively, there are two main reasons this might happen. One is *increasing returns to the use of one input.*[11] For example in the maquiladora case, the fixed costs of establishing a recruiting, selection, and training network in one location might make it more productive for a firm to expand its operations in one location than to spread them across two. The other is *negative productivity interactions between inputs*: that is, a situation where adding a worker of one type can *reduce* the marginal productivity of the other type.[12] Real-world examples might include workers who speak different languages, or groups of workers who dislike each other.

What is the optimal input mix when inputs are antagonists in the production process? Now, in contrast to the isoquants in Figures 12.3 and 12.4, the isoquants get *steeper* as we move from left to right; thus, in a sense, they are "pulled" away

[11] Mathematically, increasing returns to input i means that the second partial derivative, F_{ii}, is positive.

[12] Mathematically, this amounts to $F_{12} < 0$ in the production function $Q = F(L_1, L_2)$, where subscripts of F indicate partial derivatives. $Q = (L_1^2 + L_2^2)^{1/2}$ is an example of a production function with this property. In general, the rate of change of the (absolute value of the) slope of an isoquant (with input 1 on the horizontal axis) is given by $sign \frac{d}{dL_1}\left(\frac{F_1}{F_2}\right) = F_{11} - 2\left(\frac{F_1}{F_2}\right)F_{12} + \left(\frac{F_1}{F_2}\right)^2 F_{22}$. Thus, the isoquant can become steeper as L_1 increases either because F_{11} or F_{12} are positive, or because F_{12} is negative.

Antagonistic Inputs and the Economics of Discrimination

Economics Nobelist Gary Becker (1971) applied the preceding theory to think about the consequences of **co-worker discrimination** for labor markets. If workers' distastes for interacting across racial lines give rise to isoquants with an increasing MRS, then Result 12.6 suggests that profit-maximizing employers will want to *segregate* their workplaces on racial lines. I have heard similar arguments from employers who say that they prefer segregating their production processes by *gender* to avoid what they expect to be productivity-reducing interactions (such as "flirting") across genders. Although it is possible that some of these negative between-group interactions are real, segregated workplace policies have also been used by employers for other reasons, such as facilitating monopsonistic wage discrimination of the type studied in Section 17.1.

from the origin instead of toward it. As a result, the optimal input mix, as in the case of the linear production function, is once again always a corner solution where only one worker type is hired. (It's not hard to show this yourself: just draw a graph like Figure 12.3 where the isoquant gets steeper moving from left to right.) Thus, the optimal solution is again at a corner, just as it was when workers worked independently.

☑ **RESULT 12.7**

When Two Inputs Are Antagonists in the Production Process

In this case, the optimal hiring mix again consists of corner solutions, where the optimal input mix responds *sharply or discontinuously* to changes in the relative cost of different types of labor. Just as in the case of independent production, as the type of worker a firm is using (say Type 1) gradually gets more expensive, a cost-minimizing firm should make no changes to its input mix until w_1/w_2 hits a critical point. At that point, the firm should replace all its Type-1 workers with Type 2s.

Chapter Summary

- ☐ When a firm using two labor types has a linear production function, $Q = d_1L_1 + d_2L_2$, all workers' productivities are independent of each other. In this case, a cost-minimizing employer should hire *only* the type with the highest "bang per buck," that is, the type with the highest productivity-to-wage ratio, MP/w.

- ☐ With a linear production function (and more generally when workers are perfect substitutes in production), cost-minimizing firms' hiring policies respond *abruptly* to wage changes, switching from hiring only one type to hiring only the other when the two types' relative wages (w_1/w_2) cross a threshold. These sorts of "abrupt" responses also occur when inputs are antagonists in production.

☐ When two different labor types are imperfect substitutes in production, a cost-minimizing employer should pick a "some-of-each" worker mix that equates the marginal bang per buck (*MP/w*) earned on each worker type. Cost-minimizing firms that follow this rule will adjust their input mix *smoothly* as relative wages (w_1/w_2) change, substituting away from inputs that have become relatively more expensive and toward the other input.

Discussion Questions

1. If two inputs work independently, must they be equally productive?
2. Think of two labor types in a firm you have once worked for. In your opinion, are they perfect substitutes, imperfect substitutes, or antagonists? If they are not perfect substitutes, describe some ways in which the two labor types affect each other's productivities.
3. Imagine that a fast-food firm has the option of hiring either high-school graduates or high-school dropouts as front-line workers and that the local going wages of these two groups are $12 and $9, respectively. Now suppose the local minimum wage has just been raised from $8 to $10 per hour. Based on the analysis in this chapter, how is this change likely to affect the firm's demand for high-school graduates?

Suggestions for Further Reading

For a more complete discussion of a cost-minimizing firm's optimal input mix, consult any intermediate microeconomics textbook. For a more advanced treatment of the economics of labor demand, see Hamermesh (1993). Gary Becker's (1971) book describes not only the idea of co-worker discrimination introduced in this chapter but several other sources of discrimination as well.

References

Becker, G. (1971). *The economics of discrimination* (2nd ed.). Chicago: University of Chicago Press.

Hamermesh, D. (1993). *Labor demand.* Princeton, NJ: Princeton University Press.

Schnepel, K. (2017). Good jobs and recidivism. *Economic Journal.* doi:10.1111/ecoj.12415

13 Risky versus Safe Workers

Implicitly, Chapter 12's analysis of which worker type to hire assumed that each workers' productivity was (a) known in advance to the firm and (b) the same for each worker of a given type. Those assumptions allowed us to compare the costs of hiring different mixes of workers and find the profit-maximizing mix in a simple way. But how do things change when the productivity of individual workers is not known in advance? For example, two workers (or types of workers) might have the same *expected* productivity, but there might be much more *uncertainty* regarding one worker, or worker type, than the other. More generally, how should a profit-maximizing firm change its recruiting policy when workers' productivity is hard to predict at the time of hire? This is the question we study in this chapter. We begin with a simple example.

13.1 A Base Case Example: Risky Workers and the Principle of Option Value

Imagine that you are a risk neutral employer, choosing between two employees for a sales position. Each employee will stay with you for (at most) 10 years and must be paid $50,000 per year. One worker, whom we'll call the "safe" worker, will produce net revenues of $100,000 per year, each year, for sure. As we explained when we discussed the meaning of a 100% commission rate in Section 3.3, "net revenues" or "net sales" refer to revenues net of all costs *except* the salesperson's pay. The other worker, whom we'll call the "risky" worker, could turn out to be either a "lemon" or a "peach." If this worker turns out to be a peach (the "good" type), that person will earn you net revenues of $300,000 per year. If the worker turns out to be a lemon (the "bad" type), that person will give you net revenues of *minus* $100,000 per year. At the time of hiring, you don't know whether the risky worker is a lemon or a peach: the chances are 50/50. For the sake of simplicity, we'll assume you learn the risky worker's type after the person has been with your firm for 2 years. At that time you are free to dismiss the worker at no cost to the firm.

In the preceding example, which worker should you hire?

A first thing to notice about our base case example is that by construction, the *expected* annual net revenues of the two workers is the same: 0.5($300,000) + 0.5(−$100,000) = $100,000. Realizing this, you might be tempted to answer the previous question as follows: "Well, because the two workers yield the same expected profits, but there is more uncertainty surrounding the risky worker, you should always hire the safe worker." Although this may feel correct, it's not, for at least two reasons. The more trivial reason, of course, is that we've assumed you are a *risk neutral* employer. So, by assumption, you should be indifferent between two options with the same expected return but different levels of risk. The more fundamental reason is that even though the two workers have the same expected net revenues per year they are with you, the *expected present value of hiring them* is not the same. This is because—once you learn the risky worker's type—you can make a choice (i.e., keep or dismiss them) that affects their long-term impact on your profits. In other words, risky workers have *option value* (or if you prefer "upside" risk or potential) that safe workers don't.[1]

Taking this option value into account, which worker should you hire? As it turns out, the answer is very simple: Under the stated conditions, a risk-neutral employer should always prefer the risky worker over the safe worker.

RESULT 13.1

Employers Should Prefer Risky Workers if There Are No Dismissal Costs

When it is costless to dismiss risky workers, a risk-neutral employer should always strictly prefer a risky to a safe worker with the same expected per-period productivity.

To demonstrate Result 13.1, we'll work out the value of hiring the risky and the safe worker under a variety of assumptions using the spreadsheet shown in Figure 13.1. Figure 13.1 shows the spreadsheet using its base case parameter values, where we assume the firm discounts future profits at a rate of 20% per year, its annual quit rate is 20%, and dismissal costs are zero. To explore what happens with other parameter values, you can download a copy of the spreadsheet and experiment with different values to see how the answers change.[2] We'll

[1] Option value is widely used concept in financial economics; as you may know, options (to buy or sell a particular stock at a certain price in the future) are traded on financial markets and can command high prices. Here, the valuable option is the option to keep (or dismiss) a worker, whose future value—just like stocks—is uncertain.

[2] Spreadsheets are available at http://www.econ.ucsb.edu/~pjkuhn/Ec152/Spreadsheets/Spreadsheets.htm.

discuss these changes later in this section, but first let's work on understanding the spreadsheet and the formulas it uses.

The box in the top left of the spreadsheet allows you to input three parameter values that are common to both worker types: the firm's discount rate, the workers' turnover rate, and the cost of dismissing a worker. To the right of the values that you can input, I have indicated the base case values for these parameters in **bold**. This is just for convenience: When I ask you to "set the parameters at their base case values," you will have that information readily available. Although we've discussed discounting and turnover before, what do we mean by "firing costs" in Figure 13.1? These are the costs of dismissing a worker who turns out to be a "lemon," which include some factors internal to the firm such as a possible loss in the morale of remaining workers and costs of finding and training replacement workers. They also include factors imposed on the firm by a variety of employment protection laws (EPLs).

We'll study the effects of EPLs on firms' hiring decisions in detail later in this chapter; for now, we'll assume that there are no relevant EPLs. Thus, Figure 13.1 sets dismissal costs equal to zero.

DEFINITION 13.1 **Employment protection laws** (EPLs) refer to any law or regulation that limits employers' ability to fire or lay off workers. Examples include requirements for advance notice of termination, mandatory severance pay, mandatory legal procedures for termination, and various forms of unjust dismissal regulations.

The next two boxes in Figure 13.1 let you input the characteristics of the safe and risky workers. Using the information we've already provided, the box on the right computes the expected net sales from a risky worker using the formula

$$\text{Expected net sales} = p(\text{Sales if Good}) + (1-p)(\text{Sales if Bad}), \quad \textbf{(13.1)}$$

where p is the probability the risky worker turns out to be the good type. If you like, you can experiment with the downloaded version of the spreadsheet to see how the risky worker's expected annual sales change as you change these assumptions, and how that compares to the safe worker.

Finally, the main panel in Figure 13.1 shows the sales and salary of each type of worker over the 10-year period they might be in the firm and totals up the expected present value (EPV) of hiring each worker type over that entire 10-year horizon. To see how this works, let's start with the safe worker. Column (4) shows that all safe workers who are still with the firm produce net sales of \$50,000 per year. But what are the chances that a safe worker who is hired this year is still with the firm in each of the subsequent years? Assuming that a fixed share, θ, of workers quit every year, the spreadsheet calculates the share of workers that are still around in year t using the recursive formula:

$$N_t = (1 - \theta)N_{t-1}, \quad \textbf{(13.2)}$$

HIRING RISKY WORKERS—SPREADSHEET EXAMPLE

In this example, "bad" workers are detected after TWO periods

Discount	Rate =	0.2	**0.2**
Quit	Rate =	0.2	**0.2**
Firing	Cost =	0	**0**

"Safe" Worker Characteristics:	actual	base case
Sales:	100	**100**
Salary:	50	**50**

"Risky" Worker Characteristics:		actual	base case
Sales if	Bad:	–100	**–100**
Sales if	Good:	300	**300**
Probability (Good)		0.5	**0.5**
Salary:		50	**50**
Expected Sales:		100	**100**

Safe Worker							Risky Worker						
(1)	(2)	(3)	(4)	(5)	(6)	(7)	(1)	(2)	(3)	(4)	(5)	(6)	(7)
Year	**Sales**	**Salary**	**Sales-Salary**	**Share of workers who haven't quit (R)**	**Sales-Salary after quits**	**EPV(Sales-Salary) after quits**	**Sales If Bad**	**Salary if Bad**	**Sales If Good**	**Salary if Good**	**Sales - Salary - Firing Costs**	**Sales-Salary-FC after quits**	**EPV(Sales-Salary-FC) after quits**
1	100	50	50	1.000	50.0	50.0	–100	50	300	50	50	50.0	50.0
2	100	50	50	0.800	40.0	33.3	–100	50	300	50	50	40.0	33.3
3	100	50	50	0.640	32.0	22.2	0	0	300	50	125	80.0	55.6
4	100	50	50	0.512	25.6	14.8	0	0	300	50	125	64.0	37.0
5	100	50	50	0.410	20.5	9.9	0	0	300	50	125	51.2	24.7
6	100	50	50	0.328	16.4	6.6	0	0	300	50	125	41.0	16.5
7	100	50	50	0.262	13.1	4.4	0	0	300	50	125	32.8	11.0
8	100	50	50	0.210	10.5	2.9	0	0	300	50	125	26.2	7.3
9	100	50	50	0.168	8.4	2.0	0	0	300	50	125	21.0	4.9
10	100	50	50	0.134	6.7	1.3	0	0	300	50	125	16.8	3.3
SUM	**1000**	**500**	**500**		**223**	**147**	**–200**	**100**	**3000**	**500**	**1100**	**423**	**243**

FIGURE 13.1. Effects of Hiring Risky Workers

Note: All magnitudes are in thousands of dollars. "Base case" parameter values are in **bold**. Total expected profits are highlighted in gray.

where N_t is the number of workers still in the firm today (as a share of the initial population you hired), N_{t-1} is the number you had last year, and θ is the annual quit rate. (If you like, you can also think of $1 - \theta$ as the firm's *retention rate*, i.e., the probability any given worker is still there, 1 year later.) According to Column (5), if the quit rate is 20% per year, only 13.4% of your original workforce will be with you after 10 years have passed.[3] Put another way, column (5) gives the probability that a worker who was hired in year 1 is still in the firm in year *t*.

In Column (6), we multiply Column (4) by the share of workers who are still in the firm in Column (5). This captures the fact that you only earn profits from the salespeople who are still with you; thus, when turnover is accounted for, hiring a safe worker today yields you only $20,500 in additional sales 5 years from now. Next, Column (7) takes the present value of Column (6) using the standard formula:

$$PV(x,t) = \frac{x}{(1+r)^{t-1}}, \tag{13.3}$$

where *x* is the amount of income earned in year *t*, and *r* is the real rate of interest (per year).[4] Put another way, we assume that your firm discounts profits earned in the future at the real rate of interest that is available to it. Using Equation 13.3, the spreadsheet calculates that the present value of the $20,500 produced by your remaining salespeople 5 years in the future is only $9,900. In the bottom row of Figure 13.1, we total up Column (7) to learn that after salaries are paid and after quits are taken into account, hiring a safe worker today yields $147,000 in expected discounted net profits for the firm over the next 10 years.

The remainder of Figure 13.1 repeats the preceding exercise for the risky worker. Most of the analysis is the same, but there are some key differences. First of all, Columns (1) and (3) (for the risky worker) now show that this worker's sales depend on which type the worker turns out to be. Moreover, because the firm learns the worker's type after 2 years (and because it makes sense to dismiss all the workers who turn out to be lemons), the firm neither gets sales revenues from nor pays a salary to bad workers starting in Year 3. Taking this into account, Column (5) computes the firm's *expected* sales minus salary from hiring a risky worker in Years 3 through 10 using the formula

$$E(\text{Sales} - \text{Salary}) = p(\text{Sales if Good} - \text{Salary if Good}). \tag{13.4}$$

---

[3] Some firms, including some fast-food restaurants, have turnover rates much higher than 20%, meaning than almost none of their employees remain the same from year to year. Notice also that Equation 13.2 assumes a constant 20% quit rate *over the entire course of the employee's career.* In most firms, however, workers tend to have *declining quit hazards*: The chances they will quit in any given month or year (given they haven't quit yet) go down the longer they have been in a firm. If you like, you can modify the spreadsheet to allow for this. None of the main results in this section will change.

[4] Note that profits in the first year—Year 1—are not discounted in Equation 13.3. This implicitly assumes that profits are earned at the beginning of the year, a convention we'll use throughout this book. If you prefer to think of profits as being earned at the end of the year, just change $t - 1$ in the formula to t. None of the main results in this section will change. If you are unfamiliar with the idea of discounting and calculating the present value of an income stream, consult any introductory economics textbook.

In other words, if you hire a risky worker today, there's a 50% chance $(1 - p)$ that worker will turn out to be a lemon. If that happens, you'll fire that person at the end of Year 2 and earn zero net profits from the worker in Years 3 through 10.[5] In addition, there's a 50% chance the worker will turn out to be a peach, in which case that person will earn you \$300,000 − \$50,000 = \$250,000. Overall, because this only happens half the time, your expected profits in Year 3 from hiring a risky worker today are \$125,000.

As we did for safe workers, Columns (6) and (7) adjust Column (5) for employee turnover and discounting, respectively, yielding a total bottom line expected present value of profits [EPV(Π)] of \$243,000. Because this is much higher than the EPV(Π) from a safe worker, a profit-maximizing firm should hire the risky worker in our base case example. The intuitive reason, already discussed, is that risky workers have option value: It makes sense to take a chance on them, because (with zero firing costs) you don't have to keep them if they don't work out!

13.2 Changing Assumptions: When Are Risky Workers the Better Bet?

What happens when we change the assumptions of our base case scenario? If you download the spreadsheet, you can find out for yourself by experimenting with different values for all the parameters: the discount rate, the quit rate, the cost of firing "bad" workers, and the probability a risky worker is a lemon, among others. If you do so, here are a few additional lessons you can learn.

Effects of Discount Rate, Turnover, and Worker Productivity

First, it is easy to show that *the relative value of the risky worker falls as the discount rate rises* (to see this, just type in any number between 0.2 and 1.0 in the discount rate box in the top left).[6] This makes sense because relative to safe workers, risky workers are an investment that pays off in the future. So firms who care more about the future should value risky workers more. For exactly the same reason, *the relative value of the risky worker falls as the worker turnover rate rises*: It doesn't make sense to invest in identifying potential peaches if they are going to quit anyway. Importantly, however, notice that (as long we keep the workers' productivities at their base case values) even though both discounting and turnover reduce the risky worker's appeal, they never eliminate it: the risky

[5] You might wonder how it can be that, in our example, the "bad" risky workers are actually reducing the firm's profits in Years 1 and 2, but the firm isn't able to fire them yet. Essentially, our assumption that no one can be dismissed until Year 3 is meant to capture the idea that both actual worker performance and our measures of it can be quite noisy, especially early in a worker's career. Thus the "bad" workers are present in the firm (and hurting it) during this assessment period, but the firm doesn't yet know who they are. For a recent formal model of the process via which employers learn their workers' ability over time, see Kahn and Lange (2014).

[6] A discount rate of 1 means firms place zero weight on future profits (i.e., on anything beyond Year 1). Therefore, it doesn't makes sense to consider higher values than 1 for the discount rate.

worker is preferred to the safe worker no matter how high we raise the discount or turnover rate! (Go ahead and experiment—you may need to display more decimal places to be sure. . . .[7]) The reason is that—by assumption—the safe and risky worker have the same expected productivity even *before* you learn the risky worker's "type." So even if you only care about the first year, your EPV(Π) is still no worse with a risky than with a safe worker.

☑ RESULT 13.2

Risky Workers May Be Preferred Even When They Are Less Productive

As long as the difference in expected productivity is not too large, a risk-neutral employer can prefer a risky worker to a safe worker even when the risky worker has a *lower* expected per-period productivity.

To see this, restore all the parameter values in the spreadsheet to their base case levels, then experiment by reducing the productivity of the risky worker in the "bad" state below minus $100,000. You'll see that the firm still prefers the risky worker even when "lemons" cause a loss of $200,000, that is, when risky workers' *expected* productivity is 50 (which is only *half* of the safe worker's expected productivity!). If you experiment with different values, you'll see that the risky worker's advantage disappears when productivity, if the worker turns out "bad," is about –216. The remarkable fact that employers can prefer risky workers with lower expected productivity than a safe worker is another illustration of those workers' option value.

Effects of Riskiness and Dismissal Costs

To explore the effect of a worker's "riskiness" on his or her attractiveness to the employer, let's first reduce the risky worker's sales to minus $300,000—keeping all the other parameter values at their base case levels. Now the risky worker's expected productivity in a single year is exactly zero. Due to the worker's option value, however, the expected present value of hiring that person is still positive, at $77,000, but it is less than the expected present value of hiring the safe worker, $147,000. So the firm should hire the safe worker. Next, let's do a crazy thing: Let's make the risky worker *even riskier* (while holding the expected per-period productivity fixed at zero). Specifically, reduce the "bad" worker's productivity to –$500,000 and raise the "good" worker's productivity to +$500,000. (Statistically, this is called a *mean preserving spread* in the worker's productivity distribution, and it leaves that person's per-period expected productivity unchanged at zero.)

Amazingly, this increase in riskiness *raises* the expected present value of hiring the risky worker to $205,000. Now the employer prefers the risky worker

[7] And remember that—like the discount rate—the highest quit rate it makes sense to consider is 1. This means that all workers quit at the end of their first year with the company.

again! The reason of course is again related to option value: After Year 2, the firm only keeps the risky worker if that person turns out to be a peach: the worker's value as a lemon is irrelevant. Thus, the increased upside potential more than makes up for the increased downside risk. Indeed, this principle is very well known in financial markets: Options on risky stocks are typically worth more than options on otherwise comparable safe stocks because the value of risky stocks fluctuates more. The increased value of the risky worker as that person gets riskier illustrates the same principle. To summarize:

☑ RESULT 13.3

Holding Expected Productivity Constant, the Relative Value of the Risky Worker Increases With How Risky They Are

How do changes in firing costs affect the attractiveness of the risky worker? To explore this question, let's continue with our example where the risky worker's productivity equals –$500,000 if bad and +$500,000 if good. Now experiment by raising the level of firing costs above zero. You will find that it starts to make more sense to hire the safe worker once firing costs rise above about $175,000. This makes sense: If it is costly or difficult to get rid of underperforming workers, firms should be less willing to take a chance on risky prospects who might not work out in the end.[8]

☑ RESULT 13.4

Dismissal Costs Make Risky Workers Less Attractive

The relative value of hiring the risky worker falls as firing costs rise. In cases where the risky worker's expected per-period productivity is below the safe worker's, increasing the level of firing costs can make the risky worker less attractive than the safe worker.

One illustration of the effects of dismissal costs on risk-taking in the hiring process involves academic tenure. At most research-intensive universities in the United States, a newly hired assistant professor has 6 years in which to prove him- or herself to be a capable researcher and teacher. At the end of that period, a strict "up-or-out" rule applies: Assistant professors who attain the standard are retained and granted

[8] Although Result 13.4 is correct as stated, its illustration in the downloadable spreadsheet is actually a bit of an oversimplification. This is because the calculations in the spreadsheet ignore yet another option available to a firm: the option to *retain* an underperforming worker. Specifically, the spreadsheet simply *assumes* that the firm will fire all workers who turn out to be "bad." But if firing costs are high enough, it may actually be more profitable to *retain* underperforming workers than to fire them. When that happens, firing costs still make firms reluctant to hire risky workers, but they do this for a slightly different reason. This option is explored in one of the discussion questions for this chapter.

Unintended Effects of Higher Dismissal Costs: Did the Americans with Disabilities Act Hurt Disabled Workers?

The Americans with Disabilities Act (ADA) became law in 1991. With a goal of increasing employment among the disabled, the law requires employers to accommodate disabled workers and outlaws discrimination against them in hiring, firing, and pay. An important aspect of how the law is enforced is an employee's right to sue an employer for disability-based discrimination. Because workers rarely sue firms for not hiring them, and because suits for disability-based pay discrimination are also relatively rare, in practice, one of the most important facets of the ADA is its effects on dismissal costs: Employers put themselves at risk of a lawsuit if they dismiss a disabled worker. Because hiring a disabled worker is arguably a risky prospect for firms—their productivity may be harder to predict than the productivity of a non-disabled worker—Result 13.4 suggests that the ADA could have had the unintended effect of making firms less willing to "take a chance" on hiring a disabled worker.

Interestingly, this is exactly what economists Daron Acemoglu and Joshua Angrist found in their 2001 study of the ADA's employment effects, conducted 10 years after the ADA came into effect. For men of all working ages and women under 40, the authors found a sharp drop in the employment of disabled workers after the ADA was implemented. The authors also show that other labor policy changes taking place at this time cannot easily account for this drop, and that the decline in disabled workers' employment was largest in states with more ADA-related discrimination charges. Although not 100% conclusive that the ADA was the main reason why disabled workers' employment rates fell after 1991, Acemoglu and Angrist's analysis suggests that policymakers should be aware of possible unintended effects of employment protection laws, especially when those laws apply to workers that firms might see as "risky" prospects.

tenure while the rest are terminated. In practice, however, it can be much harder to deny tenure at some universities than others. Unsurprisingly, universities where it is very easy to deny tenure (take, for example, top schools like Princeton, where only about 1 in 10 assistant professors is awarded tenure) can afford to hire much riskier new assistant professors than universities where tenure is hard to deny. The focus at top schools is on star potential, so high-risk candidates working on far-fetched ideas are very desirable. If those far-fetched ideas don't work out, the university can just deny tenure. Universities where it is hard to deny tenure have a strong incentive to behave in a more risk-averse way in the hiring process.

Effects of Employer Risk Aversion, the Probationary Period, and Employment Protection Laws

In addition to the parameters you can experiment with in our spreadsheet, a number of additional factors also affect a profit-maximizing firm's choice between risky and safe workers. One of these is employer risk aversion: In general, compared to risk-neutral firms, risk-averse firms will be less attracted to risky workers; however, it is still possible for risk-averse firms to prefer risky workers to safe workers of equal or lower expected productivity. These employers just need to weigh their aversion to additional risk against the higher option value of risky workers.[9] Another factor is the length of the worker's probationary period, that is, the amount of time it takes for the employer to learn the risky worker's true type. As you can easily demonstrate by modifying the spreadsheet so that it takes 3 or 4 years to learn the risky worker's type, the relative value of the risky worker falls when this probationary period gets longer.

Other factors firms consider include various forms of employment protection laws, including mandated severance pay, legal procedures, and mandatory advance notice of a worker termination.[10] Legal requirements for firms to pay severance to laid-off workers are common in many European countries and can be quite costly. For example, Belgian firms have been required to pay 18 months of salary to long-service white-collar workers when terminating their employment. In France, prior approval from a judge is required for many private sector job terminations, a process that can take considerable time and money. In addition, many countries, including the United States, require firms to give workers advance notice of certain kinds of terminations.[11] A final important form of employment protection in the United States is wrongful discharge laws, which prevent firms from laying workers off for a variety of specified reasons (see, e.g., Autor, Donohue, and Schwab, 2006). In all of these cases, we might expect employers to react to higher dismissal costs by being more reluctant to "take a chance" on hiring risky workers. EPLs can have many other effects, however, some of which—including the possibility of increased training and innovation—may be beneficial to both workers and firms. We discuss some of these factors in Section 19.4.

Who Can Observe Your Employees' Job Performance, and Why Does This Matter?

A final set of parameters in our model are the **wages** paid to workers. In the example so far, we have made the very simple (but perhaps unrealistic) assumption that all workers—whether risky or safe, peaches or lemons—are paid the same wage ($50,000). Not surprisingly, this means that firms really like it when their risky workers turn out to be peaches: These workers produce $300,000 in net revenues but are paid only $50,000. Is this realistic? As it turns out, the answer depends to a large extent on a key feature of labor markets, specifically, whether workers' productivity is *public* or *private information*.

---

[9] A simple way to extend our spreadsheet model to accommodate employer risk aversion is simply to think of the payoffs to the employer in that table as utility payoffs rather than dollars. Then we can incorporate the idea that the employer may be more sensitive to losses than gains by just assigning bigger negative numbers to the firm's payoffs when the risky worker is a lemon. In this sense, our spreadsheet model applies both to risk-averse and risk-neutral employers.

[10] Although some of these restrictions officially apply only to layoffs (which are employment reductions due to a lack of available work) and not to dismissals of individual workers for underperformance, the difficulty of establishing an employer's true rationale for terminating a worker means that these public policies tend to affect the type of firing costs we're thinking of in this section too.

[11] Descriptions of these and other EPLs in number of countries are available in Kuhn (2002).

Take a Chance on Me, Please! Under-Hiring in an Online Labor Market

In 2012, oDesk was the world's largest online labor market—a site where employers can hire workers anywhere in the world to perform a variety of tasks that can be delivered online. Tasks on oDesk vary from writing computer code; to designing a website, poster, or ad campaign; to simple data entry. A key feature of oDesk is that every employee's performance ratings from all his previous oDesk employers are easily available to new employers on his profile page. Thus, oDesk is a classic example of a labor market where workers' job performance is public information.

Interestingly, a recent study of oDesk workers by Amanda Pallais (2014) shows that this public information can lead to problems: Because all other employers will know that a new worker I just took a chance on is a true gem (and can hire them away from me with little more than the click of a mouse), many employers on oDesk are reluctant to try out new workers. In essence, hiring new workers (thereby revealing to the market which are the good ones) creates a *public good*: It benefits the worker and other firms but not the firm taking the initial chance on the worker. And if you've studied public economics, you'll know that private markets don't do a good job of providing public goods.

As it happens, this is exactly what Pallais found when she hired 952 randomly selected workers on oDesk, giving them honest, public evaluations that were either detailed or coarse. Both hiring workers *and* providing more detailed evaluations substantially improved the workers' subsequent employment outcomes. Pallais also calculates that firms do *too little experimentation* with risky, new workers on oDesk, suggesting that the oDesk marketplace could be made more efficient by introducing policies (such as introductory subsidies) that encourage firms to try out new workers more frequently.

Personnel economists say that a worker's productivity is *private information* when only the worker's current employer knows their true productivity. An example might be a star-quality administrative assistant: It might indeed be possible to pay such a worker much less than that worker's productivity because other firms have no way of knowing the worker is a star. On the other hand, worker productivity is *public information* when other potential employers also know a worker's performance. Well-known examples include scientists (whose publication record, patent, and citation counts are publicly available), professional athletes, and CEOs of publicly held companies (whose companies must disclose detailed financial information). When worker productivity is public information, risky workers are less valuable to firms than when it is private information. That is because in the public case, other firms can easily bid workers away from their original employer when the market learns they are "peaches."[12] The upshot is Result 13.5.

[12] This argument implicitly assumes that the "good" worker's skills—which are worth $300,000 in the original firm—are portable to other firms. In other words, that they are *general skills*. We study the difference between general and specific skills in Chapter 19. Like private information, specific skills tend to tie workers to firms, which increases firms' incentives to invest both in identifying *and* training their best workers.

☑ RESULT 13.5

When Hiring Risky Workers Is Less Attractive

This is the case for employers in labor markets where employee productivity is *public information* than when it is *private*. If other firms can see you have successfully hired a "star," they have a strong incentive to poach those workers from you. Although this is good news, ex post, for the "peaches," it reduces a firm's incentive to take a chance on risky workers in the first place.

Chapter Summary

- ☐ In a situation where workers who don't work out can be dismissed, risky workers have option value to a firm.
- ☐ This option value makes risky workers more valuable than safe workers with the same expected per-period productivity and can even make them more valuable than safe workers with higher expected productivity.
- ☐ Risky workers' option value (and therefore their attractiveness to employers) increases with how risky they are and declines with the level of dismissal costs.
- ☐ Risky workers are less valuable to employers in labor markets where workers' productivity is public information (i.e., is visible to other potential employers). In these markets, firms may be reluctant to take a chance on workers who are uncertain prospects but have considerable upside potential.

Discussion Questions

1. Tenure is a form of employment protection that applies to some professors and teachers. Drawing on the discussion in this chapter, what would be some benefits and costs of abolishing it?
2. List all the factors (turnover rate, firing costs, etc.) that affect a firm's choice between risky and safe workers. Which of these factors make risky workers more attractive to the firm, and which have the opposite effect?
3. What is a mean-preserving spread in a worker's productivity distribution? How does it affect the attractiveness of risky workers to employers?
4. Apart from risky workers and the stock market, can you think of other examples where people or firms are willing to pay money for the option to do something in the future? (One hint: Think about the last time you bought an airline ticket or booked a hotel room.) Discuss how your willingness to pay for these options depends on the relevant amount of uncertainty.

Suggestions for Further Reading

For more on employment protection laws, Bentolila and Bertola (1990) is one of the first studies of EPLs. It asks whether EPLs can reasonably be held responsible for poor European macroeconomic performance. My (Kuhn, 2002) book on employment protection describes employment protection laws in 10 developed countries. Jones and Kuhn (1995) show that mandated advance notice of termination reduces unemployment among laid-off workers by allowing some of them to find a new job before they are terminated. Autor et al. (2006) provide evidence suggesting that wrongful dismissal laws reduce employment growth in U.S. states that adopt them. Kugler, Autor, and Kerr (2007) and Dougherty, Frisancho Robles, and Krishna (2014) find that EPLs reduce productivity in the United States and India, respectively. Button (in press) summarizes empirical research on the employment effects of EPLs since Acemoglu and Angrist's 2001 article and reminds us that EPLs can also raise employment of protected workers by making it harder to fire them. Empirically, he estimates that a 2001 expansion of employment protections for disabled workers in California *increased* their employment rates.

Finally, using data from the United States, United Kingdom, France, and Germany, Acharya, Baghai, and Subramanian (2013, 2014) find that wrongful dismissal laws *increase* innovation, at least in certain highly innovative sectors. The authors argue that this is because wrongful dismissal laws prevent employers from taking advantage of employee innovators after they have produced a successful product. We'll return to this idea in Chapter 19 when we discuss firm-specific skills and the holdup problem.

References

Acemoglu, D., & Angrist, J. D. (2001). Consequences of employment protection? The case of the Americans with Disabilities Act. *Journal of Political Economy, 109,* 915–957.

Acharya, V. V., Baghai, R. P., & Subramanian, K. V. (2013). Labor laws and innovation. *Journal of Law and Economics, 56,* 997–1037.

Acharya, V. V., Baghai, R. P., & Subramanian, K. V. (2014). Wrongful discharge laws and innovation. *Review of Financial Studies, 27,* 301–346.

Autor, D. H., Donohue, J. J., III, & Schwab, S. J. (2006). The costs of wrongful-discharge laws. *Review of Economics and Statistics, 88,* 211–231.

Bentolila, S. & Bertola, G. (1990). Firing costs and labour demand: How bad is Eurosclerosis? *Review of Economic Studies, 57,* 381–402.

Button, P. (in press). Expanding employment discrimination protections for individuals with disabilities: Evidence from California. *Industrial and Labor Relations Review.*

Dougherty, S., Frisancho, V., & Krishna, K. (2014). State-level labor reform and firm-level productivity in India. *India Policy Forum, 10*(1), 1-56.

Jones, S. R. G., & Kuhn, P. (1995). Mandatory notice and unemployment. *Journal of Labor Economics, 13,* 599–622.

Kahn, L., & Lange, F. (2014). Employer learning, productivity and the earnings distribution: Evidence from performance measures. *Review of Economic Studies, 81,* 1575–1613.

Kugler, A., Autor, D., & Kerr, B. (2007). Do employment protections reduce productivity? Evidence from U.S. states. *Economic Journal, 117,* F189–F217.

Kuhn, P. (Ed.). (2002). *Losing work, moving on: International perspectives on worker displacement.* Kalamazoo, MI: W. E. Upjohn Institute for Employment Research.

Pallais, A. (2014). Inefficient hiring in entry-level labor markets. *American Economic Review, 104,* 3565–3599.

14 Recruitment: Formal versus Informal? Broad versus Narrow?

Having decided which broad categories of workers to target with their recruiting efforts, how should employers go about actually finding and hiring workers? To answer this question, a firm facing a job vacancy actually has to make three types of decisions. The first is *whether* to post an ad and solicit job applicants. Important alternatives to such "formal" recruiting efforts are informal methods, such as asking your existing workforce to *refer* candidates, and hiring *internally*, that is, promoting an insider. Assuming you do recruit formally, the second question concerns pool size: How many applications should you solicit, and how many candidates should you interview? Among other options, larger *applicant* pools can be secured by searching longer and in more places; larger *interview* pools can be had by setting a lower bar for callbacks. Third, a recruiter needs to choose workers from the pool that has been collected. Here, some important questions include whether to engage in various types of *testing* and how much *discretion* to give to human recruiters. In sum, firms have to decide (a) whether to go "fishing" in the external labor market; (b) how wide a net to cast, and (c) how to pick the best fish from the net. We consider questions (a) and (b) in this chapter. Chapter 15 considers question (c), and Chapter 16 discusses how to avoid various forms of bias in the entire process.

14.1 Formal versus Informal Channels

The first question facing firms seeking new workers is whether to proceed formally, by placing a job ad announcing the details of the vacancy and the type of worker being sought, or whether to proceed more informally by asking one's existing workers to recommend people they know (or, of course, by a combination of these approaches). Interestingly, although quite a bit is known about the role of informal contacts in helping *workers* find jobs, less is known about the role of networks and informal contacts versus other approaches in *firms'* recruiting activities.

On the worker side, for example, we know that "contacting friends and relatives about jobs" is *not* the most common search method for unemployed workers (Kuhn & Mansour, 2014). Other methods, such as looking at ads and contacting firms directly, are used considerably more. Despite that, a consensus estimate is that at least half of all jobs are *found* through informal contacts (Topa, 2011), suggesting that such contacts are very effective when they are available. This idea is supported by evidence that applicants who are referred by a firm's current employees are much more likely to receive an offer than other applicants.[1] And, although it was long thought—somewhat paradoxically—that "weak ties" (acquaintances) were actually more useful to workers than strong ties (family and friends) in finding jobs (Granovetter, 1995), we now know that is not quite true. All in all, whereas much remains to be learned about the relative effectiveness of different job search strategies for workers, what we do know suggests that informal contacts, when available, are very helpful to workers.

What Type of Connections Really Help Workers? Evidence from Facebook

In a seminal study of 54 people's job-finding activities and outcomes, sociologist Mark Granovetter (1973) noticed that more people found their jobs via acquaintances than friends. This idea became known as **the strength of weak ties**. The idea was that your close friends are less helpful in locating new jobs *because they tend to know the same things (people, firms, job opportunities) as you do*. Thus, these strong ties provide relatively little new information. Weak ties, on the other hand, form bridges to new information and are therefore more helpful to workers in locating new jobs.

Despite being received as wisdom for decades, Granovetter's (1973) famous study confused two important concepts: (a) how are most jobs found? versus (b) which type of tie—strong or weak—is actually more likely to get you a job? In other words, if you had the option of one more LinkedIn contact, would you rather that person be a close friend or an acquaintance?

In a recent study of U.S. Facebook users, Laura Gee, Jason Jones, and Moire Burke (2017) explore this crucial distinction. Consistent with Granovetter's (1973) result, Gee et al. find that more people get new jobs where their acquaintances work than where their closer friends work. However, this is not because it's better to have an acquaintance than a friend. It's just because people have *more* acquaintances than friends. In fact, it's better (for job finding) to add one close friend than one more acquaintance—the exact opposite of what Granovetter concluded! Contrary to Granovetter's information hypothesis, the new information associated with a weak tie is more than outweighed by the fact that weak ties are likely to be less relevant to you and may be less willing to do you a favor.

[1] See, for example, Fernandez and Weinberg (1997); Petersen, Saporta. and Seidel (2000); Brown, Setren, and Topa (2016); and Burks, Cowgill, Hoffman, and Housman (2015). Related, Glitz (2017) has shown that unemployed jobseekers who have a larger number of employed former co-workers have better job search outcomes.

Turning now to our main question in this section, what are the advantages and disadvantages to *firms* of using formal methods, such as posting an ad or using a placement service, versus informal networks to recruit new workers? Of course, one possible advantage of informal methods is their low cost: If a good result can be achieved just by asking your existing workers to recommend a friend, why go through the trouble and expense of placing an ad, sifting through potentially hundreds of applications, then interviewing a handful of candidates? Another possible advantage is that a firm's existing workers might value the opportunity to recommend their friends; allowing them to do so may improve their job satisfaction and reduce their turnover. These things noted, probably the most important potential advantage of informal recruiting methods is that they might yield better workers than formal methods. Is that in fact the case?

Are Referred Workers More Productive? Evidence from oDesk

Suppose that Paul, a programmer at MicroStyle, has recommended his friend Lakshmi for a job at the company. Can MicroStyle reasonably expect Lakshmi to be a better employee than a (non-referred) candidate drawn at random from MicroStyle's applicant pool? Although this might seem like a simple question, it is not, for at least two reasons. The first is that a worker is more than a resume: Any human resources manager will tell you that resumes, although useful, are not very accurate predictors of who will perform well in a job. So, to answer this question properly, we need to do more than just compare the resumes of the two types of candidates: We need evidence on *actual job performance* of referred versus non-referred applicants. This is harder to come by.

Second, although a number of studies have compared the turnover and job performance of referred and non-referred workers after they are hired, comparing the productivity of the workers who are ultimately *hired* by a firm does not reveal whether a typical referred *applicant* is better than a non-referred applicant.[2] To see this, suppose that, on average, referred applicants to MicroStyle are known to be of higher quality than non-referred applicants. Then it makes good sense for MicroStyle to be more careful, or *choosier*, when hiring from its pool of non-referred applicants than from the pool of referrals. (For example, it might insist on a higher level of credentials like education and experience when choosing from the non-referred pool.) If MicroStyle does that, then the relatively small share of non-referred applicants who actually get hired might perform just as well as the larger share of referred applicants who are hired, even though the average referred *applicant* is better than the average non-referred applicant.[3] For this reason, comparing the productivity of referred versus non-referred *hires* doesn't tell us what we want to know either. Somehow we need information on

[2] Brown et al. (2016), Holzer (1987), Simon and Warner (1992), Datcher (1983), and Burks et al. (2015) compare turnover rates of referred versus non-referred applicants. Castilla (2005), Blau (1990), and Burks et al. (2015) compare the productivity of referred and non-referred applicants.

[3] Even controlling for resume quality, existing evidence shows that referred workers are in fact more likely than non-referred workers to be hired (e.g., Fernandez & Weinberg, 1997; Burks et al., 2015).

the actual productivity of all referred and non-referred applicants to a firm, regardless of whether the firm actually ends up hiring them!

Although this is not the sort of data that emerges from the regular operations of any typical firm, it is something we can learn by conducting a field experiment. Indeed, this is exactly what Amanda Pallais and Amy Sands (2016) did when they hired workers on oDesk.[4] Specifically, Pallais and Sands first used a job ad to hire a group of workers to do a short task. Next they posted a new job ad for a different type of work, and at the same time asked the workers they'd hired previously to recommend people for this new job. Finally, they hired *everyone* who applied to this new job, whether they had been referred or not, and measured their job performance. Assessing performance was easy because the task—visiting an airline website each day and recording certain information on it—was quite standardized.

What was the result? Simply put, the referred workers performed better in three distinct senses. First, they were less likely to quit than non-referred workers. Second, they had better resumes, that is, higher ratings from past employers, more experience, and so forth. Finally, referred workers also performed better than non-referred workers with resumes of the same quality. This means that being referred by a co-worker conveys positive information to employers *above and beyond what the employer can learn from the worker's resume.* In sum, see Result 14.1:

☑ RESULT 14.1

Referred Workers Are More Productive

In Pallais and Sands's (2016) oDesk experiment, job candidates who were referred by existing workers were less likely to quit and were more productive than an average non-referred applicant. This is true even when comparing referred and non-referred workers with equally good resumes.

Results similar to Pallais and Sands's (2016) have been found in other contexts as well. For example, Meta Brown, Elizabeth Setren, and Giorgio Topa (2016) found that informal referrals outperform other hires in a large financial services company, as do Burks et al. (2015) in a study of nine large firms in the call center, trucking, and high-tech industries. Both of these studies, however, suffer from the drawback—mentioned previously—that they can only look at the productivities of workers who were actually *hired* via the two different methods. Using a countrywide Swedish dataset, Lena Hensvik and Oskar N. Skans (2016) show that firms recruit workers with better military draft test scores but shorter schooling when hiring previous colleagues of current employees. This makes sense: Any employer can see a worker's educational qualifications on the resume, but only friends are able to recommend people who are "smarter than they look on paper."

[4] oDesk is the largest online labor market. See Section 13.2 for more information.

If referred workers are more productive than other job applicants, should employers hire *only* referred workers? Aside from the obvious reason that there might not be enough referred workers for the firm's needs, there's a second important reason this doesn't make sense. After all, even if the average non-referred worker is less productive, choosing *carefully* from that group can still yield workers who are as good, or better, than a typical referred worker. Thus, the correct interpretation of Result 14.1 is that in most cases, firms should hire both types of workers, but should *screen non-referred candidates more closely*, just as we imagined in our MicroStyle example. For example, employers might insist on higher observed credentials when hiring from the non-referred pool, while overlooking some blemishes on referred workers' resumes.[5]

☑ RESULT 14.2

Screen Non-Referred Workers More Carefully

Result 14.1 does not imply that firms should hire only referred workers. Instead, the profit-maximizing response to Result 14.1 is for employers' firms to examine resumes from both referred and non-referred groups, but to apply higher standards when choosing from the non-referred group.

Of course, in some situations, the profit-maximizing standard for non-referred workers is so high that none are ultimately hired; but in most cases, employers will likely find it optimal to hire some workers from both groups.

When and Why Are Referred Workers More Productive?

If referred workers are indeed more productive than other job applicants, what factors might account for that difference? An obvious potential advantage we've already discussed is *selection*: Referrals might yield better workers. But that's not the only reason referred workers might perform better than non-referred workers. Indeed, a second reason why referred workers might outperform others is called *peer influence* in Pallais and Sands's (2016) article. Returning to our MicroStyle example, peer influence refers to a case where Lakshmi (the referred worker) is no more able than a non-referred worker, but *decides to work harder or more conscientiously because Paul has referred her.* After all, if she and Paul are friends, she will not want Paul to look bad (and perhaps miss out on a raise). Indeed, Paul might also exert some peer pressure on Lakshmi to ensure that she lives up to the potential he told MicroStyle she had. Put another way, friendship between workers might reduce *moral hazard* in the principal–agent relationship, that is, it could improve worker *motivation*, not just selection.

[5] To illustrate this, Pallais and Sands (2014) calculated what would happen if—instead of hiring *everyone* as they did in their experiment—they chose a profit-maximizing mix of referred and non-referred candidates. Under this optimal "some-of-each" strategy, they would hire relatively few non-referred workers, but those non-referred workers would have very high quality resumes. These high observable qualifications would make up for their lack of harder-to-measure qualifications, with the result that the ultimate job performance of referred and non-referred *hires* would be the same.

A third reason, *team production*, also involves the referred worker "upping her game" because she was referred, but this time *only if she is working directly with her referrer* (Paul). For example, suppose that Paul and Lakshmi are on the same product development team. Because she is working directly with a friend, Lakshmi may have an extra incentive to perform well because she and Paul will share the same team bonus, and she cares about Paul. Put differently, friends who work together may be better at solving the *free-rider problem* inherent in team production (studied in Part 5 of this book) than strangers are.

How important are each of these three factors in explaining the superior performance of referred workers on oDesk? Pallais and Sands (2016) answer this question by doing different versions of their experiment. In the simplest version, the referrers and the workers they referred performed their tasks—visiting airline websites—in isolation from each other.[6] In fact, to minimize any possible interactions, each referred worker was told that her referrer would never know how she performed. Referrers were told that they would be judged only on their own merits, not on the performance of their referrals. Thus, this version of the experiment measures the pure *selection effect* of referrals: Because the referred and referring workers were isolated from each other after the referral was made, neither peer influence nor team production can explain why referred workers were more productive in that experiment.[7]

Next, to assess the impact of peer pressure, Pallais and Sands (2016) conducted a modified version of their experiment on a different set of workers.[8] Here, instead of isolating referrers and referred workers from each other, each referrer received a daily update on the referral's performance after each day of work and was told that the referrer's promotion prospects might depend on the referral's performance. Referred workers knew these updates were being sent. Perhaps surprisingly, the referred workers' performance in this treatment wasn't very different from Pallais and Sand's simplest experiment. At least in this context, then, the added peer pressure of upholding your recommender's reputation was not an important advantage of hiring through referrals.

Finally, to assess the effects of team production, Pallais and Sands (2016) did a third experiment where instead of working individually, the referrer and referred workers were hired to collaborate (via a chat box) on a joint project. The joint task was to create a single, shared slogan for a public service announcement. In some cases, the referred worker was paired with someone the worker didn't know; in other cases, the worker was paired with the referrer. Here, the authors

[6] This version is called "*Treatment 2 of the individual experiment*" in Pallais-Sands's paper.

[7] To eliminate even the remote possibility that referred workers may have faced some subtle peer pressure, Pallais and Sands (2014) also ran a supplemental experiment 4 months later. Here, they made separate job offers to all referred and non-referred workers in the initial experiment on behalf of a new firm. Neither the referred or non-referred workers knew that this new job offer was connected with the original experiment. Despite this, the referred workers exhibited substantially higher performance and lower turnover than non-referred workers. This is strong evidence of a pure selection effect of referrals—referred workers perform better than non-referred ones *no matter where they work*.

[8] This version is called "*Treatment 1 of the individual experiment*."

found that referrals improved team production.[9] This suggests that creating well-functioning teams may be another real benefit of hiring via referrals.

RESULT 14.3

Sources of the Referred-Worker Productivity Advantage

Three distinct reasons why referred workers might outperform other job applicants are *selection, peer influence,* and *team production.* In Pallais and Sands's (2016) oDesk experiment, only selection and team production had important effects. Of course, the relative importance of these three channels might be different in other contexts.

Some other findings from Pallais and Sands's (2016) experiments concern which types of referrals were most productive. These patterns held across all their experiments and show that although referrals are more productive, not all referrals are created equal. First, the authors found that *workers referred by high-performing workers* performed better than workers referred by low performers. Part of this is simply because referrers tend to refer workers with resumes similar to their own: Referrers with stronger resumes on average provide referrals with stronger resumes. But even controlling for the quality of workers' resumes, workers referred by high performers tended to perform better themselves.

Second, the *strength of the referrer–referral relationship* also affects the performance of the referred worker. To measure tie strength, Pallais and Sands (2016) asked the referrers three questions about their relationship with their referral: how well they know their referral, how many friends they have in common, and how often they interact. They found that referrals who have strong ties to their referrers perform better. Interestingly, this was true even though referrers who didn't know their referral well tended to compensate for this by picking referrals who looked better on paper than referrers who didn't know their referral as well. Result 14.4 summarizes this.

RESULT 14.4

When Are Referrals Especially Productive?

In Pallais and Sands's (2016) oDesk experiment, referred job candidates were especially productive when

- working on a team with their referrer;
- they were referred by a high-performing worker; and
- they were referred by someone who knew them well.

A Few Cautions

We conclude our discussion of Pallais and Sands's (2016) referrals experiment with some cautions. An obvious one is that oDesk is a special labor market that

[9] Team productivity was assessed using a variety of measures, including whether the announcement was actually submitted, and whether it met certain objective criteria (e.g. number of words and the use of specific words) that were requested by the experimenters.

may not be representative of more "traditional" labor markets. Indeed, one important feature of oDesk is that workers are probably less strongly tied to employers because it's very easy to switch employers at the click of a mouse. This may make selection and peer influence less important than elsewhere. For example, if oDesk workers are less concerned with remaining in good standing with their current employers, their incentive to refer talented workers or to pressure their referrals to perform well may be weaker. If that is true, Pallais and Sands's results will actually *underestimate* the strength of selection and peer pressure effects of referrals in more "traditional" labor markets.

Another caveat is that it is easy to imagine situations where hiring via referrals is a bad idea. For example, as we'll show in Part 5, workers who are compensated on a relative basis (e.g., workers who would compete with the new hires for promotions or bonuses) actually have an incentive to recommend *low-quality* co-workers. Also, later in the book, we'll study two situations (collusion in tournaments and ratchet effects) where workers have an incentive to pressure each other to *reduce* effort. Hiring friends of existing workers could facilitate this type of collusion between workers. Indeed, this might explain why governments and other bureaucracies (which are arguably more vulnerable to ratchet effects) frequently insist on formal, anonymous hiring procedures in lieu of informal connections. Thus, there may be important situations where formal hiring procedures yield better results than hiring friends of your current workers. Result 14.5 summarizes.

☑ RESULT 14.5

When to Avoid Referrals

Referral-based hiring may not be a good idea

(a) when workers are paid according to relative performance (because relative performance pay creates an incentive to recommend low-ability workers); and

(b) in cases (like ratchet effects) where friendships between workers make it easier for workers to collude by reducing effort levels.

Filling Higher-Ranked Positions: Internal versus External Recruitment

When filling positions above the entry level, organizations could decide to recruit an external candidate, or they could promote someone from within the organization. What are the pros and cons of these two approaches?

An obvious advantage of promoting insiders is that they understand the company and its organizational culture, and they are likely to have accumulated some valuable firm-specific skills (see Section 19.4). Second, a corporate *policy* of promoting insiders also incentivizes the *acquisition* of firm-specific skills because workers can be more confident of staying with the organization long term. Third, an internal promotion policy can increase *work incentives*: As we'll argue in Part 4, competition for promotions can be an important incentive device in many firms. Put another way, it may be optimal for companies to *bias* promotion competitions in favor of insiders (i.e., to prefer insiders to equally qualified outsiders for senior positions) as a way of strengthening work incentives for the firm's existing employees.

External recruitment also has advantages. For example, outsiders may bring fresh ideas, and may be less influenced by internal politics than insiders. Second, the pool of potential job candidates is larger for external recruitment: By considering a wider range of candidates, the organization improves its options beyond what may be a small pool of internal candidates. Third, external hiring fills one vacancy without creating another, whereas internal hiring opens up a vacancy that must be filled at lower levels of the organization. Fourth, turning to incentive effects, although the reward of internal promotion may be an important work incentive for insiders, the relatively small pool of internal competitors may make insiders complacent. As we'll discuss in detail in Part 4, insiders may even collude to keep effort levels low. In situations like these, firms may need to reserve the option of hiring an outsider, to keep the competition for promotions sufficiently stiff.

A final difference between hiring from the inside or outside is the fact that compared to insiders who have been in the firm for years, outsiders are a relatively unknown quantity. Put another way, outsiders are *riskier workers* because it is typically harder to predict their performance in the new job. Of course, as we showed in Chapter 13, this riskiness is not necessarily a disadvantage: if the value of finding an employee with star qualities is high in this job, taking a chance on the higher-variance outsider might in fact be the better option. On the other hand, if the costs and disruption associated with replacing an underperforming candidate is high, insiders may be preferred.

Summarizing the preceding discussion, although both internal and external candidates have advantages, a corporate policy of hiring mostly from within, but reserving the option to bring in external candidates if the internal pool is small or weak, seems to combine the best of both worlds. As it turns out, this is also consistent with the available evidence: Whereas most firms hire both internally and externally, evidence consistently shows that *external hires look better on paper than internal hires* for similar positions (Baker, Gibbs, & Holmström, 1994; Chan, 2006; DeVaro, Kauhanen, & Valmari, 2015). Importantly, as we discussed this evidence does *not* imply that external hires are more productive and should be used more often. Instead, it suggests that employers may be optimally *biasing promotion contests against outsiders*—thus, only going for the outsider if that person is much better than the best internal candidate. One possible reason for such a policy, as we've already discussed, is to enhance the work incentives of the company's own workers.

14.2 How Wide a Net to Cast? Searching Narrowly versus Broadly

Suppose you are an employer who has just received 100 applications for an open position. After some preliminary screening that eliminates obviously unqualified applicants, you are left with 20 resumes that all look pretty similar. Learning more about these remaining applicants' quality is now going to take some extra effort, for example, by doing additional research or by calling some or all of them in for an interview. How many should you subject to additional analysis? How many should you interview?

Alternatively, suppose you've just learned that you need to hire a new accountant because an existing worker has quit. You've decided to post an ad (perhaps because your informal search channels haven't yielded any results), and you need to set a closing date for applications. Knowing that, on average, 10 applications come in per week, how far out should you set the deadline? Finally, suppose you are writing the job ad for this position. If you stipulate that the job requires a Certified Public Accountant (CPA) credential, you know you'll get only (say) 10 applications, all with that credential. If you don't specify this, you'll get more than 10 applications, not all of which will be CPAs. Despite their lack of that specific credential, however, some of these other applicants, on closer examination, might prove to be the best person for the job. What should you do?

All the situations just mentioned are examples of cases where an employer must choose between searching narrowly (looking only at a smaller set of candidates, who might be more qualified *in expectation*), and casting a wider net, which can be costly, either because more candidates must be interviewed or because the firm might have to wait longer to fill its vacancy. In this section, we'll study two examples of this *optimal-scope-of-search* problem. Although the examples are specific, they illustrate some broad principles that are useful to keep in mind in designing any recruiting strategy. We'll start with (a simplified version of) the "how many candidates to interview" question.

How Many Applicants Should You Interview?

Let's return to the case of an employer who has narrowed down an applicant pool for a 2-year skilled contract position to 20 resumes that all look pretty similar. It's time to move on to the interview stage, and interviewing all 20 is impractical, in terms of both time and expense involved. A simple way to pose the "how broadly to search" question here is to ask how many of these candidates to bring in for an interview.

To make the problem more concrete, suppose that the *expected net productivity* of each of these 20 candidates over the entire duration of the contract is given by u = \$100,000. Importantly, this \$100,000 is not the worker's total productivity but the difference between what the worker produces and what he or she is paid for the entire contract. You should also think of it as subtracting out any losses due to the fact the candidate might not accept your job offer, or (more important) that he/she might quit before the contract is completed.[10] For brevity, we'll sometimes refer to net productivity as just worker "productivity" or "quality" in the rest of this section, but please bear in mind the qualifications as we go.

Note also that the \$100,000 in the previous paragraph is an average, or *expected value*: Job applicants differ in quality, and we'll assume the firm can

[10] Our simple model assumes the firm picks the "best" worker from the pool of applicants, where "best" means the highest *net* productivity. Because turnover reduces profits earned on a worker, applicants with the highest qualifications may not have the highest net productivity if they are more likely to be bid away by another firm either before or after they are hired.

learn their individual quality by interviewing them. To formalize this idea, let's assume that the *standard deviation* (σ) of net productivity among the candidates in your hiring pool equals \$25,000 in our baseline example.[11] Finally, suppose that the total cost of interviewing a candidate (including the use of existing staff time, checking references, perhaps flying in a candidate, background checks, etc.) is given by c = \$5,000. Assuming that you hire the candidate who emerges as the best from your set of interviews, how many candidates should you interview?[12] Mathematically, the firm's expected profits can be written

$$E(\Pi) = Emax(Q; N) - cN, \tag{14.1}$$

where N is the number of candidates interviewed and $Emax(Q; N)$ is the expected quality (Q) of the best candidate in a sample of N candidates.

Fortunately, for the distribution of productivities we'll use in our example, there's a simple formula for $Emax(Q; N)$:

$$Emax(Q; N) = u + k\,\sigma \log N, \tag{14.2}$$

where k is a constant and log N is the natural logarithm of N.[13]

Figure 14.1 graphs Equation 14.2 for our baseline example (u = \$100,000, c = \$5,000, σ = \$25,000; as well as an alternative, higher value of σ [\$50,000]. All dollar amounts in Figure 14.1 are in tens of thousands). Figure 14.1 has a number of noteworthy features. First, notice that both curves pass through the point (1, u). This reflects the simple fact that if you only interview one candidate, he will automatically be the best one! His expected productivity is just the expected value of a randomly selected worker from your pool of applicants, u. Second, both *Emax* curves increase with N, but at a decreasing rate. This reflects the fact that on average, the *best* worker in a sample of two workers drawn at random from a pool is better than the average in the pool. And of course, the more workers you sample from the pool, the better the best of them is likely to be. Eventually, though, an extra draw from the pool isn't going to help very much: the best worker in a sample of 101 is not likely to be much better than the best in a sample of 100.

---

[11] Standard deviation is a widely used measure of the amount of variability in a population; see any introductory statistics textbook for an explanation. For the productivity distribution in our example, a standard deviation of \$25,000 means that about 92% of the applicants will have net productivity between \$60,000 and \$140,000, with the rest falling outside that range. When σ rises to \$50,000, only 64% of applicants have net productivity between \$60,000 and \$140,000, with the rest falling outside that range.

[12] Importantly, by posing our question this way, we are assuming that our firm is pursuing a *non-sequential*, or "batch" search strategy, where it first chooses how many candidates to interview, *then* picks the best candidate from the pool. An alternative approach is a sequential strategy in which a firm first decides on how good a candidate they want, then keeps accepting and evaluating applications until a satisfactory one arrives. Interestingly, empirical studies of the actual recruiting process (Van Ours & Ridder, 1992, 1993; Van Ommeren & Russo, 2014) are more supportive of the "batch" model we use here, at least when employers use formal methods involving advertised vacancies.

[13] $k = \sqrt{6}/\pi$. For the statistically inclined, Equation 14.2 is the formula for the expected value of the maximum of N independent draws from a Type-1 extreme value, or Gumbel distribution (Gumbel, 1935). We use the Gumbel distribution because it has a very simple formula for the expected value of the maximum. Interestingly, no explicit formula even exists for the normal distribution.

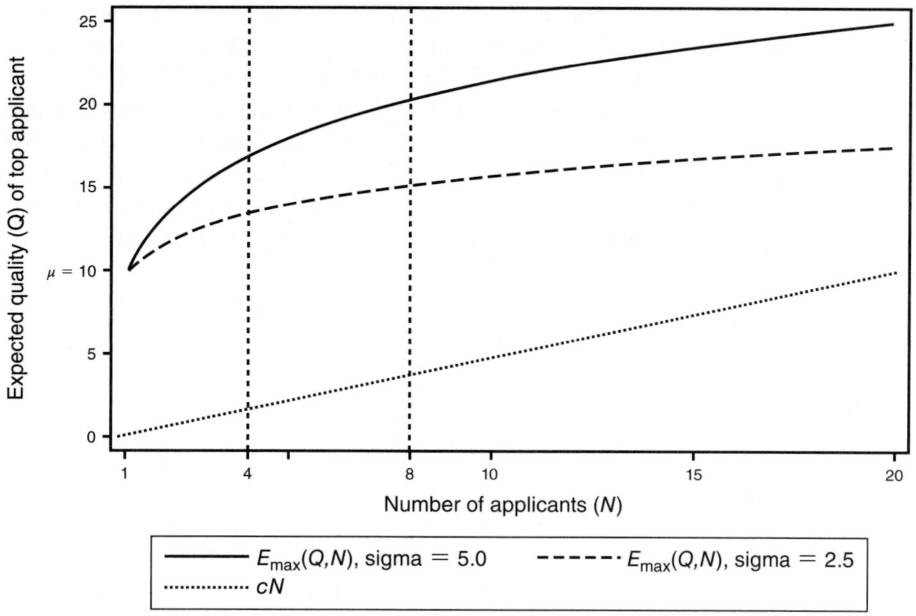

FIGURE 14.1. Expected Quality of the Best Applicant and Screening Costs as a Function of Sample Size

That is why the *Emax* curves in Figure 14.1 increase at a decreasing rate: There are *diminishing returns to* interviewing additional applicants.[14]

Finally, notice that when the standard deviation of applicant quality (σ) rises from \$25,000 to \$50,000, not only is the *Emax* curve higher, it is also steeper. The fact that the curve is higher reflects the principle of option value we discovered in Chapter 13: Greater uncertainty about worker quality is actually a good thing if you have the option of only keeping (or in this case hiring) the best ones! The fact that the curve is *steeper* means that *the marginal benefit of interviewing an extra candidate is higher when there is greater variation in applicant quality.* This makes sense: Extra opportunities to pick from the pool are worth more if the values of the workers in the pool are more different from each other.

Figure 14.1 also shows the total cost of interviewing applicants (*cN*), which is just c = \$5,000 times the number of candidates interviewed. Profits are maximized where the gap between the *Emax* and *cN* curves is greatest; this means the firm should interview four candidates when σ = \$25,000 and eight candidates when σ = \$50,000. By a familiar logic (recall, e.g., Figure 2.1), this is where the slopes of the *Emax* and *cN* curves are equal. Although it is not shown in Figure 14.1 (to reduce clutter), it is also easy to see that raising the cost of interviewing a candidate, *c*, makes the *cN* curve steeper and reduces the optimal number of interviews.

[14] Whereas Equation 14.2 is for the specific case of the Gumbel distribution, the fact that there are diminishing returns to sample size when seeking the maximum is a much more general property.

Finally, using the insights from Figure 14.1, it is interesting to ask how we might expect optimal recruiting strategies to vary with a job's **skill requirements**. Of course, if the only difference between skilled and unskilled jobs is that workers in more demanding jobs produce more revenues for the firm, then Figure 14.1 makes it clear that firms should interview the same number of candidates when recruiting for skilled versus unskilled positions. That's because a higher level of expected productivity (u) just shifts the *Emax* curve up vertically, without changing its slope at any point. This reasoning, however, seems to miss the main point of what we say when a job requires a higher level of skills. Indeed, to clarify the concept of skill requirements, it's helpful to introduce a concept that will come in handy at a number of points in the book.

DEFINITION 14.1 A worker's ability matters more in Job A than in Job B if the output gap between any two workers of different ability is greater in Job A than in Job B.

It's common in personnel economics (and also seems sensible in practice) to assume that jobs with higher skill requirements (i.e., jobs that require higher levels of education, formal training, or experience), as well as jobs that are higher up in a firm's hierarchy, are jobs in which ability matters more. Thus, from the patient's (and hospital's) perspective, the difference between a good and bad doctor probably matters more than the difference between a good and bad nurse, and even more than the difference between a good and bad cafeteria worker. Diagrammatically, we think the relationship between ability and performance in the high- and low-skill jobs looks like Figure 14.2.

According to Figure 14.2, the output gap between two workers, one with high ability A^H and the other with low ability A^L (given by the difference in the slopes of the two curves) is greater in jobs requiring more skill. The key implication of this assumption for the model in Figure 14.1 is that in addition to producing more output on average (u), we also expect jobs with higher skill requirements to have a higher σ: The difference in *output* between two candidates with the same ability gap between them will be greater in the skilled job. It follows that—as long as the cost of evaluating workers, c, doesn't *also* rise too much with skill requirements—we would expect firms to search more broadly (i.e., interview more candidates) when recruiting for skilled rather than unskilled positions. Result 14.6 sums up all these results.

RESULT 14.6 **The Optimal Number of Candidates to Interview**

In a simple optimal recruiting model, the profit-maximizing number of candidates to interview

- decreases when the cost of interviewing a candidate (c) increases;
- increases when the amount of uncertainty about applicant quality (σ) increases; and
- increases when a job's skill level rises, unless c increases very rapidly with skill demands.

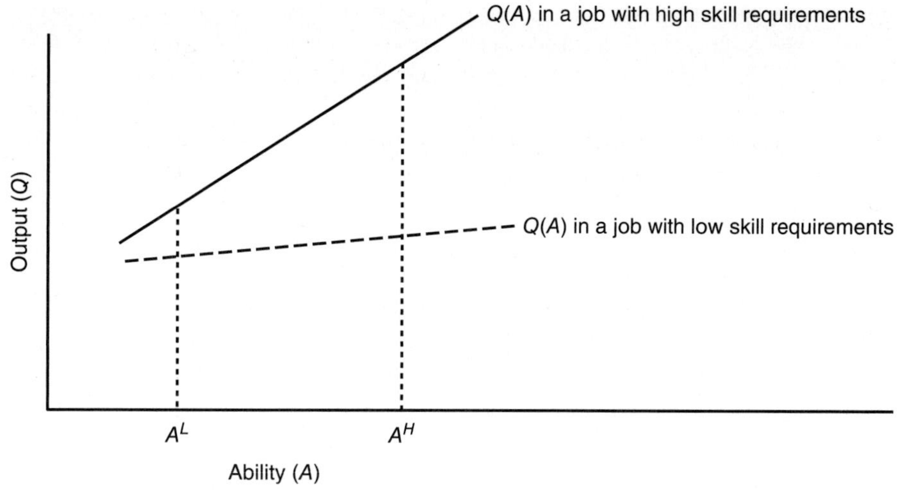

FIGURE 14.2. Output as a Function of Ability in Jobs with High versus Low Skill Requirements When Ability Matters More in Skilled Jobs

If you would like to explore these results in more detail, a downloadable spreadsheet is available on the book's website.[15] The spreadsheet does all the calculations underlying Figure 14.1 explicitly and allows you to experiment with any parameter values you like, not just those used in our example.

How Broadly Should You Target a Job Ad?

Now let's consider a related question that comes up at an earlier stage of the recruiting process: Assuming a firm is advertising for a position, how should it formulate the ad? Imagine, for example, that you need to hire an accountant and are deciding what level of required credentials, if any, to list in the ad. If you stipulate that the job requires a CPA, you know you'll get only 10 applications, all with that credential. If you don't specify this, you'll get more applications, not all of which will be CPAs. Despite their lack of that specific credential, however, some of these other applicants, on closer examination, might prove to be the best person for the job. What should you do?[16]

As it turns out, we can study this question using a simple extension of the optimal-number-of-interviews problem we just studied in Figure 14.1. The answer is worked out in the spreadsheet displayed in Figure 14.3. The *narrow*

[15] As noted previously, all spreadsheets are available at http://www.econ.ucsb.edu/~pjkuhn/Ec152/Spreadsheets/Spreadsheets.htm.

[16] A closely related question to this ad-targeting question is the problem of *where to draw the line* in deciding how many people to *interview*. Suppose, for example, that a recruiter has sorted a batch of resumes into three groups: A (highly promising), B (possibly good), and C (obvious rejects). Then the question of whether to interview only the A group, or both the A and B groups, is mathematically identical to the question studied in this section.

BROAD VERSUS NARROW SEARCH STRATEGIES—SPREADSHEET EXAMPLE		
		Baseline Values
Group A's expected net productvity (u^A):	10	**10**
Group B's expected net productvity (u^B):	8	**8**
Standard deviation of productivity (σ):	2.5	**2.5**
Application processing cost (c):	0.1	**0.1**
Number of applicants in each group (N):	10	**10**
Narrow Search Strategy (consider only the As):		
Expected Net Productivity of the Best Applicant:	14.488	
Total processing costs (cN):	1.000	
Expected Profits:	**13.488**	
Broad Search Strategy (consider both the As and the Bs):		
Expected Net Productivity of the Best Applicant:	15.085	
Total processing costs (cN):	2.000	
Expected Profits:	**13.085**	

FIGURE 14.3. Payoffs to Narrow versus Broad Search Strategies

Note: All financial magnitudes are in tens of thousands of dollars.

search strategy in Figure 14.3 is to invite only the "A" group (CPAs) to apply, then hire the best applicant from that pool of 10 applicants. Using Equation 14.2, the spreadsheet calculates the expected profit from this strategy. The only differences from Figure 14.1 are that we know in advance how many applications we'll get (10), and a change in parameter values: c has been reduced from $5,000 to $1,000 to reflect the fact that the expected cost of processing an application is less than doing an interview.

The *broad* search strategy in Figure 14.3 is *not* to specify in advance that you're only interested in CPAs. In Figure 14.3, we assume this yields 10 additional applicants (the "B" group), bringing the total to 20; but these 10 additional applicants are less qualified on average than the 10 CPAs. In fact, we assume they are on average 20% less qualified, with a net expected revenue of $80,000 instead of $100,000. To calculate the expected value of this strategy, the spreadsheet uses the formula developed by Kuhn and Shen (2013) for the expected value of the best overall candidate drawn from two applicant pools with different average productivities.

Figure 14.3 shows, first of all, that even though the B group is less productive on average than the A's, the expected net productivity of the best applicant is *always* greater in the broad search strategy. (Feel free to verify this yourself by downloading the spreadsheet and experimenting.) This is because there's always a chance that the best applicant is a B, and inviting the B's to apply gives you a chance to find those candidates.[17] In our baseline example, however (where $c = \$1{,}000$), the increase in the expected value of the best candidate from considering the B's doesn't compensate for the extra cost of processing their applications; so the firm's profit-maximizing strategy is to search narrowly—invite only CPAs to apply. This result changes, however, if we make *any one* (or more) of the following changes: cut application processing costs (e.g., to \$500), make the B's more productive on average (say, \$93,000), raise the standard deviation of applicant quality (to about \$34,000 or more), or if we reduce the total number of applications of each type (N) that are available (from 10 to five or fewer).

RESULT 14.7

When to Search Broadly versus Narrowly

Consider the profit-maximizing choice between a targeted search strategy, where a firm considers only candidates with a specific set of credentials, and a broader strategy that also looks at a wider pool whose *expected* productivity is not as high (but might still contain some exceptional candidates). The broader search strategy is more likely to be the profit-maximizing choice when

- the expected productivity gap between the two applicant pools is low;
- the cost of processing additional applications (c) is low;
- the standard deviation of applicant quality (σ) is high;
- applications are scarce overall (N is low); and
- job skill requirements are high (provided c isn't too much higher in skilled jobs).

The intuition behind the first two parts of Result 14.7 is pretty straightforward. Turning to the third, the positive effect of greater uncertainty regarding applicant quality (σ) follows from Result 14.6: In general, firms will want to interview more candidates when σ is high because the marginal return from considering one more candidate is higher. The fact that the "B" candidates are less productive on average than the "A" candidates in this example doesn't change this fact. For reasons discussed earlier, this effect of σ also suggests that firms might be more willing to search broadly for skilled than unskilled jobs, at least if c isn't too much higher in skilled jobs. Finally, the effect of N reflects a fundamental truth about labor markets: *Firms can't be picky about whom they hire when workers are hard to get.* When relatively few applications are available from the worker types a firm thinks are best, it's profit maximizing to broaden one's search strategy to consider additional groups.

[17] Our example assumes that *explicitly* specifying that you want a CPA does not raise the number of CPAs who apply. If that were the case, it would be an extra benefit of the "narrow," targeted search strategy.

Searching Narrowly or Broadly: Explicit Gender Discrimination in Chinese Job Ads

Because advertising that a firm prefers either a male or female job candidate is usually illegal in the United States and other developed countries, you might be surprised to learn that it is a perfectly acceptable and common practice in many countries, including China. For example, statistics compiled by China's Ministry of Human Resources and Social Security from 2011 indicate that employers explicitly designated 36.5% of their vacancies as "male" and 32.0% as "female," with the remainder not having a specific gender preference assigned (Kuhn & Shen, 2013). To understand this phenomenon, Kuhn and Shen collected data from one of China's largest job boards (*Zhaopin.com*) and used Figure 14.3's simple model of broad versus narrow search to study *when* job ads request a specific gender. Interestingly, Kuhn and Shen found that gender-targeted job ads (of *either* type, male or female) were much less common in jobs requiring high levels of skill (such as a college degree, or a high level of experience) than in less-skilled jobs. They speculate that this might be due, in part, to the idea that (individual) *ability matters more* in skilled jobs (higher σ), and to the likelihood that fewer applications are usually available for skilled than unskilled positions (lower N). *Whichever* gender firms might actually prefer for the job, Kuhn and Shen's model suggests that firms should be less willing to confine their search to their preferred gender when the job's skill demands are high. If this is true, the trend toward rising skill requirements may be a potent force discouraging explicit sex discrimination in China and other rapidly industrializing nations.

Chapter Summary

- ☐ One important alternative to a formal external search for new employees is asking existing employees for referrals. Recent evidence (Pallais & Sands, 2016) confirms a long-held belief that referred workers perform better on average than other job applicants. When this is the case, profit-maximizing employers should respond by imposing higher standards on regular job applicants than on referred workers.

- ☐ A second alternative to external search is promoting an internal candidate. Evidence shows that external hires tend to be more qualified than internal hires for similar vacancies. This suggests that most firms bias promotion contests in favor of insiders, perhaps as part of an optimal policy to motivate insiders.

- ☐ The optimal number of candidates to interview to fill a vacancy is higher: as the cost of interviewing falls, as the variance of applicant quality rises, and (most likely) as the job's skill level rises. Broadening the search to worker pools that are less likely to yield the best candidate is optimal under the same conditions. Broadening the search in this way also makes sense when the productivity gap between the pools is low and when applications are scarce overall.

Discussion Questions

1. Some employers give their existing workers a bonus if they recommend someone they know for a job and that person is hired. Is this always a good idea? Under what conditions might it not be a good idea?

2. LinkedIn and similar professional networking sites have greatly increased the size of many workers' informal networks. At the same time, they have made a worker's job performance much more easily available to other employers. Discuss LinkedIn's possible effects on labor markets based on the discussion in Sections 13.2 and 14.1.

3. Result 14.6 says that employers should interview more candidates when the amount of uncertainty regarding applicants' quality (σ) is high. What might be some examples of jobs or worker types where σ is high? Why do we typically assume that σ is higher in jobs requiring higher levels of skill?

4. A frequent recommendation made by human resource departments and employment equity officials is that recruiters should always search broadly, or "cast a wide net" to try to identify good candidates that might not otherwise come to the firm's attention. Interpret this recommendation in the light of the models in Section 14.2.

Suggestions for Further Reading

DeVaro (2016) has a nice discussion of the tradeoffs between internal promotions and external recruitment for higher-level positions. DeVaro and Morita (2013) have a formal model of the decision.

For more recent evidence on employers' use of age- and gender-targeted job ads in China and Mexico, see Kuhn, Shen, and Delgado Helleseter (2014).

All the formal models of recruiting in this chapter assume the employer first assembles a pool of applicants, then picks the best from the pool. Sometimes, however, the employer's search must proceed sequentially because candidates who are passed over at one stage may no longer be available if the employer's continued search doesn't work out. One widely studied way to model this problem—known as search "without recall" (of rejected candidates), where you interview candidates one at a time and have to decide "on the spot"—is known as the secretary problem. For an introduction, see https://en.wikipedia.org/wiki/Secretary_problem.

References

Baker, G., Gibbs, M., Holmström, B. (1994). The internal economics of the firm: Evidence from personnel data. *Quarterly Journal of Economics, 109,* 881–919. doi:10.2307/2118351

Blau, G. (1990). Exploring the mediating mechanisms affecting the relationship of recruitment source to employee performance. *Journal of Vocational Behavior, 37,* 303–320.

Brown, M., Setren, E., & Topa, G. (2016). Do informal referrals lead to better matches? Evidence from a firm's employee referral system. *Journal of Labor Economics, 34,* 161–209.

Burks, S. V., Cowgill, B., Hoffman, M., & Housman, M. (2015). The value of hiring through employee referrals. *Quarterly Journal of Economics, 130,* 805–839.

Castilla, E. J. (2005). Social networks and employee performance in a call center. *American Journal of Sociology, 110,* 1243–1283.

Chan, W. (2006). External recruitment and intrafirm mobility. *Economic Inquiry, 44,* 169–184. doi:10.1093/ei/cbj009

Datcher, L. (1983). The impact of informal networks on quit behavior. *Review of Economics and Statistics, 65,* 491–495.

DeVaro, J., Kauhanen, A., & Valmari, N. (2015, June 26–28). *Internal and external hiring: The role of prior job assignments.* Paper presented at the Fourth SOLE–EALE World Meeting, Montréal, Canada.

DeVaro, J. (2016). Internal hiring or external recruitment? *IZA World of Labor.* Retrieved from https://wol.iza.org/articles/internal-hiring-or-external-recruitment/long

DeVaro, J., & Morita, H. (2013). Internal promotion and external recruitment: A theoretical and empirical analysis. *Journal of Labor Economics, 31,* 227–269.

Fernandez, R. M., & Weinberg, N. (1997). Sifting and sorting: Personal contacts and hiring in a retail bank. *American Sociological Review, 62,* 883–902.

Gee, Laura Katherine, Jason J. Jones and Moira Burke. (2017). Social networks and labor markets: How strong ties relate to job finding on Facebook's social network. *Journal of Labor Economics, 35,* 485–518.

Glitz, A. (2017). Coworker networks in the labour market. *Labour Economics*, *44*, 218–230.

Granovetter, M. S. (1973). The strength of weak ties. *American Journal of Sociology*, *78*(6), 1360–1380.

Granovetter, M. (1995). *Getting a job: A study of contacts and careers.* Chicago: University of Chicago Press.

Gumbel, E. J. (1935). Les valeurs extrêmes des distributions statistiques. *Ann. Inst. Henri Poincaré*, *5*(2), 115–158.

Hensvik, L., & Nordström Skans, O. (2016). Social networks, employee selection and labor market outcomes. *Journal of Labor Economics, 34,* 825–867.

Holzer, H. J. (1987). *Hiring procedures in the firm: Their economic determinants and outcomes* (NBER Working Paper No. 2185). Cambridge, MA: The National Bureau of Economic Research.

Kuhn, P., & Mansour, H. (2014) Is Internet job search still ineffective? *Economic Journal, 124,* 1213–1233.

Kuhn, P., & Shen, K. (2013). Gender discrimination in job ads: Evidence from China. *Quarterly Journal of Economics, 128,* 287–336.

Kuhn, P., Shen, K., & Delgado Helleseter, M. (2014). *Employers' age and gender preferences: Direct evidence from four job boards.* Unpublished manuscript, Department of Economics, University of California, Santa Barbara.

Pallais, A., & Sands, E. G. (2016). Why the referential treatment? Evidence from field experiments on referrals. *Journal of Political Economy*, *124*, 1793–1828.

Petersen, T., Saporta, I., & Seidel, M.-D. L. (2000). Offering a job: Meritocracy and social networks. *American Journal of Sociology, 106,* 763–816.

Simon, C. J., & Warner, J. T. (1992). Matchmaker, matchmaker: The effect of old boy networks on job match quality, earnings, and tenure. *Journal of Labor Economics, 10,* 306–330.

Topa, G. (2011). Labor markets and referrals. *Handbook of Social Economics, 1,* 1193–1221.

Van Ommeren, J., & Russo, G. (2014). Firm Recruitment Behaviour: Sequential or Non-sequential Search? *Oxford Bulletin of Economics and Statistics*, *76*(3), 432–455.

Van Ours, J., & Ridder, G. (1992). Vacancies and the recruitment of new employees. *Journal of Labor Economics, 10,* 138–155.

Van Ours, J., & Ridder, G. (1993). Vacancy durations: Search or selection? *Oxford Bulletin of Economics and Statistics, 55,* 187–198.

15 Choosing from the Pool: Testing, Discretion, and Self-Selection

Once you've identified a set of candidates, what's the best way to choose among them? One option is to conduct one or more formal tests. Employers in the United States use tests extensively, not just in hiring, but also for promotion, initial placements, career counseling, and training eligibility. Tests that are used include performing job-related tasks; tests of physical ability (for jobs such as firefighting and military combat); psychological tests of cognitive ability, honesty, and personality; medical exams; and drug tests. Consulting public databases to view candidates' credit scores and criminal records, or even looking at their Facebook pages, can also be considered a type of test.[1]

15.1 When to Test

Under what conditions does it make sense to test a group of applicants for the presence of a desirable (or undesirable) characteristic? Economic reasoning argues that *testing is likely to be most useful under the following conditions*:

- The test is **cheap to administer**. Importantly, cost considerations include not just out-of-pocket costs to the employer but the disutility of an intrusive test to workers as well.
- The test is **accurate**, where accuracy refers to both Type-I error (the chances of hiring someone who is unqualified) and Type-II error (the chances of overlooking a "star"). Which of these is most important depends—among other things—on the firm's production process. For example, if the costs of

[1] Wozniak (2015), Weaver (2015), Doleac and Hansen (2016), and Baert (2015) study the effects of drug testing, credit score lookups, criminal record tests, and Facebook lookups on the hiring process.

having "one bad apple" are disastrous, an employer is likely to focus more on minimizing Type-I error.[2]

- The test is **valid**. In the psychological testing literature, a test is *valid* if it measures the construct you want it to measure. Thus, for example, if honesty and punctuality are what you need most in your cashiers, a test for intelligence will not be valid.
- Your applicant pool has a **high variance in abilities**. If the workers in your applicant pool are all pretty similar in terms of their likely job performance, testing them may be a waste of money.
- **The worker is likely to stay** with you for a long time. As we learned in our discussion of risky versus safe workers in Chapter 13, worker selection is an *investment* that continues to pay off only as long as the selected worker remains with the firm. Thus, investments in testing are more likely to pay off for long-tenure than short-tenure workers.
- **Firing costs are high**. Again, as we discussed in Chapter 13, hiring mistakes are easy to undo when firing costs are low. When it's hard to dismiss underperforming workers, it's rational for employers to invest more in testing candidates prior to hiring them in the first place.
- When the main **alternatives to testing** discussed at the end of this chapter (monitoring workers, probationary periods, labor market intermediaries, and inducing self-selection) **are not practical** or effective.

Civil Rights Implications of Employee Testing in the United States

In the United States, civil rights law has important implications for companies' uses of testing in personnel decisions. Specifically, regardless of whether the employer *intends* to discriminate or not, using a test that has a *disparate impact* on certain protected groups (including women, men, older workers, people with disabilities, racial and religious groups and veterans) could expose a company to a civil rights lawsuit. While tests with disparate impact are permitted if the employer can prove the tests are job-related, proving this could be costly. The 1991 Civil Rights Act also *prohibits* score adjustments, group-specific cutoffs, and alteration of test scores based on the demographics of the test-takers; thus it rules out any sort of *affirmative action* in the use of test results. Together, these factors may limit the usefulness of some employee testing procedures.

[2] In classical statistics, a Type-I error is the incorrect rejection of a true null hypothesis. In our context, that would be incorrectly rejecting the null hypothesis that the applicant was unqualified.

15.2 Effectiveness of Employee Testing Procedures

Although test accuracy and validity are clearly important, how effective are the most widely used employment screening tests in predicting workers' productivity after they are hired? Perhaps surprisingly, relatively little is known about this question. One barrier to knowledge is that the testing procedures and statistical methods used by many companies who market the tests are *proprietary*. Thus, it's often not possible for an external researcher to replicate the tests and see if they perform as advertised. Second, and related, internal researchers at testing companies have strong incentives to report only the positive results of their tests.

Recently, however, Mitchell Hoffman, Lisa Kahn, and Danielle Li (2015) obtained access to employee performance information from 15 client firms of a company that provides online job testing services.[3] These client firms all employed low-skilled service workers. In this industry, training takes several weeks, and a median new hire only remains on the job for about 3 months. Thus, the companies all place a high value on hiring workers who will end up staying on the job. Accordingly, Hoffman et al. use the length of time employees stay on the job as their main indicator of whether workers were well selected.

Hiring at these 15 firms was done by HR managers, whose *primary duty* was filling available slots. As testing was gradually introduced at the various locations, these managers were given each candidate's test results in a very simple format: The manager was told if the applicant was in the highest-scoring, the middle, or the lowest-scoring group. Importantly, however, managers *didn't have to hire according to these test results*. Instead, managers were free to use their discretion to hire anyone they wanted, just as they had done before testing was introduced at their location.

To measure the effectiveness of this test (or, equivalently, the effectiveness of the managers' *discretion*), the researchers looked at what happened when managers decided to "override" the recommendations of the test. Specifically, managers were said to override the test when they hired a member of the middle-scoring group but passed over a member of the highest-scoring group, or when they picked someone in the lowest-scoring group over someone in one of the other two groups. As it turns out, managers did this quite frequently, and some managers and hiring locations made more such exceptions than others.

After controlling for differences in the composition of different applicant pools, hiring times, and locations, the researchers found that on average, managers who made frequent exceptions to the test's results hired workers who remained on the job for significantly *less* time than other managers. Hoffman et al. (2015) were also able to examine the ultimate performance of workers who were passed over by managers, when (some of) those workers were hired at a later date. They found that workers from the top-scoring group who were passed over in one month but hired at a later date were more productive *than the workers for whom they were originally passed over*. Specifically, they stayed in their jobs about 8% longer than

[3] The job test used by the employers in Hoffman et al.'s (2015) study consists of an online questionnaire about technical skills, personality, cognitive skills, fit for the job, and various job scenarios.

people from the middle-scoring group who were hired before them from the same applicant pool. Members of the highest- and middle-scoring groups who were passed over and eventually hired stayed about 24% and 17% longer, respectively, than members of the lowest-scoring group for whom they had been passed over.

All in all, the performance of job candidates who were hired by managerial discretion that overrode the "hard" evidence of a proprietary hiring test shows that this test *did indeed have value* over and above the discretionary system previously used by the firms in Hoffman et al.'s (2015) study. Indeed, Hoffman et al.'s study suggests that the 15 companies in this study would have done better by eliminating discretion by their HR managers entirely and by replacing this component of their jobs by a simple testing algorithm.

RESULT 15.1

Effects of Managerial Discretion in Hiring: Evidence from Low-Skilled Service Jobs

Hoffman et al.'s (2015) study of hiring for low-skilled service jobs found that experienced HR managers who frequently used their discretion to override the results of a proprietary skills test hired workers who performed *worse* than workers hired by other managers.

Discretion versus Algorithms in an Online Labor Market: Evidence from oDesk

Additional evidence on the advantages of using computer algorithms in the employee selection process comes from John Horton's (2017) field experiment on oDesk. In the experiment, which started in June 2011, oDesk chose a random sample of new employers on the site and sent them suggestions of up to six recommended workers they might wish to consider for their recently posted job opening. These worker recommendations were made using a statistical model based on historical oDesk hiring data. The model suggested workers (a) who had relevant experience to the job in question, (b) appeared to be of high ability, and (c) appeared to be available for work (e.g., based on having recently completed a job on oDesk).

Interestingly, employers who randomly received algorithmically recommended workers for technical jobs fared very well in Horton's (2017) experiment: Their vacancies had a 20% higher fill rate compared to other employers. Interestingly (and in contrast to the effects of co-workers' recommendations we studied in Section 14.1, which do seem to identify higher quality candidates), this was not because the recommended workers' resumes were typically better than the kinds of workers employers recruit "on their own" by scrolling and filtering the worker profiles on oDesk. Instead, the recruiters who did not receive suggested workers *simply had more trouble finding a capable and available worker on the job site.* Once again, Horton's study shows how technical improvements in search and screening algorithms can improve on humans' abilities to find employees who are a good match for a job vacancy.

Hoffman et al.'s (2015) results suggest that relatively standard job tests can outperform human managers in at least some aspects of the employee recruitment process and in certain settings. Of course, Hoffman et al.'s results pertain to a relatively standardized setting involving less-skilled workers who turn over frequently; results in more complex and higher-stakes settings might be quite different.

15.3 Alternatives to Testing

As we've already noted, one alternative to testing is to **monitor and incentivize workers** *after* they've been hired. There actually two senses in which this is true. The first is that screening people to identify their intrinsic motivation or commitment to the organization's mission is less necessary if workers can be motivated by financial incentives after they are hired. For this reason, we might expect screening to be more important in situations where performance is hard to measure. Second, strong incentives directly imply that employers *won't care as much* about a worker's ability or effort after he or she is hired. To see this, consider the hairdresser who leases a chair from a shop-owner and keeps everything he or she makes, that is, who faces a 100% commission rate. In this extreme case, the shop owner won't care as much about whether the hairdresser works very slowly: Identifying the ablest and hardest-working employees is less important when the employees themselves rather than the principal bear the cost of low output.[4] Although this is an extreme case, the logic implies that employee testing is generally less important in work environments characterized by high levels of monetary performance incentives.[5]

A second alternative to explicit testing is a **probationary period**, that is, a fixed-duration "up-or-out" period at the start of the employment relationship where the worker simply tries to do the job. If the worker performs adequately, that worker is retained; otherwise the employment relationship ends. Probationary periods make sense when "bad" workers can't do much damage and when a cheap and relevant test isn't available. Here, the probationary period essentially functions as a kind of "test," because the best way to figure out how good you're likely to be at a job is to just watch you do the job. Indeed, in some less-skilled, low-paying jobs, very little testing takes place, and workers are simply dismissed as soon as it's apparent they're not well suited for the job.

A third alternative to testing is to use **labor market intermediaries**, such as temporary help agencies, headhunters, or other certifying agencies to prescreen your applicants. To the extent that finding and evaluating employees is a specialized skill, this makes some sense: Why should all firms try to handle this

[4] Of course, even in this extreme case of 100% commissions, there are reasons why the shop owner will care about who rents the chair. These include ensuring the shop's reputation for quality and fast service. Still, the impact of the hairdresser's performance on the shop owner's profits is much smaller under a franchise contract than if the hairdresser was hired as an employee.

[5] There's even a third reason why high incentives make testing less necessary: High incentives will cause workers who know they have high abilities to *self-select* into a firm. We have more to say about self-selection as an alternative to testing later in this section.

function internally, when their strengths and core competencies lie elsewhere? Put another way, hiring prescreened workers from a temporary help agency (and keeping them if they work out) amounts to *outsourcing* the recruitment process, an option that has become increasingly common in the U.S. labor market. For example, in 2015, 1.6% of all U.S. workers were employed by temporary help agency firms; a further 3.1% were provided to other firms by a contract firm. Thus, about 4.7% (or almost one in every 20) of all U.S. workers *were not recruited by the firm where they actually work*. This compares to 2.3% of all U.S. workers in both 1995 and 2005 (Katz & Krueger, 2016, Table 2). How does this increasingly important method of employee recruiting actually work?

In a study of U.S. temporary help supply (THS) firms, Autor (2001) found that these firms used an ingenious mix of policies to (a) sort and screen workers more accurately than their client firms, and (b) profit from this activity—from "selling" their workers to client firms at a high markup—before the screened workers were bid away from their new employers into more permanent work arrangements. According to Autor, the temporary help firms' strategy relied on more than just having better tests than were generally available. Instead, a crucial component of their screening strategy was the *free, unrestricted computer skills training* they offered to their workers.[6] This training served two functions. First, it induced *positive self-selection* of workers into THS firms. This is because abler workers (who find it easier to learn new things) will be more attracted to firms that offer free learning opportunities, even at a low starting wage. Second, by *monitoring their trainees' progress during the training process*, the THS firms are able to gather additional information about each worker's potential—information that the worker may not have been aware of. Together, these practices give the THS firm information about workers that is not available to other employers. Thus, THS firms essentially produce and sell information about worker quality to their clients.

Additional evidence that labor market intermediaries can reduce information frictions in labor markets by prescreening workers comes from two recent studies of oDesk—the online labor market we've already encountered in Pallais's (2014) study of inexperienced workers (Section 13.2), Pallais and Sands's (2016) study of referred workers (Section 14.1), and Horton's (2017) study of algorithmic recommendations in this section. Because oDesk employers typically hire workers they have never heard of on another continent, one might expect employers to have a high demand for accurate information on worker quality. Interestingly, despite oDesk's relatively effective review-based reputation system (Wood-Doughty, 2016), Stanton and Thomas (2015) noticed that more than 1,100 small autonomous intermediary organizations, which called themselves *outsourcing agencies*, entered the oDesk market within its first few years.

[6] Because these are general skills, their free provision by THS firms would seem to violate Becker's (1964) famous dictum that general training will always be paid for by workers, not by firms (see Section 19.3). In his article, Autor (2001) carefully explains how THS firms are, however, able to surmount the obstacles to general skill provision by employers that Becker pointed out.

Outsourcing agencies are usually founded by workers who have had a successful oDesk career; these founders then bring additional inexperienced workers into the market as affiliates of their agency. Around 30% of non-U.S. oDesk workers are affiliated with one of these agencies. For example, one fairly typical agency is called qCode, with 17 affiliates at the time of Stanton and Thomas's study. Like most agencies, qCode affiliates know each other offline and share similar backgrounds. In *qCode*'s case, almost all the affiliates are located in the same Siberian city and attended the same local university there. They specialize in technical job tasks. When perusing a worker's profile, oDesk employers can see not only the worker's past evaluations but also see the worker's agency affiliation status plus the average feedback score for all current and past members of that worker's *agency*. In their quantitative analysis, Stanton and Thomas (2015) show that workers affiliated with an agency have substantially higher job-finding probabilities and wages at the beginning of their careers compared to similar workers without an agency affiliation. This advantage declines at later stages of workers' careers, as the quality of nonaffiliated workers who remain on oDesk becomes apparent to employers.

In sum, agencies emerged organically on oDesk to solve an information problem that made it particularly hard for able, inexperienced workers to "be discovered" by the labor market (this is precisely the problem Pallais [2014] identified in Section 13.2). Essentially, like temporary help firms, agencies screen workers and communicate the results to employers. oDesk employers benefit from using agencies because they provide important assurances that inexperienced workers are in fact qualified to do the jobs they are being considered for.

RESULT 15.2 **Labor Market Intermediation**

Autor (2001) argues that temporary help service (THS) firms in the United States successfully screen workers by combining testing with free general skills training. This combination allows THS firms to better identify high-productivity workers than many firms can do on their own and to profit from this information by charging a substantial markup to their clients.

Stanton and Thomas (2015) show that labor market intermediaries in the form of *agencies* organically emerged on oDesk as a way of effectively identifying high-quality inexperienced workers to employers.

15.4 Self-Selection

A final alternative to testing involves **inducing self-selection** by workers, that is, structuring compensation (and other features of the work environment) in such a way that attracts workers with the qualities a firm desires and discourages other types of workers from applying. Importantly, although it seems logical that offering a *more generous* compensation package will attract better applicants, that is not the question we're considering here.[7] Here, we focus on a different question: Keeping the overall level of compensation fixed, are there ways to change the *structure* of pay (or other aspects of the workplace) in a way that induces a desired type of selection to occur?

Inducing self-selection has both advantages and disadvantages relative to testing. Advantages include the fact that—because they don't change the overall generosity of the pay package—many self-selection mechanisms have no direct cost to the employer. Self-selection mechanisms also take advantage of private information that workers may have about themselves that might not be revealed by a costly test. On the downside, self-selection mechanisms can only reveal information that workers already have about themselves. Well-designed tests, on the other hand, can sometimes reveal strengths and weaknesses of which a worker was not even aware.

To illustrate how employers can induce self-selection among job applicants, we use a simple example.[8] Consider a firm that wants to hire workers for two periods of equal length—Periods 1 and 2. If hired by this firm, all workers produce $q = 6$ units of output (net revenue) in each period. (To focus on selection issues, there is no cost of effort.) Every worker's best outside option is given by $v = 3$ in each period. However, because the job takes some time to learn, the firm must pay a training cost of $c = 5$ for every worker who is employed in the first period.[9] Finally, imagine that there are two types of workers who might apply to work at this firm. Once hired in Period 1, Type-A workers will all stay with the firm for Period 2, as long as the firm continues to pay them at least their outside option, v. Type-B workers will leave the firm at the end of Period 1 no matter what. Because workers are costly to train, the firm has an obvious interest in attracting the Type-As and avoiding the Type-Bs. However, *only the workers themselves know their own type*, and we're assuming that there is no practical test that can be administered that will get workers to reveal this information. Can firms design their compensation package in a way that encourages only the A's to apply?

To appreciate the firm's problem, let's imagine that firms have pay policies that tell workers, when they are hired, how much they can expect to earn in both periods they're with the firm. Denote this wage package—essentially the *contract* a firm is offering a worker—by the ordered pair (w_1, w_2). If neither workers nor firms discount the future, the present value of the utility (PVU) experienced by the two worker types, depending on whether they accept the offered contract are the following:

$$\text{Type-A } PVU \text{ if accept} = w_1 + w_2; \tag{15.1}$$

$$\text{Type-A } PVU \text{ if reject} = 2v; \tag{15.2}$$

$$\text{Type-B } PVU \text{ if accept} = w_1 + v; \tag{15.3}$$

$$\text{Type-B } PVU \text{ if reject} = 2v. \tag{15.4}$$

---

[7] We consider the profit-maximizing level of overall pay generosity in detail in Chapter 17.

[8] Our example is a much-simplified version of the one in Salop and Salop (1976).

[9] You can think of c either as an out-of-pocket cost to the employer or just as reflecting a low level of output during the first period when the worker is learning the job. Thus, our model is equivalent to one where there are no training costs ($c = 0$) but output (q) varies over time, that is, where $(q_1, q_2) = (1, 6)$.

This allows us to describe the conditions under which either type of worker will accept any given wage contract, (w_1, w_2), that the employer might offer:

$$\text{Type-As accept if and only if } w_1 + w_2 \geq 2v. \tag{15.5}$$

$$\text{Type-Bs accept if and only if } w_1 \geq v. \tag{15.6}$$

Thus, Type-As' acceptance decision depends on the *total amount they earn* over Periods 1 and 2. Type Bs only care about what they're paid in Period 1. As we'll see, firms who cleverly exploit this fact—that the two worker types *care about different things*—will be able to induce only the types they want, in this case the A's, to apply to their job ads.

What will the firm's profits be from different contracts? Clearly, if a worker of either type rejects the firm's contract, the firm will not employ that worker and will therefore earn zero profits from him or her. If a worker accepts, the resulting present values of profits ($PV\Pi$) are

$$PV\Pi \text{ from a Type-A worker} = (q - c - w_1) + q - w_2 = 2q - w_1 - w_2 - c. \tag{15.7}$$

$$PV\Pi \text{ from a Type-B worker} = q - w_1 - c. \tag{15.8}$$

With these formulas in hand, let's now imagine—for the sake of argument—that the firm has decided to offer only contracts with a *flat wage profile*, that is, contracts in which workers are paid the same in their first and second periods with the firm, $w_1 = w_2 \equiv w$. Now, Type-A workers only accept contracts worth $2w \geq 2v$ (i.e., with $w \geq v$), and the same is true for Type-B workers.[10] If both types of workers can earn $v = 3$ per period at other firms, it follows that *the least generous flat-wage contract that either type of worker will accept pays $w = 3$ in both periods*. What will the firm's profits be in that instance? Assuming there are equal numbers of A and B workers who might apply (or for simplicity, just one of each), combined profit from the two worker types will be

$$PV\Pi = [2q - 2w - c] + [q - w - c] = 3(q - w) - 2c = 3(6 - 3) - 2(5) = -1, \tag{15.9}$$

so the firm loses money. Essentially, the costs of training the Type-Bs who quit after Period 1 outweigh the returns to training the Type-As who stay. Further, because any contract that offers $w < 3$ attracts no workers, and any contract that pays $w > 3$ (thus attracting both worker types) loses even more money, *there is no way a firm can make money using a flat wage contract in our example*. The firm's inability to tell which workers will stay and which will quit makes it impossible to operate.

Now, let's relax our assumption of a flat wage contract, and assume that instead of offering $(w_1, w_2) = (3, 3)$, the firm announces that any worker who stays with the firm will be paid 2 in his first period and 4 in his second period: $(w_1, w_2) = (2, 4)$.

---

[10] For simplicity, this book uses the standard assumption in mechanism design theory, that agents (and principals) accept contracts that offer them the same utility they can get elsewhere. The analysis is essentially unchanged if we assume that only *some* agents accept when they are indifferent; the essential assumption to the current analysis is that no one will take a contract that leaves them strictly worse off than their next best alternative.

Thus, the overall generosity of the wage contract is in this sense unchanged, but compensation has been *backloaded* using a *rising wage profile*. What happens now?

Type-A workers' utility if they accept this contract now equals $w_1 + w_2 = 2 + 4 = 6$. This is the same as under the flat wage contract (3, 3) because the Type As *don't care when they get paid*—either today or tomorrow is O.K. Because these workers receive $2v = 6$ if they reject the firm's contract, they're still indifferent between accepting and rejecting, as before. But Type-B workers' utility if they accept this contract now equals $w_1 + v = 2 + 3 = 5$, which is less than their alternative, $2v = 6$. Thus, Type-Bs will reject this new, rising wage profile. In sum, *by changing the structure of the pay package in a way that keeps it attractive to workers with characteristics the firm values (in this case, permanence) but makes it less attractive to other worker types, the firm can induce voluntary self-selection*: only the Type-As will apply.

What will the firm's profits be now? It won't hire any B's because none apply. For every A that applies, the firm will now earn

$$PV\Pi = 2q - w_1 - w_2 - c = 2(6) - 2 - 4 - 5 = 1. \qquad \textbf{(15.10)}$$

Thus, by structuring its compensation package to induce workers to reveal information that some workers would prefer to keep private (in this case, their intentions to quit), the firm has found a way to operate profitably. Further, because both worker types are just as well off under this new wage contract (2, 4) than they were under the flat profile (3, 3), the new policy is what economists call a *Pareto improvement* over the old: It makes at least one party (in this case, the firm) better off without harming anyone else.[11]

☑ RESULT 15.3

Backloaded Wage Contracts Induce Self-Selection of Low-Turnover Job Applicants

A simple theoretical model based on Salop and Salop (1976) shows that employers who are concerned about worker turnover can induce low-turnover workers to apply, and deter high-turnover workers from applying, by offering employment contracts with low starting wages but with *built-in raises* (as long as the worker remains at the firm). Inducing worker self-selection in this way can improve economic efficiency by making it possible for firms to operate profitably in situations where that might not be possible otherwise.

Rising wage profiles are just one example of how backloaded compensation schemes (which hold back some of the worker's pay till later in the career, contingent on the worker remaining with the firm) can increase employee commitment. Other examples are stock options and pensions with delayed vesting dates.

[11] Indeed, by changing the firm's policy a little bit (e.g., by offering [2, 4.5] instead of [2, 4]), it is possible to share these gains in economic efficiency from inducing self-selection more widely: Now both the firm and the Type-A workers are strictly better off than under the flat wage profile. To see this, and to experiment with other possible pay policies on your own, download the spreadsheet for this problem at http://econ.ucsb.edu/~pjkuhn/Ec152/Spreadsheets/Spreadsheets.htm.

The preceding example has shown how firms can attract applicants with a desirable characteristic (in this case, low expected turnover) by designing a compensation policy that appeals disproportionately to people with that characteristic (in this case, backloaded pay). Whether consciously or not, this is something that firms do all the time; it is an important but sometimes overlooked influence on the applicant pools that firms are able to attract and hence on the types of employees firms are eventually able to hire. For example, we have already shown that firms who offer *incentive pay* attract *abler workers* (the Safelite case—Section 8.2). And as we just argued, firms that subject all new hires to a *probationary up-or-out period* also attract *abler workers*. In our discussion of THSs, we argued that *offering training opportunities* attracts workers who *enjoy learning*. Offering *risky pay* attracts *risk-tolerant* workers (Section 9.4). In Part 4 of the book, we'll argue that paying workers on the basis of relative output (*tournaments*) attracts workers who are *confident* in their abilities and who have a *taste for competition*. In Part 5, we'll argue that shared (team-based) pay attracts underconfident, altruistic workers. Experimental evidence that many of these selection effects can take place simultaneously is provided by Dohmen and Falk (2011). Importantly, even when these aspects of compensation policy were not consciously designed by employers to induce a particular type of self-selection among job applicants, they will affect who applies to any firm.

To sum up our discussion of self-selection, one of its key *advantages* is that it makes use of private information about workers that only those workers themselves might have and that might be hard to elicit in a test. Examples that might be relevant to our turnover example include plans to retire soon, to move to another city, or to go back to school. A related *drawback* is that self-selection relies on workers' perceptions of themselves, which may not be accurate. For example, as we'll see in our analysis of tournaments in Part 4, many people are overconfident in their own abilities; thus, letting people self-select into tournaments can lead to over-entry. In cases like these, a well-designed test may reveal better information (to workers *themselves* as well as firms) than a self-selection mechanism.

Finally, even though we introduced our discussion of self-selection as an *alternative* to testing, it's important to note that these two processes can work together as well. Specifically, *announcing* a testing strategy can *induce* worker self-selection: For example, drug users may choose not to apply to firms who publicize their drug-testing policy.[12] The key, general implication is that firms should not necessarily abandon tests that end up detecting only a small number of "bad apples"! In some cases, the main value of the test is to *change the mix of who chooses to apply* in the first place.

---

[12] Of course, announcing a drug test also allows users to cheat, for example, by temporarily curtailing their drug use. Thus, announcing tests may not be best policy when tests are easy for workers to defeat.

Chapter Summary

- ☐ Job testing can take many forms, including tests of physical ability, psychological tests of cognitive ability, honesty, and personality; medical exams; drug tests; and consulting public databases. Testing is more useful when a test is cheap to administer, accurate, and valid; when candidates have a high variance in abilities; when workers are likely to stay for a long time; and when firing costs are high.

- ☐ Hoffman et al.'s (2015) study shows that a proprietary job test for low-skilled workers outperformed the discretion of HR managers in identifying successful hires.

- ☐ The main alternatives to employee testing are monitoring workers after they're hired, probationary periods, using labor market intermediaries, and inducing self-selection. Inducing self-selection means designing compensation and other features of the workplace in ways that disproportionately attract candidates with a desired quality. For example, backloaded wage contracts are more likely to attract low-turnover workers and may not appeal to workers who expect to quit.

Discussion Questions

1. Some U.S. universities have recently prohibited their admissions staff from consulting applicants' Facebook pages. Referring to the "when to test" criteria in Section 15.3, discuss whether you think this is a good idea for universities.
2. Have you ever been required to take a job test to apply for a job? Referring to the "when to test" criteria in Section 15.3, discuss whether the test you took was likely a useful one for the job.
3. Do you know anyone (including yourself) who has worked for a temporary help services agency (such as Kelly Services or Randstad)? Did they test you and/or train you (or the person you know)? When selling your services to their clients, do you think they had a better idea of your capabilities than the firm would have if it saw your resume? Why or why not? Do you know how much the agency charged for your services? How does that compare with what you were paid, and why do you think the client firm was willing to pay the difference?

Suggestions for Further Reading

For more on how backloaded compensation can affect workers' incentives, see Lazear (1979).

In Section 5.6, we argued that convex reward schemes, like those faced by many salespeople, induce timing gaming. But what types of workers do these schemes attract? Larkin and Leider (2012) show that they attract overconfident workers, which may benefit employers under some conditions.

References

Autor, D. B. (2001). Why do temporary help firms provide free general skills training? *Quarterly Journal of Economics, 116,* 1409–1448.

Baert, S. (2015). *Do they find you on Facebook? Facebook profile picture and hiring chances* (IZA Discussion Paper No. 9584). Bonn, Germany: Institute for the Study of Labor.

Becker, G. S. (1964). *Human capital.* Chicago: University of Chicago Press.

Dohmen, T., & Falk, A. (2011). Performance pay and multidimensional sorting: Productivity, preferences, and gender. *American Economic Review, 101,* 556–590.

Doleac, J. L., & Hansen, B. (2016). *Does "ban the box" help or hurt low-skilled workers? Statistical discrimination and employment outcomes when criminal histories are hidden* (NBER Working Paper No. 22469). Cambridge, MA: The National Bureau of Economic Research.

Hoffman, M., Kahn, L. B., & Li, D. (2015). *Discretion in hiring* (NBER Working Paper No. 21709). Cambridge, MA: The National Bureau of Economic Research.

Horton, J. J. (2017). The effects of algorithmic labor market recommendations: evidence from a field experiment. *Journal of Labor Economics, 35*(2), 345–385.

Katz, L. F., & Krueger, A. B. (2016). *The rise and nature of alternative work arrangements in the United States, 1995–2015* (NBER Working Paper No. 22667). Cambridge, MA: The National Bureau of Economic Research.

Larkin, I., & Leider, S. (2012). Incentive schemes, sorting and behavioral biases of employees: Experimental evidence. *American Economic Journal: Microeconomics, 4,* 184–214.

Lazear, E. P. (1979). Why is there mandatory retirement? *Journal of Political Economy, 87,* 1261–1284.

Pallais, A. (2014). Inefficient hiring in entry-level labor markets. *American Economic Review, 104,* 3565–3599.

Pallais, A., & Sands, E. G. (2016). Why the referential treatment? Evidence from field experiments on referrals. *Journal of Political Economy, 124,* 1793–1828.

Salop, J., & Salop, S. (1976). Self-selection and turnover in the labor market. *Quarterly Journal of Economics, 90,* 619–627.

Stanton, C., & Thomas, C. (2015). Landing the first job: The value of intermediaries in online hiring. *Review of Economic Studies, 83*(2), 810–854.

Wozniak, A. (2015). Discrimination and the effects of drug testing on black employment. *Review of Economics and Statistics, 97(3), 548–566.*

Weaver, A. (2015). Is Credit Status a Good Signal of Productivity? *Industrial and Labor Relations Review, 68*(4), 742–770.

Wood-Doughty, A. (2016). *Do employers learn from public, subjective, performance reviews?* Unpublished manuscript, Department of Economics, University of California, Santa Barbara.

16 Avoiding Bias

The idea that employees should be hired, promoted, paid, and fired based on their performance—and not on their race, sex, caste, religion, or ethnicity—seems like a simple rule that happily marries the employer's self-interest with morality: "Hiring the best" without regard to these criteria seems like the most profitable strategy and also seems ethically the "right" thing to do. Unfortunately, things are not always quite so simple. In practice, defining and identifying the "best" candidate can be a murky exercise in which poor information and unconscious biases can affect the judgment even when evaluators are trying their very best to be objective. And situations can arise where the profitable thing to do is not necessarily the "right" thing. In this chapter, we'll define *discrimination* and provide some evidence that it does indeed characterize the hiring process in real firms. We then discuss the various possible *causes* of discrimination, as well as its *effects* on firms, on workers, and on social welfare. We close with a brief discussion of how employers can profitably avoid the most harmful forms of discrimination in the hiring and employee-evaluation process.

DEFINITION 16.1 Employment **discrimination** refers to the use of legally prohibited or morally objectionable criteria in any decision affecting employees, including hiring, promotion, wage setting, and layoffs.

In the United States, race, color, religion, national origin, age, sex, pregnancy, disability, and veteran status are the main criteria whose use in employee evaluation is either prohibited or strictly limited by law.

Even in situations where the use of these criteria (and of some others, like sexual orientation and obesity) is not legally prohibited, using them may be viewed by customers, investors, employees, and others as unfair or morally objectionable.

Notably, with the possible exceptions of religion, pregnancy, and veteran status, the prohibited criteria for hiring in the U.S. are *ascriptive* characteristics, in the sense that they are personal characteristics we are born with and cannot change. In part, this may reflect a shared value that it is fair to judge people on the basis of their *achievements* (such as education, training, and experience) but not on the basis of immutable factors that are outside their control.

16.1 Detecting Discrimination in Hiring

How common is it for employers to take race or sex *into account* in deciding whether to hire someone? To convincingly demonstrate that an employer is basing personnel decisions on these legally "protected" characteristics (rather than on the multitude of other qualifications and abilities that could be correlated with them), we should ideally compare employers' responses to candidates who are *identical in all other respects* except their race or sex. Although this sounds impossible, it is in fact the basis of one of the most widely used tools for measuring discrimination in recruiting: the *resume audit study*. In a resume audit study, researchers randomly submit fictitious resumes that are identical except for a prohibited characteristic to a large sample of job ads, and keep track of the number of callbacks received by the various resumes.[1]

Probably the best known resume audit study is Bertrand and Mullainathan's (2004) study of racial discrimination in hiring in the United States. Bertrand and Mullainathan sent fictitious resumes to help-wanted ads for white-collar jobs (specifically sales, administrative support, clerical services, and customer services) in Boston and Chicago newspapers. To manipulate the applicants' perceived race, resumes were randomly assigned African American names (such as Lakisha and Jamal) or white-sounding ones (like Emily and Greg).[2] "white" names received 50% more callbacks for interviews *than identical resumes* with a "black" name. Notably, the authors were able to show that this difference did not result from a tendency of employers to infer an applicant's

[1] Clearly, resume audit studies can only detect discrimination in *callbacks*, which are not the same as hires or job offers. To study job offers, researchers have conducted *interview audits* where pairs of actors (of different races or sexes) who are trained to behave identically apply in person for jobs, for housing, or attempt to buy a car. For example, Neumark (1996) sent young men and women to apply in person for restaurant jobs. Another way to study discrimination in recruiting is known as a Goldberg Paradigm experiment (Goldberg, 1968). Here, experimental subjects (usually college students or HR professionals) are asked to rate candidates for a job they know is fictitious. See Dover, Major, and Kaiser (2016) for an interesting recent application.

[2] To decide on which names are uniquely African American and which are uniquely white, the authors used name frequency data calculated from birth certificates to identify the most distinctive black and white names. To ensure that these names were widely *perceived* as either white or black, the authors then asked a group of survey respondents to guess the race associated with them. In case you are interested, the five most "white-sounding" male names that emerged from this process were Brad, Greg, Jay, Todd, and Brett. The five most "black-sounding" male names were Jermaine, Darrell, Jamal, Kareem, and Hakim; all are highly predictive of perceived race. Bertrand and Mullainathan's (2004) Table A1 has a complete list of all the names they used, including the female names.

social class from the name. This large racial gap in callbacks did not vary across occupation, industry, and employer size.

Resume audit studies of racial and ethnic employment discrimination have now been conducted in wide variety of settings. For example, Peru, Galarza and Yamada (2014) compare whites to indigenous applicants. Maurer-Fazio (2012) compares Han, Mongolian, and Tibetan applicants in China; whereas Booth, Leigh, and Varganova (2011) compare whites to Chinese in Australia. Baert, Cockx, Gheyle, and Vandamme (2015) compare immigrants to non-immigrants in Belgium; and Oreopoulos (2011) studies Canadian employers' responses to Asian-sounding names. Other applicant characteristics that have been studied using resume audits include age (Neumark, Burn, & Button, 2015), sexual orientation (Ahmed, Andersson, & Hammarstedt, 2013), caste and religion (Banerjee, Bertrand, Datta, & Mullainathan, 2009), sex (Carlsson, 2011), and motherhood (Petit, 2007). Audit-type studies have also detected racial and ethnic discrimination in non-labor-market contexts, including housing markets (Ewens, Tomlin, & Wang, 2014), the used-car market (Zussman, 2013), peer-to-peer lending (Pope & Sydnor, 2011), rides on Uber and Lyft (Ge, Knittel, MacKenzie, & Zoepf, 2016), and professors' attention to students (Milkman, Akinola, & Chugh, 2012).

☑ RESULT 16.1

Evidence of Discrimination in Hiring

Bertrand and Mullainathan's (2004) resume audit study of racial discrimination in the United States showed that resumes with distinctively white names received 50% more callbacks for interviews than identical resumes with distinctively black names.

Large callback gaps have also been detected by resume audit studies in a number of other contexts, for example, against Asian-sounding names in Canada, homosexuals in Sweden, and older women in the United States.

16.2 Why Does Discrimination Occur?

Discrimination in hiring (in the sense defined previously) can result from the *conscious* decisions of recruiters for at least four different reasons.[3] One of the first to be discussed in the economics literature is the **tastes or preferences of employer recruiters** themselves. For example, the person doing the hiring may prefer to interact with members of her or his own ethnic group, or may have a distaste for employing members of another group. Preferences of this

[3] The causes of discrimination discussed in this section refer to reasons why an employer might prefer to hire one type of worker over another *for a job that has a fixed wage attached to it.* For a discussion of discrimination in wage setting, see Section 17.2.

type have been openly expressed in a number of countries and periods of time and could help explain some of the large effects detected by Bertrand and Mullainathan (2004) during a period when it was no longer socially acceptable to express such preferences.[4] Preferences that favor in-group members over out-group members may be closely connected with humans' propensity to quickly and easily *identify* with a group, which we discuss further in Section 25.3.

A second possibility is the **tastes or preferences of the firm's customers or employees.** For example, even an unbiased recruiter or firm owner may be reluctant to hire a low-caste worker for sales jobs in India if the owner reasonably expects the customers to be averse to interacting with low-caste salespeople. Similarly (although largely absent today) there was considerable evidence of fan discrimination in favor of white players in the National Basketball Association in the 1980s: Teams that hired white players over better-performing black players earned higher fan revenues (Kahn, 2009). Turning to co-worker discrimination, a rational employer may be reluctant to hire an openly gay worker if the employer expects this to cause serious disruption among the existing workers. Together, the tastes of owners, customers, and co-workers are key elements of Gary Becker's (1971) famous theory of discrimination, which we've already encountered in Section 12.2.

A third possibility is **unbiased employer beliefs** about the relative productivities of two groups. For example, it is common for Chinese electronics producers to actively prefer (and sometimes explicitly request) women as assembly workers. This is because women on average have better fine motor skills than men (Baker & Cornelson, 2016). In these cases, a publicly observable characteristic (such as race, age, or sex) serves as an easy but imprecise substitute for a *test* that measures a skill the employer values. (Of course, in some of these cases, it may be more effective for the employer to actually test applicants directly for the skills they need rather than using demographics as a proxy for them.) In any case, employers who base hiring decisions on, say, race, sex, or age as a signal of a skill or productive attribute that is correlated with race, sex, or age are engaging in what economists call *statistical discrimination*.

[4] Although it is hard to measure preferences that people are reluctant to reveal publicly, it is not impossible. One useful approach is *list randomization* in attitude surveys. Here, survey researchers give respondents a list of, say, four noncontroversial statements, like "I had cereal for breakfast" or "I like hot dogs" and ask the subjects to report only the *number* of these statements they agreed with. The researchers then give a different, randomly selected set of subjects the same list, plus one controversial question like "I would be upset if an African American family moved next door," and ask those persons only for the total number of statements they agreed with. By comparing the number of agreements between the two random samples, researchers can determine how many people agree with the controversial statement. Importantly, in this approach, *no one* (including the interviewer) can know how a given subject answered the controversial statement, thus reducing subjects' reluctance to express preferences they fear would be disapproved of. List randomization has demonstrated high levels of conscious racial discrimination (Kuklinski, Cobb, & Gilens, 1997) and anti-gay sentiment (Coffman, Coffman, & Marzilli Ericson, 2016) in the United States.

DEFINITION 16.2 **Statistical discrimination** is a preference for hiring an individual from one group over an individual from another group, which is based on a statistically unbiased belief that the *average* productivities of the two groups are different for the job in question.

For example, if it is objectively true that women, on average, have better fine motor skills than men, a company that decides to recruit only women for fine assembly jobs without evaluating the fine motor skills of *individual* candidates is engaging in statistical discrimination.

One way to test for whether employers are engaging in statistical discrimination is to randomly include more detailed information about qualifications an employer might value on resumes in resume audit studies. For example, Bertrand and Mullainathan (2004) created two types of resumes for each race in their study: Higher quality resumes had more labor market experience, fewer holes in their employment history, more certifications and honors, and were more likely to have an email address. If employers are *inferring* these higher qualifications when they see a white name on a resume, employers' tendency to favor white resumes over black ones should be smaller when both the black and white resumes indicate that the worker has those qualifications. In Bertrand and Mullainathan's study, that was not the case: Employers' tendency to favor white names was actually somewhat higher among high-quality resumes, suggesting that statistical discrimination was not the employers' main motive for discriminating in this case. Importantly, though, Bertrand and Mullainathan's test only reveals whether employers are inferring the characteristics the researcher has added to the resumes—not other, less quantifiable skills—from the applicant's race or gender.

What aspects of the resume-screening process might explain *why* resumes with black-sounding names get fewer callbacks in studies like Bertrand and Mullainathan's (2004)? In an ingenious study that sheds light on how employers treat resumes from different groups, Bartoš, Bauer, Chytilová, and Matějka (2016) created personal websites and resumes for fictitious applicants and submitted job applications containing hyperlinks to these resumes in both Germany and the Czech Republic. This allowed the researchers to track the exact number of visitors to the (fictitious) applicants' personal profiles and to measure the share of employers who decided to actually read the applicant's resume. They found that employers were less likely to open and read the resumes of applicants with minority-sounding names (Turkish in Germany; Asian and Roma in the Czech Republic) in both countries. The fact that *minorities' resumes are less likely to be read* has important implications for the *self-fulfilling* nature of statistical discrimination, which we discuss in more detail following. Essentially, if a worker's application isn't even read, having high qualifications won't help. Thus, workers who expect to be overlooked on the basis of their ethnicity in the hiring process have little incentive to work hard to improve their qualifications.[5]

Fourth, employers could be making personnel decisions based on **biased beliefs** (where "biased" is used in the statistical sense). In a statistical sense, beliefs are biased when the employer's estimate of the *average* ability in a group differs from the group's true average ability. Historically, common wisdom about the types of jobs (say) women are capable of performing has been quite different from what we know today, suggesting that earlier beliefs were inaccurate. And in Chapter 23, we'll present some evidence that most people (and especially men) systematically overestimate their *own* ability relative to others. These beliefs are persistent and only partially responsive to contradictory evidence. Thus, biased (or ill-informed) beliefs about the relative capabilities of different groups could also affect some recruiting decisions.

In addition to these four reasons for *consciously* taking race, gender, or other "prohibited" characteristics into account, unconscious factors can also affect recruiters' decisions, especially in cases where many decisions must be made quickly, and when precise and reliable predictors of job performance are not available. One way to measure such unconscious factors is called the *Implicit Association Test* (IAT; Greenwald, McGhee, & Schwartz, 1998). This computer-based test measures the strength of a person's unconscious association between two broad concepts (such as being "good" or "bad" on the one hand, and Republican or Democrat on the other). The test is based on the fact that people can categorize objects or concepts more quickly when the concepts feel "naturally" associated to them. These tests routinely reveal, for example, that it's more natural for both men and women to associate men with careers and women with families than the other way around.

Evidence that such implicit associations may matter in the workplace includes a recent study of NBA referees by Joseph Price and Justin Wolfers (2010). These referees make split-second decisions, where unconscious factors can plausibly play a larger role. Based on a very large sample, the authors found that more personal fouls are awarded against players when they are officiated by an opposite-race officiating crew than when they are officiated by an own-race crew. In fact, these biases are large enough to affect the outcome of an appreciable number of basketball games. In a more typical employment context, Dan-Olof Rooth (2010) finds that Swedish recruiters who exhibit unconscious attitudes and stereotypes toward Arab-Muslim men according to the IAT are substantially less likely to invite those men to interviews than recruiters without such unconscious stereotypes. Interestingly, the recruiters who exhibited the strongest unconscious

---

[5] Even though it may have undesirable consequences for the labor market as a whole, employers' treatment of minority resumes in Bartoš et al.'s (2016) experiment may be a rational allocation of employers' scarce attention. This interpretation stems from Bartoš et al.'s results on *apartment rental* applications, where they found that landlords actually spent *more* effort acquiring additional information about minority applicants. This makes sense because only a minority of candidates are selected in a typical hiring situation, whereas only a minority of applicants are *rejected* in a typical apartment rental. Thus, a rational *employer* will focus attention only on the candidates that employer expects to be the best, while a rational *landlord* should scrutinize the candidates he or she expects to be the worst most closely.

biases were frequently not the ones who were aware of them, or who were willing to openly report a bias to a survey researcher. In other words, even recruiters who do not wish to take race or gender into account often do so unconsciously.

RESULT 16.2

Causes of Discrimination in Hiring

Discrimination (as defined previously and as measured in resume audit studies) can result from at least four different types of conscious behaviors: (1) employer or recruiter tastes; (2) co-worker or customer tastes; (3) unbiased beliefs of employers/recruiters; and (4) biased beliefs of employers/recruiters. Of these, (1) and (2) are commonly called *taste-based discrimination*, and (3) is called *statistical discrimination.*

Discrimination can also result from unconscious behaviors, especially in split-second decisions. Unconscious tendencies to favor one group over another can be detected by the Implicit Association Test (IAT) and are sometimes called *implicit discrimination.* Price and Wolfers (2010) provide convincing evidence of implicit racial discrimination by NBA referees; and Rooth (2010) connects IAT-based measures of unconscious attitudes toward Arab-Muslim men to the decisions of Swedish recruiters.

16.3 Consequences of Discrimination

Having defined employment discrimination and discussed its possible causes, we now turn to its consequences: What are the likely effects of considering race, sex, and other "prohibited" characteristics in HR decisions on profits, worker well-being, fairness, and economic efficiency? As you might expect, the consequences depend a lot on the underlying causes of the discriminatory behavior: Is it driven by conscious distastes, unbiased beliefs, or unconscious associations? We consider the various causes in turn.

First, almost by definition, discrimination that arises from **recruiters' tastes**, from **biased beliefs**, or from **unconscious factors** is probably bad for profits in most cases. Because these criteria involve selecting workers for reasons other than the workers' qualifications and likely job performance, recruiters who use them will hire a less-qualified workforce than recruiters who don't. As Becker (1971) pointed out, firms who engage in these practices will underperform and should eventually be forced out of competitive markets. Thus, market forces should operate to eliminate at least certain forms of discrimination. Not surprisingly, many high-performing firms can and do try hard to limit the effects of these factors on their recruiting practices.

Unfortunately, Becker's (1971) "market forces" argument does not apply to discrimination that is caused by **customer or co-worker tastes**. Building owners who indulge their white customers' tastes not to have black neighbors will likely earn higher, not lower, profits than owners who refuse to discriminate. In the 1950s and 60s, owners of Southern textile mills who tried to hire black workers risked considerable disruption, morale problems, and even sabotage from their exclusively white workforces (Heckman & Payner, 1989). And in the 1980s, NBA teams that did not cater to their fans' preferences for white players paid a price in terms of attendance. In these cases, business owners who would personally prefer not to discriminate face a trade-off between doing "the right thing" and maximizing their own profits.

Finally, what are the consequences of **statistical discrimination** for firms and workers? In some cases, like our Chinese electronics example, statistical discrimination could benefit both firms and workers by more efficiently matching workers to jobs where they are more productive.[6] A trivial example would be a case where a woman is needed to play a female role in a movie. More generally, as long as there are plenty of well-paying jobs available for all types of workers, it may be beneficial to both firms and workers to have employers use gender or other ascriptive characteristics as a low-cost way to allocate people to different tasks.

The idea that statistical discrimination could benefit both firms and workers comes, however, with an important *caveat* that relates to our discussion of employee training in Chapter 19: Statistical discrimination blunts workers' incentives to invest in skills. More specifically, making personnel decisions based on ascriptive characteristics that are *correlated with skills*, rather than based *on the skills themselves*, reduces workers' incentives to invest in skills: If I, as a worker, know I will be judged on the basis of average skills of the group I belong to rather than on my personal skills, I have no incentive to work hard to better myself. Such reductions in investment can hurt both workers and employers. Importantly, this reasoning applies both to workers who are *favored* by discriminatory policies and to those who are disfavored: The boss's nephew who is guaranteed a promotion regardless of how qualified he is has reduced incentives to qualify himself, just like the female or minority worker who knows she'll never get the promotion. In sum, even though it may be tempting and profitable in the short run to make personnel decisions based on ascriptive characteristics, in many cases there are good long-run reasons for firms to avoid that "shortcut" and pay the extra costs to evaluate workers' individual skills for hiring and promotion decisions.

Another way of expressing this idea is that discrimination against a group, even if it is purely statistically motivated, may be a *self-fulfilling prophecy* in the sense that it induces members of the group to *rationally* fulfill employers' low expectations by choosing not to invest in skills.[7]

---

[6] Because there may in fact be a quick and easy way to test for manual dexterity that is directly relevant to assembly jobs—just hire the worker for a trial period and see how he or she performs!—statistical discrimination may not be the best explanation for why gender is used in this context. Monopsonistic wage discrimination (see Section 17.2) may be a better explanation, or even a peculiar form of co-worker discrimination: For a variety of reasons (some of them cultural), it may be easier to manage workplaces that are homogeneous in terms of gender.

[7] For models of self-reinforcing employer beliefs about groups of workers, see Arrow (1973), Lundberg and Startz (1983), or Coate and Loury (1993). Notably, for these models to explain persistent wage and productivity gaps between groups, they must give rise to a situation where employers are motivated to *evaluate* members of one group (so they can distinguish productive from unproductive members of that group), while not evaluating the other. Only that way will the former group retain its incentives to invest in skills. (If neither group is evaluated, neither will invest.)

Discrimination as a Self-Fulfilling Prophecy: Evidence from French Grocery Stores and Israeli Schools

In a field study of cashiers in a French grocery store chain, Glover, Pallais, and Pariente (2017) measured managers' bias against African-origin workers using the Implicit Association Test. Using the fact that cashiers' work schedules were assigned independently of cashiers' origins and managers' characteristics, Glover et al. found that the implicit attitudes of the manager affected the job performance of his or her supervisees: minority cashiers, but not majority cashiers, were absent more often, spent less time at work, scanned items more slowly, and took more time between customers when they were assigned to a biased manager. In contrast, when working with an unbiased manager, minorities performed significantly better than majority workers. Thus, discrimination can *cause* poor employee performance, not just *reflect* the employer's expectation of poor performance!

In a similar vein but very different context, Lavy and Sand (2015) estimated the effect of Tel-Aviv primary school teachers' gender biases on boys' and girls' academic achievements later in life. They measured teachers' gender biases by comparing their average marking of boys' and girls' in a classroom exam to the respective means in a blind national exam marked anonymously and took advantage of the fact that these teachers and students were randomly assigned to classes within a given grade and a primary school. According to Lavy and Sand, being assigned to a more gender-biased teacher in primary school affected students' subject choices and course performance in high school, with potential implications for their college majors and careers. Again, encountering discrimination at one point in time *caused* reduced achievement at a later date.

In addition to the "economic" mechanism of reduced investments in training, discrimination may affect worker productivity through other, more "psychological" mechanisms. These include *stereotype threat effects* (Steele & Aronson, 1995), *Pygmalion effects* (Rosenthal & Jacobson, 1968), and *Golem effects*. The stereotype threat effect refers to evidence that *simply being perceived by someone else* through the lens of a negative stereotype can disrupt cognitive performance, for example, by creating a sense of pressure or anxiety. For example, Steele and Aronson's (1995) seminal lab experiment showed that simply asking test takers to indicate their race before taking a cognitive skills test significantly undermines African Americans' performance. This negative effect was much weaker when the researchers convinced the test takers that the test was not being used to measure their abilities, suggesting that a fear of being judged (or fulfilling a racial stereotype) was the cause of African Americans' reduced performance. Closely related, Pygmalion effects (Rosenthal & Jacobson, 1968) refer to the positive effect of a leader's high expectations on a group's performance; and Golem effects to the negative effect of low expectations (Reynolds, 2007). Both of these have been extensively studied by psychologists, most often in the classroom. All three effects, however, are channels where evidence has shown that expectations of a group's behavior can be self-fulfilling, thus either creating or reinforcing pre-existing performance gaps. These effects can be significant costs of statistical discrimination.

☑ RESULT 16.3

Consequences of Discrimination in Hiring

The likely consequences of discrimination for firms and workers depend on its causes. Almost by definition, discrimination that is based on *firm or recruiter tastes, biased beliefs*, or *unconscious attitudes* is likely to reduce profits and to hurt the group that is discriminated against.

Discrimination that is based on *customer or co-worker tastes*, however, likely raises profits, at least in the short run. Here, employers may face an ethical dilemma between rejecting customer or co-worker tastes the employer may find objectionable and making more money.

Engaging in *statistical discrimination* (i.e., discrimination based on *unbiased beliefs*) has more complex consequences. In the short term, it raises profits. However, in the longer term, it can be harmful both to firms engaging in it and to society as a whole. This is because making hiring and other HR decisions on the basis of a person's membership in a group rather than that person's individual qualifications reduces the incentives of both the favored and the unfavored groups to improve their qualifications.

16.4 Reducing Bias in Employee Evaluation

As we argued previously, reducing or eliminating certain types of bias from the employee evaluation process can be both ethically desirable *and* beneficial to employers' short-run or longer run profits. What are some HR policy options for reducing such biases, and what do we currently know about their effectiveness? In this section, we'll discuss three main options: changing the *recruiters' decision environment*, *monitoring recruiters*, and *"blind" recruiting strategies*.

Anyone who has been involved in the hiring process knows that even with the best digital applicant tracking systems to prescreen and organize applications, recruiting is often hard work. Sifting through large numbers of resumes that differ in many ways, weighing all candidates' strengths and weaknesses, and finally coming up with a short list, especially when you're subject to competing demands on your time, makes it very tempting to use any sort of shortcut, including relying on stereotypes or emotional "gut reactions," to make a quick and easy decision. Psychologists have formalized this idea of using shortcuts to make quick decisions as the difference between *System 1 and System 2 cognitive functioning* (Stanovich & West, 2000). System 1 decision-making refers to our intuitive system, which is typically fast, automatic, effortless, implicit, and emotional. System 2 refers to reasoning that is slower, conscious, effortful, explicit, and logical. In general, System 2 decisions tend to be of higher quality (e.g., from the point of view of identifying the best-performing candidate) but require the use of more time and cognitive resources.

Under what conditions are people more likely to make thoughtful, System 2, decisions? Perhaps unsurprisingly, a large body of psychological research on *judges*' objectivity has shown that circumstances that are tiring (e.g., long hours, fatigue), stressful (e.g., heavy, backlogged, or very diverse caseloads; loud construction noise; threats to physical safety; popular or political pressure about a particular decision; emergency or crisis situations), can adversely affect decision quality (Eells & Showalter, 1994; Hartley & Adams, 1974; Keinan, 1987). One important way in which decisions are compromised in these situations is via an increased reliance on stereotypes. Similar experimental results on "shooter bias" (discerning whether a shooter in a videogame is holding a gun or a nonthreatening object), finds that laboratory subjects' disproportionate tendency to shoot black avatars is exacerbated when the subjects are tired (Ma et al., 2013), rushed (Payne, 2006), or cannot see well (Payne, Shimizu, & Jacoby, 2005).

Overall, considerable evidence on decision-making in multiple contexts suggests that recruiters are likely to be less influenced by unconscious biases (like those revealed by the IAT) or to use stereotypes to take conscious shortcuts when they are under less time pressure and less stressed. Thus, a simple and often-overlooked way to reduce bias in hiring is simply to change the **decision environment** to give recruiters access to the time and quiet needed to make System 2 instead of System 1 decisions.

Did Your Judge Just Have Lunch? Then You Can Get Out of Jail! Evidence of Decision Environment Effects on Israeli Parole Judges

The job of a parole judge is to decide whether a prisoner's behavior has been good enough to warrant his supervised release into the community ("parole"). In this situation, the "easy" decision for a judge is just to refuse parole regardless of the merits of the prisoner's case: Judges can get into big trouble for releasing dangerous offenders, but judges experience essentially no negative consequences for keeping a well-behaved prisoner in jail. Although we would like to believe that "what a judge had for breakfast" should not affect how carefully he decides his cases, a fascinating recent study of the behavior of eight highly experienced Israeli parole judges by Danziger, Levav, and Avnaim-Pesso (2011) suggests otherwise.

Every day, each of these judges considers between 14 and 35 cases, spending an average of 6 min on each decision. The decisions come to the judges in essentially random order, over which the judges have no control. The judges' workday is divided into three sessions, with food breaks in between the sessions. In cases heard during the first 15 min of each session, the judges granted parole about 65% of the time. Remarkably, as the judges made more and more decisions within a session, the parole rate fell steadily, dropping almost to zero in the last 15 min before each scheduled food break.

Danziger et al. (2011) argue that these striking trends occur because repeated decision-making drains the judges' mental resources, tempting them to make the easiest, least-informed, or "default" choice of denying parole. If the quality of decisions made by experienced judges is so strongly influenced by how recently they had a meal break, it seems plausible that real recruiters might not make the most objective and well-informed decisions when making large numbers of them under severe time pressure.

A second approach to improving decision quality in recruiting is to **monitor the recruiters**, for example, by periodically assessing the recruiters' performance using objective measures of the workers they hire, as in Hoffman, Kahn, and Li's (2015) study (see Section 15.2). This type of assessment can help companies to train effective recruiters, and if necessary to assign less-effective recruiters to other tasks in the organization. Finally, where appropriate, it may be optimal to reduce the discretion of human recruiters (who can become tired and vulnerable to Type-I thinking) by testing and other algorithmic systems, or even to outsource much of the employee selection process to intermediaries who specialize in these activities, as we discussed in Section 15.3.

Effects of Decision Monitoring on Discrimination: Evidence from Major League Baseball

Major league baseball (MLB) umpires make scores of split-second decisions when they call pitches in every game. In a rigorous, quantitative study of these decisions, Parsons, Sulaeman, Yates, and Hamermesh (2011) found that in MLB as a whole, umpires slightly favor pitchers of their own race by expanding the strike zone when faced by an own-race pitcher. More importantly for our purposes here was *when* and *where* these umpire biases were present: they *only* occurred in ballparks without computerized QuesTrec cameras, which provide more objective measures of each pitch's location. In parks without QuesTrec cameras, biases were strongest in games that had low attendance and for pitches that weren't pivotal for an at-bat; again, these are situations where the umpire's decisions are being scrutinized less closely. Parsons et al.'s study demonstrates that closer monitoring of decision-makers can improve the quality of their decisions and (pardon the pun) "level the playing field" by eliminating the effects of conscious or unconscious racial biases.

Parsons et al.'s (2011) study also has an important implication for how we measure discrimination. Specifically, they found that *pitchers responded to umpires' biases* by more frequently targeting their pitches at the borders of the strike zone when facing an own-race umpire. Pitches in that "fuzzy" region are called balls nearly as frequently as they are called strikes, allowing the umpire to employ maximum subjectivity. To use a baseball term, especially in low-scrutiny situations, pitchers try to "paint the corners" when facing own-race umpires, a practice that tends to improve the performance statistics of majority pitchers (because they face own-race umpires more frequently than minority pitchers do). As a result, *even the apparently objective statistics* (like earned run average) we typically use to measure pitchers' performance are biased against minority pitchers. Put another way, when worker productivity is measured subjectively, and when these measurements are biased by discrimination, employers may mistakenly conclude that minorities are less productive than other workers when in fact they are not.

A third and final HRM policy aimed at limiting biases in hiring is **blind recruiting**. Blind recruiting refers to various ways of concealing a worker's sex, race, or age from recruiters at certain (usually earlier) stages of the recruitment process. To illustrate, a well-known success story for blind recruiting methods is Claudia Goldin and Cecilia Rouse's (2000) study of auditions for the major U.S. symphony orchestras. Starting in the 1970s and 1980s, most of the major orchestras introduced screens to the process, where players performed behind a screen that concealed their identity from the judges. Controlling for each musician's own quality by using a fixed-effects regression (which essentially compares the same musician's success when that musician auditions with vs. without a screen), Goldin and Rouse found that the screen increases the probability a woman will be advanced out of a preliminary round, and greatly enhances the likelihood a female contestant will be the winner in a final round. Overall, the authors estimate that the screens caused a large increase in the percentage of major orchestra musicians who are female (and presumably improved the quality of the orchestras because the women won in blinded competitions).

Various forms of anonymous application procedures (AAPs) have been introduced and evaluated in other contexts. For example, in a study of 3,529 applications to 109 positions in Swedish local public sector administration, Aslund and Skans (2012) found, like Goldin and Rouse (2000), that AAP increased the interview rates of both women and individuals of non-Western origin. Only women, however, received more job offers under AAP. In a large study of French companies, Behaghel, Crépon, and Le Barbanchon (2015) found that these procedures *reduced* the hiring of minority candidates, most likely because the firms in their sample—all of whom had volunteered to experiment with anonymous recruiting—actually tried to favor minorities when applicants' minority status was not concealed.[8]

Finally, in a related context, Jennifer Doleac and Benjamin Hansen (2016) study the effects of "ban the box" (BTB) policies adopted by some U.S. states. These policies prevent employers from conducting criminal background checks until late in the job application process; one of their goals was to reduce racial disparities in employment. Instead, the opposite happened: BTB reduced the probability of being employed by 5.1% for young, low-skilled black men, and by 2.9% for young, low-skilled Hispanic men. Thus, removing information about one job qualification (whether the applicant has a criminal record) induced employers to rely *more* on something else—in this case, race—as a signal of that qualification, that is, it increased the amount of race-based statistical discrimination, as we might expect. Doleac and Hansen's results thus illustrate an important *caveat* affecting all types of blind recruiting policies: *restricting employers' access to certain pieces of information may induce employers to rely more on other worker characteristics that signal the missing information.* As a result, in Doleac and Hansen's case, the BTB "cure" may have been worse than the disease it was intended to eliminate.

[8] Krause, Rinne, and Zimmermann (2012) summarize the effects of additional experiments with anonymized job applications in Sweden, the Netherlands, and Germany.

RESULT 16.4

Policies to Reduce Discrimination in Hiring

Three main HRM policies with the potential to reduce hiring discrimination are changing the *recruiter's decision environment*, *monitoring the recruiter*, and *blind recruiting*.

Removing distracting environmental influences, such as long hours, frequent decisions, and other sources of stress, has been shown to reduce judges' reliance on stereotypes in making decisions. This suggests that reduced time pressure on recruiters may have similar effects.

Monitoring of decisions has been shown to eliminate racial bias among baseball umpires, though the effectiveness and practicality of similar policies in the workplace are unclear.

Blind recruiting has been very successful in some applications (orchestra musicians) but can have unexpected and undesired consequences in others. For example, hiding criminal record information from employers in state-level, ban-the-box policies *reduced* the employment of young, low-skilled black men (Doleac & Hansen, 2016). This happened because "blinding" some attributes incentivizes employers to rely on other attributes to try to infer the missing information. In this case, employers appear to have used race as a signal for criminality.

Threatened Majorities: Unintended Side Effects of Corporate Diversity Messages

A common practice used by large U.S. employers to signal their willingness to fairly consider female and minority applicants is a *diversity message*, for example, statements in job ads such as "At [company name], we respect and honor employees of all races, religions, genders, sexual orientations, disabilities, and ages. In recognition of these efforts we were recently named a diversity leader by [industry association]." In a recent study of the effects of such messages on the recruitment process, Tessa L. Dover, Brenda Major, and Cheryl R. Kaiser (2016) found that pro-diversity messages not only make white men believe that women and minorities are being treated fairly, they also raise the share of white men who believe that they themselves are being treated unfairly.

In the experiment, young white men on a college campus participated in a hiring simulation for an entry-level job at a fictional technology firm. For half of the "applicants," the firm's recruitment materials contained a diversity statement similar to the one just mentioned. For the other half, the materials did not mention diversity. In all other ways, the firm was described identically. All of the applicants then underwent a standardized job interview while their performance was videotaped and their cardiovascular stress responses were measured. Compared to white men interviewing at the company that did not mention diversity, white men interviewing for the pro-diversity company expected more unfair treatment and discrimination against whites. They also *performed more*

(continued)

poorly in the job interview as judged by independent raters, and their cardiovascular responses during the interview revealed that they were more stressed.

Thus it appears that pro-diversity messages signaled to these white men that they might be discriminated against. These concerns interfered with their interview performance and caused their bodies to respond as if they were under threat, in the same way that minorities respond physically when exposed to *stereotype threat* situations. This effect occurred regardless of the men's political ideology, their attitudes toward minority groups, their beliefs about the prevalence of discrimination against whites, or their beliefs about the fairness of the world. Dover et al.'s (2016) results provide additional evidence for the *stereotype threat effect*: Expectations of discrimination can *cause* poor interview performance. They also suggest that negative responses to diversity statements may be widespread among white men, including many who endorse the tenets of diversity and inclusion.

Overall, Dover et al.'s (2016) results suggest an important downside to corporate diversity initiatives that might help explain their relatively lackluster success to date: When people feel threatened, they may resist efforts to make the workplace more inclusive. Indeed, according to Dover et al., "to date, diversity initiatives' strongest accomplishment may actually be protecting the organization from litigation—*not* protecting the interests of underrepresented groups." Thus, to be effective, existing diversity initiatives may need to be changed, or to be replaced by approaches that are experienced as less threatening to majority workers.

Chapter Summary

- ☐ Employment discrimination refers to the use of certain criteria, including race, religion, and sex, in HR decisions. Discrimination in the recruiting process can be detected using resume audit studies, such as Bertrand and Mullainathan (2004). This study of white-collar employers in Boston and Chicago showed that resumes with distinctively white names received 50% more callbacks than identical resumes with a black-sounding name.

- ☐ Discrimination as defined previously can be due to at least four types of conscious factors—employer tastes, co-worker or customer tastes, unbiased beliefs about productivity, and biased beliefs. Discrimination that results from (statistically) unbiased beliefs about productivity differentials between groups is known as statistical discrimination. Discrimination that results from unconscious associations is known as implicit discrimination and can be detected by an implicit association test (IAT).

- ☐ Discrimination that is due to employer tastes, biased beliefs, or unconscious associations likely reduces profits. Discrimination that results from customer or co-worker tastes, or from unbiased beliefs (statistical discrimination), may increase profits, at least in the short run. Statistical discrimination has long-run costs to both firms and society as a whole, however, because it reduces the incentives of both the favored and the unfavored groups to improve their qualifications.

- Three ways to reduce bias in evaluating resumes are changing the recruiters' decision environment, monitoring recruiters, and "blind" recruiting strategies. Although there have been some success stories involving these strategies, their effectiveness and practicality in wider settings remains unclear.

Discussion Questions

1. When subjected to the current qualifying tests for combat in the U.S. Army, much fewer women pass the test than men, but some individuals do. In contrast to some other employment contexts, however, testing people for combat jobs is a long, difficult and very expensive process for the military. Although the U.S. Military is still gathering data on this question, suppose it turns out that women's pass rate is a consistent 5% in large samples, that the cost of testing is $100,000 per candidate, and the military values a successfully trained combat soldier at $1 million dollars (over and above what the soldier is paid; these are just made-up numbers, designed to pose a question). With these numbers, on average, 20 female candidates need to be evaluated, at a total cost of 20 * $100,000 = $2 million dollars, to produce a worker worth $1 million dollars to the military. If these turn out to be the right numbers, would you support an official policy (which, by definition, is a form of statistical discrimination) of excluding women from consideration for combat jobs in the U.S. military? Why or why not?

2. Blind recruiting methods appear to have been a success in the labor market for orchestra musicians. Can you think of any other contexts in which such methods might be practical?

3. This is a question about discrimination based on co-worker tastes. Suppose (for the sake of argument) that you are an employer with a workforce that is heavily female, and the employees like it that way. They find it easier to have conversations that would be awkward with a man in the workplace; and they enjoy the supportive, all-female atmosphere. After interviewing a number of candidates, you find that the best-qualified candidate is a man; but you believe that the morale of your *existing* employees (and thus their productivity and your profits) would fall if you hired him. Would you hire him? Is it ethical *not* to hire him? Would your answers change if we switched the genders in this example, so the incumbent workers were all men? Why or why not?

Suggestions for Further Reading

Useful and up-to-date summaries of the literature on discrimination in hiring and other contexts are provided by Bertrand and Duflo (2017), Neumark (2016), and Lahey and Beasley (2016).

For an excellent study of whether racial bias affects death sentencing in U.S. courts, see Alesina and Ferrara (2014).

For more recent evaluations of the Implicit Association Test (IAT), see Greenwald, Poehlman, Uhlmann, and Banaji (2009); and Oswald, Mitchell, Blanton, Jaccard, and Tetlock (2013). Bertrand, Chugh, and Mullainathan (2005) provide a nice introduction to the IAT for economists.

For formal economic models of self-fulfilling beliefs about group productivity, see Arrow (1973), Lundberg and Startz (1983), or Coate and Loury (1993).

For more on job testing and minority workers, see Autor and Scarborough (2008), Weaver (2015), and Wozniak (2015).

References

Ahmed, A. M., Andersson, L., & Hammarstedt, M. (2013). Are gay men and lesbians discriminated against in the hiring process? *Southern Economic Journal, 79,* 565–585.

Alesina, A., & La Ferrara, E. (2014). A test of racial bias in capital sentencing. *American Economic Review, 104,* 3397–3433.

Arrow, K. J. (1973). The theory of discrimination. *Discrimination in Labor Markets, 3*(10), 3–33.

Aslund, O., & Nordstrom Skans, O. (2012). Do anonymous job application procedures level the playing field? *Industrial and Labor Relations Review, 65,* 82–107.

Autor, D. H., & Scarborough, D. (2008). Does job testing harm minority workers? Evidence from retail establishments. *Quarterly Journal of Economics, 123,* 219–277.

Baert, S., Cockx, B., Gheyle, N., & Vandamme, C. (2015). Is there less discrimination in occupations where recruitment is difficult? *ILR Review, 68*(3), 467–500.

Baker, M., & Cornelson, K. (2016). *Gender based occupational segregation and sex differences in sensory, motor and spatial aptitudes* (NBER Working Paper No. 22248). Cambridge, MA: The National Bureau of Economic Research.

Banerjee, A., Bertrand, M., Datta, S., & Mullainathan, S. (2009). Labor market discrimination in Delhi: Evidence from a field experiment. *Journal of Comparative Economics, 37*(1), 14–27.

Bartoš, V., Bauer, M., Chytilová, J., & Matějka, F. (2016). Attention discrimination: theory and field experiments. *American Economic Review, 106,* 1437–1475.

Becker, G. (1971). *The economics of discrimination* (2nd ed.). Chicago: University of Chicago Press.

Behaghel, L., Crépon, B., & Le Barbanchon, T. (2015). Unintended effects of anonymous résumés. *American Economic Journal: Applied Economics, 7*(3), 1–27. doi:10.1257/app.20140185

Bertrand, M., & Mullainathan, S. (2004). Are Emily and Greg more employable than Lakisha and Jamal? A field experiment on labor market discrimination. *American Economic Review, 94,* 991–1013.

Bertrand, M., Chugh, D., & Mullainathan, S. (2005). Implicit discrimination. *American Economic Review, 95,* 94–98.

Bertrand, M., & Duflo, E. (2017). Field experiments on discrimination. *Handbook of Economic Field Experiments, 1*, 309–393.

Booth, A. L., Leigh, A., & Varganova, E. (2011). Does ethnic discrimination vary across minority groups? Evidence from a field experiment. *Oxford Bulletin of Economics and Statistics, 74,* 547–573.

Carlsson, M. (2011). Does hiring discrimination cause gender segregation in the Swedish labor market? *Feminist Economics, 17*(3), 71–102.

Coate, S., & Loury, G. C. (1993). Will affirmative action eliminate negative stereotypes? *American Economic Review, 83,* 1220–1240.

Coffman, K. B., Coffman, L. C., & Ericson, K. M. M. (2016). The size of the lgbt population and the magnitude of antigay sentiment are substantially underestimated. *Management Science.* doi:10.1287/mnsc.2016.2503

Danziger, S., Levav, J., Avnaim-Pesso, L. (2011). Extraneous factors in judicial decisions. *Proceedings of the National Academy of Sciences, 108*(17), 6889–6892.

Doleac, J. L., & Hansen, B. (2016). *Does "Ban the box" help or hurt low-skilled workers? Statistical discrimination and employment outcomes when criminal histories are hidden* (NBER Working Paper No. 22469). Cambridge, MA: The National Bureau of Economic Research.

Dover, T., Major, B., & Kaiser, C. R. (2016). Members of high-status groups are threatened by pro-diversity organizational messages. *Journal of Experimental Social Psychology, 62,* 58–67. doi:10.1016/j.jesp.2015.10.006

Eells, T. D., & Showalter, C. R. (1994). Work-related stress in American trial judges. *Journal of the American Academy of Psychiatry and the Law Online, 22*(1), 71–83.

Ewens, M., Tomlin, B., & Choon Wang, L. (2014). Statistical discrimination or prejudice? A large sample field experiment. *Review of Economics and Statistics, 96,* 119–134.

Galarza M., & Yamada, G. (2014). Labor market discrimination in Lima, Peru: Evidence from a field experiment. *World Development, 58,* 83–94.

Ge, Y., Knittel, C. R., MacKenzie, D., & Zoepf, S. (2016). *Racial and gender discrimination in transportation network companies* (NBER Working Paper No. 22776). Cambridge, MA: The National Bureau of Economic Research.

Glover, D., Pallais, A., & Pariente, W. (2017). Discrimination as a self-fulfilling prophecy: Evidence from French grocery stores. *Quarterly Journal of Economics, 132*(3), 1219–1260.

Goldberg, P. (1968). Are women prejudiced against women? *Society, 5*(5), 28–30.

Goldin, C., & Rouse, C. (2000). Orchestrating impartiality: The impact of blind auditions on female musicians. *American Economic Review, 90,* 715–741.

Greenwald, A. G., McGhee, D. E., & Schwartz, J. L. K. (1998). Measuring individual differences in implicit cognition: The Implicit Association Test. *Journal of Personality and Social Psychology, 74,* 1464–1480.

Greenwald, A. G., Poehlman, T. A., Uhlmann, E. L., & Banaji, M. (2009). Understanding and using the Implicit Association Test: III. Meta-analysis of predictive validity. *Journal of Personality and Social Psychology, 97,* 17–41.

Hartley, L. R., & Adams, R. G. (1974). Effect of noise on the Stroop Test. *Journal of Experimental Psychology, 102,* 62–66.

Heckman, J. J., & Payner, B. S. (1989). Determining the impact of federal antidiscrimination policy on the economic status of Blacks: A study of South Carolina. *American Economic Review, 79*(1), 138–177.

Hoffman, M., Kahn, L. B., & Li, D. (2015). *Discretion in hiring* (NBER Working Paper No. 21709). Cambridge, MA: The National Bureau of Economic Research.

Kahn, L. (2009, January). *The economics of discrimination: Evidence from basketball* (IZA Discussion Paper No. 3987). Bonn, Germany: Institute for the Study of Labor.

Keinan, G. (1987). Decision making under stress: Scanning of alternatives under controllable and uncontrollable threats. *Journal of Personality and Social Psychology, 52,* 639–644.

Krause, A., Rinne, U., & Zimmermann, K. (2012). Anonymous job applications in Europe. *IZA Journal of European Labor Studies, 1,* 1–20.

Kuklinski, J. H., Cobb, M. D., & Gilens, M. (1997). Racial attitudes and the "New South." *Journal of Politics, 59,* 323–349.

Lahey, J., & Beasley, R. (2016). *Technical aspects of correspondence studies* (NBER Working Paper No. 22818). Cambridge, MA: The National Bureau of Economic Research.

Lavy, V. & Sand, E. (2015). *On the origins of gender human capital gaps: Short and long term consequences of teachers' stereotypical biases* (NBER Working Paper No. 20909). Cambridge, MA: The National Bureau of Economic Research.

Lundberg, S. J., & Startz, R. (1983). Private discrimination and social intervention in competitive labor markets. *American Economic Review, 73,* 340–347.

Ma, D. S., Correll, J., Wittenbrink, B., Bar-Anan, Y., Srirarm, N., & Nosek, B. A. (2013). When fatigue turns deadly: The association between fatigue and racial bias in the decision to shoot. *Basic and Applied Social Psychology, 35,* 515–524.

Maurer-Fazio, M. (2012). Ethnic discrimination in China's Internet job board labor market. *IZA Journal of Migration, 1*(12), 1–24.

Milkman, K. L., Akinola, M., & Chugh, D. (2012). Temporal distance and discrimination: An audit study in Academia. *Psychological Science, 23,* 710–717.

Neumark, D. (1996). Sex discrimination in restaurant hiring: An audit study. *Quarterly Journal of Economics, 111,* 915–941.

Neumark, D. (2016). *Experimental research on labor market discrimination* (NBER Working Paper No. 22022). Cambridge, MA: The National Bureau of Economic Research.

Neumark, D., Burn, I., & Button, P. (2015, October). *Is it harder for older workers to find jobs? New and improved evidence from a field experiment* (NBER Working Paper No. 21669). Cambridge, MA: The National Bureau of Economic Research.

Oreopoulos, P. (2011). Why do skilled immigrants struggle in the labor market? A field experiment with thirteen thousand resumes. *American Economic Journal: Economic Policy, 3*(4), 148–171.

Oswald, F., Mitchell, G., Blanton, H., Jaccard, J., & Tetlock, P. E. (2013). Predicting ethnic and racial discrimination: A meta-analysis of IAT criterion studies. *Journal of Personality and Social Psychology, 105,* 171–192.

Parsons, C., Sulaeman, J., Yates, M., & Hamermesh, D. S. (2011). Strike three: Discrimination, incentives and evaluation. *American Economic Review, 101,* 1410–1435.

Payne, B. K. (2006). Weapon bias: Split-second decisions and unintended stereotyping. *Current Directions in Psychological Science, 15,* 287–291.

Payne, B. K., Shimizu, Y., & Jacoby, L. L. (2005). Mental control and visual illusions: Toward explaining race-biased weapon misidentifications. *Journal of Experimental Social Psychology, 41*(1), 36–47.

Petit, P. (2007). The effects of age and family constraints on gender hiring discrimination: A field experiment in the French financial sector. *Labour Economics, 14,* 371–391.

Pope, D. G., & Sydnor, J. R. (2011). What's in a picture? Evidence of discrimination from Prosper.com. *Journal of Human Resources, 46,* 53–92.

Price, J., & Wolfers, J. (2010). Racial discrimination among NBA referees. *Quarterly Journal of Economics, 125,* 1859–1887.

Reynolds, D. (2007). Restraining Golem and harnessing Pygmalion in the classroom: A laboratory study of managerial expectations and task design. *Academy of Management Learning and Education, 6,* 475–483.

Rooth, D.-O. (2010). Automatic associations and discrimination in hiring: Real world evidence. *Labour Economics, 17,* 523–534.

Rosenthal, R., & Jacobson, L. (1968). Pygmalion in the classroom. *Urban Review, 3*(1), 16–20.

Stanovich, K. E., & West, R. F. (2000). Individual differences in reasoning: Implications for the rationality debate?. *Behavioral and Brain Sciences, 23*(5), 645–665.

Steele, C. M., & Aronson, J. (1995). Stereotype threat and the intellectual test performance of African Americans. *Journal of Personality and Social Psychology, 69*(5), 797.

Wozniak, A. (2015). Discrimination and the effects of drug testing on black employment. *Review of Economics and Statistics, 97(3), 548–566.*

Weaver, A. (2015). Is Credit Status a Good Signal of Productivity? *Industrial and Labor Relations Review, 68*(4), 742–770.

Zussman, A. (2013). Ethnic discrimination: Lessons from the Israeli online market for used cars. *Economic Journal, 123*(572), F433–F468.

17 Setting Pay Levels: Monopsony Models

Overall, how generous should a firm's compensation package be to maximize its profits? So far, in modeling principal–agent interactions in this book, we've answered this question in a rather unrealistic way. Specifically, in Part 1's model of one principal and one agent, the profit-maximizing contract was *just* generous enough to get the agent to take the job. (Technically, the contract just had to satisfy the agent's *participation constraint*, $U \geq U^{alt}$ in Equation 3.7.) Paying any less than this meant the principal didn't hire anyone, and paying any more was just giving money away to the single agent.

This is, of course, pretty unrealistic. In real firms, wage setting is not such an all-or-nothing decision, for at least two reasons. One is that employers typically hire many workers, not just one; in most of these cases, the *number* of workers who are attracted to (and stay in) the firm will likely vary smoothly, rather than abruptly, with the generosity of a firm's compensation policy. Second, even when a firm is dealing with a single worker, it is unrealistic to assume that firm knows the exact value of the worker's next best alternative. In this case, the employer's assessment of the *probability* the worker will accept a firm's job offer will also increase smoothly with the generosity of the firm's offer. In both these more realistic cases, a profit-maximizing employer faces a trade-off: Raising pay costs money, but it might buy the firm more workers, better workers, happier workers, more productive workers, and workers who don't quit so often. That is the trade-off we study in this chapter.

Broadly speaking, labor and personnel economists refer to the situations studied in this chapter as cases of *monopsony* in labor markets.[1] Monopsony

[1] The word "monopsony" comes from the Greek words for "single buyer" and was coined by the British economist Joan Robinson in her 1933 book, *The Economics of Imperfect Competition*. She used it to describe a labor market with only one employer. Nowadays it refers to any situation in which employers face a smooth trade-off between the number or quality of workers they can attract and the generosity of the compensation package they offer. In other words, the "monopsony" trade-off applies to almost every firm.

models are the focus of this chapter. In Chapter 18, we'll consider the effects of pay levels on worker *discipline*—another important consideration when choosing how much to pay.

17.1 Optimal Exploitation: Pay Levels and the Elasticity of Labor Supply

To construct a simple model of optimal pay generosity, let's consider a firm hiring workers, each of whom produces the same amount of net revenue, Q. Because we are abstracting from effort decisions in this part of the text, each worker's utility depends only on one thing: the total wage, w, the firm pays that worker.[2] Under these conditions, as already suggested, you can think of the simple mathematics we'll do in this section in two distinct ways (the mathematical results apply to both interpretations).

Specifically, in the *many-worker interpretation* of the mathematics, we consider a firm that is (implicitly) deciding how many workers to hire by setting its offered wage, which applies to all workers. In this interpretation, the offered wage is w, the number of workers hired is N, which increases with w via the smoothly increasing *labor supply function* $N(w)$. In the *single-worker* interpretation, a risk-neutral firm is deciding on how high a take-it-or-leave-it wage offer (w) to make to single worker. But in contrast to the models in Part 1 of the book, the firm doesn't know the *exact* value of the worker's best outside option, or *reservation wage*. We model this uncertainty by imagining a smoothly increasing function $N(w)$ denoting the *probability* the worker will accept the firm's offer as a function of the offered wage. The results derived in the following apply equally to both the single- and many-worker interpretations; but in most of our discussion, we'll use the terminology of the many-worker interpretation.

Mathematically, under the preceding assumptions, the firm's decision is just to find the level of w that maximizes profits, which are given by

$$\Pi = (Q - w)\, N(w). \tag{17.1}$$

In words, each worker who is hired produces net revenues of Q but is paid w. Thus, the firm earns a profit of $(Q - w)$ on each worker hired. Total profits are just profits per worker times the number of workers hired, $N(w)$. The quantity $(Q - w)$ is sometimes called the *absolute (wage) markdown*, or if you prefer *absolute exploitation*. It's just the gap between what each worker produces and what that worker is paid.

As it turns out, there's a simple yet totally general solution to the maximization problem in Equation 17.1 that was discovered by British economists John Hicks (1932) and Joan Robinson (1933). Both were among the most influential

[2] One way to think about this is that workers get no disutility from working. Another is that effort does cause some disutility, but the amount of effort associated with working is the same regardless of how much the worker is paid. Thus, the only aspect of the job that matters to the worker—in deciding whether to take the job or not—is what it pays.

economists of the early 20th century; Hicks won the first British Nobel Prize in 1972; Robinson is still known for her pioneering work in the economics of imperfect competition. These authors showed that the profit maximizing wage is given by a simple equation:

RESULT 17.1

The Profit-Maximizing Wage

The profit maximizing wage for a firm facing an upward-sloping labor supply curve is given by the formula

$$w = \frac{\eta}{1+\eta} Q, \tag{17.2}$$

where η (a Greek letter, pronounced "ate a," as in "I ate a sandwich") represents the *elasticity of labor supply* to that firm.

DEFINITION 17.1

Elasticity is a measure of the responsiveness of one quantity to changes in another. Elasticity measures are frequently used by economists in a variety of contexts. A key application in personnel economics is the (firm-level) *labor supply elasticity*, η, which is defined as the percentage change in labor supplied that is caused by a 1% change in the wage the firm pays, that is,

η = *percent change in labor (N) supplied/percent change in wage (w) offered.*

High values of the labor supply elasticity mean that labor supply is very sensitive to the offered wage; in this case, small wage increases attract a lot more workers (and small wage cuts cause a lot of workers to quit). When the labor supply elasticity is low, the number of workers a firm can hire (or retain) is not very sensitive to the offered wage.

For small changes in the offered wage, the labor supply elasticity can be defined using calculus as

$$\eta = \frac{w}{N} \times \frac{dN}{dw} = \frac{d \log N}{d \log w}.$$

Equation 17.2 expresses the profit-maximizing wage as a fraction of the worker's productivity.[3] To see how it works, notice that the profit-maximizing wage equals zero when labor supply is completely inelastic ($\eta = 0$). This is because cutting the offered wage doesn't cause any of the firm's workers to leave;

[3] To derive Equation 17.2, simply differentiate Equation 17.1 with respect to the wage and set the result equal to zero, yielding the first-order condition for a maximum: $d\Pi/dw = -N + (Q - w)(dN/dw) = 0$. Notice that this just balances the marginal *cost* of a wage increase (the fact that you have to pay a higher wage to each of N workers) against its marginal benefits (you get to hire dN/dw additional workers and earn a profit of $Q - w$ on each one of them). Rearranging this first-order condition [and using the definition of η as $(w/N)(dN/dw)$] yields Equation 17.2.

they will all stay, even at a wage of zero. At the other extreme, workers must be paid their full productivity ($w = Q$) when labor supply is infinitely elastic.[4] In this case, cutting the wage even one penny means *all* of a firm's workers will quit, so firms have no choice but to pay workers their full productivity and earn zero profits. In between these extremes, the profit-maximizing wage rises from zero (complete exploitation) to Q (zero exploitation) as the labor supply elasticity rises. In sum, we have Result 17.2:

☑ RESULT 17.2

The Profit-Maximizing Wage Increases with the Elasticity of Labor Supply to the Firm

The simple theory of monopsony in labor markets predicts that profit-maximizing firms will exploit workers most (i.e., pay the lowest wages, relative to productivity) when the elasticity of labor supply to the firm is low. The intuition is simple: When the labor supply elasticity is low, firms won't lose as many workers when they cut wages. In contrast, a high level of labor supply elasticity represents a case where many workers have outside options that are comparable in value to what the current firm is offering.

Effects of Labor Supply Elasticity on the Profit-Maximizing Wage in an Imaginary Company

To understand in a little more detail how Equation 17.2 works, you can download the spreadsheet that is reproduced in Figure 17.1.[5] This spreadsheet calculates the profits of an imaginary firm in which each of up to 100 workers produces net revenues of $Q = \$10$ each. The firm faces a labor supply curve given by the equation

$$N = Kw^{\eta}, \tag{17.3}$$

where η is the elasticity of labor supply.[6] In the spreadsheet, I've chosen the value of the constant K in a special way: K is automatically calculated such that regardless of the labor supply elasticity, the firm will always hire 100 workers if it sets a wage of 10. If you like, you can think of a firm that has a current stock of 100 workers and is paying each one of them his or her full productivity. It is now asking itself, "What will happen to my labor force and my profits as I cut my wage below 10?" And perhaps more importantly, "How far should I cut to maximize my profits?"

---

[4] $\eta/(1+\eta)$ approaches 1 as η approaches infinity.

[5] Spreadsheets are available at http://econ.ucsb.edu/~pjkuhn/Ec152/Spreadsheets/Spreadsheets.htm.

[6] The labor supply curve in Equation 17.3 is a widely used, convenient type of equation called a *constant elasticity* supply equation. This just means that the (percentage) sensitivity of labor supplied to wages is the same at all points on the labor supply curve. The quickest way to verify that the parameter η represents the labor supply elasticity at all points for this curve is to take logs of the curve, then differentiate: $\log N = \log K + \eta \log w$; therefore, $d\log N/d\log w = \eta$.

Optimal Wage Setting with an Upward-Sloping Labor Supply Curve–Spreadsheet Example

Productivity (Q) = 10

Labor supply elasticity (η) = 2

Labor supply function: $N = K^*(w^{\eta})$, where $K = 100/(10^{\eta})$

Note: the spreadsheet automatically picks K to ensure that 100 workers are always available when the wage = 10:

K = 1

Profit-maximizing wage (from the formula, $w = Q^*\eta/(1+\eta)$): 6.67

wage (w)	number of workers (N)	profits ($\pi = (Q-w)^*N$)
0	0	0
0.5	0.25	2
1	1.00	9
1.5	2.25	19
2	4.00	32
2.5	6.25	47
3	9.00	63
3.5	12.25	80
4	16.00	96
4.5	20.25	111
5	25.00	125
5.5	30.25	136
6	36.00	144
6.5	42.25	148
7	49.00	147
7.5	56.25	141
8	64.00	128
8.5	72.25	108
9	81.00	81
9.5	90.25	45
10	100.00	0

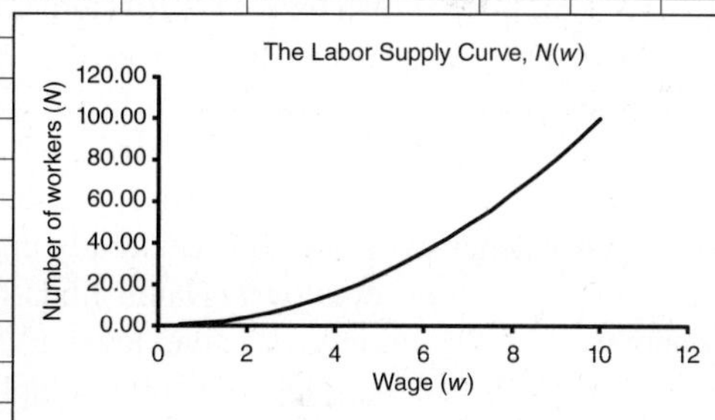

FIGURE 17.1. Effects of Labor Supply Elasticity on the Profit-Maximizing Wage

For any given value of labor supply elasticity, the spreadsheet will plot for you the labor supply curve faced by this firm. Experimenting with various values, you'll see that when the supply elasticity is low, not many workers quit when the wage is cut. For example, when $\eta = 0.2$, the firm can cut its wage down to 4 (i.e., it can pay workers only 40% of what they produce) and still retain 80% of its original 100-worker labor force. When $\eta = 0.5$, only 60% of workers remain at a wage of 4. This number falls to 40% when $\eta = 1$, to under 20% when $\eta = 2$, and effectively to zero when $\eta = 5$. As you raise the labor supply elasticity beyond that, the supply curve becomes closer and closer to vertical near the quantity $N = 100$. This means that the firm loses essentially all its labor force even for infinitesimal wage cuts below 10. This is, of course, the extreme case of perfectly competitive labor markets where all firms are wage takers, which is the standard model in most labor economics textbooks.

Are Competitive Labor Markets Good or Bad for Workers?

Although it's sometimes claimed that competitive labor markets drive wages down, workers' right to quit at any time when a better opportunity arises—and to do so without providing either a reason or advance notice—is a key and perhaps unappreciated source of workers' economic power. It is this right that keeps wages high when the labor supply elasticity (a measure of labor market competitiveness) is high. Indeed, the economic power associated with workers' freedom to quit is dramatically illustrated by employers' historical attempts to restrict those rights.

For example, Suresh Naidu (2010) studies the effect of **anti-enticement laws** on worker mobility and wages in the postbellum U.S. South. Anti-enticement laws were fines imposed on employers for the offense of recruiting a sharecropper or other worker who was already under contract to another employer. Naidu finds that increases in the enticement fine lowered the mobility of black sharecroppers across employers. Higher fines also reduced workers' wages and their rate of wage growth (because moving to better jobs is an important way to improve one's wages). The effects of anti-enticement laws are a dramatic illustration of the power of worker mobility to keep wages high.

Much more recently, high-tech employees of Apple, Google, Intel, Intuit, Lucasfilm, and Pixar launched a class action suit against their employers, accusing the companies of entering into agreements to (1) not recruit each other's employees; (2) provide notification when making an offer to another's employee (without the knowledge or consent of that employee); and (3) cap pay packages offered to prospective employees at the initial offer, all with the intent to reduce employee compensation and mobility. According to the plaintiffs, "as additional companies joined the alleged conspiracy, competition among participating companies for labor decreased. Compensation of defendants' employees was less than what would have been paid in a properly functioning labor market where employers compete for workers." On January 15, 2015, Apple, Google, Intel, and Adobe agreed to a $415 million settlement, subject to judicial approval (Lief, Cabraser, Heimann, & Bernstein, 2015). Despite the general tendency of the business community to support freely competitive markets in general, it appears these firms were willing to break the law to eliminate competition in their own labor markets!

Next, let's apply and check the formula in Equation 17.2. For any labor supply elasticity you choose, the cell highlighted in yellow (in the spreadsheet) calculates the profit-maximizing wage using that formula. Some elasticity values you might try out (because the answers work out to nice round numbers) are $\eta = 0.25, 0.333, 0.5, 1, 2, 4, 9,$ and 19. As you do this, you'll find that the profit-maximizing wage rises from \$2.00 to \$9.50. The rest of the table just illustrates and verifies this result by calculating labor supply and total profits for 20 candidate values of the offered wage for any elasticity value you choose. For the suggested elasticity values above, you'll see that the profit-maximizing wage in the yellow cell will match one of the 20 round numbers in the wage column of the table. Another thing you might notice is that the *maximized level of profits* falls as labor supply elasticity rises: Firms don't like competitive labor markets because good outside options for workers limit the firm's ability to exploit them by cutting wages!

Simple monopsony models like the ones in Equation 17.2 have been proposed as explanations for a number of well-known phenomena in labor markets. These include the fact that, across the world, wages for comparable work are higher in larger cities than smaller ones, and higher in cities than the countryside. Although a number of other factors also contribute to this phenomenon, Manning (2010) presents evidence suggesting that the greater level of labor market competition in cities also plays a role: Workers have many more alternative options in cities, placing stricter limits on employers' wage-setting power. Other researchers have applied monopsony models to the study of labor markets with a small number of key employers, such as markets for teachers (Falch, 2010, 2011; Ransom & Sims, 2010) and nurses (Staiger, Spetz, & Phibbs, 2010). Monopsony power has also been proposed as an explanation for why some immigrants—especially those whose mobility across employers is limited—are paid less than citizens and permanent residents. Examples include Depew, Norlander, and Sørensen's (2013) study of H1-B visa holders in the United States (who cannot switch employers within the United States without getting a new visa); U.S. undocumented workers (Hotchkiss & Quispe-Agnoli, 2012); and immigrants to Germany (Hirsch & Jahn, 2015).

Wages and Benefits: The Economics of Compensating Wage Differentials

Aside from wages and effort, jobs have many other features that workers care about, including location, hours, working conditions, schedules, safety, job security, and a wide array of benefits like sick time, health insurance, and retirement benefits. For the most part, when we talk about wage-setting

Can Monopsony Explain Why Women Are Paid Less than Men?

Possibly the earliest and most famous application of a monopsony model to labor markets is Joan Robinson's (1933) proposal that gender differences in the firm-level labor supply elasticity, η, might help explain the gender wage gap in many economies: If men are more likely to react to low pay by switching to another employer than women are, profit-maximizing employers can get away with paying equally qualified women less than men. Recently, Barth and Dale-Olsen (2009); Ransom and Oaxaca (2010); and Hirsch, Schank, and Schnabel (2010) tested this idea and found that men's quit rates were indeed more sensitive to wages than women's. Possible reasons include men's greater ability or willingness to move geographically to improve their labor market options. If true, this greater willingness to relocate would protect men from exploitation to a greater extent than women, who might be more tied to a location for family reasons.

in this chapter, what we really mean is the *overall attractiveness* of the job package, including all these features, most of which (like wages) are costly for the employer to provide. Indeed, economists since Adam Smith have argued that workers may be willing to pay for desirable job features by accepting a lower wage. Following Smith, economists refer to wage differentials between jobs that reflect differences in jobs' non-wage aspects as *compensating differentials.*

Economists have been trying to estimate the amount of wages that workers are willing to sacrifice in return for desirable job attributes for decades. One of the most convincing estimates, however, is a recent field experiment by Alex Mas and Amanda Pallais (in press). During the application process to staff a national call center, Mas and Pallais randomly offered applicants choices between traditional Monday-to-Friday, 9 a.m. to 5 p.m. office positions and alternatives. These alternatives included flexible scheduling, working from home, and positions that give the employer discretion over scheduling. The authors also randomly varied the wage difference between the traditional schedule and these alternatives, allowing them to estimate workers' willingness to pay for these alternatives. Mas and Pallais found that although the great majority of workers are not willing to pay for flexible scheduling, some workers care intensely about it and are willing to sacrifice a significant amount of wages to avoid it. However,

How Highly Do Workers Value Their Own Lives? Evidence from "The Deadliest Catch"

To estimate workers' valuation of job safety, Kurt Lavetti (2016) surveyed commercial fishing deckhands who worked in the Alaskan Bering Sea between 2003 and 2009, one of the world's most dangerous jobs. Because the risk associated with these jobs varies sharply over time (in a way that workers can predict before they sign up with a captain), and because wage contracts between hands and captains last only a few weeks or few months, Lavetti was able to measure differences in wages paid between the same captain–deckhand pairs under different safety conditions. Lavetti finds that deckhands' hourly wages were highly seasonal, ranging from $25 per hour in June and July to around $50 per hour in December and January. Suggestively, this pattern very closely tracks the fatality risk, which varies from about 1 death per 1,000 worker-years in the summer to over 6 deaths per 1,000 worker-years in the winter. Lavetti is able to rule out a preference for working in better weather as the explanation for this pattern by exploiting La Nina weather patterns, which can raise the fatality rate within a season, and which have similar effects on wages. Overall, Lavetti estimates that—based on their willingness to accept higher wages in return for a higher risk of death—Alaskan deckhands value their lives at about 6.6 million dollars. Calculations like these, of the value of a statistical life that is revealed by trade-offs real workers are willing to make, are widely used in cost–benefit analyses and in the courts (to award damages). Compared to most previous estimates, however, Lavetti's are probably the most convincing ones available (though they apply, admittedly, to a very special population).

the average worker is willing to give up 20% of wages to avoid a schedule set by an employer on a week's notice. Perhaps unsurprisingly, women—especially those with young children—were willing to pay considerably more to avoid this, and for the option of working from home. Whereas women's willingness to sacrifice wages in return for more control over their own schedules has been advanced as a possible explanation of the gender wage gap, Mas and Pallais note that the compensating differentials they estimate are not large or prevalent enough to explain much of the gender wage gap.

17.2 Does It Really Matter What You Pay? Finding a Pay Level Niche

Could there ever be a circumstance where a firm's profits *do not depend on how much it pays*? Although this seems hard to believe, a closer look at the last section's simple monopsony model suggests, in fact, that there may be important, real-world situations where this is true. To see this, it helps to study the solution to the last section's model graphically. We do that in Figure 17.2, which shows three isoprofit curves for the firm, between w (a bad to the firm) and N (a good). Just like the agent's indifference curves between income and effort in Figure 1.3, these curves show that the *firm's* well-being (profits) now increase to the northwest. The equation for each of these isoprofit curves comes directly from rearranging Equation 17.1 to get

$$N = \Pi/(Q - w). \tag{17.4}$$

Equation 17.4 tells us how N, the number of workers required to achieve any target level of profits (Π), varies with the wage the firm offers. For example, suppose the desired level of profits is \$100 and worker productivity, Q, is \$10. Then if the wage is \$9.99, the firm needs to hire 100/0.01 = 10,000 workers to earn a profit of \$100. At a wage of \$5.00, the firm only needs 100/(10 – 5) = 20 workers. At a wage of 0, it would only need 10 workers.

Figure 17.2 also shows an example of a labor supply function facing the firm; the specific curve shown there is a straight line through the origin. Like all such curves, it has a labor supply elasticity, η, of exactly 1.[7] For a firm maximizing its profits subject to this supply curve, we can find a solution the same way we did in Figure 2.3: at a tangency point with the highest attainable isoprofit curve. As you can verify from the spreadsheet or directly from Equation 17.2, in this case profits are maximized when workers are paid exactly half their productivity, that is, when $w = Q/2$. It's also pretty easy to visualize what happens for alternative values of η: as η rises above 1, the labor supply curve in Figure 17.2 gets steeper, shifting the tangency point to the right, at a higher wage. The opposite happens as η falls below 1. This is just another way of illustrating Result 17.2.

[7] To verify this, you can set $\eta = 1$ in the spreadsheet corresponding to Figure 17.1.

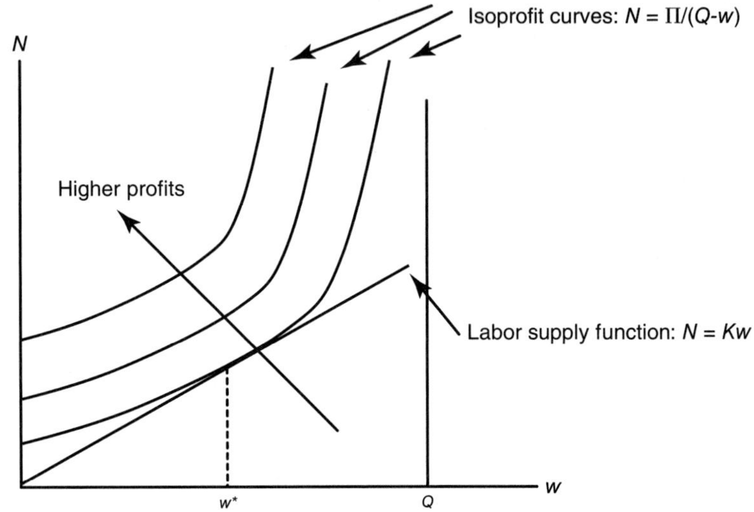

FIGURE 17.2. Profit-Maximizing Pay Generosity: Example with $\eta = 1$

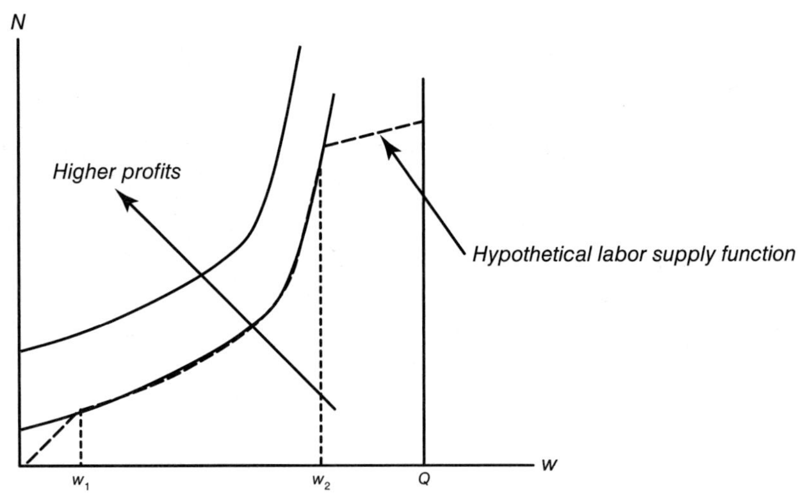

FIGURE 17.3. An Example Where Pay Doesn't Matter: Any Wage between w_1 and w_2 Yields the Same Level of Profits

With the apparatus of Figure 17.2 in hand, we can now return to the question posed at the start of this section: *Are there circumstances in which firms might be completely indifferent as to what wage they pay*? As it turns out, Figure 17.3 shows an example where this is actually the case.

In Figure 17.3, the bold, dashed labor supply curve facing an individual firm coincides with an isoprofit curve over a range of wages, from w_1 to w_2. As a result, the firm's profit-maximizing wage is actually *any* wage between w_1 and w_2: They all yield the same level of profits. Although this might seem like a strange type of labor supply curve, nothing in the theory of monopsony or labor supply rules it out.[8] More importantly, Figure 17.3's labor supply function is actually a phenomenon we'd *expect* to see in certain types of labor markets.

The first economists to demonstrate that a labor supply curve like the one in Figure 17.3 might be a feature of real labor markets were Kenneth Burdett and Dale Mortensen (1998). Mortensen was awarded the 2010 Nobel prize for this and other work on equilibrium in labor markets. Burdett and Mortensen visualized a labor market in which there were many firms competing to hire the same group of workers. Each firm adopts a policy of picking some wage level and paying that amount to all its workers. A key feature of the market envisioned by Burdett and Mortensen is that there are *search frictions*—in this case, the authors imagined that opportunities for workers to move to new firms only arrive occasionally. In markets like this, *each firm faces an upward-sloping labor supply curve because the more it pays, the fewer of its workers will move on to better paying employers when the opportunity arises.* Further, there are good reasons to expect this labor supply to look exactly like the one in Figure 17.3, where the gain to offering a higher wage (which takes the form of a reduction in a firm's quit rate) *exactly matches* the direct cost of raising the wage.[9] Another way of saying this is Result 17.3.

☑ RESULT 17.3

Under Some Circumstances, Wage Increases Can Pay for Themselves by Making It Easier to Hire and Retain Workers

If the labor supply curve has the shape predicted by search models like Burdett and Mortensen's (1998) and as illustrated in Figure 17.3, it is possible for higher wages to attract just enough extra labor to balance the cost of paying those extra wages, leaving profits unchanged. Under these circumstances, high-wage employers can coexist with, and do just as well as, low-wage employers.

Result 17.3 has an interesting implication for firms who might be deciding how well to pay: in the long run, *it may not matter* (from the point of view of your own profits) whether a firm pays well or badly! Paying badly may save money in wages, but it raises the costs of hiring and turnover. Paying more

[8] Notice that this contrasts with consumer demand theory, where there's a logical reason to expect the consumer's budget constraint to be linear in most cases.

[9] The reason relates directly to entry and exit decisions of firms and to the coexistence of firms paying different wages in a competitive market. Essentially, if all firms have access to the same production technology (say they are supermarkets, which have a highly standardized technology), the only way that two firms paying different wages can coexist in the long run is if they earn the same level of profits.

Costco versus Sam's Club: High- versus Low-Wage Strategies in Retail

In a recent *Harvard Business Review* article, Zeynep Ton (2012) summarizes over 10 years of her research on the performance of retailers like Costco, QuikTrip convenience stores, Mercadona (a Spanish family-owned supermarket chain), and Trader Joe's supermarkets who adopt a high-wage, low-turnover strategy, and of their competitors who pay considerably less. For example, in the "wholesale club" retail segment, employees earn about 40% more at Costco than at Sam's Club, Costco's closest competitor (operated by Walmart). At Trader Joe's (a California-based food chain), the starting wage for a full-time employee is $40,000 to $60,000 per year, more than twice what some competitors offer. The wages and benefits at QuikTrip are so good that the chain has been named one of Fortune's "100 Best Companies to Work For" every year since 2003. All of Mercadona's employees are permanent, and more than 85% are salaried full-timers.

Given these huge wage differences, one might expect that the aforementioned retailers would have to charge higher prices, and/or earn lower profits, than their low-wage competitors. Ton, however, finds that these companies had among the *lowest* prices in their industries, solid financial performance, and better customer service than their competitors. In addition, these high-wage retailers offered workers more training, better benefits, and more convenient schedules than their competitors. Ton's in-depth study of the retail industry dramatically illustrates how high- and low-wage employers can coexist, and why paying higher wages is not necessarily a recipe for losing money, even in a highly competitive, low-margin sector like retail sales.

may seem risky, but could easily benefit a firm in enough ways to make up for the extra costs. Essentially, a firm's choice of a wage may not affect how profitable it is but may simply determine which *pay niche* it occupies in the local labor market.[10]

Industry studies like Zeynep Ton's (2012) work on retail also identify at least three additional factors (besides lower turnover) that can make up for the costs of paying higher wages. One of these is in fact the central concept of this part of the book: selection! Indeed, it seems highly likely that higher wages buy a firm not only more workers, but *more productive* workers.[11] As Ton shows, it's easier to recruit and retain *good* workers if you pay better. Second, as we show in Chapter 18,

[10] It might be tempting to conclude from Result 17.3 that passing a law that forced *all* employers to pay better could make workers better off without costing firms anything. Unfortunately this is not necessarily true because in Burdett and Mortensen's (1998) model, the advantages reaped by the high-wage firms derive not from their high *absolute* wages but from their high wages *relative* to other employers in the local labor market: If all firms raised their wages together, every firm's costs of doing business would rise, and *no* firm would find it any easier to recruit workers than before.

[11] To incorporate this into Section 17.1's simple model of optimal wage-setting, simply make $Q(w)$ be an increasing function in Equation 17.1. In that expanded model, the optimal wage will depend on both the quantity- and *quality*-elasticities of labor supply.

more generous pay might have an effect on effort and job performance of a firm's *existing* workers via a mechanism economists call an *efficiency wage effect*. Finally, the lower turnover achieved by paying better means it makes more sense to train your employees; this can also raise the productivity of your existing workers. We study the interaction between employee turnover and firms' optimal training strategies in Chapter 19.

Chapter Summary

- ☐ The profit-maximizing generosity of pay for a firm is an increasing function of the elasticity of labor supply to that firm. In competitive (high-elasticity) labor markets, firms cannot pay workers much less than their productivity because quits are very sensitive to wages. When labor supply elasticity is low, firms have considerable monopsony power and can pay low wages without losing many workers.

- ☐ In some labor market equilibrium models like Burdett and Mortensen's (1998), low- and high-wage employers can coexist in the same industry and locality, earning similar profits. In these situations, the higher compensation costs of the high-wage employers are balanced by the advantages of lower turnover, lower absenteeism, abler workers, and higher levels of employee effort. Thus, employers can choose to adopt a high- or low-wage strategy. It may not be possible for all employers to pick the former, however, because some of the advantages of paying high wages are only when wages are high relative to workers' other labor market options.

Discussion Questions

1. Imagine you operate a relatively low-wage franchise business in town, paying \$10 an hr while most of your competitors are paying \$12. Describe how your labor force is likely to differ from other firms in your industry in terms of education, training, absenteeism, turnover, and job performance.

2. Now imagine you are contemplating raising your wage to \$12 an hr. If you did so, are there any other company policies you might want to change at the same time? How would you expect the aforementioned features of your labor force to change? Under what conditions is this wage increase likely to be a good or a bad idea for your business?

3. How would your answer to the preceding question change if, instead of just your business raising its wage, a minimum wage law was passed requiring all employers in your town to pay at least \$12 per hr?

Suggestions for Further Reading

Readers interested in a broad and engaging survey of the monopsony literature will enjoy Alan Manning's 2003 book, *Monopsony in Motion*. For a business perspective on high- versus low-wage strategies, Zeynep Ton's (2012) *Harvard Business Review* article makes interesting reading.

For more on measuring the value of a statistical life, see Viscusi and Aldy (2003). Additional evidence on how much workers value the flexibility and stability of their hours, and on how this affects gender wage differences (and college major selection), see Wiswall and Zafar (in press).

References

Barth, E., & Dale-Olsen, H. (2009). Monopsonistic discrimination, worker turnover, and the gender wage gap. *Labour Economics, 16,* 589–597.

Burdett, K., & Mortensen, D. T. (1998). Wage differentials, employer size, and unemployment. *International Economic Review, 39,* 257–273.

Depew, B., Norlander, P., & Sørensen, T. A. (2013). *Flight of the H-1B: Inter-firm mobility and return migration patterns for skilled guest workers* (IZA Discussion Paper No. 7456). Bonn, Germany: Institute for the Study of Labor.

Falch, T. (2010). The elasticity of labor supply at the establishment level. *Journal of Labor Economics, 28,* 237–266.

Falch, T. (2011). Teacher mobility responses to wage changes: Evidence from a quasi-natural experiment. *American Economic Review (Papers and Proceedings), 101,* 460–465.

Hicks, J. R. (1932). *The theory of wages*. London: Macmillan (2nd ed.).

Hirsch, B., Schank, T., & Schnabel, C. (2010). Differences in labor supply to monopsonistic firms and the gender pay gap: An empirical analysis using linked employer–employee data from Germany. *Journal of Labor Economics, 28,* 291–330.

Hirsch, B., & Jahn, E. J. (2015). Is there monopsonistic discrimination against immigrants? *Industrial and Labor Relations Review, 68*(3), 501–528.

Hotchkiss, J. L., & Quispe-Agnoli, M. (2012). *Employer monopsony power in the labor market for undocumented workers* (Working Paper No. 2009-14d). Atlanta, GA: Federal Reserve Bank of Atlanta.

Lavetti, K. (2016). *The estimation of compensating wage differentials: Lessons from the deadliest catch.* Unpublished manuscript. Department of Economics, Ohio State University, Columbus, OH.

Lief, Cabraser, Heimann, & Bernstein. (2015). *Case center: High tech employees class action lawsuit.* Retrieved January 28, 2015 at https://www.lieffcabraser.com/antitrust/high-tech-employees/

Manning, A. (2003). *Monopsony in motion: Imperfect competition in labor markets.* Princeton, NJ: Princeton University Press.

Manning, A. (2010). The plant size-place effect: Agglomeration and monopsony in labour markets. *Journal of Economic Geography, 10,* 717–744.

Mas, A., & Pallais, A. (in press). Valuing alternative work arrangements. *American Economic Review.*

Naidu, S. (2010). Recruitment restrictions and labor markets: Evidence from the postbellum U.S. South. *Journal of Labor Economics, 28,* 413–445.

Ransom, M. R., & Oaxaca, R. L. (2010). New market power models and sex differences in pay. *Journal of Labor Economics, 28,* 267–289.

Ransom, M. R., & Sims, D. P. (2010). Estimating the firm's labor supply curve in a "new monopsony" framework: Schoolteachers in Missouri. *Journal of Labor Economics, 28,* 331–355.

Robinson, J. V. (1933). *The economics of imperfect competition.* London: MacMillan.

Staiger, D. O., Spetz, J., & Phibbs, C. S. (2010). Is there monopsony power in the labor market? Evidence from a natural experiment. *Journal of Labor Economics, 28,* 211–236.

Ton, Z. (2012, January–February). Why good jobs are good for retailers. *Harvard Business Review,* 125–131. Retrieved from https://hbr.org/2012/01/why-good-jobs-are-good-for-retailers

Viscusi, W. K., & Aldy, J. E. (2003). The value of a statistical life: A critical review of market estimates throughout the world. *Journal of Risk and Uncertainty, 27*(1), 5–76.

Wiswall, M., & Zafar, B. (in press). Preference for the workplace, human capital, and gender. *Quarterly Journal of Economics.*

18 Setting Pay Levels: Efficiency Wage Models

Economists use the term "efficiency wages" to refer to the idea that paying a worker a higher wage might *cause* that worker to become more productive. There are at least three main ways this might happen. Probably the earliest to be discussed was in the context of developing countries, where it was argued that higher wages could have a direct effect on workers' productivity by improving their nutrition and health. Although this might be an important mechanism in low-wage economies, we won't study it in this book. A second way that higher wages could raise productivity is via a reciprocity mechanism, like the ones we studied in Chapter 10: Workers might respond to higher pay by voluntarily providing more effort, perhaps for fairness-related reasons. In this book, we'll call such wages *reciprocity-based* or *fairness-based* efficiency wages. Finally, in any firm that has a policy of dismissing workers caught shirking, higher wages help deter shirking because they raise the cost of job loss. We refer to wages that are high for this reason as *rational, shirking-based* efficiency wages. Firms may also change the *structure* of compensation to deter shirking, without necessarily raising the level of overall pay. These ideas are studied in Chapter 18.

18.1 Shirking and Dismissals: High Pay as a Worker Discipline Device

Our starting point in developing these models is Becker's (1974) model of optimal monitoring in Chapter 6, where we considered an agent who can only pick two effort levels: E^* ("working") or 0 ("shirking"). We denoted the agent's direct benefit to shirking by B and the cost his shirking imposes on the firm by G.

The probability that a shirking worker is detected was denoted by p, which we'll now assume is just a fixed number. In Chapter 6, we denoted the penalty the firm imposed on shirking workers by F (the "fine") and argued that whenever a firm could save on monitoring expenses by raising F, it should make F as high as possible.

In this section, we'll make one small tweak to Chapter 6's model of shirking and examine its consequences. Specifically, we'll assume that instead of imposing fines on shirking workers, firms deal with shirkers via a very simple policy: they just fire anyone caught shirking. (In most cases, this is the highest penalty a firm can impose on a worker anyway.) If that is a firm's policy, under what conditions will a rational worker shirk?

If the firm pays each of its workers a wage w, then under Chapter 6's assumptions, a nonshirking worker can count on receiving w for sure. A shirking worker, on the other hand, will have an expected utility of

$$EU^{shirk} = (1 - p)w + pw^{alt} + B, \tag{18.1}$$

where p is the probability the worker is caught (and therefore fired), and w^{alt} is the value of what the worker earns if fired. (Note that w^{alt} depends both on what the worker can earn in another firm and on how much time that person might spend unemployed until another job is found.) Thus a rational worker will refrain from shirking if and only if

$$w \geq (1 - p)w + pw^{alt} + B, \text{ or}$$

$$w \geq w^{alt} + B/p. \tag{18.2}$$

A simple but profound implication of the no-shirking condition in Equation 18.2 is Result 18.1.

RESULT 18.1

Efficiency Wages in a Rational Shirking Model

A policy of dismissing shirkers can only be effective if a firm pays strictly *more* than its workers will receive if they are dismissed, that is, if $w > w^{alt}$. Wages that are deliberately set by firms to be "'better than the market" with the intent of preventing shirking are efficiency wages of the rational-shirking type.

A (perhaps paradoxical) implication is that higher wages can be an effective disciplinary device: They mean that workers have more to lose if they are caught shirking.

One set of situations in which employers might consider using efficiency wages of the preceding type is jobs where mistakes or inattention by workers can cause great damage to capital equipment, human lives, or a company's reputation. Examples might include airplane pilots, crane operators, and CEOs. Put another way, Result 18.1 suggests that jobs that involve a lot of *responsibility* should be paid more, regardless of whether those jobs require a great deal of skill. Indeed, as it turns out, the *job evaluation schemes* described in Section 10.7 that are used by many large employers to set their internal pay policies attach considerable weight to a job's level of responsibility. An efficiency-wage-based desire to make sure those workers have a lot to lose if they shirk may help explain these high levels of pay. It may also help explain a strong temptation for corporate boards to pay their CEOs *better* than what the competition is offering.

Unemployment as A Worker Discipline Device

Imagine for a moment an economy where unemployment was so low that any worker who was fired from a job could immediately find another job that was just as good. In that economy, Result 18.1 has the paradoxical implication that the only way for a firm to prevent shirking is to pay better than other firms. Because it is impossible for all the employers to be "above average," this suggests that some level of *unemployment* might actually be a necessary feature of a capitalist economy. Without it, maintaining worker discipline would be a challenge. This idea is explored in depth by economists Carl Shapiro and Joseph Stiglitz (1984), though it can also be found in the writings of Karl Marx (1867), who argued in *Das Kapital* that a "reserve army of the unemployed" was required to enforce worker discipline in capitalist economies.

Whether a significant level of unemployment is an *essential* component of worker discipline is of course an unresolved question: As we've already seen in Chapter 2, there are many other ways to motivate workers besides the fear of dismissal. But an important lesson of Shapiro and Stiglitz's (1984; and Marx's, 1867) model is that employers can probably expect problems of worker discipline to be less severe in bad economic times when unemployment is high. Interestingly, that is exactly what was found by Lazear, Shaw, and Stanton (2016) in a recent study of a large U.S. services company from before, during, and after the recent Great Recession. Using data on 23,000 of the company's employees who perform exactly the same moderately skilled job at workplaces around the United States, the authors found that individual workers' productivity rose when unemployment in their state was high and explain this result using a rational-shirking model. The authors also argue that the historically large *increase* in labor productivity during the Great Recession might have been caused, in part, by higher effort levels of workers who had more than usual to fear from losing their jobs.

Is Teacher Tenure Harmful to Students? Evidence from Chicago and Washington, DC

A contentious feature of many public school teachers' contracts in the United States is the fact that after a short qualifying period, it can be extremely difficult to dismiss teachers for poor performance. This has led to many calls for the abolishment of "teacher tenure" and to a recent court case in which a Los Angeles County Superior Court judge ruled that California's 2-year tenure system was unconstitutional. According to the judge, California's policy—which made it very hard to dismiss incompetent teachers—violated students' civil rights because it disproportionately exposed low-income students to incompetent teachers.

But what is the evidence that giving teachers job security—thus eliminating the work incentives associated with the threat of job loss—actually reduces teacher performance? In one recent study, Brian Jacob (2013) studies the consequences of a 2004 collective bargaining agreement between the Chicago Public Schools and Chicago Teachers Union that gave principals the flexibility to dismiss teachers with less than 5 years of experience for *any* reason, and without the elaborate documentation and hearing process typical in many large, urban school districts. Jacob found that this new policy reduced annual teacher absences by roughly 10% and reduced the number of teachers with 15 or more annual absences by 20%. The effects were strongest among teachers in elementary schools and in low-achieving, predominantly African American high schools.

Thomas Dee and James Wyckoff (2015) conducted a similar study of IMPACT, the controversial teacher-evaluation system introduced in the District of Columbia Public Schools in 2009. Focusing on teachers whose performance evaluations put them at a significant risk of dismissal under the new system, the authors found that dismissal threats affected both teacher performance *and* their quit rates. Specifically, raising the threat of dismissal for poor performance increased the quit rate of low-performing teachers by more than 50%. Increased accountability also improved the performance of the at-risk teachers who remained by 0.27 of a teacher-level standard deviation.

Both Jacob's (2013) and Dee and Wyckoff's (2015) studies focus on public school teachers in underperforming U.S. schools, so their results may not generalize to other contexts. The results do illustrate, however, another possible cost of the employment protection laws we discussed in Section 13.1: Removing the threat of dismissal can increase shirking by workers.

18.2 Effects of Pay Levels on Worker Selection and Motivation: Evidence

So far in Part 3, we have identified at least three possible benefits that might accrue to a firm that raises the generosity of its pay package. First, higher wages can make it easier to hire and to retain workers of a given quality. Second, higher wages are likely to attract and retain *better*-qualified workers. And finally, higher wages—at least when combined with a credible threat of dismissal for low performance—can incentivize a firm's existing workers to improve their job performance.

But how important are the above effects in real firms? And can these effects ever be strong enough for wage increases to "pay for themselves" (i.e., to raise profits)? In this section, we'll review three empirical studies that look at this question. Two come from the U.S. auto industry, and one comes from the education system.

Henry Ford's Famous Five-Dollar Day: Was It Good for the Company?

The Ford Motor Company was founded in 1903, in an era when many small automobile companies built a small numbers of cars by hand using skilled craftsmen. While Ford started out producing cars this way, by 1913, the company revolutionized automobile manufacturing by introducing assembly line production. Among other advantages, the assembly line replaced skilled craftsmen by much lower-wage, less-skilled workers who could be trained to do simple tasks quickly. Using these workers (many of whom were immigrants with limited English), Ford now had 14,000 assembly line workers, producing 248,000 cars per year.

Ford's revolutionary movement to low-cost, low-skill workers came at a cost, however. Employee turnover under the new assembly line model was roughly 370%! This meant that, on average, 50,000 workers would need to be hired each year to maintain a workforce of 14,000. To put it another way, the average worker only stayed with Ford Motor Co. for a little over 3 months, creating massive costs in terms of finding, hiring, and training new workers. In addition, Ford's fluid workforce and low wages created another problem: absenteeism. On any given day, one out of every 10 Ford workers didn't show up for work. This created quality and production flow problems because each assembly line worker was assigned to perform a very specific task. Thus, when workers failed to show up, other workers would often need to be shuffled around the factory, doing work that they were less accustomed to.

In January of 1914, Ford decided to do something radical (and perhaps hard to imagine today) to combat these problems. Essentially overnight, he **doubled** the company's base wage rate from $2.50 per day to $5.00 per day. Although there were some qualifications—related mostly to the fact that Ford could now afford to be much more selective in picking its workers—the wage increase applied to essentially all production workers in the firm.[1]

What happened after this sudden change in company policy? In a quantitative study of historical company data, Daniel Raff and Lawrence Summers (1987) document some dramatic changes. Absenteeism fell from 10% to 2.5%, a reduction of three-fourths. Consistent with the monopsony model, Ford's quit rate fell by 87% between March 1913 and March 1914 (from 400% to 22%). Thus, rather than staying for 3 months, the average Ford worker could now be expected to stay at his job for 4½ years. Finally, productivity rose between 40% and 70%

[1] To qualify for the higher wage, a worker had to be a man over the age of 22 who was with the firm at least 6 months. Ford hoped to retain the most stable workers, especially those responsible for a family.

when the five-dollar day was introduced. Although the authors weren't able to pin down exactly which of these changes (selection of better workers, reduced turnover, reduced absenteeism, or increased effort) accounted for most of this productivity increase, it seems likely that at least a portion was due to abler workers moving to Ford, possibly from other auto manufacturers in Detroit.

Did Ford's five-dollar day "pay for itself"? Here, Raff and Summers's (1987) evidence is a bit more mixed. Profits grew in 1914, but it's important to remember that Ford was a successfully growing company during this entire period, including the years just before the five-dollar day was introduced. In fact, profits grew at a slightly *slower* pace in 1914 than in previous years. Despite this, the authors argue from other data that the longer term net effect on profits was indeed positive, something that Henry Ford truly believed. Indeed, Ford was very clear that the *motivation* for his massive pay increase was to raise profits. For example, although he was always at great pains to avoid capricious discharges of his workers, Ford was also careful to maintain the threat that inefficient workers would be discharged after wages rose. In explaining the five-dollar day, Ford said, "There was . . . no charity in any way involved. . . . We wanted to pay these wages so that the business would be on a lasting foundation. We were building for the future. A low wage business is always insecure. . . . The payment of five dollars a day for an eight hour day was one of the finest cost cutting moves we ever made" (Henry Ford, quoted in Raff & Summers, 1987, p. S59).

Wages and Shirking in the 1980s: More Evidence from the Auto Industry

In a more recent study of efficiency wages in the U.S. auto industry, Peter Cappelli and Keith Chauvin (1991) analyze data from 78 manufacturing plants of the same company in 1982. These 78 factories were distributed around the United States. Because all the workers belonged to the same union, wages were identical across all of the company's plants.[2] This fact, in combination with the fact that the company operated plants in very different labor markets across the United States, allowed the authors to test a key feature of both monopsony and efficiency wage theory: that a key determinant of employee recruitment, retention, and shirking is a worker's wage *relative* to his best alternative. Even though the company paid the same wage everywhere, this relative wage varied dramatically across the company's plants, ranging from a high level in places like South Carolina (where, say, \$45,000 per year would be an extremely good wage) to Michigan, where the same wage was comparable to what many other firms were paying. Thus, Cappelli and Chauvin asked whether—as suggested by efficiency wage theory—shirking is lower in plants located in low-wage states, where the company's wage premium over the local labor market was much higher.

[2] Wages were also essentially independent of seniority. Basically, the union contract stipulated a common wage for all the company's production workers, regardless of where in the United States they were employed.

Cappelli and Chauvin (1991) measured shirking by the rate of disciplinary dismissals in a plant; this is a reliable and objective measure because the union contract imposed the exact same regulations and procedures for dismissal of workers across all plants. Using regression analysis, they then asked whether a high wage premium was associated with fewer disciplinary dismissals. The authors also control for the local unemployment rate to see if it affects shirking decisions, as suggested by Shapiro and Stiglitz's (1984) model.

Cappelli and Chauvin (1991) indeed found that plants that pay better relative to the local labor market experience significantly less worker shirking. The same is true for plants located in high-employment areas. The authors also attempted to calculate whether the reduction in shirking from a $1 per hour wage increase would be large enough to cover the costs of the wage increase. Because dismissal procedures are very costly at this company, and because the actions taken by shirking workers can cause considerable economic damage in a capital-intensive assembly line environment (shutting down the line for any amount of time means none of the workers on it produce anything!), Cappelli and Chauvin conclude that this is certainly possible, though it's hard to nail down precisely.

The Equity Project's $125,000 Year: Can Large Increases in Teacher Pay Improve Educational Outcomes?

Whereas U.S. schools have tried many different ways to improve teacher and student performance, one idea that was not pursued until recently was dramatically raising teacher pay. In 2009, however, a new charter middle school (Grades 5–8) embracing this philosophy was opened in New York City's Washington Heights neighborhood. Called *The Equity Project* (TEP), this school was labeled by the *New York Times* as one of the country's "most closely watched educational experiments." TEP operated on the same per-student budget as other New York City public schools but spent dramatically less on administrative personnel and operated with larger class sizes (about 31 students compared to about 27). The resulting savings were used to pay teachers much more than other schools: TEP teachers received a base salary of $125,000, plus weekly professional development and a bonus based on schoolwide performance. In comparison, the median salary for New York City district teachers in TEP's geographic area was $75,092 in 2012–2013.

Several years after TEP was established, and 1 year after its first 5th-grade class graduated from 8th grade, Furgeson, McCullough, Wolfendale, and Gill (2014) studied its effects on student achievement. Although the school experienced some growing pains in its first 2 years of operation, by the 2012–2013 school year, TEP's cumulative impacts on students' achievement were consistently positive. By the time they graduated, TEP students had test score gains equal to an additional 1.6 years of school in math and an additional 0.4 years of school in English, compared to New York City students in similar schools.

Importantly, TEP's success was not the result of "cherry-picking" its students. In fact, the school admitted students using a lottery that favors students in its neighborhood and low-achieving students. Compared to students in nearby schools, TEP students had similar 4th-grade test scores and had a similar socio-economic background. TEP's success was not the result of selectively "pushing" low-achieving students out the door either: Its attrition rate was similar to other comparable New York City schools. So why did TEP succeed? According to Furgeson et al. (2014), TEP devoted a lot of resources to recruiting and identifying the best teachers, to continuous training, and evaluation of teachers (including a mandatory 6-week summer institute). In addition, TEP's high salaries probably helped the school recruit talented teachers and may also have allowed the school to set such high expectations of teacher performance. TEP also held teachers accountable: More than a third of TEP teachers were not rehired after their 1st year. Thus, it seems possible that TEP's high salary, combined with the very real possibility of not being rehired, generated a strong efficiency wage effect on effort.

Although TEP remains a small demonstration project in its early stages, its experience demonstrates once again that wage increases, even though an obvious direct cost to employers, can also have substantial beneficial effects on employee performance, at least if they are accompanied by significant increases in expectations and training and by the prospect of job loss if those expectations are not met.

18.3 Deferred Compensation as an Incentive and Retention Tool

In the last two sections, we discussed high wages (combined with a policy of firing shirkers) as a worker discipline device. Although high wages can indeed deter shirking, from the principal's point of view, they are of course a rather *expensive* way to accomplish that goal. In this section, we explore some ways to change the *structure* of compensation in a way that deters shirking while keeping the overall level of pay fixed.[3] All of these changes, which could reduce shirking at no direct cost to the employer, involve some form of *deferred* compensation, that is, they are arrangements in which the employer decides to "hold back" some of a worker's pay until later in the employment relationship. As we'll see, these solutions can also reduce shirking, but they raise some new problems as well. For example, they might incentivize *employers* to behave dishonestly, or distort workers' incentives to retire at the socially optimal time.

Modeling Shirking in a Multiperiod Context

To understand how deferred compensation might change a worker's decision to shirk, we need a model in which the principal and agent interact more than once. To that end, let's imagine a single worker (call her Amira) who is attached to a

[3] Notice that we also considered the effects of compensation structure (including how wage payments are allocated over time) in Section 15.4. There, the focus was on how compensation structure affects the *type* of worker that is attracted to the firm. Here, we focus on the effects of compensation structure on workers' effort choices, and on worker retention (i.e., on quit rates).

firm (call it Netpix) for T periods. We'll think of a period as lasting 1 year. Netpix pays its workers a wage of w_t, which be different each year. For now, we'll ignore the issue of quits: Amira stays with Netpix from Period 1 through Period T unless she is fired. As in Section 18.1, the worker's effort decision is dichotomous: In each year, she simply decides whether to work or shirk. If Amira works, she produces a fixed amount, Q. If she shirks, her output for the entire year is zero.

If Amira shirks, we now assume (for simplicity) that she's caught with certainty ($p = 1$ in the language of Section 18.1). Although all shirkers are caught, they're not detected immediately: Specifically, we assume that shirkers are caught in the *middle of the year*.[4] This means that a shirking worker will still be paid for half of the year in which that worker shirks, despite producing no output. Shirking confers a one-time benefit, B, to the worker, which can be thought of as the dollar value of the extra leisure that person enjoys until caught. In our example, we'll set $B = 50$, as shorthand for \$50,000. If she's fired, Amira goes to another job (her next best option), and stays there until Period T, where she is paid w_t^{alt} each year. Thus, each period the worker must choose whether to work (in which case the worker gets to stay with the firm for 1 more year, with the possibility of either working or shirking in the future), or to shirk, in which case the worker will get fired in the middle of the year and spend the rest of his or her career (up to Period T) outside the firm. Mathematically, a rational worker thus compares the present values of two income streams to decide whether to work or shirk in each period. To simplify our present-value calculations, we'll assume that workers don't discount the future (i.e., that $\delta = \beta = 1$: see Section 9.7).

More precisely, if Amira shirks in Period t, the present value of her utility (PVU) from that period forward will be[5]

$$\text{PVU}_t^{shirk} = 50 + 0.5 \times (w_t^{alt} + w_t) + w_{t+1}^{alt} + \ldots + w_T^{alt}, \qquad \textbf{(18.3)}$$

where 50 is the one-shot gain from shirking, and the second term in the expression incorporates the assumption that shirkers are caught and dismissed in the middle of the year.

If Amira works in Period t, the present value of her utility from that period forward will be

$$PVU_t^{work} = w_t + V_{t+1}, \qquad \textbf{(18.4)}$$

where V_{t+1} is the value (to the worker) of still being with the original firm (Netpix) at the beginning of Period $t + 1$. We'll work this out for each year in our examples following.

To see how the timing of compensation affects the worker's shirking decision, we'll work with the three-period example laid out in Table 18.1.

[4] If shirkers were caught immediately, their lack of effort wouldn't hurt the firm; thus, shirking would no longer be a problem.

[5] As in Section 15.3, we'll continue to measure utility when working by the wage income received. Disutility of effort enters the model via the parameter B, which is the value of extra leisure enjoyed when a worker decides to shirk.

TABLE 18.1 PRESENT VALUES OF UTILITY (PVU) FROM WORKING VERSUS SHIRKING: THE CONSTANT-WAGE CASE

PERIOD	OUTPUT (IF WORK)	WAGE (W_T)	OUTSIDE WAGE (W_T^{ALT})	REMAINING *PVU* FROM WORKING	REMAINING PVU FROM SHIRKING
1	100	100	70	100 + 235 = **335**	50 + 0.5(100 + 70) + 70 + 70 = **275**
2	100	100	70	100 + 135 = **235**	50 + 0.5(100 + 70) + 70 = **205**
3	100	100	70	**100**	50 + 0.5(100 + 70) = **135**

Table 18.1 considers the constant-wage case in which a worker who produces \$100,000 of value per year is paid that full amount in each of her 3 years at the company. To see whether (and *when*) she's likely to shirk, we proceed (as we did in the basic principal–agent problem) by *backwards induction*, starting with Year 3.

Suppose, then, Amira has made it to the start of Year 3 without shirking. If she "works" in Year 3, she won't get fired and will earn a wage of 100. If she shirks, she'll get an immediate benefit of $B = 50$ from shirking, and will earn a total of 0.5(100 + 70) = 85 in wages, because she'll be fired in the middle of the year. This adds up to 135, so **she'll definitely shirk in her final year** with the company *if she sticks around that long.*

What will Amira do in Year 2, assuming she's with Netpix at the start of that year? Using the same logic as before, if she shirks, she'll get an immediate benefit of 50; earn 85 in Year 2, and 70 in Period 3; for a total present value of 205. If she works, she'll get 100 in Year 2, plus the value of still being with the firm at the start of Year 3, V_3. What's V_3? Well, we just worked out that the best thing to do in Year 3 if she's still with Netpix is to shirk, which is worth 135. Thus, the value of working in Year 2 is 100 + 135 = 235, which is better than shirking, so **working is best in Year 2**.

Finally, what will Amira do in Period 1? If she shirks then, she'll spend most of the next 3 years outside the firm, earning a *PVU* of 275. If she works, she'll earn 100 in Period 3 and do the best she can from there on, receiving $V_2 = 235$, for a total *PVU* of 335. **Thus, working is best in Year 1**. To sum up, Amira's best plan, faced with a constant wage schedule of 100 per year, is to work in her first 2 years on the job and slack off in her last year.

How will her employer, Netpix, feel about Amira's plan? If Amira carries out her plan, she'll receive a total of 250 in wages from the company and produce 200 in output (because she produces nothing in the first half of Year 3 before getting caught). It follows that **Netpix would lose money by offering Amira this job and won't offer it to her.** Importantly, this end result is *economically inefficient*: Amira ends up working outside Netpix for the entire 3 years, producing and earning \$70,000 per year instead of the \$100,000 she would produce with the company. Although she would *like* to convince Netpix before she joins the company that she won't slack off in her final year with them, this can be hard to do. As we argued in Section 10.2, effort is noncontractible in most realistic situations, that is, promises not to shirk at a future date are almost impossible to enforce in any courts. Put another way, *the knowledge that rational workers will be tempted to shirk in the future can eliminate the possibility of mutually beneficial exchange between firms and those workers.*[6]

Bonding as a Shirking Deterrent

One way out of the previous dilemma is for our worker (Amira) to *post a bond* before she starts working with Netpix. Imagine, for example, that Amira deposits \$50,000 into an account that she agrees to forfeit to the employer if she commits a fireable offence before the end of her 3-year contract. The consequences of shirking in each year of her Netpix career are now shown in Table 18.2.[7]

Now, it makes sense for Amira to work in all three periods. In Year 3, for example, she earns 135 (as in the previous example) if she shirks. If she works, however, she gets 100 + 50 = 150 because her \$50,000 bond is returned to her. Working backwards as we did before, we see that working is the best strategy in all three periods.[8]

Thus, Amira is made better off by being able to post a bond: Netpix can now be confident that Amira won't shirk if Netpix hires her. Economic efficiency is increased because Amira is now working in the place (Netpix) where she's most productive. And although Netpix is indifferent between the scenarios in Tables 18.1 and 18.2 (it makes zero profits either way), it's easy to show that Netpix can also be made better off if Amira is able to post a bond. To see this, replace the wage profile (100, 100, 100) by the profile (95, 95, 95) in Table 18.2. If you work through the example, Amira still refrains from shirking and will earn a *total* PVU from working of 335 − 50 (the cost of the bond) = 285. Netpix will earn a total profit of 3 × 5 = 15. So, both parties are better off than without the bond, when Amira earns 210 and Netpix earns zero profits.

In the United States, explicit bonds are available for a wide variety of occupations, including auto dealers, contractors, notaries public, auctioneers, house cleaners, driving instructors, guard services, and truck drivers. In most of these cases, the bond is not an upfront payment made by the worker, as we've assumed

[6] You might argue that our Netpix example is a bit artificial because any worker nearing the end of a 3-year contract may rationally refrain from shirking in the hopes of being offered another contract. That's absolutely correct, but it follows from our use of a three-period example to simplify the calculations. More generally, whenever an employee knows that he has relatively little time left with his employer (whether due to impending retirement, labor force withdrawal, or an expected move to another employer), his incentives to refrain from shirking—which derive mainly from the present value of continuing his relationship with the current employer—become compromised, leading to the problems we study here.

[7] Notice that the \$50,000 bond does not appear in Table 18.2's calculations for period 1. That's because the bond must be paid before the worker can start the job. Once she has accepted the job and paid the bond, a rational Amira's shirking decisions will depend only on how shirking affects her chances of getting that money back.

[8] Although we have assumed a bond of 50 (exactly equal to the value of shirking to the worker), any bond above 35 will prevent shirking in this example.

TABLE 18.2 PRESENT VALUES OF UTILITY (PVU) FROM WORKING VERSUS SHIRKING, WITH BONDING

PERIOD	OUTPUT (IF WORK)	WAGE (W_T)	OUTSIDE WAGE (W_T^{ALT})	REMAINING *PVU* FROM WORKING	REMAINING PVU FROM SHIRKING
1	100	100	70	100 + 250 = **350**	50 + 0.5(100 + 70) + 70 + 70 = **275**
2	100	100	70	100 + 150 = **250**	50 + 0.5(100 + 70) + 70 = **205**
3	100	100	70	100 + 50 = **150**	50 + 0.5(100 + 70) = **135**

to simplify matters. Instead it's essentially an insurance policy purchased for an annual fee by the worker (or his employer) from a *surety company.* Surety companies investigate potential workers and only bond those they feel have a sufficiently low risk of violating their employment contracts.[9] Here, the worker's loss from violating her bond is the strong likelihood that no surety company will bond her again. As our theoretical example suggests, bonded status can make workers much more attractive to employers, landing them good jobs they might not otherwise qualify for.[10]

Deferred Compensation as a Shirking Deterrent

Although bonding is used in some jobs, it is not very common. One potential reason is that an alternative solution exists. In particular, instead of requiring an upfront payment from Amira or involving a surety company, Netpix can implicitly *manufacture* a bond by offering Amira an *upward-sloping wage contract.* Put another way, Netpix can *take the bond out of Amira's early-career wages* (by underpaying her relative to her productivity), and pay Amira back by overpaying her later (*if* she's still with the company). The idea is distinct from, but related to the idea of implicitly making sales workers "pay for their jobs" by taking the job fee ($-a$) out of the first few units they sell (see Section 3.3).

This strategy is illustrated in Table 18.3, which assumes that instead of the wage profile (100, 100, 100), Amira is now paid the profile (20, 100, 180) with the same total value, just different timing. The high rate of pay in her final period now deters Amira from shirking in that period, and the *anticipation of high pay if she makes it to her final period* deters her from shirking in earlier periods. Thus, by deferring some of Amira's compensation, we've worked out a way for her to be employed at Netpix, where she is $30,000 more productive per year than she is anywhere else.

---

[9] Bonds that prevent a worker from quitting are prohibited in some jurisdictions.

[10] Wikipedia has a very helpful article on https://en.wikipedia.org/wiki/Surety_bonds.

TABLE 18.3 PRESENT VALUES OF UTILITY FROM WORKING VERSUS SHIRKING, WITH DEFERRED COMPENSATION

PERIOD	OUTPUT (IF WORK)	WAGE (W_T)	OUTSIDE WAGE (W_T^{ALT})	REMAINING *PVU* FROM WORKING	REMAINING PVU FROM SHIRKING
1	100	20	70	20 + 280 = **300**	50 + 0.5(20 + 70) + 70 + 70 = **235**
2	100	100	70	100 + 180 = **280**	50 + 0.5(100 + 70) + 70 = **205**
3	100	180	70	**180**	50 + 0.5(180 + 70) = **175**

To summarize, deferred compensation means paying workers less than they produce when they're young (junior) and more than they produce when they're older (senior). Notably, firms that use deferred compensation *give workers raises just for accumulating seniority*: In Table 18.3, Amira's pay rises rapidly over the years despite the fact that her productivity remains fixed at 100 per year. Although awarding raises purely for seniority (independently of performance) is sometimes seen as a sign of lax or lazy management, that is not the case here. True, older workers are overpaid relative to what they produce, but these high pay levels essentially function as *prizes* (for staying with the firm and not getting fired) that the firm has promised to pay when young workers agreed to join the firm at a low starting wage.

Are these types of deferred compensation contracts common in the real world? Although it's hard to know without clean and accurate measures of individual worker productivity over their entire careers with a firm, the notion that new hires "work their butts off" for low pay while older workers who have received seniority-based pay increases might not be pulling their full weight seems plausible in some contexts.[11] Again, although little hard evidence exists, some examples that are frequently cited are law firms and universities. Traditionally, young lawyers are hired by law firms and work extremely long hours for relatively low pay until they become partners. Although partners play important roles in the practice (including bringing in new business), they arguably have a much nicer life than the new hires and are paid much more. In the same way, young scientists work extremely long hours at low wages as postdocs and assistant professors. In doing so, they are—at least in part—motivated by the high pay and job security associated with eventually landing a tenured position.

[11] Supporting evidence for this idea comes from studies of displaced workers: workers who permanently lose their jobs due to plant closures or large-scale layoffs. Among displaced workers, those with many years of service at the company that closed suffer much larger wage losses than junior workers, suggesting that the older workers were overpaid relative to their market alternatives (see, e.g., Jacobson, Lalonde, & Sullivan, 1993). This pattern could, however, result from other factors as well, such as a higher level of firm-specific skills among senior workers.

RESULT 18.2

Bonding and Deferred Compensation as Shirking Deterrents

In long-term employment relationships, workers' desires to keep working for a firm can be an important deterrent to shirking. The value of this deterrent, however, diminishes as workers approach the end of their relationship with a firm. If firms anticipate this, they may be unwilling to hire some workers in the first place, even though those workers would be more productive in their firm than anywhere else.

Two solutions to this problem are employee bonding and deferred compensation, combined with a policy of dismissing shirkers. Implemented correctly, these policies can reduce shirking by changing the structure of pay over time, without increasing the total amount of pay.

Bonding, Deferred Compensation, and Quits

So far in this section, we've argued that bonding and deferred compensation—combined with a policy of dismissing shirkers—can prevent shirking. By the very same arguments, it also follows that bonding and deferred compensation can reduce employee *quits*: Holding back some pay till the worker has remained with the firm for a certain period provides an obvious incentive not to quit until the held-back pay has been received. Indeed, reduced worker turnover—a central component of an effective employee selection strategy—may be the most important benefit of a deferred-compensation strategy.

Again, although measuring the employee-retention effects of deferred compensation is difficult, some well-known deferred-compensation practices are deliberately designed to limit employee turnover. One of the best examples is employee stock options, which typically do not vest until the worker has remained with the firm for a certain amount of time. In the technology sector, where turnover of top employees with valuable technical knowledge can be very costly, non-vested stock options are widely used, in combination with other practices like non-compete agreements, to limit worker turnover.

RESULT 18.3

Bonding and Deferred Compensation as Quit Deterrents

For the same reasons that bonding and deferred compensation can reduce shirking, they can also reduce voluntary turnover of employees without requiring an increase in the total amount of pay. Employee stock options that don't vest until a worker has accumulated a minimum period of service are an important example of this practice.

Deferred Compensation and the Retirement Decision

So far in this section, we've made the case *in favor of* deferred compensation. We now turn our attention to some problems with these schemes, the first of which is that deferred compensation can distort workers' retirement decisions,

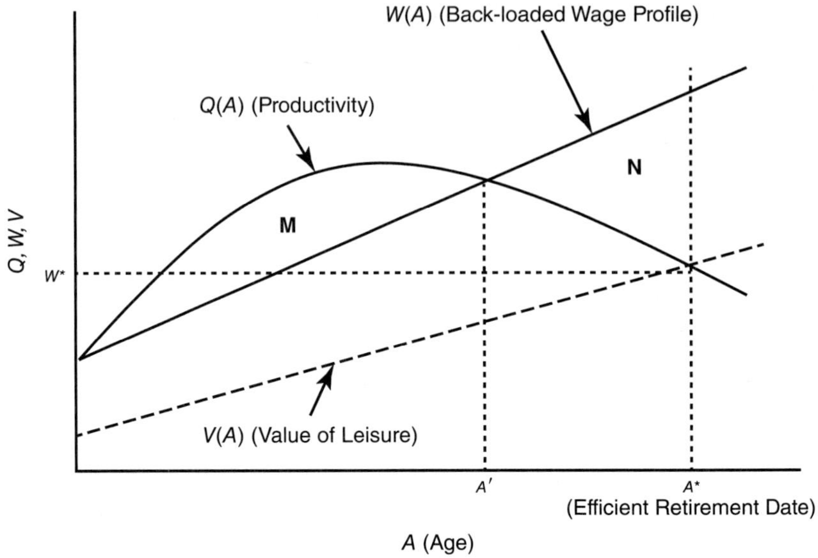

FIGURE 18.1. Deferred Compensation and Retirement Incentives

incentivizing workers to remain on their jobs beyond the economically efficient retirement date. This idea, first and famously exposited by Lazear (1979), is illustrated in Figure 18.1.

Figure 18.1 illustrates a lifetime productivity profile, $Q(A)$, that is relatively typical: Productivity starts out at a low level when a worker (call him Tony) enters the labor force; increases as he acquires skills, connections, and experience; then eventually starts to decline. Although some of this decline may be due to the physiology of aging, it is also rational for employees to invest less in keeping their skills up to date as they approach retirement.[12] Figure 18.1 also shows a hypothetical value-of-leisure profile, $V(A)$, which is increasing over time; $V(A)$ represents the utility value to Tony of no longer being employed. Although it seems natural to think of $V(A)$ as rising with age—again, in part, for the physiological reason that work gets more painful with age—an increasing $V(A)$ function is not at all essential to our argument.

Now, suppose first that Tony is self-employed, or (equivalently) that he works for a firm that pays him exactly what he produces in each year of his

[12] Whereas a hump-shaped $Q(A)$ function is pretty ubiquitous, the age of peak productivity may vary substantially across professions. For example, the peak may be in the early teens for Olympic gymnasts, and quite late in life for politicians and historians. The hump can shift over time as well: Jones and Weinberg (2011), for example, show that in contrast to Einstein's famous early-life achievements, chemists and physicists now "peak" much later in life.

life. Thus, Tony's lifetime wage profile coincides with his productivity profile, *Q*(*A*). When will Tony retire? Tony will retire at age *A**, which is the point at which his earnings from working no longer outweigh his enjoyment from not working. Assuming that *Q*(*A*) also represents the value to society of what Tony produces in his job, *A** is also the *economically efficient* retirement age for Tony.

Things change, however, if Tony works for a company that deliberately holds back some of his compensation to later ages, as a way of reducing Tony's incentives to shirk and increasing his loyalty to the company. To see this, imagine that Tony faces the backloaded wage profile, *W*(*A*), which underpays him (relative to his productivity) when he's young and overpays him when he's older. If areas M and N in the figure are equal (adjusting for discounting), then the wage profile *W*(*A*) has the same present value as the profile *Q*(*A*), though that is not essential to our argument either. Faced with the wage profile *W*(*A*), when will Tony retire? Unless his employer can force him to retire at age *A**, or unless it can cut his wage dramatically (down to *W**) when he reaches age *A**, he'll want to keep working well beyond his efficient retirement age! That's because Tony's wage at that age vastly overstates his true value to the company. In fact, Tony's wage begins to exceed his true value to the company at the age *A'*, which means the company would prefer he retires even earlier than the efficient age, *A**.

How can employers and workers avoid this problem? If they wish to defer some of the worker's compensation, one attractive option might be to include a *mandatory retirement age* in the worker's employment contract. Of course, if the mandatory age is set in advance, this is less than a perfect solution because older workers may differ considerably in their productivity (*Q*) and their value of leisure (*V*).[13] Another serious (but country-specific) problem is that mandatory retirement clauses are not legal in U.S. employment contracts.[14] These clauses can have large effects on older workers: For example, Holgersson and Thögersen (2002) show that the 1994 prohibition of compulsory retirement for professors dramatically reduced their retirement rates.

A third option could be to structure workers' retirement benefits so as to incentivize workers to retire at an efficient age. For example, a worker's pension could be an increasing function of seniority, which *stops* increasing after age 65. This ensures that the worker has plenty of incentive to work *until* age 65 (as the pension continues to increase), but once age 65 is reached, the marginal benefits of working longer are lessened.[15]

---

[13] Giving the employer discretion over the worker's retirement date doesn't help either because (as noted) opportunistic employers will have an incentive to retire their workers *too young*, that is, at age *A'* in Figure 18.1.

[14] Trying to induce retirement by dramatically cutting wages is also prohibited.

[15] As defined-contribution retirement plans have all but replaced traditional pensions in the United States, employers' options to make such adjustments are now much more limited than they were.

RESULT 18.4

Deferred Compensation and Retirement Incentives

An important side effect of backloaded wage profiles is that they can *send the wrong signals to older workers about when they should retire.* Because older workers are overpaid relative to their productivity under such profiles, they'll want to keep working beyond their efficient retirement age.

Mandatory retirement clauses in employment contracts are (imperfect) solutions to this problem, though they are prohibited in some countries, including the United States. Another solution is designing pension plans to induce retirement at efficient ages.

Deferred Compensation and Employers' Incentives

So far in our discussion of deferred compensation, we've assumed that workers are the only parties who might break their end of the employment bargain, either by shirking, or by quitting earlier than the employer would like. To address those problems, we've argued that it might be efficient for employers to "hold back" some of workers' pay till later in the employment relationship. Thus, we were implicitly assuming that employers' concerns with their reputations (or some other factor) are strong enough to ensure that employers keep up their end of the employment contract. However, especially under deferred-compensation arrangements like those described here, the incentives for employers to renege on their promises can be very high.

For example, consider a firm with an aging workforce, like many manufacturing companies in the U.S. Rust Belt during the late 20th century. Having promised to overpay its older workers (relative to their productivity), such a company might now face a situation where most of its workers are paid more than they produce. Indeed, *any* firm using deferred compensation will want to fire all of its workers older than age A' in Figure 18.1. Although that might be hard to do explicitly (e.g., age-based layoffs are prohibited by the U.S.'s Age Discrimination in Employment Act), there are other ways to accomplish the same goal. For example, the company could disproportionately claim that its older workers were shirking. Because firing shirkers is consistent with deferred-compensation contracts, it would be very hard to prove that the firm was reneging on its obligations to its workers. Alternatively, if older workers were a large majority, the company could simply go out of business to avoid further losses associated with its implicit promises. A final option is to agree to a hostile takeover, merger, or a leveraged buyout from companies like Bain Capital. As Shleifer and Summers (1989) argued in an influential article, such acquisitions allow the new owners to violate implicit contracts made by the previous owners, essentially with impunity. According to Shleifer and Summers, at least part of the profit-enhancing impacts of such leveraged buyouts is not due to better management but is a result of reneging on deferred-compensation agreements made by the previous owners.

RESULT 18.5

Deferred Compensation and Breach of Trust by Employers

Deferred-compensation arrangements create incentives for *employers* to violate implicit labor contracts by avoiding their obligations to their older workers. These violations can take various forms, including disproportionately laying off or firing older workers, going out of business, or corporate takeovers.

Given these incentives, workers who are considering a job that (explicitly or implicitly) defers some of their pay should carefully consider the employer's incentives and abilities to honor those commitments in the future.

Deferred Compensation and Workers' Reputations

Having discussed employers' reputations for upholding their commitments, we conclude this section with a brief discussion of *workers'* reputations. To that end, suppose that a worker's *propensity to shirk* is a relatively permanent characteristic and that other employers can observe whether a worker was fired for cause from a previous job.[16] If that is true, or if outside employers have other ways of observing an employee's productivity at previous jobs, then arrangements such as bonds, deferred compensation, or even incentive pay schemes like piece rates and bonuses may be unnecessary. Even without these devices, *workers are disciplined by their reputation in the labor market* because future employers will avoid known shirkers.

Personnel economists refer to the idea that people work hard early in their careers to build reputations as nonshirkers as "career concerns." Interestingly, the idea dates back to a seminar article by Eugena Fama (1980) in which he argued that incentive pay schemes for CEOs—which have exploded in size and popularity since then—may be *unnecessary*. After all, in some sense, a CEO's job performance is known to the entire world: It's the stock market performance of the company while he's in charge. If that's the case, then the best CEOs will be rewarded by generous job offers from other (and likely larger) companies, providing strong incentives to perform well even in the absence of incentive pay. Thus, when a worker's job performance is public information, the labor market for workers provides strong incentives to supply effort, even in firms that offer no incentive pay at all. Of course, the degree to which workers' performance information is public varies substantially across jobs and industries, and the preceding argument applies mostly to young workers (who are building reputations and have a career with several potential job changes ahead of them).

[16] This is less obvious than it may seem. For a variety of reasons, it can be hard for new employers to know why an applicant's previous job ended. Aside from the applicant's obvious incentives to obscure this information (e.g., by blaming "policy disagreements" for the termination or simply not including the job on his resume), previous employers can also be complicit, for example, by promising a good recommendation letter in return for a resignation. More generally, objectively assigning blame to one side can be impossible even for well-intentioned parties.

We consider the effort-eliciting role of workers' reputations in more detail when we study *market-based tournaments* in Section 22.4. Here, we conclude by noting that—in addition to all the other incentive mechanisms we've studied so far—workers' concerns for their labor market reputations are an important motivator in some work settings. In those settings (for example, in academia where every scientist's publication record is easily accessed on the web, and where "star" performers can receive generous offers from other employers), performance pay within companies may not be necessary.

RESULT 18.6 **Workers' Career Concerns as a Discipline Device**

When information about individual workers' job performance is widely available to other employers, future wage and job offers from other employers may incentivize workers on their current jobs to the point where *neither deferred compensation nor incentive pay may be necessary.* Such *worker reputation effects* are more effective near the start of workers' careers, when their value to future employers is more sensitive to their current performance.

Chapter Summary

- ☐ High wages can act as an effective worker discipline device in rational shirking-based efficiency wage models, but only if the employer maintains a consistent policy of dismissing shirkers.

- ☐ Evidence from Ford Motors in 1914, from the U.S. auto industry in the 1980s, and from a New York City public school all show that large wage increases can have a number of beneficial effects listed previously, including lower turnover, lower absenteeism, abler workers, and higher levels of employee effort.

- ☐ Deferring some of the worker's compensation can increase the power of high wages as a worker discipline device and can reduce employee turnover as well.

- ☐ Deferred compensation, however, can distort workers' retirement decisions and creates incentives for employers to renege on their long-term obligations to their workers.

- ☐ If workers' job performance or their records of being fired for cause are known to other employers, neither deferred compensation nor any of the incentive pay schemes we study in Parts 1, 2, 4, and 5 of the book may be necessary. The wider labor market will reward hard workers without any need for individual employers to incentivize their workers.

Discussion Questions

1. What are the pros and cons of allowing employers to offer employment contracts with mandatory retirement provisions?
2. Consider a firm that has had a long tradition of job security for its senior workers, plus a practice of paying its most senior workers more than the value of their productivity. Overall, business conditions are still about the same as when those workers were hired. Is it ethical for the firm to lay these senior workers off? Discuss whether such a decision is always in a firm's long-term interests, and under what circumstances it is economically efficient.
3. In this chapter, we noted that employers who operate deferred-compensation arrangements might have incentives to renege on those arrangements in other ways, such as mischaracterizing the true reason for firing older workers, going out of business, or participating in a leveraged buyout that cuts older workers' benefits. Referring to Shleifer and Summers' (1988) discussion of this issue, in your view are existing legal remedies, the company's economic prospects, and the employer's concern for its reputation sufficient to deter these opportunistic actions in most circumstances?

Suggestions for Further Reading

For empirical evidence that firms defer workers' compensation, see Medoff and Abraham (1980); Kotlikoff and Gokhale (1992); and Guiso, Pistaferri, and Schivardi (2013).

For models of career concerns, see Akerlof (1976) and Gibbons and Murphy (1992).

For evidence that career concerns motivate workers, see Chevalier and Ellison (1999); Cullen and Mazzeo (2008); Landers, Rebitzer, and Taylor (1996); and Lim, Berk, Sensoy, and Weisbach (2016) for studies of mutual fund managers, public school principals, lawyers, and hedge fund managers, respectively.

For the seminal paper on efficiency wages, see Shapiro and Stiglitz (1984). There are also interesting comments and replies to it in the September and December 1985 issues of the *American Economic Review*.

For experimental evidence on Shapiro and Stiglitz's (and Marx's) idea that equilibrium unemployment in a labor market can emerge from the interactions of employers' attempts to discipline their workers, see Fehr, Kirchsteiger, and Riedl (1996).

For direct evidence that wage increases raise the quality of workers that can be hired, see Giuliano's (2013) study of teenage employment at a large U.S. retail firm.

References

Akerlof, G. A. (1976). The economics of caste and of the rat race and other woeful tales. *Quarterly Journal of Economics, 90,* 599–617.

Holgersson, C., & Thögersen, S. (2002). Did the elimination of mandatory retirement affect faculty retirement? *American Economic Review, 92*(4), 957–980.

Becker, G. S. (1974). Crime and punishment: An economic approach. In G. S. Becker & W. M. Landes (Eds.), *Essays in the economics of crime and punishment.* Cambridge, MA: National Bureau of Economic Research. Retrieved from http://www.nber.org/chapters/c3625.pdf

Cappelli, P., & Chauvin, K. (1991). An interplant test of the efficiency wage hypothesis. *Quarterly Journal of Economics, 106,* 769–787.

Chevalier, J., & Ellison, G. (1999). Career concerns of mutual fund managers. *Quarterly Journal of Economics, 114,* 389–432.

Cullen, J., & Mazzeo, M. (2008). *Implicit performance awards: An empirical analysis of the labor market for public school principals.* Unpublished manuscript, Department of Economics, University of California, San Diego.

Dee, T. S., & Wyckoff, J. (2015). Incentives, selection, and teacher performance: Evidence from IMPACT. *Journal of Policy Analysis and Management, 34*(2), 267–297.

Fama, E. F. (1980). Agency problems and the theory of the firm. *Journal of Political Economy, 88,* 288–307.

Fehr, E., Kirchsteiger, G., & Riedl, A. (1996). Involuntary unemployment and non-compensating wage differentials in an experimental labour market. *Economic Journal, 106*(434), 106–121.

Furgeson, J., McCullough, M., Wolfendale, C., & Gill, B. (2014, October). *The Equity Project Charter School: Impacts on student achievement.* Cambridge, MA: Mathematica Policy Research.

Gibbons, R., & Murphy, K. J. (1992). Optimal incentive contracts in the presence of career concerns: Theory and evidence. *Journal of Political Economy, 100,* 468–505.

Guiso, L., Pistaferri, L., & Schivardi, F. (2013). Credit within the firm. *Review of Economic Studies, 80*(1), 211–247.

Jacob, B. A. (2013). The effect of employment protection on worker effort: Evidence from public schooling. *Journal of Labor Economics, 31,* 727–761.

Jacobson, L. S., Lalonde, R. J., & Sullivan, D. G. (1993). Earnings losses of displaced workers. *American Economic Review, 83*(4), 685–709.

Jones, B., & Weinberg, B. (2011, November 22). Age dynamics in scientific creativity. *Proceedings of the National Academy of the Sciences, 108,* 910–914.

Kotlikoff, L. J., & Gokhale, J. (1992). Estimating a firm's age-productivity profile using the present value of workers' earnings. *Quarterly Journal of Economics, 107,* 1215–1242.

Landers, R. M, Rebitzer, J. B., & Taylor, L. J. (1996). Rat race redux: Adverse selection in the determination of work hours in law firms. *American Economic Review, 86,* 329–348.

Lazear, E. P. (1979). Why is there mandatory retirement? *Journal of Political Economy, 87,* 1261–1284.

Lazear, E. P., Shaw, K. L., & Stanton, C. (2016). Making do with less: working harder during recessions. *Journal of Labor Economics*, *34*(S1), S333–S360.

Lim, J., Sensoy, B. A., & Weisbach, M. S. (2016). Indirect incentives of hedge fund managers. *Journal of Finance*, *71*(2), 871–918.

Marx, K. (1867). das Kapital, vol. 1. *Marx/Engels: Werke, 23.*

Medoff, J. L., & Abraham, K. G. (980). Experience, performance, and earnings. *Quarterly Journal of Economics, 95,* 703–736.

Raff, D. M. G., & Summers, L. H. (1987). Did Henry Ford pay efficiency wages? *Journal of Labor Economics, 5*(4), Part 2, S57–S86.

Shapiro, C., & Stiglitz, J. E. (1984). Equilibrium unemployment as a worker discipline device. *American Economic Review, 74,* 433–444.

Shleifer, A., & Summers, L. H. (1988). Breach of trust in hostile takeovers. In A. J. Auerbach (Ed.), *Corporate takeovers: Causes and consequences.* Chicago: University of Chicago Press.

19 Training

As we learned in Part 1, when a firm needs a product or service, it may either "buy" the product from an outside source, or "make" it in-house. This logic also applies to the firm's workforce: Should the firm "buy" workers who come pre-trained with useful skills, or "make" skilled workers by hiring low-skill workers and training them in-house? In Chapter 19, we will discuss this question and many others related to worker training. As a warm-up exercise, we'll start in Section 19.1 by studying a training decision made by most workers before they enter the labor market: whether to attend college. This is a relatively simple human capital investment decision to analyze because the training decision primarily affects just one person—the potential student—who is also the investment's primary beneficiary.

In the remainder of the chapter, we study investments in the training of workers who are already attached to a firm. Here, both workers and firms may bear part of the costs of acquiring certain skills, and benefit from the added productivity those skills yield. Thus, in addition to asking whether the investment should be made, we also need to figure out which party—the worker or the firm—should pay for it and reap its rewards to maximize economic efficiency. Finally, we will consider a richer context in which workers and firms can decide *how many* skills to train, rather than just *how intensely* to train a single skill.

19.1 When to Train? An Education Example

Of all the types of training that make workers more valuable to their employers, some of the most important are investments made before a worker even enters the labor market, including investments in health, education, and even in migration to a better labor market. In this section, we'll study a worker's decision to make a pre-labor-market investment of this type. We do this partly to remind ourselves of the importance of a healthy, well-educated labor force to any modern economy, but (as noted) also as a warmup exercise for the study of training investments that are made inside firms. An advantage of this exercise is that it illustrates many of the main features of the training decision while avoiding some important complications that we'll study later in this chapter.

To that end, consider the case of Sam, who has just graduated from high school at age 18. Sam is thinking of taking a 1-year-long welding course right after graduation. Tuition costs \$20,000, and it's a full-time program so he can't hold down a paying job while he's in the program. Sam estimates that his annual earnings if he qualifies as a welder will be \$35,000 compared to \$30,000 if he doesn't (for simplicity, we'll assume all these numbers are after taxes). He doesn't have any savings, but he's able to get a student loan at a rate of 8% per year. To keep the math simple, let's imagine that if he graduates, Samuel plans to be a welder until he's 35. After that, his welding skills will be useless and he'll earn the same amount whether he went to welding school or not. Sam is pretty confident that he'd enjoy welding work about the same as any other kind of work (and about the same as any time spent in welding school), so he cares only about the financial consequences of his training decision. Should Sam go to welding school?

A naïve answer to Sam's question is that it's obvious he should go—after all, the program costs \$20,000, and he'll recoup that amount in just four years from the \$5,000 in extra annual earnings it buys him. The rest is gravy, right? As you might guess, there are at least two serious problems with this answer. The first is that it ignores the biggest component of Sam's total cost of going to welding school: He won't be able to work for a year. Once we count Sam's \$30,000 *opportunity cost* of going to school, we realize that the training actually costs him \$50,000. The second problem with this answer is that it ignores the interest Sam will need to pay on his student loan, which could be substantial at an 8% annual rate.

The correct way to answer Sam's question is the same way any investor or business should evaluate an investment opportunity: Calculate the expected present values of the two options and pick the highest one. In Sam's case, he is choosing between the income streams shown in Figure 19.1. The present value (at age 18) of Sam's income stream without training is

$$PV^N = \sum_{t=0}^{17} \frac{Y_t^N}{(1+r)^t}, \tag{19.1}$$

where r is the interest rate (8% in our base case example), t is Sam's age minus 18 (so $t = 17$ when he's 35), and Y_t^N is his income in Year t if he doesn't train (30 in every year in our example).[1]

[1] Equation 19.1 continues the convention we established in Equation 13.3 of not discounting the first year of income in a stream.

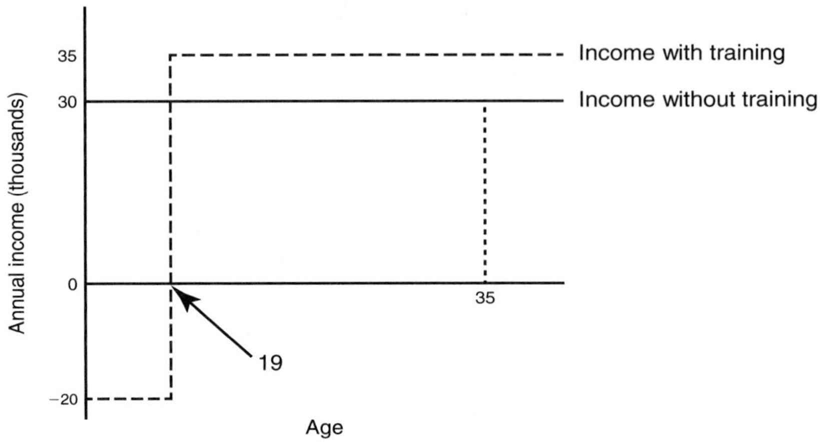

FIGURE 19.1. Hypothetical Income Streams with and without Training

The present value of Sam's income stream if he trains is given by

$$PV^T = \sum_{t=0}^{17} \frac{Y_t^T}{(1+r)^t}, \tag{19.2}$$

where Y_t^T is his income in Year t if he trains (−\$20,000 in Year 0 and +\$35,000 in all other years).

The present values of these two income streams are worked out in the spreadsheet shown in Figure 19.2. Perhaps surprisingly, you'll notice that from a financial point of view, Sam's investment in a welding course doesn't quite pay off, yielding an income stream with a present value of about \$299,257 compared to \$303,649 without the course.

Of course, this conclusion depends very much on the parameters of the problem. You can verify this by changing the parameter values in the spreadsheet yourself, with the following results.[2] Sam's training investment (and training investments in general) becomes more attractive when training is more effective (to see this, raise Sam's earnings as a welder to \$36,000 and welding school will pay off), when training's direct costs fall (starting at the base case, cut tuition to \$15,000), when training's *indirect* costs fall (cut his earnings without the training to \$29,000), and when the interest rate on the funds to finance the investment falls (reduce the student loan rate to 6%). By making small changes to the spreadsheet you can also easily show that training becomes more attractive the longer a time horizon you have to reap the rewards from your investment (simply imagine Sam welds till he's 40 years old; or conversely, consider whether training is a good investment for a 60-year-old Sam). And of course a shorter training period is also beneficial if it yields the same results. Finally, investments in training become less attractive as

[2] Spreadsheets are available at http://econ.ucsb.edu/~pjkuhn/Ec152/Spreadsheets/Spreadsheets.htm.

you become less likely to *use* the training in the future. This could happen either if there's a chance Sam might quit welding (and go back to a non-welding job paying $30,000) before he turns 35, or if he leaves the labor market altogether, for example, to care for a young child. To build these into the spreadsheet, you can use the approach we took for quits in the risky workers spreadsheet in Figure 13.1.

TRAINING—SPREADSHEET EXAMPLE

In this example, Sam is making decisions at age 18 that affect his earnings up to age 35

Interest Rate =	0.08	**0.08**
Tuition Cost =	20	**20**
Annual earnings without training =	30	**30**
Annual earnings with training =	35	**35**

		Without Training		With Training	
(1)	(2)	(3)	(4)	(5)	(6)
Age	**Year (t)**	**Income**	**PV(Income)**	**Income**	**PV(Income)**
18	0	30	30.00	−20	−20.00
19	1	30	27.78	35	32.41
20	2	30	25.72	35	30.01
21	3	30	23.81	35	27.78
22	4	30	22.05	35	25.73
23	5	30	20.42	35	23.82
24	6	30	18.91	35	22.06
25	7	30	17.50	35	20.42
26	8	30	16.21	35	18.91
27	9	30	15.01	35	17.51
28	10	30	13.90	35	16.21
29	11	30	12.87	35	15.01
30	12	30	11.91	35	13.90
31	13	30	11.03	35	12.87
32	14	30	10.21	35	11.92
33	15	30	9.46	35	11.03
34	16	30	8.76	35	10.22
35	17	30	8.11	35	9.46
SUM			303.649		299.257

FIGURE 19.2. Present Value of Income with and without Training

Notes: All earnings and tuition costs are measured in thousands of dollars. Base case parameter values indicated in bold.

RESULT 19.1 **Worker-Financed Investments in Education or Training**

Investments made by workers in their own education or training are more likely to pay off

- the higher the effectiveness of the training;
- the lower the direct and opportunity costs of training;
- the lower the interest on funds used to finance the training;
- the shorter the training period;
- the longer the time horizon over which the returns to training can be reaped;
- the more likely the worker continues to use the skill that was learned; and
- the more likely the worker is to remain in the labor market.

19.2 Training in Firms: When Is It Efficient?

Having worked out the conditions under which a worker should invest in training before entering the labor market, let's turn our attention to the slightly more complicated case of training decisions that are made after a worker has become attached to a firm. To explore this situation, let's consider the case of Sarah, a new employee in a CountriBank office whose productivity with and without a company training module is shown in Figure 19.3. If the company offers no special training, a new worker like Sarah produces Q^N as long as she stays with the company. After an initial training period that lasts until T^*, a trained worker produces more than this, Q_1^T. During the training period, however, Sarah's productivity is much lower, at Q_0^T. This reduced productivity can take a number of forms, including Sarah's time away from her main task, the time of the workers assigned to train Sarah, and the mistakes Sarah makes (or customers she alienates) while learning the ropes of an unfamiliar task.

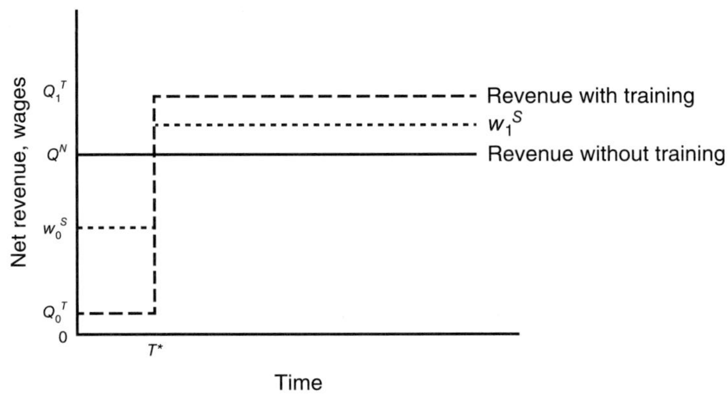

FIGURE 19.3. Hypothetical Revenue and Wage Streams with and without Training

Note: The line consisting of short dashes is a wage profile with 50–50 sharing of the costs and benefits of training.

Most of the factors affecting whether CountriBank should assign Sarah to the type of training described in Figure 19.3 are the same ones considered by Sam in his welding school decision. One key difference, however, is that the optimal training decision in the CountriBank case now depends on the *type* of training in a way that wasn't relevant before. To illustrate that, we first need to define two distinct types of skills that might be provided by the company's training program.

DEFINITION 19.1 **General skills** are skills that are useful both to a worker's current employer and in relevant employment opportunities at other employers.

Examples of general skills CountriBank might teach Sarah include general customer relations skills; proficiency with widely used software like Microsoft Office, Java, or C++; technical writing skills; basic bookkeeping skills; and familiarity with common financial products such as checking accounts, car loans, mortgage loans, and mutual funds. Other examples of general skills probably include basic literacy, numeracy, and widely recognized certifications in areas ranging from welding and plumbing to accountancy and web administration.

DEFINITION 19.2 **Firm-specific skills** are skills that are useful only if an employee stays with the current employer.

Examples of firm-specific skills include knowledge of a company's internal hierarchy, procedures, personalities, culture, and politics. Also included are any skills that are not widely used in a worker's relevant labor market. An example might be highly idiosyncratic (and perhaps obsolete) company software, but even a welding certificate can be a firm-specific skill if a worker lives in an area where welding jobs are rare and the worker is not willing or able to relocate.

Under what conditions should Sarah be assigned to the training program described in Figure 19.3? To answer this question, we'll begin by ignoring any possible conflict of interest between workers and firms and simply asking which of the two productivity paths in Figure 19.3 yield the highest present value. In other words, we'll ask whether the investment in Sarah's training pays off by making Sarah more productive, ignoring for the moment how these productivity gains are shared between Sarah and CountriBank. The answer to that question is provided in Result 19.2.

Result 19.2 reflects the important fact that firm-specific skills become useless when a worker leaves her current firm. General skills, on the other hand, retain their value when a worker switches firms but do lose their value when a worker leaves the labor market.[3] To interpret Result 19.2, recall that it refers only

[3] It is of course possible for some skills learned on the job to remain valuable in the home. A restaurant chef can be a better home cook, for example, and a skilled construction worker can do his or her own house repairs. As an approximation, however, the assumption that most job skills lose their value when a person is no longer working for pay seems reasonable.

to the conditions under which training investments are *economically efficient* in the sense that they maximize the sum of profits and utility, or social surplus as defined in Definition 4.1. As we'll see in the next section, a number of complications might prevent actual arrangements between workers and firms from being this efficient, especially when training is firm specific.

RESULT 19.2 **Training in Firms**

1. Investments in the training of employed workers are more likely to pay off
   - the higher the effectiveness of the training ($Q_1^T - Q^N$ in Figure 19.3);
   - the lower the direct and indirect costs of training ($Q^N - Q_0^T$);
   - the lower the interest on funds used to finance the training (*r*);
   - the shorter the training period (T^*); and
   - the longer the time horizon over which the returns to training can be reaped.
2. The value of acquiring *general skills* increases with the worker's expected future *labor force attachment*.
3. The value of acquiring *firm-specific skills* increases with the worker's expected *retention rate* at the firm where that worker was trained.

19.3 Training in Firms: Who Should Pay?

Now, let's turn to the question of who should pay for Sarah's training, or equivalently, *what should Sarah's wage be* during the training and post-training periods? As it turns out, this depends on whether the skills CountriBank is teaching her are general or firm specific. We'll start with the case of **general training** by thinking through the consequences of three alternative ways of dividing up training's costs and gains. Our analysis of both the general and specific training cases is based on Gary Becker's (1964) classic analysis.

First, let's suppose the firm pays for Sarah's training. What we mean by this is that even though she is much less productive during her training period, Sarah still gets paid the same as a new worker who receives no training, $w = Q^N$. Thus, by absorbing the cost of training Sarah, CountriBank takes a loss on her of $Q^N - Q_0^T$ during the training period. The reward for the firm is that it continues to pay Sarah Q^N after she's trained, making a profit of $Q_1^T - Q^N$. In other words, if the firm pays for Sarah's training, her wage profile over time just coincides with the solid line in Figure 19.3—she continues to get the same wage before and after training, with the firm absorbing both the costs and gains from training her.

Will this arrangement work if Sarah's training gives her a perfectly portable, general skill? The answer is clearly "no" because a trained Sarah is now capable of producing Q_1^T at a variety of relevant employers, whereas CountriBank is paying her only Q^N. Because other employers can make money by paying Sarah any wage between Q^N and Q_1^T, and because this could constitute a nice raise for Sarah, it seems likely that a trained Sarah would leave CountriBank under these circumstances. As a result, CountriBank will run a loss on training Sarah, as it paid the costs but didn't recoup the gains. Anticipating this, we would expect CountriBank (and indeed any employer) to be wary of paying for the general training of its workers.

Next, let's ask what would happen if CountriBank required Sarah to share in the costs and returns from her general training, for example, by splitting both of them fifty-fifty. In this case, Sarah's wage during the training and post-training periods would be w_0^S and w_1^S, respectively, in Figure 19.3, where each of these wages splits the difference between her productivity with and without training in the relevant period. Thus, Sarah's wage profile rises over time but not as much as her productivity increases. Does this solve the problem described in the previous paragraph (that a trained Sarah will leave)? Clearly not because even though her post-training wage is better than the previous case ($w_1^S > Q^N$), other employers can still easily bid her away from CountriBank and make a profit. Thus, sharing the costs and benefits does not work either.

By now, it should be apparent that the only workable solution to financing *general* training (at least in a free labor market where workers can quit whenever a better opportunity arises) is an arrangement where workers pay all the costs *and* receive all the rewards. In this "worker pays" scenario, Sarah's wage profile coincides with her actual productivity (Q_0^T and Q_1^T), thus rising steeply over her career. Notably, this also incentivizes Sarah to get the training, and—because it avoids the "poaching" problem associated with the previous two scenarios—finally makes it in her employer's interest to train her.

☑ **RESULT 19.3**

Workers Should Pay for General Training

In Becker's (1964) model of general training, the efficient (and in many cases the only feasible) way to finance general training is for the worker to pay all the costs and reap all the rewards in the form of a higher post-training wage.

If we return for a moment to the example of Sam and his welding course, Result 19.3 makes a great deal of sense: Even if Sam was already an employee of a company that needed qualified welders, it could be quite risky for Sam's company to pay for his welding course, unless the company could somehow write a contract that obliges Sam to return to the company for a minimum period of time afterward, or at least to reimburse the company for his training costs if he leaves. While such "training contracts" may appear to violate laws prohibiting indentured servitude, Hoffman and Burks (2017) recently noted that U.S. courts generally permit these contracts when it is clear they promote the public good by increasing investment in training. According to the authors, training contracts have also been used for firefighters, pilots, mechanics, salesmen, paramedics, electricians, accountants, teachers, flight attendants, bank workers, repairmen,

Starbucks' College Achievement Plan: So Why Do Some Employers Pay for College?

On June 15, 2014, the Starbucks Corporation announced the introduction of the *Starbucks College Achievement Plan*. Under the plan, all benefits-eligible Starbucks workers in the United States can receive financial support for taking online, for-credit courses offered by Arizona State University. Freshmen and Sophomores receive a partial scholarship and need-based financial aid, while Juniors and Seniors receive reimbursement for all tuition payments per block of credits successfully completed. Participants in the program are paid their usual rate for time worked while enrolled in the program and have no commitment to remain at Starbucks past graduation (Starbucks, 2014). And although Starbucks' plan is novel by tying benefits to online education at a particular university, a study by Peter Cappelli (2004) indicates that employer tuition assistance for college education is in fact quite common in the United States. For example, as many as one-third of undergraduates in fields like business and engineering receive financial assistance from their employers. Among adults enrolled in post-secondary education in degree- or credential-granting programs, 24% were receiving tuition assistance from an employer, and 53% were either receiving tuition support or paid time off.

Because post-secondary education is probably a very general skill, how can we make sense of these policies in light of Result 19.3? Cappelli (2004) considers a number of possible explanations, but his analysis suggests two as the most likely. First, most tuition assistance programs (TAPs) require workers to be with the firm for a certain amount of time to be eligible. (In Starbucks' case, a minimum number of hours must be worked to become *benefits eligible*.) Thus, by offering a reward for staying with the firm for a certain period of time, TAPs may reduce turnover *during the period before training begins*. This incentive is an example of the deferred-wage incentives we studied in Section 18.3 and is absent in Becker's model (in part because he doesn't consider a pre-training, "qualifying" period). Second, turnover may also fall *while the employees are receiving tuition assistance* because employees would lose this valuable benefit by quitting. Of course, this reduction in turnover will only benefit the employer if (a) enough workers stay *after* training at a low enough wage to let the firm recoup its tuition costs, or (b) Starbucks is able to earn profits on workers even while the workers are earning credits, despite paying the workers' tuition costs.

Are scenarios (a) and (b) plausible ones? Cappelli (2004) argues that (a) could be true simply because most real-world labor markets have more *frictions* than we are assuming in this section. Some workers may have sufficiently limited outside options, so they will stay with their original firm even after receiving general training. Cappelli argues that (b) might be true because of TAP's effect on worker *self-selection* (i.e., the types of effects discussed in Section 15.4). Specifically, if high-performing workers are more likely to *sign up* for TAP programs, the TAP may pay for itself even before the training is even completed. In this way, the TAP is a better tool for reducing employee turnover than an across-the-board wage increase because it only appeals to a subset of workers—the college motivated—the firm is more interested in retaining.

Alternative Skill Maintenance, Unions, and Job Security

Although labor economists traditionally talk only about two skill types—general, which are useful both inside and outside the current firm, and specific, which are useful only inside the current firm—there is of course a third logical possibility: **alternative skills**. Alternative skills are not used in one's current firm but may be valuable elsewhere, for example, if you lose your job. Examples might be writing or math skills for someone whose current job doesn't require much of either activity. Without some effort, these skills can easily depreciate or atrophy if they are not used.

Arthur Sweetman and I (Kuhn & Sweetman, 1999) introduce this idea and use it to understand differences in what happens to union and nonunionized workers when they permanently lose their jobs. Although both types of workers suffer wage losses when they lose a job, nonunion workers' postdisplacement wages are positively correlated with the amount of time the worker spent on their previous job. This suggests that some of the skills acquired on the previous job are general, that is, they are portable into the worker's next job. For (formerly) unionized workers, though, the opposite is true: The longer they spent in their previous job, the *lower* are their postdisplacement wages.

In the article (Kuhn & Sweetman, 1999), we argue that differences in **alternative skill maintenance** might explain this intriguing pattern: Not only do union jobs typically use a narrower range of skills, most unionized workers (rationally) expect their jobs to be very secure. Accordingly, there is little incentive for unionized workers to invest effort in maintaining skills they're not using on their current job. Unfortunately, when those secure union jobs do disappear, older unionized workers tend to be very vulnerable. Kuhn and Sweetman's results suggest another possible cost of Employment Protection Laws (EPLs): They may discourage workers from maintaining their alternative skills, making them very vulnerable if a job loss should ever occur.

A key lesson for workers is, if you're in a job that uses a very narrow skill set, beware! You might want to devote some effort to maintaining important alternative capabilities, just in case that job disappears.

firm-sponsored MBAs, and social workers.[4] In these specific situations, training contracts may thus be a viable way for firms to pay for workers' general training.

Finally, let's work out who is likely to pay for **firm-specific** training. Mathematically, the only way this differs from the case of general training is in the level of Sarah's post-training productivity if she goes to another employer. In the case of general training, Sarah's outside productivity was Q_1^T in Figure 19.3; now it is just Q^N (because the newly acquired skills are useless outside CountriBank).

[4] In their study, Hoffman and Burks (2017) analyze data on training contracts used by long-haul trucking firms. These contracts impose a financial penalty on workers who quit within 12–18 months of receiving company-financed training. According to the authors, the contracts significantly reduced quitting, particularly when workers were close to the end of their contracts.

Everything else in our example (such as Sarah's pre-training productivity) remains unchanged. With this in mind, let's now ask how the three financing schemes described earlier perform in the case of firm-specific training.

In the "firm pays" scenario, Sarah is paid Q^N both before and after her training. Thus, the firm loses money on Sarah while she's in training, and profits afterwards. But because Sarah's post-training wage now equals her productivity at other firms, there is no longer any strong incentive for other firms to poach her away from CountriBank. That said, this "firm pays 100%" approach leaves CountriBank highly vulnerable to small changes in Sarah's preferences, or in her perceived value to other employers after she's trained. Essentially, any random new opportunity that is just a little better than Q^N will induce Sarah to leave CountriBank. This uncertainty about Sarah's outside options has two undesirable consequences. First, it means CountriBank can expect to lose money from training Sarah, making it reluctant to train her in the first place. Second, paying Sarah only Q^N after she's trained is economically inefficient. That's because Sarah will quit more often than she should (from the point of view of maximizing total surplus in Definition 4.1). Specifically, at a post-training wage of Q^N, Sarah will quit whenever her wage outside the firm exceeds Q^N. Thus, it is quite possible that she'll choose to move from her current firm—where she produces Q_1^T—to a firm where she produces much less than that. (This happens whenever her outside productivity is between Q^N and Q_1^T.) These quits are wasteful *because they benefit Sarah less than they hurt her initial employer.*

RESULT 19.4

If Firms Pay the Full Cost of Firm-Specific Training, Trained Workers Are Likely to Quit Too Often

Anticipating this, firms will be reluctant to offer training opportunities. If there is any uncertainty in the value of a worker's outside options after being trained, a "firm pays all" financing plan for firm-specific training risks wasting valuable investments in training by generating excessive quits: Too often, workers will leave for other firms where their firm-specific skills are not used. Because quits by trained workers are highly costly to firms under a "firm pays all" plan, firms will avoid offering training opportunities under this financing plan even when the training would raise the sum of profits and worker utility.

Now let's turn to the opposite extreme of a "worker pays all" scenario, which worked quite well in the case of general training. Here, Sarah's post-training wage is Q_1^T, which eliminates the problem of her being wastefully bid away by low-value, outside offers. However, this new scheme now leaves *Sarah* vulnerable, in a parallel fashion to CountriBank's vulnerability in the previous scenario. Specifically, if there is even a small amount of uncertainty in Sarah's *value to her current employer* (i.e., in the value of Q_1^T), CountriBank will be tempted to lay her off in situations where she shouldn't be. Suppose, for example, that despite expectations, her post-training productivity is just a little less than Q_1^T. Now, CountriBank will be better off firing Sarah (and earning zero profits) than by keeping her on at a loss.

Firing Sarah in this situation, however, is socially wasteful, because it will cause her productivity to fall from just under Q_1^T down to Q^N).[5] Put another way, these layoffs are wasteful *because they hurt the worker more than they benefit the firm.* Anticipating these sorts of problems, Sarah might (understandably) be unwilling to pay the full cost of learning a skill that is only valuable to her current employer.

RESULT 19.5

If Workers Pay the Full Cost of Firm-Specific Training, Trained Workers Are Likely to Be Laid Off Too Often

Anticipating this, workers will be reluctant to accept training opportunities when they are offered. If there is any uncertainty in the value of a worker's future value to her original firm, a "worker pays all" financing plan for firm-specific training risks wasting valuable skills by generating excessive layoffs: Too often, workers will be forced to move to other firms where their firm-specific skills are not used. Because layoffs are highly costly to workers under a "worker pays all" plan, workers will decline training opportunities even when they would raise the sum of profits and worker utility.

Because both the extreme "worker pays all" and "firm pays all" schemes have important vulnerabilities in the case of firm-specific training, Becker (1964) argued that the only viable solution for financing firm-specific investments in training is one that avoids the worst aspects of both extremes by sharing the costs and benefits. Although the optimal sharing rate will not necessarily be the 50:50 split depicted in Figure 19.3—that will depend on the relative amount of uncertainty in the worker's outside options compared to the uncertainty in her within-firm productivity—some sharing will generally be better than either extreme solution.[6]

RESULT 19.6

Financing Firm-Specific Training

According to Becker's (1964) model, the efficient (and only likely) way to finance firm-specific training is for the worker and firm to share both the costs and the benefits. The worker's optimal share is larger the higher the uncertainty in outside options, and the firm's optimal share is larger the higher the uncertainty in the training's effectiveness.

[5] An astute reader will notice that this begs an important question: If Sarah's training turns out to be less effective than expected, doesn't it make more sense just to renegotiate her post-training wage than to kick her out the door? It might, but in this section, we'll focus only on employment contracts that promise a particular post-training wage, which is often the case in large firms with standardized pay policies. More importantly, allowing for *ex-post*-wage renegotiation actually creates an entirely new set of problems—holdup—that we'll cover in Section 19.4.

[6] Hashimoto and Yu (1980) and Hall and Lazear (1984) provide a formal analysis of Becker's cost-sharing solution to the specific investments problem. MacLeod and Malcomson (1993) propose a related solution that allows for renegotiation only in certain circumstances.

Specific to What? Occupation-, Industry-, and Location-Specific Skills

In this chapter, we've placed a lot of emphasis on the distinction between firm-specific and general skills. That's because what really matters for training decisions and wage setting is whether the skills acquired would be useful *outside the firm where they were learned.* That said, skills can be specific to other contexts too. For example, even if a skill is not firm specific, it could be *occupation specific*, that is, specific to a given type of work (e.g., skills in sales or in web management). Or it could be specific to a given *industry* such as petrochemicals or education. A number of skills, including language and familiarity with tax laws and business culture, can be *country or location specific.* Economists studying worker mobility have documented that crossing each of these boundaries tends to result in wage losses for workers, suggesting that some skills are not portable across them (see, e.g., Neal, 1995, and Parent, 2000, for industry; Poletaev & Robinson, 2008, and Kambourov & Manovskii, 2009, for occupation; and Chiswick & Miller, 2014, for language). More recently, some economists have argued that what really matters for workers' ability to switch employers is the specific *mix* of tasks they do, such that workers who have unusual mixes of skills have a harder time moving (Lazear, 2009; Gathmann & Schoenberg, 2010). Although all of these factors affect a worker's outside options, as we have already argued, the most important distinction for wage setting and training decisions is the extent to which workers can easily find a job with another employer that uses all or most of the skills they have acquired.

19.4 Firm-Specific Training and the Holdup Problem

A natural question that arises from the last section's discussion is whether investments in firm-specific training might be less problematic if firms and workers were able to bargain a little more flexibly about wages after the training has occurred. For example, suppose that Sarah is tempted to leave after training because she has received a wage offer that's better than her current wage. If that outside wage offer is less than her productivity on her current job, wouldn't it be in her current employer's interest to consider matching or bettering it, instead of sticking to the agreed-on, post-training wage and watching her go?

Interestingly, whereas *ex-post* negotiations like the preceding one can eliminate some inefficient separations, allowing for this kind of bargaining can also create some serious disincentives to invest in specific training in the first place. The problem that arises is called the *holdup problem* and has received considerable attention in economics since Paul Grout (1984) stated the problem so clearly. As it happens, Grout's example was not about worker training but about a firm making investments in their plant and equipment. The logic is the same, though, so we'll introduce the holdup idea using Grout's example.

DEFINITION 19.3 An economic relationship between two parties generates **economic rents** when the relationship generates enough revenue to pay both parties what they can earn in their next best activity, and *then some.* This difference between the total revenues available to be divided between the parties and their best outside option is defined as the economic rents associated with the relationship.

Imagine a unionized firm that is thinking of upgrading the machines in an aging factory. Column (1) in Table 19.1 shows the productivity, wages, and profits earned from a representative worker before the investment in new equipment. By construction, both workers and firms earn zero *economic rents* in this situation: The old equipment is just good enough to produce enough output to pay the worker what he could earn elsewhere and leave the firm with a zero economic profit (thus making it indifferent between being in business or not).[7] Another way of saying there are no rents is to say there is absolutely no room for wage negotiation in column (1) of Table 19.1: Even though the firm is unionized, there is nothing the union can do to secure a wage above the firm's break-even wage of £20,000. Any wage above £20,000 would cause the firm to shut down.

Now let's imagine that Grout's (1984) firm is contemplating a *relationship-specific* investment in its plant. By installing new machinery, it can double the output of an average worker from £20,000 to £40,000. Because the new machines cost £15,000, this seems like a good investment. The problem with the machines, however, is that they are custom built: They are only useful in producing the particular type of widget this firm produces. These means that the

TABLE 19.1 HYPOTHETICAL PRODUCTIVITY, WAGES, AND PROFITS PER WORKER WITH AND WITHOUT INVESTMENT IN NEW MACHINERY (£)

	WITHOUT INVESTMENT	WITH INVESTMENT
	(1)	(2)
Worker's productivity	20,000	40,000
Investment cost	0	15,000
Alternative wage	20,000	20,000
Wage under "split the diff"	20,000	30,000
Profits	0	-5,000
Profits + wages	20,000	25,000

[7] Economic profits are defined as the gap between a firm's revenues and *all* its costs, including the opportunity costs of capital, labor, and the entrepreneur's own time. Thus, economic profits equal zero when a firm is indifferent between operating and not. For more on the difference between economic profits and accounting profits, see any introductory economics textbook.

machines, once installed in the factory, have no resale value, making them a relationship-specific investment.[8]

Column (2) of Table 19.1 shows what happens if the firm invests in the new machinery if wages are determined by negotiation between the firm and union *after* the machines are in place. With the machines in place, the firm now produces £20,000 in economic rents that are up for grabs in negotiations with the union. More precisely, once the machines are in place, the firm will want to stay in business for any wage less than £40,000; and workers are willing to work for any wage above £20,000. (The £15,000 investment is a sunk cost that is no longer relevant.) Thus, any wage between £20,000 and £40,000 will keep the firm in business. If the union and firm are equally powerful negotiators, they'll end up splitting this rent equally at a wage of £30,000. The result, of course is that the firm ends up losing money on its relationship-specific investment! Anticipating this, *a smart firm will never make such an investment, even though it is economically efficient* (because it raises the sum of profits and wages). This notion, that relationship-specific investments can be held hostage after they are made—in a way that can destroy the incentive to make the investment—is called the holdup problem.

DEFINITION 19.4 The **holdup problem** refers to a situation where relationship-specific investments create rents whose division can be bargained over *after* the investments have been made. When the (expected) outcomes of that bargaining process prevent socially efficient investments from being made in the first place, a holdup problem is said to exist.

Besides capital investments in unionized plants, holdup problems come up in other areas of economics too. One example that's probably all too familiar is the curious case of printer cartridges: Once you've bought a printer, you have to use a very specific replacement cartridge that in most cases you can only buy from the company that sold you the printer. This makes the original printer a relationship-specific investment (specific to your relationship with HP, Brother, or whomever). Thus, although printers tend to be very cheap, cartridges cost a fortune. One interpretation is that companies are *holding customers hostage* after they buy a piece of equipment that can only be used with their cartridges.[9] Another common example

[8] If you don't like the assumption of a unique, custom-built machine, you can imagine that the costs of uninstalling, moving, and re-installing these machines in another firm is prohibitive. The only thing that truly matters for the relationship specificity of the firm's investment is that the new equipment *can only be used in conjunction with the union.* Thus, if the firm could sell the entire plant (including the new machines) to a new owner who could easily operate it with non-union workers, the machines would no longer be a relationship-specific investment.

[9] This begs the question of why some company doesn't start a new line of printers that cost more up front but have cheap cartridges. If customers believe the company will keep the cost of cartridges low, they should surely be interested. Alternatively, new industry entrants have tried to profit just by offering "compatible" cartridges at a lower cost. In response, it appears that the "legacy" printer companies have retaliated by warning consumers that the "knockoff" cartridges are unreliable and could void the customer's printer warranty. Threats and counterthreats like these are emblematic of hold-up situations that arise whenever relationship-specific investments have been made.

is in business-to-business dealings such as joint ventures and franchises. Many such cooperative ventures require two or more companies to make major investments up front that are essentially useless outside the new partnership. If the division of the spoils is not carefully laid out up front, *rational* fear that future bargaining over economic rents will eliminate one's returns from making relationship-specific investments can prevent economically efficient projects from ever starting.

Returning to the topic of this chapter, how might holdup affect workers' investments in firm-specific skills? Applying Grout's (1984) logic to this case suggests that *workers* who make firm-specific training investments should be wary if there's any chance the firm might hold these investments hostage later. For example, suppose Sarah has worked hard to learn a skill that's only useful at CountriBank and is now expecting a raise to w_1^S in Figure 19.3 as a reward for her efforts and a reflection of her new, higher value to the firm. A simple way for CountriBank to hold her hostage is just to claim that business has been poorer than expected, so the firm can no longer afford to pay her the promised post-training wage of w_1^S. If the skills she has acquired are only useful in CountriBank, there is nothing Sarah can do![10]

☑ **RESULT 19.7**

Holdup and Investments in Firm-Specific Training

Workers who are asked to bear some of the cost of acquiring firm-specific skills should be aware that those investments are vulnerable to holdup by firms. This is not an issue if firms negotiate in good faith and if they honor both the spirit and letter of implicit and explicit training and pay agreements. Opportunistic firms, firms in financial distress, as well as firms that have been taken over by new owners, however, may be very tempted to push workers hard in extracting relationship-specific rents after workers have invested in firm-specific skills.

An interesting implication of Result 19.7 is that the EPLs whose negative consequences we studied in Section 13.1 could have an unexpected *beneficial* effect on workers' incentives to invest in firm-specific skills. A recent experimental study by Anderhub, Königstein and Kübler (2003) illustrates this. Even in a context where the "worker" subjects have good reason to expect their employers to *want* to retain them in a future period, Anderhub et al. found that giving workers a *contractual guarantee of future employment* increased their investments in firm-specific training. Additional empirical support for this idea comes from two recent studies of innovative activity by employees—which can be a highly relationship-specific investment—by Acharya, Baghai, and Subramanian (2013, 2014). Looking at the effects of country-level changes in dismissal laws in the

[10] Of course, if the firm wishes to maintain a reputation as a good employer, it might refrain from actions like these. But reputational considerations are not always effective remedies for holdup problems. We discussed the important effect of firms' reputations on long-term relationships between workers and firms in Section 18.3.

United States, the United Kingdom, France, and Germany, their 2013 study shows that stronger dismissal protection can enhance employees' innovative efforts by reducing employers' ability to act in bad faith after the worker has produced an innovation. Acharya et al.'s 2014 study finds similar results for the effects of changes in wrongful discharge laws across the United States. MacLeod and Nakavachara (2007) also study the effects of EPLs across the United States, finding that a *good faith rule,* which requires employers to compensate employees as they have agreed and to avoid dismissing employees opportunistically, has consistently positive effects on the employment of skilled workers but not on unskilled workers. This makes sense if skilled workers are more likely to make significant firm-specific investments that can be taken advantage of by opportunistic employers.

In sum, this section has shown that (legitimate) concerns about being "held up" by an investment partner can compromise incentives to make relationship-specific investments in a number of contexts, including workers' investments in firm-specific skills. Our analysis yields some general lessons for anyone contemplating making a relationship-specific investment (such as buying a

Holdup in *Modern Warfare:* Problems for Employee Innovators

Even when there are clear agreements on who holds the patents and copyrights, the relationships between innovators and their employers can generate rents that are "up for grabs" after an innovation has succeeded. Given the logic of holdup, this can create significant problems (with each attempting to hold the other hostage) when the innovators "hit a home run," and a large pool of rents is created.

A recent illustration of the problem involves two of the most successful video game developers in history: Jason West and Vince Zampella. As employees of Activision in the late 2000s, they created two video game franchises, *Call Of Duty* and *Modern Warfare,* that became the most successful in the industry. Together, they generated billions of dollars in revenue for Activision and created a diehard fan base in the millions. In November 2009, after over 2 years of nearly around-the-clock work, West and Zampella delivered *Modern Warfare 2* to Activision, at which time the game had already achieved over $1 billion in advance sales. But just weeks before West and Zampella were to receive the royalties for *Modern Warfare 2,* Activision fired them. In a lawsuit, West and Zampella claimed that Activision's intention in firing them was to avoid paying them the royalties they had rightfully earned.

In its counterclaim Activision claimed that West and Zampella engaged in various tactics designed to increase their own bargaining power with Activision. These included threatening to bring production of *Modern Warfare 2* to a stop, delaying preproduction on *Modern Warfare 3,* engaging in discussions with Activision's closest competitor, and encouraging their own employees at Activision to follow them to that competitor.

When large economic rents are created from the combined efforts of multiple parties, holdup can be a serious problem. Knowing this, both innovators and the companies that employ them may be less willing to invest in innovative ventures than is socially optimal.

Non-Compete Agreements for Physicians: A Remedy for Holdup by Employees?

Non-compete agreements (NCAs) are contracts that prohibit a worker from competing against a firm for a specified period of time after leaving it. Structured correctly, such contracts are legal in the United States and are commonly used in number of industries, especially where trade secrets may be involved. NCAs remain controversial, however, in part because of their resemblance to anti-enticement laws used in the post-bellum U.S. South (see Section 17.1). Still, Lavetti and Simon (2014) argue that U.S. physicians actually *benefit* when they sign an NCA. Such agreements *prevent the doctors themselves* from holding up their employers (by threatening to leave and take their patient base with them). Eliminating this risk, according to Lavetti and Simon, improves investment incentives for both doctors and their employers, with the result that doctors with NCAs are 27% more productive, earn 14% higher wages, and have much higher earnings growth than comparable physicians without NCAs.

franchise or starting a business partnership). Specifically, if you are considering entering this type of relationship, you should first *anticipate the future bargaining power of your partner.* Once you're in a relationship that you've both invested in, your partner will have a greater ability to inflict economic pain on you than that person does now. Second, if possible, try to *secure clear cost and revenue sharing agreements in advance* so these can't become objects of negotiation later. Finally, planning relationships like these will proceed more smoothly if you can also put yourself in your partner's shoes. Specifically, understand your partner's own legitimate concerns about future vulnerability. Your partner, too, has a right to be concerned about how you will use your future bargaining power; so don't be insulted if that person, too, asks for some things to be spelled out up front. Keeping these three simple principles in mind may help you navigate the challenging world of relationship-specific business investments a little better.

19.5 Costs and Benefits of Multiskilling

So far in this chapter we've worked out *when* it makes economic sense for a worker to invest in learning a particular skill, and we've worked out *who should pay* for training depending on the type of skill that's acquired. One question we haven't yet addressed is *how broadly* workers should be trained. In some jobs and workplaces, such as traditional assembly lines or the telephone sales workers in Section 7.1's CTrip study, workers are trained very narrowly—they learn one basic task and perform it repeatedly. Other companies train even entry-level workers in a wide variety of skills, sometimes deliberately rotating workers into different parts of the company just to familiarize them with a variety of tasks. Whereas the costs of all this additional training are obvious, are there some important offsetting benefits that might explain why some firms choose to multiskill?

In an insightful article on Japanese HRM practices, Lorne Carmichael and Bentley Macleod (1993) argue that a policy of multiskilling one's workers is well matched to workplaces where *continuous process innovation* is important.

DEFINITION 19.5 **Continuous process innovation** refers to productivity-improving changes in the way things are done in a workplace that do *not* involve changes in physical capital, information technology, or replacement of workers. Continuous process innovation involves fine-tuning machines, procedures, and work organization; is usually gradual; and often results from employee actions or suggestions because employees are the most likely people to see day-to-day sources of inefficiency and to see simple ways they might be eliminated.

Although the idea of continuous process innovation originated in manufacturing, it applies to all workplaces. *Any* employee idea for making things work better, faster, or smoother with existing resources (including things like changing the workflow in a virtual office, or suggesting a more effective way to engage with customers) is a type of process innovation.

Why, according to Carmichael and Macleod (1993), is multiskilling especially useful in this context? To see this, consider a worker who knows how to perform only one narrow task in a company and who has just noticed a way to accomplish the task with fewer hours or workers. What are that worker's incentives to tell the employer about this idea? Although the worker might be rewarded for doing so, there is also a danger that that worker will be put out of a job because the one thing that person knows how to do is no longer in such high demand. And while an employer might *promise* to reward the worker's idea, it is not unreasonable to expect narrowly trained workers to be skeptical of such promises. If they are, they'll be reluctant to share information about labor-saving improvements when *their own labor* is being saved. So, how can a firm credibly convince its workers that their jobs will not be in danger if they suggest or make labor-saving changes in work organization?

According to Carmichael and Macleod (1993), Japanese manufacturing firms solved this problem decades ago via an explicit *multiskilling* strategy. Even though it was costly and time-consuming, new employees were regularly rotated through a variety of positions and divisions, acquiring a wide range of skills early in their careers. Secure in the knowledge that *even if they completely eliminated their current job,* there would be many other things they could do in the firm, workers were not only more willing to share labor-saving ideas, they would simply go ahead and implement them. In fact, many of these companies facilitated this type of employee innovation by providing paid work time for employees to consult with each other about ways to improve operations. According to the authors, multiskilling also made workers more willing to embrace new technologies that were introduced *by the company*. Firms that practiced multiskilling, according to Carmichael and Macleod, also made important, public commitments to give their workers long-term job security. As suggested by Result 19.2, this security then resulted in an increase in workers' willingness to invest in firm-specific skills.[11] Perhaps paradoxically (and at odds with the ideas of Section 19.4), guaranteeing workers job security can create a virtuous circle that raises workers' productivity!

DEFINITION 19.6 **Japan's New HRM paradigm** refers to a system of management that combines job security, multiskilling, ongoing worker-initiated process innovation, high voluntary investments in firm-specific skills, and a high level of worker acceptance of technological change. This "new" paradigm is widely credited with Japan's victory over U.S. automakers in the 1970s and 1980s.

Chapter Summary

- ☐ In general, the payoffs to investments in training increase with the length of the period over which the returns to training can be reaped, with the probability the worker remains in the labor market (for general training), and with the probability the worker remains in the current firm (for firm-specific training).
- ☐ In general, the payoffs to investments in training decrease with the direct and opportunity costs of training, with the interest rate, and with the length of the training period.
- ☐ According to Becker's (1964) model, firms should never pay for workers' general training, whereas firms and workers should split the costs and benefits from firm-specific training.
- ☐ The fact that many firms do pay for their workers to attend college (a general skill), may be explained by a number of considerations not included in Becker's model, including the use of tuition assistance plans as a selection device to retain high-quality workers (Cappelli, 2004).

[11] My favorite example of these skills is the father of a coauthor of mine who spent his entire career in the Toyota research department perfecting their formula for beige paint! Could you imagine investing in such a firm-specific skill if your job was not secure?

- ☐ The holdup problem arises when parties to a relationship-specific investment (like firm-specific training) bargain over the rents created by that investment after it has been made. If workers expect this type of bargaining to occur, they may be reluctant to make firm-specific investments. This may be an especially important consideration for employee innovators.

Discussion Questions

1. In contrast to Chapters 13 and 18 which identified some costs of EPLs, this chapter suggests at least two reasons why EPLs (or a commitment by a firm to provide job security) might raise worker productivity. What are those two reasons? Based on all their potential costs and benefits, under what conditions do you think EPLs are most likely to be harmful? When are they more likely be beneficial?
2. What is the last time you thought of a way to make things work better or more smoothly at your workplace? Did you share this idea with your employer or co-workers? Why or why not? What changes in your workplace might make you more willing to share efficiency-improving or labor-saving ideas with your employer?
3. Does your employer assist some of its workers with the costs of college tuition, or with other forms of education or training that take place outside the workplace? How can workers qualify for such assistance—is there a formal process or are decisions made on a case-by-case basis? Are workers expected to remain with the firm after training is complete? Drawing on the discussion in this chapter, explain why you think your employer has chosen its policy.

Suggestions for Further Reading

If you are interested in how U.S. labor law restricts firms' abilities to dismiss and lay off workers, MacLeod and Nakavachara (2007) provide a detailed and deep discussion. Cappelli's (2004) paper on why employers pay for college is a very readable and insightful update on Becker's classic discussion.

References

Acharya, V. V., Baghai, R. P., & Subramanian, K. V. (2013). Labor laws and innovation. *Journal of Law and Economics, 56,* 997–1037.

Acharya, V. V., Baghai, R. P., & Subramanian, K. V. (2014). Wrongful discharge laws and innovation. *Review of Financial Studies, 27,* 301–346.

Anderhub, V., Königstein, M., & Kübler, D. (2003). Long-term work contracts versus sequential spot markets: experimental evidence on firm-specific investment. *Labour Economics, 10*(4), 407–425.

Becker, G. S. (1964). *Human capital.* Chicago: University of Chicago Press.

Cappelli, P. (2004). Why do employers pay for college? *Journal of Econometrics, 121*(1), 213–241.

Carmichael, H. L., & MacLeod, W. B. (1993). Multiskilling, technical change and the Japanese firm. *Economic Journal, 103*(416), 142–160.

Chiswick, B. R., & Miller, P. W. (2014). International migration and the economics of language. In B. Chiswick & P. Miller (Eds.), *Handbook on the Economics of International Migration: The Immigrants* (pp. 211–269). Amsterdam, Netherlands: Elsevier.

Gathmann, C., & Schoenberg, U. (2010). How general is human capital? A task-based approach. *Journal of Labor Economics, 28,* 1–49.

Grout, P. A. (1984). Investment and wages in the absence of binding contracts: A Nash bargaining approach. *Econometrica: Journal of the Econometric Society*, 449–460.

Hall, R. E., & Lazear, E. P. (1984). The excess sensitivity of layoffs and quits to demand. *Journal of Labor Economics, 2*(2), 233–257.

Hashimoto, M., & Yu, B. T. (1980). Specific capital, employment contracts, and wage rigidity. *Bell Journal of Economics*, 536–549.

Hoffman, M. & Burks, S. V. (2017). *Training Contracts, Employee Turnover, and the Returns from Firm-sponsored General Training* (NBER Working Paper No. 23247). Cambridge, MA: The National Bureau of Economic Research.

Kambourov, G., & Manovskii, I. (2009). Occupational specificity of human capital. *International Economic Review, 50,* 63–115.

Kuhn, P., & Arthur Sweetman, L. (1999, October). Vulnerable seniors: Unions, tenure, and wages following permanent job loss. *Journal of Labor Economics, 17,* 671–693.

Lavetti, K., & Simon, C. (2014). *Buying loyalty: Theory and evidence from physicians.* Working paper, Department of Economics, Ohio State University, Columbus, OH.

Lazear, E. (2009). Firm-specific human capital: A skill-weights approach. *Journal of Political* Economy, *117,* 914–940.

MacLeod, W. B., & Malcomson, J. M. (1993). Investments, holdup, and the form of market contracts. *American Economic Review*, 811–837.

MacLeod, W. B., & Nakavachara, V. (2007). Can wrongful discharge law enhance employment? *Economic Journal, 117*(521), F218–F278.

Neal, D. (1995). Industry-specific capital: Evidence from displaced workers. *Journal of Labor Economics, 13,* 653–677.

Parent, D. (2000). Industry-specific capital and the wage profile: Evidence from the National Longitudinal Survey of Youth and the Panel Study of Income Dynamics. *Journal of Labor Economics, 18,* 306–323.

Poletaev, M., & Robinson, C. (2008). Human capital specificity: Evidence from the *Dictionary of Occupational Titles* and displaced worker surveys, 1984–2000. *Journal of Labor Economics, 26,* 387–420.

Starbucks. (n.d.). *Starbucks College Achievement Plan.* Retrieved January 29, 2015, from https://www.starbucks.com/careers/college-plan

Part 4
Competition in the Workplace: The Economics of Relative Rewards

In many aspects of life, people are evaluated and rewarded not just for their absolute performance but on their performance relative to others. Examples include students who are "graded on a curve," students competing for a fixed number of slots on entrance exams like China's *gaokao* or Korea's CSAT, research teams competing to submit a patent, sports teams competing for a championship, crowdsourcing of ideas or innovations, or any situation where workers are assessed and rewarded relative to their co-workers.

In workplaces, one of the most common situations where relative performance matters is when workers in a given job category compete against each other for promotion to a limited number of higher-ranked positions. Another would be competition for lump sum cash bonuses or prizes that are awarded only to the top performer(s) in a group. Economists refer to competitions for a fixed number of prizes as *tournaments*. But other forms of relative rewards can also be important in workplaces. These include situations where a manager is given a fixed total budget for merit pay and has to divide it among all the employees in the division, the *stack ranking* (or "rank and yank") system famously advocated by Jack Welch (former General Electric CEO), and indeed any rating or reward system that compares workers to each other.

In this part, we'll study all these reward schemes. We start by developing a simple economic model of a tournament between employees for a fixed prize (which could be either a bonus or a promotion). We then apply the theoretical insights from this model to a number of real-world uses of relative performance evaluation, ranging from contract farming to the pay of mutual fund managers and professional golfers. In doing so, we'll address the following questions: What are the intended *and* unintended effects of relative reward schemes on worker behavior? What is the optimal structure of a relative reward scheme (e.g., how big should the prize be in a tournament, and should there be more than one prize)? When should firms use relative rewards, and when are they a bad idea?

Overall, we'll learn that relative reward schemes have some important benefits, such as economizing on employee evaluation and insulating workers from certain types of risks, but also some key pitfalls, such as reducing workers' incentives to cooperate with each other and incentivizing some workers to take excessive risks. Understanding these costs and benefits provides useful guidelines for when relative pay is likely to be a good or a bad idea in a particular work setting.

A Simple Model of Tournaments

20

If you've ever been graded "on a curve" or worked hard to outshine your coworkers and win a promotion, you've participated in what economists call a *tournament.* What are the advantages and disadvantages of using tournaments to motivate workers? In Chapter 20, we begin our analysis of that question by showing that under some simple circumstances, tournaments can be just as efficient as the individual pay-for-performance schemes we studied in Part 2. In other, more special cases, for example among risk averse workers facing common productivity shocks, tournaments can even be more socially efficient than individual rewards. That said, tournaments introduce strategic considerations into workers' effort decisions, in the sense that each worker's optimal effort now depends on *how hard he expects his competitors to work.* This makes it harder for workers to choose effort levels and tends to create greater variability in worker performance under tournaments than under comparable piece rates.

20.1 The Basic Elements of a Two-Player Tournament

We begin our study of tournaments by introducing a formal model of a simple tournament in which two agents compete to win a single bonus. Consider a principal employing two agents, 1 and 2, whose production functions are given by

$$Q_1 = d_1E_1 + \varepsilon_1 \tag{20.1}$$

and

$$Q_2 = d_2E_2 + \varepsilon_2, \tag{20.2}$$

where E_i is worker i's effort, d_i is a productivity parameter, Q_i is worker i's measured output (or "performance"), and the random variable ε_i is worker i's luck. As we have always done, let the agents' disutility-of-effort functions be given by $V(E_i)$, with V' and $V'' > 0$.

One familiar way the principal might compensate these two workers is via *individual* incentive contracts that link each worker's pay to his or her own performance. If these contracts are linear (i.e., if $Y_i = a_i + b_i Q_i$ for $i = 1, 2$), then all the results in Part 1 of the book will apply. We've already studied a large number of issues that affect the optimal design of individual piece rate contracts like these.

A different way to motivate these two workers is to give both workers a certain level of base pay, a, let them work, then pay a bonus of size S to the worker whose performance turns out to be best.[1] In other words, the principal could offer the following contracts to its two workers:

$$Y_1 = \begin{cases} a & \text{if } Q_1 < Q_2 \\ a + S & \text{if } Q_1 > Q_2 \end{cases} \tag{20.3}$$

and

$$Y_2 = \begin{cases} a & \text{if } Q_2 < Q_1 \\ a + S & \text{if } Q_2 > Q_1. \end{cases} \tag{20.4}$$

Thus, the two workers compete to produce the highest output, Q, then the loser gets a and the winner gets $a + S$.[2] It is common to refer to the difference between these two payoffs, S, as the *prize spread* in this tournament. Although we have described S as a bonus, economists also use tournament theory to think about promotions and promotion ladders in firms. In that case, you should think of S as the total value to the worker of being promoted to the next rung in the firm's hierarchy.

With these basic elements of the tournament specified, we can now pose the following two questions. First, given that we have decided to pay the workers using a tournament, what is the best way to do it (i.e., what are the socially efficient values of a and S)? Second, is there any advantage (or disadvantage) to paying workers via a tournament versus individual piece rates? In other words, if we define *social surplus* as the sum of profits and utility (as in Definition 4.1), does the optimal tournament generate more or less social surplus than the

[1] While a (the pay of the non-winners) is typically positive in most real-world promotion contests, nothing in the logic of tournaments requires it to be, for the same reason that a can be negative in an optimal piece rate contract. Looking beyond the workplace, we do sometimes observe negative levels of a, such as the entry fees in professional blackjack or poker tournaments.

[2] If there's a tie between the two workers (i.e., $Q_1 = Q_2$), we can suppose that the principal flips a coin to award the prize. For the types of luck distributions we study in this chapter, ties happen with essentially zero probability (because the ε's are drawn from a continuous distribution). Therefore, to save clutter, we don't include this possibility in our formal analysis. Nothing would change, however, if we assumed ties were resolved by a coin toss.

optimal piece rate system? The answer to this question will help us understand whether (or when) it makes more sense to reward people based on their relative or their absolute performance.

We'll answer these questions in the first part of this chapter for a specific, simple case of the two-player tournament model described previously. Specifically, we'll use our baseline cost-of-effort function $V(E_i) = E_i^2/2$, assume that both workers are equally able ($d_1 = d_2 = d$), and assume an especially tractable form of luck, described following. Toward the end of the chapter, we'll discuss how the results change when we relax the assumptions of this simple model. To anticipate the results, we'll show that in this simple, baseline case, tournaments and piece rates are equivalent in the sense that neither can outperform the other. This equivalence breaks down when we change the assumptions, so that sometimes tournaments outperform piece rates, whereas in other cases, piece rates are better. Distinguishing those cases will be our task in the rest of Part 4.

20.2 Effort and the Probability of Winning the Promotion

Tournaments motivate workers because working harder increases a worker's chances of winning the prize. But in any competitive situation, my chances of winning also depend on the efforts of my competitors. As a basis for our formal model of tournaments, in this section we work out exactly how a player's chances of winning a competition depend on *both* the competitors' efforts in a simple, base-case example.

We begin by being more precise about how lady luck affects the outputs of our two agents after they have decided how much effort to commit to their jobs. Notice first that according to Equations 20.1 and 20.2 and the definition of the contest, Worker 1 wins the contest if and only if

$$d(E_1 - E_2) > (\varepsilon_2 - \varepsilon_1). \tag{20.5}$$

(Recall that both workers are equally able, by assumption, so $d_1 = d_2 = d$.) This makes sense: Worker 1 wins if the expected output gap resulting from his relative effort, $d(E_1 - E_2)$, outweighs Worker 2's relative luck, $(\varepsilon_2 - \varepsilon_1)$. Next, to keep things as simple as possible, let's assume that Worker 2's relative luck ($\varepsilon \equiv \varepsilon_2 - \varepsilon_1$) follows a *uniform distribution* on the interval [−5, 5]. Although this sounds complicated, it's not. What it means, loosely speaking, is that "nature" picks a real number between −5 and +5, with all real numbers having an equal chance of being selected. Because the range of possible values is symmetric around zero, nature is fair to the two contestants in the sense that the expected value of ε (i.e., of the advantage conferred on Agent 2) is zero. A little more precisely, the *probability density function* of a uniform distribution on [−5, 5] is a constant, as shown in Figure 20.1.

One convenient consequence of this simple distribution is that the chance that a draw of ε lies between any two adjacent integers (e.g., between 2 and 3) is

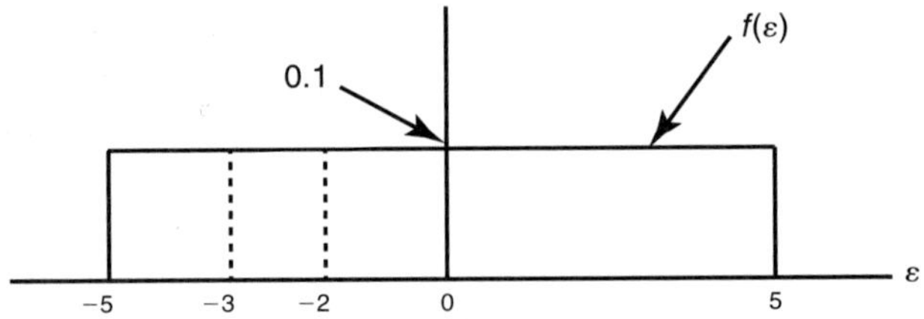

FIGURE 20.1. The Probability Density Function (pdf), f(ε), of a Uniform Distribution on the Interval [–5, 5]

Notes: The area under a pdf between any two values of ε gives the probability that nature picks a number between those two values. For example, the chances of picking a number between -3 and -2 are given by 1 (the base of the rectangle) times 0.1 (its height) = 0.1, or 1 in 10.

10%. The chances that nature draws a negative number ($\varepsilon < 0$) are 50%, and the chances that ε is less than any number x between −5 and +5 are given by

$$\text{Prob}\ (\varepsilon < x) = 0.5 + 0.1x. \tag{20.6}$$

Combining Equation 20.5 and 20.6, we can calculate the probability that worker 1 wins as

$$\text{Prob (1 wins)} = \text{Prob}\ [\varepsilon < d(E_1 - E_2)] = 0.5 + 0.1d(E_1 - E_2). \tag{20.7}$$

This also makes sense: The probability that Worker 1 wins the promotion depends positively on that worker's own effort but negatively on Worker 2's effort. If both agents put in the same effort ($E_1 = E_2$), then regardless of whether that effort is high or low, the agents each have an even chance of winning [Prob (1 wins) = 0.5]. If Worker 1 works harder than Worker 2, then Worker 1 will have a better chance of winning than Worker 2 [Prob (1 wins) > 0.5].

To illustrate the effects of the two workers' effort choices on the probability that Worker 1 wins, Figure 20.2 graphs this relationship for an example where $d = 1$.

A final detail in understanding the effects of agents' efforts on their chances of winning concerns the employer's measurement technology. A simple way to model the effects of this technology is by changing the range of the luck distribution from [–5, +5] to a general range given by [$-R/2$, $+R/2$]. Thus, if $R = 10$, Worker 2's relative luck, ε, can take on any value between –5 and +5, as shown in Figure 20.1 where the density of the distribution (the height of the curve) equals 0.10. If R on the other hand equals 20, ε can take on any value between –10 and +10, and the density becomes 0.05 (1/20) instead of 0.10. Thus, higher values of R correspond to a greater spread, or dispersion, in the distribution of relative luck, which would be the case if the firm's measurement technology was less accurate, or *noisier.* When productivity measurement is noisier, the same level of effect can give rise to a wider range of measured output levels than before. For this more general case, we have Result 20.1.

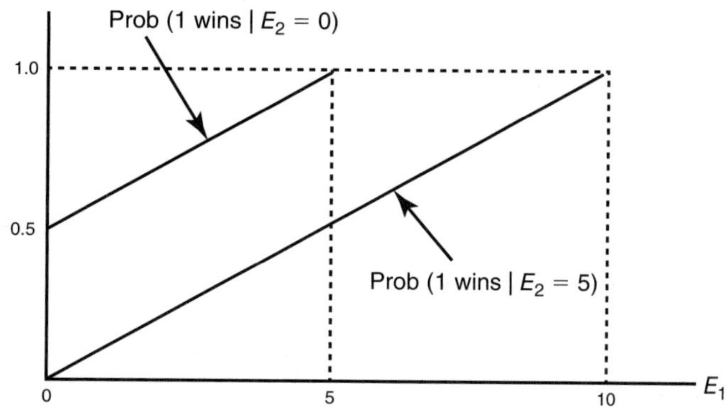

FIGURE 20.2. The Probability That Worker 1 Wins, as a Function of Both Workers' Effort Levels (Example of $d = 1$)

Notes: Using Equation 20.7, when Worker 2 does nothing ($E_2 = 0$), Worker 1 has a 50% chance of winning if Worker 1 does nothing also. As Worker 1 raises the effort to above 0 (keeping E_2 at 0), Worker 1's chances of winning rise above 50%. When Worker 2 chooses $E_2 = 5$, Worker 1 has no chance of winning if Worker 1 picks $E_1 = 0$. If Worker 1 raises the effort to 5 (keeping E_2 at 5), Worker 1 achieves an even chance of winning; choosing $E_1 > 5$ raises Worker 1's chances of winning above 50%.

RESULT 20.1

Effects of Worker Effort on the Probability of Winning a Tournament

When two agents, i and j, have the same ability (d), and the distribution of their relative luck ($\varepsilon_2 - \varepsilon_1$) is uniform on the interval [$-R/2$, $+R/2$], the probability that worker i will win the promotion can be written as

$$p_i(E_i, E_j) = 0.5 + \alpha d(E_i - E_j), \tag{20.8}$$

where $\alpha = 1/R$ is the density of the uniform distribution. R, the range of the distribution, measures the importance of luck in the production or productivity measurement technology.

Let's conclude this section by summarizing the determinants of who wins the contest, as laid out in Equation 20.8. First, the probability that a worker wins rises when that worker's own effort increases and falls when the other worker's effort increases. Second, the probability of winning doesn't depend on the players' absolute effort levels, only on the difference between them ($E_i - E_j$). This leads to the interesting possibility that if the two workers could agree to cut both their effort levels by the same amount, neither worker's chances of winning would change; these workers would both be better off because they still get the same expected pay but work less hard. We discuss this type of collusion in Chapter 21. Third, note that (by design in our baseline example) the contest we have designed is both *fair* and *symmetric.*

DEFINITION 20.1 A contest is **fair** if all agents who produce the same output (Q) have an equal chance of winning.

DEFINITION 20.2 A contest is **symmetric** if it is fair *and* if all agents have the same productivity (*d*) and the same cost-of-effort function *V*(*E*).

In symmetric, two-player contests, two workers who exert the same effort will have equal chances of winning, that is, 50%. Fourth, in a tournament, the marginal effect of effort on the probability of winning (αd) increases with the *precision* with which output is measured, $\alpha = 1/R$. For intuition, consider the decision of an employee who is considering whether or not to work a bit harder in an office setting. If productivity measurement is very precise, then the worker knows that such extra effort is likely to be noticed: It won't be in vain. In a very imprecise world, however, the worker might assume that any extra effort will go unrecognized, reducing that worker's incentives to work. Last, the marginal effect of effort on the probability of winning also rises with the workers' productivity (d).

20.3 The Agents' Problem: Optimal Individual Effort, Given the Contest Rules

As we learned in Part 1, principal–agent models need to be solved via *backwards induction*: We can't figure out what the best contract is until we first work out how the agent(s) would respond to *every possible contract* an agent might face. Accordingly, our next step in modeling tournaments is to study the agents' problem: How hard do we expect each agent to work when facing a tournament described by the ordered pair (a, S)?

Taking a and S as given, let the disutility of effort be $E_i^2/2$. Then the expected utility of Agent 1 is

$$EU_1 = p_1(E_1, E_2)[a+S] + [1 - p_1(E_1, E_2)]\, a - E_1^2/2 \tag{20.9}$$

$$= a + p_1(E_1, E_2)\, S - E_1^2/2 \tag{20.10}$$

$$= a + [0.5 + \alpha d(E_1 - E_2)]\, S - E_1^2/2. \tag{20.11}$$

Agent 1's problem is to choose the effort, E_1, to maximize his own utility (EU_1), taking as given the rules of the contract (a and S) and how hard Agent 1 expects Worker 2 to work (E_2).

Taking the derivative of Equation 20.11 with respect to E_1 and treating Worker 2's effort as given, the first-order condition for a maximum is $\alpha dS - E_1 = 0$. Re-arranging, worker 1's optimal effort is

$$E_1 = \alpha dS. \tag{20.12}$$

The effect of each parameter on optimal effort should be intuitive. First of all, effort is independent of a. This is similar to the piece rate problem in Part 1, where we found that rational self-interested agents' effort choices should be unaffected by the level of base pay. Second, optimal effort increases with the prize spread, S, with worker productivity, d, and with the precision of the firm's performance measurement system, α. This makes sense: When the prize spread increases, the principal is raising the stakes, which naturally motivates workers. Similar logic applies to higher levels of d and α. An interesting consequence is that because effort is the product of α, d, and S, a firm with a noisy measurement system can always compensate for it by raising S. Thus, imprecise output measures are not necessarily a problem in tournaments. Third, because exactly the same math applies to Worker 2 as Worker 1, Worker 2's effort will also be given by $E_2 = \alpha dS$. In other words, we have Result 20.2.

☑ RESULT 20.2 **Effort and Luck in Symmetric Tournaments**

In a symmetric tournament, all agents optimally pick the same level of effort. They therefore all have the same chance of winning.

Although it seems intuitive (and fair) that the winner should be the hardest worker, Result 20.2 shows that this is not in fact the case in fair tournaments between equally matched opponents. Because the agents optimally work equally hard, the winner of a *symmetric* tournament is determined purely by luck—that is, by whether nature picks a high or low value of ε. Despite this, note that the tournament is doing exactly what it is designed to do: eliciting high levels of effort from both competitors.

Finally, even though Agent 1's chances of winning the contest depend on Agent 2's effort, notice that E_2 does not appear in Equation 20.12. Importantly, this property—that *Agent 1's optimal effort choice does not depend on how hard Agent 1 expects Agent 2 to work*—is a special feature of the baseline example we have chosen to solve in this chapter. In the language of game theory, agents' optimal effort choices are dominant strategies only if the distribution of relative luck is uniform.[3] We discuss what happens when the agents' optimal efforts are interdependent in Section 20.6.

20.4 Efficiency: Which Effort Levels Maximize the Size of the Pie?

As we discussed in Chapter 4, socially efficient contracts maximize the sum of the firm's profits and the workers' utilities. This constitutes the total "pie"

[3] A choice (i.e., an effort level) is a dominant strategy for player i if it is player i's best choice *regardless of the choices made by all the other players.*

that can be divided between workers and firms using the lump sum transfer, *a*, that flows between them. Regardless of how we feel about distributional issues between workers and firms, there are good reasons to want contracts to be socially efficient because improvements in efficiency always create an opportunity to make both firms *and* workers better off. In this section, we find the socially efficient effort levels in our baseline example (where the production functions are given by $Q_i = dE_i + \varepsilon_i$, and effort cost functions equal $E_i^2/2$). Once we have those effort levels, Section 20.5 will design a tournament that induces workers to choose exactly those effort levels.

The firm's expected profits from running a tournament in our example are given by

$$E(\Pi) = Q_1 + Q_2 - 2a - S = dE_1 + dE_2 - 2a - S. \quad \textbf{(20.13)}$$

Total expected revenues from the two workers are $Q_1 + Q_2$. (The "relative luck" term ε doesn't appear because it has an expected value of zero.) Both workers receive the base pay, *a*, but only the winner receives the bonus, *S*.

By the same logic, total expected utility for the two workers is given by

$$EU_1 + EU_2 = 2a + S - E_1^2/2 - E_2^2/2. \quad \textbf{(20.14)}$$

Adding Equation 20.13 and 20.14 yields

$$\text{Total surplus} = W = d(E_1 + E_2) - E_1^2/2 - E_2^2/2. \quad \textbf{(20.15)}$$

Notice that—just as in Section 4.2—the cash payments flowing between firms and workers, *a* and *S*, drop out (these just divide the pie between the three parties). Making the pie as big as possible therefore means maximizing the difference between the total output that is produced, $d(E_1 + E_2)$, and the total disutility of producing it. Notice also that—aside from the fact that there are now two workers—this is exactly the same definition of social welfare that we used in the case of individual piece rates in Definition 4.1. The welfare *criterion* we are trying to maximize does not depend on the institutional arrangements (piece rates, tournaments, or something else) we are using. Instead, these institutions are just different *tools* we are using to try to achieve the same goal.

Differentiating Equation 20.15 with respect to the two effort levels and setting them equal to zero yields the first-order conditions

$$d - E_1 = 0, \quad \textbf{(20.16)}$$

and

$$d - E_2 = 0. \quad \textbf{(20.17)}$$

Solving these two equations for effort, we get that $E_i = d$ for $i = 1, 2$. Summing up is Result 20.3.

RESULT 20.3

Economically Efficient Effort Levels

Regardless of how the worker is paid, the economically efficient level of effort from a worker with expected productivity $Q_i = dE_i$, and effort disutility $V_i = E_i^2/2$ is given by

$$E_i^* = d. \quad \textbf{(20.18)}$$

20.5 Achieving Efficiency with the Optimal Tournament

Having set our goal—getting both workers to pick socially efficient effort levels—let's now design a contest between them that achieves exactly that. One point of this exercise is to show that optimal contests can look very much like an arrangement we often see in firms: a group of workers are all guaranteed a certain positive level of base pay, $a > 0$, while the best-performing member of the group receives an additional bonus or promotion with positive value S. Second, the exercise yields values of utility, profits, and other outcomes that can be compared to what happens under efficient piece rates in the next section. To make things really concrete, we'll work with a very specific example: In this section and the next, we therefore set $\alpha = 0.1$ and $d = 4$.

Using Result 20.3 ($E_i^* = d$), we now know that our goal is to induce both workers to pick $E_i = 4$. Using Equation 20.5, our two agent's effort choices given the contest rules are $E_1^* = E_2^* = 4 = \alpha dS = 0.1(4)S = 0.4S$. Rearranging, we see

TABLE 20.1 UTILITY, PROFITS, AND OTHER OUTCOMES UNDER EFFICIENT TOURNAMENTS AND PIECE RATES

	(1)	(2)
	Socially Efficient Tournament ($a = 9$ and $S = 10$)	Socially Efficient Individual Piece Rates ($a = -2$ and $b = 1$)
Worker's Expected Output (Q)	$= dE + \text{E}(\varepsilon)$ $= 4(4) + 0$ $= 16$	$= dE$ $= 16$
Worker's Expected Income (Y)	$= a + 0.5S$ $= 9 + 0.5(10)$ $= 14$	$= a + bdE$ $= -2 + 16$ $= 14$
Worker's Expected Utility (U)	$= a + 0.5S - E^2/2$ $= 14 - 4^2/2 = 6$	$= a + bdE - E^2/2$ $= -2 + 16 - 4^2/2 = 6$
Expected Profits Per Worker (Π)	= Expected output − Expected wage $= 16 - 14$ $= 2$	= Expected output − Expected wage $= 16 - 14$ $= 2$

Note: $\text{E}(\varepsilon)$ denotes the expected value of epsilon.

that to induce this choice, S must equal 10. With $E_i = 4$, each worker will produce $Q_i = dE = 16$ units of output in expectation. Supposing in addition (the reason will soon be clear) that we give workers a base pay of $a = 9$, we can now work out the exact levels of workers' income and utility and the firm's profits in this socially efficient tournament. The results are displayed in column (1) of Table 20.1. In sum, when we set the prize spread, S, to induce efficient effort levels; and when we pay each worker a base pay of $a = 9$, each worker will produce an expected output of 16 units, have a total expected income of 14 units, and an expected utility of 6. The firm will earn an expected profit of 2 units per worker employed.

20.6 A Theorem: The Equivalence of Tournaments and Piece Rates

Now that we've completely characterized output, income, utility, and profits in a socially efficient tournament, we're in a position to compare efficient tournaments to efficient piece rates. To that end, let's now suppose that instead of competing for a promotion, each of the two workers in the previous example (where $d = 4$ and $V(E) = E^2/2$) was compensated via an ordinary piece rate. Recall that under this scheme, Worker 1's expected income would be given by $Y_1 = a + bdE_1$, and that the socially efficient piece rate is $b = 1$. Last, suppose that $a = -2$ in this piece rate contract. How will utility, profits, and other outcomes compare to the efficient tournament?

Faced with this piece rate contract, both workers will now choose $E^* = 4$. Why? Under the piece rate, Worker 1's expected utility is $a + bdE_1 - E_1^2/2$. As we did in Chapter 2, maximizing this yields the familiar result that $E^* = bd = 1(4)$. Column (2) of Table 20.1 works out the remaining outcomes, all of which are *identical* to the tournament outcomes in column (2). This illustrates the Tournaments Equivalence Theorem.

☑ RESULT 20.4

The Equivalence Between Tournaments and Piece Rates

By appropriately choosing the parameters of the contract (a and b in the case of piece rates; a and S in the case of tournaments), any overall outcome (i.e., any combination of output, effort, worker utility, and firm profits) that can be generated by one type of contract can *also* be generated by the other. These outcomes include the socially efficient one, which maximizes profits plus utility. This result *requires all workers to be risk neutral.*

One important implication of Result 20.4 is that tournaments can economize on employee monitoring and evaluation costs: To see this, suppose that an employer can't observe the workers' output well, but the employer can observe workers' *relative* output with some error (i.e., assign rough *ranks* to workers). As long as workers are risk neutral, Result 20.4 says that the firm and its workers can do just as well with a tournament as with a piece rate. Indeed, because—as we already noted—the employer can always compensate for imprecise measurement by raising the prize spread, tournaments can work just as well as piece rates even with noisy assessments of relative productivity.

The theory of tournaments might also help explain a fact that many of us seem to take for granted: Workers often receive big raises when they are promoted. Such raises are, however, rather hard to understand in more familiar economic models (like those in most labor economics texts), which argue that workers are always paid their marginal product: It's hard to imagine that a worker who gets a 50% raise on promotion from assistant manager to chief manager becomes 50% more productive overnight. However, if promotions are seen as a prize for which the assistant managers compete, these large salary jumps are easier to understand.

Although we illustrated Result 20.4's equivalence theorem in a very simple example, the theorem applies in a much more general set of circumstances. For example, the equivalence of piece rates and tournaments does not depend on our use of a linear production function, a quadratic disutility-of-effort function, or the assumption of only two agents. Also, with one important proviso, Result 20.4 does not depend on our very special assumption that the players' relative luck follows a uniform distribution. The proviso is that for essentially all luck distributions other than the one we have studied, the agents' (privately) optimal effort levels will not be dominant strategies as they were in Section 20.3. In these other cases, a player's optimal effort level will depend on what that person expects co-worker(s) to do, complicating the agent's choice problem if we continue to assume that the agents all make their effort decisions at the same time. Theoretically, economists often forecast how agents will behave in situations like this by assuming the agents are able to arrive at a *Nash equilibrium* of their actions. As it turns out, the equivalence theorem between tournaments and piece rates extends to these other luck distributions, provided we are willing to assume the agents' (interdependent) effort decisions are Nash equilibrium choices.

DEFINITION 20.3 **Nash equilibrium**, a core concept in game theory, is simply an outcome where no agent can improve his choice, given the choices of all the other agents. In a two-person tournament, a Nash equilibrium of the effort game between the agents can be found by (a) deriving Agent 1's preferred choice for every possible effort level of Agent 2: $E_1{}^* = f^1(E_2)$; (b) deriving Agent 2's preferred choice for every possible effort level of Agent 1: $E_2{}^* = f^2(E_1)$; then (c) finding the intersections (there could be more than one) of these two *reaction functions* in (E_1, E_2) space. These intersections identify effort choices that are utility maximizing for both agents *and* are consistent with each other, in the sense that each agent behaves as the other expects him to.

Unfortunately it is not always easy for groups of real people engaged in strategic interactions to converge on a Nash equilibrium: In addition to being cognitively demanding, it requires all the players to know each other's preferences and to be confident that all the other players are just as well-informed and rational. Because that is hardly guaranteed, actual behavior in real tournaments tends to be quite a bit more variable (both over time and across people) than Nash equilibrium predicts. Still, some experiments show that, at least on average, agents in these situations do make Nash equilibrium choices; so Nash behavior provides at least a rough guide to average behavior.[4] Summarizing is Result 20.5.

RESULT 20.5

Strategic Considerations Make Effort Choices in Tournaments Harder to Predict than Under Individual Piece Rates

When agents' optimal effort choices are not dominant strategies, selecting optimal effort requires agents to *forecast* their co-workers' effort choices. Because this is difficult and often inaccurate, actual agent behavior tends to be more variable and unpredictable in a tournament than under a theoretically equivalent piece rate scheme.

20.7 Some Extensions: Many Players, Prizes, and Stages

In this section, we briefly explore how the results derived earlier in this chapter change when we make our model of tournaments more realistic in a number of ways. We start by asking how things change when there are more than just two contestants.

Many Players

Probably the most important thing to know about multiplayer tournaments is that they can be modeled in exactly the same way we've been doing so far. Most of the results we've derived, including Results 20.2 through 20.5, continue to apply. One interesting new question that arises with multiple players, however, is the following: Keeping everything else (including the total size of the single, winning prize, S) the same, how does adding more equally able contestants change the effort levels of the players in a tournament? As I've learned by informally asking people (including economists), it turns out that different people have quite different intuitions about what should happen.

One very sensible intuition follows from Result 20.2: Because all equally able agents have the same chance of winning the prize in equilibrium, each one will have a smaller chance of winning as more contestants are added. This very intuitive *1/N effect* reduces each agent's incentives to work as the number of competitors increases. On the other hand, let's not forget Adam Smith's famous intuition that increased competition can make us work harder. To see this, consider

[4] See, for example, Bull, Schotter, and Weigelt (1987).

the extreme case of a competition with only one player (e.g., an automatic promotion after a year in the job). Because that player is guaranteed to "win," the player has no incentive to work at all. Adding a competitor will certainly raise the incentives to work; and adding two competitors might do so even more (because now the player has to work hard enough to beat two people instead of just one to win). This second, *competition effect* tends to raise effort levels as contestants are added, while keeping the single prize constant in value.[5] In sum is Result 20.6.

☑ RESULT 20.6

Adding More Contestants to a Competition for a Single, Fixed Prize May Raise or Lower Agents' Optimal Effort Levels

This is because of two opposing effects that occur as contestants are added: a 1/*N effect* that reduces efforts and a *competition effect* that raises efforts. An interesting implication for employers is that *allowing more workers to compete for a prize can increase work incentives without the need to make the prize any bigger.*

Prize Structure

Another issue that arises once we begin to think about tournaments with more than two players is the question of optimal *prize structure*. For example, in a tournament with three players, should there be a single "top" prize for the best performer only, or should there also be a smaller second prize? Perhaps surprisingly, there is still a lot that economists don't know about questions like these; for example, it was only recently proved that a single, top prize is the best motivator in an important class of tournaments called Tullock Contests (Tullock, 1987; Schweinzer & Segev, 2012).[6] Psychological factors may also affect optimal prize structure. For example, in addition to the widely publicized jackpot prizes, most large lotteries (which can have millions of contestants) also offer a large number of smaller prizes. This may be a form of positive, variable reinforcement that induces players to keep buying tickets.

Finally, getting prize structure right can be critical in contests where there are substantial *ability differences* between players. Consider, for example, a multiplayer competition where one player is so dominant that he or she is almost guaranteed to win the top prize. If there are no prizes for coming in second, third, or lower, none of the lower-ranked players will have much incentive to supply effort: The top prize has been taken "out of competition" by the presence of a superstar. Indeed, Jennifer Brown (2011) shows that reallocating money from the top prize to the second prize raises lower-ranked players' efforts when there's a dominant player in the game. We'll study tournaments with unevenly matched players in much more detail in Chapter 22.

---

[5] List, Van Soest, Stoop, and Zhou (2014) show that these two effects exactly cancel each other out when agents have uniformly distributed, *independent* luck. In addition, they show that the 1/*N* effect dominates when the density of the luck variable is decreasing, and they provide lab and field evidence (the latter from a fishing tournament) in support of these predictions.

[6] In Tullock contests, a player's chance of winning is given by the ratio of that player's effort to the sum of all the other players' efforts. For additional details, see Dechenaux, Kovenock, and Sheremeta (2015).

Sequential and Multistage Contests

The tournament models we have studied so far are *simultaneous-move games* in the sense that all the agents in a competition must choose their effort levels without knowledge of other workers' choices or luck. The motivation for this assumption is to capture the essence of Yogi Berra's insightful dictum on the game of baseball: "It ain't over till it's over."[7] In other words, even if competitors (say, for a promotion) are picking effort levels and experiencing luck over a continuous period of time, a player can't know all the actions and luck that will be experienced by that player's competitors until the game is over, that is, until the time when neither player can do anything anymore. Thus, in this sense, most real contests are at least in part simultaneous-move games because the players have to make choices without complete knowledge of their competitors' actions and luck. This will be especially true in workplace tournaments where—in contrast to sports where everyone knows the score during the course of the game—workers may not have a good idea of "who's ahead" at any particular time during the competition.

DEFINITION 20.4 In a **simultaneous-move game**, all the participants must choose their actions without any knowledge of the other player's actions.

That said, there are many real competitions where competitors do see some aspect of their competitors' previous effort decisions (and luck realizations) when picking their own effort. Examples include monthly sales tournaments (at least when workers know something about each other's sales during the month), most promotion tournaments, and almost all sports (with the possible exception of "one-shot" events like the 100 m sprint!). As you might expect, economists and others have modeled these types of competitions in several ways, the simplest of which is a *sequential contest*. For example, if the agents in Section 20.3 took turns in selecting their effort levels (either by just moving once each, or by going back and forth any finite number of times), that would be a sequential contest. In contrast to simultaneous-move contests (which are solved by finding a Nash equilibrium of the game played by the agents with each other), sequential contests are solved by backwards induction.[8] Notice, by the way, that backwards induction is not necessary in the special case of the uniform relative luck distribution studied at the start of this chapter: Here, because the agents' optimal effort choices don't depend on each other's efforts, agents will behave identically whether they move first, second, or simultaneously with the other player.

---

[7] Berra's famous quote was made in July 1973 when Berra's Mets trailed the Chicago Cubs by 9½ games in the National League East. The Mets rallied to clinch the division title in their second-to-last game of the regular season. For more Yogi wisdom, see https://en.wikipedia.org/wiki/Yogi_Berra.

[8] For example, in the case of two agents taking one turn each, Agent 1 (the first mover) first figures out how to expect Agent 2 to respond to *every possible level* of Agent 1's effort (E_1). Once Agent 2's expected Stage-2 behavior has been worked out, Agent 1 can then decide on an optimal effort level. The logic is identical to the sequential interaction between the principal and agents described in Section 1.7, and to the Stackelberg duopoly games that are often discussed in intermediate microeconomics.

DEFINITION 20.5 In a sequential contest, the players take turns choosing their effort levels according to some prespecified rule. In cases where players move more than once, the winner of a sequential contest is determined by adding up each player's total performance in all periods of the game. The winner is the player with the highest total performance.

Sequential contests become especially interesting and relevant to real-world competitions when the players experience some luck each time they choose an effort level, and when their competitors can see the results of this luck [e.g., by observing their competitor's current performance ($Q = dE + \varepsilon$) during the course of a repeated interaction]. An obvious example is when both players can see the current score of a game, which reflects the effort *and* luck of both players up to that point. Whenever luck matters in this way, and whenever feedback of this sort is available to players, a fundamental transformation occurs: Even when both players are evenly matched at the start of a sequential game, random luck in the early stages almost always turns what was a symmetric contest into an asymmetric one. To win the game, a team that is seven points behind has to beat the other team by more than seven points during the rest of the game to win. Thus, there is a close link between *asymmetric contests* (i.e., contests that start out being biased in favor of one player or the other) and sequential contests (which become asymmetric as soon as one player takes a lead over the other).

RESULT 20.7

Sequential Contests and Asymmetric Contests

If luck affects contestants' performance, and if contestants can observe each other's performance during the course of a sequential contest, *essentially all sequential contests—even those between equally matched players—become asymmetric competitions after they start.* Agents who experience good luck early have an advantage in the remaining competition for the purely mechanical reason that they are now "ahead": They don't need to perform as well as the other player during the rest of the game to win.

We will study asymmetric contests in much more detail in Chapter 22, but it may be of interest to highlight some of the questions that arise when differences in effort or luck in early phases of a contest make the later phases asymmetric. For example, we might expect that players who move later (followers) will tend to *take it easy* when their competitor(s) had bad luck early in the game. In addition to taking it easy, followers who find themselves ahead could also become more *cautious*, taking actions to *reduce the role of luck* in the rest of the game. For example, they might "run out the clock" in basketball or American football. Both of these responses by players who find themselves ahead in the game—working less hard and becoming more cautious—are realistic possibilities in promotion tournaments, raising the issue of how much feedback employers should give their workers on interim performance. Indeed, if feedback sometimes reveals that the contest has essentially already been decided, withholding feedback may be a very useful way to prevent likely winners from "coasting"—and likely losers from "giving up"—near the end of the evaluation period.

RESULT 20.8 **Feedback in Sequential Contests**

It may not always be optimal for principals to provide interim information (feedback) on the relative performance of agents in a sequential contest. This is because when agents learn that one is very far ahead of the other, both agents may reduce their efforts relative to a situation where they think *both* players still have a realistic chance of winning.

DEFINITION 20.6 A **multistage contest** is a *series of contests* between multiple players where the overall winner depends in some way on the *number of contests won.* One example is a *round-robin tournament,* where each player plays against every other, and the overall winner has the most wins.

A second type of multistage contest that is probably much more relevant to the workplace is the *elimination tournament*, where a large initial pool of contestants is narrowed down with only the winners of early rounds advancing to later rounds. Promotion ladders inside firms share these features and have been studied as such since Rosen's famous 1986 article.

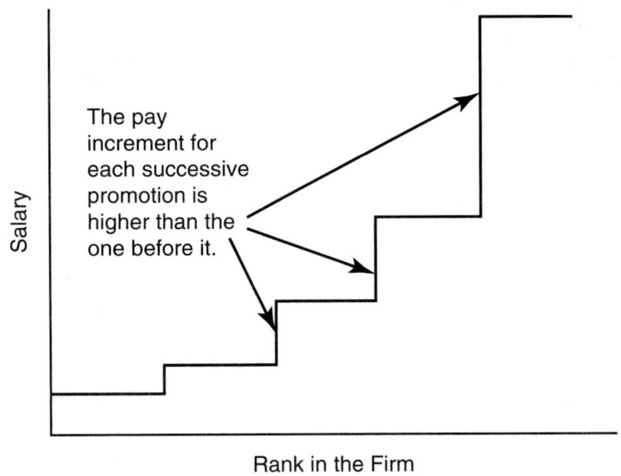

FIGURE 20.3. A Large Corporation's Typical Salary Scale

Prize Structure in Elimination Tournaments: CEO Pay and the FIFA World Cup

In a seminal article, University of Chicago economist Sherwin Rosen (1986) argued that *promotion ladders* can be usefully thought of as a type of elimination tournament. Because in many organizations it is important—if not essential—to win promotions at lower levels of the firm's hierarchy to be promoted to higher ranks, the employees who make it to the top are usually the ones who have won a series of earlier promotions inside the same firm.

When firms operate this way, Rosen noticed that the total reward from winning any given promotion has two distinct components: (1) the raise that is earned for the current promotion and (2) the fact that winning this promotion gives you the *right to compete* for higher-level promotions. This second component, sometimes called the *option value* of winning, is not present in a single-stage contest and (by the same logic) is not present in the competition for the highest position in the firm.

Given this logic, Rosen noticed that *there may not be any need to attach raises to promotions at lower ranks at all*: The option value of early promotions alone might be sufficient to motivate people to compete for them. Indeed, prizes in sports elimination tournaments are often very small in the early rounds compared to later levels. For example, in the 2014 FIFA World Cup in Brazil, teams advancing from the first round (of 32 teams) to the next (but not advancing beyond that) earned an extra $1 million compared to those who lost in the first round. In contrast, the gap between first and second prize was 35 − 25 = $10 million. This prize structure bears a strong resemblance to the salary structure in many large companies, shown in Figure 20.3, with large increases near the top of the ladder and much smaller ones further down.

To explain this pattern, Rosen noted that like the World Cup, the "final" few promotions in a firm's ladder *have no option value*. Near the bottom of the hierarchy, the future opportunities attached to a promotion may be a substantial reward in themselves, so not much extra cash is needed to induce workers to compete for such promotions. At the top, a larger amount of cash is required to motivate workers because these few remaining promotions do not open up a path to higher ranks. Of course, this may not be the *only* reason why CEO pay is so high—or why it has increased so much in recent decades—but Rosen argues that it could be a contributing factor.

Continuous Relative Reward Systems

The tournaments we have studied so far are a type of relative reward system because they remunerate employees on the basis of the relative instead of their absolute performance. They do so by awarding a lump sum prize to the top (or the top few) performers in a group of employees. But tournaments are not the only form of relative reward schemes. In particular, it is possible to pay people for their relative performance in a way that links each person's pay more smoothly to his or her relative performance. For example, in a two-person contest, each person, i, could be paid $Y_i = a + b(Q_i - Q_j)$, where Q_j is the output of the other worker. In this scheme, each worker is paid b dollars for every dollar of output that exceeds the other worker's output. This could be generalized to a larger number of workers with the pay policy $Y_i = a + b(Q_i - \overline{Q})$, where $\overline{Q}$ is the mean output of all the workers in a comparison group.[9]

DEFINITION 20.7 In a **continuous relative reward system,** each participant's pay is a continuous function of that worker's relative performance. For example, if a worker's relative performance is the difference between performance Q_i and the group's average performance $\overline{Q}$, the pay policy $Y_i = a + b(Q_i - \overline{Q})$ would be a continuous relative reward scheme.

Promotions as Signals: The Problem of the Star Administrative Assistant

Because they interact with their employees on a regular basis, most employers probably know more about their own employees' abilities than they know about other firms' workers. Whenever employers have this type of *private information* about their workers, promotions may have a cost to employers that we have ignored so far in this chapter. Specifically, if high-ability workers are more likely to win promotion contests, and if other potential employers can see that a worker has been promoted, then promoting a worker will reveal new information to other employers: that the promoted worker was the best in her pool of co-workers. This problem—that promotions might reveal employers' private information about *who the good workers are* to other firms—was first studied by Cornell economist Michael Waldman in 1984.

In his article, Waldman (1984) demonstrates two potential consequences of the scenario just described, the first of which is **underpromotion:** Compared to a world in which accurate information on each employee's productivity is freely available to all potential employers (as in professional sports and scientific research, where player performance and publication databases can be searched by anyone), employers will promote fewer workers. Able, low-level workers are sometimes concealed from other firms by not promoting them to avoid these top performers being hired away, or "poached." Put another way, employers have an incentive to keep the top performers in their lower ranks (e.g., a star administrative assistant) *invisible* to other firms.

Second, when firms actually do promote workers, they will need to **give promoted workers large raises**. This is not because the workers have suddenly *become* more productive but because the act of promotion *reveals* to other potential employers that the worker has a high level of ability and potential. Wages must therefore jump upward to prevent promoted workers from being poached by other employers. Notice that this is a different (and complementary) explanation for why wages jump at promotion from the one advanced in Section 20.6, where we argued that promotions can be seen as prizes designed to motivate workers to supply effort.

[9] Interestingly, continuous relative reward schemes are actually somewhat easier to model theoretically than tournaments because they avoid the need to model how the probability of winning a lump sum reward depends on the efforts of all the agents as we did in Section 20.2.

Examples of continuous relative reward schemes include the policy of grading students "on a curve." In this policy, the class's average grade is set in advance, so a student's grade depends only on his performance relative to his classmates. Workplace examples include any situation where a worker's peers are used as a standard against which to judge an individual's performance, as well as any policy that links pay to average peer performance or to a worker's rank in some comparison group. Pay schemes with at least one of these properties are quite common, and we will study a number of them later in this part of the book. Examples will include contract farming, agricultural labor, and mutual fund managers.

20. 8 Tournaments with Risk-Averse Agents

How do the results of this chapter—including Result 20.4 on equivalence—change if agents are risk averse rather than risk neutral? Although it might seem intuitive that risk-averse workers will dislike tournaments, a little reflection reveals that working under a tournament does not necessarily expose a worker to more risk than working under an individual piece rate. To see this, consider the pay distributions associated with the two schemes in Figure 20.4. If a worker's output is given by $Q = dE + \varepsilon$, her pay under a linear individual piece rate will be given by $Y = a + bdE + b\varepsilon$. If, in turn, the random variable ε has a bell-shaped distribution (like a normal distribution, e.g.), then for any given level of effort, the distribution of the worker's possible pay levels will be given by the bell-shaped curve in Figure 20.4. Most of the time, the worker's pay will be in a range of values near the middle of the distribution (say, between a and $a + S$), but every once in a while (when the worker's luck is either very good or very bad) the worker could end up with very low or high levels of pay outside that range.

RESULT 20.9 The Relative Riskiness of Tournament versus Piece Rate Pay

Because tournaments eliminate the chance of receiving extreme levels of pay, they do not necessarily increase a worker's compensation risk compared to individual piece rates. Thus it is possible, but not guaranteed, that a risk-averse worker would prefer a tournament-based pay scheme to an individual piece rate scheme offering the same expected value of income.

In a tournament, however, the worker's pay can take on only two values: a if the worker loses, and $a + S$ if the worker wins. Although this adds to the riskiness of pay by eliminating the possibility of ever being paid some number between a and $a + S$, it also reduces the riskiness of pay by eliminating the chance the worker will ever learn less than a (or more than $a + S$). Thus, it is quite possible that a risk-averse worker might prefer a tournament to an individual piece

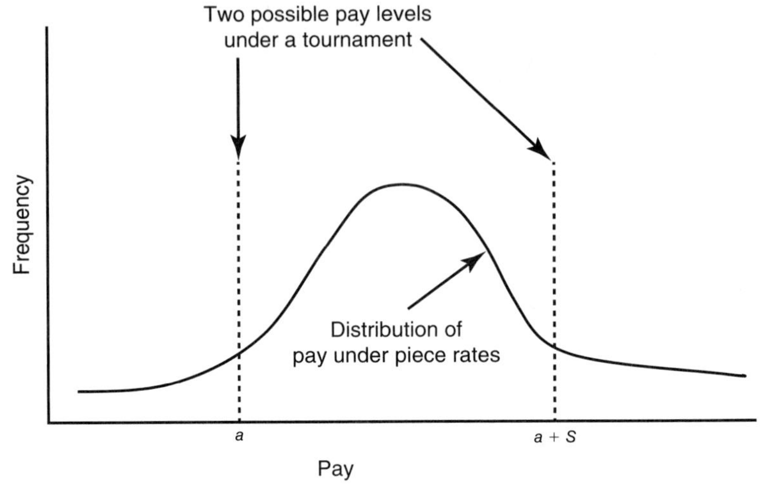

FIGURE 20.4. The Distribution of Pay Under Tournaments versus Piece Rates

rate because the tournament guarantees that the worst thing that can ever happen to pay is that the worker doesn't win the prize for being best in the group.[10] Thus, purely on the basis of which pay scheme exposes workers to more risk, it is not immediately obvious that tournaments are riskier for workers than individual pay schemes.

On the other hand, an additional source of uncertainty associated with tournaments may make them less attractive to risk-averse workers. Specifically, in contrast to individual piece rates, in tournaments, a worker's pay depends on a co-worker's performance, which can be hard to predict due to the strategic considerations described in Result 20.5. Second, even if we could be sure that all workers choose Nash equilibrium effort levels, workers may not have a good idea of how able their competitors are likely to be. This is especially important when people are deciding whether or not to enter a competition—a topic we return to in Chapter 23.

A second reason why risk-averse workers might prefer relative to absolute reward systems applies equally to tournaments and to continuous relative reward schemes. This is the fact that relative reward schemes by their very nature automatically insure workers against common shocks to their productivity.

[10] This downside risk of individual piece rates can however be mitigated by pay policies such as Safelite's PPP policy that guarantees a minimum pay level (subject of course to keeping one's job). See Chapter 8.

DEFINITION 20.8 **Common productivity shocks** are random events that affect the output of all workers in a group the same way. For example, if the "luck" variables ε_1 and ε_2 in Equations 20.1 and 20.2 were given by

$$\varepsilon_1 = \mu + \nu_1 \text{ and } \varepsilon_2 = \mu + \nu_2,$$

the random variable μ would be considered a common shock, while the independent random variables ν_1 and ν_2 would be considered idiosyncratic, or worker-specific shocks.

Common shocks occur in wide variety of workplace contexts. For example, the monthly sales of all the car salespeople at a dealership tend to rise when the local economy is doing well, when the weather is good, and when the government introduces a new subsidy for fuel-efficient vehicles. The productivity of all the data entry workers or customer relations agents in an office tends to fall when the computer network slows down, when an important set of files has been corrupted, or when new government regulations increase record-keeping requirements. All the wheat farmers in a county suffer when the rains don't come, all the Uber drivers in a city experience a surge in their revenues when there's a convention in town, and all the manufacturing workers in the United States produce less revenues for their employers when the U.S. dollar appreciates vis-à-vis the currencies of the countries where their products are sold. All of these common shocks can lead to sizable and random fluctuations in a worker's output that are no fault of the worker: Output may fall considerably even though workers continue to supply the same amount of effort. If risk-averse workers in these situations are paid an individual piece rate like those studied in Part 1, these workers could have highly unpredictable earnings, which they will dislike.

A useful and appealing feature of tournaments and other relative reward schemes is that they automatically insure risk-averse workers against common productivity shocks. For example, if the main sales incentive in a car dealership is a $5,000 bonus for the employee with the *highest* sales in a given month, workers will not be penalized when the group as a whole has a bad month.[11] Further, this insurance doesn't blunt workers' incentives to sell cars because the insurance is only against events (rain, economic downturns) that are outside an individual worker's control. And finally, since risk-averse workers should be willing to sacrifice some wages for this extra security, relative pay schemes have the potential to make both workers and employers better off than pay schemes that depend on a worker's absolute performance only.

[11] Essentially, by comparing workers to each other, relative reward schemes automatically make contracts state contingent in the way recommended for risk-averse workers in Section 5.2: If this month's sales target is your co-workers' average performance, the target in Figure 5.1 is *automatically* reduced in bad times. This might help explain why we rarely observe employee pay plans that are explicitly linked to measures of weather, local business conditions, or other common factors.

RESULT 20.10

Tournaments and Other Relative Pay Schemes Insure Workers Against Common Shocks to Their Productivity

Whenever workers are paid on the basis of their relative instead of their absolute performance, they will not be financially penalized by negative shocks, such as bad weather or poor business conditions, that reduce the productivity of all workers in their comparison group.

20.9 Relative Pay Schemes in Action: The Market for Broilers

Chickens that are raised for meat (as opposed to egg laying) are called broilers in the United States. As it turns out, the market for broilers is a classic principal–agent problem that nicely illustrates the ability of relative reward schemes to insulate risk-averse agents against common productivity shocks. The main facts and concepts are presented in an article by Knoeber (1989). The system he describes, sometimes known as contract farming, is also widely used in some other agricultural contexts, including the market for eggs, turkey, and pork.

A principal in the U.S. broiler industry is a large company such as *Perdue* or *Tyson*, known as an integrator. Instead of raising chickens themselves, integrators write contracts with many individual farmers, known as growers, to do this work. Every 6 to 9 weeks, the integrator sends a new batch of chicks to a grower, whose job it is to house and feed them until they are ready to be sold for slaughter. Importantly, the integrator also supplies (at its own expense) all the chicks' feed and any necessary veterinary services during this period. The process is illustrated in Figure 20.5.

How are the growers compensated in this arrangement? At the end of the "growing" period, integrators pay the growers a certain amount per pound of broiler produced. To encourage the growers to care for the chicks in a way that economizes on feed and vet services, this price depends on the amount of feed

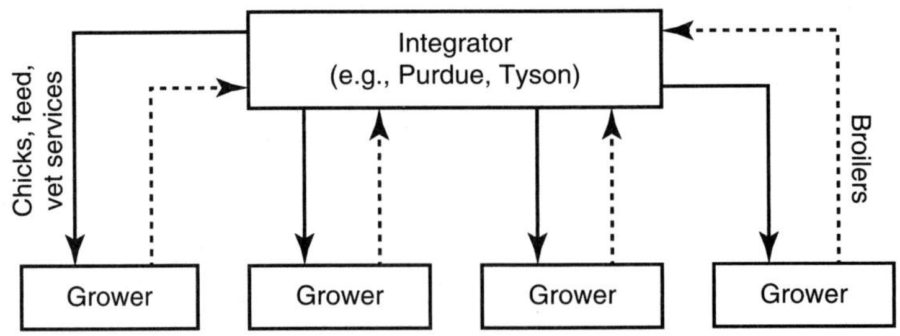

FIGURE 20.5. Organization of the Broiler Market

and vet services used, with low-cost producers receiving a higher price. The interesting feature for our purposes is that the price a grower gets depends not on absolute costs but only on relative cost performance, compared to a dozen or so other growers in the area (about a 20-mile radius). This is a continuous relative reward scheme where each grower's performance is benchmarked relative to the other growers in the local geographic area.

Why are relative rewards used in this market? To understand this, Knoeber (1989) first rules out a few possible explanations. First, he notes that relative assessment of growers in this market is not part of a promotion ladder (like those discussed in Section 20.7) because contract growers are almost never hired as employees by the big integrator companies. Knoeber also notes that this relative pay policy doesn't save on measurement and monitoring expenses (as we argued in Section 20.6) because the company maintains detailed cost and performance records regardless. Thus, he argues that the relative reward scheme is designed to incentivize risk-averse growers to save costs while insuring them against common productivity shocks. Indeed, we expect growers to be risk averse because they are typically family farmers who take out large loans to build barns and buy equipment. Having a more predictable income stream would seem to be quite valuable to them.

What are the productivity shocks that affect growers in this market? These include fluctuations in weather (which affect how much chicks eat) and local disease outbreaks (which can consume a lot of expensive veterinary services). Also important is the breed of chicks that has been supplied to the growers. Integrators are constantly experimenting with new feed formulas and new breeds of chicks in an effort to produce faster-growing, healthier chicks; and some breeds inevitably turn out to be cheaper to raise than others. Because tying growers' pay to the random results of Tyson's feed and breeding experiments (and weather and local disease outbreaks) exposes them to unnecessary risk, Knoeber (1989) argues that eliminating this risk by comparing growers to others who are exposed to the same chicks, feed, and weather makes them better off. Indeed, Knoeber calculates that payment by relative output eliminates about half the potential variance in growers' income, without compromising incentives in any significant way.

Knoeber (1989) points out that are some other advantages to using relative pay in broiler production as well. One is that the system facilitates innovation: By insulating growers from the risk associated with new breeds of chicks and types of feed, relative pay lowers the costs to integrators of experimenting with new methods. Another is that the reward formula adapts more easily than straight piece rates do to technological progress affecting all growers the same way: If technical improvements make it cheaper and easier for everyone to raise chicks, the piece rate per pound will eventually need to be adjusted downward (a problem we'll consider in detail when we study the ratchet effect). This periodic adjustment won't be necessary if growers are paid on a relative basis only.

Finally, consider one incentive problem in principal–agent relationships that we haven't yet discussed: principals' incentives to honestly assess the productivity of their agents. If agents' productivity isn't completely visible to both agents and principals, unscrupulous principals paying piece rates have an incentive to underreport their workers' true productivity (because then they will owe agents less money). Although one hopes that most employers avoid such behavior voluntarily to maintain a good reputation, employers who use relative reward schemes are not subject to this temptation in the first place. To see this, notice that a firm running a tournament between two workers commits in advance to pay a total amount of $2a + S$ to its workers, regardless of how either worker performs. Thus, performance evaluation in a tournament only affects how a fixed amount of pay is distributed among workers, so the firm cannot save money by misrepresenting workers' performance. This final advantage of relative pay schemes should be particularly useful in contexts where employers may not be able to rely on strong reputations for honest evaluation of their agents' performance, such as new firms or markets with a lot of employer turnover.

RESULT 20.11 **Additional Advantages of Relative Pay Schemes**

In addition to insuring workers against common shocks, relative pay schemes

1. Facilitate the principal's ability to experiment with new production methods by sheltering workers' pay from the effects of these experiments.
2. Reduce the need to continually adjust piece rates when innovations raise productivity levels.
3. Eliminate any temptation by principals to misrepresent workers' true productivity levels.

Chapter Summary

- Tournaments are an alternative to piece rates as a way to motivate workers. They work by giving prizes to the top performer(s) in a group.
- Under certain conditions (including worker risk neutrality) tournaments can theoretically deliver identical results to any set of individual piece rates, though tournaments are more affected by strategic interactions between workers than piece rates are.
- Tournaments may economize on the cost of measuring employee performance because they can function with just an imprecise measure of relative performance.
- Elimination tournaments are a type of multistage contest that can be used to model promotion ladders in firms.

- ☐ Continuous relative reward systems differ from tournaments by linking pay continuously rather than discontinuously to relative performance.

- ☐ Both tournaments and continuous relative reward systems automatically insure workers against common shocks to their productivity.

Discussion Questions

1. Are you convinced by Professor Rosen's argument for why raises at the top of the corporate hierarchy are so high? Why or why not? What important features of the job market for top executives does his analysis ignore?
2. In this chapter, we gave two reasons for why wages tend to jump upward when workers are promoted. What are they, and can you think of any others?

Suggestions for Further Reading

For additional analysis of optimal prize structure in contests, see Moldovanu and Sela (2001), Szymanski and Valletti (2005), and Schweinzer and Segev (2012).

For additional analysis and evidence on multistage contests, see Harbaugh and Klumpp (2005), Gilsdorf and Sukhatme (2008), Fu and Lu (2012), and Groh, Moldovanu, Sela, and Sunde (2012). Konrad (2009) provides a useful review of this literature, with applications to political competitions and innovation races as well as personnel economics.

For additional analysis of employers' incentives to keep high-performing workers in their lower ranks invisible, see Milgrom and Oster (1987), Bernhardt and Scoones (1993), Bernhardt (1995), and DeVaro and Waldman (2012).

For more on contract farming, see National Public Radio's story retrieved from http://www.npr.org/blogs/thesalt/2014/02/20/279040721/the-system-that-supplies-our-chickens-pits-farmer-against-farmer.

References

Bernhardt, D., & Scoones, D. (1993). Promotion, turnover, and preemptive wage offers. *American Economic Review, 83,* 771–791.

Bernhardt. D. (1995). Strategic promotion and compensation. *Review of Economic Studies, 62,* 315–339.

Brown, J. (2011). Quitters never win: The (adverse) incentive effects of competing with superstars. *Journal of Political Economy, 119,* 982–1013.

Bull, C., Schotter, A., & Weigelt, K. (1987). Tournaments and piece rates: An experimental study. *Journal of Political Economy, 95,* 1–33.

Dechenaux, E., Kovenock, D., & Sheremeta, R. M. (2015). A survey of experimental research on contests, all-pay auctions and tournaments. *Experimental Economics, 18,* 609–669. doi:10.1007/s10683-014-9421-0

DeVaro, J., & Waldman, M. (2012). The signaling role of promotions: Further theory and empirical evidence. *Journal of Labor Economics, 30*(1), 91–147.

Fu, Q., & Lu, J. (2012). The optimal multi-stage contests. *Economic Theory, 51,* 351–382.

Gilsdorf, K. F., & Sukhatme, V. (2008). Testing Rosen's sequential elimination tournament model: Incentives and player performance in professional tennis. *Journal of Sports Economics, 9,* 287–303.

Groh, C., Moldovanu, B., Sela, A., & Sunde, U. (2012). Optimal seedings in elimination tournaments. *Economic Theory, 49,* 59–80.

Harbaugh, R., & Klumpp, T. (2005). Early round upsets and championship blowouts. *Economic Inquiry, 43,* 316–329.

Knoeber, C. R. (1989). A real game of chicken: Contracts, tournaments, and the production of broilers. *Journal of Law, Economics and Organization, 5*(2), 271–292.

Konrad, K. (2009). *Strategy and dynamics in contests.* Oxford, England: Oxford University Press.

List, J., Van Soest, D., Stoop, J., & Zhou, H. (2014, March). *On the role of group size in tournaments: Theory and evidence from lab and field experiments* (NBER Working Paper No. 20008). Cambridge, MA: National Bureau of Economic Research.

Milgrom, P., & Oster, S. (1987). Job discrimination, market forces, and the invisibility hypothesis. *Quarterly Journal of Economics, 102,* 453–476.

Moldovanu, B., & Sela, A. (2001). The optimal allocation of prizes in contests. *American Economic Review, 91,* 542–558.

Rosen, S. (1986). Prizes and incentives in elimination tournaments. *American Economic Review, 76,* 701–715.

Schweinzer, P., & Segev, E. (2012, October). The optimal prize structure of symmetric Tullock contests. *Public Choice, 153*(1), 69–82.

Tullock, G. (1967). The welfare costs of tariffs, monopolies, and theft. *Economic Inquiry, 5*(3), 224–232.

Szymanski, S., & Valletti, T. M. (2005). Incentive effects of second prizes. *European Journal of Political Economy, 21,* 467–481.

Waldman, M. (1984). Job assignments, signaling, and efficiency. *Rand Journal of Economics, 2*(Summer), 255–267.

Some Caveats: Sabotage, Collusion, and Risk-Taking in Tournaments

21

In Chapter 20 we showed that tournament incentive schemes can be just as efficient as piece rates, and can even have additional benefits, such as insulating risk-averse workers from common productivity shocks. However, tournament-based pay can also create some new problems that do not arise when people are paid only on the basis of their own absolute performance. In Chapter 21, we study three such problems.

First, we'll see that introducing competition to the workplace can backfire by turning what was once a friendly, cooperative work environment into one where co-workers refuse to help each other, or worse—actively *sabotage* each other. Second, tournaments incentivize workers to *collude* against the employer by attempting to collectively reduce their effort levels. Finally, tournaments distort workers' incentives to take *risks*: workers who are lagging far behind in a competition have an incentive to take excessive risks in order to win, because they have nothing to lose. By the same token, workers who are ahead might take fewer risks than the employer would want them to, just to preserve their expected victory.

21.1 Helping and Sabotage in Tournaments

Imagine that you and a co-worker, Ted, operate the customer relations division of PropMan, a property management company in your city. Because local knowledge is important, the two of you serve different parts of the city: east and west. Your work is independent, but you and Ted both rely on the company's database software to look up and manage information on your properties, clients, and contractors (tradespeople who come in to fix problems in the properties). Every year, both you and Ted are evaluated for your customer satisfaction using assessment tools like the *Net Promoter Score* or *Key Performance Indicators* based on a sample of your customer interactions. If your customer satisfaction index exceeds a certain target, you will receive a $5,000 bonus at the end of the year. The same is true for Ted.

Now imagine that you have just discovered a great new way to use the company's database that helps you provide much better service to your customers. It's a simple, easy-to-communicate idea—once you see it, you get it. No one else in your office knows this yet. Ted has been having some trouble pulling up the information he needs quickly on the system and he comes by your desk asking for some advice.

Do you share your new discovery with Ted? In this situation, I'm guessing that you will. Doing so requires almost no effort on your part and might help Ted earn a $5,000 bonus at the end of the year. Assuming you win also, you might even celebrate your winnings together at year end. And who knows, maybe Ted will give you a useful suggestion in the future (he's well connected with local tradespeople, for example). He is a nice guy and it's both pleasant and useful to be on good terms with your office mates.

Finally, let's imagine that PropMan changes its pay policy. Inspired by the success of relative-pay schemes in other industries (like contract farming), the company switches to a tournament scheme. Instead of awarding each employee $5,000 if they reach their own goal, next year the worker with the best score gets a $10,000 annual bonus and the other gets no bonus. Will you share your useful new discovery with Ted now? My guess is that you won't. Although the idea is easy to communicate, giving Ted the information raises his chances of getting the bonus, thus potentially costing you $10,000. So you might not let on that you've found this great new trick. More subtly, because Ted understands your situation and may not want to put you into an awkward position, he might not even ask you for help. You won't ask him either. Indeed, the whole atmosphere of the workplace can change, and useful information that could raise both workers' performance won't be shared. And it's much less likely that you and Ted will be celebrating together at the end of the year.

The story of Ted and PropMan illustrates a key weakness of relative performance evaluation—it *penalizes* workers for helping each other. Because helping includes not just information sharing but training and active cooperation on tasks, we would expect all these activities to languish under relative reward schemes. By the same logic and even more perversely, relative reward schemes—by their very nature—create incentives for workers to take actions that reduce each other's performance, or at least to reduce the boss's *perception* of each other's performance: that is, to engage in *sabotage*. For example, if the stakes are very high and you are in close competition with Ted for the best score, you might be tempted to spread a negative rumor among Ted's customers, or even post a negative, anonymous review of Ted's performance on Yelp.

Although the Ted and PropMan story is plausible, it is fictitious. Is there any evidence that workers could be induced to engage in sabotage by relative performance incentives? A compelling study of student workers at a prestigious liberal arts college in the Northeastern United States shows that they can.

Donations from alumni and other supporters play a vital role in the finances of many U.S. liberal arts colleges. As one way of maintaining contact with these supporters, colleges sometimes send out personalized letters with handwritten addresses to signal that individual care was taken. In an article published in 2010, two professors at Middlebury College in picturesque rural Vermont paid 160 students to prepare letters of this kind for a period of 30 min. By randomly exposing the students to different pay schemes, Professors Carpenter and Matthews and their co-author John Schirm (2010) measured the effect of tournament-based pay on job performance, as well as on sabotage. In their context, sabotage took the form of negatively evaluating one's co-workers' performance in a way that reduced the co-workers' pay, a phenomenon the authors call "office politics."

DEFINITION 21.1 **Office politics** refers to the practice of trying to negatively influence your employer's perception of a co-worker's job performance for the purpose of improving your chances of success in a tournament or other relative reward scheme.

In Carpenter et al.'s (2010) experiment, there were eight student subjects per session. Each student had a computer, a work table, an "output box," access to a shared printer, and a list of names and addresses. The subjects were instructed to complete a form letter with names and addresses from a list, print the letter, stuff it into an envelope, *hand* address the envelope, and then add the envelope to the output box. After the end of the production period, all the participants examined each other's output boxes. They counted the number of completed envelopes and rated the quality of a randomly selected envelope on a scale from 0 to 1. Thus, if an envelope was rated as 0.7, it counted as 0.7 quality-adjusted envelopes, with a perfect envelope counting as 1 quality-adjusted envelope. In all the treatments, quality was also measured in two additional ways: first by the experimenters and second by a U.S. postal service letter carrier, who presumably has a high level of experience in gauging the quality of a sealed envelope.

In Carpenter et al.'s (2010) *baseline treatment,* 40 randomly selected workers received a simple piece rate. Pay was $1 for each quality-adjusted envelope produced, using the experimenter's assessment of quality. A second group of 40 students was exposed to the *tournament treatment.* Importantly, subjects in this treatment were entitled to the same piece rate payments that were used in the baseline treatment. The only difference was that *in addition*, the worker with the highest number of quality-adjusted envelopes in that worker's group of eight workers received a bonus of $25. Thus, incentives were stronger and more generous in the tournament treatment than the baseline treatment because the experimenters simply added a new bonus on top of the piece rate incentives already available.

The third treatment was called a *tournament with sabotage*; it was identical to the tournament treatment except for which measure of quality-adjusted output was used to calculate a student's pay. Now, each student's pay (and rank in the tournament) was based on the mean assessment of that student's work by seven co-workers plus the supervisor. Thus, subjects now had an opportunity to sabotage each other by misreporting the quality and quantity of envelopes produced by their co-workers. Finally, for completeness, the authors ran a treatment that allowed for sabotage when workers received the piece rate scheme that was used in the baseline treatment. Because workers had no incentives to sabotage each other here, they did not do so: The results were indistinguishable from the baseline treatment. Accordingly, Carpenter et al. (2010) just included these workers in the baseline group when reporting their results.

The results of Carpenter et al.'s (2010) experiment are displayed in Table 21.1. In discussing them, we'll first look at how the treatments affected workers' *evaluations* of each other's outputs, that is, the results of the peer review process in this workplace. We'll then turn to how the treatments affected the workers' actual, objective performance as measured by the postal worker. Finally, we'll ask how introducing the relative incentive plan affected the well-being of the employer and the workers in this experiment.

Treatment Effects on How Workers Rated Each Other's Work

Comparing Rows 2 and 3 of Table 21.1, we see first that under the baseline (piece rate) treatment, the student workers assessed each other's output *more generously* than the "objective" postal worker did (11.74 > 11.12). Under purely individual compensation, subjects have nothing to gain by underreporting (or denigrating) each other's output. Instead, it seems the students were being nice to each other: After all, it costs a worker nothing to exaggerate his colleague's performance but helps his colleague. In the basic tournament treatment [column (2)], however, workers were now less generous than an objective measure: 11.34 < 12.30. Although subjects still had nothing to gain financially from misreporting each other's output in this treatment, perhaps the competitive atmosphere of the tournament led them to rate their co-workers' performance more negatively.

Finally, in the *tournament with sabotage* treatment where peer evaluations did affect workers' chances of winning the bonus, subjects dramatically underestimated their co-workers' outputs. According to column (3) of Table 21.1, co-workers rated quality-adjusted output as 7.60, while the objective third party evaluated output to be 9.63. Perhaps surprisingly—especially

TABLE 21.1 THREE MEASURES OF OUTPUT IN CARPENTER, MATTHEWS, AND SCHIRM'S (2010) ENVELOPE-STUFFING EXPERIMENT, BY TREATMENT

	(1)	(2)	(3)
	Baseline Treatment (Piece Rate)	**Tournament** Treatment	**Tournament with Sabotage** Treatment
1. "Raw" output: Number of envelopes, as counted by postal worker	13.65	14.78	12.30
2. Total quality-adjusted output, as **assessed by postal worker**	11.12	12.30	9.63
3. Total quality-adjusted output, as **assessed by the subject's peers**	11.74	11.34	7.60

when we remind ourselves of the high admissions standards at many liberal arts colleges—sabotage by peers in this treatment was not restricted to "shading" one's essentially subjective estimate of an envelope's quality. Subjects also undercounted the number of envelopes in each other's output bins, thus misreporting a clearly objective measure of output. As a result of this "brazen" sabotage, only 50% of peers' raw envelope *counts* were correct in the tournament-with-sabotage treatment compared with 80% under straight piece rates.

In addition to being brazen, the sabotage observed in Carpenter et al.'s (2010) experiment with tournament-based pay had another key feature: It was **directed**. Importantly, subjects didn't underestimate all their peers' performance equally; instead, workers were much more likely to undercount a colleague's output *if that colleague produced more envelopes than they did*. This result greatly strengthens the argument that Carpenter et. al.'s subjects were rationally responding to the incentives inherent in tournament-based pay rather than perhaps reacting emotionally to the competitive tournament environment. When the prize only goes to the top performer in your work group, sabotage leads to financial gain only when it is directed at people who are likely to outperform you.

DEFINITION 21.2 **Directed sabotage** is taking an action that reduces the actual or perceived output of a colleague who is performing better than you to raise your own chances of winning a tournament prize.

RESULT 21.1

Introducing Prizes for Top-Performing Workers Can Lead to Directed Sabotage by Workers

In Carpenter et al.'s (2010) experiment, sabotage took the form of negative peer evaluations: Workers understated both the quality and quantity of their peers' work. Consistent with rational responses by workers to tournament incentives, workers directed their sabotage only at co-workers with higher performance levels.

Treatment Effects on Objectively Measured Output

How did different incentive schemes affect workers' *actual* performance, as measured by an objective third party (the postal worker)? As expected, simply strengthening incentives by adding a prize (without introducing peer evaluations) raises both the quality and quantity of output as assessed by an objective observer. This can be seen by comparing the "piece-rate" and "tournament" payment schemes in row 2 of Table 21.1: Objective output rose from 11.12 to 12.30. The opposite is true, however, when workers had the option of sabotaging each other using the peer review process. Adding a prize in this environment dramatically reduced not only *measured* output, but actual, objective output as well. Objective output now falls to 9.63, which is well below piece rate output even though the firm is offering stronger incentives than in the straight piece rate treatment. The most likely explanation is that workers (rationally) anticipate that their competitors will "undervalue" their work when pay depends on relative performance. This reduces every worker's marginal returns to effort.

RESULT 21.2

Introducing Prizes for Top-Performing Workers Can Also Reduce Objectively Measured Employee Performance

In Carpenter et al.'s (2010) experiment, it appears that the expectation that their work would be sabotaged reduced workers' effort levels and thereby their actual job performance.

Treatment Effects on Worker and Employer Well-Being

What is the effect of introducing a bonus for top performers into a workplace where sabotage is possible (i.e., of moving from the baseline treatment to the tournament-with-sabotage treatment) on the employer's well-being? Even though the employer in Carpenter et al.'s (2010) experiment is not a for-profit enterprise, it is not too hard to work this out. To see how, imagine that the expected value to the college (in terms of donor relations and future gifts) of one quality-adjusted envelope is r dollars. Because in all the treatments, the college has chosen to pay students at least \$1 per quality-adjusted envelope, it seems reasonable to assume that $r > 1$. Importantly, when $r > 1$, the principal always prefers more output to less, which seems highly reasonable.

We can now compute the principal's *per-worker* "profits" under the piece rate and tournament-with-sabotage schemes as follows:

$$\text{Profits under piece rates} = r(E^P) - 1(E^P) = (r-1)E^P. \qquad \textbf{(21.1)}$$

$$\begin{aligned}\text{Profits under tournaments with sabotage} &= r(E^T) - 1(E^T) - \$3.12 \\ &= (r-1)E^T - \$3.12, \qquad \textbf{(21.2)}\end{aligned}$$

where E^P and E^T are the number of envelopes produced per worker under the piece rate and tournament-with-sabotage treatments. In Equation 21.1, profits under piece rates are calculated as the value of output minus the value of piece rate payments to workers. In Equation 21.2, profits under tournaments with sabotage equal the value of output, minus piece rate payments, minus \$3.12 = \$25/8 which is the per-worker cost of the \$25 prize. Subtracting Equation 21.1 from 21.2 gives the effect of introducing the tournament on profits:

$$\text{Effect of tournament on profits} = (r-1)\,(E^T - E^P) - \$3.12 < 0. \qquad \textbf{(21.3)}$$

Profits fall when the tournament was introduced because output falls ($E^T - E^P < 0$), while the employer has to subtract the additional cost of paying the tournament prize.

Sabotage at Harvard Law

When I was an economics PhD student in the Harvard economics department, I had to visit the Harvard Law School library (which was just next door to the economics department) to look up some data on tax rates. Because the book I needed was not in the stacks where it should have been, I asked a librarian if it might be checked out, on reserve, or unavailable for some other reason. Her response was both immediate and astonishing: "Oh, a student must have hidden it in the stacks somewhere." When I asked her to explain what she meant, I got an unexpected lesson in the capacity for competitive reward schemes to lead to sabotage.

Harvard Law is a fiercely competitive environment. Among the most coveted prizes for these elite students are a small number of internships with judges in the U.S. Supreme Court and Court of Appeals. Because these (and some other highly sought-after positions) are fixed in number, Harvard Law students are engaged in a tournament with each other: If others do worse on their course assignments, I will have a better chance of getting a prize. According to my librarian, hiding useful books from each other (by deliberately mis-shelving them in the library) was a common form of sabotage.

But was this form of sabotage destructive? If it was, why would such a prestigious institution allow it to continue to the point where it was well known? I can only speculate, but one might argue that—in contrast to many workplaces where collaboration is essential—Harvard Law students were being trained to work in a highly adversarial profession. Perhaps knowing how and when to undermine your opponents is a desirable trait in certain environments!

Next, let's turn to the workers' utility. Per-worker utility under the piece rate and tournament-with-sabotage schemes can be written

$$\text{Utility under piece rates} = 1(E^P) - vE^P = (1 - v)E^P. \tag{21.4}$$

$$\begin{aligned}\text{Expected utility under tournaments with sabotage} &= 1(E^T) + \$3.12 - vE^T \\ &= (1 - v)E^T + \$3.12.\end{aligned} \tag{21.5}$$

In Equation 21.4, utility under piece rates is calculated as the piece rate payments received minus the worker's cost of effort. Equation 21.5 calculates utility under tournaments with sabotage as piece rate payments received, plus the expected value of the prize, minus the cost of effort. Analogous to r (the value of a unit of output to the employer), v is the (cash equivalent) effort cost to the worker of producing a quality-adjusted envelope. Because the workers in our experiment supply positive levels of effort in the baseline treatment (where the piece rate equals \$1), it makes sense that v must be *less* than 1 for workers.[1]

---

[1] In our notation v is the average effort cost per envelope the worker chooses to supply. If v were greater than 1, workers would be better off not supplying any envelopes, because they are only paid one dollar per envelope.

Subtracting Equation 21.4 from 21.5 gives the effect of introducing the tournament on workers' expected utility:

$$\text{Effect of tournament on expected utility} = (1 - v)(E^T - E^P) + \$3.12 > 0. \quad \textbf{(21.6)}$$

Despite the presence of sabotage, expected utility *rises* when the tournament is introduced because the worker now works less hard ($E^T - E^P < 0$) and now has a chance of winning a prize worth \$3.12 in expectation.

☑ RESULT 21.3

Effects of a Tournament on Profits and Utility When Sabotage Is Possible

In Carpenter et al.'s (2010) envelope-stuffing experiment, introducing a cash prize for top-performing workers made the employer worse off but made workers better off. Profits fell because output fell and because the prize cost money. Utility rose because of the newly available prize money and a lower level of worker effort.

Treatment Effects on Social Welfare (Profits Plus Utility)

So far we have shown that introducing a prize for the top performer into a workplace where sabotage is possible reduced profits but raised workers' expected utility. But how do these gains in workers' utility compare to the firm's losses? Put another way, did introducing the bonus raise social welfare, defined as the sum of profits plus utility? To work this out, we add up Equations 21.3 and 21.6 to get

$$\text{Effect of tournament on profits + utility} = (r - v)\,(E^T - E^P) < 0. \quad \textbf{(21.7)}$$

Notice that when we add the equations, the changes in payments to workers (both the piece rates and the prizes) subtract out: These are just cash transfers between firms and workers, and their size does not affect the sum of profits plus utility. The only terms left are the employer's valuation of the change in output, $r(E^T - E^P)$, which is negative because employers prefer more envelopes to less, and the worker's valuation of the change in output, $v(E^T - E^P)$, which is positive

☑ RESULT 21.4

Effect of a Tournament on Economic Efficiency When Sabotage Is Possible

In Carpenter et al.'s (2010) envelope-stuffing experiment, introducing a cash prize for top-performing workers into a work environment where sabotage is possible reduced social welfare, defined as the sum of profits plus utility. Social welfare fell because the increase in worker utility was smaller than the drop in the employer's profits. Essentially, the expectation of sabotage reduced workers' incentives to supply effort to a socially suboptimal level.

because she prefers less effort to more. However, because completed envelopes are worth more to the employer than they cost workers to produce ($r > 1 > v$: otherwise it wouldn't make sense for the employer to hire these workers in the first place), the fall in profits outweighs the increase in utility. Thus, social welfare falls.

Carpenter et al.'s (2010) experiment raises some important cautions regarding the use of tournament-based incentive schemes in the workplace. Among the most important is the simple but powerful idea that tournaments reduce workers' incentives to cooperate with each other. Thus, employers should think very

Other Responses to Competition in the Workplace: Quits and Specialization

Bo Cowgill (2015) studies the effects of competition for promotions at large white-collar technology and services company. Employees at the firm are mostly software engineers, product managers, sales, marketing, and support staff. Promotions permanently raise a worker's base salary by 20%, but company policy dictates that no more than 10% of employees in a unit can be promoted in competitions that occur twice per year. Because workers are evaluated every quarter, Cowgill can create an index of how close the promotion race is for every employee in the company: If all the workers in your unit had very similar scores in the last quarter, the race is close. If the scores are very different, then the likely winners of the promotion won't depend so much on how hard people work in the current quarter. Cowgill has access to a wide array of performance and activity measures because the company's highly computerized environment logs workers' activities in considerable detail.

In line with our theoretical expectations, Cowgill (2015) finds that workers in highly competitive (closely matched) promotion contests work longer and harder, without any decline in quality of output produced. At the same time, those workers were less helpful to their colleagues: Fewer workers were nominated by their colleagues for "peer cooperation" bonuses, and workers were less meticulous in documenting their work. (Written documentation, such as "commenting" your computer code, makes life much easier for your colleagues.) Employees in highly competitive contests were also more likely to quit the company, presumably because outside options were more attractive relative to a situation where especially hard work was required to advance.

The most interesting and unexpected effects of a competitive workplace, however, were increased specialization of the employees' activities. Because the jobs at the company were multidimensional, workers faced with intense competition were able to specialize much more in a smaller set of tasks that were different from their co-workers'. Why did they do this? One possible interpretation is that, by making themselves harder to compare to their peers (because they are now doing different things), workers were engaging in the sorts of noise-enhancing obfuscation discussed in Section 21.3. A more charitable interpretation is that the increased competition encouraged workers to specialize in the activities they were best at, that is, in their comparative advantage. In this interpretation, stiffer workplace competition had an unexpected benefit that has not been documented before.

carefully about using tournaments in any workplace where worker cooperation and information sharing is an important aspect to production. If a tournament is absolutely necessary, options that could limit sabotage include reducing the prize spread. Another is to include measures of worker cooperation in job performance criteria. This can be difficult (and almost paradoxical) to implement—workers will be competing to be more helpful to their peers than their peers are to them!—but might create *some* incentives for workers to cooperate.

A final and more direct takeaway from Carpenter et al.'s (2010) experiment is that tournaments and peer performance evaluation should probably never be used together. Having workers grade each other in a tournament practically begs workers to undervalue each other's performance.

21.2 Collusion in Tournaments

In the last section, we argued that relative pay schemes can lead workers to cooperate too little with each other. In this section, we'll show that the opposite is also possible: Relative pay schemes can lead to *too much* cooperation between workers—at least too much cooperation of the "wrong" kind from the employer's point of view!

A Fictitious Example: Jim and Jamal

To see this, let's consider an example of Jim and Jamal: two salespeople at an auto dealership. Aside from a fixed payment that does not depend on the number of cars they sell, the only incentive pay Jim and Jamal can receive is a $1,000 prize that goes to the worker with the highest sales each month. The dealership hopes that this will encourage both Jim and Jamal to work hard, but the workers—who happen to be friends—might react differently. The friends, who are equally able, realize that if they both work their very hardest, each will receive their base pay and have a 50/50 chance of winning the prize each month. If they both work a more moderate amount, going home at 5 p.m. every day and spending more time with their kids and family, they will still receive their base pay, and each will *still* have a 50/50 chance of winning the prize. So, why shouldn't they take it easier?

In the preceding story, the two workers are **colluding** against their employer by agreeing to a coordinated reduction in effort. Collusion, of course, happens in other contexts as well, such as the members of the once-powerful OPEC cartel (the Organization of Petroleum-Exporting Countries) conspiring to keep oil production low; employers in Silicon Valley conspiring to keep salaries low (see the box, "Are Competitive Labor Markets Good or Bad for Workers" in Section 17.1); and bid-rigging in auctions for items like oil, radio spectrum, airport landing rights, and government contracts, where buyers have an incentive to collude to keep bids low, and sellers to keep bids high. As in all these cases, collusion leads to gains for the colluding parties (Jim and Jamal) while hurting others (the auto dealership in our example). Collusive agreements, however, are vulnerable because they create incentives for the colluding parties to cheat on each other.

For example, knowing that Jamal has agreed to take it easy, Jim may be tempted to put in just a little more effort, especially if that would have a big impact on his chances of winning the prize. By the same logic, members of the OPEC cartel have the incentive to surreptitiously exceed their production quotas; indeed, these incentives to cheat have contributed to the organization's eventual decline into irrelevance today.

Collusion in the Field: Evidence from Fruit Pickers

Is there any evidence that relative pay schemes can backfire by encouraging output-reducing collusive arrangements between workers? A 2005 study of farm-workers by Oriana Bandiera, Iwan Barankay, and Imran Rasul shows that they can. Bandiera et al. studied an English berry farm that hires temporary workers every summer to pick fruit. Most of the workers come from Eastern European countries, live in housing provided by the farm, and many of them establish close friendships over the course of a season. As part of their study, Bandiera et al. collected data on these friendship networks, which play an important role in the study. Like the Safelite auto glass repairers we studied in Chapter 8, the berry pickers on Bandiera et al.'s farm work independently: A worker's ability to do the job does not depend in any important way on whether others are doing theirs. Output was measured in kilograms of fruit picked (with some adjustment for quality).

As we discussed in Section 5.2, a common problem with piece rate incentive schemes is that they can expose workers to a high level of compensation risk when production is uncertain. This was also an issue on Bandiera et al.'s (2005) berry farm. Because field conditions and the amount of fruit available to pick varied substantially from day to day (and field to field), paying workers a straight piece rate per kilogram of fruit produced would expose these low-income workers to large day-to-day fluctuations in pay due to no fault of their own. In the years before Bandiera et al.'s study year (2002), however, the farm had developed an informal way to handle this problem. Every morning, the farm manager surveyed the fields to be picked that day, and assigned a piece rate for each field based on the manager's best estimate of field conditions. The rate per kilo was low if fruit was plentiful and easy to pick and high under more challenging conditions.[2] This way, if a worker put in an honest day's work each day, the take-home pay wouldn't vary too much from day to day. In sum, before the 2002 season, a worker's total pay for a day was given by bK_i, where K_i is the kilograms the individual i picked, and b is that day's piece rate (in £), which was set before the start of each day by the field manager.

In the first half of the 2002 season, the farm tried to formalize this system of adjusting piece rates (making them more generous on difficult days) by using the average output of all the workers on the field at the end of the day as an "objective" measure of field conditions. In addition to formalizing the guesswork involved in picking a piece rate at the beginning of the day, the farm's motivation

[2] Notice that this arrangement is effectively a *state-contingent contract*, like the ones we studied as a possible contracting option when workers were risk averse in Section 5.2. It differs from the optimal contracts described there because the piece rate (b) is state contingent, not the level of base pay (a).

for the new system was the same as the one behind the successful use of relative incentives in U.S. contract farming we studied in Section 20.9: "It allowed them to difference out common productivity shocks, such as those derived from weather and field conditions" (Bandiera et al., 2002, p. 927), thus reducing the day-to-day random variation in workers' earnings.

In this new scheme, the field manager announced an *expected* b at the start of the workday to give workers some guidance, but the actual b was determined at the end of the day according to the following formula:

$$b = \overline{w} / \overline{K}, \tag{21.8}$$

where $\overline{w}$ is the target level of daily earnings the company wanted an *average* worker to earn (this did not change from day to day). $\overline{K}$ was the average kilos picked by all the workers that day. Thus, if the firm's target level of earnings for an average worker was £50 per day, and average output on the field *today* was 40 kg, the piece rate paid to *all* workers today would be £50/40 kg = £1.25 per kg picked. With this piece rate, a worker who picked the average amount for that day ($K_i = \overline{K}$) earned $\overline{w}$, or £50. Above-average workers earned more than £50 and below-average workers less.

Because workers were now evaluated and paid relative to the average performance of their entire work group, this new arrangement was a *continuous relative reward system* (see Definition 20.7). And as in all relative reward systems, one worker's choice to work hard hurts his co-workers. In the current context, this is because worker i's working hard raises not only i's own output K_i, but $\overline{K}$ as well. Via Equation 21.8, this reduces the piece rate paid to *all* the other workers on the same field that day.

Halfway through the 2002 season, the farm in Bandiera et al.'s (2005) study abruptly abandoned this new, relative incentive scheme and went back to the old, "guesswork" system where the field manager set the day's piece rate in advance based on her best guess of field conditions. To see why, consider the statistics in Table 21.2. First and most importantly, hourly productivity rose dramatically, from 5.01 to 7.98 (an increase of 59%) when the farm *abandoned* the relative pay scheme. Total kilos picked per day also increased substantially. All this occurred in the absence of significant changes in inputs: neither average hours worked per day nor the average number of workers in the field on a given day changed significantly. Finally, costs didn't rise: Workers' average daily pay levels didn't change significantly either. In sum, at least based on aggregate statistics before and after relative incentives were abandoned, the farm was better off (with more fruit to sell) and workers were worse off, receiving the same pay as before for more work.

Before jumping to conclusions about the effects of relative pay, however, it is important to rule out other possible causes of this change in output in the middle of the 2002 season. The authors were very aware of this, and so they controlled for a number of potential alternative explanations. First, the authors are able to rule out differences in the quality of the fields that were picked in the two halves of the season. This was achieved by using field fixed effects (an econometric tool introduced in Section 7.2). Second, the firm may have used

TABLE 21.2 MEASURES OF OUTPUT AND INPUTS IN BANDIERA ET AL.'S (2005) FRUIT-PICKING STUDY

	(1) RELATIVE INCENTIVE SCHEME (FIRST HALF OF 2002 SEASON)	(2) TRADITIONAL PIECE RATE SCHEME (SECOND HALF OF 2002 SEASON)	(3) DIFFERENCE
Productivity measures:			
Kilograms picked per hour	5.01	7.98	2.97*
Kilograms picked per day	Confidential	Confidential	23.2*
Input measures:			
Total hours worked per day	Confidential	Confidential	−4.75
Workers per field	41.1	38.1	−3.11
Cost measures:			
Daily pay	Confidential	Confidential	1.80

Note: * = statistically different from zero at the at the 1% level.

better workers later in the season: this was addressed using worker fixed effects and by adding a control for worker experience. Third, the authors addressed the important issue of seasonality. Because the pay policy was changed mid-season, it is possible that simple seasonality accounts for higher output levels later in the season. To control for this, the authors collected data from a different season (2004), during which the farm's pay policy was unchanged. This allows for a particular day and month to be compared against itself in a different year, when a different payment method was used. Finally, it should be noted that throughout the study, the focus was on the quantity of fruit picked; but quality may be changing as well. However, there was no rise in misclassification of fruit after piece rates were introduced.

Why Was Productivity Lower with Relative Incentives?

The farm's brief experiment with the relative pay scheme reduced productivity: Why did this happen? Bandiera et al. (2005) dug into the data to find out *under what circumstances* the output gap between the pay regimes was the biggest. This yielded an important clue: Under relative incentives (but not under piece rates), a worker's output was 21% lower when working on a field with five or more of the worker's friends than when working only with strangers. This suggests one of two causes: either altruism or collusion.

Altruism is a possible explanation because working hard under a competitive pay scheme directly hurts one's co-workers. Perhaps workers voluntarily "held back" when working under a competitive pay scheme with their friends to avoid reducing their friends' piece rates via Equation 21.8 (by raising $\overline{K}$).[3] Alternatively, perhaps the friends were simply colluding to keep output low and the piece rate high for their mutual benefit. This also makes sense, especially if it is easier for friends than strangers to maintain collusive arrangements. But which one is it? Is there any way to distinguish between altruism and collusion?

To answer this question, the authors turned to a well known theoretical result that applies to collusion in any context: Collusive agreements are much easier to enforce if the colluders can accurately observe each other's behavior. For example, if it was easy for all countries to see how much oil each one was selling (i.e., if there was no secret black market for oil), OPEC would probably be much stronger than it is today because the members could easily punish quota violators. The same principle applies in the berry field: If I can see how often you are filling your basket, I can easily tell whether you are sticking to our deal to both "take it easy."

As it turns out, since most of the berries picked on Bandiera et al.'s (2005) farm grew low to the ground, most of the time it was easy for workers on the same field to keep track of each other's output. That was not the case, however, when the workers were picking "Type 2" berries, which grow on tall bushes. And as it turns out, when friends worked together picking Type 2 berries, they did not restrict their output under the relative incentives scheme. Thus, Bandiera et al. conclude that collusion and not altruism is the most likely explanation for the fact that relative incentives reduced output on their berry farm.

RESULT 21.5

Collusion in Tournaments

Bandiera et al.'s (2005) fruit farm study shows that collusion can occur when workers compete in tournaments. The authors also show that collusion is more common when workers *know each other*, and that collusion is possible only when workers can *observe each other's output*.

Collusion to restrict output makes workers better off at the employers' expense and can make tournaments or other relative pay schemes less effective than individual incentives.

Result 21.5 has a number of implications for HRM that apply to any workplace, not just fruit farms. First, it's probably a bad idea to use relative performance pay when collusion is easy for workers to enforce (e.g., in small work groups where workers know each other well, where they can observe each other's efforts, and where they expect to stay together a long time). If a tournament is unavoidable, employers can limit collusion by using larger work groups, by keeping worker performance information confidential, and by periodically reshuffling work groups. Interestingly, this is exactly what is done by the principals (integrators) in Section 20.9's contract farming example! Farmers (agents) are not told who

[3] Of course, workers also have a purely selfish reason for holding back effort under the farm's relative incentive scheme: They would also undercut their *own* piece rate by working hard. But this effect is very small in magnitude in a typical work group of 40 workers. Also, it is present whether or not one's friends are on the field.

Ratchet Effects: Another Cause of Output Restriction

A common problem faced by employers is the question of *job design;* just how many duties could be assigned to a particular position before it becomes impossible for the worker to perform the job well? In many cases, employers don't have a good idea of how hard various duties really are, so they might be tempted to experiment with different job requirements to see how a given worker or group of workers performs. If they do a good job, the job is clearly easy to do, so the firm can assign a larger set of duties.

The problems with this should be readily apparent: If the extra duties aren't combined with some reward, such as a pay increase or a higher promotion chance, workers who do a good job will be rewarded with a more onerous set of duties and nothing else. This creates an incentive for workers to restrict output, thereby concealing from firms the true difficulty of their jobs. This well-known phenomenon is called the *ratchet effect* and has been studied in a wide variety of contexts, including workplaces. See this chapter's suggestions for further reading if you'd like to learn more.

The ratchet effect can give rise to output restrictions even in contexts where workers are not paid according to their relative performance. Some of the most vividly documented examples are still those documented by industrial sociologist Stanley Mathewson (1931) in the 1930s in his many interviews of non-unionized manufacturing workers.

they are competing with, and groups are reshuffled periodically. A final option, in the context of promotions as tournament prizes, is for firms to reserve the right to award the "promotion" to an outsider. This way, if the insiders collude too much, none will be promoted, and the outsider will get the desirable high-level job.

21.3 Tournaments and Risk-Taking

Suppose that you and I are competing for a promotion, and I have already picked my effort level. Specifically, you know that I will be putting in 10 units of effort in the competition. Because you and I are equally able and the contest is fair, you know that by putting in 10 units of effort yourself, you could guarantee yourself a 50/50 chance of winning the promotion. Alternatively, suppose that by expending just one unit of effort you could increase the role of luck (ε) in the tournament so much that the winner is determined purely by luck—effort no longer has anything to do with it.[4] If you could do this without being detected, and if you are a neoclassical economic agent who does not experience guilt, you might consider this a very attractive option: By spending one unit of effort to muddy the waters,

[4] In the model of Section 20.2, this would mean taking an action that raises the range, R, of the relative luck distribution to a very high level. For a formal model of risk-taking in tournaments, see Hvide (2002).

you achieve the same result (a 50/50 chance of winning) as by spending 10 units of effort to produce output.

The preceding example illustrates another potential pitfall of tournaments: If agents can take actions that increase the role of luck in the production (or evaluation) process, they will be tempted to take those actions in lieu of exerting productive work effort. For example, a manager might decide to invest in a high-risk project or hiring an excessively risky worker. In the world of sports, risk-increasing actions include pulling the goalie in ice hockey and throwing a "Hail Mary" pass in American football. Actions that raise the role of luck also include obfuscation, that is, making it hard for the principal to tell who is doing a better job by hiding or destroying information.

Whereas incentives to "win by luck" instead of by effort exist in all tournaments, including symmetric ones, they are especially strong in uneven situations where one agent who (perhaps due to low ability or simply because of being behind in a competition) has only a small chance of "winning by effort." In those cases, why wouldn't the agent throw a "Hail Mary" pass in the off chance of winning? By the same logic, agents who are far enough ahead in a competition can have the opposite incentive: they may be motivated to take actions that reduce or eliminate the role of luck to preserve their lead, such as not passing the ball, not taking shots, and generally just "running down the clock."[5]

RESULT 21.6

Risk-Taking in Tournaments

If agents can take low-cost actions that increase the role of luck in tournaments, they will be tempted to take such actions to increase the chances of winning the prize "by luck" rather than by exerting productive effort.

Incentives to take such risk-enhancing actions are especially attractive to agents who are less able or who are behind in a sequential contest. Agents who are ahead, on the other hand, may even have an incentive to take risk-reducing actions, such as "running down the clock" in the least risky way possible.

Although the previous examples are commonplace in the world of sports, is there any evidence from the business world that tournament-based pay can induce agents, especially those who are behind in a competition, to undertake risky actions that are not in the principal's interests? Brown, Harlow, and Starks's study of mutual fund managers, published in the *Journal of Finance* in 1996, provides exactly that.

Mutual fund managers invest pools of savings that have been entrusted to their care by investors. With the amounts that have been invested, the managers choose stocks, bonds, and other assets to achieve goals specific to their fund class—such as growth, income, or preservation of principal. In most cases, a fund manager's pay for a given calendar year is a simple percentage of the total

[5] There is in fact good evidence of this in business as well: In another study of contract farming for broilers, Knoeber and Thurman (1994) show that the higher ability farmers choose less risky strategies.

assets he or she manages. Despite this simple piece rate formula, however, managers' pay has a tournament component, and this component was especially important during the 1976–1991 period studied by Brown et al. (1996).

The tournament element is a consequence of how funds are rated (by rating agencies like *Morningstar* and others) and of how investors tend to move their money between funds. Essentially, all the funds' investment performances are ranked, with each fund compared to others in its asset class, and these rankings were published in a highly visible format in major newspapers at the end of each calendar year. In response to these rankings, investors tended to move large amounts of money out of low-ranked funds and into higher-ranks ones. Top-ranked funds often received large inflows of cash, which raised their managers' pay substantially.

Given this environment, Brown et al. (1996) put themselves into the mindset of a manager whose fund was lagging behind median performance in the asset class in the latter half of the year. Because such a manager had little chance of becoming the top manager for the year by investing wisely, he or she might be tempted to try to "win by luck" instead, that is, to choose high-risk investments that might just pay off big. If it didn't pay off, relatively little was lost because the rewards going to lower performing managers weren't all that different from each other.[6] Even though such actions might not be in the interests of investors—who are promised a certain level of risk when buying a particular type of fund—Brown et al. found that indeed, managers who were behind at mid-year increased the riskiness of their portfolios. Interestingly, these effects were largest for managers of smaller, newer funds with a less established track record. As we might expect, established managers with a solid reputation did not fear losing investors because of one bad year. But the "new kids on the block" took risky actions to try to salvage a bad year.

☑ **RESULT 21.7**

Risky Choices by Mutual Fund Managers

In their study of mutual fund managers—who could expect a large increase in pay from being the top-ranked fund in their class at year end—Brown, Harlow, and Starks (1996) found that fund managers who were behind at mid-year increased the riskiness of their portfolios for the remainder of the year. They did this not just passively (by holding on to losing stocks), but actively, by selling safe assets and buying riskier ones.

The largest increases in portfolio risk were found among young, inexperienced managers without an established record who had the most to lose from a year of subpar performance.

A final interesting feature of Brown et al.'s (1996) results is the methods managers used to raise riskiness of their portfolios. Because the riskiness of a

[6] There is actually a second reason—besides tournaments—why low-performing mutual fund managers had an incentive to take more risks later in the year. Most managers were guaranteed a certain minimum salary for the year, regardless of how poorly their portfolio performed. Thus, many low-performing managers literally had nothing to lose by taking greater risks near the end of the year.

stock rises with its ratio of debt to equity, stocks that decline in value automatically become riskier simply because the denominator of this expression falls. Thus, a low-performing manager could raise the riskiness of a portfolio just by passively hanging on to losing stocks. As it turns out, however, Brown et al. were able to show that managers did more than this. Specifically, by simulating how an unmanaged portfolio would perform, the authors were able

The Thrill of the Chase: Intrinsic Rewards from Winning

In the models of tournaments we have studied so far, the only reason agents exert effort is because the winner receives a financial reward. But what if people are willing to exert effort purely for the joy of winning? After all, many people work hard to win games and contests of all sorts that have no financial rewards. Many of us even seem to derive pleasure from beating a computer that isn't even playing its best!

Evidence that people (and other animals) will work hard purely for the joy of winning includes Coffey and Maloney's (2010) analysis of data from horse and dog (greyhound) racing. In accordance with standard tournament theory, Coffey and Maloney found that (controlling for track condition, weather, the average ability of the contestants, and other possible confounding factors) horses ran faster when the prize money was higher. They also ran faster in the "stretch"—the straight section at the end when horses were close together when entering the stretch. Dogs, however, did not respond to the amount of prize money (they had no way of knowing that and didn't have a jockey!); but, like the horses, the dog also ran faster in the stretch when the race was close. Thus, it appears that dogs, like humans, might be willing to work hard just for the pure joy of winning a competition!

One way to study intrinsic rewards from competition on human workers' effort is to give workers information about their relative performance that was not previously available. When Blanes i Vidal and Nossol (2011) did this in a German wholesale/retail company, they found that productivity in filling orders increased by about 6%. In a 3-year randomized trial with full-time furniture salespeople, however, Barankay (2012) found that removing the information about performance ranks increased sales performance by 11%. He argued that the rank information discouraged low-ranking workers and led them to direct their efforts to other aspects of their jobs. Finally, Charness, Masclet, and Villeval (2014) found that informing laboratory subjects about their relative performance raised not only their effort levels but also raised the amount by which they sabotaged their co-workers and artificially inflated their own performance scores.

Altogether, the evidence on whether (and when) humans' pure taste for winning (or for attaining a higher, publicly announced rank, i.e., status) can raise effort levels in the workplace remains mixed. This is an important question, however. For example, if it were true that simply telling workers their performance ranked raised all workers' effort levels, this would constitute a "free" way for employers to get extra effort from their workforce (subject only to the proviso that people still want to work at the company). That said, many very successful employers deliberately abstain from giving workers their relative performance information for "morale"-related reasons (which could include concerns about workers' helping behavior and sabotage activities). Additional research on the intrinsic rewards to competition would seem to be warranted.

to show that low-performing managers were making active decisions to raise the riskiness of their portfolios by selling safe stocks and buying riskier ones. Thus, it appears their actions were conscious decisions, not just a result of laziness or neglect.

The implications of Brown et al.'s (1996) study for personnel policy are relatively straightforward: Companies should be aware that tournament-based pay schemes incentivize workers—especially low-performing ones—to take actions that increase the riskiness of the production process, or that obfuscate performance measures: that is, that make it harder for the principal to rank workers' performance. Thus employers might wish to avoid tournament-based pay in situations where actions like this are possible. If tournaments are unavoidable, firms should consider limiting the agent's discretion over risk or penalizing a high level of variance in the agent's performance.

Chapter Summary

- ☐ Sabotage can occur and cooperation between workers may be reduced when workers compete in tournaments. These effects can be large enough to make tournaments a less effective incentive scheme than piece rates.
- ☐ Relative reward schemes also create incentives for collusion among workers to keep output and effort low. Collusion is easier to maintain when workers know each other well and can monitor each other's job performance.
- ☐ When workers can take actions that increase the random noise with which output is produced or measured, tournaments can create incentives to take such actions, to "win by luck" instead of "winning by effort." Such risk-increasing strategies are most attractive to workers who would otherwise have little chance of winning the tournament, such as low-ability workers or workers who are behind in a multiperiod competition.

Discussion Questions

1. In some environments, it is hard to measure workers' performance on anything other than a relative scale. For example, common and unmeasurable factors may be so important that it's really hard to know what constitutes a good level of performance: All we can really know is how workers performed relative to each other. Or, a new technology has just been invented, and no one really knows how effective it can be when used correctly and carefully. Given that a principal in this situation has no choice but to measure performance on a relative scale, what problems would you advise her to look out for?
2. What actions might the principal in the preceding example take to avoid or mitigate each one of the aforementioned problems?

3. You are in a small upper-division class with only 10 total students, and you are all quite friendly with each other. The professor tells the class that the upcoming final exam next week will be graded purely on a curve, such that grades will be assigned based on how far above or below the class average each student scores. One of your classmates suggests that you should all agree to spend the weekend relaxing instead of studying. Does this collusion have a good chance of working? How would things change if the class had 50 students instead? What if studying required publicly checking into the library in a way that all your classmates could see?

Suggestions for Further Reading

In an additional analysis of contract farming, Knoeber and Thurman (1994) show that less-able broiler producers adopt riskier strategies. Hvide and Kristiansen's (2003) theoretical study of hiring competitions shows that incentives to win by obfuscation and other noise-enhancing activities exist in this context as well. According to the authors, incentives to obfuscate can be reduced by having fewer contestants and by restricting contestant quality via minimum (or maximum) qualifications for entry.

Carmichael and MacLeod (2000); Charness, Kuhn, and Villeval (2011); and Gibbons (1987) all study ratchet effects; and Mathewson (1931) illustrates them with vivid interview examples from a manufacturing plant. Chapter 3 is especially relevant.

For a theoretical analysis of how intrinsic rewards from winning and other emotional reactions by workers might affect the optimal design of tournaments, see Grund and Sliwka (2005), and Kräkel (2008).

References

Bandiera, O., Barankay, I., & Rasul, I. (2005). Social preferences and the response to incentives: Evidence from personnel data. *Quarterly Journal of Economics, 120,* 917–962.

Barankay, I. (2012). *Rank incentives: Evidence from a randomized workplace experiment.* Unpublished manuscript, Management Department, The Wharton School of Business, University of Pennsylvania, Philadelphia, PA.

Blanes i Vidal, J., & Nossol, M. (2011). Tournaments without prizes: Evidence from personnel records. *Management Science, 57,* 1721–1736.

Brown, K. C., Harlow, W. V., & Starks, L. T. (1996). Of tournaments and temptations: An analysis of managerial incentives in the mutual fund industry. *Journal of Finance, 51*(1), 85–110.

Carpenter, J., Matthews, P. H., & Schirm, J. (2010). Tournaments and office politics: Evidence from a real effort experiment. *American Economic Review, 100,* 504–517.

Carmichael, L., & MacLeod, W. B. (2000). Worker cooperation and the ratchet effect. *Journal of Labor Economics, 18,* 1–19.

Charness, G., Kuhn, P., & Villeval, M-C. (2011). Competition and the ratchet effect. *Journal of Labor Economics, 29,* 513–547.

Charness, G., Masclet, D., & Villeval, M. C. (2013). The dark side of competition for status. *Management Science, 60*(1), 38–55.

Coffey, B. & Maloney, M. T. (2010). The Thrill of Victory: Measuring the Incentive to Win. *Journal of Labor Economics, 28*(1), 87–112.

Cowgill, B. (2015). *Competition and Productivity in Employee Promotion Contests.* Unpublished manuscript, Columbia Business School, Columbia University, New York, NY.

Gibbons, R. (1987). Piece rate incentive schemes. *Journal of Labor Economics, 5,* 413–429.

Grund, C., & Sliwka, D. (2005). Envy and compassion in tournaments. *Journal of Economics and Management Strategy, 14*(1), 187–207.

Hvide, H. K. (2002). Tournament rewards and risk taking. *Journal of Labor Economics, 20,* 877–898.

Hvide, H. K., & Kristiansen, E. G. (2003). Risk taking in selection contests. *Games and Economic Behavior, 42,* 172–179.

Knoeber, C. R., & Thurman, W. N. (1994). Testing the theory of tournaments: An empirical analysis of broiler production. *Journal of Labor Economics, 12*(2), 155–179.

Kräkel, M. (2008). Emotions in tournaments. *Journal of Economic Behavior and Organization, 67,* 204–214.

Mathewson, S. (1931). *Restriction of output among unorganized workers.* New York: Viking Press.

22 Unfair and Uneven Tournaments

So far in this part, we've focused on tournaments that are both **fair—**in the sense that contestants who *perform* equally well (produce the same amount of output, Q) have an equal chance of being awarded the prize—and **symmetric** (in the sense that all contestants have the same ability [d] and the same cost-of-effort function, $V[E]$). In this chapter, we study what happens when either one of these assumptions is violated. In other words we will study **asymmetric** tournaments (see Definitions 20.1 and 20.2). How well (if at all) do tournaments work as an incentive scheme when the contestants are unevenly matched, or when the contest itself is biased toward or against certain contestants? Sections 22.1–22.3 answer these questions for the case of one-shot competitions. In Section 22.4, we discuss how the results change when we turn our attention to multistage elimination tournaments such as promotion ladders.

22.1 Effort and the Probability of Winning the Tournament

The first key theoretical result about asymmetric tournaments is that they are less effective at eliciting effort from contestants than symmetric tournaments. To see this, consider again the relationship between a contestant's effort and that person's probability of winning the tournament, which we derived for the special case of a uniform distribution of relative luck in Section 20.2. For this special case, the relationship is illustrated in Figure 22.1.

Figure 22.1 shows Player 1's chances of winning the tournament as a function of his own effort, E_1, holding Player 2's effort fixed at E_2. When $E_1 < A$, Player 1 has no chance of winning; and when $E_1 > B$, he wins for sure. For effort levels between A and B, Player 1's chances of winning increase linearly with

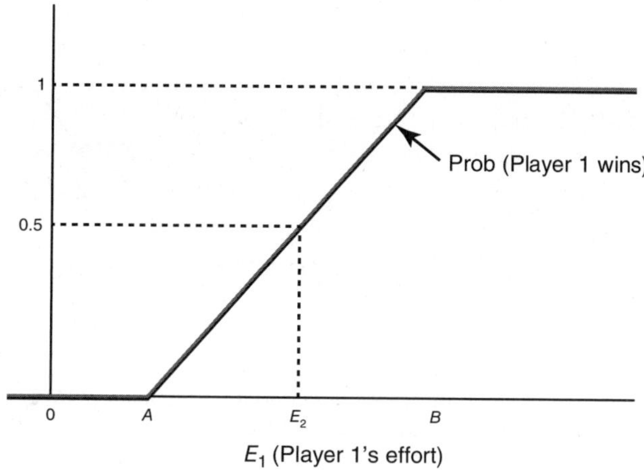

FIGURE 22.1. Effort and the Probability of Tournament Victory for a Uniform Relative Luck Distribution

his own effort.[1] And because the contest is symmetric, both players have a 50% chance of winning when $E_1 = E_2$.

For more realistic distributions of luck (such as the normal distribution, e.g.), the relationship between effort and the chances of success takes a similar but smoother form, illustrated in Figure 22.2.[2] Here, Player 1 has a small but nonzero chance of winning even when exerting zero effort, and a small but nonzero chance of losing (by luck) even when working much harder than Player 2. Still, at low effort levels (around point *A*), Player 1's chances of winning are not very sensitive to that person's effort levels (the slope of the curve is positive, but not very steep). The same is true at very high effort levels, around point *B*. In contrast, Player 1's chances of winning are the most sensitive to effort when exerting a similar effort level to Player 2, that is, when E_1 is approximately equal to E_2.

How does the relationship in Figure 22.2 change when the tournament is not symmetric? To see this, imagine first that instead of being equally able, Player 1 is much less able than Player 2. If you like, you can imagine you are Player 1 and your opponent in a round of golf is Tiger Woods in his superstar days. In general, competing against an abler player has the effect of shifting the Prob (Player 1 wins) function in Figure 22.2 horizontally, to the right, as shown in Figure 22.3.

[1] The slope of this relationship changes discontinuously at *A* and *B* because of a special feature of the uniform distribution: It has minimum and maximum values beyond which ε can never go.

[2] One widely used function for the Prob(Win) function that looks like Figure 22.2 is the urn-balls function: Prob (1 Wins) $= E_1/(E_1 + E_2)$. Here, effort is analogous to purchasing balls at a cost of $V(E)$ and placing them in an urn. Nature then picks one ball at random to determine the winner of the contest. Thus, if both players purchase the same number of balls, each has a 50% chance of winning. Tournaments of this form are sometimes called Tullock tournaments, after economist Gordon Tullock, who pioneered their application to the study of political contests (Tullock, 1967).

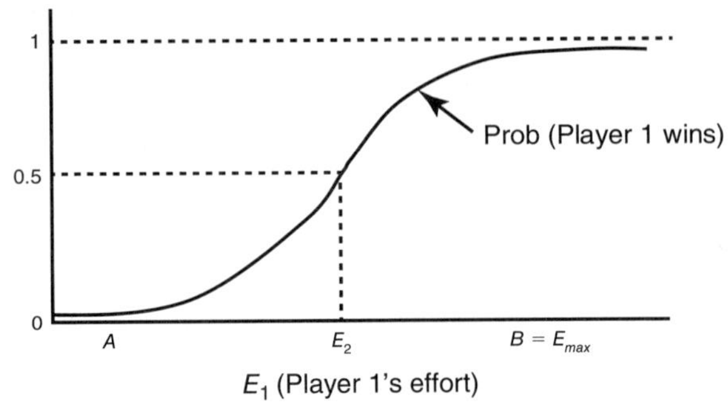

FIGURE 22.2. Effort and the Probability of Tournament Victory for a More Typical Luck Distribution, Such as a Normal Distribution (Symmetric Tournament)

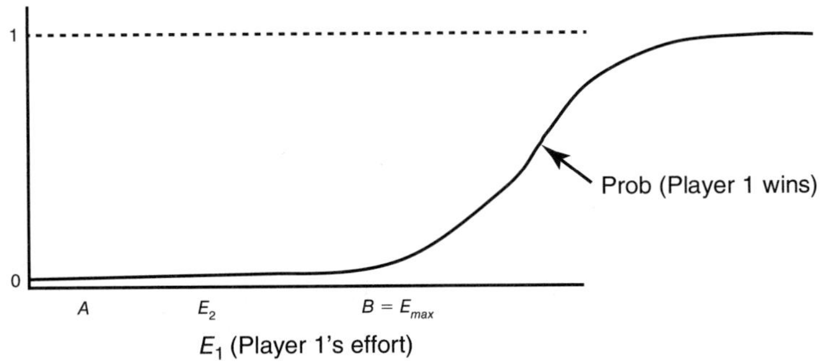

FIGURE 22.3. Effort and the Probability of Tournament Victory for a More Typical Luck Distribution, Such as a Normal Distribution (Player 1 Is Much Less Able)

Because the curve is upward sloping, this reduces Player 1's chances of winning at every possible level of effort chosen. Now, if you match Tiger Woods's effort level, you have only a very low chance of winning (say 0.01 for the sake of argument). Even at your highest feasible effort level E_{max} (suppose this is equal to B, which would have almost guaranteed you victory in an even contest), you still have almost no chance of winning.

Now let's turn the tables—what if you are Tiger Woods playing golf against an ordinary human? Now, as Figure 22.4 shows, the Prob (Player 1 wins) function is shifted dramatically to the left, with most of it now out of the picture. Player 1 now has at least (say) a 99% chance of winning, regardless of what Player 1 does. Thus, even though Figures 22.3 and 22.4 look very different, they share one crucial feature: For both players in a highly uneven tournament, the chances of winning don't really depend very much on how hard they work! Tiger Woods wins pretty much regardless of how hard he tries, and you lose even if

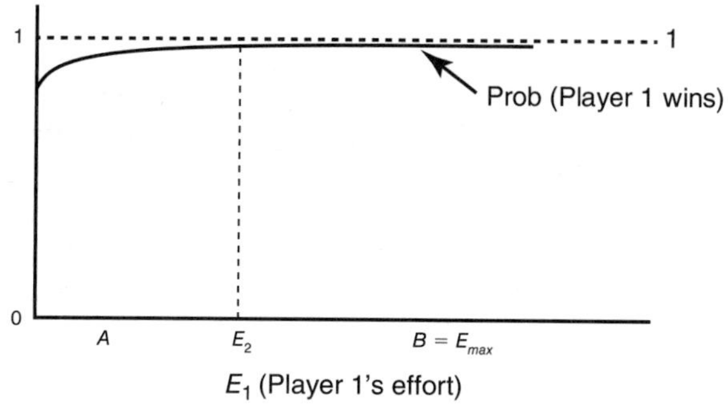

FIGURE 22.4. Effort and the Probability of Tournament Victory for a More Typical Luck Distribution, Such as a Normal Distribution (Player 1 Is Much More Able)

you exert the maximum possible effort you are capable of. Thus, both players actually have low incentives to try their best, in contrast to the even contest in Figure 22.2, where the Prob (Player 1 wins) curve is very steep in the feasible range of effort levels.

Putting the intuition from Figures 22.3 through 22.4 together, we have Result 22.1.

> **RESULT 22.1**
>
> **Incentives to Supply Effort in Asymmetric Tournaments**
>
> For any given level of the tournament prize (S), both players' incentives to supply effort are lower in an asymmetric tournament than in a symmetric one. When **players differ significantly in ability**, the abler player's incentives are blunted because that player is very likely to win no matter how hard he or she works. The less-able player's incentives are blunted because that player is extremely unlikely to win, regardless of how hard he or she works.
>
> The same logic applies when contestants are equally able but the contest's rules are **unfair**. (Imagine the competition for a promotion in a nepotistic firm involving the boss's nephew.) Now the person the tournament is biased against has low incentives because that player has very little chance of winning, and the boss's nephew can easily coast to victory without trying very hard.

22.2 Evidence on Asymmetric Tournaments: The Tiger Woods Effect

Although the theoretical arguments in Section 22.1 seem pretty compelling, is there any real-world evidence that effort levels are lower in asymmetric than symmetric tournaments? This question was addressed in a study of golf tournaments by Jennifer Brown (2011), a professor at the Sauder School of Business at the University of British Columbia. Brown's study took advantage of two important features of that sport, the first of which is that it had a universally acknowledged dominant player for a significant period of time. Between 1996 and 2006, Tiger Woods finished first in 54 of the 219 tournaments he competed in. He made the top three in 92 of these tournaments and the top 10 in 132 of them. He was Player of the Year eight times, and his average score of about 11 below par was consistently far below the average of the top-20-ranked players (about 4 below par).[3] Thus, if other players (even the very best of them) knew that Tiger was playing in a given tournament, they knew that their chances of winning the top prize had just declined significantly.

Second, although it is standard sports rhetoric for players to say that they "always play their best" regardless of the conditions, stakes, or opposition, to test our theory of tournaments, it is important that this rhetoric *not* be true. If players always supply the same level of effort, their performance will not depend on whether tournaments are evenly or unevenly matched. Thus, to test our model of asymmetric tournaments, we need to look at a situation where (a) *effort matters* for the outcome, and (b) players *don't* always exert their maximum effort.

In her article, Brown (2011) makes a convincing case for both these points. During a competition, she argues that extra attention to the "lie" of the field, the target, the weather, and club selection can make a big difference. Even more relevant to our model, a player's activities before a competition also matter considerably; these include studying the course, playing practice rounds, and hitting balls on the driving range. Further, these actions (like effort in our theoretical model) can be very costly to players. Because players can receive high fees for attending corporate outings just before a tournament (ranging from $100,000/day for David Love III to $1,000,000/day for Tiger), the *financial opportunity cost* of spending a day preparing for the tournament can be very high. Thus it seems reasonable to imagine that players don't always do "everything possible" to prepare for and win a tournament, especially when their chances of winning are not so high to begin with.

To assess whether effort levels are lower in asymmetric golf tournaments, Brown (2011) then collected data on all the players in 269 PGA tournaments from 1999 to 2006. Each of these players was ranked according to the Official World Golf Rankings. To let her statistically control for factors (other than the evenness of the competition) affecting players' performance, she also collected weather data for all the golf courses in each tournament, each tournament's TV viewership data from all the major networks, PGA ticket sales, and a host of other variables.[4] Using regression analysis to hold all these other factors constant, Brown then asked whether the performance of players other than Tiger was different in tournaments

---

[3] Nongolfers, please note that the winner of a golf tournament is the player with the *lowest* score (fewest strokes).

[4] Econometrically inclined readers and golf geeks may wish to know that Brown's (2011) statistical controls included a player's rank, a fixed effect for every possible player-course combination, and the following controls for each event: whether it was a major tournament, temperature and wind speed, total rain in the past 3 days, total purse, field quality, TV viewership, and total in-person attendance.

where Woods played compared to tournaments where he was absent. The answer was striking: Tiger's closest competitors (players ranked 1–20) made on average about three more strokes when Tiger was playing than when he was absent. The gap for lower-ranked players was even higher. Result 22.2 summarizes.

RESULT 22.2

Performance in Asymmetric Tournaments: Evidence from Professional Golf

Jennifer Brown's 2011 study of professional golf tournaments shows that Tiger Woods's competitors performed significantly worse in tournaments where Tiger was absent than when he was present. This suggests Woods's competitors reduced their effort levels in response to the unevenness of the competition: Tiger's presence meant that effectively, the top prize had been taken out of competition, so all the other players were essentially competing to win the second and lower prizes only.

Bad Field Advantages, Marital Problems and Psychological Pressure: Competing Explanations for Tiger Wood's Superstar Effect?

Despite the detailed list of statistical controls in Brown's (2011) study, you may not be entirely convinced that the "superstar effect" she documents—that is, the lower performance of Woods's competitors in his presence than his absence—was due to a rational reduction in effort on their part. In fact, I would be delighted if you were still skeptical because that is the mark of a good social scientist!

At least two important competing explanations for Brown's (2011) main result seem worth considering. The first is that there is something special about the tournaments Tiger chose not to attend (other than Tiger's presence itself) that tends to improve the other players' performance. After all, Tiger's presence on the course is not a randomly assigned treatment variable of the sort we discussed in Section 7.1. For example, it could be the case that Tiger is the sort of player that performs better in adverse conditions (soggy field, rambunctious crowd, etc.), that is, that he has a **bad field advantage** or simply prefers to play in challenging conditions. If Brown's statistical controls for these conditions are imperfect, then her results may simply be picking up the fact that Tiger is more likely to be present on days when field conditions are bad (and all the players tend to perform worse) than when they are good. If so, Tiger's presence would not be *causing* other players to perform worse at all. To address this possibility, Brown takes advantage of two episodes that removed Tiger from the field over which he arguably had no control: his knee surgery in June 2008 and his highly publicized **marital difficulties** between November 2009 and April 2010. As it turns out, the improvement in other players' performance during these absences was the same as during Tiger's other absences, suggesting that the estimated superstar effect is not spurious.

(continued)

A second possibility is that the reactions of Tiger Woods's competitors to his presence are **emotional** rather than rational (similar to the negative "choking" effects of high stakes documented by Ariely, Gneezy, Loewenstein, and Mazar, 2009, in Section 9.3). But, as Brown (2011) notes, putting Woods on the field actually *reduces* the financial stakes for the other players. Further, her statistical controls for TV viewership and attendance should account for any psychological pressure associated with the higher visibility of tournaments where Tiger is playing. Finally, most of the media attention focused on Tiger anyway, and players paired with Woods (who would receive much more fan attention) played no differently from other players. Thus, it is hard to think of a convincing "emotional" story to explain Brown's estimated superstar effect.

22.3 Addressing Ability Differences in Tournaments: Leagues, Handicaps, and Affirmative Action

In the previous section, we showed that for a given amount of total prize money, S, asymmetric contests induce less effort from both (or indeed all) agents in a competition. It follows that using an asymmetric contest (when a more symmetric alternative is available) will reduce profits, either because less effort is supplied or because a higher prize must be offered to generate the same level of effort.[5] In this section, we ask how a smart principal or employer can avoid these drawbacks of asymmetric contests.

A first, obvious piece of advice applies to situations where a group of competitors *is* equally able. Even if we ignore any profit-harming, negative emotional reactions that an unfair tournament might unleash among agents, the simple tournament theory in Section 22.1 tells us that it is never in the employer's interest to make contests between equally able agents unfair because this elicits less effort for the same cost. Thus, scrupulously avoiding bias—including its subtler and unconscious forms discussed in Section 16.4—is not just an ethically appealing strategy but a *profit-maximizing* one also. According to the basic theory of tournaments, even a *perception* of bias is predicted to reduce the motivation of both the person who is harmed by the perceived bias *and* the person who is favored by it.

☑ RESULT 22.3 Contests Between Equally Able Agents Should Be Fair

In one-shot competitions between workers who are equally able, profits will be maximized only when the rules of the contest are fair and are *perceived* to be fair. "Fair" in this context just means that the agent with the best measured performance should win the prize (and that any ties are resolved by flipping a fair coin).

[5] It is also possible to show that making a contest asymmetric (e.g., by making the rules unfair) can be socially inefficient as well.

But what can employers do in a more typical situation where the employee pool includes workers of varying ability levels? If it is important to use tournaments in this context, another solution is to group workers into pools of roughly similar ability, then run a fair tournament within each group. This is, of course, a widely used strategy in competitive sports. Many team sports organize competition into different leagues, within which the competition is relatively even. Individual sports do the same, and also stratify competition by weight classes, age (especially for children), and sex, in part to ensure even competition (and thus higher effort and more interesting games) between more evenly matched opponents. In the workplace, this can amount to something as simple as comparing workers of equal experience or similar exposure to training programs when assessing and rewarding relative performance.

☑ **RESULT 22.4**

Leagues Can Improve Competition by Homogenizing Pools of Competitors

When a group of workers has *unequal abilities*, and when tournament-based pay is necessary, employers should consider organizing competitions into relatively *homogenous leagues*. This ensures not only that all workers have a chance to win a bonus, but also that *all workers are at risk of not winning* if they do not perform to a certain standard.

Finally, what can be done when workers differ in ability and it is not practical to group them into homogeneous leagues (e.g., because there are just too few workers for this to be effective)? If employers still need to use tournament-based incentives, yet another sports analogy offers a potential solution: handicaps and point spreads. For example, there is in fact a frequently used way to make a golf match between me and Tiger Woods interesting: let's put up some prize money and impose a 50-stroke handicap on Tiger. Now, to win the money, Tiger needs to beat me by 50 strokes. This could be interesting after all. . . . By the same logic, readers who place bets on actual or fantasy sports will be familiar with the idea of a point spread, which requires the favored team to beat its opponent by a fixed number of points to earn a monetary prize for the bettor.

Handicaps (which in some contexts can be considered a form of *affirmative action*, or AA) illustrate the important distinction between *evenness* and *fairness* in tournaments. As Result 22.3 stated, *even* tournaments (i.e., tournaments between equally able agents) should be *fair*, that is, to maximize profits, firms should not require a point spread for either party to win. But when contestants are *unevenly* matched in terms of ability, the profit-maximizing policy can frequently involve making the rules *unfair* by introducing a handicap or point spread. This gives the less-able contestants a leg up or "head start," thereby increasing all agents' incentives to supply effort. In short, to maximize profits, in most cases *uneven* tournaments should also be *unfair*.

RESULT 22.5

Handicaps or Affirmative Action Can Raise Effort Levels in Tournaments Between Differently Abled Players

When running a competition between unequally matched competitors is inevitable, all players' incentives can be strengthened (at no cost to the principal) by giving the abler contestants a handicap or requiring them to beat a point spread to win the prize. In these competitions, a less-able agent can win the prize even when his job performance is strictly inferior to another agent's.

Although they solve one problem, affirmative action and handicaps may introduce other problems. For example, they may create morale problems if they are viewed as unfair by a firm's abler workers. Other possibilities that have been studied include *mismatch effects* (when less-able workers are promoted into jobs for which they are underqualified) and the possibility of creating *negative stereotypes* (where all persons from a group that benefits from AA are perceived to have succeeded *only* because of the advantage conferred by AA). Recent evidence on mismatch effects from college admissions is discussed in Section 22.3; Coate and Loury (1993) provide a fascinating analysis of the complex potential effects of affirmative action on stereotyping.

Although Result 22.5 suggests that affirmative action can improve work incentives when used correctly, is there any empirical evidence that this can actually happen in real life? In a study published in 2013, Caterina Calsamiglia, Joerg Franke, and Pedro Rey-Biel studied the effects of AA in tournaments between Spanish schoolchildren. The children, drawn from Grades 4 and 6 in two similar schools, were asked to solve simple (4 x 4) Sudoku problems. Each competition was between two students, with one student drawn from each school, and the winner in each pair won a €7 voucher that could be used for books or other school supplies. To induce "ability" differences in these tournaments, Calsamiglia et al. took advantage of the fact that the students at one of the schools (the "experienced" school) had had considerable practice doing these problems in the weeks leading up to the experiment, whereas students in the "non-experienced" school had not.

Calsamiglia et al. (2013) randomly assigned these student pairs into three main treatments. In the first treatment (NK), the students did not know there was a difference in preparation between the two schools. In the second (K) treatment, all the students were told that one school had practiced these problems and the other had not. Finally, in the AA treatment, students knew there was a difference in preparation and were informed that the students from the less-prepared school would get a certain number of "bonus" or free sudokus in the scoring. In some pairs, an eight-sudoku bonus was given; in others, 20 free sudokus were given to students from the less-prepared school. Thus, to win the €7 voucher in the AA treatment, a student from the better prepared school would have to beat a competitor by either eight or 20 sudokus.

The effects of affirmative action in Calsamiglia et al.'s (2013) experiment are revealed by comparing the K and AA treatments. Consistent with the theoretical prediction in Result 22.5, introducing handicaps (AA) significantly increased the average performance of the students from the less-prepared school. Perhaps, as suggested by Figure 22.3, these students felt they had no chance of winning without the bonus, and the bonus was enough to give them a "fair" shot at winning the prize. Introducing handicaps also raised the performance (number of correctly completed sudokus) of the students from the experienced school, but this increase was not statistically significant.

Some additional insight into how and why Calsamiglia et al.'s (2013) AA scheme affected students' behavior and well-being is available when we look at exactly *which* students at each school changed their performance the most when AA was used. Using data from the students' practice session before the experiment (which gave the children a chance to get used to the problems but didn't count toward their score), the authors were able to rank all the students in each school by their individual performance. Because students were ranked only against others from their same school, these rankings were unaffected by the amount of preparation each school offered and represented a more "fundamental" form of ability than the differences induced by teaching sudokus at one school but not the other. If we rank students according to this measure of ability, which students' behavior was most affected by the AA policy?

As it turns out, AA increased the performance of two specific groups of students only: less-able students in the experienced school and abler students in the inexperienced school, while other student types were unaffected. Given the logic of tournaments, this makes sense: Top students at the experienced school were unaffected by AA, as they could be confident of winning even in the presence of AA. Low-performing students at the inexperienced school were unaffected because even with AA, they had little chance of beating a randomly selected student from the better school. On the other hand, bright students at the less-prepared school really responded to AA: The bonus finally gave them a chance to win against the better prepared school. Anticipating this, low-ranked students at the prepared school now had a strong incentive to "pull up their socks" because they now faced a realistic threat from the less-prepared school. In essence, the biggest beneficiaries of affirmative action were bright students in "bad" schools, and the biggest losers were not-so-bright students in "good" schools. Both groups of students, however, were induced to work harder by the AA policy. Whatever else may be true about AA schemes, their introduction into this environment did not induce their beneficiaries to "take it easy" (as a result of the extra free points they were given). Instead, the opportunity provided by AA induced AA's beneficiaries to work harder by bringing a goal within their reach.[6]

---

[6] In their study of contract farming for broilers, Knoeber and Thurman (1994) show that the large integrators (such as Perdue and Tyson) seem to have figured this out: When using relative performance to reward growers, the integrators try to reduce ability mixing in comparison groups as much as possible. When that is not possible, they handicap growers of unequal ability. Schotter and Weigelt (1992) study equal opportunity and AA remedies for tournament asymmetries in a laboratory.

Selecting the Best: Does Affirmative Action Reduce Tournaments' Selection Efficiency?

As we'll discuss in Section 22.3, in addition to eliciting effort from contestants, many tournaments serve another function as well: *identifying* the ablest contestants so that they can be put into positions where that ability is put to the best possible use (such as a higher rank in the organization). Because handicapping a tournament reduces the chances that the best competitor will win, could handicapping lead to undesirable results by putting less-able people into positions for which they are not fully qualified?

Although this is possible, the answer to this question depends on a number of factors. First, handicapped tournaments can be used to incentivize workers (or students) without tying the prizes to promotions that do not make sense. There is nothing in the logic of handicapping a competition that forces organizers to put winners in jobs for which they are not qualified. Second, the selection efficiency of handicapped tournaments depends on the type of ability one is trying to identify. If the goal of Calsamiglia et al.'s (2013) contests with Spanish schoolchildren is to identify the children who are best at solving mini-sudokus on the day of the test, then those children are the ones with the best absolute scores, not the winners of the handicapped tournaments. If, however, the goal is to identify the children with the best "raw" mathematical ability (so we can offer them a more advanced math program), then we might indeed be quite interested in the children who performed well (but not at the very top) despite the lack of any instruction at their school.

Thus, whether it makes sense to promote winners of a handicapped tournament into positions that demand higher ability is an empirical question that depends in part on the context, the type of ability (current or potential) that is most relevant, and whether it is feasible for less-prepared but high-potential candidates to make up their deficits in preparation when put into a more demanding environment.

In the context of U.S. higher education, the question of how well students who benefit from affirmative action perform when admitted to highly competitive universities is called the *mismatch hypothesis*. For a recent, careful study of this question, see Arcidiacono, Aucejo, and Hotz (2016), who studied California universities during a period when racial preferences for admission were in place. They found that less-prepared minorities at higher ranked campuses had lower persistence rates in science and took longer to graduate, and estimate that this same group of students would have higher science graduation rates had they attended lower ranked campuses.

22.4 Ability Differences in Multistage Contests and Promotion Ladders

In the one-shot competitions we have studied so far in this chapter, ability differences between competitors are predicted to have a straightforward effect: They should reduce the total amount of effort elicited by any given amount of prize money (S). This effect, as we argued, can be counteracted by various changes in compensation policy, including leagues, handicaps, AA, and raising the amount of prize money itself.

Most competitions, however, do not occur in isolation. Promotion to assistant manager puts a worker into the running for the manager position. Winning the division title lets you compete in the national final. And even if a competition is not explicitly connected to any other competitions, winning it may reveal important information to others about just how talented you really are. How do ability differences affect agents' behavior in these more complex environments? And how do they affect the optimal structure of multistage contests? In this section, we'll work through four key examples to show that ability differences can have quite different and complex effects in these dynamic contexts.

Example 1: Ability Differences in Elimination Tournaments in the Symmetric Ignorance Case

A convenient place to start is Sherwin Rosen's (1986) model of promotion ladders, which we briefly introduced in Section 20.7. A little more formally, Rosen imagines an initial group of 2^n competitors in an n-stage pairwise elimination tournament. For example, if we start with eight competitors, the contest will have $n = 3$ levels. Here, all eight workers first receive a base payment (the equivalent of a in the one-stage contest) of W_0 dollars. The four winners in Stage 1 of the competition are all paid an additional award of W_1, the two winners in Stage 2 receive an additional W_2 dollars, and the winner of the final stage receives an additional W_3 dollars. If you like, you can think of the W_s as the wages attached to different ranks of the firm, and the gaps between them, for example. $S_1 = W_1 - W_0$ and so forth, as the *raises* associated with each successive promotion.

Importantly, Rosen's (1986) goal is to design a series of raises $(S_1, S_2, \ldots S_n)$ that **maintain agents' effort levels throughout the tournament**, that is, that guarantee that the surviving players' effort levels will not drop as the end of the tournament approaches. Although maintaining effort levels is not the only thing a contest designer is likely to care about, it seems like a very reasonable goal to try to achieve.[7] For example, if the decisions made at higher ranks of the organization are more consequential than decisions at lower ranks (i.e., if "ability matters more" for job performance at higher ranks—see Definition 14.1), we will want to make sure that workers who are promoted to the highest ranks are working at least as hard as those below them.

In Section 20.7, we described Rosen's (1986) theoretical results for the case in which all workers in the competition are known to have the same ability. In that case, Rosen shows that for effort to remain constant across all the ranks, all the raises but the last one (S_n) must be the same, and the last one must be strictly larger than all the others. All these calculations take the option value of

[7] Ultimately, we want any compensation structure, including promotion tournaments, to be socially efficient, that is, to maximize the sum of profits and utility. Perhaps surprisingly, relatively little of the recent theoretical research on sequential contests (especially in the field of Operations Research) studies their social efficiency properties, partly because it is challenging to derive general mathematical results.

promotions into account, and the lack of option value at the end means that the last prize must be bigger to maintain incentives. If we want effort to *increase* as workers move up the ranks, the size of the raises must rise across the ranks, with an especially large jump again at the top level, as shown in Figure 20.3.[8]

Now, let's ask how these results change when workers are not equally able. The simplest case to consider is the one Rosen (1986) calls **symmetric ignorance**: Everybody knows that the starting pool of workers has a mix of abilities, but nobody knows "who's who."[9] Thus, at the beginning of the tournament, all the competitors look the same; but as the competition goes, on everyone (workers and employers both) can infer something about which workers are the most talented by observing which ones survive. Although luck affects the outcome of every single competition, on average, the "fittest" tend to survive as the competition progresses, so the pool of remaining players gets more and more talented as we move up the ladder. How does this process affect the optimal prize structure described previously?

Happily, Professor Rosen works this out in Section V of his famous article. Key to his insight is the idea (which extends our reasoning in Section 22.1) that *ability differences reduce effort even when the players don't know which one of them is the most able.* To see this, imagine you must play a game against a randomly drawn opponent: If a coin comes up "heads," the opponent is so much better than you that your effort is irrelevant to whether you win. If the coin comes up tails, the opponent is so much worse than you that your effort is again irrelevant—you will win for sure. Thus, we should see low effort in a highly mixed contestant pool even when no one knows "who's who" in the pool.

Now let's apply this idea to an elimination tournament where there are two types of players: high and low ability (H and L). Suppose also that H is rare in the entry-level pool, and that there are enough stages in the tournament that we can be quite sure that the two finalists are both of H. For example, you might imagine that only one in 10 workers in the initial pool of competitors is an H type, but there's a 90% chance each finalist is an H. All of this is common knowledge.

How does this "weeding out" of less-able players affect effort levels and optimal prize structure for the tournament? At the entry level, there isn't much contestant heterogeneity: Each player knows that there's a 90% chance of being an L, and a 90% chance the opponent is an L. Thus, most players will be evenly matched in the early stages, which should motivate them to work hard. A large raise for the first promotion is thus not required to motivate workers. Heterogeneity in the

---

[8] Because Rosen's (1986) model assumes pairwise elimination, every promotion contest is between just two workers. If the number of players competing for the promotion changes as we move up the ladder (e.g., 30 production workers might compete for the foreman job, whereas only five vice presidents might compete for president), the optimal size of raises could change across the ranks for this reason as well.

[9] This case is simpler than the one where the tournament designer (and presumably the workers also) already knows something about which workers are best when the contest starts for at least two important reasons. First, there is no *seeding* decision to be made at the start: All workers look exactly the same, so the principal has no way to match them up in any specific way. Second, despite the fact that workers differ in ability, information and competition are symmetric at every level of the tournament: All anyone knows about the workers in the kth stage of competition is the simple fact that they have survived that long.

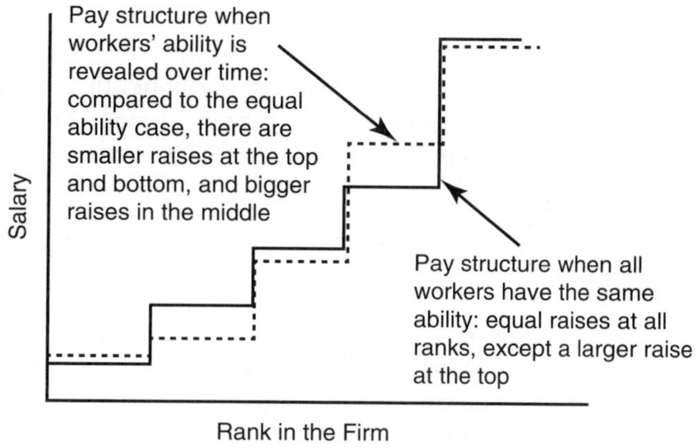

FIGURE 22.5. Effort-Maintaining Wage Structures in Rosen's (1986) Symmetric Ignorance Model

population of surviving workers will be highest when enough contestants have been eliminated so that the pool is likely to be about evenly split between Ls and Hs: Now, whether you win depends more on which type of opponent you're (randomly) matched with than on how hard you work.[10] Thus, to motivate workers at these intermediate stages, larger raises must be attached to promotions. Finally, as we get closer to the end of the competition, "survival of the fittest" ensures that almost all the remaining contestants are H workers and therefore evenly matched with each other again. Now a smaller prize spread will do the trick again. The end result of this process is depicted in Figure 22.5.[11]

RESULT 22.6

Effects of Survival of the Fittest on Optimal Prize Structure in Elimination Tournaments

The end result of the *ability-learning process* in Rosen's symmetric ignorance model is that—compared to a contest where all workers are known to have the same ability—the promotion-based raises that are needed to maintain effort as workers move up the promotion ladder will be smaller near the bottom and the top of the hierarchy and larger in the middle.

---

[10] Recall that matching has to be random in the symmetric ignorance case because all the contestants who have reached a given stage of the tournament "look the same" to everyone—there is no way to systematically match them, even if we wanted to.

[11] The key feature of Rosen's (1986) example—that heterogeneity in the contestant pool first rises then falls as the tournament progresses—does not necessarily generalize to cases with more than two types of workers where the results will depend on the shape of the ability distribution. Rosen's example is best thought of as an illustration of how selection and motivation can interact over the course of an elimination tournament.

Rosen's (1986) elegant model is one example of how a tournament's tendency to *select* the most talented workers interacts with its ability to *motivate* workers—the two central themes of our book. In the example, as in real life, both of these factors interact to influence the design of the optimal contract between principals and agents (in this case the prize structure in an elimination tournament).

Example 2: What If *All* We Care About Is Selection? Selection Contests

In Rosen's (1986) model, employers (and workers themselves) learn which workers are the most able by observing how workers progress through an elimination tournament. But in a sense this learning is a *by-product* of a system (the pairwise elimination tournament) that the firm is using to motivate its workers. What if the employer's main objective is just to learn which worker is the best, or to learn *all* the workers' ability levels so as to assign them optimally to different ranks in the firm?

DEFINITION 22.1 Contests that are designed exclusively for the purposes of learning workers' abilities are called **selection contests.**

Selection contests may be appropriate models for a number of important real-world decisions. Outside personnel economics, applications include choosing a country's Olympic team, finding the best treatment for a disease, and elections. For example, the U.S. presidential primary elections are an elimination tournament whose main goal is hopefully *not* to encourage all the candidates to spend large amounts of effort and money in the campaign but to select the best candidate. In personnel economics, selection contest models help us think about promotion and selection decisions in contexts where either (a) workers' efforts aren't affected by the structure of the tournament, or (b) the principal doesn't care about effort. One example is the hiring decision, where the goal is just to hire the best person, not to encourage workers to lobby hard to get the job. In Section 14.2, we studied a number of simple ways to select the best candidate from a pool; models of selection contests let us consider a much broader set of possible mechanisms, such as elimination tournaments where large numbers of applications are processed in several stages. Another example is any case where the firm has devised other methods (such as piece rates, performance bonus, stock options, and the threat of dismissal) to ensure optimal effort levels so the raises associated with promotions are a negligible part of the overall incentive package. This could arguably describe a large number of workplaces.[12]

[12] The fact that an employer does not rely on promotion-linked raises to incentivize workers does not imply that it won't give promoted workers a raise. For example, raises might be required just to compensate workers for the extra difficulty—greater responsibility, longer hours, increased stress, and so forth—associated with a higher ranked position. Or, as we will argue in Example 3, the labor market might *force* employers to attach raises to promotions.

What is known about selection contests? One question we might ask is which type of contest maximizes the expected ability of the ultimate winner. Ryvkin (2010) compares three tournament types: a one-shot *contest* where everybody competes in the same pool; a binary *elimination tournament* where players are randomly paired up at the start, then winners compete with winners until one candidate is left; and a *round-robin tournament* where every player competes with every other, and the overall winner is the one with the most wins. Perhaps not surprisingly, the expected quality of the overall winner is lowest in the one-shot contest, higher in the elimination tournament, and highest in the round-robin format. But this is largely because of the difference in the number of competitions: 1, $log_2(N)$, and $N(N-1)/2$, respectively. If tournaments are costly to run, principals will need to trade off the greater selection efficiency of the multistage methods against their higher costs. Perhaps this is why the "middle" option (elimination tournaments) seems to best describe many firms' actual recruiting methods. Much more remains to be learned, however, about the best way to design selection contests when it is costly to run additional stages of the selection process.[13]

Margaret Meyer (1991) considers a fourth type of selection contest, specifically a *multistage contest* (Definition 20.6) where a pair of workers competes multiple times before one of them is promoted to a job where it is more important to have high ability. This promotion decision is based on the combined results of all their matches. In Meyer's model, workers always supply the same level of effort; each match just provides another piece of information on which worker is likely the better one. If you like, you can think of these matches as quarterly or annual performance evaluations. Meyer imagines that higher level decision makers in the organization—who award the promotions—can only observe the number of matches each worker won. In this situation, Meyer shows that higher officials might want to instruct their subordinates to systematically *bias* the competitions *against the early laggard* (i.e., the worker who does worse in the first few comparisons).

How, exactly, might competitions be biased in this way? One possibility is to instruct middle managers to systematically assign the early laggards to more challenging tasks, or to assign them more "nonpromotable" duties that take time away from activities that demonstrate their abilities. Another is to instruct middle managers to handicap early leaders when awarding "victories." Essentially, high-level management is saying this to middle managers: "Unless a trailing candidate beats a leader by a wide-enough margin to *reverse* your assessment about which one is the better worker, I don't need to know about it." Essentially, this makes trailing candidates "invisible" to higher management unless those candidates score a sufficiently convincing upset. This may seem unfair, but as Meyer shows, it can be an efficient way for attention-strapped top management to gather information.[14]

---

[13] Ryvkin and Ortmann (2006) describe two main types of costs in running tournaments and provide some simulation results for how they can affect the optimal structure of selection tournaments.

[14] It also makes sense in other contexts: Top officials at the U.S. National Institutes of Health do not need to stay informed about research on every drug that is being evaluated for a certain disease. If a drug has already failed a few trials, officials only need to hear about it again if it scores a surprising upset victory over alternatives in subsequent tests.

RESULT 22.7

Invisible Trailing Contestants In Multistage Selection Contests

In multistage selection contests, Margaret Meyer (1991) shows that it may be optimal for time- and attention-constrained higher managers to instruct mid-level managers to bias promotion contests in favor of early leaders, and thus against workers who fall behind early on. Essentially, this creates "invisible" trailing candidates who can only command the attention of higher ranks if they outperform their co-workers by a large amount.

Notice that Result 22.7's recommendation—to bias the contest against workers who are *behind* in multistage contests—contrasts with Result 22.5, which recommends a bias against the abler worker in one-stage competitions.

Example 3: Optimal Grouping in Market-Based Tournaments

A simplifying feature of Examples 1 and 2 is the assumption that all the workers "look the same" to the employer at the start of the promotion or selection process. Thus, an employer who has a large enough pool of workers at the entry level to run multiple parallel competitions does not need to decide how to group the workers into competitions. This changes when employers already know something about "who's who" at the very start—employers now need to know whether it is better, for example, to put all the new workers with "star" potential into a "fast-track" promotion pool and let them "fight it out" or to mix up all the pools and give everyone a chance to (eventually) compete for the top spot.

According to Result 22.1, we might expect that maximum effort (for the same prize money) will always be obtained when the contestant pools are as homogeneous as possible. But Result 22.1 applies to a one-shot tournament where the employer sets a fixed prize, S, in advance. In this example, we'll show that heterogeneous contestant pools can sometimes elicit more effort than homogeneous pools in an important type of tournament we haven't studied yet: market-based tournaments. Although the market-based tournament we study here has only one stage of competition, we include it in our study of multistage contests because the wages of promoted workers are determined by a stage consisting of market-level interactions between workers and outside employers that occur after the competition has taken place. As we'll see, in market-based tournaments, the size of the prize received by the victor is determined not by the firm but *by the labor market*. This can create an advantage for *heterogeneous* contestant pools.

We begin by considering a firm with a pool of workers of mixed abilities. The employer has some idea of which workers are the best, but this information is imprecise. Running a contest between the workers, however, reveals some additional information about who really are the better workers. If outside employers see the results of this contest (i.e., they see who is promoted), then as we argued in Section 20.7, promotions can act as **signals**, encouraging outside employers to lure promoted workers away with higher wages and forcing the original firm to match those raises. In other words, instead of being something the original firm *has promised to offer* to incentivize its workers, the tournament prize, *S,* may be something that firm is *forced* to offer by the labor market.

DEFINITION 22.2 Tournaments in which workers work hard not just to win a cash prize, but to demonstrate to a wider labor market that they are highly skilled, are called **market-based tournaments**.

Market-based tournaments are one example of the role of **career concerns**—that is, workers' attempts to shape the labor market's **beliefs** about them—in incentivizing workers. Economists use a variety of **employer learning models** to think about how current and future employers update their beliefs about workers' abilities by observing workers' past performance. See this chapter's Suggestions for Further Reading for more information about these ideas.

In an interesting recent model of market-based tournaments, Marc and Oliver Gürtler (2015) show that heterogeneity in the pool of workers competing for a promotion can actually *raise* workers' effort levels instead of reducing them. This is because in market-based tournaments, the rewards to promotion, *S*, reflect *what the market has learned* about the tournament winner's ability. Thus, prize spreads (and therefore work incentives) will be higher when the results of a contest are particularly *informative*.

Under what conditions are contest results are especially informative? If two contestants we initially thought were equally strong (say Goliath A and Goliath B) compete in a fight, and Goliath A wins, we infer that Goliath A was maybe a bit stronger than Goliath B after all, and update our beliefs a little. But if David beats Goliath (i.e., the player we expected to be weaker beats the stronger), we update our beliefs about *both* those players' abilities a lot: **Upsets are informative**. To make a long story short, Gürtler and Gürtler (2015) show that under the right conditions, grouping contestants together into heterogeneous pools (where there is considerable ability variation inside each pool) can elicit more effort from workers than homogeneous pools because heterogeneous pools allow for upsets. Now, the "Davids" have a chance to beat a Goliath, thereby earning a huge raise. And the Goliaths will work extra hard to avoid losing to a David because this would hurt them substantially.

☑ RESULT 22.8

Ability Differences Between Players Can Raise Effort Levels in the Early Stages of Market-Based Tournaments, By Affecting the Beliefs of Alternative Employers

This is because heterogeneity in contestant pools creates the possibility of **upsets**, which are especially informative about contestants' true abilities. Because labor markets will reward workers who are discovered to be more able whether the original employer likes it or not, contestants will be motivated to work hard both to achieve and to prevent upsets.

Example 4: Grouping, Seeding, and Option Value in Promotion Ladders

As we noted in Example 1, incentives in multistage elimination tournaments are more complex than in one-shot tournaments because of option value: The reward to winning early stages includes not just the prize for that stage, but also (often more importantly) the option to compete in later stages. In this environment, the way that competitors are grouped in early stages affects not only their chances of advancing but whom they are likely to compete with in later stages, thereby affecting the option value of winning early. Could these changes in option value also make heterogeneous pools an attractive choice?

Rudi Stracke and Uwe Sunde explore the implications of option value for contestant grouping decisions in a 2014 paper. Although they establish a number of results about the effects of heterogeneity on effort in elimination tournaments, the quickest way to see how option value can make heterogeneity valuable is by considering a specific example based on their work.[15] Before getting into the details, however, it is helpful to distinguish two distinct aspects of multistage tournament design that do not come up in simpler contests.

DEFINITION 22.3 In multistage elimination tournaments, workers who are assigned to different promotion pools never compete with one another. **Pools, promotion ladders,** or **competitions** are analogous to leagues in sports, where a group of contestants compete against each other in a certain order, but rarely compete with people outside the group. If a company runs multiple promotion pools, it can decide whether to have homogeneous pools (where the contestants within each pool are as similar to each other in ability as possible), heterogeneous pools (where they are as different as possible), or an allocation somewhere between these extremes.

Suppose there is some heterogeneity in a pool of workers that has started a multistage elimination tournament. Then the administrator of the tournament needs to decide which workers compete with each other in the first round. In this **seeding** decision, the company can decide to have **homogeneous seeding** (where the first contestants to be paired up are as similar to each other in ability as possible), **heterogeneous seeding** (where these contestants are as different as possible), or something in between.

With these definitions in hand, let's now imagine a firm that has just hired eight employees, who can be of two types: L or H. Everybody knows that four of the workers have low ability L and the rest have high ability H, and everybody knows which worker is which type. Thus, in contrast to Rosen's (1986) symmetric heterogeneity model and to Gürtler and Gürtler's (2015) market-based tournament model, competition between workers does not reveal any information. Imagine

[15] Rosen (1986) considers examples similar to Stracke and Sunde's (2014) in Section IV.

also that the employer is running two parallel promotion ladders, or promotion pools, containing four workers each. In each of these pools, there is a two-stage competition to determine the overall winner. In the first stage, four entry-level workers engage in pairwise competitions for promotion to the middle rank in the firm; in the final stage the two winners of those competitions compete against each other for promotion to the top rank.[16] Each promotion has a fixed cash prize associated with it, which can differ between the two competition levels. Finally, assume that when faced by the same competitor in a one-shot contest, H workers always supply more effort than L workers because H workers have a lower marginal cost of effort.

Now let's compare two different ways the entry-level employees could be sorted into promotion pools. In the *homogeneous pools* case, the workers are perfectly sorted into two pools before the competitions begin: One pool contains four high-type workers (HHHH), and the other contains four low-type workers (LLLL). In the *heterogeneous pools* case, both pools are mixed, with two workers of each type in each pool (HHLL). The main question we want to answer in this example is, "Can a policy of constructing heterogeneous promotion pools ever elicit higher worker effort levels than a homogeneous-pools policy?"

In order to answer this question, we need to make an assumption about seeding in the case where promotion pools are heterogeneous. To demonstrate our main result as simply as possible, we will assume that in the heterogeneous pools case, the two H workers compete with each other (HH) and the two L workers compete with each other (LL). In other words, the firm has chosen a *homogeneous seeding* policy.

Based on our discussion of one-shot contests in Sections 22.1–22.3, you might think that the homogeneous pools organization is likely to yield the most effort by all workers. This is because all workers are evenly matched in both stages, although that is not the case with heterogeneous pools. But this logic ignores the option value of promotion. With homogeneous pools, the option value of winning the first promotion is always another competition against a person of your own ability. In our heterogeneous-pools case, however, the option value of winning the first promotion for an L worker is a second-stage competition against an H worker, which the L worker is likely to lose. For H workers, the option value is a guaranteed to be a competition against an L worker, which the H worker is likely to win. Thus, *heterogeneous contestant pools raise the option value of winning early stages for the H workers while reducing it for L workers.* In their paper, Stracke and Sunde (2014) show that the resulting extra first-stage effort among the H workers will in general outweigh the lost output among the L players because H players' output is more sensitive to incentives.

---

[16] Taken literally, this assumes that the firm has an up-or-out promotion policy (like the tenure decision at universities, the partnership decision at law firms, or tennis tournaments). However, models like this can be used to study more familiar workplace contexts, like those where early losers remain employed at lower ranks. To do this, we simply need to interpret the prizes as the total *career* income associated with attaining each rank, as opposed to a lump-sum cash prize.

Thus, on average across all the workers types, first-stage effort is higher in the heterogeneous pools case.[17]

RESULT 22.9

Ability Differences Between Players Can Raise Effort Levels in the Early Stages of Elimination Tournaments By Affecting Players' Option Values

In the example studied by Stracke and Sunde (2014), mixing up the contestant pools by ability in the early stages raises the option value of winning an early stage. This is because higher ability workers now face weaker competition in later stages and therefore have a greater incentive to make it to the later stages. In some cases, this extra early effort can be enough to raise the total effort expended by all players across both stages of the tournament.

Putting all this together, compared to the homogeneous pools case, elimination tournaments with heterogeneous pools have lower overall effort in the second stage (due to uneven competition) but higher overall effort in the first stage (due to higher option values). Heterogeneous tournaments elicit more effort overall when the latter effect outweighs the former, and Stracke and Sunde (2014) provide examples where that happens.

Stracke and Sunde (2014) also consider the consequences of heterogeneous versus homogeneous pools for the **selection efficiency** of tournaments. In the homogeneous pools case, we know for sure that one H worker and one L worker will emerge as overall winners at the end of the elimination tournament. In our heterogeneous pools case, each of the two final matchups pits one H worker against one L worker. Because the H workers are more likely to win these contests, heterogeneous pools are more likely than homogeneous pools to produce H workers as overall winners. If it's important to the firm to have the best person rise to the top of the hierarchy, this may be a second advantage of a heterogeneous promotion pools policy.[18]

RESULT 22.10

Compared to Homogeneous Contestant Pools, Mixed-Ability Contestant Pools Can Raise the Expected Share of Final Winners Who Are of High Ability, H

---

[17] In Stracke and Sunde's (2014) notation, the incentive effect of the heterogeneous pool on effort (relative to the homogeneous pool) is given by Δx_1^* = HHLL vs. HHHH for H workers, and by Δx_1^* = HHLL vs. LLLL for L workers.

[18] Of course, the firm doesn't have to assign the winner of the homogeneous multistage tournament among L workers [LLLL in Stracke & Sunde's (2014) example] to a high rank in the organization; they could just get a cash prize. This reminds us that it is not always optimal for employers to use the same tool (a tournament) both to assign workers to tasks or ranks in the organization and to motivate them to work hard. Existing models of promotion tournaments sometimes lump these together, however.

Seeding in Elimination Tournaments: The Case of Tennis

In addition to grouping heterogeneous contestants into different tournaments, organizers of elimination tournaments who have advance knowledge of the contestants' relative ability also have to decide how to match up the players in the opening stage *within* each tournament. In other words, they must decide how to *seed* each tournament.

Interestingly, although Result 22.1 (for one-shot contests) suggests that matching pairs as evenly as possible might maximize efforts, many real-world elimination tournaments do the exact opposite. For example, in most tennis tournaments, the top two players (1 and 2 seeds) are placed in separate brackets, but then the 3 and 4 seeds are assigned to their brackets randomly, and so too are seeds 5 through 8, and so on. Thus, the designers take special steps to ensure that the best players are *not* matched with each other in early stages. In other words, tennis tournaments enforce a *heterogeneous seeding* policy.

One important reason why tournament organizers might prefer heterogeneous seeding is *selection* efficiency: organizers might place a high value on ensuring that the best players survive into the final stages of the competition. In the case of sports tournaments, this probably maximizes overall excitement and expected fan revenues (in part by keeping them engaged longer). In the workplace, heterogeneous early matchups raise the chances that the ablest worker will rise to the highest rank of the firm.

Chapter Summary

- ☐ In one-shot competitions between workers who are equally able, profits will be maximized only when the rules of the contest are fair.
- ☐ In one-shot competitions between workers with different abilities, effort levels of all competitors can usually be increased for the same prize money by grouping players into homogeneous leagues or by handicapping the abler worker.
- ☐ In addition to eliciting effort from workers, multistage tournaments can also provide new information on which workers are the most able. This allows employers to make better decisions on which workers to assign to jobs where "ability matters more." Although tournaments with multiple stages generally provide more precise information, they are also costlier to run.

- ☐ In contrast to one-shot competitions, grouping competitors into homogeneous ability pools is not always optimal in multistage tournaments. In market-based tournaments, greater heterogeneity in early matches increases the risk of upsets, which can be highly motivating.

- ☐ In elimination tournaments, knowing that a later stage will have mixed abilities raises abler players' motivation to advance to those stages. Also, mixing players up in early stages raises the chances that the ablest players survive into the final stages, thereby raising selection efficiency.

Discussion Questions

1. In our discussion of Stracke and Sunde's (2014) paper, we assumed that the seeding in the heterogeneous pools case was HHLL; in other words the two H workers were matched in the first stage, as were the two L workers. How would the results change if the heterogeneous pools case used mixed-ability matches (HLHL) instead?
2. In a recent study of basketball games titled "Can Losing Lead to Winning?," Berger and Pope (2011) find that being slightly behind at halftime actually *increases* a team's chances of winning the game. This conflicts with this chapter's results that any asymmetry in a contest should reduce effort levels. What other behavioral phenomena discussed in this book might account for Berger and Pope's finding?
3. In your current or most recent job, was the prospect of winning a promotion an important motivator for you? In which types of jobs are promotions likely to be an important motivator?
4. Elimination tournaments in sports, including National Football League playoffs, National Basketball Association and National Collegiate Athletic Association college basketball, and World Cup soccer, use a variety of rules to seed the competition. Some of them even do re-seeding at higher levels to match, for example, the highest ranked surviving seed with the lowest. What do think might motivate these different approaches?

Suggestions for Further Reading

For evidence that ability differences reduce effort in professional tennis, see Sunde (2009). For more on tournament selection efficiency from golf tournaments, see Brown and Minor (2014).

For additional information in market-based tournaments, see Waldman (2013).

For more on the effects of workers' career concerns (i.e., establishing a reputation as being a good worker), see Akerlof (1976); Fama (1980); Gibbons and Murphy (1992); Landers, Rebitzer, and Taylor (1996); and Chevalier and Ellison (1999).

For additional examples of employer learning models, see Altonji and Pierret (2001); Kahn and Lange (2014); and MacLeod, Riehl, Saavedra, and Urquiola (2017).

References

Akerlof, G. A. (1976). The economics of caste and of the rat race and other woeful tales. *Quarterly Journal of Economics, 90,* 599–617.

Altonji, J., & Pierret, C. (2001). Employer learning and statistical discrimination. *Quarterly Journal of Economics, 116,* 313–350.

Arcidiacono, P., Aucejo, E. M., & Hotz, V. J. (2016). University differences in the graduation of minorities in STEM fields: Evidence from California. *American Economic Review, 106,* 525–562. Retrieved from http://dx.doi.org/10.1257/aer.20130626

Ariely, D., Gneezy, U., Loewenstein, G., & Mazar, N. (2009). Large stakes and big mistakes. *Review of Economic Studies, 76,* 451–469.

Berger, J., & Pope, D. G. (2011). Can losing lead to winning? *Management Science, 57,* 817–827.

Brown, J. (2011). Quitters never win: The (adverse) incentive effects of competing with superstars. *Journal of Political Economy, 119,* 982–1013.

Brown, J., & Minor, D. B. (2014). Selecting the best? Spillover and shadows in elimination tournaments. *Management Science, 60*(12), 3087–3102.

Calsamiglia, C., Franke, J., & Rey-Biel, P. (2013). The incentive effects of affirmative action in a real-effort tournament. *Journal of Public Economics, 98,* 15–31.

Chevalier, J., & Ellison, G. (1999). Career concerns of mutual fund managers. *Quarterly Journal of Economics, 114,* 389–432.

Coate, S., & Loury, G. (1993). Will Affirmative Action Eliminate Negative Stereotypes? A*merican Economic Review, 83*(5), 1220–1240.

Fama, E. F. (1980). Agency problems and the theory of the firm. *Journal of Political Economy, 88*(2), 288–307.

Gibbons, R., & Murphy, K. J. (1992). Optimal incentive contracts in the presence of career concerns: Theory and evidence. *Journal of Political Economy, 100,* 468–505.

Gürtler, M., & Gürtler, O. (2015). The optimality of heterogeneous tournaments. *Journal of Labor Economics, 33,* 1007–1042.

Kahn, L., & Lange, F. (2014). Employer learning, productivity and the earnings distribution: Evidence from performance measures. *Review of Economic Studies, 81,* 1575–1613.

Knoeber, C. R., & Thurman, W. N. (1994). Testing the theory of tournaments: An empirical analysis of broiler production. *Journal of Labor Economics, 12*(2), 155–179.

Landers, R. M., Rebitzer, J. B., & Taylor, L. J. (1996). Rat race redux: Adverse selection in the determination of work hours in law firms. *American Economic Review, 86,* 329–348.

MacLeod, W. B., Riehl, E., Saavedra, J. E., & Urquiola, M. (2017). The big sort: College reputation and labor market outcomes. *American Economics Journal: Applied Economics*, *9*(3), 223–261.

Meyer, M. A. (1991). Learning from coarse information: Biased contests and career profiles. *Review of Economic Studies, 58,* 15–41.

Rosen, S. (1986). Prizes and incentives in elimination tournaments. *American Economic Review, 76,* 701–715.

Ryvkin, D. (2010). The selection efficiency of tournaments. *European Journal of Operational Research, 206,* 667–675.

Ryvkin, D., & Ortmann, A. (2006). Three prominent tournament formats: Predictive power and costs. *CERGE-EI Working Paper Series, 303*, 1–33.

Schotter, A., & Weigelt, K. (1992). Asymmetric tournaments, equal opportunity laws, and affirmative action: Some experimental results. *Quarterly Journal of Economics, 107,* 511–539.

Stracke, R., & Sunde, U. (2014). *Dynamic Incentive Effects of Heterogeneity in Multi-Stage Promotion Contests* (IZA Working Paper No. 7880). Bonn, Germany: Institute for the Study of Labor.

Sunde, U. (2009). Heterogeneity and performance in tournaments: A test for incentive effects using professional tennis data. *Applied Economics, 41,* 3199–3208.

Tullock, G. (1967). The welfare costs of tariffs, monopolies, and theft. *Economic Inquiry*, *5*(3), 224–232.

Waldman, M. (2013). Classic promotion tournaments versus market-based tournaments. *International Journal of Industrial Organization, 31,* 198–210.

23 Who Wants to Compete? Selection into Tournaments

Some occupations, like working in a law practice, at a hedge fund, as a ballerina, or as an athlete, are widely perceived to involve more inter-worker competition than others. Likewise, some companies and workplaces have a reputation for a more "dog-eat-dog" culture than others, which may be created and reinforced by rules that allocate raises, promotions, and layoffs on the basis of relative performance. What types of workers are attracted to competitive, tournament-oriented workplaces? Are those always the types of workers the employers want to have? And do workers always make the best choices for themselves when deciding what type of workplace to enter?

In this chapter, we address these questions in three stages. First, we ask what economic theory predicts about who should be attracted to tournaments. Second, we'll look at how the evidence on selection into tournaments stacks up against those theoretical predictions. Finally, we look specifically at gender differences in the choice to enter competitive environments. These differences have been widely studied, and may have significant implications for women's careers and for firms' abilities to retain a diverse pool of employees, especially at higher levels of the organization.

23.1 Ability, Risk Aversion, and Tournament Entry

Economic theory suggests at least five attributes of workers that should affect their choice to enter a competitive pay environment. First and most obvious are tastes for competition itself, of the sort we discussed in Section 21.3: People who enjoy competition for its own sake should be more likely to enter tournaments. Second, as we noted in Section 20.8, risk-averse people might either be more or less attracted to tournaments. On the one hand, tournaments should attract risk-averse workers when there are common shocks to the production process.

On the other hand, tournaments also expose workers to additional risk related to the fact that their pay depends on their co-worker's performance, which is unpredictable. Thus, at least when common shocks are unimportant, we might expect risk-averse workers to avoid tournaments.

The third factor is the effect of ability: Compared to a situation where pay is fixed, or to an individual piece rate where a worker is paid what he or she produces, we would expect abler workers to be more attracted to a tournament than less-able workers: The tournament is more attractive to talented workers because they are more likely to win. Fourth, and closely related, is a worker's assessment of the *competitors'* ability: If a worker thinks the competitors are not very strong, energetic, smart, or talented, that worker will want to play against them in a tournament for money. By the same token, workers who are *overconfident* (i.e., who overestimate their true relative ability) will be attracted to tournaments, and underconfident workers will avoid them.[1]

Finally, simply being in a competitive environment (with the same total and marginal financial incentives as a noncompetitive environment) could affect a worker's performance. Will the worker respond to competition by "upping her or his game," like the greyhounds in Section 21.3; or will that worker become discouraged, intimidated, or choke like the Indian villagers in Section 9.3? We refer to changes in an individual's performance when that person moves from a noncompetitive into a competitive environment as the *response to competition*; these responses can vary across people, just as risk aversion and ability can vary as well.

☑ RESULT 23.1

Who Should Be Attracted to Tournaments?

Simple economic models suggest that competitive pay environments should be most attractive to workers who *enjoy* competition, who *respond well* to competition, and who think they are *more able* than their competitors. Risk aversion has an ambiguous predicted effect on tournament entry but is more likely to raise entry when there are common shocks to production.

So far, evidence on the role of the preceding factors on selection into competitive pay environments is relatively limited. The few studies that have been done seem to support the main predictions summarized in Result 23.1. For example, Leuven, Oosterbeek, Sonnemans, and van der Klaauw (2011) conducted

[1] All these predictions about the effect of ability are for a prize of a fixed size. In their seminal article, Lazear and Rosen (1981, Section IV) pose a different question: Suppose an employer sets the total value of pay in a tournament such that the employer just breaks even when workers of a certain targeted ability level decide to enter. If the employer then allows anyone to sign up for the competition, less-able workers will want to join (because they still have a chance of "winning by luck"), causing the employer to lose money. To prevent this, Lazear and Rosen argue that employers will need to restrict admission to the contests for the big prizes, for example, by making them win a number of previous rounds. This is another possible rationale for using elimination tournaments to allocate promotions.

an experiment in an introductory microeconomics class where students were allowed to self-select into one of three competitions with different prize levels: €1,000, €3,000, and €5,000. The student with the highest grade in each competition won the prize. In this situation, you might ask yourself, "Why would anyone choose to enter the €1,000 competition instead of the €5,000 competition when there is no entry fee for any of the competitions?" A little theoretical reflection on equilibrium self-selection into tournaments, however, yields an answer: since abler students will have a better chance at winning the top prize, we'd expect them to disproportionately choose the higher-stakes tournaments. Anticipating this, it can be rational for lower-ability students to choose the low-stakes competitions, where they at least have a chance of winning.[2]

Consistent with this theory, the authors found that the ablest students (based on their performance in previous courses) self-selected into the highest-prize tournaments, and that average grades were much higher in the high-prize competitions. Perhaps more interestingly, none of this difference in grades between the competitions was due to higher levels of effort when prizes were higher—the *entire* performance gap was due to differences in who chose to join which contest. Leuven et al.'s (2011) experiment illustrates an important selection effect of tournaments: Tournaments with large prize spreads (i.e., jobs with chances for big promotions) are likely to attract more qualified workers.

In a series of laboratory experiments, Eriksson, Teyssier, and Villeval (2009) let subjects choose between tournament-based pay and an individual piece rate with equal expected value. Consistent with Result 23.1, they found that underconfident subjects avoided the tournament; risk-averse workers also avoided competition. Also of interest, performance under *both* individual pay and tournament pay was higher when subjects were free to choose which scheme to join than when they were randomly assigned to a scheme. This suggests that allowing workers to choose whether to enter competitive pay environments can be beneficial.[3] In a broader study of selection into different pay schemes, Dohmen and Falk (2011) also found that tournaments attract overconfident workers and workers who are less risk averse.

Finally, in a study focused on the effects of overconfidence, Camerer and Lovallo (1999) studied the decisions of students at the Wharton Business School and the University of Chicago to enter a competitive environment. Specifically, they modeled the decision to enter a competitive industry in which the payoff per entrant decreased with the number of entrants. The twist in Camerer and Lovallo's study that makes it interesting for our purposes was that a subject's payoff if that person entered the "industry" also depended on how the subject ranked relative to competitors on a test of sports trivia. This allowed Camerer and Lovallo to measure each prospective contestant's actual and perceived relative ability, and to see how these factors affected entry.

[2] A similar process where persons of similar ability tend to self-select into homogeneous groups without any central coordination can occur in the process of forming work teams, or even marriages. See the discussion of assortative matching and equilibrium team formation in Chapter 27.

[3] Notice that this benefit from allowing self-selection contrasts with the concerns about over-entry of low-ability workers raised by Lazear and Rosen (1981).

Camerer and Lovallo's (1999) results were dramatic. Not only were overconfident subjects more likely to enter the competition, *a large majority of their subjects were overconfident*. Although this may have been a consequence of their subject pool (some of whom were MBA students in a highly competitive program), it had important consequences: Entrants earned positive profits in only 3 out of 48 possible cases! In other words, high levels of overconfidence among business-oriented students at highly competitive U.S. universities led to dramatic rates of *over-entry* into competitive environments. Although there are a number of other important explanations for the high failure rate of new business ventures in all countries, Camerer and Lovallo suggest that systematic overconfidence may be a contributing factor.[4]

RESULT 23.2 **Evidence on Tournament Entry**

Available experimental results show that, consistent with the predictions in Result 23.1, people who have a high assessment of their own relative ability (i.e. "confident" and "overconfident" people) are more likely to enter tournaments. In all available studies, higher levels of risk aversion seem to deter tournament entry.

23.2 Gender, Confidence, and Competitiveness

Although women make up about 47% of the U.S. workforce, in 2015, they accounted for only 14.2% of the top five leadership positions in S&P 500 companies and only 4.8% of the CEOs.[5] Women are also highly underrepresented in top political positions in almost all nations. Although a large number of factors have been shown to contribute to this gap, one set of factors that has only recently received significant attention are the individual characteristics outlined in Result 23.1: tastes for competition, behavioral responses to competition, risk aversion, and confidence. Are there significant gender differences in these personal characteristics? If so, can they help explain why—even in societies where women have unprecedented economic freedoms compared to earlier generations—women remain highly underrepresented at the top ranks of highly competitive organizations?

[4] Students in Camerer and Lovallo's (1999) experiment overestimated their own relative ability even when they knew that all participants in the experiment had been informed that high performance on sports trivia would improve earnings in the experiment. This tendency to ignore the factors that led your competitors to enter a tournament is known as *reference group neglect* and could have important consequences in elimination tournaments. Specifically, if competitors fail to account for the fact that everyone who makes it to the same rank in an elimination tournament had to win all their previous rounds, they may incorrectly interpret their own wins as evidence they are likely to be better than their *current* opponent.

[5] Egan (2015).

Niederle and Vesterlund's Study: The Roles of Preferences and Confidence

In a highly cited early study of gender and self-selection into tournaments, Muriel Niederle and Lise Vesterlund (2007) conducted a real-effort laboratory experiment where groups of four students (always composed of two men and two women) add up sets of two-digit numbers. Although this is a mundane task, it suits the study well because output is easily measured, and men and women generally perform this task equally well. In Part 1 of the experiment, subjects were paid a simple piece rate of 50 cents per correct answer after a set amount of time had expired. Then they were told the number of correct questions they answered. This gave the subjects familiarity with the task and potentially allowed them to gauge how good they might be compared to others.

In Part 2 of the experiment, subjects competed in a tournament with the other three members of their group. This tournament was designed to yield exactly the same expected earnings as the piece rate if competitors are equally able (and therefore have a one-in-four chance of winning): The person with the most correct answers received \$2.00 *per correct answer*; the others got nothing. Again, after performing the task, the subjects were told only the number of questions they answered correctly—not whether they won. That information was only provided at the very end of the experiment, after all tasks had been completed.

Finally, in Part 3, the students worked again, but this time they were allowed to choose how they would be paid for their performance before starting to work: They could pick either the piece rate method used in Part 1 or the tournament method used in Part 2.[6] Here, the gender differences were dramatic: 73% of the men, but only 35% of women, chose the tournament.

What explains this difference? As we've already noted, actual performance in Part 1 was the same for men and women, so gender differences in ability can't explain men's higher rate of tournament entry. Indeed, because the genders were equally able, most of the men who chose to enter the tournament ended up losing money: They would have done better, given their ability, to choose the individual piece rate because their chances of winning the tournament were minimal. Could it be that, despite equal performance in Part 1, men *responded to* competition better than women to competition by raising their Part 2 performance? No, because the authors found essentially no performance differences for either gender between the piece rate and tournament. Could gender differences in risk aversion explain the result? As it turns out, gender differences in risk aversion have been measured in many studies, and although they exist, they are much too small to explain the dramatic tournament-entry gap in Niederle and Vesterlund's (2007) study.

If *actual* differences in ability at this task can't explain men's high tournament entry rates, what about differences in *perceived* ability, or "confidence"? To assess the effects of confidence, subjects were paid \$1 if they correctly predicted their

[6] To address the fact that members of a group will typically not all make the same choice, the performance of subjects who chose tournament pay in Part 3 was compared with the performance of their group members in Part 2, when all members of the group were competing against each other.

rank in the tournament. Interestingly, 75% of the men thought they were the best in their group of four (a mathematical absurdity), while 43% of women did. Thus, although both men and women were overconfident, men were much more overconfident. Further, the authors found that men's higher levels of overconfidence can statistically account for a substantial share of the gender gap in tournament entry in their study. Still, even when comparing equally confident men and women, men continued to enter the tournament more frequently. Niederle and Vesterlund (2007) attributed this remaining gap to gender differences in tastes for competition.

RESULT 23.3

Gender Differences in Tournament Entry in Niederle and Vesterlund's (2007) Experiment

When experimental subjects could choose between receiving an individual piece rate and entering a tournament of equal expected value, Niederle and Vesterlund (2007) found that men were much more likely than women to choose the tournament. This difference in behavior cannot be explained by gender differences in ability at the task, by gender differences in the response to competition, or by gender differences in risk aversion. Instead, the main factors accounting for the gap are (a) a much higher level of overconfidence among men in their own ability, and (b) a gender gap in tastes for competition.

What are the implications of Niederle and Vesterlund's (2007) results for human resources management? Although no HR decision should ever be based on the results of a single experiment on college students, the experiment does suggest that able women may disproportionately self-select out of tournament-based reward schemes; employers might want to consider this when deciding whether to use competitive pay schemes. Second, the experiment shows that the average college-age man is highly overconfident. At least in this experiment, these men would have made considerably more money if they based their decisions on more realistic (and more modest) assessments of their own ability. Whether such high levels of overconfidence hurt or help men more generally in their careers is an interesting question that deserves further study.[7]

Since Niederle and Vesterlund's (2007) study, a number of other authors have replicated and extended their main result. For example, Datta Gupta, Poulsen, and Villeval (2013) also find that men are more likely to choose tournament-based pay over a piece rate than women are. The authors were able to narrow this gap by raising the prize spread and by letting participants choose the gender of their competitors, but neither of these changes eliminated the gap. Interestingly, men's willingness to compete was accentuated even further if they knew they would be

[7] Although overconfidence hurt men financially in Niederle and Vesterlund's (2007) experiment, it is not at all clear that overconfidence is a liability in the broader labor market. For example, overconfidence can be helpful if it motivates higher effort levels, not just for the individual but teammates as well. Also, Heller (2014) provides an interesting example of why a risk-averse principal might prefer to hire overconfident agents.

Can Overconfidence Hurt Men? Evidence from the Stock Market

Theoretical models of the stock market predict that overconfident investors trade excessively—frequently changing the stocks in their portfolio because they believe they are "better than the market" at guessing which companies are likely to do well in the future. Psychological research also shows that, in areas like finance, men are more overconfident than women; thus, theory predicts that male investors should trade more excessively than women.

In a widely cited study, Barber and Odean (2001) tested this prediction using account data for over 35,000 households from a large discount brokerage. Focusing on common-stock investments, they found that men traded 45% more than women. Furthermore, they were able to estimate the effect of this gender difference in trading on the returns earned on the investments. Rather than increasing their returns (as it would if men's more frequent trading was driven by access to better information), trading *reduces* men's net returns by 2.65 percentage points a year as opposed to 1.72 percentage points for women. Thus, according to Barber and Odean, the stock market appears to be an environment where men's greater overconfidence actually harms them financially.

competing against a woman. Garratt, Weinberger, and Johnson (2013) studied athletes' choices in a charity road race in Santa Barbara—the *State Street Mile*—which gives participants the option to choose between two different levels of competition. Although women were again less likely to pick the higher level of competition, this difference was largely confined to older women. Highly qualified young women were not deterred from competition at all. Whether these young women will remain as interested in competition as they age is an interesting and important question.

Additional Evidence: The Roles of Biology and Culture

In a recent laboratory study, Wozniak, Harbaugh, and Mayr (2014) present some evidence suggesting that biology may also play a role in explaining gender differences in competitiveness. Motivated by a substantial literature showing that economic decisions are affected by hormones, and by the fact that both estrogen and progesterone fluctuate substantially and in a predictable way over the menstrual cycle, these authors asked whether women's preferences for competitive pay environments varied over their cycles. Consistent with other studies, the authors found that women on average were more reluctant to choose tournament-based pay than men. Most of this gap, however, comes from women who are in the low-hormone phase of their menstrual cycle. Women in the high-hormone phase were much more likely to compete than women in the low phase, but still not quite as likely as men.

In addition to identifying a possible role for biology, Wozniak et al. (2014) also identified a powerful role of *information* in explaining (and potentially eliminating) gender differences in competitiveness. Specifically, if both men and women have biased beliefs about their relative ability—with men being more overconfident than women—what would happen if we simply gave all workers accurate, objective feedback about their relative performance in previous competitions? If the experimental subjects treat this information seriously, it should eliminate the gender gap in confidence (because objective performance was the same, on average, for women and men) and eliminate the gender gap in tournament entry. Interestingly, that is exactly what happened: Simply providing a small amount of objective performance feedback eliminated even the large gender differences in competitiveness that were observed during the low-hormone phase of the menstrual cycle. This result may have interesting implications for companies' decisions to provide relative performance information to workers: Although this information can sometimes have negative consequences (see Barankay, 2012; and Charness, Masclet, and Villeval, 2014, in Section 21.3's discussion of intrinsic rewards), providing rank feedback can also encourage the efforts of talented, underconfident workers.

A final fascinating study of this question highlights the role of *culture* in accounting for gender gaps in competitiveness. Specifically, Gneezy, Leonard, and List (2009) studied gender differences in selecting into competitive environments across two distinct societies: the Maasai in Tanzania and the Khasi in India. Of these, the Maasai are considered a textbook example of a patriarchal society, whereas the Khasi are matrilineal.[8] These differences in how the societies are organized lead to large gender differences in power and decision-making across the two societies. For example, anthropologists interviewing Khasi men have been told "We are sick of playing the roles of breeding bulls and baby-sitters." Quotes from Maasai women included "Men treat us like donkeys."

The experimental task was to toss a tennis ball into a bucket that was 3 m away.[9] Participants were informed that they had 10 chances. All tasks were performed in a situation where only the experimenter and the subject could see the subject's performance. The *only* decision made by the subjects was whether he or she would be paid 20 rupees for every successful throw (i.e., a piece rate) or 60 rupees for every successful throw *if* he or she outperformed an anonymous, randomly selected person from their village (a tournament).[10] In the patriarchal society, Gneezy et al. (2009) observed similar results to those obtained from U.S. and European subjects: Maasai men chose to compete at roughly twice the rate as Maasai women. Fascinatingly, however, this result was reversed among the Khasi, where women choose the competitive environment more often than Khasi men. Because biological gender differences are the same in these two societies, Gneezy et al.'s (2009) experiment provides dramatic evidence that culture can have a large effect on which gender is the more competitive one. Because company cultures can vary a great deal, this suggests that changing corporate cultures might have dramatic effects on women's decisions to compete for higher ranked positions.

---

[8] In a matrilineal society, inheritance and clan membership follow the female lineage, from mothers to daughters. In the Khasi case, family life is organized around the mother's house, which is headed by the grandmother who lives with her unmarried daughters, her youngest daughter (even if she is married), and her youngest daughter's children. The youngest daughter never leaves and eventually becomes the head of the household; older daughters usually form separate households adjacent to their mother's household.

[9] Because neither male nor female subjects had any experience with this task, the authors expected no actual gender differences in actual task performance, and none were found in the experiment.

[10] Maasai participants received the equivalent amount in Tanzanian shillings.

RESULT 23.4

Biology, Information, Culture and the Gender Gap in Competitiveness

In a laboratory experiment, Wozniak et al. (2014) show that a substantial share of the gender gap in tournament entry comes from women who are in the low-hormone phase of their menstrual cycle. The same authors, however, show that even this "biologically based" gap can be eliminated by simply giving both men and women accurate feedback about their relative performance. Gneezy et al. (2009) show that women are more competitive than men in a matrilineal society. Together, these studies suggest that although biology may play a role, the gender gap in competitiveness is highly sensitive to contextual factors such as culture and information.

Gender Differences in the Response to Competitive Pressure: Evidence from the World's Most Competitive Exam

Although Niederle and Vesterlund (2007) found that neither men's nor women's task performance responded much to competition, a number of other, careful studies have observed such responses. For example, Gneezy, Niederle, and Rustichini (2003) found that increasing the competitiveness of a laboratory pay-for-performance task environment led to significant increases in men's performance but no change in women's. Gneezy and Rustichini (2004) found a similar effect in foot races involving 9- and 10-year-old Israeli schoolchildren: Boys' race times improved when they were running against someone else, although girls' times didn't change.

A particularly dramatic and consequential setting where such gender differences might matter, however, is in access to higher education. This is especially true in China, where graduating from a top university is seen as opening up a world of opportunities, and where admission to universities depends almost exclusively on a student's performance on a single, high-stakes test. Indeed, China's National College Entrance Exam (the *gaokao*), is widely regarded as "the world's most competitive exam."

In a recent paper, Cai, Lu, Pong, and Zhong (2016) use data from the *gaokao* to study whether men respond better to competitive pressure than women. To measure how students respond to pressure, the authors compare the students' performance on the actual exam to their performance on the low-stakes mock exam held 2 months earlier. Cai et al. find that compared to male students, females underperform on the high-stakes *gaokao*. In other words, comparing male and female students who performed equally on the low-stakes test, female students performed significantly worse on the actual *gaokao*. This gap is substantial: It reduces women's chances of qualifying for a Tier 1 university by 15%. The authors also show that (a) this gap is larger in subgroups of students where the stakes matter more; and (b) compared to males, females performed worse on the afternoon exam when they experienced a negative surprise in their morning performance. These additional results strengthen the case that gender differences in performance under pressure affect *gaokao* scores, with a quantitatively large impact on the share of women who win places in China's top tier universities.

Chapter Summary

- ☐ Consistent with simple theoretical predictions, all the available evidence suggests that workers who have a high assessment of their own relative ability are more likely to enter tournaments.
- ☐ This means that tournaments not only tend to attract abler workers, they also tend to attract overconfident workers. Because the average worker is somewhat overconfident, excessive tournament entry can sometimes occur (Camerer & Lovallo, 1999).
- ☐ There is considerable evidence that women are less likely to select tournament-based pay than equally capable men in Western societies. One important cause of this gap is a gender gap in confidence: Women are less (over)confident than men, on average.
- ☐ Although biological factors may also play a role, simple informational interventions (like objective performance feedback) and culture can eliminate and even reverse any biological differences that may exist.

Discussion Questions

1. Consider a simple task like hitting a target with a ball or answering movie trivia questions, and two identifiable groups in your classroom (men vs. women, tall vs. short, alphabetical order of the last name, etc.).[11] Design a simple experiment to (a) measure each person's assessment of relative ability at the task, (b) measure each person's actual ability, (c) measure the average level of overconfidence in the class, and (d) determine which of the two groups is more overconfident for this task.
2. Can you think of any tasks for which women might be more overconfident than men?
3. Could overconfidence ever be a beneficial trait? What might be some examples where overconfidence can lead to financial gains?

Suggestions for Further Reading

Are you interested in how to design tournaments to attract high-ability candidates? Commentators who lament the quality of teachers in some countries sometimes point to the very limited promotion opportunities in that profession—the ratio of principals to teachers is very low—as a possible cause. Others claim that higher

[11] In the economics profession, it has been shown that authors whose last name falls early in the alphabet tend to do better professionally. The most likely explanation is our profession's convention of always listing the authors of a paper in alphabetical order.

overall pay levels or greater meritocracy in *awarding* promotions play a more important role. Motivated by these questions, Morgan, Sisak, and Vardy (2012) theoretically model the ability of three features of promotion contests—the base wage, the number of promotion opportunities, and the role of merit (as opposed to factors like seniority or nepotism)—in awarding promotions. They find that higher levels of meritocracy always succeed in attracting more able candidates, although that is not necessarily true for higher base pay levels or increased promotion chances.

In other research on how men and women respond to competition, Lavy (2013) and Paserman (2010) study high school teachers and professional tennis players, respectively, and find little gender difference. Studies that focus on real-world academic settings show that men appear to outperform women when competitive pressures are higher, although the opposite is true in less competitive settings. See, for example, Azmat, Calsamiglia, and Iriberri (2014); Morin (2013); Ors, Palomino, and Peyrache (2013); Attali, Neeman, and Schlosser (2011); and Jurajda and Munich (2011).

References

Attali, Y., Neeman, Z., & Schlosser, A. (2011). *Rise to the challenge or not give a damn: Differential performance in high vs. low-stakes tests* (IZA Discussion Paper No. 5693). Bonn, Germany: Institute for the Study of Labor.

Azmat, G., Calsamiglia, C., & Iriberri, N. (2014). Gender difference in response to big stakes. *Journal of the European Economic Association, 14*(6), 1372–1400.

Barankay, I. (2012). *Rank incentives: Evidence from a randomized workplace experiment.* Unpublished manuscript, Management Department, The Wharton School of Business, University of Pennsylvania, Philadelphia, PA.

Barber, B. M., & Odean, T. (2001). Boys will be boys: Gender, overconfidence, and common stock investment. *Quarterly Journal of Economics, 116,* 261–292.

Cai, X., Lu, Y., Pan, J., & Zhong, S. (2016). *Gender gap under pressure: Evidence from China's National College Entrance Examination.* Unpublished manuscript, Department of Economics, National University of Singapore, Singapore.

Camerer, C., & Lovallo, D. (1999). Overconfidence and excess entry: An experimental approach. *American Economic Review, 89,* 306–318.

Charness, G., Masclet, D., & Villeval, M. C. (2014). The dark side of competition for status. *Management Science, 60,* 38–55.

Datta Gupta, N., Poulsen, A., & Villeval, M. C. (2013). Gender matching and competitiveness: Experimental evidence. *Economic Inquiry, 51,* 816–835.

Dohmen, T., & Falk, A. (2011). Performance pay and multidimensional sorting: Productivity, preferences, and gender. *American Economic Review, 101,* 556–590.

Egan, M. (2016). Still missing: Female business leaders. *CNNMoney*, March 25, 2015. Retrieved from http://money.cnn.com/2015/03/24/investing/female-ceo-pipeline-leadership/index.html

Eriksson, T., Teyssier, S., & Villeval, M. C. (2009). Self-selection and the efficiency of tournaments. *Economic Inquiry, 47,* 530–548.

Garratt, R. J., Weinberger, C., & Johnson, N. (2013). The state street mile: Age and gender differences in competition aversion in the field. *Economic Inquiry, 51,* 806–815.

Gneezy, U., & Rustichini, A. (2004). Gender and competition at a young age. *American Economic Review, 94,* 377–381.

Gneezy, U., Leonard, K. L., & List, J. A. (2009). Gender differences in competition: Evidence from a matrilineal and a patriarchal society. *Econometrica, 77,* 1637–1664.

Gneezy, U., Niederle, M., & Rustichini, A. (2003). Performance in competitive environments: Gender differences. *Quarterly Journal of Economics, 118,* 1049–1074.

Heller, Y. (2014). Overconfidence and diversification. *American Economic Journal: Microeconomics, 6*(1), 134–153.

Jurajda, S., & Munich, D. (2011). Gender gap in performance under competitive pressure: Admissions to Czech universities. *American Economic Review: Papers & Proceedings, 101,* 514–518.

Lavy, V. (2013). Gender differences in market competitiveness in a real workplace: Evidence from performance-based pay tournaments among teachers. *Economic Journal, 123,* 540–573.

Lazear, E., & Rosen, S. (1981). Rank-order tournaments as optimum labor contracts. *Journal of Political Economy, 89,* 841–864.

Leuven, E., Oosterbeek, H., Sonnemans, J., & van der Klaauw, B. (2011). Incentives versus sorting in tournaments: Evidence from a field experiment. *Journal of Labor Economics, 29,* 637–658.

Morgan, J., Sisak, D., & Vardy, F. (2012). *On the merits of meritocracy.* Unpublished manuscript, Department of Economics, University of California, Berkeley.

Morin, L. P. (2013). Do men and women respond differently to competition? Evidence from a major education reform. *Journal of Labor Economics*, *33*(2), 443–491.

Niederle, M., & Vesterlund, L. (2007). Do women shy away from competition? Do men compete too much? *Quarterly Journal of Economics, 122,* 1067–1101.

Ors, E., Palomino, F., & Peyrache, E. (2013). Performance gender gap: Does competition matter? *Journal of Labor Economics, 31,* 443–499.

Paserman, D. M. (2010). *Gender differences in performance in competitive environments? Evidence from professional tennis players.* Working Paper. Department of Economics, Boston University, Boston, MA.

Wozniak, D., Harbaugh, W. T., & Mayr, U. (2014). The menstrual cycle and performance feedback alter gender differences in competitive choices. *Journal of Labor Economics, 32,* 161–198.

Part 5
The Economics of Teams

Imagine yourself as an instructor in a university course. You have decided to give an assignment to your class, which involves writing a research report. One way to organize this project is to ask each student to work independently and submit his or her own paper for grading. Another approach is to put the students into groups and require each group submit a joint report. Your objective is to maximize the total amount of learning that occurs. Although your students like to learn, you believe that they will be more motivated when they know that their successful efforts will be rewarded with a higher grade. What should you do?

Whenever a group of people (whether students, workers, or friends) works together on a project whose result depends on the efforts of all the group's members, personnel economists consider that a *team production* problem. When the reward received by individual team members (in the preceding example, the grade) depends—at least in part—on the *entire* team's performance, *team-based pay,* or *team-based rewards* are said to exist. Examples of team production include team sports, workplace teams, clubs, co-authorships, movie crews, and even couples or families. In most of these situations, team-based rewards also exist. Teams are fundamentally different from the tournaments we studied in the last part of the book because they are *cooperative* rather than competitive in the following sense:

In a tournament, having a hard-working or very able co-worker makes you worse off. In a team, as we'll see, workers generally *benefit* from having abler and harder working teammates.

In this part of the book, we'll study the two main questions in personnel economics—how to motivate and how to select workers—in the twin contexts of team production and team pay. We'll also suggest some answers to the instructor's dilemma described previously: What are the advantages and disadvantages of team pay and production, and under what circumstances might a team-based rewards system work better or worse than an individualized system? As we'll see, these circumstances depend (among other things) on whether there are substantial ability differences among the team members and on the nature of the team production process.

One key disadvantage of team-based rewards is their potential to induce *free-riding* among team members. Free-riding, or the "*1/N*" problem, refers to the fact that under many team-based reward schemes, group members may not fully take into account the benefits that their own high effort levels would generate for their co-workers. This leads group members to select inefficiently low effort levels. On the other hand, we'll identify important benefits of group production, including the opportunity for workers with different skills and strengths to specialize in the tasks they do best, to share useful information, and to help each other. Perhaps more surprising, we'll see that team-based pay creates monetary *incentives* for workers to engage in all these collaborative activities. Another advantage of team-based pay is that—like tournaments—it can also reduce the amount of monitoring and performance measurement the principal needs to do, for two main reasons. First, under team pay, team members have an incentive to "do the principal's job" by monitoring and disciplining *each other.* Second, if only each group's total output needs to be measured, bundling workers into groups means that the principal doesn't need to make as many assessments. In our example of the course instructor, choosing a group assignment reduces the number of papers that have to be graded.

Finally, we'll study worker *selection* into team-based production environments. In this regard, we'll show that there is a lot of wisdom in Groucho Marx's famous dictum, "I refuse to join any club that would have me as a member." Put another way, teams looking to add new members must cope with the fact that the people who most want to join will typically be less able than the team's current members. This *adverse self-selection into teams* contrasts starkly with the positive self-selection we observed in tournaments, where people with high (actual or perceived) ability are more prone to enter competitions. Closely related, when workers are allowed to self-sort into teams, there will be a tendency for the "best to pair with the best"—a form of *assortative matching* that has also been studied in marriage markets. Whether this type of team formation is in the employer's interests depends very much on the nature of its production process. For example, if you, as an instructor, want to maximize the amount of learning that occurs, you might prefer to match the best-prepared students with the least-prepared. On the other hand, if your goal is to produce a single superstar paper, you may want to match "the best with the best."

Incentives in Teams and the Free-Rider Problem

24

In this chapter we introduce our study of teams in the workplace by constructing a simple mathematical model of *team production* and *team-based pay*. Although paying a group of workers as a team may foster cooperation that can benefit a workplace, this payment scheme also has a fundamental drawback: *the free-rider problem*. If you've ever played on a sports team or worked a school group project where one person seems to hardly try at all, you've experienced this problem first hand. In the context of a workplace, this problem is caused because workers who produce additional financial value for the team do not reap the full benefits of their efforts: Effort costs are borne by the individual, but the rewards are shared by all. Although this problem can be difficult to solve, we will learn that under certain circumstances, carefully designed team incentives can eliminate the free-rider problem and restore economic efficiency.

24.1 Structure of the Team Production Problem

Imagine a group of N workers who are working together to produce a joint product. This product can be almost anything—for example, a written report, a meal served to a restaurant customer, a movie, the amount and quality of steel that rolls off a production line, or a comfortable and timely airline flight between two cities. For the sake of argument, imagine that we can summarize the output produced by this group of workers by a single number, Q. As we did in the basic principal–agent problem, we'll think of Q as the *net revenues* produced by this group of workers, which depend on both the quality and quantity of the goods or services they produce in a given period of time.[1]

[1] As before, Q is net of all costs, including materials and overhead, *except* payments to the workers themselves.

In Chapter 12, we used a powerful tool—the production function—to describe how a firm's output depends on the amount and quality of inputs that it hires. In this part of the book, we'll use a production function to describe the relationship between the *effort* levels of all the workers in a group and the group's total output. Specifically, we'll assume that Q is given by

$$Q = F(E_1, E_2, E_3, \ldots, E_N), \quad \textbf{(24.1)}$$

where E_i is the effort of group member i, and F is the production function.

DEFINITION 24.1 **Team production** occurs whenever a group of workers produces a product, Q, whose value depends on the effort levels of all the group's members. Mathematically, this relationship is described by a **production function**, as in Equation 24.1.

As we discussed in Chapter 12, production functions can take a variety of forms depending on the nature of the production process. For example, if two group members work independently (e.g., each serving different customers in a call center), then the most appropriate production function is a *linear production function*:

$$Q = d_1E_1 + d_2E_2, \quad \textbf{(24.2)}$$

where Q is the total output produced by the group, and d_i is the *ability* of group member i. As we noted when we introduced this function in Equation 12.1, in a linear production function, *neither worker's productivity depends on how hard the colleague works.* We'll explore other types of team production functions later in this chapter.

Given that a group of workers is engaged in team production, how might those workers be compensated? In some situations, it might be possible to pay each team member according to individual effort, or on personal "contribution" to the group's overall performance. For example, if an employer can measure E_1 and E_2, the employer could announce that the two members of a team will be paid according to the reward schedules $Y_1 = a_1 + b_1E_1$ and $Y_2 = a_2 + b_2E_2$. If so, we could think of E_1 and E_2 as the observable "outputs" of the two workers, and apply all the reasoning and mathematics we developed in Part 1 of the book. Putting this a little more formally is Result 24.1.

RESULT 24.1 **Team Production when Each Agent's Effort, E, Is Contractible**

If the pay of each member of a team can be linked to that individual's own effort or "contribution" to the group, incentivizing workers in teams poses no special theoretical problems relative to incentivizing individual workers. The optimal contract simply links each person's pay, Y_i, to individual effort, E_i. By appropriately linking each person's own pay to member's efforts via piece rates like those derived in Part 1, rational, self-interested team members can theoretically be induced to supply socially efficient effort levels.

Although Result 24.1 provides a useful point of departure for our study of teams, it assumes away one of the key challenges in motivating teams of workers: In many, if not most, cases, the only available (or the only *contractible*) performance measure on which the group members' pay can be based is the output of the entire group, Q. For example, in the classroom assignment discussed in Part 5's Introduction, the instructor typically only observes the quality of the assignment that is ultimately handed in. The instructor has no way of knowing which of the group members did most or all of the work and has no choice but to assign the same grade to all the members. When economists (unlike many other researchers) publish papers, it is traditional to list all the authors in alphabetical order, regardless of which one did most of the work. Thus readers (who "reward" authors by citing their papers) also see only the group's total output. At higher levels of an organization, the head office may need to allocate resources (and rewards) to different divisions without having any knowledge of which executives in each unit were the key to success or failure. All of these situations are cases of *team-based pay*:

DEFINITION 24.2 **Team-based pay** refers to a situation where the pay of the individual members of a work group depends, at least in part, on the performance of the *entire team*. Pay schemes that are **purely team based** link each member's pay *only* to the group's overall performance. Thus, they take the form

$$Y_1 = R_1(Q),\ Y_2 = R_2(Q),\ \ldots,\ Y_N = R_N(Q), \quad \textbf{(24.3)}$$

where R_i is a function stipulating team member i's pay as a function of the entire group's output, Q.

In view of Result 24.1, we will restrict our attention in this chapter to *purely* team-based pay schemes. This allows us to focus on the special problems inherent in incentivizing workers in teams, where it's often hard to separately assess the members' contributions. In doing so, it's important to note that some of these problems can be mitigated by combining team incentives with individual incentives like those we studied in Parts 1 through 4.

Just as a group's production function can take a variety of forms, a principal might consider using different types of team-based pay schemes. For example, one widely used group pay scheme is the *equal-sharing rule*:

$$Y_1 = Y_2 = Y_3 = \ldots = Y_N = Q/N. \quad \textbf{(24.4)}$$

Under an equal-sharing rule, the total output, Q, produced by the entire group is shared equally among all the members, regardless of what Q turns out to be, and regardless of which members worked the hardest. This would be the case, for example, if all the wait staff at a coffee shop divided the contents of the tip jar equally.

Even if each individual's pay can only depend on the group's total output, it does not follow that all the group members must be paid the same. For example, a principal (or the group of workers themselves) could decide to use a more general *sharing rule* of the form

$$Y_i = \alpha_i Q,\ i = 1, 2, \ldots, N, \tag{24.5}$$

where $\sum_{i=1}^{N} \alpha_i = 1$. Thus, a *sharing rule* divides the group's output among the workers, but not necessarily in equal shares. For example, the shift supervisor might receive a larger share of the day's tips than the other employees, perhaps because that person is in a position with more responsibilities.

Team-based pay schemes don't have to be strictly proportional to output, either. For example, each team member could face the same pay scheme given by

$$Y_1 = Y_2 = Y_3 = \ldots = Y_N = a + bQ. \tag{24.6}$$

Equation 24.6 describes a *group piece rate* (with intercept a and slope b) that links *each worker's* pay to the *group's* output. Unlike a sharing rule, however, a group piece rate can have a non-zero intercept, a.

Team-based pay schedules don't even have to be linear. For example, a common nonlinear team-based pay scheme is a team bonus. For example, the following pay scheme

$$\begin{aligned} Y_1 = Y_2 = Y_3 = \ldots = Y_N &= a \text{ if } Q < Q_{min} \\ Y_1 = Y_2 = Y_3 = \ldots = Y_N &= a + B \text{ if } Q \geq Q_{min} \end{aligned} \tag{24.7}$$

pays every member of the group an amount, a, regardless of whether the group attains its production target, Q_{min}. If the group meets or exceeds the target, every member receives an additional bonus, B.

A final important distinction among group pay schemes refers to the sense in which they balance the group's budget. Specifically, we can design pay schemes that guarantee the budget will be balanced regardless of how the group performs or that will only balance the budget in a more limited set of circumstances:

DEFINITION 24.3

A team-based pay scheme is said to satisfy **strong budget balancing** if it guarantees that the total amount paid to all the team members, $\sum_{i=1}^{N} Y_i$, equals the total amount produced by the group, Q, *for all possible values of* Q. In other words, regardless of how much output is produced by the team, the pay scheme automatically divides all of that output (and no more *or* less) between the team members.

A team-based pay scheme satisfies **weak budget balancing** if it guarantees that the total amount paid to all the team members, $\sum_{i=1}^{N} Y_i$, equals the total amount produced by the group, Q, *for at least one possible value of* Q. The weakly balanced schemes we will study are typically designed to "balance out" at a level of output that the group (or a principal) would like to achieve, for example, the economically efficient level.

By construction, any sharing rule (whether equal or not) satisfies strong budget balancing. The two remaining team pay schemes discussed previously (group piece rates with $a \neq 0$ and team bonuses) cannot satisfy strong budget balancing. To see this, suppose that a team facing a group piece rate with $a > 0$ failed to produce any output, that is, $Q = 0$. (Perhaps they didn't win the contract to build 100 aircraft.) According to the compensation rule in Equation 24.6 they would—perhaps very reasonably—still be paid a positive amount for their efforts. Or, suppose a work group exceeded its target output for the group bonus described in Equation 24.7. If this bonus was designed so that the budget balances when workers achieve the goal (i.e., if $a + B = Q_{min}$), any work group that exceeds its output target will be paid strictly less than it produces.

In sum, team-based pay schemes can take a variety of forms. Indeed, it's not hard to think of additional pay schemes that combine two or more of the features described previously, and a number of such "hybrid" schemes are sometimes used in the real world. In the next few sections, however, we'll focus on the four schemes described previously—sharing rules (both equal and unequal), linear piece rates, and group bonuses—and assess their potential to elicit efficient effort levels from a group of agents.

24.2 Efficiency: Which Effort Levels Maximize the Size of the Pie?

To assess the performance of the various types of team-based pay, it's helpful to first establish a standard against which we can compare them. As in previous parts of the book, we'll use economic efficiency as our criterion. Therefore, to assess how "good" a pay scheme is, we'll just add together the well-being of all the parties involved. In the case of team production, this amounts to adding up the utilities of all the team's members.[2] So, to establish a standard, this section asks, "If we could somehow make every team member pick the exact effort level we wanted, what effort levels would we assign to maximize the sum of the agents' utilities?"

To keep the mathematics as simple as possible, we'll assume until further notice that there are N agents who do not interact in production and are all equally able. Therefore the baseline production function in this part of the book is given by

$$Q = E_1 + E_2 + E_3 + \ldots + E_N. \quad \textbf{(24.8)}$$

[2] Notice that in our most basic model of team production, *there is no principal*: The contract (i.e., the pay scheme) is just an agreement among all the agents about how to share the fruits of their labors. As we move through Part 5 of this book, however, we'll eventually identify six different reasons why a team of agents might, in fact, want to designate a special person as a principal, boss, or manager and give them special responsibilities (see Section 26.3 for a summary). Doing so helps us think more clearly about precisely "what do bosses do?" in organizations, and how their most important functions might differ depending on the type of work environment being considered.

We also assume that all of the agents have the same, baseline utility function we defined in Chapter 1, that is, that $U_i = Y_i - V(E_i) = Y_i - E_i^2/2$, where Y_i is worker *i*'s total pay. Together, the production function in Equation 24.8 and this baseline utility function will serve as our base-case model of team production.

In this base-case model, the sum of all the workers' utilities is

$$W = \sum_{i=1}^{N} [Y_i - V(E_i)] = \sum_{i=1}^{N} Y_i - \sum_{i=1}^{N} V(E_i). \tag{24.9}$$

Next, assume that the total amount the agents are paid must add up to the total amount of output that is produced, that is, that

$$\sum_{i=1}^{N} Y_i = Q. \tag{24.10}$$

Substituting Equations 24.10 and 24.8 into Equation 24.9 means that the sum of workers' utilities can be written as

$$W = \sum_{i=1}^{N} U_i = [E_1 - E_1^2/2] + [E_2 - E_2^2/2] + \ldots + [E_N - E_N^2/2]. \tag{24.11}$$

Which effort levels make W as large as possible? According to Equation 24.11, Worker 1's effort should make $E_1 - E_1^2/2$ as large as possible, Worker 2's effort should make $E_2 - E_2^2/2$ as large as possible, and so on. From Chapter 2 (or directly by finding the level of E_i that maximizes $E_i - E_i^2/2$), this means that the socially optimal level of effort is given by $E_i = 1$ for every worker.

RESULT 24.2

Economically Efficient Effort Levels in Team Production (Base Case)

Under our *base-case assumptions* for team production ($Q = E_1 + E_2 + E_3 + \ldots + E_N$, and $U_i = Y_i - E_i^2/2$), the socially optimal level of effort for every member of the group satisfies $\mathbf{E_i = 1}$. In other words, if the workers want to maximize the sum of their utilities, each worker should contribute exactly one unit of effort.

If Result 24.2 describes what a reasonable group of workers would want every member of the group to do, how does this compare to what we would expect an economically rational group of workers to do under various team-based pay schemes? We turn to this question in Section 24.3.

24.3 Sharing Rules and the Free-Rider (1/*N*) Problem

In this section, we derive the effort levels we'd expect a team of workers to select if they were paid according to a sharing rule. Recall that under a sharing rule (as defined in Equation 24.5), each team member's pay depends only on the entire group's output via a compensation function, $Y_i = \alpha_i Q$, where α_i is Worker *i*'s share of the group's output, and all the shares add up to one. For most of this section, we'll focus on the equal-sharing rule, $Y_i = Q/N$, where N is the number of members in the team (defined in Equation 24.4), but we'll consider unequal sharing rules toward the end of the section. Finally, recall that by construction, all sharing rules satisfy strong budget balancing (see Definition 24.3).

To work out how we expect team members to behave under an equal-sharing rule, imagine for simplicity that the team members cannot communicate when making their effort decisions, and that they know they will never interact with each other again. (We'll discuss what happens when these things change later.) So that we can make comparisons, we'll continue to use the "base-case" assumptions of the previous section. Because all the workers face exactly the same decision, we'll focus on "Worker 1's" decision, then apply the result to all the other workers.

Substituting the production function (Equation 24.8) into the compensation function (Equation 24.4), then substituting the compensation function into the utility function ($U_i = Y_i - E_i^2/2$), we can express Worker 1's utility as a function of all the workers' efforts as

$$U_1 = (E_1 + E_2 + \ldots + E_N)/N - E_1^2/2 =$$

$$E_1/N - E_1^2/2 + (E_2 + \ldots + E_N)/N. \quad \textbf{(24.12)}$$

Because Worker 1 has no control over the other workers' decisions, all Worker 1 can do is to select the effort, E_1, to maximize utility, taking the other workers' efforts as given. Thus, Worker 1 should select E_1 to maximize $E_1/N - E_1^2/2$. Using our usual methods, the solution is given by $E_1{}^* = 1/N$. By symmetry, all the other workers will face the same cost–benefit trade-off and make the same decision.

☑ RESULT 24.3

Equilibrium Effort Levels under an Equal-Sharing Rule (Base Case)

Under our base-case assumptions for team production, the *actual* effort levels that would be selected by rational, self-interested workers who are paid according to an equal sharing rule are given by $\mathbf{E_i = 1/N}$, where N is the number of workers on the team.

Thus, if there are 5 workers on a team, each will supply one-fifth of a unit of effort, and the entire team will produce only a single unit of output. This contrasts with the socially efficient levels of effort, which are 1 for each worker. If the workers could somehow agree to all "just do the right thing," the team as a whole would produce 5 units of output instead of the single unit induced by the equal-sharing rule. To see the intuition behind Result 24.3, consider what happens to the group's output, Q, and to Worker i's pay, when Worker i chooses to raise the effort level by a small amount, holding all the other workers' efforts fixed. When Worker i produces \$1 more of net revenues, the group's total output rises by \$1. Under an equal-sharing rule, however, Worker i's own pay, however, only rises by \$1/5 or 20 cents. Thus, $(N - 1)/N = 80\%$ of Worker i's additional output is paid not to Worker i, but to teammates. Unless Worker i cares about the teammates' utility, Worker i will thus select an effort level as if facing a flat tax of 80% on everything that worker produces.

DEFINITION 24.4 **The free-rider problem** refers to the fact that whenever the members of a group are paid according to an equal-sharing rule, each member only receives 1/Nth of the marginal financial benefit that member creates for the group by working a little harder. Thus, although all members of the group would *like* their teammates to work harder, all economically rational team members will ignore the benefits their efforts bestow on their colleagues. As a result, the entire group is predicted to choose inefficiently low levels of effort and output.

Result 24.3 implies that the severity of the free-rider problem increases with the number of group members, N. In a group of two workers under an equal-sharing rule, each worker still receives 50 cents out of each extra dollar earned for the group. In a group of 100 workers, each worker only gets a penny. This has an important implication for the incentive effects of company-wide bonuses and profit-sharing schemes. Although these schemes are sometimes argued to

Free-Riding, Public Goods, and the Environment

Although we have developed our model of free-riding in the context of a work group, the free-rider problem is much more general than that. Indeed it applies to a wide variety of situations where what is best for an individual member of a group is not best for the group as a whole. One example where we can use our formal model almost exactly as it stands is the case of pollution.

To see this, imagine a group of N identical homeowners around a lake, each of whom benefits equally from being able to swim and fish in a clean lake. Denote the quality of the lake by Q. Each house discharges liquid waste that eventually makes its way into the lake, but that can be abated by each homeowner at a cost, $V(E_i)$, where E_i is the dollar amount invested in abatement by household i. If $Q(E_1, E_2 \ldots, E_N)$ is the production function for lake quality, the sum of the households' utilities is given by $NQ(E_1, E_2, \ldots, E_N) - \sum_{i=1}^{N} V(E_i)$. (Remember that *every* homeowner gets a benefit of Q from being able to enjoy a clean lake.) Maximizing this sum using our baseline production and cost-of-effort functions implies an economically efficient abatement investment of $E = N$ for every homeowner.

If Homeowner 1 is selfish, however, without an enforceable agreement among the residents he will choose E_1 to maximize $Q(E_1, E_2, \ldots, E_N) - V(E_i)$, which means he'll pick $E_1 = 1$. Thus, as in our group-pay example with an equal-sharing rule, selfish individuals will contribute $1/N$ as much as they should toward a common goal. Here, the free-riding problem results not from a particular reward-sharing rule that the group has chosen but from the simple fact that a clean environment is a *public good* from which all group members benefit. In general, rational, selfish individuals will make suboptimal voluntary contributions to public goods because the benefit of contributing is shared by all while the costs are borne by each individual.

incentivize workers, the simple mathematics of team-based pay suggests that any such incentive effects are likely to be miniscule. Consider, for example, a company with 10,000 production workers whose production function is given by $Q = \sum_{i=1}^{10,000} E_i$. An incentive plan that distributed the net revenues produced by this group equally among its members would give each worker one penny for every $100 of value created, for an effective tax rate of 99.99%. This is a very weak financial incentive to work hard.[3]

Although the case of a few homeowners around a lake may seem unimportant, exactly the same model applies to nations' investments in reducing greenhouse gas emissions into the atmosphere, or to nations' efforts to reduce overfishing in the world's oceans. Another application is to charitable contributions: Whenever a musician "passes the hat" after a performance, when National Public Radio solicits contributions, or when a church collects money from its members, the members are in a situation where they want others to contribute (because they value the service) but would rather not contribute themselves. All of these situations induce a temptation to free-ride which, in turn, can lead to underprovision of a good that everyone values. One solution to this problem, of course, is compulsory taxation to fund important public goods like police, roads, bridges, and national defense. Of course, because work effort is harder to measure than cash contributions, this solution is not really available for workplace teams.

Having demonstrated that equal-sharing rules lead to free-riding, we now turn to the case of unequal sharing rules of the form $Y_i = \alpha_i Q$, where $\sum_{i=1}^{N} \alpha_i = 1$. At first glance, this might seem like a way out of the free-riding dilemma: After all, isn't the main problem with the equal-sharing rule the fact that everyone receives the same share of the pie regardless of how hard they work? Re-doing the math underlying Result 24.3, however, shows that this is not the case.

RESULT 24.4

Equilibrium Effort Levels under an Unequal-Sharing Rule (Base Case)

Under our base-case assumptions for team production, the effort levels that would be selected by rational, self-interested workers who are paid according to an unequal-sharing rule, $Y_i = \alpha_i Q$, are given by $\mathbf{E}_i = \alpha_i$. Because $\sum_{i=1}^{N} \alpha_i = 1$, it follows that the team as a whole will produce just one unit of output, which is the same as under the equal-sharing rule.

Results 24.3 and 24.4 together imply that any sharing rule, whether equal or not—in other words, any group pay scheme that satisfies strong budget balancing—creates a "1/N" or "free-riding" problem in group production. In sum,

[3] That said, Carpenter, Robbett, and Akbar (2016) suggest an alternative way that company-wide profit-sharing plans could be effective: Even though these plans may be ineffective in raising workers' effort levels directly, they may provide enough of an incentive for people to *report their co-workers for shirking*. This underscores the important point that team incentives not only have direct effects on effort but also incentivize workers to monitor each other.

The Unscrupulous Diner's Dilemma: Free-Riding at Lunch

A question that often comes up when a group of people eat out together is how to settle the bill: Should all diners pay the costs of their own meals, or should the group just divide the total bill equally? Because dividing the bill equally is a kind of equal sharing rule, it can also induce a sort of free-riding. To see this, let $B(F_i)$ be Diner *i*'s benefit (taste, nutrition, etc.) from consuming F_i dollars of restaurant food. If each individual pays for her or his own meal, each will choose F_i to maximize $B(F_i) - F_i$. Assuming diners get diminishing marginal benefits from additional food ($B'' < 0$), each diner will set $B'(F_i) = 1$, and this will be economically efficient because each person fully internalizes the cost of their own food consumption. If we introduce equal sharing of the bill, each diner will choose F_i to maximize $F_i - \frac{\sum_{i=1}^{N} F_i}{N}$. Each diner will therefore set $B'(F_i) = 1/N$ and eat more (because of the diminishing marginal benefits from food). After all, under the equal-pay rule, the marginal cost to Diner *i* of ordering a \$10 dessert in a group of 8 diners is only \$1.25! Thus, we might expect diners to order (inefficiently) more food if they know the bill will be shared equally.

To test this prediction, Uri Gneezy, Ernan Haruvy, and Hadas Yafe (2004) paid Israeli university students to have lunch together at a restaurant near the Technion University campus in Haifa, Israel. Groups of six students were invited to appear at the restaurant just before lunch. Each group consisted of three men and three women; the authors tried to ensure that no group members knew each other before the experiment. On arrival, all participants received a set of written instructions and were told that the experimenters would pay them 80 NIS (or about \$20 U.S. at the time) for participating. All subjects were asked to maintain strict silence while they read the instructions and filled out a written questionnaire. All were informed that they would be asked to write down their order from the restaurant menu during the last part of the silent period. The only difference between the groups was that some groups were told they would each pay for their own meal, while others were told that the bill would be shared equally among the six diners.

Consistent with the theory of free-riding, subjects ordered more food under the even-split treatment than the individual-pay treatment. Although the difference in the average number of items ordered was quite small (1.87 vs. 1.67), the difference in the amount spent by each diner was considerable (50.9 vs. 37.3 NIS, or about U.S. \$12.73 vs. \$9.33 at the time). Thus, subjects spent about 36% more money under the even-split treatment. Importantly, in other parts of the experiment where subjects where given a choice between the individual- and equal-pay systems, a large majority selected individual pay, suggesting that the equal-pay system was economically inefficient—it made most group members worse off.

compared to the equal-sharing rule, unequal-sharing rules can only reallocate effort among team members; they cannot raise the total amount of effort.

As we'll see in the next section, the source of free-riding isn't the equality in the sharing rule but the strong budget balancing associated with the use of any sharing rule. Perhaps paradoxically, the "fiscally responsible" approach of ensuring that the group's budget will balance "no matter what" blunts incentives and leads to free-riding.

We conclude this section by discussing how things change when we move beyond the very specific set of assumptions we've used to model effort choices in teams so far. Although the exact optimal and equilibrium effort levels ($E = 1$ and $E = 1/N$, respectively) will of course change, we first note that Result 24.4—that any sharing rule leads to free-riding—generalizes to any cost-of-effort function, $V(E)$, that generates finite levels of effort. It also generalizes to most realistic production functions, with an important proviso: Any production function in which the team members' marginal products depend on each other's efforts—which includes most realistic team production functions—introduce a strategic element to agents' behavior: In these cases, each agent's privately optimal effort choice now depends on how hard she expects her teammates to work.[4] As we'll see in Chapter 26, predicting workers' behavior in these situations is trickier, but—unless workers' efforts are highly complementary—agents should again select inefficiently low effort levels under any sharing rule. Chapter 26 will also explore how our basic results change when we allow team members to communicate when making effort choices and when there are ability differences between workers. Interestingly, in contrast to tournaments, ability differences are often helpful in a team setting.

Finally, how do the results change when we allow for repeated interactions among team members, rather than the "one-shot" interaction we studied here? Although people might act differently in reality, it may be surprising to note that our baseline model's prediction that free-riding will occur does not change as long as rational agents know they will interact a fixed, finite number of times.[5] When agents do not know how many times they will interact in the future, rational agents who are harmed by their co-workers' free-riding in one interaction may sometimes find it optimal to punish their co-workers by shirking themselves. These dynamic interactions between team members can sometimes be effectively used to prevent free-riding. We'll study some of these processes in Chapter 25.

24.4 Group Piece Rates, Group Bonuses, and Free-Riding in Teams

In the last section, we showed that *any* sharing rule—whether equal or not—should lead rational, selfish team members to free-ride. In this section, we consider two other group pay schemes—group piece rates and group bonuses—and

[4] Put another way, when the team production function is given by Equation 24.8, and agents are paid according to a proportional sharing rule like Equation 24.5, each agent's privately optimal effort choice is a *dominant strategy.* Thus, the linear production function assumption in teams plays the same role as the *uniform relative luck* assumption in tournaments, which we used in Part 4 of the book to simplify the agents' choice problem.

[5] The easiest way to see this is to reduce the worker's decision to a binary one ("work" vs. "shirk") as we did in Chapter 6. Then the team members' effort choice problem becomes a simple *prisoner's dilemma* game. There is a large literature on prisoner's dilemma games, with many established results including the fact that shirking is the only subgame perfect equilibrium in a finitely repeated prisoner's dilemma. For additional information, consult an introductory game theory textbook, such as Spaniel (2011) and the accompanying YouTube videos.

show that in contrast, these schemes *can* prevent free-riding if they are correctly designed. Perhaps surprisingly, this is precisely because—unlike sharing rules—these schemes do not satisfy strong budget balancing. Thus, *abandoning* the "fiscally conservative" approach that ensures the budget will be balanced *no matter how the group performs* can dramatically improve incentives and economic efficiency. Interestingly, this creates the potential for one team member to assume a special role of *promising to absorb the group's shortfalls and surpluses.* This special team member might be considered the team's "manager" or "principal." This "budget-breaking" role is the first of *six leadership functions* we shall identify in this part for why teams can benefit from appointing a manager. Deriving these distinct functions of leadership from first principles (as we do here) helps us think a bit more clearly about their role in organizations.

Group Piece Rates

In the last section, each individual's pay was assumed to be $Y_i = Q/N$, or $Y_i = \alpha_i Q$. But these sharing rules are just special cases (without an intercept) of a linear reward schedule based on the *group's* output, $Y_i = a_i + b_i Q$, that is, of a group piece rate system. (Notice that in a group piece rate scheme, each team member could in principle have a different pay intercept a_i, and a different slope term b_i.) Using our baseline production and effort-cost functions, Worker 1's utility under a group piece rate is just

$$U_1 = a_1 + b_1(E_1 + E_2 + \dots + E_N) - E_1^2/2. \qquad \textbf{(24.13)}$$

Maximizing Equation 24.13 with respect to E_1 yields a utility-maximizing effort level of $E_1{*} = b_1$.

Can a group piece rate scheme be designed so as to eliminate free-riding, that is, to induce each team member to pick the socially efficient effort level of $E_i{*}$? Of course! The mathematics of the problem says that all we need to do is to set $b_i = 1$ for every team member. In other words, the group piece rate must ensure that *each* team member's own pay must increase by \$1 for every \$1 increase in the *entire group's* output. Of course, a pay scheme of this form $Y_i = a_i + Q$ cannot possibly satisfy the group budget constraint, $\sum_{i=1}^{N} Y_i = Q$, for all potential values of Q, because under this scheme, total payments to workers will rise by N dollars for every extra dollar of the team's total output. If there were three workers, for example, an efficient team piece rate would require paying out \$3 (\$1 to each worker) for each additional dollar's worth of output produced by the group.

Are efficient team piece rates, therefore, totally impractical, and will they always result in massive losses for a team or team leader who uses them? Actually they will not. To see this, imagine that a principal (or the team as a whole) first designates a desired target output M. For the sake of argument, let's set this target equal to the socially efficient group output, which is given by $M = N$ (the number of group members) under our baseline assumptions. Now, impose the following group pay scheme: If the group's total output equals M (the efficient level where every worker contributes one unit of effort), each worker is paid an equal share of the team's output (i.e., \$1), and the team just breaks even. If total output is \$1 short of M, however, then the principal will cut *every* worker's pay by \$1 and keep the difference. For a \$2 shortfall, each member is docked \$2, and so on. As a result, the level of a (each person's compensation if the group's output turns out to be *zero*) will in general be a large negative number. On the other hand, for every dollar that the group's output exceeds M, the principal promises to pay every worker an extra \$1, *losing* \$$N$ − \$1 in the process. Mathematically, this contract has the form

$$Y_i = 1 + (Q - M) = -(M - 1) + Q. \qquad \textbf{(24.14)}$$

Thus, it is a linear group piece rate with intercept $-(M - 1)$ and a slope of 1, where M is the target level of the group's output.

Will this contract work? As long as every team member believes the principal will honor the preceding contract, every team member should work *exactly* the efficient amount and the principal will just break even. For example, suppose $N = 5$. Actual group output under an equal-sharing rule equals 1, with each member setting effort = 1/5. To induce social efficiency, however, the principal sets a target group output of 5 (the efficient level). If that target is exactly attained, each team member is paid \$1, so the group just breaks even. For every \$1 the group's output deviates from 5 (whether up or down), each team member's pay changes by \$1. Applying Equation 24.14, this pay scheme is just $Y_i = -4 + Q$, with a piece rate, $b = 1$, for every agent. To ensure that the group's budget balances when each worker "does his part," the group needs to charge an admission fee of \$4. Figure 24.1 illustrates the old (budget-balancing) and new (budget-breaking) contracts diagrammatically.

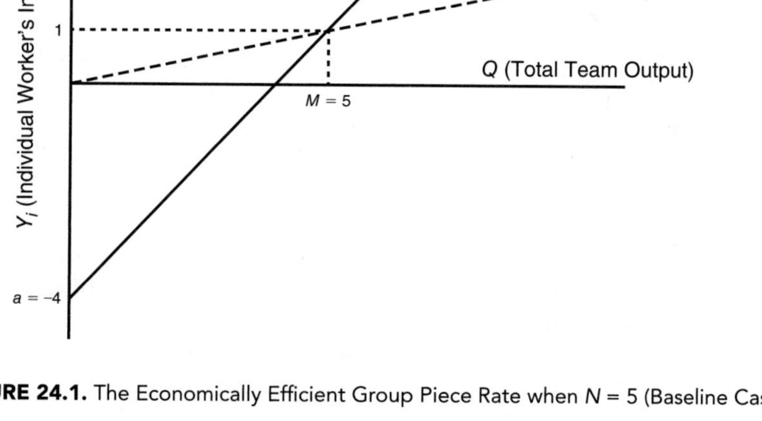

FIGURE 24.1. The Economically Efficient Group Piece Rate when $N = 5$ (Baseline Case)

In Figure 24.1, the dashed line, $Y_i = Q/5$, plays two roles: First, it gives the amount each worker would be paid for each level of group output if a five-member group adopted an equal-sharing rule. Second, it shows the group's budget constraint: The height of the curve shows the amount the group *can afford* to pay each member if the group's budget must balance at every possible output level. The bold, solid line shows the economically efficient group piece rate, derived previously. Like the equal-sharing rule, this scheme balances the budget if each member selects the efficient amount of effort (yielding a group output of $Q = 5$). Unlike the equal-sharing rule, however, this scheme does not balance the budget for other possible output levels. When the group produces less than 5 units of output, the efficient scheme runs a surplus because each worker is paid less than the budget-balancing amount. When the group's output exceeds 5 units, the efficient scheme runs a deficit by promising to pay each worker more than the budget-balancing amount.

In sum, to attain efficient effort in teams of rational, selfish agents using a group piece rate, some entity—be it a designated team member or a third party we might call a principal or an entrepreneur—has to commit to a compensation rule that will "break the budget" whenever the group does not perform as it is expected to. This rule provides strong incentives by "overpaying" the group when they produce more than the efficient amount and underpaying them when they produce less. Although such a scheme imposes risks on the principal, it also ensures that the group's budget will balance as long as the principal is correct in her expectations of what agents will do. In a classic article, 2016 Nobelist Bengt Holmstrom (1982) proposed that committing to "budget-breaking" incentive schemes like these (and bearing the risks associated with them) is an important function of entrepreneurs (or principals) in a free-enterprise system.[6]

☑ RESULT 24.5 **Group Piece Rates**

Rational, self-interested team members can be induced to select economically efficient effort levels using a linear group piece rate scheme like Equation 24.14 or Figure 24.1, which pays *each* worker $1 extra for every extra $1 the entire group produces. Although such schemes cannot achieve strong budget balancing, they can be designed to balance the budget "in equilibrium," that is, if the group as a whole produces the efficient output level. Typically, this requires that agents pay substantial amounts for access to a job.

To operate such a scheme, some entity (i.e., a "principal" or entrepreneur) needs to commit to absorb any budget shortfalls or surpluses that occur if the group does not attain its target.

A final noteworthy property of efficient group piece rates concerns the incentives of the principals who have decided to offer such policies. In particular, note that the incentive scheme $Y_i = -4 + Q/N$ creates a strong incentive for the principal

[6] The general idea behind these schemes can be traced back to Groves (1973).

to misrepresent how well the group actually performed, and indeed to sabotage the group's efforts: By reducing the group's output below 5, a principal can cut each member's pay according to the contract schedule and earn a profit. Thus, schemes of this nature can only hope to function when workers are convinced that principals will honestly evaluate the group's output. Smart workers should be reluctant to work for opportunistic principals offering such pay schemes.

Group Bonus Schemes

Another way to compensate a group of workers is to promise every member of the group a bonus, *B*, if the group achieves a certain target output level, *M*. This bonus is paid in addition to each worker's base pay, *a*, which is received even if the target is not achieved, as shown in Figure 24.2.

The bold step function in Figure 24.2 is a group bonus scheme of the form described in Equation 24.7. As in Figure 24.1, the dashed line is the budget constraint, showing the amount each worker must be paid if the budget is to balance at that level of output. Like the group piece rate, the group bonus is designed to balance the budget if the group attains the efficient, target output level. Thus, $a + B = Q^*/N$, where $Q^* = M$ is the *economically efficient* output for the entire group. At other group output levels, however, the budget does not typically balance.[7] For the scheme in Figure 24.2 to work, the bonus, *B*, has to be large enough to ensure that each worker prefers to provide the efficient effort level, rather than just "settling for" base pay, *a*.

An important distinction between group bonus and group piece rate schemes is that group bonus schemes introduce *strategic considerations* into workers' effort decisions. To see this, consider again the case of a five-member team ($N = 5$) with our baseline production and utility functions, $Q = E_1 + E_2 + E_3 + E_4 + E_5$ and $U_i = Y_i - E_i^2/2$. As we've already shown, the economically

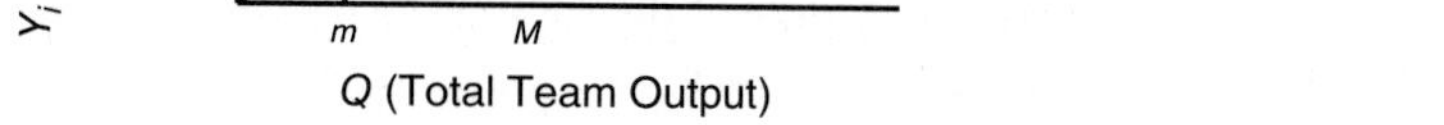

FIGURE 24.2. A Group Bonus Scheme

[7] The group as a whole is underpaid if $Q > M$ or if $m < Q < M$, and overpaid if $Q < m$. Now, in contrast to the group piece rate, the entrepreneur earns a profit if the group overperforms expectations, which should reduce or eliminate unscrupulous entrepreneurs' incentives to sabotage the group.

efficient effort level for each agent is $E_i^* = 1$, so let's try to achieve efficiency by setting $Q^* = 5$ as our target output level by announcing a group bonus plan, $(a, B) = (0, 1)$. Thus, each agent is paid nothing ($a = 0$) if the group as a whole produces less than five units of output, and each agent is paid $Y_i = 1$ if the group produces five or more units. This way, the group's budget will balance if each team member "does his part" by supplying one unit of effort. Notice, incidentally, that this particular group bonus scheme (with $a = 0$) is *less generous* than the equal-sharing rule in Figure 24.2 in the sense that pays either the same or strictly less than equal sharing at every possible level of output.

To understand the strategic considerations facing the members of a team under this group bonus plan, consider the utility-maximizing effort choices facing one of the members (say, Agent 5). Suppose first, for the sake of argument, that Agent 5 expects four teammates to contribute half a unit of effort each ($E_i = 0.5$), for a total of two units from the four teammates together. Because the team as a whole needs to produce five units of output for the group bonus to be paid, this means that Agent 5 will get a bonus if and only if that agent supplies at least three units of effort. Assuming Agent 5 is purely self-interested, what's that person's utility-maximizing choice?

If Agent 5 supplies less than three units of effort, the group won't attain its target, and Agent 5 will attain a payoff of $0 - (E_5)^2/2$. Therefore (because this payoff decreases as effort increases), if Agent 5 plans to supply less than three units of effort, that agent's best choice is to supply no effort at all and earn a payoff of zero. On the other hand, if Agent 5 supplies three or more units of effort, the group will attain its target and Agent 5 will earn a payoff of $1 - (E_5)^2/2$. So (by the same logic), if Agent 5 plans to supply *at least* three units of effort, the best choice is to supply *exactly* three units, earning a payoff of exactly $1 - (3)^2/2 = -3.5$. Thus, Agent 5's best choice is to supply zero effort. To summarize, if Agent 5 expects four teammates, as a group, to supply two units of effort, Agent 5's best choice is to shirk completely and supply no effort at all.

Now suppose that Agent 5 believes that the four co-workers, as a group, will supply one unit of effort each (which happens to be the economically efficient level). Now the group bonus will be paid if Agent 5 supplies one or more units of effort. Using the same logic as previously, Agent 5's best choice now is to supply exactly one unit of effort, attaining a utility of $1 - (1)^2/2 = 0.5$. To summarize, if Agent 5 expects four teammates, as a group, to each supply one unit of effort, *Agent 5's best choice is also to supply one unit of effort.*

Comparing the last two paragraphs, we have just demonstrated the *strategic* nature of workers' decision problem under a group piece rate: *Worker 5's utility-maximizing effort choice depends on what that worker expects co-workers to do.* Because the co-workers' behavior can be hard to forecast, in general, it will be trickier for workers to make effort decisions in a group bonus scheme than in other situations like individual or group piece rates.

The strategic complications with group bonuses, however, go even beyond this. In many cases, when an individual agent's optimal decision depends on other agents' decisions, there is a set of actions by all the agents that are mutually consistent; such a set of actions is called a **Nash equilibrium** of the game among the agents (Definition 20.3).[8] When there is only one set of consistent actions (as there was, e.g., in some of the tournament games we studied in Part 4), this unique Nash equilibrium is often quite a good predictor of how real people will behave. In the case of group bonuses, however, in most cases there are *at least two Nash equilibria*. One is for every agent to supply the economically efficient effort level ($E_i = 1$). (This is a Nash equilibrium because the argument we applied to Agent 5 previously applies to all the other agents too: If everyone else chooses $E_i = 1$, then that is your best choice also.) The other Nash equilibrium is for every agent to supply zero effort: if everyone else chooses $E_i = 0$, then that is your best choice too. Because there are at least two Nash equilibria, it will not be obvious—even to extremely smart agents who understand game theory—to figure out how to act. This *coordination problem* is the "bad news" about group bonuses.

☑ RESULT 24.6

Group Bonuses

In contrast to output sharing rules, group bonuses *can* be designed so that it is a Nash equilibrium for all agents to supply economically efficient effort levels, while simultaneously balancing the group's budget in equilibrium. Interestingly, such group bonus plans are typically less generous to employees than a budget-balancing sharing rule in the sense that they *withhold* output from the group if the group underperforms its target. Some entity such as a principal or entrepreneur must commit to withhold or even destroy such undistributed output for the group bonus to work.

A potential disadvantage of group bonuses is that they introduce a strategic element to workers' decisions: Because it only pays to "do your part" when others do theirs, agents now need to forecast their teammates' behavior to decide whether it pays to work. Further complicating matters, even agents who are sophisticated enough to figure out which combinations of all the workers' effort levels are mutually consistent (and therefore a Nash equilibrium to the effort game among the workers) won't know what to do! That's because, in the case of group bonuses, there are usually *multiple* Nash equilibria to this game. The problem of making group decisions in the presence of multiple Nash equilibria is generally referred to as a coordination problem; we'll explore it in greater detail in Chapter 26.

---

[8] Readers familiar with game theory will recognize that the qualifier "in most cases" refers to the fact that a Nash equilibrium in pure strategies is not guaranteed, even though an equilibrium in mixed strategies is.

The Pirate's Tale: An Extreme Case of Withholding Output when a Group Underperforms

A fictitious story that personnel economists sometimes tell to illustrate the principle of withholding output to improve group performance involves a pirate ship that just weathered a severe storm. The ship contained a lockbox full of compartments, each of which contained a crew member's life savings (presumably in gold ducats). During the storm, the contents of the compartments all got mixed together.

Because there was no written record of each person's balance, the ship's captain faced a dilemma: how to get each sailor to honestly report the amount of his own savings, so the total could be divided up correctly again. The temptation for each sailor to cheat by exaggerating his savings is obvious. But having studied personnel economics, the brilliant captain announced the following policy: each sailor would privately report his savings to the captain, after which the captain added up the amounts. If the total reported amount exceeded the amount in the box, the captain said he would throw the entire box overboard.

In the reporting game among the pirates induced by the captain's policy—just as in the effort game among workers in a team—there are two types of Nash equilibria: in one, pirates don't tell the truth (after all, there's no point in being truthful if you don't expect your shipmates to do so); in the other, everyone is honest. But notice that—at least in the pirates' case—even if the other pirates lie, you have nothing to lose by telling the truth yourself. Thus, at least in the story, the pirates (all of whom are outlaws by profession) were all induced to behave truthfully by a policy that not only withheld, but committed to *destroy* wealth if a specific goal was not attained by the group.

Why do group bonuses make full cooperation a Nash equilibrium to the "effort game" among workers? Intuitively, they do this because they *create* "interdependencies" (or complementarities, as we shall call them) between workers' decisions in a situation where none existed before: Now, it is actually in my interest to supply efficient effort if, but only if, my teammates do so as well. We'll return to this important idea when we study the Koret garment factory in Chapter 25 and when we study the effects of complementarities in the team production function in Chapter 26.

The pirate's tale also illustrates a final, important limitation of group bonuses: As with any bonus scheme, these schemes can lose their effectiveness (and possibly lead to a significant waste of resources) when there is a significant degree of *randomness* in the group production process, for example if the group's production function took the form $Q = \sum_{i=1}^{N} E_i + \varepsilon$, where ε is a random variable. In the pirates' case, the faulty memory of just one well-intentioned crew member could lead to the destruction of the entire group's wealth. More realistically, simple bad luck could rob an entire group of engineers or salespeople of a well-deserved group bonus. This suggests that real-world group bonuses might need to be limited in size when employees are very risk averse, and that the threshold for group bonuses should be set sufficiently low that bad luck doesn't "rob" workers of a well-deserved bonus too frequently.

Chapter Summary

- ☐ This chapter theoretically studies the case of a principal employing a group of agents where the principal can only observe the total output, Q, produced by the entire group. The agents are assumed to be rational and self-interested, and they only interact with each other once. All agents must choose their effort levels simultaneously.

- ☐ We assess the ability of three broad types of reward schedules—sharing rules, group piece rates, and group bonuses—to induce team members to supply economically efficient levels of effort. All of these schemes use only the group's overall performance to set individual members' wages.

- ☐ We find that *no* sharing rule can induce efficient effort because under any sharing rule, the individual team members receive only a fraction of the returns to their effort but bear all the costs. This is an example of the free-rider problem, which appears in many contexts, including pollution, public goods, and charitable giving where individual and group interests diverge.

- ☐ Unlike sharing rules, properly designed group piece rates can induce rational, self-interested agents to supply economically efficient effort levels. As in Part 1's single-agent case, the efficient group piece rate has a slope of $b = 1$. In this context, however, $b = 1$ means that *each* team member's pay must rise by \$1 when the entire group's output rises by \$1. It follows that efficient group piece rates *cannot* balance the group's budget for all possible output levels (i.e., they can't satisfy strong budget balancing). The resulting need to have a principal who absorbs surpluses and shortfalls could create incentives for unscrupulous principals to sabotage or misrepresent the group's output.

- ☐ Properly designed group bonuses can also induce rational, self-interested agents to supply economically efficient effort levels. A possible advantage of group bonuses over the efficient group piece rate is that principals now make a profit when the group exceeds its target output; this eliminates principals' incentives to sabotage or misrepresent output. A disadvantage is that group bonuses introduce a strategic element to agents' decisions: Each agent's preferred effort level now depends on how hard that agent expects co-workers to work. This gives rise to coordination problems between workers, which we will study in Chapter 26.

Discussion Questions

1. Consider an employee who has been granted an option to buy a certain number, n, of his company's shares at a certain future date, for a predetermined strike price, p^*. Notice that this option is worthless unless the company's stock price rises above p^*. Thinking of the entire company as the

worker's "team" and the team's overall performance (Q) as just the stock price p, derive the equation for the employee's compensation rule $Y(Q)$ that is implied by this stock option grant. Does it correspond to any of the four compensation rules introduced in Section 24.1? If yes, which one? If no, discuss how it differs from all of those rules. How much free-riding would you expect that such a rule would induce? Which workers in a company is a stock option plan most likely to motivate?

2. Look up gainsharing online. Compare gainsharing to the stock options discussed previously. Based on the theoretical models developed in this chapter, would you expect gainsharing to be an effective remedy for free-riding in workplace teams?

3. Consider a group of homeowners around a lake who want to improve the quality of the shared access road to their community. Imagine that each owner gets the same benefit, $B(Q)$, from an access road, where B is a benefit function with diminishing marginal returns ($B' > 0$, $B'' < 0$), and Q is the total amount of money spent on the road. Thus, $Q = E_1 + E_2 + \ldots + EN$, where E_i is the dollar amount contributed by household i to the road budget. Mathematically describe the socially optimal contribution of each homeowner, and each homeowner's predicted contribution, when each is simply asked to contribute as much as the homeowner wants. Provide exact solutions for the case where the utility function is given by $B(Q) = ln(Q)$, showing that in this case, each individual will contribute exactly $1/N$th of what the homeowner should.

4. In our description of the unscrupulous diner's dilemma, we argued that a rational self-interested diner will order more food if the bill is shared equally than if each person pays for their own meal. This is because the diner sets $B'(F_i) = 1/N$ in the former case, and $B'(F_i) = 1$ in the latter. Using a diagram, show *why* F_i must be higher when the bill is shared if there are diminishing marginal benefits from food consumption, that is, if $B'' < 0$.

5. In our discussion of group bonuses in Figure 24.2, we said that "the bonus has to be large enough to ensure that each worker prefers to provide the efficient effort level, rather than just 'settling for' base pay, a." How big is this, exactly? To check whether the bonus drawn in Figure 24.2 is big enough, add some indifference curves into the figure, just as we did in our analysis of Safelite's PPP plan in Figure 8.1. Show that the bonus in the figure is big enough to induce efficient effort if the highest indifference curve attainable by "settling" for base pay passes below the point $(M, a + B)$ in Figure 24.2. Explain. How might your answer differ for high- versus low-ability workers?

6. Return to Section 24.4's example of a five-person team facing a group bonus scheme $(a, B) = (0, 1)$ with a target output of $Q^* = 5$. Using our baseline production and utility functions, we demonstrated there that if Agents 1 through 4 each contributed one unit of effort (for a total of four units), it would then also be in Agent 5's purely selfish interest to also supply one unit of effort.

Now, assume instead that as a group, Agent 5's four colleagues supply only 3.7 units of effort (so they "underperform" relative to the economically efficient level). Your assignment is to show two things. First, show that Agent 5's optimal effort level is now $E_5 = 1.3$. In other words, it pays Agent 5 to supply more effort than before by "making up" for his colleagues' shortfall. Put another way, if Agent 5's colleagues get the group close enough to its goal, it pays Agent 5 to "do some of his teammates' work for them." But how close is "close enough"? Your second task is to show that it pays Agent 5 to make up for the teammates' underperformance if and only if the four teammates supply at least $5 - \sqrt{2} \approx 3.59$ units of effort.

7. Despite Gneezy et al.'s (2004) experimental results in the Israeli restaurant, it is very common for groups of friends to agree to share the bill equally when they eat out together. Using ideas from economics and game theory, discuss why a group might choose to share the bill equally despite the free-riding that it might create.

Suggestions for Further Reading

Many of the theoretical results in this chapter were developed in Holmstrom's (1982) classic article, "Moral Hazard in Teams." One of the earliest empirical studies of moral hazard in teams is Nalbantian and Schotter's (1997) laboratory study, who found that free-riding does indeed happen in six-member teams and that effort levels can be increased by adding elements of competition between workers.

For a more recent field study, see Blimpo (2014) who shows that a group bonus incentive (for teams of four high school students) is just as effective at raising performance on a national standardized exam as a similarly sized individual bonus. Blimpo's results suggest that free-riding may not be as serious an issue in many real-world contexts as the models in this chapter suggest. In Chapters 25 and 26, we'll encounter a number of reasons why that might indeed be the case.

In this chapter, we argued that one reason why "a team of agents needs a principal" is budget breaking: Incentives can be considerably strengthened if one person agrees to enforce a set of compensation rules and to absorb any budgetary surpluses or shortfalls if the team does not perform as hoped. For an alternative theory for why there are principals, see Alchian and Demsetz (1972), who argued that the principal's main function is to try to measure each member's contribution to the team's output. To incentivize the principal to do this well, Alchian and Demsetz argue that the principal should be given the right to keep any extra output that principal is able to extract from the team.

In this chapter, we have argued that in many situations, firms use team-based pay simply because it is unavoidable—high-quality measures of individual workers' performance simply don't exist. Another possible reason for team-based pay, however, could stem from workers' preferences for fairness and equality with their co-workers. See Rey-Biel (2008) and Englmaier and Wambach (2010) for explorations of this idea.

References

Alchian, A. A., & Demsetz, H. (1972). Production, information costs, and economic organization. *American Economic Review, 62,* 777–795.

Blimpo, M. P. (2014). Team incentives for education in developing countries: A randomized field experiment in Benin. *American Economic Journal: Applied Economics, 6*(4), 90–109. doi:10.1257/app.6.4.90

Carpenter, J. P., Robbett, A., & Akbar, P. (2016, May). *Profit sharing and peer reporting* (IZA Discussion Paper No. 9946). Bonn, Germany: Institute for the Study of Labor.

Englmaier, F., & Wambach, A. (2010). Optimal incentive contracts under inequity aversion. *Games and Economic Behavior, 69*(2), 312–328.

Gneezy, U., Haruvy, E., & Yafe, H. (2004). The inefficiency of splitting the bill. *Economic Journal, 114*(495), 265–280.

Groves, T. (1973). Incentives in teams. *Econometrica, 41,* 617–631.

Holmstrom, B. (1982). Moral hazard in teams. *Bell Journal of Economics, 13,* 324–340.

Nalbantian, H., & Schotter, A. (1997). Productivity under group incentives: An experimental study. *American Economic Review, 87,* 314–341.

Rey-Biel, P. (2008). Inequity aversion and team incentives. *Scandinavian Journal of Economics, 110*(2), 297-320.

Spaniel, W. (2011, September 3). *Game theory 101: The Complete Textbook.* CreateSpace.

25 Team Production in Practice

The free-rider problem described in Chapter 24 describes a dilemma faced by every work group: Members want the work to be done, but (all else equal) would prefer that it be done by someone else! In that chapter, we asked how we'd expect rational, self-interested group members to choose effort levels in a highly abstract "baseline" situation. The most important aspects of this situation were the assumptions that (1) workers interact only once, (2) workers' reward schedules can only depend on the entire group's performance, (3) workers can't communicate with each other, (4) all workers are equally able, and (5) workers' marginal productivities are independent of each other's efforts. If the group's compensation rule has to satisfy strong budget balancing, Chapter 24 showed that rational, self-interested agents will always choose to free ride, choosing effort levels that are below the economically efficient level. Chapter 24 also presented evidence that free-riding occurs in a real-world situation that satisfies most of the assumptions of the baseline model: A situation where people who do not know each other split the bill in a restaurant.

Real work groups, of course, are *immensely* more complicated than Chapter 24's baseline model: They are typically composed of workers who interact and communicate repeatedly, who differ in ability, and whose efforts complement (or substitute for) each other in the production of output. In the next two chapters, we'll study effort choices in more realistic work groups by asking how things change when we relax Chapter 24's strict assumptions. In Chapter 26, we'll focus mainly on assumptions (4) and (5). We'll define the different ways in which workers' productivities can interact in groups and study how these interactions, along with ability differences between workers, affect free-riding.

In this chapter, we'll focus mainly, though not exclusively, on assumptions (1)-(3). In doing so, we'll discover one of the most important advantages of team-based pay that was assumed away in Chapter 24: If workers can see (and react to) *each other's* effort levels, the members of a work group possess important information and influence that is unavailable to a principal who sees only the group's total output. For example, when two students submit a joint project to a professor, the students probably know much more about who really did the work than the professor does. Further, because the students' rewards are team based, they actually have an incentive to *encourage and discipline each other.* Thus, the informal mutual monitoring, rewards, and punishment that take place *within* work groups could be a powerful force against free-riding. Perhaps this is one of the reasons why—despite the concerns raised in Chapter 24—teams are widely used in workplaces and why team-based pay is an increasingly important component of compensation. For example, Lawler and Mohrman (2003) report that the share of Fortune 1000 companies using work-group or team incentives for more than a fifth of their workers more than doubled, from 21% to 51%, between 1990 and 2002.[1]

Our discussion in this chapter is organized around three empirical studies of teams. Each of these studies, in turn, takes an additional step away from Chapter 24's abstract model and toward the complex world of real work groups. The first study is a laboratory experiment where "effort" is just a number selected by participants who can't communicate. It provides convincing evidence (a) that punishment of free-riders by peers can discipline groups and (b) that emotions—not just rational calculations—play a key role in motivating these punishments. Second, we turn to a field experiment where effort is real physical exercise and participants interact in person over a period of almost two months. It shows how, under the right circumstances and despite the potential for free-riding, peer pressure can actually make team-based pay a *more* effective incentive device than individual incentives. Finally, we study the effects of a team-based pay scheme that was introduced into an operating factory. Among other lessons, it shows that team-based pay can have benefits that go beyond employees' mutual monitoring and effort choices. These benefits include helping behavior, information sharing, and mutual training that take place within work groups. Overall—despite Chapter 24's pessimistic message about free-riding—Chapter 25 shows us that team-based pay can be a powerful incentive device *because it harnesses information and influence available to members of a work group that might never be available to a principal who is not directly engaged in the production process.*

25.1 Altruistic Punishment and Team Performance

In this section, we'll describe the results of a lab experiment that puts people into a situation that is very similar to Chapter 24's base-case model of team production. This situation is called a **linear public goods game**, or a **linear voluntary contribution mechanism (VCM)**. In this game, we consider a group of N workers, each of whom has the utility function:

$$U_i = Y_i - E_i, \tag{25.1}$$

[1] Scientific research has also become much more team based over the past several decades (Wuchty, Jones, & Uzzi, 2007).

where Y_i is Worker *i*'s total pay and E_i is effort. Notice that there is no increasing marginal disutility of effort in this example; in fact, an alternative interpretation of E_i, if you like, is just putting money into a pot for a common group project (as in Chapter 24's *public goods* example).

The group's production function is given by

$$Q = d(E_1 + E_2 + E_3 + \ldots + E_N), \tag{25.2}$$

where $d > 1$ is a productivity parameter.[2]

Finally, imagine that each worker can supply a maximum possible effort of *M* units and that all the workers are paid according to the equal-sharing rule:

$$Y_i = Q/N. \tag{25.3}$$

DEFINITION 25.1 The group production problem described by Equations 25.1–25.3 is known as the **linear voluntary contribution mechanism** (linear VCM). In addition to studying group production, the linear VCM is widely used to study public goods provision and charitable donations because it is natural to think of E_i as the total amount of money each person donates to a group account. $E_1 + E_2 + \ldots + E_N$ is then the total amount of money collected, and Q is the value of the public good that money can buy. The productivity parameter, *d*, captures the idea that there's some efficiency advantage to working together or to pooling financial resources. In the public goods context, *M* can be thought of as the total amount of money each agent has available to spend on the joint project. Any money not contributed to the project is assumed to benefit the agent directly because it can be spent on other things.

RESULT 25.1

Efficiency and Equilibrium in the Linear VCM

1. When $d > 1$, the *economically efficient* contribution level (E_i) in the linear VCM is for all group members to contribute the *maximum possible amount* (*M*) to the group project.
2. When $d < N$, the *individually rational* contribution level (E_i) in the linear VCM is for all group members to contribute *nothing* (i.e., $E_i = 0$) to the group project. Indeed, when $d < N$, $E_i = 0$ is the *dominant strategy* for every member of the group.

Result 25.1 is not hard to prove with the tools we used in Chapter 24 and is also pretty intuitive: If each dollar donated by a member creates $d >$ \$1 inside the group account, it makes sense for all the group members to agree to put all their

[2] If $d \leq 1$, there is no point in team production (or in putting money into a group account): The money (or effort) is more valuable outside the account than inside.

money in the group account, then split the proceeds equally. But if each member makes a contribution decision in isolation, that member will realize that each dollar contributed will only raise the individual's payoff by d/N dollars. Thus, unless the productivity advantages of group production are *enormous* (i.e., unless $d > N$), each member's dominant strategy is to free ride and contribute nothing.[3]

In a study published in *Nature,* Ernst Fehr and Simon Gächter (2002) implemented exactly the VCM described previously in a laboratory setting. Specifically, they grouped all their subjects into teams of $N = 4$ "workers" each, and gave each subject an endowment of $M = 20$ lab dollars every time he or she interacted with his/her teammates. In each interaction (or "round" of the experiment), each member simultaneously chose how many of the 20 lab dollars to put into the group's account. Once these "effort" (or contribution) decisions were made, the experimenters added up the total amount contributed by the four group members and multiplied that total by a productivity parameter (d) equal to 1.6. The group's total output, $Q = 1.6(E_1 + E_2 + E_3 + E_4)$ was then divided equally and paid to the group's members. At the end of each of these rounds, the members were informed of the contributions made by the other three members of their group and of their total payoff earned in that round.

Importantly, even though Fehr and Gächter's (2002) subjects played this "team production" game six times in a row, the authors reshuffled the subjects in such a way that no two subjects were ever in the same group more than once. Because the subjects were made aware of this, this creates the condition of *no repeated interactions* in Chapter 24's baseline model.

If humans are selfish, rational maximizers, how would we expect them to play this "team production" game? According to Result 24.1, no subject should ever put money into the group account. To see this in the context of Fehr and Gächter's (2002) experiment, notice that Subject 1's payoff from the experimenter is given by an endowment ($M = 20$), minus the subject's contribution to the group account (E_1), plus a one-fourth share of the group's output: $Q = 1.6 (E_1 + E_2 + E_3 + E_4)$. Mathematically,

$$\begin{aligned} U_1 &= 20 - E_1 + 1.6(E_1 + E_2 + E_3 + E_4)/4 \\ &= 20 - E_1 + 1.6(E_1)/4 + 1.6(E_2 + E_3 + E_4)/4 \\ &= 20 - E_1 + 0.4E_1 + 0.4(E_2 + E_3 + E_4) \\ &= 20 - 0.6E_1 + 0.4(E_2 + E_3 + E_4). \end{aligned} \tag{25.4}$$

Thus, although it is nice for Agent 1 when Agents 2, 3, and 4 contribute to the group account (each dollar they contribute raises Agent 1's payoff by 40 cents), Agent 1's net private reward from contributing \$1 to the group account is *minus* 60 cents. This is true no matter how much the other agents contribute. Thus, Agent 1's dominant strategy is to contribute nothing, and the same logic applies to the other agents as well.

---

[3] To appreciate how large the group's productivity advantages have to be to make positive voluntary contributions pay, notice that in a group of two workers, working together would need to double *each worker's* productivity. In a group of 10 workers, every single worker would need to be 10 times more productive in the team than when working alone.

Fehr and Gächter's results for the previous experiment are shown in Figure 25.1—specifically, in the right-hand side of panel (a), and in the left-hand side of panel (b). According to Figure 25.1, the first few times the subjects interacted in the standard linear VCM, the average contribution was about 10 lab dollars. This is more than predicted by the neoclassical model (zero) but less than the economically efficient amount (20). Perhaps subjects experimented with the idea of being "nice" or "socially responsible" at first. As they acquired experience with the VCM game, however, contributions tailed off, ending at about 5 lab dollars after six rounds. Because many other experimenters have studied the linear VCM game, we know that these findings are pretty typical:

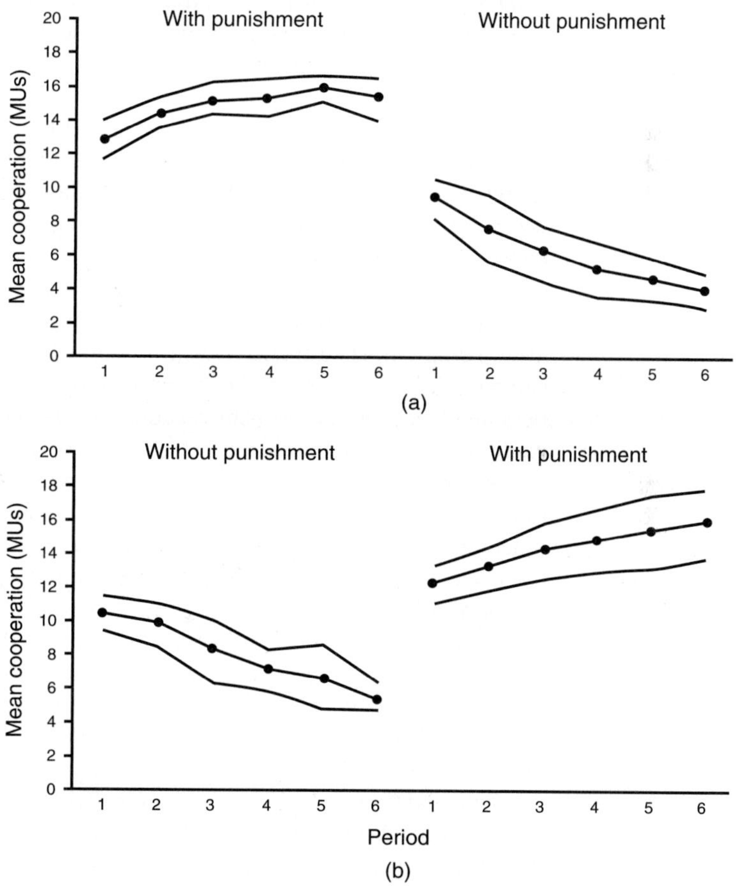

FIGURE 25.1. Group Account Contributions in Fehr and Gachter's (2002) VCM Experiment

Vertical axis shows the subjects' mean contributions to the group account, with the 95% confidence interval. In the (a) sessions, punishment options were available to subjects for the first six periods, then unavailable in the next six. In the (b) sessions, this order was reversed.

Eventually, contributions converge toward zero as more and more rounds are played. Thus, consistent with the simplest neoclassical economic model, complete free-riding eventually emerges as subjects realize that cooperation doesn't pay in this environment.

The real contribution of Fehr and Gächter's (2002) experiment, however, is what they did next. By making one small change to the standard VCM experiment, they dramatically changed the results. This change introduced a very limited and specific opportunity for their subjects to *interact more than once*. Specifically, after each of the six rounds, the experimenters now gave each agent the opportunity, for a cost, to "punish" any other agent in their group. For every lab dollar an agent spent on punishment, that agent could reduce another agent's payoff by three lab dollars. Each agent could spend up to 10 lab dollars on punishment per round and was allowed to allocate punishments to three co-workers in any way the agent wished. Like their contribution decisions, agents made their punishment decisions simultaneously without being allowed to communicate.

Before describing Fehr and Gächter's (2002) results when punishment was allowed, it's worth thinking through how we might expect rational, selfish agents to behave in this situation. Importantly, although there are circumstances in which it is rational to incur a personal cost to punish others (any judge or dictator knows this!), all of these situations involve *repeated interactions* between parties. For example, if subjects in the experiment can see you punishing someone who made a low contribution, they might make a higher contribution next time to avoid being punished themselves. But these sorts of interactions—where agents can try to develop a reputation for punishing free-riders—*can never happen* in Fehr and Gächter's experiment because no two workers are ever in the same production group more than once.

As a result, we should never expect rational, selfish agents to punish anyone in Fehr and Gächter's (2002) "punishment" treatments. Punishment reduces the other worker's payoff (which a rational agent should not care about) at a cost to the agent (which the agent dislikes) with no possibility of influencing the behavior of others the agent might interact with in the future (because no one who experiences or observes the agent's behavior will ever interact with that agent again). Indeed, the only people who could possibly gain when an agent punishes someone are the *other* experimental subjects who will interact with the punished worker later in the experiment. For this reason, any punishment that does occur in Fehr and Gächter's experiment is in a sense *altruistic*.

Fehr and Gächter's (2002) findings in their "punishment" treatments are shown on the left-hand side of Figure 25.1's panel *a*, and on the right-hand side of panel *b*. According to the figure, the first few times the subjects interacted, the average contribution was a little higher than in the baseline treatment (at about 12 lab dollars, compared to 10 in the baseline VCM). Thus, even in their very first interaction, subjects appear to have anticipated that low contributions might expose them to punishment. Further, in stark contrast to the standard linear VCM, subjects' contributions *increased* after the first round, ending up at around 16 lab dollars (i.e., 80% of the maximum possible and socially efficient level) by last (sixth) round.

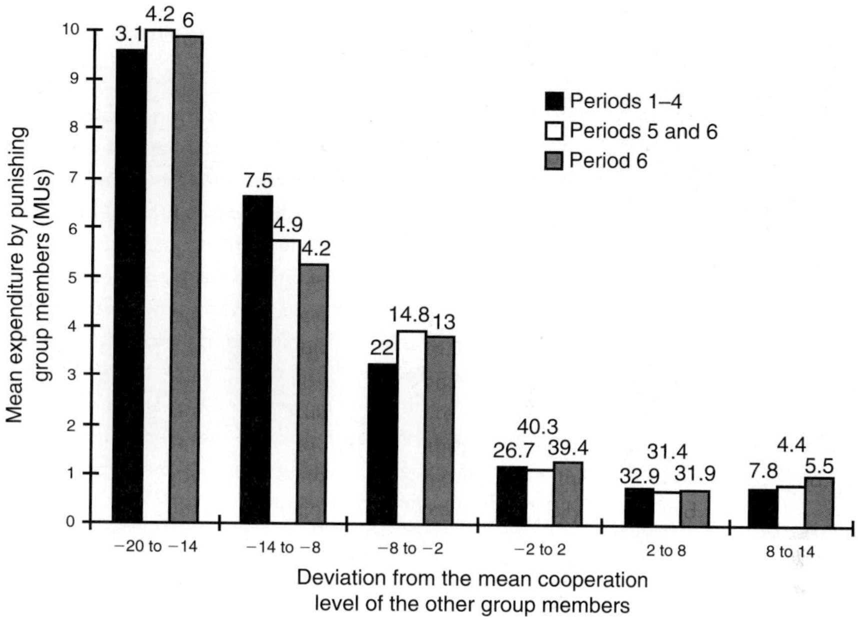

FIGURE 25.2. Expenditures on Punishment in Fehr and Gächter's (2002) VCM Experiment

Vertical axis shows the mean expenditure on punishment as a function of the difference between the punishee's contribution to the group account and the mean contribution of the other group members. The numbers above the bars indicate the share of the observations on which each bar is based. For example, in Periods 1–4, 3.1% of subjects contributed between 20 and 14 lab dollars less than the average of the others in their group.

Whom did subjects punish in Fehr and Gächter's (2002) team production experiment? As you might expect, subjects directed their punishments almost exclusively at the "free-riders" on their team. This is dramatically illustrated by Figure 25.2, which shows that teams spent about 10 lab dollars punishing agents who contributed 14–20 lab dollars less than their teammates. (Remember that a free-rider could be punished by more than one teammate.) This compares to less than one lab dollar spent on workers whose contribution was near or above the group's average.

Why did subjects punish free-riders in Fehr and Gächter's (2002) team production game? To learn a little more about this, the authors conducted a follow-up questionnaire asking people about their motivations. *Anger* was the most commonly reported rationale for punishing others. Notably, subjects also said they *expected* to be the object of others' anger if they made a low contribution, suggesting that fear of punishment explains the lack of shirking in the experiment. Summing up the results of Fehr and Gächter's team production experiment is Result 25.2.

Result 25.2 illustrates how *repeated interactions* among team members can dramatically change the amount of free-riding that occurs. In Fehr and Gächter's (2002) experiment, the only repeated interactions that were allowed took the form

RESULT 25.2

Free-Riding in a Laboratory Experiment with and without Punishment Opportunities

Fehr and Gächter (2002) conducted a standard team production laboratory experiment (linear VCM) where agents were not allowed to punish each other. After subjects acquired experience with the game, effort levels converged toward zero, indicating a high level of free-riding. This behavior is consistent with rational, self-interested behavior by the agents.

When Fehr and Gächter changed the experiment to let agents punish each other at a cost, effort levels trended, instead, toward the maximum possible (and economically efficient) level. This behavior is *inconsistent* with rational, self-interested behavior by the agents.

Based on *which* subjects were punished and the subjects' own reported motivations, *anger against free-riders* and the *expectation that anger would be directed at free-riders* appear to be the best explanations of why cooperation was higher when peer punishment was allowed.

of costly punishments that team members could choose to inflict on each other.[4] Although punishing co-workers can be in the interests of rational, self-interested workers when the same group of workers engages in team production repeatedly, Fehr and Gächter show that punishment occurs and is effective *even when workers know they will never interact again*—a situation in which punishment is never rational. Thus it appears that an *emotional* factor—anger—may improve group function and economic efficiency in groups. Whether and how human emotions like anger at shirkers have evolved—either biologically or culturally—because they improve the functioning of groups is a fascinating question that has recently been explored by anthropologists and other social scientists (see, e.g., Henrich, Boyd, Bowles, Camerer, & Fehr, 2001; Henrich et al., 2005, 2010).

25.2 Can Team-Based Pay Outperform Individual Pay? Peer Pressure on Campus

In Chapter 24, we argued theoretically that free-riding could be a major problem with team-based pay. In the Section 25.1, however, we presented results from Fehr

[4] Another important form of repeated interaction is, of course, simply playing the team production "game" repeatedly with the same co-workers (day after day, or year after year). In that case, workers have another way to punish each other, that is, simply by withdrawing their own future effort in retaliation for low effort today. An advantage of this type of punishment is that instead of being costly to the punisher, an effort reduction constitutes an immediate *benefit* to the punisher. Thus it is less costly to inflict. A disadvantage, especially in larger groups, is that shirking hurts the entire group: It cannot be directed specifically at the free-riders. When a worker shirks to protest another's free-riding, even hard-working co-workers will be hurt by the shirking.

and Gächter's (2002) lab experiment showing that a stylized form of "peer pressure"—voluntarily inflicted cash punishments by team members—could eliminate some, but not all, of the free-riding problem. One thing Fehr and Gächter's study did not do, however, was to compare team-based pay to individualized pay. Is it possible that—despite our concerns about free-riding—peer pressure in teams can make team pay a *more* effective means of eliciting effort than a comparable individual pay scheme?

That is the question addressed in a study of undergraduate students at the University of California, Santa Barbara, where I teach economics. In the study, Philip Babcock, Kelly Bedard, Gary Charness, John Hartman, and Heather Royer (2015) paid students to attend the 24-hr study room in the UCSB library. To earn credit for one visit, a student had to spend at least 40 consecutive minutes in the room between 11 a.m. and 7 p.m., Monday–Friday (when the experimenters were present to monitor attendance). After an initial group of students had all agreed to participate and received a show-up fee, some of the students were randomly assigned to the *individual treatment*. Students in this treatment received $2 for each time they visited the study room in a 2-week period, up to four visits. If they visited four or more times, they received an additional bonus of $25.

Other students were randomly assigned to the *team treatment*. Each of these students was randomly matched to a single teammate, to whom they were introduced face-to-face. Teammates stood next to each other during the sign-up process and were required to exchange names and email addresses. As in the individual treatment, students in the team treatment received $2 for each visit they made to the study room. Both team members were also eligible for a $25 bonus, but this bonus was paid only if *both* team members made four or more visits. Team members were not required to remain in contact after they were introduced and were not required to visit the study room at the same time. Notice that this team incentive scheme is less generous than the individual scheme because it sets a higher bar for receiving the bonus (both you and your teammate must visit four times) and is the same in all other respects.

How would we expect the behavior of dispassionate, rational, self-interested students to differ between Babcock et al.'s (2015) individual and team treatments? To work this out, suppose that p is the probability your partner completes all four visits in the 2-week period, and note that p cannot exceed one. Next, graph the agent's budget constraint in Figure 25.3. Under individual incentives, pay rises by $2 for each visit up to and including three visits, then jumps to $4 \times 2 + 25 = \$33$ if a fourth visit is made. Under group incentives, pay rises by $2 for each visit up to and including three visits, then *expected* pay (because it depends on the *probability* of your partner completing 4 visits) jumps to $4 \times 2 + 25p \leq \$33$, if a fourth visit is made. So, unless students can be 100% sure their teammates will fulfil their quota of four visits, the students' reward for making the fourth visit is smaller in Babcock et al.'s team treatment than in the individual treatment.

The indifference curves in Figure 25.3 represent a rational individual who chooses to make four visits under the individual treatment, and fewer than four in the team treatment, for the simple reason that the expected bonus from the fourth visit is smaller in the team treatment. Although it is possible to draw

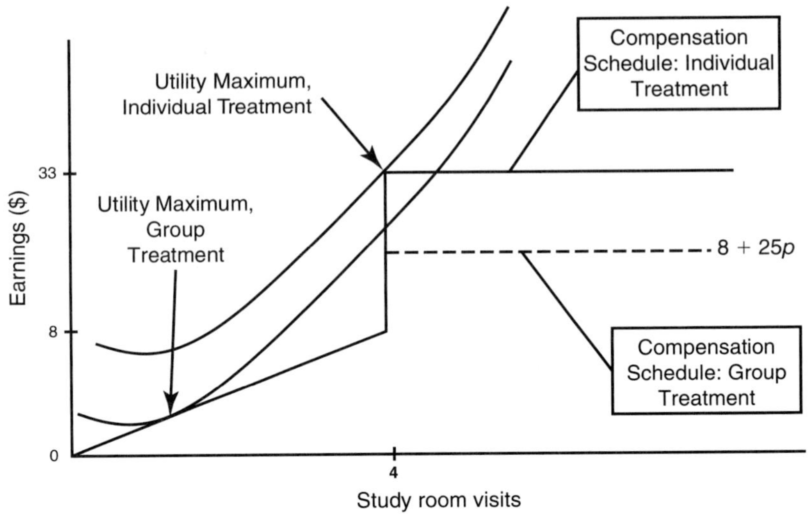

FIGURE 25.3. Pay Schedules and Indifference Curves in Babcock et al.'s (2015) Pay-for-Study Experiment

Kelly Bedard, Philip Babcock, Gary Charness, John Hartman, and Heather Royer. "Letting Down the Team? Evidence of Social Effects of Teams" Journal of the European Economic Association, 2015: 841–870. Reproduced with permission Oxford University Press.

RESULT 25.3

Predicted Effort Levels in Babcock et al.'s (2015) Pay-for-Study Experiment

Babcock et al. (2015) paid students to attend a study room in two alternative ways: an individual bonus and a group bonus. Because the group bonus was paid only if *both* team members achieved the target attendance level, rational, self-interested workers should visit the study room less often under the team bonus than under the individual bonus.

(non-crossing) indifference curves that yield identical choices in the two treatments, it is not possible to draw an indifference map under which rational, dispassionate students would work more under team than individual incentives.

What did the students actually do in Babcock et al.'s (2015) experiment? The main results are shown in Table 25.1. Contrary to the prediction in Result 25.3, students made more study room visits in the *team* than in the individual treatment, visiting an average of 2.7 times compared to 2.3 times. Of the team-pay students, 69% visited at least once compared to 58% of the individual-pay students. Both these differences were highly statistically significant. Team-pay students were also slightly more likely to visit at least four times (i.e., enough to qualify for the bonus), though this difference was not statistically significant.

TABLE 25.1 STUDY ROOM VISITS BY STUDENTS IN BABCOCK ET AL.'S (2015) CAMPUS EXPERIMENT, BY TREATMENT

	NUMBER OF VISITS	SHARE VISITING AT LEAST ONCE	SHARE VISITING AT LEAST 4 TIMES
Individual Treatment	2.332	0.582	0.460
Team Treatment	2.729	0.691	0.529

Why did UCSB students respond more positively to Babcock et al.'s (2015) team-based incentives than their individual incentives? If you think about this for a bit, quite a few explanations might come to mind. For example, students may have felt some *altruism* toward their teammate, so perhaps they made an extra effort to help the teammate earn money. Or maybe they wanted to avoid the *guilt* associated with preventing their teammate from earning $25. Perhaps having an assigned teammate made it *easier to visit* the study room because they could attend together and make it a more social experience. In addition, students may have received *praise* and other positive reinforcement from teammates, or feared *negative reactions* from their teammates if they didn't visit.

Which of the preceding factors were the most important? To learn more about this, Babcock et al. (2015) conducted some additional experiments, and also collected data in an exit interview. In one additional experiment, the authors re-ran the team treatment with just one change: Students did not know the identity of their teammate. In this *anonymous team treatment*, students were matched to a random, undisclosed student from another class. Interestingly, this dramatically changed the results: Now, consistent with the rational behavior predictions from Result 25.3 and Figure 25.3, students assigned to the team treatment visited the study room much less frequently than students in the individual treatment. This suggests that factors associated with *personal interaction*, such as positive or negative reinforcement, create the high effort levels in the main team treatment. If subjects enjoyed helping strangers (*pure altruism*) or experienced *guilt* when disappointing strangers, visits in the anonymous treatment would have exceeded visits in the individual treatment, which was not the case.

In another experiment, Babcock et al. (2015) explained the rules of the individual and team treatments to the students, then let the students *choose* which treatment they would receive. Which one do you think they picked? As it turns out, *almost all (97%) of the students picked the individual treatment over the team treatment*! This is very strong evidence that the high effort levels in the team treatment are not the result of factors that *raise* students' utilities, like the opportunity to help a classmate earn money, or utility from visiting the study hall together.[5] Instead, the results from Babcock et al.'s choice treatment

[5] Actually, teammates rarely visited the study room together—additional evidence that utility from shared visits was not a key consideration.

strongly suggest that avoiding *unpleasant* feedback, or avoiding *guilt* associated with disappointing *someone you know*, is the main explanation for the higher output levels in the team treatment.

The previous reasoning is also supported by the authors' exit-survey results. In the survey, participants who attended the study room four or more times were asked *why* they did so; they could check as many answers as applied. For the most part, students in the various experiments and treatments gave the same reasons for their choices, with one key exception: 55% of team-treatment members said they attended four or more times *so as not to disappoint their partner*, compared to only 28% of anonymous-team-treatment members.

RESULT 25.4

Actual Effort Levels in Babcock et al.'s (2015) Pay-for-Study Experiment

Contrary to the prediction in Result 25.3, students attended the study hall *more* often in Babcock et al.'s team treatment than their individual treatment.

Additional experiments and exit interviews conducted by the authors suggest that this was not because students derived positive utility from helping their teammates earn extra money, or because students enjoyed "working together."

Instead, the most likely explanation appears to be a desire to avoid encountering negative feedback from, or experiencing guilt associated with, disappointing a person the student knows, both of which might be considered forms of *peer pressure*.

Babcock et al.'s (2015) field experiment results suggest that—despite concerns about possible free-riding in teams—peer pressure can make team-based pay a *more effective* incentive device than a comparable individual incentive scheme. Babcock et al.'s results are especially convincing because, as we have noted, the group incentive scheme they use—although similar in all respects but one—is actually *less generous* and has *weaker marginal monetary incentives* than their individual incentive scheme. Thus, the experimenters were able to elicit more effort from their subjects *while spending less money* using the team-based scheme, compared to individualized-reward setting.

Although it is possible to find a best-selling management consultant who advocates almost any HRM policy one is interested in, it is still of interest to note that Babcock et al.'s (2015) results have been echoed in the management literature. For example, best-selling management consultant Patrick Lencioni (2002) argued that "more than any policy or system, there is nothing like the fear of letting down respected teammates that motivates people to improve their performance." Indeed, a deeply felt sense of duty toward peers is often cited by soldiers—who are engaged in perhaps the ultimate form of "team production"—as their main source of motivation, even when the strategic or political goals of their operations may have become dubious.

The Surprising Subtlety of Peer Pressure: How Is Pressure Actually Exerted?

Babcock et al.'s (2015) experiment shows that peer pressure can raise effort levels in teams. But how does this actually work? What are workers actually doing or saying to their teammates to urge them to work harder? A number of recent experiments have suggested that workers may need to do very little to have this effect on their teammates. For example, in a laboratory experiment, Masclet, Noussair, Tucker, and Villeval (2003) found that simply indicating (on a scale from 0 to 10) how much you approved or disapproved of an anonymous teammate's contribution had the potential to increase contributions: No financial punishments of the sort studied in Fehr and Gächter's (2002) experiment were needed. In fact, peer pressure can be exerted even when no words are uttered, as in Mas and Moretti's (2008)'s classic study of supermarket cashiers. Mas and Moretti found that cashiers worked harder when their performance was *visible* to other, high-performing cashiers (located behind them in the line of checkout counters). In Falk and Ichino's (2006) envelope-stuffing experiment, the mere *physical presence* of a more-productive employee raised workers' effort levels. More recently and even more dramatically, Corgnet, Hernán González, and Rassenti (2015) studied anonymous groups of workers paid according to an equal sharing rule for doing a task at a computer. In their experiment, simply knowing that one's screen was being observed by an anonymous member of their own team (with no other consequences) increased workers' output enough to completely eliminate free-riding: Team incentives worked just as well as individual incentives. The lesson from all these studies is that peer pressure may be quite easy and costless for workers to exert on each other. If true, this helps us understand why small groups of workers can often function remarkably well, despite the threat of free-riding that has been identified by economic theory.

Does Babcock et al.'s (2015) ability to elicit more effort at less cost using a group bonus than an individual bonus suggest that employers should use team bonuses more frequently? Aside from the usual cautions one should mention—for example, that Babcock et al. is just one study in a very particular environment with very limited interactions among team members—an additional, special caution is required here. In particular, recall that when offered a choice, *Babcock et al.'s subjects avoided the team treatment like the plague!* This strongly suggests that, although peer pressure associated with team pay raises effort levels, it also *reduces worker utility*. In the language of Part 1, the negative peer pressure associated with team pay may make it harder for employers to satisfy workers' *participation constraint*. In layman's language, employers who create an environment where workers encounter high levels of peer pressure may find it hard to attract workers. Indeed, some workers may be easier to attract and retain if they know their pay will not depend on the actions of a co-worker and if they know their actions will never directly affect a co-worker's pay. Smart employers should consider this fact before thoughtlessly implementing a team bonus scheme.

RESULT 25.5 **Peer Pressure and Worker Utility**

Babcock et al.'s (2015) experiment shows that peer pressure has some important advantages for employers in team-based production environments: Peer pressure can raise workers' effort levels at little or no financial cost to the firm.

Babcock et al.'s experiment also reveals an important cost to employers who encourage or tolerate a work environment with high levels of peer pressure. Because many workers may dislike peer pressure, such firms may find it harder to attract and retain workers.

25.3 Team Incentives in a Garment Factory: Why So Successful?

As a skeptical reader (and I hope you are one!) you may very reasonably react to the previous studies in this chapter with some reservations: Can experiments in the economics laboratory or small-stakes field experiments with college students really tell us anything about the effects of team-based incentives in real workplaces? If we are to be convinced that team-based pay can overcome the free-rider problem in a more realistic setting, it would be helpful to study the introduction of team pay into an actual workplace. Although such field studies rarely allow us to identify the causal effects of compensation policies as convincingly as randomized controlled trials do, they provide an important window into how teams work in the infinitely more complex world of real workplaces.

Fortunately for our purposes, Barton H. Hamilton, Jack A. Nickerson, and Hideo Owan (2003) conducted a classic study of team-based pay in a garment factory operated by the Koret company, located in Napa, California. Between 1995 and 1997, this factory switched all its 288 production workers from individual piece rates to a group pay system. Because the company had been paying its workers on an individual piecework basis before the change, it already had high-quality data on its workers' output before the change and continued to collect it afterward. This data made Hamilton et al.'s study possible.

Interestingly, Koret's switch to team-based pay was *not* motivated by an expectation that group pay would raise productivity. Instead, it was the company's way of adapting to a changing retail market for clothing: As electronic communications and inventory systems improved during the 1990s, it became possible for stores to monitor real-time sales of individual products and to adjust their orders quickly in response to customer demand. Thus, for the first time, retailers could know that the orange (but not the blue) sweater in a certain product line was selling like hotcakes, and transmit an order for additional orange sweaters to the manufacturer with a request for immediate delivery. To accommodate such requests, Koret and many other clothing manufacturers switched from their old, large-batch, manufacturing system, called the progressive bundling system (PBS) to a new, *just-in-time*, *module-based* system where teams of six or seven workers produced a small batch of items on request, producing the entire garment from start to finish within the group.

In a little more detail, under the old, PBS system, each worker sat at her own machine, took an item out of a large bin, completed her task (say, adding the sleeves), then put the finished item into another large bin that was wheeled to a worker in a different area of the plant for the next task (say, adding the buttons). This generated a large volume of work in progress (WIP): that is, unfinished clothing that sat in bins as the item slowly moved between workers. After the change, *the existing machines* in the factory were moved into modules with one machine of each type, so that a group of six or seven workers could perform all the sewing operations for the same garment. Due to their proximity, these workers were able to communicate easily and were given the freedom to organize the production of their garment in any way they liked. In sum, the production system changed from one in which each worker worked largely in isolation to one of *group production*.

A second feature of the new system was the replacement of the large, WIP bins that moved around the entire factory by a *kanban* within each group. In general, the term *kanban* refers to an inventory-control system for a supply chain, originally developed by Taiichi Ohno, an industrial engineer at Toyota.[6] Although the *kanban* can take many forms in different workplaces, in Koret's context, it took the very simple form of a wooden stick (i.e., a dowel) on which unfinished articles were hung as they moved between the team members. From the point of view of inventory control, the key feature of this stick is the fact that—unlike the old bins—it could only hold a very small number of items. From the point of view of *incentives in teams*, the key consequence of the stick's small capacity was that it *created complementarities* between workers: If there is nothing on the *kanban* for me to work on, I can't do my job! In the language of economics, the *kanban* creates a situation where the marginal productivity of each worker's effort depends positively on co-workers' efforts. We'll explore complementarities more formally in Chapter 26; but for our purposes, we simply note that they increase workers' incentives to monitor, encourage, and discipline each other.

The third and final feature of the Koret's new production system was the replacement of the individual piece rate system by *team-based pay*. Instead of being paid for individual output, each worker was now paid an equal share of the group's output. Importantly, from the view of measuring the causal impact of Koret's HRM policy changes, these three items—team production, the *kanban*, and team-based pay—were the only substantial changes in the production environment at Koret during this time. Because the exact same machines were used, we know that the quality and quantity of the capital these workers were working with did not change. The same is true of the workers themselves (almost all of whom stayed with the company) and the materials that were used. Thus, Hamilton et al. (2003) were able to estimate the combined effect of introducing these three policies at Koret, holding other features of the workplace fixed. As shorthand, we'll refer to this *policy package* simply as "teams" following.

---

[6] Kanban is a very well-known term in the auto industry. In fact, The Daily Kanban is a widely read auto industry news blog. http://dailykanban.com/.

DEFINITION 25.2 The team-based production system introduced at the Koret apparel factory between 1995 and 1997 consisted of three main elements:

1. **Group production:** Machines were relocated so that groups of 6 to 7 workers could produce an entire garment from start to finish, and communicate and organize work as they desired within those groups.
2. Tight **inventory control:** A *kanban* was used to tightly limit the amount of WIP that could be stored within each group. This created strong *complementarities* between the workers' efforts.
3. **Team-based pay:** Members of each team were paid according to a *strict equal sharing rule*: No matter which team member did the most work or acted as an informal leader, all team members received the same pay, which depended only on the group's total output.

In the Koret context, we refer to the entire HRM policy bundle outlined here simply as "teams" or the "team system."

Because Koret is a real-world production environment, it's not surprising that they didn't change the entire factory to the new system overnight. So workers didn't feel threatened or confused, the policy at first was that workers could voluntarily switch from the old (PBS) method to the new (module production) system at will. In fact, the first eight teams consisted of volunteers. Furthermore, until the entire plant switched to team production, team members could return to PBS at will. Last, team members could be voted off if their teammates didn't want to have them on their team.

To estimate the effect of teams on worker productivity, Hamilton et al. (2003) examined weekly productivity data for every worker employed at Koret before and after the switch to teams had been completed. Because—just as in Lazear's (2000) study of incentive pay at Safelite from Chapter 8—teams were adopted on a staggered basis and data was available on each worker's productivity before and after the change, Hamilton et al. estimated the productivity effects of teams using regression methods. To estimate the effects of teams on the *average productivity of all the workers employed* at Koret, Hamilton et al. estimated the regression equation:

$$\ln(Q_{ij}) = \alpha + \beta \times Team_{ij} + M_j + \Sigma_j \gamma_j X_{ij} + \varepsilon_{ij}. \quad \textbf{(25.5)}$$

The left-hand side of Equation 25.5 is the natural logarithm of Worker i's mean output in Week j. The dummy variable $Team_{ij}$ equals one if Worker i was on a team that week and zero otherwise. The control variables X_{ij} include the worker's age in Week j and monthly retail apparel sales in the United States. As an additional control for seasonal factors, the regression included a complete set of month fixed effects, M_j, just as in Lazear's (2000) approach. When Hamilton et al.

(2003) estimated Equation 25.5, they obtained a value of $\beta = 0.178$, indicating that the use of teams at Koret led to a productivity *increase* of approximately 18% after accounting for a worker's age and cyclical factors.

To estimate the effect of teams on the *amount by which team productivity raised a typical worker's productivity* at Koret, Hamilton et al. (2003) estimated the regression equation:

$$ln(Q_{ij}) = \alpha + \beta \times Team_{ij} + M_j + \Sigma_j \gamma_j X_{ij} + W_i + \varepsilon_{ij}. \quad \textbf{(25.6)}$$

The only difference between Equations 25.5 and 25.6 is the addition of W_i, which is a fixed effect for each worker.[7] Thus, after allowing for the same seasonal effects and time trends as Equation 25.5, Equation 25.6 estimates β *by comparing the output of the same worker before and after joining a team.* Any effects of teams on productivity that operate through worker self-selection (with, e.g., either the best or the worst workers joining teams first) will now be absorbed into the person effects (W_i) and are thus removed from our estimate of β. Put a different way, Equation 25.6's estimate of β is a *within-worker* estimate of the change in productivity due to teams.

The estimated value of β in Equation 25.6 was 0.136, indicating that controlling for seasonal factors and time trends, the productivity of a typical Koret worker increased by about 14% when that worker joined a team. Like the estimate of β in Equation 25.5, this effect is highly statistically significant and amounts to (0.136/0.178 =) 82% of the overall increase. Thus, about 100 − 82 = 18% of the increase in productivity associated with teams at Koret reflects the systematic selection of high-ability workers under the PBS system into teams. Thus, somewhat surprisingly, the workers who were most attracted to teams at Koret were disproportionately of high ability.[8]

RESULT 25.6

Teams Raised Productivity at Koret

Controlling for seasonal factors and a time trend, the introduction of teams at Koret raised total productivity by 18%. Of this effect, about 14% was an increase in the productivity of individual workers before versus after joining a team. The remaining 4% was a result of positive selection into teams: The workers who performed best under the old PBS system were more likely than other workers to join teams.

Why did productivity rise under the team system at Koret? Isn't this surprising, in view of Chapter 24's predictions that free-riding could be a dangerous consequence of team production, especially when an equal-sharing rule is used?

[7] See the discussion of Lazear's (2000) Safelite study in Section 8.1 for an explanation of fixed effects in regressions.

[8] Hamilton et al. (2003) also present direct evidence of this, showing that the first workers to volunteer for teams at Koret were the ones with higher output under the old PBS system.

Peer Pressure Without Team Pay: Supermarket Cashiers, Envelope Stuffers, and the Wide Prevalence of Peer Effects

One of this chapter's key arguments has been that team-based pay motivates workers to apply peer pressure to their teammates. But peer pressure can also play an important role in other work settings, even where team pay is not used. In Mas and Moretti's (2008) supermarket cashier study (discussed earlier), the workers' pay didn't depend on their team's performance, so the peer pressure effects they observed must have been motivated by something else. One possibility is the cashiers' *workload*: Because all the customers eventually have to get checked out, work that is not done by one cashier must be done by her shift-mates.

Another very common situation where peer pressure may emerge even without team pay is any situation where workers' efforts are complementary in the production process and where workers are rewarded based on their *individual* performance: If underperformance by my teammates reduces my personal productivity (and hence my pay), I will have an incentive to pressure my teammates into doing a better job.

Effects of peer pressure on worker performance have even been observed when *neither* of the previous factors (interdependent workloads or complementarity in production) is present, for example, in Falk and Ichino's (2006) envelope-stuffing experiment. Here, the mere presence of a high-performing worker in the same room raised workers' performance, even though both workers worked and were paid completely independently. The important lesson from all these observations is that *the informal peer interactions that take place within workplace teams, although largely invisible to employers, may in fact be an important but underappreciated part of the work incentive system in many workplaces.*

One reason you might already suspect—based on the previous two studies in this chapter—is peer pressure: When each worker's pay depends on teammates' output (as it does under an equal sharing rule), team members have a strong incentive to monitor and pressure each other to "do their part." These incentives were accentuated by Koret's *kanban* system, which increased the interdependence between the workers. More direct evidence that peer pressure was important comes from Hamilton et al.'s (2003) interviews with the workers, who reportedly pushed each other to work hard (often by joking) and caught quality problems more quickly than a supervisor would. Indeed, Koret's managers reported that under the team system, workers "were more aggressive than management at disciplining team members."[9]

Hamilton et al. (2003) also identified an additional mechanism that appears to have raised the productivity of teams at Koret: changes in *helping behavior*, in *information sharing*, and in *mutual training* among workers. In interviews, the workers said that they could produce faster and with higher quality on teams. Workers

[9] Team members may also have been disciplined by a fear of being voted off their team, though it is not clear how often this happened at Koret, especially after the entire plant moved to the team system.

said it was easier to share tasks, to shift tasks, and to "figure out easier ways to sew."[10] To see why workers might be more willing to share information under team pay, consider the incentives of a highly capable worker under the team system versus the individual piece rate system. Under the latter, she has no financial incentive to share her special knowledge and expertise with her less-able co-workers. But in a team, her pay will increase if she can make her *teammates* more productive. Thus, she now has financial incentives to share her knowledge and to take time and effort to train her teammates. These financial incentives to help your co-workers under team pay contrast starkly with tournament-based pay, which (as we noted in Section 21.1) actively *discourages* helping behavior among workers.

To assess whether the increased incentives for information sharing and training can explain the productivity advantages of the team system at Koret, Hamilton et al. (2003) divided the teams that were formed into two categories: homogeneous teams (composed of workers whose productivity was roughly similar to each other under the old PBS system) and heterogeneous teams (where PBS performance was very different among the members). If peer training is important, we should see the largest productivity gains from the team system in the *heterogeneous* teams. This is because the team's best members will have more information they can impart to the rest of the team. Interestingly, this is exactly what Hamilton et al. found. Also consistent with the peer training hypothesis, they found that the productivity of a team depended much more on the (pre-team) performance of its ablest member than on that of its least able member.[11]

☑ RESULT 25.7

Explanations for the Productivity Increase at Koret

In addition to mutual monitoring and peer pressure, evidence suggests that increases in *helping behavior, information sharing,* and *mutual training* among workers contributed to the productivity advantages of teams at Koret. These processes have more scope to raise productivity in heterogeneous teams than in homogeneous teams, and that is exactly where the biggest increases in productivity occurred.

A key implication of all three studies of teams in this chapter is that despite concerns about free-riding, *team incentives may be an effective way to harness information possessed by workers that is not easily available to management.* As Chapter 24 showed, if the only reliable information available to management is the output of the entire group, the only types of contracts that can remedy

[10] Workers also said they found teams "more interesting and fun." This suggests yet another reason why teams may have raised productivity: The *intrinsic rewards* to work may have risen, thereby diminishing the marginal cost of effort and raising effort levels.

[11] It's not at all obvious that we should expect this. For example, we would expect the *least*-able worker's ability to be the most important if the team has a *weakest link* production function. We will study weakest-link team production functions in Section 26.2.

Identity in Teams and the Nike Swoosh

Many Nike employees, including the company's founder, Phil Knight, have the company's trademark "swoosh" tattooed on their left calves as a sign of group membership and camaraderie (Camerer & Malmendier, 2007). Can apparently meaningless (not to mention costly and painful!) symbols of this type improve the functioning of teams?

Social identity theory, developed by Henri Tajfel and John Turner (1979), argues that rather than acting as isolated, self-interested economic agents, human beings naturally and easily categorize themselves as belonging to an overlapping set of groups, defined, for example, by friendship, family, politics, religion, gender, ethnicity, occupation, and other categories. This tendency to identify with groups matters for personnel economics because humans behave differently toward members of "their" group than toward others. Thus, if the Nike swoosh creates a sense of belonging to the company, it could conceivably make employees care more about their co-workers and increase their motivation to achieve a common goal. Thus, it could help solve the free-rider problem.

Although it would be very challenging to prove (or disprove) the hypothesis that Nike swoosh tattoos improve productivity or profits at Nike, hundreds of experiments in social psychology show (a) that it is very easy to create a sense of group identity among people; and (b) that once such a sense of identity has been created, people behave more favorably toward group members ("insiders") than toward strangers or toward members of other groups.

To create groups that people identify with in a laboratory setting, any one of several surprisingly "minimal" procedures works. These include having people wear t-shirts of the same color (Morita & Servátka, 2013), grouping them according to their preference between two similar pieces of abstract art (Tajfel, Billig, Bundy, & Flament, 1971), or just randomly assigning them to two groups with different "color" names (e.g., a "blue" and a "maize" group—Chen & Li, 2009).

Once such "minimal" groups are formed, laboratory subjects immediately behave differently toward in-group and out-group members in economically meaningful ways. For example, compared to their interactions with outsiders, experimental subjects show more charity to in-group members who are less well-off than themselves, show less envy of in-group members who are better off than themselves, are more likely to reward an in-group member for good behavior, and are less likely to punish an in-group member for misbehavior (Chen & Li, 2009). Most importantly from this chapter's perspective, Chen and Li (2009) show that experimental subjects are significantly more likely to choose actions that maximize the *sum* of payoffs of the members of their group. In other words, people are more likely to make *economically efficient* choices (such as *not* free-riding on their teammates) when interacting with members of a group they identify with. If such "minimal" interventions can create a sense of group identity with economically meaningful effects, it is not hard to imagine that companies that make large investments in creating a strong sense of group identity (or company "mission") might indeed reap a real economic reward from those investments.

Competition between Teams: A Study of Political Contributions

So far in this book, we've considered workers' incentives to cooperate (in teams) and to compete (in tournaments) separately. But human society is full of examples of competition *between* teams, in situations ranging from sports, business, and politics, to war. Indeed, competition between companies—such as between United and American Airlines, or between Apple, Google, and Microsoft—is in many ways the lifeblood of a thriving capitalist economy. Together, these examples suggest that this "hybrid" incentive scheme—where groups of people compete against other groups for a reward—might be a particularly effective incentive scheme for our species. As it turns out, existing evidence from laboratory and other studies confirm that competition with another team is a highly effective way to motivate team members. For example, an early study of several different forms of team incentives (Nalbantian & Schotter, 1997) found that **team tournaments** were by far the most effective at increasing effort.

More recently and dramatically, the incentive effects of competition between teams was illustrated in Augenblick and Cunha's (2015) field experiment on political contributions in the United States. Augenblick and Cunha mailed 10,000 postcards to potential donors to the 2008 campaign of a Democratic candidate for the U.S. House of Representatives. The postcards were all identical except for a single, prominent, randomly assigned sentence that read either "Your contribution can make a big difference" (the *control* treatment), "Small Democratic contributions have been averaging $28" (the *cooperative* treatment), or "Small Republican contributions have been averaging $28" (the *competitive* treatment). Strikingly, contribution rates in the *competitive* treatment were 34% higher than the *cooperative* treatment and 86% higher than in the *control* treatment. Thus, framing political donations as a *competition between your group and another group* increased the extent to which people *cooperated* with members of their own group.

The political contributions studied by Augenblick and Cunha (2015) are a real-world example of **intergroup public goods games** (IPGs), which were defined by Rapoport and Bornstein (1987) and are commonly used in laboratory research. In these games, individuals in two groups choose contribution amounts, and members of the group with the largest total amount of contributions are given a larger reward than members of the other party. The surprising effectiveness of IPGs suggests (as I suspect any summer camp counsellor already knows) that setting up group competitions may be a particularly effective way to motivate people.

free-riding are extreme ones that violate strong budget balancing, like a group piece rate with a slope of one or a large group bonus. If workers, however, have a better idea of which team members are doing their part, team-based pay incentivizes them to use this information in various ways. This includes praising hard workers, applying peer pressure on shirkers, helping each other, sharing information, and training each other. As the empirical studies in this chapter have shown, these positive incentives embedded in team pay can sometimes be strong enough to outweigh the possible disadvantage of free-riding. The positive incentives for workers to help each other under team-based pay also contrast starkly with incentives that tournaments create for workers to sabotage each other. For all these reasons, team-based pay may be an attractive compensation option to consider, especially in production environments where it is important for workers to cooperate and to share information.

Chapter Summary

- This chapter describes three empirical studies that show that teams can function surprisingly well, despite the free-rider problem identified by economic theory.

- Fehr and Gächter (2002) study the linear public goods game, or linear VCM, in the laboratory. This game puts agents into a specific version of the team production problem we studied theoretically in Chapter 24: a version with a linear disutility-of-effort function (Equation 25.1), a linear production function (Equation 25.2), and an equal-sharing rule (Equation 25.3) for pay. As predicted by that model, Fehr and Gächter find that agents free ride a lot. When the experiment is changed, however, to allow agents to punish each other (by paying money to reduce another agent's payoff), they find that free-riding is almost eliminated: Agents choose to punish free-riders at their own expense. Because the experiment was structured so that no agent ever interacts with the same agent more than once, these punishments cannot be explained by a rational desire to change the punished agents' behavior for one's own future benefit. For that reason, Fehr and Gächter call it altruistic punishment. The main motivation for altruistic punishment among Fehr and Gächter's agents, however, appears to be an emotional one: anger at free-riders.

- Babcock et al. (2015) paid UCSB students to attend a study room in two alternative ways: an individual bonus ($25 if you attended at least four times), or a group bonus ($25 if *both you and your teammate* attended at least four times). Because it is harder to earn the group bonus than the individual bonus, rational agents should on average make fewer visits under the team incentive scheme, that is, they should free ride. In contrast, Babcock et al. found that students made more visits under the group bonus. Thus, the experimenters were able to elicit more study effort from students at a lower cost using a team bonus than an individual bonus! Further investigations revealed that this increase in effort was generated more by a desire to avoid guilt or negative feedback from their partner than from altruistic pleasure associated with helping the partner. Indeed, when offered a choice, students strongly preferred the individual bonus scheme over the group bonus scheme. This suggests that peer pressure can have a downside for employers: Workers may avoid workplaces known to expose them to high levels of peer pressure.

- Hamilton et al. (2003) studied the introduction of team production and team-based pay at the Koret garment factory between 1995 and 1997. Like the two previous studies, and in contrast to the predictions of Chapter 24, the authors found that the new, team-based system raised productivity, by 18%. In addition to mutual monitoring and peer pressure (which were encouraged by a low-inventory *kanban* system that increases the interdependence among the workers), Hamilton et al. identified some additional mechanisms via which team pay increased productivity: higher levels of helping behavior, information sharing, and mutual training (all of which are incentivized by an output-sharing rule). Evidence for these processes comes from the fact that productivity increases from team pay were greatest among teams with a wide mix of abilities (i.e., heterogeneous teams): In these teams, there is likely more information that can be transferred from the most- to the least-productive workers.

- All in all, this chapter illustrates the power of a number of mechanisms—mutual monitoring, peer punishment, peer pressure, helping behavior, information sharing, and mutual training—to improve productivity under team-based pay. All of these mechanisms take advantage of information possessed by workers (e.g., about each other's performance or about how best to do a specific job) that is not easily available to management. In some circumstances, these mechanisms can be strong enough to completely eliminate free-riding and generate higher levels of output than the individualized reward systems studied in Parts 1 and 2 of the book.

Discussion Questions

1. Imagine you are doing a joint project for a course in which five of you will receive the same grade. One of the members of your group is doing nothing at all. After the course is over, you don't expect you will interact with this student again. List all the strategies you can think of that might be considered to induce this student to "do his or her part" before the project is submitted. Which ones have we discussed in this book and which ones haven't we? Which ones would you recommend, and which ones would you expect to work? How, if at all, would your answer change if you knew you would have to do a joint project with this student three more times before graduating?
2. In Babcock et al.'s (2015) experiment on college students' study room attendance, there are two types of reasons why students might be motivated to work harder in the "group incentives" treatment. One is a desire to avoid something negative, like a feeling of disapproval or unpleasant comments from a teammate; another is the "positive" opportunity to visit the room together and to help another student earn money and improve his or her grades. Why do the authors conclude that the "negative" motivations described previously were more important?

3. Imagine you are in a repeated group production and pay situation with the same group of workers. Two alternative ways you can try to "discipline" your teammates are (a) to have a policy of shirking (selecting zero effort) the next time you interact if any one of your teammates shirks today, or (b) expending some costly effort after each period to punish any teammate who has shirked. Discuss the advantages and disadvantages of these two strategies.

4. Compare the incentives for helping your co-workers, for sharing information with your co-workers, and for sabotaging your co-workers under tournament-based versus team-based incentive schemes.

5. Have you ever participated in a team-building exercise in a workplace, school, or voluntary organization? Do you think this made a difference to the performance of the team, or was it a waste of time? Why?

Suggestions for Further Reading

Ananish Chaudhuri (2011) provides a recent survey of cooperation in public goods experiments, like the VCM.

Additional lab experiments that study the role of peer punishment in sustaining group cooperation include Masclet et al. (2003) and Falk, Fehr, and Fischbacher (2005). A different form of punishment—voting members off a team, or expulsion—is studied by Cinyabuguma, Page, and Putterman (2005).

An early formal model of peer pressure as a source of incentives in groups was developed by Kandel and Lazear (1992). For additional field studies of the effects of peer pressure in teams, see Knez and Simester's (2001) study of firm-wide incentives at Continental Airlines, and David C. Chan's (2016) study of emergency department physicians.

For additional evidence on the power of competition between teams, see Bornstein and Ben-Yossef (1994); and Bornstein, Gneezy, and Nagel (2002).

For an excellent experimental study that shows the economic effects of group identity, see Chen and Li (2009).

For clean evidence that group-building activities—such as engaging in non-work-related conversation or a group problem-solving activity—contribute to higher levels of cooperation in the linear public goods game, see Eckel & Grossman (2005).

References

Augenblick, N., & Cunha, J. M. (2015). Competition and cooperation in a public goods game: A field experiment. *Economic Inquiry, 53,* 574–588.

Bedard, K., Babcock, P., Charness, G., Hartman, J., & Royer, H. (2015). Letting down the team? Evidence of social effects of teams. *Journal of the European Economic Association, 13,* 841–870.

Bornstein, G., & *Ben-Yossef,* M. (*1994*). Cooperation in intergroup and single-group social dilemmas. *Journal of Experimental Social Psychology, 30,* 52–67.

Bornstein, G., Gneezy, U., & Nagel, R. (2002). The effect of intergroup competition on group coordination: An experimental study. *Games and Economic Behavior, 41,* 1–25.

Camerer, C. F., & Malmendier, U. (2007). Behavioral economics of organizations. In P. Diamond & H. Vartiainen (Eds.), *Behavioral economics and its applications* (pp. 235–290). Princeton, NJ: Princeton University Press.

Chan, D. C. (2016). Teamwork and moral hazard: Evidence from the emergency department. *Journal of Political Economy, 124,* 734–770.

Chaudhuri, A. (2011). Sustaining cooperation in laboratory public goods experiments: A selective survey of the literature. *Experimental Economics, 14,* 47–83.

Chen, Y., & Xin Li, S. (2009). Group identity and social preferences. *American Economic Review, 99,* 431–457.

Cinyabuguma, M., Page, T., & Putterman, L. (2005). Cooperation under the threat of expulsion in a public goods experiment. *Journal of Public Economics, 89,* 1421–1435.

Corgnet, B., Hernán González, R., & Rassenti, S. (2015). Peer pressure and moral hazard in teams. *Review of Behavioral Economics. 2*(4), 379–403.

Eckel, C. C., & Grossman, P. J. (2005). Managing diversity by creating team identity. *Journal of Economic Behavior and Organization, 58,* 371–392.

Falk, A., & Ichino, A. (2006). Clean evidence on peer effects. *Journal of Labor Economics, 24,* 39–58.

Falk, A., Fehr, E., & Fischbacher, U. (2005). Driving forces behind informal sanctions. *Econometrica, 73,* 2017–2030.

Fehr, E., & Gächter, S. (2002). Altruistic punishment in humans. *Nature, 415*(6868), 137–140.

Hamilton, B. H., Nickerson, J. A., & Owan, H. (2003). Team incentives and worker heterogeneity: An empirical analysis of the impact of teams on productivity and participation. *Journal of Political Economy, 111*(3), 465–497.

Henrich, J., Boyd, R., Bowles, S., Camerer, C., & Fehr, E. (2001). *Cooperation, reciprocity and punishment in fifteen small scale societies* (Working Paper 2001-01-007). Santa Fe, NM: Santa Fe Institute.

Henrich, J., Boyd, R., Bowles, S., Camerer, C., Fehr, E., Gintis, H., . . . & Henrich, N. S. (2005). "Economic man" in cross-cultural perspective: Behavioral experiments in 15 small-scale societies. *Behavioral and Brain Sciences, 28,* 795–855.

Henrich, J., Ensminger, J., McElreath, R., Barr, A., Barrett, C., Bolyanatz, A., . . . & Lesorogol, C. (2010). Markets, religion, community size, and the evolution of fairness and punishment. *Science, 327,* 1480–1484.

Kandel, E., & Lazear, E. P. (1992). Peer pressure and partnerships. *Journal of Political Economy, 100*(4), 801–817.

Knez, M., & Simester, D. (2001). Firm-wide incentives and mutual monitoring at Continental Airlines. *Journal of Labor Economics, 19,* 743–772.

Lawler, E. E., III, & Mohrman, S. A. (2003). Pay practices in Fortune 1000 corporations. *WorldatWork Journal*, *12*(4), 45–54.

Lazear, E. P. (2000). Performance pay and productivity. *American Economic Review, 90*(3), 1346–1361.

Lencioni, P. (2002). *The five dysfunctions of a team: A leadership fable.* San Francisco: Jossey-Bass.

Mas, A., & Moretti, E. (2009). Peers at work. *American Economic Review, 99,* 112–145.

Masclet, D., Noussair, C., Tucker, S., & Villeval, M. C. (2003). Monetary and nonmonetary punishment in the voluntary contributions mechanism. *American Economic Review, 93,* 366–380.

Morita, H., & Servátka, M. (2013). Group identity and relation-specific investment: An experimental investigation. *European Economic Review, 58,* 95–109.

Nalbantian, H., & Schotter, A. (1997). Productivity under group incentives: An experimental study. *American Economic Review, 87,* 314–341.

Rapoport, A., & Bornstein, G. (1987). Intergroup competition for the provision of binary public goods. *Psychological Review, 94,* 291–299.

Tajfel, H., & Turner, J. (1979). An integrative theory of intergroup conflict. In S. Worchel & W. Austin (Eds.), *The social psychology of intergroup relations* (pp. 33–47). Monterey, CA: Brooks/Cole.

Tajfel, H., Billig, M., Bundy, R., & Flament, C. L. (1971). Social categorization and inter-group behavior. *European Journal of Social Psychology, 1*(2), 149–178.

Wuchty, S., Jones, B. F., & Uzzi, B. (2007). The increasing dominance of teams in production of knowledge. *Science, 316,* 1036–1039.

Complementarity, Substitutability, and Ability Differences in Teams

26

So far in Part 5, our theoretical models have assumed that the team's output is produced according to our baseline production function, $Q = E_1 + E_2 + \ldots + E_N$. By using this function, we automatically assumed that all the team members were equally productive, and that the team members' efforts did not interact in the production function. In this chapter, we relax these assumptions to consider ability differences, as well as situations where one team member's marginal productivity does depend on his teammates' efforts. Understanding the effects of productivity interactions is important because, after all, these interactions are probably the main reason why teams exist in the first place: By working together, specializing, and sharing information, teams can do things that can't be accomplished by the same people working independently. In other words, teams can be "more than the sum of their parts." As we shall see, studying productivity interactions also yields some insights on the optimal design of team incentives, and on the need for *communication* and *leadership* in teams.

26.1 Complementarity and Substitutability: Definitions and Evidence

To keep our study of productivity interactions manageable, we make an important and very helpful simplification throughout this chapter. Specifically, as we did in Chapters 6 and 18, we'll assume that every worker's effort decision is dichotomous: Each worker chooses either to shirk, thereby supplying zero units of effort, or to work, thereby supplying one unit of effort. To define the different ways that workers' efforts can interact in the team production process, we begin by defining each worker's *marginal product* in this context.

Defining Complements and Substitutes

Using our most general production function $Q = F(E_1, E_2, E_3, \ldots, E_N)$ in Equation 24.1, we can now define Worker 1's **marginal product**, F_1, as follows:

DEFINITION 26.1 For any team production function $Q = F(E_1, E_2, E_3, \ldots, E_N)$, when workers' effort choices are dichotomous (0 or 1), Worker 1's **marginal product** (MP_1) is defined as the difference in the *team's* output when Worker 1 works, compared to when Worker 1 shirks:

$$MP_1 = F_1 = F(1, E_2, E_3, \ldots, E_N) - F(0, E_2, E_3, \ldots, E_N). \quad \textbf{(26.1)}$$

Notice that, in Equation 26.1, Worker 1's marginal product can depend on the effort levels of *all teammates*. Marginal products of Workers 2 through N can be defined analogously, and in general *every worker's marginal product will depend on all teammates' effort levels*. The *way* in which team members' marginal productivities interact defines whether any two members are substitutes or complements in production:

DEFINITION 26.2 Workers i and j are **substitutes** (in the production of a variable amount of output) if additional effort by worker i (j) *reduces* the marginal productivity of worker j (i). In this case, we say that $F_{ij} < 0$.

Workers i and j are **complements** (in the production of a variable amount of output) if additional effort by worker i (j) *raises* the marginal productivity of worker j (i). In this case, we say that $F_{ij} > 0$.

Mathematically, Workers 1 and 2 are substitutes (complements) if and only if

$$F_{12} \equiv [MP_1 \text{ when } E_2 = 1] - [MP_1 \text{ when } E_2 = 0]$$
$$= [F(1, 1, \ldots) - F(0,1, \ldots)] - [F(1, 0, \ldots) - F(0, 0, \ldots)] < (>)\ 0. \quad \textbf{(26.2)}$$

When $F_{12} = 0$, Workers 1 and 2 are neither substitutes nor complements, and we shall say that they work *independently*, which is the case in the baseline team production function (Equation 24.8) that we've used so far in this part of the book.[1]

[1] Perhaps surprisingly, the property of substitutability/complementarity between two workers (or inputs to the production process) is *symmetric*: If additional effort from worker i raises worker j's marginal productivity, it must also be the case that additional effort from j raises i's marginal product. This follows from the assumption that the group's total output can be represented by a production *function* $F(E_1, E_2, E_3, \ldots, E_N)$. Readers who have taken multivariate calculus will recognize this fact as the property that the second derivatives of any function must be symmetric: $F_{ij} = F_{ji}$, for any i and j.

A simple example of substitutability and complementarity comes from team sports (or indeed from any context where a team has to beat a given target—like the number of points scored by the other team—to produce *any* output). If my team is ahead, an additional point scored by my teammates *reduces* the marginal impact of my effort on our chances of winning the game (because my teammates' efforts just put us farther ahead). Thus our efforts are *substitutes.* If my team is behind, however, an additional point scored by my teammates *raises* the marginal impact of my own effort on our chances of winning the game (because my teammates' efforts now tighten up the game by pulling us closer to the opposing team's score). Thus our efforts are *complements.*

Before turning to empirical studies of productivity interactions within teams, we note that the concepts of substitutability and complementarity in Definition 26.2 differ from the concepts in Definition 12.5. In Chapter 12, we focused on

Does Effort Complementarity And Substitutability Affect Team Members' Effort Decisions? Evidence from Professional Baseball

If professional athletes' incomes depend, at least in part, on their entire *team's* performance, then we would expect rational players' effort decisions to reflect patterns of substitutability and complementarity between player types: Athletes should work harder when complementary players perform better and should take it easier when the players they are substitutes with perform better. In a recent study of U.S. professional baseball, Eric Gould and Eyal Winter (2009) argued that a team's pitchers and hitters are substitutes with each other, while a team's hitters are complements with other hitters. In the former case, notice that if the team's hitters have opened up a 9-run lead, the pitcher's efforts don't matter quite so much to the team's chances of winning. By the same token, if the pitcher is cruising toward a no-hitter, the batters' efforts don't make quite as much of a difference. Thus we expect batters and pitchers to be substitutes in the team's production function (for winning the game): If one is doing very well, the other doesn't have to.

Turning to the interactions between batters, if the two hitters before me (in an inning) have both hit singles, my personal hitting performance has a larger impact on the team's chances of winning than if the two batters ahead of me both struck out. Thus, high performance by my teammates boosts the *marginal impact* of my own performance on the team's success, making hitters complementary with each other (at least within an inning).

To see if these patterns of substitutability and complementarity actually affect players' performance levels, Gould and Winter (2009) collected annual data on the performance of every U.S. major league baseball player from 1970 to 2003. Using regression analysis to hold constant the quality of each player's teammates, they found that if a pitcher's teammates hit well in a given season, that pitcher tended to perform more poorly. In contrast, if a hitter's teammates hit well, he tended to hit better. This evidence is consistent with the idea that (even within the same team), some members are complements with each other, while other players are substitutes for each other, and that players' effort decisions reflect these patterns.

the employer's optimal *mix* of two different *types* of labor, in a context where the two labor types had different prices and where the firm could hire as many of each type as it wished. The question there was how to produce any given amount of output at minimum cost, so the relevant definition was whether the labor types were substitutes or complements *in the production of a fixed amount of output.* In this part of the book, we are interested in a simpler type of complementarity: how the effort choices of the members of a team affect each other's productivity in a context where the team's total output adjusts as members change their effort decisions. That is why we include the phrase "in the production of a variable amount of output" in Definition 26.2. For the most part, we'll skip that modifier in this chapter and in Chapter 27, but you should be aware that the definitions of substitutes and complements in this part of the book differ from those used in Chapter 12 (and also from most intermediate microeconomics texts, which focus mostly on the issues raised in Chapter 12).

Evidence on Productivity Interactions between Team Members

How important are productivity interactions between workers (in the sense that $F_{12} \neq 0$) in real workplaces? In some cases, the existence of effort complementarities within teams is so obvious that it wouldn't even be ethical to do an experiment to measure its importance. It seems beyond question that a surgeon would perform much worse without the assistance of a qualified nurse or anesthesiologist, and that is a situation most of us would avoid if at all possible. Measures of productivity interactions are, however, available from some other contexts where inadequate performance by one team member is not quite so disastrous for the entire team.[2]

Indeed, as already suggested by Gould and Winter's (2009) baseball study, some of the best evidence of productivity interactions comes from professional sports, where detailed data is available not only on the "output" (points scored, games won, etc.) of an entire team, but of each of its members. Do certain players make their teammates more, or less productive, and are these *productivity spillovers* properly reflected in their salaries? A recent study of NBA players by Peter Arcidiacono, Josh Kinsler, and Joseph Price (2017) studies these questions and finds strong evidence of complementarities, that is, of instances where $F_{12} > 0$. Arcidiacono et al. study outcomes at the level of a team possession, which can end in one of six ways: no point is scored, or each of the team's five players can score.[3] The authors estimated a statistical model on data from 905,378 possessions and 656 unique players active in the NBA from 2006–2009. Because their model exploits information both about which players are on the court and

[2] Perhaps surprisingly, measures of productivity interactions are rare even in these contexts, but for a different reason. As we discussed in Chapter 24, in many cases, the only reliable measure of output available to principals (or researchers) is the achievement of an entire team. The contributions of the individual members (and how these contributions interact) are often hard to measure.

[3] A possession is a continuous period of time during which one team has the ball (i.e., is on offense). A typical 48-min NBA game has about 100 possessions per team, so an average possession lasts about $(48 \times 60)/200 = 14.4$ s.

Who's the Most Productive Player in the NBA? Estimates of Productivity Spillovers in Basketball

As in most professional sports, the "big data" generated in professional basketball has given rise to the highly quantitative industry of sports data science, part of which is devoted to measuring the precise value of every player to his team. Well-known existing measures of player value in the NBA include the player efficiency rating (PER)—which measures each player's per-minute productivity and is generated using a complicated formula based on box-score statistics—and the adjusted plus-minus (APM) rating, which estimates how many additional points a player contributes to a team's scoring margin compared to the league-average player. It is constructed using a fixed effects regression.

Interestingly, though, neither of these measures distinguishes a player's direct productivity (e.g., points scored) from the indirect effect he has on the team's success by *making his teammates more or less productive.* To address this limitation, Arcidiacono et al. (2017) took advantage of the fact that the members of every player's work group—the four other players on the court with him—change on a regular basis. As noted, their results show that productivity spillovers play an important role in team production; as a result, the "best" players according to traditional sports metrics (PER and APM) are not, in fact, the most valuable players in the game.

Specifically, whereas PER and APM, respectively, rank LeBron James and Dwyane Wade as the league's most valuable player in 2009/2010, Arcidiacono et al. (2017) rate Dwight Howard as the top player at more than three standard deviations above the average, with Wade in third spot and LeBron in sixth place. Howard rises to the top in Arcidiacono et al.'s ratings because he is the top ranked defensive player, almost a full standard deviation better than the next best defender.

Interestingly, despite Arcidiacono et al.'s (2017) finding that players' "helping" behavior contributes substantially to their team's success, helping behavior is not highly rewarded in NBA players' salaries. According to the authors, the monetary returns to a player's own productivity are substantially higher than the returns to helping others. Partly, this may be because—at least before Arcidiacono et al.'s method was developed—productivity spillovers were very hard to measure, while a player's own productivity is highly visible. Ardiciacono et al.'s results suggest that existing team compensation practices that reward visible individual success may be inefficient because "direct productivity is easily observed in ways that facilitating the productivity of others is not."

about which of those players scores, it is able—unlike existing measures—to distinguish between a player's own ability and his ability to help others. Arcidiacono et al.'s measure controls for the quality of the five defensive players every five-person offensive team is playing against. It also values defensive play by giving the same weight to every point *prevented* by a player as it gives to the points he scores or facilitates while on offence.

Another work environment where it is possible to measure productivity spillovers between workers is in scientific research. Much like professional athletes, the productivity of individual scientists is highly quantifiable (via publications, citations, patents, prizes, and other measures), and scientists increasingly work in groups within which helping and mentoring behavior is important. Although it is hard to measure productivity interactions using simple correlations, recently some much more convincing studies of these effects have emerged.[4] These newer studies are based on some otherwise highly unfortunate natural experiments that have affected the scientific community. For example, in a paper titled "Superstar Extinction," Pierre Azoulay, Joshua Graff Zivin, and Jilian Wang (2010) estimated the size and sign of spillovers generated by 112 eminent life scientists who died prematurely and unexpectedly, thus inflicting an effectively random, negative shock on their collaborators' access to a distinguished colleague. Following the death of such a superstar, they found the star's collaborators experienced, on average, a lasting 5% to 8% decline in their ability-adjusted publication rates. Similar effects were found by Fabian Waldinger (2010, 2012) who studied the effects of the dismissal and expulsion of prominent Jewish and other mathematics and science professors from Nazi Germany on their PhD students' and colleagues' research performance during 1930s.

A final context where high-quality evidence on productivity spillovers is available is in medical care. Recently, Ann P. Bartel, Nancy D. Beaulieu, Ciaran S. Phibbs, and Patricia W. Stone (2014) conducted a careful, quantitative study of nursing units in a large hospital system, which showed strong complementarities between the members of these small, intra-organizational work groups. The distinguishing and remarkable aspect of Bartel et al.'s findings is that *production complementarities are highly individualized* (i.e., they occur between specific persons when they are working together) and *tend to grow with shared experience* as the members of a team get to know each other and develop ways of working together. Using the length of a patient's stay after a given procedure as their measure of a team's productivity (longer stays are a negative outcome, indicating that complications occurred), the authors found that the amount of experience a nurse has acquired on a *specific nursing unit* is much more important to the unit's performance than her experience in the profession, or even in the current hospital. In addition, any type of disruption to a team's membership, such as the departure of experienced nurses and temporary replacement of team members by equally qualified contract nurses, reduced the team's performance. Even the absorption of a new team member in the absence of any departures—an event that should eventually add to the total amount of "human capital" on the team—led to a sizable, temporary reduction in productivity. In essence, Bartel et al.'s study shows that nurses are more productive *when they have served with the same peer group of nurses* for a longer period of time.

Bartel et al.'s (2014) study suggests that productivity interactions in medical teams result from processes and mechanisms that are more complex than simply

[4] Concerning correlational studies, suppose we just looked at the correlation between an individual scientist's research productivity and the research productivity of that scientist's peers (say the other professors in the department at the university). We would find a positive correlation: Top researchers tend to be in departments with top-ranked colleagues. Of course it would be a mistake to conclude that the high productivity of a Harvard scientist's peers *makes* that person more productive due to team-production effects. Instead, it is just as likely that only the best scientists get jobs at Harvard in the first place. *Selection effects* like these make it next to impossible to measure productivity interactions in most real-world contexts using correlational studies alone.

putting two workers with different skills or strengths in proximity to one another. Instead, giving workers time to get to know their co-workers raises the amount of production complementarity between them. In the authors' words:

> The essence of team production is that it involves interaction among team members, typically of the sort involving communication, knowledge sharing, and coordination. Workers may develop tacit routines that facilitate communication and coordination with coworkers, and can build relationships with coworkers that facilitate productivity-enhancing activities such as learning and mentoring. When experienced teams are disrupted, these activities that manage interdependencies and build capability are likely to be impaired (p. 233).

Bartel et al. (2014) go on to argue that the concept of productive capability embodied in a *team that has gotten to know each other well* is an under-researched but potentially important reason behind the large productivity differences that exist between work groups or between firms that appear to be identical on the surface (e.g., in terms of their workers' qualifications and the quality of their capital and information technology).

☑ RESULT 26.1

Evidence on Productivity Interactions Between Workers

Careful empirical studies of professional baseball, professional basketball, scientific research, and medical teams all provide evidence of cases where workers have positive effects on each other's productivity (i.e., of *complementarity*, where $F_{12} > 0$). The processes underlying these positive interactions include explicit "helping" behaviors on the basketball court (Arcidiacono et al., 2017), intellectual collaborations between scientists (Azoulay et al., 2010; Waldinger, 2010, 2012), and improved communication and coordination within teams of nurses who have accumulated significant amount of shared work experience (Bartel et al., 2014).

Negative productivity interactions (i.e., *substitutability*) can also exist on teams, as is illustrated by Gould and Winter's (2009) study of major league baseball: In seasons when a team's hitters are performing well, its pitchers tend to underperform; and in seasons when pitchers do well, hitters tend to underperform. This makes sense because under some circumstances, high performance by a player's teammates can make it less important for a player to perform at his best.

By now, I hope I've convinced you that workers' efforts on real teams affect each other's marginal productivities in contexts that include national sports championships, scientific discoveries, and hospital patients' health.[5] Taking that as given, the next three sections turn their attention to the *theoretical* study of workers'

[5] Another context where recent evidence has demonstrated a form of complementarity is in decision-making. Charness and Sutter (2012) review the literature on group decision-making and find that groups make better decisions than individuals, in the sense that group decisions are less subject to behavioral biases, including limitations on cognitive sophistication and self-control.

effort decisions when these interdependencies are present. How would we expect production spillovers to affect workers' effort decisions in teams and the optimal structure of team incentive schemes? In the next three sections, we'll study these questions for three different types of spillovers in turn—extreme complementarity, moderate complementarity, and substitutability. We conclude the chapter in Section 26.5, in which we discuss two related issues: optimal team size and the effects of ability differences between workers in teams.

26.2 Team Effort Choices under Extreme Complementarity

Given the relatively widespread evidence of complementarity in team production documented in the last section, our goal in this section is to build some intuition about workers' (privately) optimal effort decisions when complementarity exists. To that end, we start with the simplest (and most extreme) case of complementarity in the production function, known as the "weakest-link" production function.

DEFINITION 26.3 A team of N workers faces a **weakest-link, perfect complements, or *Leontief* production function** (after Nobelist Wassily Leontief) if the group's total output, Q, is given by the equation

$$Q = \min(d_1E_1, d_2E_2, \ldots, d_NE_N), \tag{26.3}$$

where E_i is the effort supplied by team member i, and d_i is member i's ability.

In our *baseline weakest-link production function*, we'll assume that all the team members are equally able (i.e., that $d_1 = d_2 = \ldots = d_N = D$). Thus, the group's output depends only on the lowest effort made by any of the members:

$$Q = D \times \min(E_1, E_2, \ldots, E_N). \tag{26.4}$$

A simple example might be a group of hikers or an assembly line: The entire group can only move at the speed of its slowest member. More generally, the weakest-link environment represents a situation where—in accordance with the principles of *lean production* (Krafcik, 1988)—every member is *essential* to the team. Essentially, the team succeeds if and only if all members "do their part."

If workers' effort choices are dichotomous—that is, each worker either "works" ($E_i = 1$) or shirks ($E_i = 0$)—then the baseline weakest-link production function can be simplified even further as

$$Q = 0 \text{ if } n < N,$$
$$Q = D \text{ if } n = N, \tag{26.5}$$

where n is the number of team members who choose to work (as opposed to shirking), and N is the size of the team. In the weakest-link production function, every worker's marginal product is zero unless all the other workers "work." If all the others work, however, then your effort choice is pivotal for the team, as your efforts alone can raise team's total output from zero to D. Thus, each worker's marginal productivity depends positively, and very strongly, on teammates' effort choices.

To understand team members' optimal effort choices in a weakest-link production environment, let's consider a four-person team ($N = 4$) with the baseline weakest-link production function $Q = D \times \min(E_1, E_2, E_3, E_4)$. For simplicity, set the group's productivity parameter, D, equal to 4. When effort choices are binary, the group's output can be depicted as a function of the number of agents "working" (n) in Figure 26.1.

Total output is zero unless all four workers work ($n = 4$), in which case four units are produced, as indicated by the solid line, which jumps from Q = 0 to Q = 4 as soon as $n = 4$. If the members of the team are paid according to the equal sharing rule ($Y_i = Q/N$), each member's pay, as a function of the group's total output, will be given by the line composed of long dashes: Each member gets nothing unless "everyone does their job" (i.e., unless total effort equals 4), in which case each member gets an equal share of what's produced: $Y_i = 1$.

Importantly, the equation for worker i's pay (Y_i) in Figure 26.1 is identical to the equation for worker i's pay under the group bonus plan $(a, B) = (0, 1)$ in Section 24.4. Therefore, all the conclusions we drew about optimal effort decisions there apply here as well. Specifically, any agent who expects all co-workers to "work" (i.e., to set $E_i = 1$) will also find it privately optimal to work. That said, "everybody working" is only one Nash equilibrium of the effort game among the workers: Weakest-link production processes, just like group bonuses, give rise to potentially serious coordination problems among workers.

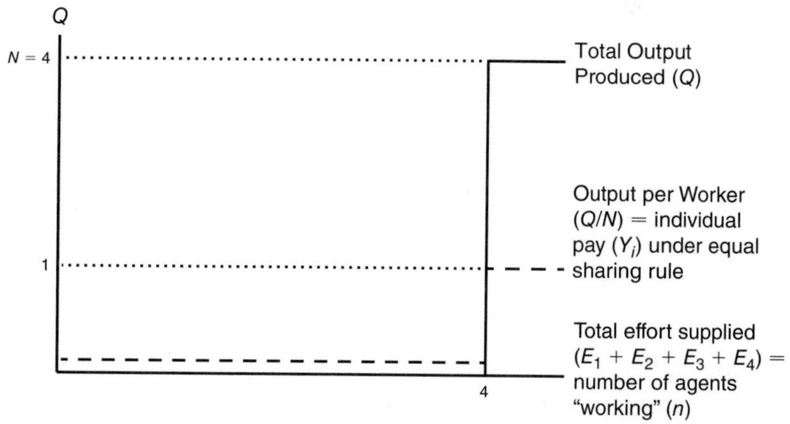

FIGURE 26.1. Output and Pay under the Baseline Weakest-Link Production Function, with $D = N = 4$

Note: Both total output and output per worker equal zero when $n < 4$.

RESULT 26.2

Predicted Effects of Weakest-Link Production Processes

When the production process exhibits extreme complementarity (i.e., a weakest-link process), it is generally a Nash equilibrium for all agents to supply economically efficient effort levels even under an equal-sharing pay rule. This happens for the same reason that group bonus pay schemes can work: when all other agents do their job, the remaining agent is pivotal, or *decisive*. By "decisive" we mean that no output is produced unless that agent chooses to "work" (as opposed to shirk).

On the downside, weakest-link production processes also create the possibility for coordination problems among the workers because high effort only pays for each worker if that worker can be quite certain that all colleagues will work hard too.

Intuitively, with weakest-link production processes, "nature" (i.e., the hard facts of the production process) is doing the same thing the principal did by implementing a group bonus in Section 24.4: withholding pay from everyone unless the group attains its target.[6] As noted before, this has both an upside and a downside (relative to other production functions): On the plus side, economic efficiency can now be a Nash equilibrium, even for pay schemes like equal sharing that satisfy strong budget balancing. On the minus side, a significant coordination problem is created among the workers: I only have a personal incentive to work if I can be sure my colleagues will also work.

How serious are these coordination problems in practice? For several decades now, economists have studied a type of laboratory game introduced by Hirshleifer (1983) called the *weakest-link voluntary contribution mechanism* (VCM). As you might expect, this game is identical to the linear VCM we studied in Section 25.1, except that the team's production function, $Q = d(E_1 + E_2 + \ldots + E_N)$ is replaced by the weakest-link function, $Q = D \times \min(E_1, E_2, \ldots, E_N)$. Experimental evidence suggests that subjects playing the weakest link VCM (much like subjects playing the basic VCM) often start out experimenting with moderate effort levels but that their behavior usually evolves toward a stable situation of "coordination failure" where all players choose the lowest possible effort level.[7]

Although this type of coordination failure may seem strange, dysfunctional companies are often described in terms of coordination failure: Individual workers (or production teams, locations, or divisions) often express a willingness to work harder and more effectively but complain that there is little point in doing so if other parts of the company won't do the same. Changing these expectations can be challenging. To shed some light on how that might be accomplished, Jordi Brandts and David Cooper (2007) conducted some lab experiments specifically focused on this *corporate turnaround* problem.

[6] The adverb "generally" in Result 26.2 refers to whether it is economically efficient for production to take place at all. Specifically, if the group productivity parameter, D, is large enough so that all members of the team will be better off by joining the team and supplying the efficient effort level (compared to not working and receiving a guaranteed payoff of zero), Result 26.2 holds.

[7] See, for example, Van Huyck, Battalio, and Beil (1990); Knez and Camerer (1994); and Weber, Camerer, and Knez (2004).

The Corporate Turnaround Game: "It's Not What You Pay, It's What You Say"

Imagine that you are a manager who is struggling to "turn around" a work team or corporation suffering from coordination failure: everyone says they're willing to change, but they can't see the point unless other parts of the organization "up their game" at the same time. What types of strategies might work? The stereotypical economist's response, of course, is "incentives": Raise the amount of money at stake for the individual workers, teams, or divisions. In contrast, organizational psychologists often stress that *communication* is essential to changing expectations in a way that workers feel confident that their additional efforts will in fact make a difference. Indeed, team members' *expectations* about what their teammates will do play a critical role in the game-theoretic models of team behavior we've just discussed. If communication can change these expectations, it could have powerful effects.

To assess the effects of incentives and communication in turning around dysfunctional teams, Brandts and Cooper (2007) assembled groups of five laboratory subjects—four workers and one manager—where the workers' production function (measured in lab pesetas) was given by $Q = 60 \times \min(E_1, E_2, E_3, E_4)$. Each worker was allowed to choose one of five possible effort levels—0, 10, 20, 30, or 40—and was encouraged to think of these as weekly hours devoted to the activity that was most productive for the group. Thus, depending on the *minimum* effort level supplied by the four team members, the group's output could be either 0, 600, 1,200, 1,800, or 2,400 lab pesetas. Each worker was endowed with 200 lab pesetas per round of the experiment and was charged 5 lab pesetas per unit of effort that worker chose to supply, so $V(E_i) = 5E_i$.

Each worker's pay was given by the function $Y_i = B \times \min(E_1, E_2, E_3, E_4)$, where B is the workers' *bonus rate*. In the main part of the experiment, each manager could choose the team's bonus rate: B could be any integer between 6 and 15. To see how this works, imagine that B was set at 15. In that case, worker i's pay can be expressed as $Y_i = 15 \times \min(E_1, E_2, E_3, E_4) = 60 \times \min(E_1, E_2, E_3, E_4)/4 = Q/4$. Thus, the most generous bonus rate the manager was allowed to choose is an equal-sharing rule that divides all the output equally among the four workers and leaves nothing for the manager. By the same logic, the least-generous bonus rate, 6, pays each of the four workers one-tenth of the group's output: $Y_i = Q/10$, leaving 60% of the group's output in the manager's hands.

Once these instructions were understood, subjects played 30 rounds of the turnaround game in their fixed, five-member "firms." For the first 10 rounds of the experiment, the workers' bonus rate was set by the experimenters at the minimum level (6). Thus the manager was strictly an observer: Managers could see their team's total output but could neither control the bonus rate nor communicate with employees. The motivation for this enforced low bonus rate was to generate coordination failure, and this was successful: As Brandts and Cooper (2007) expected, output was very low.

In the remaining 20 rounds, each manager was allowed to set his or her own bonus rate to try to "turn around" a dysfunctional team. In the "no communication" sessions, this *incentive-based* strategy was the only one the managers were allowed to use. In other sessions, Brandts and Cooper (2007) allowed each manager to communicate electronically with four workers before each round. These sessions either allowed for only one-way messages from the manager to the team of workers, or for unrestricted, two-way chat between a manager and each of her workers. No statements or commitments made by managers or workers during these chat sessions were enforced by the experimenter, so they constitute what game theorists call *cheap talk*. Because it does not change the payoffs of any player or the consequences of any actions, according to standard economic models, cheap talk should not affect the amount of output produced.

The main result of Brandts and Cooper's (2007) experiment is that *communication was much more effective than incentives in turning around dysfunctional groups*. To see this, consider first the mean key outcomes by treatment in Table 26.1. Despite the fact that managers chose to offer roughly the same financial incentives in all three treatments (an average bonus rate of between 9 and 10), effort, profits, and workers' payoffs were all much higher when managers were allowed to send nonbinding text messages to their team, and even higher when two-way communication between managers and workers was allowed. In fact, profits were more than twice as high when two-way communication was allowed, and workers' payoffs increased by (283 – 192)/192 = 47%. This dramatic improvement was possible even though the messages were unenforceable "cheap talk" between anonymous parties.

In contrast, when Brandts and Cooper (2007) used regression analysis to compare the effort levels of workers whose manager gave them a high bonus rate to workers who received a low bonus rate, they found that high levels of financial incentives did not lead to significant increases in effort. Without any increased confidence that your co-workers would raise their effort levels along with you, higher incentives just created greater frustration (about the large rewards workers *could have earned* if only their co-workers had worked harder!), without generating any extra output.[8]

TABLE 26.1 MEAN INCENTIVES, EFFORT, PROFIT, AND WORKER PAYOFFS IN BRANDTS AND COOPER'S (2007) TURNAROUND GAME EXPERIMENT

	TREATMENT		
Outcome:	No Communication	One-Way Communication (Managers to Workers)	Two-Way Communication
Bonus Rate Offered	9.3	9.3	9.9
Minimum Effort	4.1	12.7	20.1
Manager Profit	183	376	446
Employee Payoff	192	231	283

[8] Notably, these "no effect" results refer to the *level* of the bonus rate paid. *Changes* to the bonus made by individual managers did elicit higher effort levels in Brandts and Cooper's (2007) experiment, but these effects most likely result from the coordination effects of the pay raises, rather than their incentive effects: Rate increases are probably a good time for workers to experiment with raising their effort levels (in the hopes that their teammates will do the same). Thus, the raises actually function as a type of communication.

Given that communication was so successful in raising productivity in Brandts and Cooper's (2007) experiment, you might be interested to know *what exactly managers were saying* to workers that generated these gains. Although managers said many different things (including some complex, multiperiod plans that were proposed), an exhaustive analysis of the content of managers' text messages revealed that the most effective communication strategies were quite simple: Managers who requested a specific, high level of effort; who pointed out the mutual benefits of high effort; and who implied that their employees were being paid well, were the most successful.[9]

Brandts and Cooper's (2007) experiment underscores the basic fact that when workers' productivities are interdependent, coordination problems affect workers' decisions on how hard to work and how to allocate their effort. Further, *incentives alone, no matter how strong, can't solve coordination problems.* Communication, even when it is completely unenforceable "cheap talk," can make a world of difference in improving the output of a team of workers.[10]

☑ **RESULT 26.3**

Incentives versus Communication in a Corporate Turnaround Game: "It's Not What You Pay, It's What You Say"

Brandts and Cooper (2007) studied the problem of inducing a "dysfunctional" group of workers to raise their effort levels in a weakest-link production context—where coordinated increases in effort are required to generate additional output.

Perhaps surprisingly, high levels of financial work incentives that were not accompanied by communication from managers were ineffective in "turning around" these teams of laboratory subjects. Simple messages from managers (e.g., just requesting a certain effort level) however, were very effective, despite the fact that these messages were unenforceable "cheap talk." Even without any additional financial incentives, just allowing for communication between managers and workers more than doubled managers' profits while raising employees' payoffs by 47%.

---

[9] The most successful messages *from workers* to managers were the ones that encouraged managers to send exactly these types of messages to the group as a whole. (Note that workers could not communicate with each other or see each other's messages.)

[10] A reasonable response you might have to Brandts and Cooper's (2007) result is that it's irrelevant to real workplace teams: In contrast to the economics laboratory, in real work environments, both workers and managers have frequent opportunities to communicate with one another, so the coordination problems studied by Brandts and Cooper are largely irrelevant. Although it is certainly true that real workplaces offer many more *opportunities* for communication, economists would argue that these aren't always optimally exploited. And even when they are exploited, credibility problems remain. (I may be tempted to slack off even after I've promised you I'll do my best.) Coordination problems also arise *between* teams of workers (or divisions of companies) where communication channels can be quite limited; indeed, this is one of the main contexts in which coordination failures are studied.

Communication, Complexity, and Team Incentives: Complementary HRM Policies in Steel Mini-Mills

In what types of production environments are team incentives most effective? Under what conditions is it most important for employers to facilitate communication between employees? Brent Boning, Casey Ichniowski, and Kathryn Shaw (2007) addressed these questions in a detailed econometric study of rolling lines in in 34 different steel mini-mills. Steel rolling lines are a classic case of team production because few useful measures of an individual worker's performance exist, and the best and most relevant measure of output is the total *yield* of the line itself. *Yield* is the percentage of steel fed into the line that meets a quality standard when it emerges at the other end. (Steel that does not meet the standard can't be sold.) Rolling mills also exhibit almost-perfect complementarity between workers because the line can't attain the quality standard unless all team members do their part.

Boning et al. (2007) were interested in the effects of two HRM practices that were gradually adopted across the industry during the mid to late 1990s: group incentives (i.e., team-based pay) and *problem-solving teams*—that is, paid, non-production time during which workers were encouraged to meet and problem-solve about ways to make their line work better. Boning et al. found that both team-based pay and problem-solving teams raised yield but that each had a more powerful effect when used in combination with the other. Thus, the two *HRM policies were complements* (in the same sense that two workers are complements when they work "better together"). Essentially, team-based pay *incentivized* workers to share ideas about making the line work better, although problem-solving teams gave workers the *opportunity* to do so (because this was impossible to do effectively while operating the line). Boning et al. also found that this HRM *policy bundle* was much more effective in technologically complex production processes, whose products must satisfy very tight tolerances and where communication is critical, than in lines that produced simple iron bars.

Boning et al.'s (2007) study supports (with data from a real production environment) Brandts and Cooper's (2007) important idea that communication is essential in weakest-link production environments. In these environments, employers may benefit not just from incentivizing workers based on their entire team's performance but also from *facilitating communication* by providing paid time during which teams can meet and brainstorm about how to improve the production process.

Boning et al.'s (2007) study also yields an important lesson for personnel economics more broadly. Although personnel economists have studied the effects of many different HRM policies (ranging from individual incentive pay to letting employees work from home), they frequently tend to evaluate these policies in isolation from one another. Boning et al.'s results, however, clearly show that some policies may only be fully effective when implemented in conjunction with other, complementary policies. Understanding HRM policy *interactions* remains a topic we still know very little about.

26.3 Team Effort Choices under Moderate Complementarity

Now that we've studied extreme complementarity in a team's production function, we can move on to workers' effort choices under a less extreme form of complementarity. We'll start with the theory—of what we would expect rational, selfish agents to do—then move on to the evidence.

The Theory of Moderate Complementarity

The simplest way to model moderate complementarity in a team's production function is to continue to assume that all workers are identical and that effort is dichotomous (0 or 1). Because the workers are identical, the production function can be written as a function of the number of workers "working," n. In this situation, the workers are complements if the production function $F(n)$ is *increasing at an increasing rate.*[11] Other expressions for the same property (all of which are equivalent in this context) are that the function F is *strictly convex*, that it exhibits *increasing returns to scale*, or that it is *supermodular.* The idea is simply that as each additional worker starts to "do his part," not only does this result in extra output from that worker, it also makes his *colleagues* more productive because the workers interact positively in the productive process.[12]

Figure 26.2 and row 1 of Table 26.2 give an example of a production function with these properties for a three-worker team. In this production process, 20 units of output are produced even when all three agents shirk. As the number of agents truly "working" increases from 1 to 2 and 3, output rises by 20, 25, and 35 units, respectively. Thus, $F(n)$ exhibits increasing marginal returns to effort.

TABLE 26.2 EXAMPLE OF A THREE-AGENT PRODUCTION FUNCTION WITH MODERATE COMPLEMENTARITY

	NUMBER OF AGENTS "WORKING" (N)			
	0	1	2	3
1. Units of output produced, $F(n)$	20	40	65	100
2. Value of output produced, $Q = 12 \times F(n)$	\$240	\$480	\$780	\$1,200
3. Payment to worker with equal sharing rule, $Y_i = Q/3$	\$80	\$160	\$260	\$400

[11] If workers' effort choices were continuous rather than discrete, complementarity could be described mathematically by the derivatives $F'(E) > 0$, $F''(E) > 0$, where E is the total effort supplied by all the workers.

[12] A different reason why output might increase at an increasing rate with the total number of agents "working" would be if the abler agents join the group of "workers" later than the less-able workers. For now, we'll continue to assume that all workers are equally able; the effects of ability differences are explored in Section 26.4.

To figure out how workers might make their effort decisions with such a production function, assume first (for reasons that will become apparent) that the output shown in Figure 26.2 is measured in physical units, F, where F represents, say, the number of boxes of premium fettucine produced by the team. If each unit of output (box of fettucine) sells for $12 (net of all non-labor costs), the net revenues, Q produced for each level of n are given by the second row of Table 26.2.

Next, suppose that the effort cost of working, $V(1)$, equals $90, that $V(0) = 0$, and that the three workers on this team are paid according to an equal sharing rule. Thus, each team member is paid $Y_i = Q/3 = 4F$ dollars. Another way of saying the same thing is that for every $12 package of fettucine the group produces, each agent receives a "bonus rate" of $4.

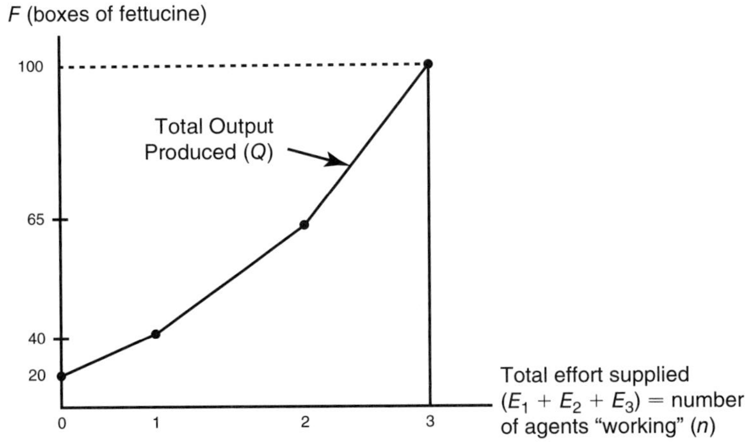

FIGURE 26.2. Team Output with Moderate Complementarity Between Workers: An Example with $N = 3$

The Challenger Space Shuttle Disaster and O-Ring Production Processes

On January 28, 1986, the NASA Space Shuttle orbiter broke apart 73 seconds into its flight, then disintegrated over the Atlantic Ocean at 11:39 Eastern Standard Time. The event caused the deaths of its seven crew members and was a dramatic setback to the U.S. space program. The space shuttle and booster system, which contain millions of components, exploded due to the failure of a single O-ring seal that was not designed to fly under the unusually cold conditions of the launch.

If we think of each Shuttle component as being produced by a distinct team, the production function for a successful Shuttle launch might be thought of as resulting from a combination of the efforts of each team and chance, as follows. Suppose that a component functions correctly *for sure* if its team "works" (i.e., supplies adequate effort), and functions with some probability $\alpha < 1$ if its team shirks. A successful launch occurs only if *all* of the shuttle's N components function correctly. Then (if the luck experienced by all the teams/components is independent), the probability of a successful launch is simply $Q = \alpha^s = \alpha^{N-n}$, where s is the number of teams that shirk, and n is the number of teams that "work." The graph following plots this function for the case of 10 teams, for three different values of α (0.7, 0.8, and 0.9). Notice that the function has exactly the increasing-returns property shown in Figure 26.2: The teams' efforts are complementary, as the chances of mission success increase at an increasing rate with the share of members "doing their part."

In economics, the concept of an "O-ring" production process was used by Michael Kremer (1993) to study how interdependence in complex production processes relates to economic development. Although useful as a theoretical tool, this simple production function is of course only a caricature of the process of building the Challenger, which has been exhaustively studied since the disaster. Rather than "shirking" by any individual team, it appears that communication problems may have been the most important contributor to this awful event.

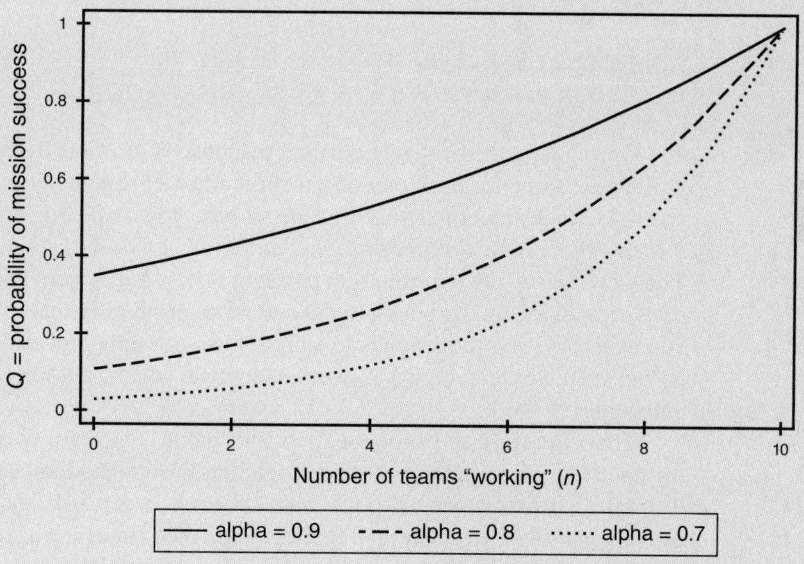

To see what we expect the agents to do, let's work through the consequences of an agent's choices in all the possible situations that agent could find herself in, just as we did for the agents facing a group bonus in Section 24.4.

First, suppose that the agent expects both of her co-workers to shirk. In that case, her utility from working will be

$$U^{work} = 4 \times F(1) - 90 = 4(40) - 90 = 70; \tag{26.6}$$

and her utility from shirking is

$$U^{shirk} = 4 \times F(0) - 0 = 4(20) = 80. \tag{26.7}$$

So, in this case, it is (privately) optimal for the agent to shirk.

If the agent expects exactly one co-worker to shirk, the agent's utility from working and shirking will be given by

$$U^{work} = 4 \times F(2) - 90 = 4(65) - 90 = 170, \tag{26.8}$$

and

$$U^{shirk} = 4 \times F(1) - 0 = 4(40) = 160. \tag{26.9}$$

Now, it is optimal to work.

Finally, if the agent expects no co-workers to shirk, the agent's utility is

$$U^{work} = 4 \times F(3) - 90 = 4(100) - 90 = 400 - 90 = 310, \tag{26.10}$$

and

$$U^{shirk} = 4 \times F(2) - 0 = 4(65) = 260. \tag{26.11}$$

Once again, the privately optimal response is to work. Because this analysis will be the same for each one of our three identical agents, it follows that in our example, under an equal sharing rule, *it pays for an agent to work if and only if the agent can be sure that at least one the two co-workers will do so as well.* Thus, in a sense, the coordination problem is now less severe than in the extreme case of weakest-link production functions, where it only makes sense to work if you expect *all* your colleagues to work. Now with only moderate complementarity between workers, it pays to work as long as you expect just one of your three colleagues to work.

That said, just as in the weakest-link game, there are two Nash equilibria to the effort game among the three workers in our moderate-complementarity example.[13] If every agent expects both co-workers to shirk, the agent will shirk as well, and these expectations will be confirmed for every agent. If every agent expects both of their co-workers to work, the agent will work, and these expectations will be confirmed for every agent too. What will happen? Theory gives us no guide; and as Brandts and Cooper's (2007) results suggest, much will depend on the quality and credibility of communication in the work team.

---

[13] We restrict our attention to pure strategy equilibria throughout this book. See any game theory textbook for a discussion of other types of equilibria, that is, mixed-strategy equilibria.

RESULT 26.4

Equilibrium Effort Levels under Moderate Complementarity and Equal Sharing

For our example of a team production function with moderate complementarity in Table 26.2 and an effort disutility of $90, there are two Nash equilibria in the effort game between the three workers when they are paid according to an equal-sharing rule. In one equilibrium, everybody shirks. In the other, everybody works. These are the same two equilibria that exist in weakest-link games, where complementarity is extreme.

In the case of moderate complementarity, however, a new and different remedy to the coordination problem becomes more practical; in short, this solution (which was proposed by Eyal Winter in 2004) can be called *leadership.* To see how Winter's proposed solution works, continue to assume that all three of the agents are equally able, that their production function is given by Table 26.2, that they can't communicate with each other, and that the only decision each of them makes is whether to "work" or "shirk." The only thing we'll change is the pay schedule; instead of the equal-sharing rule where each agent gets $4 for each $12 fettucine box the group makes (or one-third of the total each), let's *arbitrarily* assign different output shares to each of the three workers. If we label the workers by their pay levels, Worker 3 now gets $3 for each box, Worker 4 gets $4, and Worker 5 gets $5. Thus the equal sharing rule (of one-third, or 4/12 each) is replaced by an unequal rule with shares 5/12, 4/12, and 3/12.

Before studying the consequences of this scheme, we should first note that it goes strongly against the intuitive idea that *employers should not make arbitrary pay distinctions among workers.* If employers randomly pick some people to receive higher wages than others, one might expect this to violate workers' sense of fairness and reduce employee morale. But an arbitrary distinction is exactly what we are proposing here.

To see how introducing this distinction affects team members' incentives, let's once again derive each agent's optimal actions as a function of the agent's *expectations* regarding what colleagues will do. Turning first to Worker 5 (the agent with the highest piece rate), we already know that Worker 5 will want to work expecting one or both colleagues to work because that was the case when the bonus rate was 4, and we have now raised the bonus rate to 5. But what if Agent 5 expects *both* co-workers to shirk? Now, the utilities from working and shirking will be

$$U^{work} = 5 \times F(1) - 90 = 5(40) - 90 = 200 - 90 = 110 \qquad \textbf{(26.12)}$$

and

$$U^{shirk} = 5 \times F(0) - 0 = 5(20) = 100. \qquad \textbf{(26.13)}$$

Worker 5 will now choose to work, *even if no one else does*! Putting these results together, *working is a dominant strategy for Agent 5*: it is this agent's best choice, no matter what the other agents decide to do.

If everyone knows that Worker 5 can be expected to work, what will Agent 4 (the next highest-paid agent) choose? By the same argument (show this yourself as an exercise), working is an (iterated) dominant strategy for Worker 4: *Agent 4 prefers to work*, regardless of what Worker 3 does.[14]

Finally, if Workers 4 and 5 are both expected to work, Worker 3's utilities are given by

$$U^{work} = 3 \times F(3) - 90 = 3(100) - 90 = 300 - 90 = 210 \quad \textbf{(26.14)}$$

and

$$U^{shirk} = 3 \times F(2) - 0 = 3(65) = 195. \quad \textbf{(26.15)}$$

So, knowing that Workers 4 and 5 will work, Worker 3 will now prefer to work.

Putting this all together, we see that the unequal reward scheme ($Y_1 = 3F$; $Y_2 = 4F$; $Y_3 = 5F$) costs the firm exactly the same as the equal reward scheme ($Y_1 = Y_2 = Y_3 = 4F$); but the unequal payment scheme has only one Nash equilibrium: Everybody works.[15] So—at least in theory—free-rider and coordination problems have been solved!

RESULT 26.5

Equilibrium Effort Levels under Moderate Complementarity and Unequal Sharing

For our example of a team production function with moderate complementarity in Table 26.2 and an effort disutility of $90, there is only one Nash equilibrium in the effort game between the three workers when they are paid according to an appropriately designed unequal sharing rule. In this equilibrium, everybody works. Thus, the coordination problem can be solved by using an unequal sharing rule that makes arbitrary distinctions among the agents.

Evidence on Moderate Complementarity: Treating Equals Unequally

Can Winter's (2004) idea of arbitrarily paying different bonus rates to identical members of a team, or "treating equals unequally," work in practice? A recent experimental study by Sebastian Goerg, Sebastian Kube and Ro'i Zultan (2010)

[14] The term "iterated" refers to the fact that once we have established that shirking is a dominated strategy for Worker 5, we remove the possibility that Worker 5 will shirk from the set of things *the other agents believe* that Worker 5 might do.

[15] For game theory enthusiasts, we know this is the unique Nash equilibrium because of the method we used to find it: the *iterated removal of dominated strategies*. For additional details, see Spaniel's game theory video on the topic, retrieved from https://www.youtube.com/watch?v=Pp5cF4RWuU0, or the Wikipedia article on strategic dominance retrieved from https://en.wikipedia.org/wiki/Strategic_dominance.

TABLE 26.3 PERCENT OF TEAM MEMBERS CHOOSING TO WORK (AS OPPOSED TO SHIRK) IN GOERG ET AL.'S (2010) TREATING EQUALS UNEQUALLY EXPERIMENT

	TREATMENT	
Player's Individual Reward Rate	**Unequal Rewards (3, 4, and 5)**	**Equal Rewards (4 each)**
3 lab dollars	88.9%	
4 lab dollars	88.9%	72.2%
5 lab dollars	97.2%	
Mean, over all three players	91.7%	72.2%

suggests that it can, at least in the lab. In fact, Goerg et al. implemented exactly the effort game and production function described in Table 26.2 with a sample of students at the University of Bonn, Germany. Their main results are reproduced in Table 26.3.

When all three members of a team were paid equally (four lab dollars for every unit of output produced by the group), 72.2% of subjects chose to supply positive effort ($E_i = 1$). But when the team members were given different shares of the team's output ($3, $4, and $5, respectively), 91.7% of the subjects supplied positive effort.[16]

Why did unequal pay work better than equal pay in Goerg et al.'s (2010) experiment? An important clue comes from the choices made by the workers in the unequal treatment. As predicted by the classical model of purely selfish behavior, almost all (97.2%) of the workers receiving the highest rate of pay (5) worked. Because the other two workers could therefore be virtually certain that at least one of their colleagues would work, their own, purely selfish incentives to work were increased (because workers' efforts *complement* each other in the production process). To appreciate the effects of these *changes in expectations*, it is instructive to compare the behavior of the lowest paid worker in the *unequal treatment* (call him Jamal) with an average worker in the *equal treatment* (call her Kirsten). Jamal is paid less than Kirsten ($3 vs. $4) and is also paid less *fairly* than Kirsten (because, unlike Kirsten, he has been arbitrarily singled out to get a lower bonus share than his co-workers). Despite this, Jamal works harder than Kirsten! (A total of 88.9% of workers in Jamal's situation choose to work, compared to 72.2% of workers in Kirsten's.) Because Jamal's absolute

[16] Although our example has been framed as a situation where all of the revenues produced by the workers are shared among the workers (so no profits are earned under either reward scheme), it is easy to see how Goerg et al.'s (2010) experimental results are consistent with an increase in profits when the unequal (3, 4, 5) pay scheme is implemented. To see this, imagine that fettucine packages (F) sold for $15 instead of $12. If an employer allocated $12 of these $15 to the workers, the workers would behave exactly as they did in Goerg et al.'s experiment (i.e., as in Table 26.3). The employer's wage bill would be the same as well. But since significantly more workers work under unequal pay, it is very likely that more output would be produced, and profits would rise by $3 for every additional unit of output that is created.

and relative pay are both lower than Kirsten's, his higher effort levels can only be attributed to his enhanced expectations that his colleagues will actually do their jobs.

RESULT 26.6

Treating Equals Unequally: The Surprisingly Beneficial Effect of Paying Identical Workers Differently

Testing a theoretical prediction by Winter (2004), Goerg et al. (2010) arbitrarily assigned different shares of team output (i.e., different α's) to identical "workers" in a lab experiment on team production where there was moderate complementarity between the workers' efforts. Compared to a "fairer," equal-shares treatment, effort levels were higher, and free-riding lower, even among workers with lower pay.

These results are consistent with the idea that giving one worker a larger stake in the outcome can solve coordination problems in teams. Essentially, other workers benefit from the knowledge that it is now in one worker's interest to "do the job" regardless of anyone else's actions. This worker becomes a *de facto* leader, whose leadership "by example" improves the functioning of the team.

Although Result 26.6 might seem strange at first, a little reflection brings to mind some real-life examples. Suppose for instance that you want to get a group to do something, and the members' efforts are complements in that task. An example could be any task where, unless everyone pulls their weight, the quality of the final product is unacceptable—group projects in school, a football team's performance, or a synchronized swim team in the Olympics. Then, even when (from your point of view as the principal) the workers all appear to be identical, it could be in everyone's interests for you to assign one person as "leader" or "captain" and to make his or her compensation—whether financial or just symbolic—more sensitive to the group's overall performance than is the case for the other workers. By making high effort the *dominant strategy* for this person, this arbitrary distinction can help groups solve the coordination problem that is inherent in teams with complementarities.

Of course, arbitrary distinctions like those described previously are not *always* a good idea, as the studies of pay equity described in Section 10.7 have shown. To conclude this discussion, let's remind ourselves of the specific conditions under which "treating equals unequally" might make sense: this strategy should be considered when (a) workers are engaged in group production that involves *complementarities* between workers' efforts, (b) the complementarity is strong enough to cause some coordination failures but mild enough to be remediable by pay differences, and (c) workers are paid according to a sharing rule.

What Do Leaders Do? A Recap

Although the business press is replete with books and advice on "how to be an effective leader," such advice is often contradictory and frequently less than precise. Part of the reason may be that leaders perform many different functions and that the relative importance of these functions varies across organizations and positions. Indeed, the theoretical and empirical discussion in our book so far has identified as least six different tasks that a leader—who could be a "principal" or just a special, designated agent—may need to perform to solve moral hazard and selection problems in organizations. They are (with references to this book and to the key research)

1. **Measuring and monitoring** agents' performance, committing to a reward policy (contract), and implementing that policy (Parts 1 and 2; Alchian & Demsetz, 1972).
2. **Selecting personnel:** By choosing overall pay generosity and pay structure, and by actively recruiting, selecting and retaining the "right" people, managers can have large effects on organizational performance (Part 3).
3. **"Breaking budgets"**: By committing to absorb possible production shortfalls and surpluses that can occur when the group doesn't meet its targets, leaders can implement much stronger incentive schemes than plans that simply divide the "pie" (Section 24.4; Holmstrom, 1982).
4. Leaders **communicate and coordinate:** Incentives alone (whether financial or otherwise) can't make groups work effectively together when marginal returns to effort are interdependent across units of the organization. In these cases, communication from leaders can improve performance by changing workers' *expectations* of what their colleagues will do (Section 26.2; Brandts & Cooper, 2007).
5. Leaders **lead by example:** If other team members know the leader will work hard *no matter what anyone else on the team does*, this can change expectations enough to solve free-rider problems in groups when efforts are complements (Section 26.3; Winter, 2004).
6. Leaders are experts who **impart information and train others**. So far, this has been best illustrated by the informal team leaders in the Koret garment factory (Section 25.3), though there is a substantial quantitative literature on *expert leaders* that suggests that having done the jobs of those you supervise produces more effective leaders due to the expertise this generates (Goodall, 2011; Goodall, Kahn, & Oswald, 2011; Goodall & Pogrebna, 2015). We also return to this leadership role in Section 27.2 (Lazear, 2005; Lazear & Shaw, 2007).

Do Leaders Matter?

Although it seems obvious that better leaders improve the functioning of teams and organizations, this is a surprisingly difficult thing to prove with data. A key obstacle, of course, is disentangling the contribution of a leader from that of the leader's team: A great team can make even a mediocre leader look good.

Still, a few more convincing studies exist. Some take advantage of panel data that follows a large number of leaders and teams (or CEOs and companies) over a longer period of time. That way, most leaders will be exposed to a variety of different teams and we can disentangle the effect of the leader's ability from the quality of the team that leader is matched with. In this vein, Marianne Bertrand and Antoinette Schoar (2003) show that there are, indeed, significant quality differences between CEOs; and that the better CEOs tend to be located in firms with better (i.e., more "arms-length" and meritocratic) governance and to receive higher salaries. Bertrand and Schoar also show that managers tend to have a personal "style" that they carry with them as they move from firm to firm. Using the same approach within a technology-based service company, Lazear, Shaw, and Stanton (2015) study front-line supervisors ("bosses") and find that they vary a lot in effectiveness: Replacing a boss in the lower 10% of boss quality with one in the upper 10% increases a team's total output by more than adding one worker to a nine-member team. Lazear et al. also find that workers assigned to better bosses are less likely to quit.

A different approach to measuring the value of leaders is to take advantage of the rather grim "natural experiment" resulting from a leader's unexpected death. Using this approach, Jones and Olken (2005) collected data on all national leaders worldwide from 1945 to 2000 and identified the circumstances under which the leader came into and left power. Using the 57 leader transitions where the leaders' rule ended by death due to natural causes or an accident, they found that national economic growth rates change substantially and in a sustained fashion: A one standard deviation change in leader quality leads to a growth change of 1.5 percentage points per year. Applying this method to CEOs, Bennedsen, Pérez-González, and Wolfenzon (2007) found that CEOs' (but not board members') own and family deaths are strongly correlated with changes in firm operating profitability, investment, and sales growth.

A more surprising result was obtained by Ulrike Malmendier and Geoffrey Tate (2009), who studied the performance of U.S. CEOs after they receive a major award (such as "Best Manager" or "CEO of the Year") conferred by publications such as *Business Week, Forbes, Time, CNN,* and others. They found that award-winning CEOs subsequently underperformed, both relative to their prior performance and relative to a matched sample of non-winning CEOs. Despite this decline in performance, their compensation increased after the awards, both in absolute amounts and relative to other top executives in their firms. The authors attribute some of this effect to the fact that the winners spend more time on public and private activities outside their companies, such as assuming board seats or writing books. Superstar CEOs, it would appear, are bad news for shareholders.

26.4 Team Effort Choices under Substitutability

So far we've studied team production when identical team members work independently, when they are perfect complements, and when they are moderate complements. When worker's effort choices are dichotomous, the production functions in those three cases can be represented by three curves in Figure 26.3, each of which relates the number of team members who are supplying positive effort, n, to the total amount of output produced.[17] When team members work independently, output is given by our baseline team production function, $Q = d \times \text{sum}(E_i) = n$, which is a straight 45-degree line. As the degree of complementarity increases, these curves become more "convex" in shape when viewed from below (essentially "pulled" toward the southeast), until the curve assumes a "backward L" shape in the case of perfect complementarity.[18] Under perfect complementarity, no output is produced unless every worker supplies positive effort; thus, the production function can be expressed as $Q = D \times \min(E_i)$, or equivalently by the conditions $Q = 0$ if $n < N$; and $Q = D$ if $n = N$.[19]

In this section, we explore how the main results we've derived so far change when, instead of being complements, workers are substitutes in the team production function. To start that analysis, Figure 26.3 also shows the production functions for the cases of moderate and perfect substitutability. As the degree of substitutability increases, the production function is now *concave* in shape (pulled toward the northwest); thus the first few workers who chip in have higher marginal products than the remaining ones. In the extreme case of perfect substitutability, only *one* worker needs to provide positive effort for the group to attain its maximum feasible output. In this extreme case, any one of the team's N workers can do the entire team's work alone. Now, the production function jumps upward at $n = 1$ and is horizontal after that (an upside-down "L" if you like). Mathematically, this means $Q = D \times \max(E_i)$, or equivalently: $Q = 0$ if $n < 1$; $Q = D$ if $n \geq 1$.[20]

---

[17] Strictly speaking, the curves in Figure 26.3 should be a series of dots, since it is not possible, say, for 3.5 workers to work (i.e. to have $n = 3.5$). To make the Figure easier to read, however, we show the continuous curves that would connect these dots for each type of production function.

[18] In addition to appearing convex from below, *convexity* here also refers to the mathematical definition of a function. A continuous, differentiable function of a single variable is strictly convex if its second derivative (F'') is positive. In words, convexity in this context means that output is *increasing at an increasing rate* as n increases. Concavity, which will be our focus in this section, means that $F'' < 0$. Thus, output is *increasing at a decreasing rate* as n increases.

[19] In Figure 26.3, we set $D = dN$. This allows us to compare the various production functions more easily by setting the group's maximum output (when all agents are working) at the same level in all the production functions shown.

[20] A different type of intermediate case between perfect complementarity and perfect substitutability is the widely studied *threshold* production function. It is described by the conditions: $Q = 0$ if $n < n^*$; $Q = D$ if $n \geq n^*$, where n^* is the minimum number of agents who need to "work" for any output to be produced. In Figure 26.3, output now "jumps" upward at a point, n^*, somewhere between $n = 1$ and $n = N$. (In a sense, workers are now perfect complements to the left of n^* and perfect substitutes to the right.) A workplace example could be engineering teams (e.g., at Airbus or Boeing) competing for a contract: Here, the variable n is the quality of the team's proposal (which increases with the number of members providing their full effort levels). If the quality of the proposal does not attain some minimum standard (enough to win the contract), no sales are made.

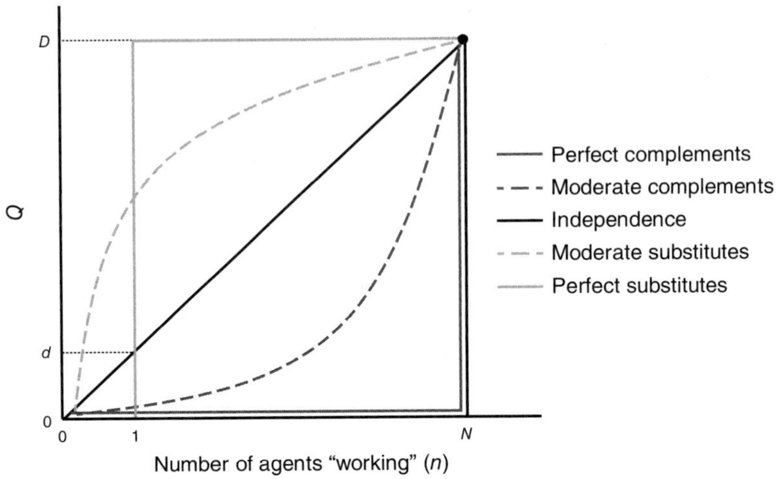

FIGURE 26.3. Team Output with Varying Degrees of Substitutability and Complementarity

Effort Choices under Moderate Substitutability

How do workers' effort decisions change when their efforts are substitutes in the team production function? Turning first to moderate substitutability, fortunately Goerg et al. (2010) also considered this case in their experiment, replacing the production function in row 2 of Table 26.2 (20, 40, 65, 100) by its "mirror image" (across the diagonal in Figure 26.3) of (20, 55, 80, 100). Notice, incidentally, that this production function *dominates* the "moderate complements" production function in the sense that output is strictly higher when $n = 1$ or 2 and the same when $n = 0$ or $n = 3$. Thus, you might expect team members—who are paid a share of the team's output—to be more motivated to supply effort when their efforts are substitutes than when they are complements. As in their "complements" treatments, Goerg et al. randomly assigned two different payment schemes: either equal rewards ($4 each) or unequal rewards ($3, $4, and $5) to the three team members of each team.

They found two main results. First, under equal pay ($4, $4, $4), effort was statistically the same under substitution as under complementarity (73.6% vs. 72.2% of subjects "worked"). Because the "substitutes" production function is more generous to workers (as argued previously), it follows that the substitutes production function is actually less effective in eliciting effort *per dollar spent* on worker compensation. Put another way, under equal pay with a moderate-substitutes production function like the dashed lighter gray line in Figure 26.3, *the principal would experience no decline in worker effort if she simply kept all the output between the moderate complements and moderate substitutes curves for herself!* This illustrates a key idea we first encountered when discussing group piece rates and bonuses in Section 24.4: The principal can benefit (and improve efficiency) by *committing to withhold output from the team* when the team fails to meet a preannounced target.

Goerg et al.'s (2010) other result is that under unequal pay ($3, $4, $5), effort was much *lower* with the "substitutes" production function than the complements production function (65.3% vs. 91.7% of subjects "worked"). Again, this is despite the greater "generosity" of the substitutes function. Thus, although unequal pay was effective in solving the free-rider and coordination problems under complementarity (as we showed in Section 26.3), it is *ineffective* under substitutability. Empirically, that's because under substitution, very few of the lowest paid workers (with a bonus rate of \$3) work. Intuitively, this occurs because even with equal pay, once two agents have decided to work, diminishing returns makes it hard to get the "last" agent to contribute work: He can only produce 20 more boxes of output, compared to 35 in the case of complements. Reducing this "last" agent's bonus rate to \$3 by introducing unequal pay reduces his motivation even further.[21]

☑ RESULT 26.7

Effort Decisions under Moderate Substitutability

Diminishing returns in the team production function make it harder to achieve full efficiency in effort provision because it is now more challenging to motivate team members to provide the "last" unit of effort needed: Not only are the marginal returns to providing this unit shared with all other workers (as always, under a sharing rule), but now the last unit of effort isn't very productive (due to diminishing returns).

Rather than mitigating the preceding problem, Winter's (2010) "unequal rewards" remedy to free-riding—which was effective when workers were complements—*exacerbates* free-riding by reducing the pay of the worker who is least likely to "chip in," that is, the lowest paid worker. Thus **Winter's *treating equals unequally* policy is not likely to improve efficiency when workers are complements.** Instead, it virtually guarantees that the lowest paid worker has no incentive to work, even if the other two workers do their part. These results are demonstrated theoretically and empirically in Goerg et al. (2010).

Effort Choices under Perfect Substitutability: "Don't Worry—Jane'll Handle It!"

Consider a team of four identical workers, each with our baseline utility function, $U_i = Y_i - E_i^2/2$. As always in this chapter, effort is dichotomous (zero or one). The team has a *perfect-substitutes* production function given by $Q = D \times \max(E_i)$, or equivalently, $Q = 0$ if $n < 1$; $Q = D$ if $n \geq 1$. Thus, D units of output are produced if one or more agents "work," and no output is produced if no agents work. The team members are paid according to an equal sharing rule.

Under these assumptions, consider worker i's utility in the event that none of his three colleagues work. In this event, the worker's effort choice is decisive for the group, and utility is given by

$$U^{work} = \frac{D}{4} - \frac{1^2}{2}, \tag{26.16}$$

and

$$U^{shirk} = 0. \tag{26.17}$$

[21] For theoretically inclined readers, Goerg et al. (2010) formalize these statements by deriving all the Nash equilibria to the effort game among workers under both substitutability and complementarity (see their Table 2). Under complementarity with unequal pay, the only (pure-strategy) Nash equilibrium has the two best-paid workers working and the worst-paid shirking. Under complementarity with equal pay, the only equilibria have two workers working and the other shirking.

Thus, it pays for him to work as long as the group's productivity parameter, D, is greater than or equal to 2. We'll assume this is true, which also means that it's economically efficient for the group's task (which requires only one worker's effort) to be completed.

Next, consider worker i's utility in the event that one or more of this worker's three colleagues work. In this event, the worker's effort choice is not decisive for the group (someone has already "done the job"), so utility is given by

$$U^{work} = \frac{D}{4} - \frac{1^2}{2}, \qquad \textbf{26.18}$$

and

$$U^{shirk} = \frac{D}{4}. \qquad \textbf{26.19}$$

Thus, it pays for worker i to shirk.

It follows that there are four distinct Nash equilibria to the effort game among these four workers: In each of these equilibria, one agent works and the other three shirk.[22] In each of these equilibria, every player's choice is optimal given what the other players do, and the players' choices are mutually consistent. But which equilibrium (if any) will occur? In other words, who will be the unlucky agent who gets stuck with doing the job? Again, the agents face a coordination problem, and it can be hard to predict how they'll solve it.

This problem—"which one of us should do the work when there are more than enough of us to do it?"—was theoretically analyzed by Diekmann (1985), who pointed out that it is a special type of public goods problem where any one person in a group can create a fixed benefit for the entire group, but everyone would rather have somebody else do it. Dickmann called the problem *the volunteer's dilemma*; examples from outside the workplace include actions like reporting a pothole or broken streetlight, assisting a motorist who has broken down, or reporting a crime that several people have witnessed. In situations like these, Diekmann argued that the *diffusion of responsibility* that arises when many potential volunteers are available actually *inhibits* helping behavior, compared to a situation where only one person is available to do the job. Thus, a broken-down motorist might be more likely to receive assistance on a deserted road than on a busy one! Other factors that inhibit volunteerism in these situations include *diffusion of blame* (blame for inaction may be less severe if you were one of many who did not take action) and a rational desire to avoid *duplication of effort*: It is wasteful for more than one person to report the same incident (or for more than one person to "work" in our four-person work team example). For this reason, we would expect the under-volunteering problem to be more severe *if bystanders can't observe each other's volunteering decisions* (as in the case of calling 911, e.g.). It could be that no one calls because "with this many onlookers, someone must already have called."

[22] Recall that we restrict our attention to pure strategies only in this book. Mixed equilibria also exist.

RESULT 26.8

Effort Decisions under Perfect Substitutability

When the team production function exhibits perfect substitutability, any one team member can do the work of the entire team. The resulting situation is an effort game between the agents known as *the volunteer's dilemma* in which every team member wants the "work" to be done but (because effort is costly) prefers that someone else do it.

Because the volunteer's dilemma has multiple Nash equilibria, coordination failures are possible, which means that group dysfunction—that is, an outcome where no one invests—is a real possibility. The existence of multiple equilibria also makes behavior hard to predict. That said, because the three factors that inhibit volunteering behavior—diffusion of responsibility, diffusion of blame, and duplication of effort—are all accentuated as the team grows in size, we expect that each individual will be less likely to "work" as the size of the team grows. Also, agents' behavior will depend on whether they can observe if others have already invested. If they can, wasteful duplication of effort can more easily be avoided.

The Bystander Effect and the Murder of Kitty Genovese

Around 3:15 a.m. on March 13, 1964, Catherine Susan "Kitty" Genovese was approaching the front door of her apartment at 82-70 Austin Street in Queens, New York, after finishing work. There, she was brutally stabbed, raped, and robbed over a period of about a half an hour by a stranger, Winston Moseley, during which she repeatedly screamed for help. At 4:15, an ambulance finally arrived, but she died en route to the hospital. Two weeks after the attack, the *New York Times* published a report claiming that 37 or 38 of Genovese's neighbors saw or heard the attack and did not call the police. In the wake of the attack, preachers, professors, and journalists debated the reasons for the neighbors' apparent indifference, citing factors that included "moral decay," "dehumanization produced by the urban environment," "alienation," "anomie," and "existential despair."

After the attack, the neighbors' inaction came to be called the *Genovese syndrome* and was investigated by a number of social scientists. One of the most convincing analyses was by two social psychologists, John Darley and Bibb Latané (1968), who argued that inaction in a group could be explained by the *rational* behavior of individuals, each of whom truly *wants* the victim to be helped. Indeed the *bystander effect* identified by Darley and Latané has become one of the best known results in social psychology. It shows that a bystander's propensity to help in situations like Genovese's declines with the number of others that he *knows are also aware* of the situation. The results have been replicated in numerous lab experiments, where participants are either alone or among a group. The experimenters stage an emergency situation (which appears genuine) and measure how long it takes the participants to intervene (if ever). Typically, the presence of others inhibits helping, often by a large margin. For example, Latané and Rodin (1969) staged

(continued)

an experiment around a woman in distress. Of the subjects who were alone in the room, 70% called out or went to help the woman after they believed she had fallen and was hurt, but when there were other people in the room, only 40% offered help.

Incidentally, although the Genovese episode generated some important social science research, it is somewhat comforting to note that the behavior of Genovese's neighbors was not quite as callous as the *Times* originally reported. As it turns out, later investigations by police and prosecutors revealed that the number of neighbors who heard or observed portions of the attack was closer to a dozen than the 37 or 38 cited in the *Times* article. Also, two of Genovese's neighbors did call the police, who were slow to arrive. In an article published after Moseley's death in prison in 2016, the *Times* admitted that its original report had been "flawed," saying "While there was no question that the attack occurred, and that some neighbors ignored cries for help, the portrayal of 38 witnesses as fully aware and unresponsive was erroneous."

But how important is the volunteer's dilemma in the workplace? At first glance, one might argue that it should be mostly irrelevant because (in contrast to situations that occur in public places) there is an easy remedy to this problem in the workplace: Just reduce the size of the team! If only one person is needed to do a particular job, why assign three people to it?[23] In many cases, this is indeed the best solution, and we will return to it in a more general way when we discuss optimal team sizes in Section 26.5.

Some "helping" jobs in organizations, however, can't be eliminated by cutting team size. For example, a work team—which needs to be larger for other reasons—might need one volunteer to take minutes at a meeting, to organize an event, to represent the team on a committee, or to a write a report. To the extent that these activities are not explicitly compensated (i.e., they are essentially "non-promotable" support tasks), and to the extent that workers have some discretion on whether to accept them, they are a form of volunteerism analogous to those described previously. Completely eliminating such tasks from any organization is probably not feasible, given the complex and imperfectly contractible nature of the employment relationship we discussed in Section 10.2.

So, how do nonpromotable support tasks get done in workplaces, and who tends to do them? In a 2015 paper titled "Breaking the Glass Ceiling with 'No': Gender Differences in Declining Requests for Non-Promotable Tasks," Lise Vesterlund, Linda Babcock, and Laurie Weingart address this question using simple laboratory experiments where subjects choose effort in precisely the

[23]Of course, this argument—of reducing team size to the minimum needed to do the job—also applies to the threshold production function, $Q = 0$ if $n < n^*$; $Q = D$ if $n \geq n^*$, where n^* is the minimum number of agents who need to "work" for any output to be produced. The coordination problems associated with wasteful duplication of effort when workers are substitutes can be eliminated by setting team size, N, *just equal to* n^* in these cases. These reductions in team size might be described as "eliminating slack" from an organization.

perfect substitutes production context described previously. Specifically, in each round of their experiment, participants from a large pool consisting of both men and women were randomly and anonymously assigned to groups of three. Members of each group were then given 2 min to make an investment (volunteering) decision. If no one in the group invested before the 2 min had elapsed, everyone earned $1. If *any* member invested before the 2-min mark, the round ended immediately, with the investor earning $1.25 and the other two group members earning $2.00 each. Thus, it is economically efficient in this game for the investment to be made, but everyone prefers that someone else make it.

How did people behave in Vesterlund et al.'s (2015) "volunteering" experiment? A first interesting feature of behavior is that *people waited until (almost literally) the last second to make their decisions*! Overall, two-thirds of investment decisions were made with less than 3 seconds remaining on the clock. This suggests that volunteering games in groups naturally lead to *procrastination* for reasons that differ from the causes of individual procrastination.[24] Who has not attended a meeting where the chair asks for volunteers and a long, uncomfortable silence ensues? Indeed, *procrastination in teams* has been studied by a number of economists.[25]

A second main result of Vesterlund et al.'s (2015) study is that—despite the potential for free-riding and coordination failures in this environment—for the most part, "the work got done." Over the course of the 10 rounds, an investment was made 84.2% of the time. Thus, in the vast majority of cases—usually with just seconds to spare—some group member stepped in and volunteered to "take one for the team" to achieve a higher payoff for all. Third, and perhaps most interestingly, who were the workers who ended up doing the nonpromotable task to help the group? To a very large extent, Vesterlund et al. found that *it was the women*. On average, women invested at 167% the rate of men (specifically, women invested 35% of the time, compared to 21% for men), a difference which is highly statistically significant.

To shed additional light on why women were much more likely to volunteer for nonpromotable helping tasks, Vesterlund et al. (2015) conducted *single-sex sessions*, where it was apparent to participants that everyone they'd be matched with would be of their own sex. If "volunteering" is an innate or culturally conditioned behavior for women, we'd expect them to volunteer just as frequently in all-female groups as in a mixed-sex group. Similarly, if men are naturally more selfish, we'd expect them to volunteer *just as little* in an all-male group as in a mixed-sex group. Put another way, we'd expect all-male teams to perform quite poorly (with investments being made less frequently than in mixed-sex groups) and all-female groups to perform especially well.

Interestingly, this is *absolutely not* what Vesterlund et al. (2015) found. Instead, single-sex groups performed quite similarly to mixed-sex groups: Comparable to the 82% investment rate in the mixed-sex sessions, the authors found

---

[24] For an excellent study of procrastination by individual workers, see Kaur, Kremer, and Mullainathan (2015).

[25] See in particular Bonatti and Hörner (2011) and Weinschenk (2016).

an investment rate of 81% in the single-sex sessions. Thus, it appears that the gender gap in helping behavior seen in Vesterlund et al.'s main experiment was not driven by a preference or personality trait that differs systematically between the sexes. Instead, the behavior is better explained by a factor that is central to our game-theoretical analysis—subjects' *expectations* of whether their teammates will "work"—which appear to be context dependent. Essentially, if women expect men to shirk in mixed-sex groups, women's rational, self-interested strategy is to make the investment. By the same token, if men expect women to *do* the work in mixed-sex groups, men's rational, self-interested strategy is to take it easy and "let Jane do it." In mixed-sex groups, it therefore appears that sex acts as a *coordinating mechanism* that helps groups converge on a particular equilibrium of a game with multiple equilibria. In single-sex groups, that device is not available. Because men can no longer assume that the women will do the work, they now step up (somebody has to do the cooking, cleaning, and sewing on a pirate ship, after all!). In all-female groups, rational women will now experiment with "being more selfish" because they are now more confident that their teammates will invest.

☑ RESULT 26.9

Gender and Nonpromotable Tasks: Vesterlund et al.'s Volunteering Experiment

The perfect-substitutes team production function is a surprisingly accurate representation of a decision that frequently arises in organizations: *Which* member of a work group will volunteer to do a task that benefits the group but has little personal benefit?

In a 2015 paper, Vesterlund et al. implement a three-person, perfect-substitutes, team production problem in the laboratory. Overall, groups performed quite efficiently, "getting the job done" over 80% of the time. Strikingly, however, the team members who ended up "doing the work" were quite disproportionately female, with women "stepping up" at 167% the rate of men. Because both women's high rate of volunteering and men's low rate disappeared when the subjects were put into single-sex groups, the preceding gender differential is not well explained by gender differences in personality, tastes, or altruism. Instead it appears that *shared expectations* (among both men and women) that women will do the "helping" tasks in mixed-sex groups are a better explanation.

Like Niederle and Vesterlund's (2007) experiment on gender and competition—which we studied in Section 23.2—Vesterlund et al.'s (2015) experiment on gender and volunteering might help explain the continuing low representation of women in high corporate, academic, and political positions. Indeed, both casual empiricism and the small amount of data that is available suggest that women are more likely to accept such non-promotable, "helping" task assignments. For example, in a survey of 350 faculty at University of Amherst,

Misra, Hickes Lundquist, Holmes, and Agiomavritis (2011) found that compared to men, women faculty spent 7.5 fewer hours per week on research—which *is* promotable—and 4.6 more hours per week on university service committees (to which lip service is given but is rarely decisive in receiving tenure or promotions). Thus, according to Vesterlund et al., to "get ahead" at the same rate as men, *women need to learn to say "no"* more frequently to requests to volunteer for nonpromotable, "helping" tasks.[26]

26.5 Effort, Ability Differences, and Optimal Team Size

In the last section, we provided a simple and extreme example of how an adjustment to team size (specifically, reducing the team to a single individual when workers are perfect substitutes) could solve coordination and free-riding problems in teams. Our first goal in this section is to consider the question of optimal team size more generally: How big should a team be? Our second goal is to study the effects of ability differences among team members: Do ability differences typically cause problems in teams (as they did in tournaments) or could ability differentials actually *improve* the functioning of teams?

Optimal Team Size

We begin our discussion of optimal team size by completely ignoring the problem of how to induce team members to supply efficient levels of effort. Put another way, we'll assume away the *moral hazard* problem of motivating the agents by assuming that everybody on the team "works" (as opposed to shirking). In this case, how large should a team be? To address this issue, we begin by what we mean by the "optimal" team size.

☑ RESULT 26.10

Ignoring Moral Hazard, the Optimal Way to Group a Pool of Identical Workers Into Teams Is to Maximize Average Product (AP) Per Member

If all agents can be counted on to provide full effort levels when they are added to a team, a profit-maximizing employer with a large pool of identical workers should group the workers into teams such that the *average product* (AP) of a team member is maximized. This grouping is also the *economically efficient* grouping.

[26] If you are interested in learning more about how to say "no" effectively and without repercussions, check out the *Forbes* magazine article on Vesterlund et al.'s *I Just Can't Say "No" Club.* https://www.forbes.com/sites/ruchikatulshyan/2016/06/28/the-i-just-cant-say-no-club-women-need-to-advance-in-their-careers/#accd71049173.

To prove Result 26.10, imagine a firm with a large group of workers (M in number) that it wants to allocate to work teams. If the firm divides its M workers into m equal teams, then (ignoring remainders) each team will have $N = M/m$ workers in it. Suppose that any team that is formed has a production function given by $Q(N)$, which can have increasing, decreasing, or constant returns to scale.[27] Then this firm's profits will be given by

$$\Pi = mQ(N) - Mw, \qquad \textbf{(26.20)}$$

where w is the wage it has to pay each (identical) worker. Using $m = M/N$, Equation 26.20 can be rewritten:

$$\Pi = M\frac{Q(N)}{N} - Mw. \qquad \textbf{(26.21)}$$

Because M and w are fixed (they don't depend on how workers are organized into groups), the way to make profits as large as possible is to choose a team size, N, such that output per worker (Q/N) is maximized. To prove that this is also the *economically efficient* team size, just replace w in Equations 26.20 and 26.21 by $V(E) = V(1)$ (the disutility of effort). Then maximizing average product also maximizes the difference between the total amount produced by all the workers and the workers' effort costs of producing that output.

RESULT 26.11

Optimal Team Size with Increasing or Decreasing Returns at All Output Levels

If the team production function has decreasing returns to scale (i.e., substitutability) at all levels of output, the optimal team size is as small as possible (i.e., one worker). In other words, the firm shouldn't group workers into teams at all.

If the team production function has increasing returns to scale (complementarity) at all levels of output, the optimal team size is as large as possible. In other words, the firm put all its M workers into a single, large team.

Perhaps the easiest way to see Result 26.11 is to consider the production functions for moderate substitutes and complements in Figure 26.3, interpreting the horizontal axis now as N (team size) rather than n (the number of workers who decide not to shirk). In each of those production functions, the average product ($AP = Q/N$) of a team member can be represented by the slope of a ray from the origin to the curve at any given team size. For the moderate-substitutes production function, this slope is greatest when the smallest possible number of

[27] Output can be written as a function of the number of team members, N, because we have assumed that every team member "works," that is, that $n = N$.

workers is employed. (It is tangent to the production function at the origin.) For the moderate-complements function, Q/N increases without limit as N rises.

DEFINITION 26.4 When the team production function exhibits increasing returns to scale at low output levels, but decreasing returns at high output levels, it is a **classical** team production function.

We use the term "classical" because this production function is closely related to the U-shaped average cost function that is taught in standard introductory economics. It is also the simplest production function that leads to an optimal team size that is neither zero nor infinity.

The solid curve in Figure 26.4 depicts a classical team production function. This team production function is intuitively appealing for two reasons. First, the increasing returns as the first few team members are added capture the idea that there can be efficiency gains from working together. These gains include the opportunity to specialize, to engage in division of labor, and to share expertise and information. Second, the diminishing returns at high output levels capture the idea that eventually, large teams become unwieldy. Workplace teams, if they exist, rarely consist of the entire company (except perhaps in an abstract sense). So, if we are to explain why most firms of any size are organized into subunits, the team production function must eventually have diminishing returns to scale.

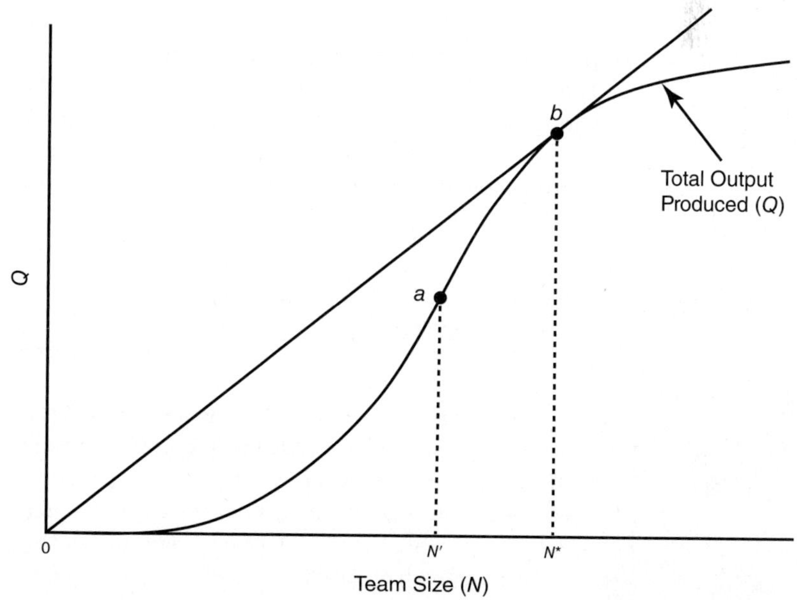

FIGURE 26.4. Economically Efficient Team Size with Identical Workers

The classical production function in Figure 26.4 has increasing returns to scale (i.e., an increasing slope) at team sizes ranging from zero up to N'. That is because point a is the function's *inflection point*, where the slope is maximized. When more than N' workers are allocated to a team, the team's production process has decreasing returns. Because the average product per team member (Q/N) at any given team size is given by the slope of a ray from the origin to the production function, average product is maximized at point b, where the ray is tangent to the production function. Thus, the optimal team size is N^* workers. Notice that N^* must be to the right of N'. Thus, *at the optimal team size, a team has decreasing returns to an additional member.*

RESULT 26.12

Optimal Team Size with a Classical Team Production Function, without Moral Hazard

If the team production function is classical and workers always supply full effort levels, the optimal team size will be at an interior point (i.e., more than one worker and less than the firm's entire workforce). At this output level, the team's production function will be subject to *diminishing returns*, that is, $Q''(N) < 0$.

We have now reached a point where we can introduce moral hazard into our discussion of optimal team size. Specifically, we now ask, "How does the preceding analysis change when we allow for the possibility that team members might not exert full effort?" As we've seen in Sections 26.3 and 26.4, when agents are paid according to a sharing rule, it is somewhat easier to motivate team members when they are complements than when they are substitutes. Thus—for essentially the same reason that it pays to reduce the group size to one person in the volunteer's dilemma—*it may make sense to reduce team size from N^* toward N' in Figure 26.4.* By eliminating the region of diminishing returns in the production function—at the cost of a relatively small reduction in average product (AP)—we might reduce shirking and coordination problems for the reasons discussed in Sections 26.3 and 26.4.

RESULT 26.13

Optimal Team Size with a Classical Team Production Function, *with* Moral Hazard

If the team production function is classical and workers can ***choose*** whether to work or shirk, the **optimal team size might be smaller than the size that maximizes AP.** In other words, it might be to the left of point N^* in Figure 26.4. By reducing or eliminating the region of the production function with diminishing returns, it may be easier to motivate agents by taking full advantage of agents' incentives to motivate and monitor each other when they are complements in the production process.

The intuition behind Result 26.13 is a more formal version of arguments that are frequently advanced in favor of the *lean production paradigm* (Krafcik, 1988). As we discussed in Section 25.3, this management philosophy deliberately *creates complementarities* among workers (e.g., using a dowel as a *kanban* in garment production) to take advantage of their incentive-enhancing properties. As Result 26.13 suggests, one key way to create these complementarities is *by reducing team size below the level that would be efficient in the absence of moral hazard concerns.*

Ability Differences and Effort Choices in Teams

In Chapter 22, we argued that ability differences between agents created problems in tournaments: When competing agents are unevenly matched, incentives to supply effort are reduced among both the abler and the less-able contestants. Possible remedies included raising the stakes, organizing contestants into "leagues" of matched ability, and "handicapping" the abler agents to tighten up the competition. Does any of this logic carry over to teams? In particular, are ability differences beneficial or problematic in teams? And if a team's ability "mix" is not optimal, is there anything (other than adjusting the mix) a principal can do to address the situation? Given the fact that complementarity is one of main reasons that teams exist, and given the last section's argument that firms will have an incentive to choose team sizes and production processes that accentuate complementarities, we restrict our discussion to team production functions with effort complementarities.[28]

As it turns out, when workers are complements, ability differences make it *easier* to attain efficient effort levels in team production. This result contrasts sharply with what we found for tournaments in Part 4. To see this, return to our analysis of effort choices in a three-agent team with moderate complementarity (the fettucine example) in Section 26.3. There, we showed that if the agents were paid according to an equal sharing rule ($4 per fettucine box each), the effort game among the three agents had two equilibria: one in which everybody works, and one in which everybody shirks.[29] In that example, however, we assumed that the agents were equally able, that is, that each agent experienced the same disutility from working (90 lab dollars).[30]

Now, let's change that example to one where the three agents have different effort costs of 70, 90, and 110 lab dollars, respectively. Thus, the average effort costs are unchanged at 90 lab dollars, but now the agents are heterogeneous, with

[28] Winter (2004) also treats the case of substitutability, but the results are much less clear and intuitive.

[29] This follows from the fact that, when any agent expects two co-workers to shirk, that agent's utility equals 80 shirking but only 70 working.

[30] The equal-ability assumption also entered our calculations in a second way, namely, that the output levels when 1 or 2 agents are working in Table 26.2 and Figure 26.2 did not depend on *which* agents were working. To keep the calculations simpler, we'll continue to assume that (i.e., that the workers are *interchangeable* in the production process) in what follows.

the first agent (called "Agent 70") being the most able.[31] If you re-do the arithmetic in Equations 26.6–26.11 starting with Agent 70, you will find that *it now pays Agent 70 to work regardless of what that agent expects colleagues to do.*[32] From this it follows (by *iterated removal of dominated strategies*) that there is now only one Nash equilibrium to the effort game in which everybody works.

RESULT 26.14

Ability Differences and Effort Decisions in Teams When Workers Are Complements

When workers are complements in production, ability differences among workers can mitigate free-riding and coordination problems. They can do this by making it a dominant strategy for the abler agents to work, thus eliminating "shirking by all" as one of the Nash equilibria of the effort game among the workers.

Intuitively, ability differences between workers play the same role as the arbitrary wage differences that we studied in Section 26.3: They can change workers' expectations of what their colleagues will do by creating at least one agent—a de facto leader—who everyone expects will work *no matter what anyone else does.* An example is the "big donor" at a fundraising event. At many such events, it is common to display a large thermometer in the hall showing the group's progress toward its goal. To the extent that the group of donors attaches a discrete value to reaching the goal (so that, e.g., \$99,999 feels qualitatively different from a \$100,000 goal), this creates a type of complementarity between their donations because each member's utility "jumps" upward when the goal is reached. But because it is hard for a small donor to feel that a donation is relevant to attaining the group's goal, it is common to ask the donors with the "deep pockets" to make their pledges first, thus raising the "temperature" that's displayed. This brings the next-richest donors into a situation where they can "make a difference," and so on, with progressively smaller donors feeling that their contribution can become relevant as the goal is approached.

To see the implications of Result 26.14 for workplaces, consider an employer with a pool of employees of varying ability who is deciding how to group these workers into teams. According to the result, if the workers are complements, total output is likely to be higher if they are organized into *mixed-ability* teams, so that each team will have one leader who changes expectations and motivates the others on the team. Notice that this is the *opposite* of the ability-homogeneous groups that are recommended by Chapter 22's tournament theory.

The previous discussion is useful if an employer has a large group of heterogeneous employees and has the flexibility to combine them into work groups in various ways. But what if an employer is stuck with a given ability mix of team

[31] We refer to agents with lower effort costs as having higher ability because they can generate more output per unit of effort than a high-effort-cost agent. In most cases, it does not matter whether we model higher ability as a higher productivity parameter (d_i) or as having lower effort costs, though it is sometimes mathematically more convenient to do it one way versus the other.

[32] If neither colleagues work, Agent 70 gets a utility of 80 if shirking and 90 working.

members that is not the optimal mix? Is there anything the employer can do with its pay policy—analogous to the handicaps used in tournaments—to remedy the situation? As it turns out, if the group is too homogeneous, we've already answered this question in Section 26.3: The employer can "manufacture" heterogeneity by introducing arbitrary wage differentials between members.[33] Finally, it's worth noting that when team members are heterogeneous in ability, Winter (2004) has shown that it is generally in the firm's interest to *accentuate* these ability differences by assigning higher bonus rates to abler workers. In a sense, this policy is also the opposite of what we found in Section 22.3 for tournaments, where moral hazard can be mitigated by using affirmative action to counteract ability differences.

RESULT 26.15 **Managing Ability Differences in Teams (Winter, 2004)**

(a) When workers are complements in production, workers should be grouped into *mixed-ability teams*, not homogeneous-ability teams, to maximize effort and output.

(b) When ability differs within teams, and workers are complements in production, the optimal pay policy allocates *higher group bonus rates to the abler team members.*

In discussing the broader implications of Result 26.15, Winter (2004) interprets the better paid, higher ability workers in his model of team production as occupying higher ranks within an organization. He also notes that—because substantial pay differences can make sense even when workers are equally able (Result 26.4)—pay differences that reinforce ability differences can lead to a situation in which even minor ability differences correspond to large differences in pay. Interestingly, this is the same outcome as in Rosen's (1986) superstar model of multi-stage promotion tournaments (see Section 20.7) though for a very different reason: motivating an *interdependent team* of workers.

Chapter Summary

- Complementarity in the context of team production means that higher effort by one worker raises the marginal productivity of others. Hard evidence of complementarity has been found in the contexts of professional sports, scientific research, and medical teams.

[33] It seems intuitive that in the opposite situation—where the group is *too heterogeneous*—a firm could counteract this by "leaning against the wind" and giving smaller bonus rates to the abler workers. To the best of my knowledge, this question has not been studied. It is also not clear that a team can have *too much* heterogeneity when workers are complements.

- ☐ Weakest-link team production functions embody an extreme form of complementarity. An advantage of these production processes (compared, say, to a linear production function) is that it is generally a Nash equilibrium for all agents to supply efficient effort levels. A disadvantage is that it can be hard for agents to coordinate on the efficient equilibrium. Brandts and Cooper's (2007) Corporate Turnaround experiment shows that a small amount of communication between principals and agents can be much more effective than higher financial incentives in these circumstances. Facilitating communication within teams by providing paid meeting time can has been shown to improve the productivity of production teams in steel mini-mills (Boning et al., 2007).

- ☐ Team production processes with moderate complementarity exhibit increasing returns to scale, like the "O-ring" process where a component has a chance of failing if its producer supplies insufficient effort. When workers are identical, Winter (2004) and Goerg et al. (2010) have shown that principals can improve the functioning of teams in these cases by arbitrarily choosing one member and paying that member a larger bonus rate than the others. This member becomes a de facto leader because it is in this person's interests to supply full effort regardless of what the others do, which mitigates coordination problems.

- ☐ Team production processes with moderate substitutability exhibit decreasing returns to scale. Here, it is typically counterproductive to introduce pay heterogeneity among identical workers.

- ☐ Extreme substitutability in production (where there are more than enough workers on the team to get the job done) can often be profitably eliminated by reducing the size of the team. When this is not possible, the teams' members face the volunteer's dilemma. Vesterlund et al.'s (2015) experiments on this dilemma show that although a volunteer is successfully identified in the vast majority of cases, women are much more likely to volunteer than men. The authors argue that this high rate of volunteering for nonpromotable tasks may help explain women's underrepresentation in higher corporate ranks.

- ☐ Ignoring moral hazard, the economically efficient allocation of a large workforce of identical workers to teams maximizes the AP of a team member. When moral hazard (i.e., the potential for free-riding) is present, employers may wish to reduce team sizes below this level to enhance the complementarities among workers within the team. In a way, this is the essence of the lean production model.

- ☐ In sharp contrast to tournaments, ability differences among team members can actually *improve* team functioning by facilitating coordination on full effort by all members. This happens for the same reason that adding pay heterogeneity can improve team performance. When there are ability differences on a team, the optimal pay policy accentuates these by giving abler members higher shares of output. This also contrasts with tournament pay policy, where mitigating ability differences via affirmative-action-type policies can improve efficiency.

Discussion Questions

1. Could Arcidiacono et al.'s (2017) approach to measuring productivity spillovers in sports be applied to beach volleyball? What special problem might arise in this case?
2. Think of a workplace or other team you have belonged to. In your estimation, are the members substitutes or complements according to the definitions in this chapter? If complementarities exist, are they between specific people, as in Bartel et al.'s (2014) study, or just between the roles people occupy? Do the complementarities grow with shared experience? Is the team of the efficient size? Why or why not?
3. What does it mean for a worker to be decisive in a weakest-link or threshold production process?
4. In many lab experiments, such as Fehr and Gächter's (2002) study of altruistic punishment, the experimenters don't let the subjects communicate with each other in any way. Sometimes the experimenters even go to great lengths to ensure that no pair of subjects interacts more than once. These conditions are clearly unrealistic, and would never occur in any real workplace team. Why, then, do the experimenters impose them? Do you think that imposing these conditions is a good idea?
5. Explain in your own words why it might sometimes make sense for employers to impose arbitrary bonus rate differentials between identical workers in a team.
6. Think of your current or most recent boss on a job. Which of the six leadership functions listed at the end of Section 26.3 did the boss perform? In your estimation, were these the most important and relevant functions for that production environment? Why or why not? Did your boss perform them adequately?
7. Describe the volunteer's dilemma. Under what conditions is it likely to be most severe?
8. In Sections 24.4, 26.2, and 26.3, we demonstrated that a worker's expectations of what her teammates were going to do were an important determinant of her (privately) optimal behavior. Suppose that you were able to influence other team members' beliefs about your own behavior by acquiring a

reputation for being (a) an incurable shirker, or (b) a diehard workaholic who never shirks. If your team exhibits a weakest-link production process, which reputation would you rather have? What if workers are extreme substitutes?

9. Look up lean production online. Which features of this management philosophy are reflected in results derived in this chapter?

10. Return to the question of optimal team size without moral hazard, which we considered in Results 26.10 through 26.12. Instead of assuming—as we did there—that the firm can form as many teams as it wants from its workforce, each with a production function of $Q(N)$, assume instead that the firm is contemplating a single new project which has that production function. To allocate workers to that project, it has to remove them from another activity where each worker produces units of output. Does the profit-maximizing team size still maximize AP? Why or why not?

11. Discuss how Results 26.12 and 26.13 change when, instead of having a classical production function, teams have a threshold production function, that is, where $Q = 0$ if $n < n^*$ and $Q = D$ if $n \geq n^*$, where n^* is the minimum number of agents who need to "work" for any output to be produced. Interpret your result in terms of designing organizations so as to "eliminate slack."

Suggestions for Further Reading

Although we have considered a variety of possible team production functions in this chapter, most are quite simple and allow for a relatively limited range of productive interactions between workers. For a theoretical and experimental analysis of team production using a much more general team production function (the CES, or constant elasticity of substitution function), see Fenig, Gallipoli, and Halevy (2015).

Although we have studied coordination problems in a team of workers selecting effort levels, these problems arise in a wide variety of other contexts, including organizational design, technology adoption and diffusion, monopolistic competition, speculative attacks on currency markets, and bank runs, to name just a few. For additional reading on coordination problems in these areas, see Schelling (1980), Friedman (1994), or Cooper (1999).

In addition to Brandts and Cooper's (2007) evidence, many experiments have shown that communication increases contributions and effort even when it is cheap talk. For additional examples, see Cooper, DeJong, Forsythe, and Ross (1992), or Charness and Dufwenberg (2006).

In Section 25.3 we noted that competition between teams can be an effective motivator. But what about cooperation between teams? After all, in an important sense all large firms consist of many teams; so firms are effectively teams of teams. Indeed, some of the most interesting applications of team theory are to the question of how to get different subunits, divisions, etc. of a larger firm to cooperate, coordinate, and share information with each other. For some interesting studies of this process, see Knez and Simester (2001) who study interactions between teams at Continental Airlines, and Feri et al.'s (2010) large-scale experiment.

For additional evidence and analysis of complementarities between HRM policies, see Ichniowski, Shaw, and Prennushi's (1997) study of steel finishing lines, and Ichniowski and Shaw (2003).

The issue of optimal and actual task allocation within teams (including who should be the "leader") is just beginning to be studied by personnel economists. For some recent analyses, see Rivas and Sutter (2011) and Cooper and Sutter (2014).

For an interesting application of our optimal team size rule in evolutionary anthropology (with evidence from Inuit hunting groups) see Smith (1985).

References

Alchian, A. A., & Demsetz, H. (1972). Production, information costs, and economic organization. *American Economic Review, 62*(5), 777–795.

Arcidiacono, P., Kinsler, J., & Price, J. (2017). Productivity spillovers in team production: Evidence from professional basketball. *Journal of Labor Economics, 35*(1), 191–225.

Azoulay, P., Graff Zivin, J. S., & Wang, J. (2010). Superstar extinction. *Quarterly Journal of Economics, 125*, 549–589.

Vesterlund, L., Babcock, L., & Weingart, L. (2015). *Breaking the glass ceiling with "no": Gender differences in declining requests for non-promotable tasks.* Unpublished manuscript, Department of Economics, University of Pittsburgh, Pittsburgh, PA.

Bartel, A. P., Beaulieu, N. D., Phibbs, C. S., & Stone, P. W. (2014). Human capital and productivity in a team environment: Evidence from the healthcare sector. *American Economic Journal: Applied Economics, 6*(2), 231–259. doi:10.1257/app.6.2.231

Bennedsen, M., Pérez-González, F., & Wolfenzon, D. (2007, March). *Do CEOs matter?* Unpublished manuscript, Stern School of Business, New York University, New York, NY.

Bertrand, M., & Schoar, A. (2003). Managing with style: The effect of managers on firm policies. *Quarterly Journal of Economics, 118*, 1169–1208.

Bonatti, A., & Hörner, J. (2011). Collaborating. *American Economic Review, 101*, 632–663. doi:10.1257/aer.101.2.632

Boning, B., Ichniowski, C., & Shaw, K. (2007). Opportunity counts: Teams and the effectiveness of production incentives. *Journal of Labor Economics, 25*, 613–650.

Brandts, J., & Cooper, D. (2007). It's what you say, not what you pay: An experimental study of the manager-employee relationship in overcoming coordination failure. *Journal of European Economic Association, 5*, 1223–1268.

Charness, G., & Dufwenberg, M. (2006). Promises and Partnership. *Econometrica, 74*(6), 1579–1601.

Charness, G., & Sutter, M. (2012). Groups make better self-interested decisions. *Journal of Economic Perspectives, 26*(3), 157–176.

Cooper, R., DeJong, D. V., Forsythe, R., & Ross, T. W. (1994). Alternative Institutions for Resolving Coordination Problems: Experimental Evidence on Forward Induction and Preplay Communication. *Problems of coordination in economic activity*, 129–146.

Cooper, Russell. (1999). *Coordination Games: Complementarities and Macroeconomics.* Cambridge, UK: Cambridge University Press.

Cooper, D. J., and Sutter, M. (2014). *Endogenous role assignment and team performance.* Unpublished manuscript, Department of Economics, Florida State University, Tallahassee, FL.

Darley, J. M., & Latané, B. (1968). Bystander intervention in emergencies: Diffusion of responsibility. *Journal of Personality and Social Psychology, 8*, 377–383.

Diekmann, A. (1985). Volunteer's dilemma. *Journal of Conflict Resolution, 29*, 605–610.

Fehr, E., & Gächter, S. (2002). Altruistic punishment in humans. *Nature, 415*(6868), 137–140.

Fenig, G., Gallipoli, G., & Halevy, Y. (2015). *Complementarity in the Private Provision of Public Goods by Homo Pecuniarius and Homo Behavioralis.* Unpublished manuscript, Vancouver School of Economics, University of British Columbia, Vancouver, BC Canada.

Feri, F., Irlenbusch, B., & Sutter, M. (2010). Efficiency Gains from Team-Based Coordination—Large-Scale Experimental Evidence. *American Economic Review, 100*(4), 1892–1912. doi: 10.1257/aer.100.4.1892

Friedman, James W., ed. (1994). *Problems of Coordination in Economic Activity.* Boston: Kluwer Academic.

Goerg, S. J., Kube, S., & Zultan, R. (2010). Treating equals unequally: Incentives in teams, workers' motivation and production technology. *Journal of Labor Economics, 28*, 747–772.

Goodall, A. (2011). Experts versus managers: A case against professionalizing management education in business schools. In W. Amann, C. Dierksmeier, M. Pirson, H. Spitzeck, & E. Kimakowitz (Eds.), *Under fire: Humanistic management education as the way forward* (pp. 122–129). London: Palgrave Macmillan.

Goodall, A., Kahn, L., & Oswald, A. (2011). Why do leaders matter? A study of expert knowledge in a superstar setting. *Journal of Economic Behavior and Organization*, *77*(3), 265–284.

Goodall, A., & Pogrebna, G. (2015). Expert leaders in a fast moving environment. *Leadership Quarterly*, *21*, 1086–1120.

Gould, E. D., & Winter, E. (2009). Interactions between workers and the technology of production: Evidence from professional baseball. *Review of Economics and Statistics*, *91*, 188–200.

Hirshleifer, J. (1983). From weakest-link to best-shot: The voluntary provision of public goods. *Public Choice*, *41*(3), 371–386.

Holmstrom, B. (1982). Moral hazard in teams. *Bell Journal of Economics*, 324–340.

Ichniowski, C., Shaw, K., & Prennushi, G. (1997). The Effects of Human Resource Management Practices on Productivity: A Study of Steel Finishing Lines. *American Economic Review*, 291–313.

Ichniowski, C., & Shaw, K. (2003). Beyond Incentive Pay: Insiders' Estimates of the Value of Complementary Human Resource Management Practices. *Journal of Economic Perspectives*, *17*(1), 155–180.

Jones, B. F., & Olken, B. A. (2005). Do leaders matter? National leadership and growth since World War II. *Quarterly Journal of Economics*, *120*, 835–864. doi:10.1093/qje/120.3.835

Kaur, S., Kremer, M., & Mullainathan, S. (2015). Self-control at work. *Journal of Political Economy*, *123*, 1227–1277.

Knez, M., & Camerer, C. F. (1994). Creating "expectational assets" in the laboratory: "weakest link" coordination games. *Strategic Management Journal*, *15*, 101–119.

Knez, M., & Simester, D. (2001). Firm-Wide Incentives and Mutual Monitoring at Continental Airlines. *Journal of Labor Economics*, *19*(4), 743–772.

Krafcik, J. F. (1988). Triumph of the lean production system. *Sloan Management Review*, 30(1): 41–52.

Kremer, M. (1993). The O-ring theory of economic development. *Quarterly Journal of Economics*, *108*(3), 551–575. doi:10.2307/2118400

Latané, B., & Rodin, J. (1969). A lady in distress: Inhibiting effects of friends and strangers on bystander intervention. *Journal of Experimental Social Psychology*, *5*(2), 189–202.

Lazear, E. P. (2005). Entrepreneurship. *Journal of Labor Economics*, *23*, 649–680. doi:10.1086/491605

Lazear, E. P., & Shaw, K. L. (2007). Personnel economics: The economist's view of human resources. *Journal of Economic Perspectives*, *21*(4), 91–114.

Lazear, E. P., Shaw, K. L., & Stanton, C. T. (2015). The value of bosses. *Journal of Labor Economics*, *33*, 823–861.

Malmendier, U., & Tate, G. (2009). Superstar CEOs. *Quarterly Journal of Economics*, *124*, 1593–1638. doi:10.1162/qjec.2009.124.4.1593

Misra, J., Lundquist, J. H., Holmes, E., & Agiomavritis, S. (2011). The ivory ceiling of service work. *Academe*, *97*(1), 22.

Niederle, M., & Vesterlund, L. (2007). Do women shy away from competition? Do men compete too much? *Quarterly Journal of Economics*, *122*, 1067–1101.

Rivas, M. F., Sutter, M. (2011). The benefits of voluntary leadership in experimental public goods games. *Economics Letters*, *112*(2), 176–178.

Rosen, S. (1986). Prizes and incentives in elimination tournaments. *American Economic Review*, *76*, 701–715.

Schelling, T. C. (1980). *The strategy of conflict.* Cambridge, MA: Harvard University Press.

Smith, E. A. (1985). Inuit Foraging Groups: Some Simple Models Incorporating Conflicts of Interest, Relatedness, and Central-Place Sharing. *Ethology and Sociobiology*, *6*(1), 27–47.

Van Huyck, J. B., Battalio, R. C., & Beil, R. O. (1990). Tacit coordination games, strategic uncertainty, and coordination failure. *American Economic Review*, *80*, 234–248.

Vesterlund, L., Babcock, L., & Weingart, L. (2015). *Breaking the glass ceiling with "no": Gender differences in declining requests for non-promotable tasks.* Unpublished manuscript, Department of Economics, University of Pittsburgh, Pittsburgh, PA.

Waldinger, F. (2010). Quality matters: The expulsion of professors and the consequences for PhD student outcomes in Nazi Germany. *Journal of Political Economy*, *118*, 787–831.

Waldinger, F. (2012). Peer effects in science: Evidence from the dismissal of scientists in Nazi Germany. *Review of Economic Studies*, *79*, 838–861.

Weber, R. A., Camerer, C. F., & Knez, M. (2004). Timing and virtual observability in ultimatum bargaining and "weak link" coordination games. *Experimental Economics*, *7*, 25–48.

Weinschenk, P. (2016). Procrastination in teams and contract design. *Games and Economic Behavior*, *98*, 264–283.

Winter, E. (2004). Incentives and discrimination. *American Economic Review*, *94*, 764–773. doi:10.1257/0002828041464434

Choosing Teams: Self-Selection and Team Assignment

27

In Section 26.5, we asked how ability differences among teammates might affect their effort decisions. In contrast to tournaments, we found that ability differences in teams could sometimes make it *easier* for principals to elicit efficient effort levels. In this chapter, we consider two additional aspects of ability differences in teams. In Section 27.1, we focus on *self-selection* into teams. There, we consider situations where workers can choose whether or not to join a team and ask two questions: First, compared to working on their own, *which* workers will prefer to work on teams? The factors we identify here also apply to workers' decisions on whether to join profit-sharing and related incentive schemes and to workers who are choosing between firms with cooperative, individualistic, or competitive cultures. Second, imagine a firm that *requires* all of its workers to *sort themselves* into teams (as in the Koret garment factory discussed in Section 25.3). Who will end up matching with whom? Under what conditions should firms assign workers to teams instead of letting them self-organize? We'll even discuss what economics has to say about perhaps the ultimate example of team formation—the process of choosing a lifetime partner in the marriage market.

In Section 27.2, we'll focus on cases where firms involuntarily assign workers to teams and ask what the optimal way to assign them is. Should workers be grouped into teams with homogeneous or heterogeneous skill levels or skill types? If team members bring different skills or information to the team, when is it most important for employers to facilitate "horizontal" communication among team members, as in the steel mini-mills we studied in Section 26.2? And finally, *how* can employers foster effective information sharing within workplace teams?

To allow us to focus on worker *selection* into teams, throughout this chapter we'll completely ignore the problem of *motivating* workers, that is, we'll ignore the moral hazard problem. In other words, as we did in most of Part 3, we'll assume that all workers provide the same level of effort regardless of whether they are on a team or work independently, and regardless of the *type* of team they are on (in particular, regardless of who their teammates are).

27.1 Who Wants to Join Teams? Ability Differences and Self-Selection

In this section, we study the factors affecting team formation among heterogeneous workers in two different ways. In the first, "partial equilibrium" approach, we imagine a pre-existing team with a certain set of members, and ask three simple questions about it: "Who would want to join that team?"; "Which of the original members would want to leave that team?"; and "Which outsiders would the current members agree to *admit* to their team?" The answers to those questions are summarized in a pair of rules we call the *Groucho Marx Rules*, named after the comedian's famous resignation message to the Delaney Club: "Please accept my resignation. I don't want to belong to any club that will accept me as a member."[1]

After exploring the surprising amount of economic insight contained in Groucho's simple statement, we will next turn our attention to the more difficult "general equilibrium" question of what we might expect to happen if, for example, an employer just asked a group of workers to sort themselves into teams of a certain size, letting those workers communicate and interact in any way they like during the process. In addition to their implications for the workplace, we'll see that models of this equilibrium self-selection process have broader implications for a wider set of issues including firm formation, marriage markets, and rising income inequality in many economies.

The section concludes by summarizing some evidence on equilibrium team formation that is literally from the "field." Specifically, in a recently published analysis of the same U.K. fruit farm they studied in Section 21.2, Bandiera, Barankay and Rasul (2013) analyzed what happened when they required all of their fruit pickers to self-organize into teams of five. The results support the main predictions of equilibrium selection models, but also show some surprising effects of team self-selection on workers' effort levels, which are typically not considered in those models.

The Groucho Marx Rules

The first and simplest question we can pose about worker self-selection into teams considers a team of N heterogeneous workers with a linear production function given by

$$Q = d_1E_1 + d_2E_2 + \dots + d_NE_N, \tag{27.1}$$

where d_i is the ability of team member i.[2] If any of these team members decides to work alone instead of on a team, we'll assume that worker produces an output

[1] Marx fans may wish to know that there are actually several versions of this quote, some of which refer to a different club. This version comes from his 1959 memoir, "Groucho and Me."

[2] Equation 27.1 generalizes the linear production function introduced in Equation 24.2 to the case of more than two workers.

of $Q_i = d_i E_i$ and is paid full productivity, $Y_i = Q_i$. Assuming that every team member always supplies one unit of effort, then the total output of this team will be given by the sum of its members' abilities:

$$Q = \sum_{i=1}^{N} d_i, \tag{27.2}$$

and the output of any member when working alone is just $Q_i = d_i$.

Now, let's ask which of the N members actually *want* to be on this team. If the members are paid according to an equal sharing rule, then team member i's pay when working on the team is given by

$$Y_i^T = \frac{\sum_{i=1}^{N} d_i}{N} \equiv \bar{d}, \tag{27.3}$$

where $\bar{d}$ is the mean ability of the team members. When working alone, person i would earn

$$Y_i^A = d_i \tag{27.4}$$

because that person's output is no longer averaged with any teammates. Equations 27.3 and 27.4 lead to the following income- and utility-maximizing decision rule for individual i:[3]

$$\text{Join the team if and only if } d_i < \bar{d}. \tag{27.5}$$

RESULT 27.1

The Groucho Marx Rule for Joining and Quitting Teams

When teams have linear production functions and members are paid according to an equal-sharing rule, people will only want to join teams whose average member is a more productive worker than they are.

Put another way, with linear production functions and an equal-sharing pay rule, all the workers with above-average ability in any team will prefer to quit and work independently instead.

The Groucho Marx rule for joining teams shows that equal sharing rules on teams create incentives for *adverse selection into teams*. Notably, this tendency for teams to attract less-able workers contrasts strongly with Results 23.1 and 23.2 on tournaments, where we noted that tournaments tend to attract contestants who think they are *abler* than their competitors. This Groucho Marx rule also suggests two important cautions for employers who may be thinking of letting workers choose between joining teams or working independently. First, if it's

[3] In this chapter, a worker's utility is maximized when income is maximized because we have assumed that all workers exert the same amount of effort no matter where they are employed.

important to have the best workers on the teams, *letting workers choose might not be the best policy*. Second, under any group pay rule (like equal sharing) that tends to equalize the pay of the members, *it may be a challenge keeping the best workers in the team environment*. In these circumstances, employers may wish to consider various types of financial and symbolic ways to recognize the special contributions of each team's top contributor(s).

Closely related to Result 27.1, consider now the effects of adding a new member on the well-being of the N team members in our example. Each member's income before the new addition is just $\overline{d}$ (the average ability of the incumbent team members), and each member's income after adding a new member is $\overline{d}^N$, the average ability of the new team of $N + 1$ members. Thus, all the incumbent team members will only want to admit new members *who bring up the average ability* of the team, that is, workers who are abler than the existing members.

☑ RESULT 27.2

The Groucho Marx Rule for Admitting Team Members

When teams have linear production functions and members are paid according to an equal-sharing rule, all the members of existing teams will agree on the following admissions policy: The team should only admit new members who are abler than the average existing member.

This second Groucho Marx rule suggests an additional *caveat* for employers: workers who belong to output-sharing teams have incentives to be too reluctant and "choosy" when admitting new members. In essence, new members might be excluded from the team even though those members would be more productive on the team than off of it. (The prospective members are excluded because the incumbents don't want to share the team's spoils with the newcomers.) This reluctance to admit newcomers is actually a well-known problem in the economics of worker-managed firms and might be one reason why such firms are so uncommon in unregulated markets.[4] The implication for employers is to be cautious when granting output-sharing teams too much control over the number and type of members they can admit.

While conveying a very widely-applicable intuition, our two Groucho Marx rules have special significance for a particular type of club (including, for example, the club of Nobel Prize winners), whose main "output" is a signal of prestige. In essence, the main thing these clubs do is certify that you belong to a group whose typical member has a particular level of wealth or accomplishment. Here, Equation 27.3—which says that each team member's utility from belonging to a team is given by the average ability of the existing members—is an especially accurate description of reality. Returning to Groucho's famous quote, joining such a group only raises Groucho's prestige if the club's members are more

[4] See Ward's (1958) and Browning's (1987) analyses of worker cooperatives for further discussion of this point.

Who Wants to Cooperate? Gender and Self-Selection into Teams

In an experiment published in 2015, Marie Claire Villeval and I (Kuhn & Villeval, 2015) studied gender differences in decisions to join teams. To allow for comparisons with decisions to join tournaments, we used a similar design to Niederle and Vesterlund's (2007) study of gender and tournament entry (see Section 23.2). Therefore, we gave subjects a choice between (a) doing a real-effort laboratory task as part of a two-person team with a linear production function and an equal-sharing pay rule, or (b) working alone and being paid for their own performance. Because teams are a *cooperative* work environment (where each worker's pay depends *positively* on a teammate's performance), we thought that both men's and women's decisions to join teams might be very different from their decisions to enter tournaments, where competition prevails.

In addition to the fact that neither men nor women free-ride on these two-worker teams, our article had two main results. First, consistent with the first Groucho Marx rule, we found strong and consistent evidence of *adverse selection* into teams: Abler participants of both genders tended to avoid teams, and participants *who thought their partner was very able* tended to join teams. As a result of this selection process, self-selected teams performed worse than randomly assembled teams and worse than the subjects who choose to avoid teams. Second, we found that *women were much more likely to choose the team environment than men.*

To understand why this happened, we asked the subjects to guess their own and their teammate's likely task performance before they made their team-entry decisions. As in Niederle and Vesterlund's (2007) "tournaments" experiment, the women in the Kuhn and Villeval (2015) experiment were less confident in their own relative abilities than men were (despite being just as good at the task as men). Importantly, *this gender difference in confidence completely explains women's higher rates of entry into team-based pay in the experiment*: In sum, women are more likely to believe they are less able than their teammates, and this belief *raises* women's (perceived) financial gain from joining a team!

distinguished than he is. But such a group would only wish to admit Groucho if it felt the opposite: that adding Groucho would raise *their* average prestige. Thus, Groucho keenly infers that offering to admit him may be a tacit admission by the group that it was not very prestigious to begin with.

Kuhn and Villeval's (2015) results have a number of implications for workplace policies. One is to shed some light on the underlying reasons for gender differences in workers' selection into cooperative versus competitive work environments. In our experiment, women's above-average, team-entry decisions were not the result of any gender differences in preferences (such as higher altruism, risk aversion, or a greater desire for pay equality). Instead, women's team-entry decisions can easily be explained as a rational, income-maximizing response to their own beliefs about their own relative ability. To the extent that these beliefs can be altered by providing accurate information, this suggests that gender differences in workplace choices may not be "set in stone" by biological or cultural factors but could instead be changed by providing accurate performance feedback, as Wozniak, Harbaugh, and Mayr (2014) argued in the case of tournaments (see Section 23.2).

Finally, just as Niederle and Vesterlund's (2007) experiment may help explain some women's avoidance of competitive work environments, Kuhn and Villeval's experiment may shed some light on some women's attraction to cooperative work environments. Indeed, in most nations, women tend to be highly overrepresented in "helping" professions like nursing, teaching, child and elder care, and social work—professions where cooperation, not competition, are essential to the production process.

The Theory of Equilibrium Team Formation

Now that we've studied individual workers' incentives to join teams, as well as team members' decisions regarding whom to admit, we can move on to a harder question: Suppose that a firm uses teams, and that—as is often the case—it allows its workers to choose their own teammates. If every worker has to be on a team, who will actually match with whom? Instructors who assign group projects encounter this situation frequently, and it also comes up in the context of company mergers, strategic coalition formation among countries or political parties, in human marriage markets, and even in mate selection in the animal kingdom.

To even begin to think about this problem formally, it helps to restrict our attention to cases where all potential teammates can be ranked along a single dimension of desirability, or "quality," and where everyone agrees on that ranking. In this case, we can define three broad ways in which members of a population can be matched into groups, or teams.

DEFINITION 27.1

Positive assortative matching occurs when agents are more likely to match with others of similar quality to themselves than with agents of a different quality. In this case, members of the same team tend to be similar to each other, although the average qualities of the teams tend to be quite different from each other. Put another way, the *within-team* variance of quality is low, although the *between-team* variance is high.

Random matching occurs when all agents are equally likely to match with each other, regardless of quality. In this case, members of the same team are no more or less similar to each other than are members of different teams.

Negative assortative matching occurs when agents are more likely to match with others of a different quality from themselves than with agents of similar quality. In this case, members of the same team tend to be different from each other, although the average qualities of the teams tend to be similar to each other. Put another way, the within-team variance of quality is high, whereas the between-team variance is low.

Loosely put, positive assortative matching occurs when "likes match with likes," and negative assortative matching occurs when "opposites attract." Although the mathematics of equilibrium team formation can become complex, and whereas theoretical predictions can depend on the precise assumptions about how matches can be made and broken, economists who have studied matching theory tend to agree on one result. Essentially, whenever the total "output" of a team or coalition must be *shared* among the members (in the sense that less-able members inevitably gain from being in the same team with abler members), *positive* assortative matching tends to occur in equilibrium.[5]

To see why, consider an even-numbered pool of N workers, all with different abilities, d_i, who have to sort themselves into teams of two. Suppose further that the output of any team that is formed just equals the sum of its members' abilities $(d_i + d_j)$, and that this is divided equally within each team. Then the utilities of team members i and j, when teamed with each other, just equal $U_i = U_j = (d_i + d_j)/2$. Now, because everyone wants to match with the most able person in the pool, the ablest person can pick any teammate that person wants. Naturally the best person will pick the second best, so the top two will match. Then the same argument applies to the third and fourth best, and so on down the list. Once all these matches are formed, no one will be able to propose an alternative match that makes both prospective teammates better off. In sum, if all workers are free to propose matches with any other worker, and if both team members must agree to any match, then the only matching pattern that can survive self-interested attempts to improve one's match is a pattern of *perfect assortative matching*.[6]

RESULT 27.3

Expected Matching Patterns when Team Members Are Paid According to an Output-Sharing Rule

When workers of heterogeneous abilities are required to self-select into teams where they are paid according to an output-sharing rule, we expect *positive assortative matching* to occur.

The perfect assortative matching predicted by the preceding thought experiment is of course an extreme result, which derives from the *frictionless* matching process that was assumed: Anyone could leave their partner without cost at any time for a better match, and everyone's ability was publicly known. In more realistic contexts, we expect matching to be positive but less than perfect.[7] The incentives for workers to invest time and effort in improving their matches, however,

[5] Mathematically, sharing refers to any situation where the utility of one member of a team depends positively on the quality of that member's teammates. This is clearly the case in teams that use any kind of output sharing rule, and in marriages where resource sharing is ubiquitous, inevitable, and moral.
[6] For theoretically inclined readers, the solution concept described in words here is a *coalition-proof Nash equilibrium*. For a simple application of this theoretical concept to workplace team formation, see Bandiera, Barankay, and Rasul (2013), whose experiment is discussed later in this section.
[7] For an interesting theoretical example of how assortative matching emerges in marriage markets with frictions, see Burdett and Coles (1997).

will be stronger (a) when the team-based component of pay is high, and (b) when the overall pool of workers to be matched is very heterogeneous (making the best person very different from the worst). Thus, we expect Result 27.4.

☑ RESULT 27.4

Expected Effects of Team-Based Pay and Ability Inequality on Matching Patterns

Theory predicts that positive assortative matching into teams should be stronger when team incentives are stronger, and when the dispersion of ability in the overall worker pool is high.

Although some of our earlier theoretical discussions of team-based financial incentives emphasized the need for these incentives to be very strong (recall, e.g., the discussion of group piece rates in Section 24.4), Result 27.4 identifies one potential *drawback* of strong team-based financial incentives. Specifically, in situations where workers are allowed to self-sort into teams, strong team-based financial incentives will affect not only workers' effort levels but will also affect *how workers sort themselves into teams.* In cases where it is economically efficient for teams to be heterogeneous—for example, because heterogeneity improves incentives or because it maximizes learning opportunities among the members—strong team incentives can be counterproductive because they may induce workers to match up with teammates who are as similar as possible to themselves in terms of ability. Indeed, to avoid this problem, in certain circumstances it may be better for employers to *assign* workers to teams rather than letting workers self-select. Of course, if workers have better information about their own capabilities and compatibilities than the employer does, involuntary assignment may also have some disadvantages as well.

Field Evidence on Equilibrium Team Formation

Is there any evidence that strengthening team incentives affects the way workers self-select into teams? As it happens, a recently published field experiment on agricultural workers by Bandiera et al. (BBR; 2013) illustrates this process. In the 2005 harvest season on the same U.K. fruit farm we studied in Section 21.2, Bandiera et al. required all of their fruit pickers to self-organize into teams of five. Teams were formed at a weekly *team exchange*, where workers could either register a list of five people who had all agreed to form a team or could form teams with other unmatched workers who attended. Team members were paid according to an equal-sharing rule that applied to the total amount of fruit their team picked every day.

At two points in the 2005 season, the experimenters increased the incentives faced by these teams. The first such increase was purely symbolic in the sense that no additional compensation was offered. Instead, the farm managers just publicized the total output of every team, so that all the workers could see which teams were the highest ranked in the firm. Section 21.3's evidence that workers have intrinsic motivations to "win" a tournament suggests that this could change workers' effort and team-formation behavior. Later in the season, the firm introduced a substantial weekly cash prize for the most productive team.

BBR's (2013) most important and novel finding was that strengthening team incentives (in either of these two ways) did indeed change the way workers sorted themselves into teams. In the first half of the season, when incentives were lowest, workers were very likely to form teams with their friends, without paying too much attention to how productive those friends were. Thus, teams didn't differ from each other too much in terms of average ability, although workers of quite different ability levels frequently found themselves on the same team. When team incentives were increased, however, workers teamed up differently. Now they were much less likely to be on the same team with their friends and tended much more to match up with workers of similar ability to themselves. Thus, the degree of positive assortative matching increased: Teams now differed substantially from each other in terms of average ability, although within teams, the workers tended to be of similar ability.

What was the effect of strengthening team incentives on total productivity on BBR's (2013) fruit farm? As we noted previously, this depends in part on whether homogeneous or heterogeneous teams are more productive in the fruit-picking context. Although mutual helping and training opportunities—a key advantage of heterogeneous teams—were minimal in BBR's context, heterogeneous teams did have one important advantage: Compared to working with strangers, working with friends—even if they weren't the ablest teammates you could find—was more effective in reducing free-riding within teams. Thus, the side effect of discouraging workers from teaming up with friends has the potential to undo the incentive-enhancing effect of stronger incentives. As it turns out, this is exactly what BBR found when teams' rank information was publicized: Total productivity *fell* by 14%. That said, the strong motivating effect of the cash bonus was sufficient to outweigh this side effect (productivity rose by 24%).

☑ RESULT 27.5

Effects of Team-Based Incentives on Team Formation Patterns and Productivity: Fruit Farm Evidence

Bandiera et al.'s (2013) study of fruit pickers shows that increasing team incentives—either symbolically, by publishing the team ranks, or financially, by introducing a bonus for the top-performing team—increased the amount of positive assortative matching in the way workers sorted themselves into teams.

Overall, providing rank information *reduced* average productivity on the fruit farm because it made workers less likely to team up with their friends. (Friendship within teams tended to reduce free-riding.) The cash bonus for the best team, however, increased productivity, as its direct motivating effect outweighed the effect of reducing the number of friends on the same work team.

Marriage as Team Formation: Assortative Matching and Income Inequality in the U.S. Marriage Market

One of the most important ways in which humans sort themselves into productive "teams" that share the fruits of their labors is in the marriage market. And although assortative marital matching can be studied for any human characteristic (including language, religion, height, race, IQ, politics, and caste, to name a few), one characteristic that has particularly important implications for economic inequality is education.

In the United States, as in most other countries, it is well known that marriages exhibit *positive assortative matching on education.* In other words, people are much more likely to marry someone with an education level similar to their own than we'd expect if matching were random. Less well known is the fact that the degree of positive assortative matching on education in U.S. marriages *has been increasing rapidly* since at least 1970 (Greenwood, Guner, Kocharkov, and Santos, 2014, 2016). Put simply, Americans today are much more likely to be married to a person of similar education to themselves than they were 50 years ago.

Why has this happened? In a clear parallel to Bandiera et al.'s (2013) fruit farm experiment, economists attribute at least some of this change to the well-known increase in wage inequality that occurred over the same period: As the earnings gap between college- and high-school-educated people rose dramatically, the *economic consequences of marrying* a college- versus high-school-educated spouse also rose. In other words, the strength of team-based financial incentives rose, leading to an increase in the degree of positive assortative matching.

An important societal consequence of the increase in positive education matching is that it has magnified the increase in income inequality *between families* (i.e., between "teams") in the United States. As college-educated men are now much more likely to be married to college-educated women, and as the wage gap between workers with and without a college education has continued to grow, the economic gap between these college-educated "power couples" and other families has become increasingly visible, with important consequences for society and politics.

Bandiera et al.'s (2013) field experiment brings us back to one of this book's main themes, that HRM policies work through at least two main channels: motivation and selection. In Bandiera et al.'s case, HRM policies that increase team incentives affected not only how hard the pickers worked within each team but also how they self-selected themselves into teams. In some cases, like the policy of publishing the team rankings, the selection effects of the policy can counteract the direct incentive effects of the policy, leading to an unexpected and undesirable result.

27.2 Skill Diversity, Information Sharing, and Team Performance

So far in our study of teams, we have examined the conditions under which workers are likely to self-select into homogeneous versus heterogeneous teams, and we have argued that heterogeneous teams might have some advantages for at least two reasons: incentives (Section 26.5) and helping behavior (Section 25.3). In this final section, we explore the role of a third factor—information sharing—in enhancing team productivity. Three main lessons emerge.

First, we present a formal argument suggesting that both heterogeneous ability levels and *disjoint information sets* have benefits for teams. Second, we compare knowledge-sharing teams that capitalize on disjoint information with another form of organization—hierarchies—and ask under what conditions either type of organization is likely to be optimal. Finally, we note that—although the sharing of disjoint information that workers bring to teams is usually desirable—it is by no means *automatic*. Here we discuss some recent empirical research from the IT industry on the decisions by members to contribute ideas to a group—research that has intriguing emerging implications for optimizing team performance.

Ability Differences, Disjoint Information, and Team Productivity

In their study of the Koret garment factory, Hamilton et al. (2003) found that teams with a greater dispersion of ability levels outperformed more homogeneous teams with the same average ability.[8] Hamilton et al. (2003) attributed this result, in part, to the greater opportunities for peer training and information sharing in heterogeneous teams: Teams with a "superstar" member can ask that person to share special skills and knowledge with the group, thereby raising the other members' performance. These opportunities may be less prevalent in teams where everyone is at the same level of competence.

A more formal version of Hamilton et al.'s (2003) argument is presented in Figure 27.1. Here we imagine a situation in which there is only one *type* of skill, or area of expertise, that is used on a team. For concreteness, it might help to think of a unit of skill as a year of experience in an area: As workers accumulate experience, they encounter new situations and learn new facts and ways of working that less-experienced workers haven't yet been exposed to. In such an environment, Figure 27.1 compares two two-worker teams, both with the same total amount of skills: 10 units, or 10 total years of experience. On the homogeneous team, both workers have 5 units of skill (years of experience); on the heterogeneous team, one worker has 7.5 years and the other has 2.5 years. Note that if the team members work independently (i.e., if the production function takes a linear form like Equation 27.2), then we would expect these two teams to be equally productive: $Q = 5 + 5$ in the homogeneous team and $Q = 7.5 + 2.5$ in the heterogeneous team.

On the other hand, if the worker with 7.5 years of experience can transmit some skills and knowledge to the less-experienced teammate (say, bringing teammate up to a skill level of 5), the heterogeneous team will soon be more productive than the homogeneous team, producing 12.5 units of output. This reasoning highlights a special feature of knowledge and information that distinguishes them from most other economic goods: Knowledge and information are *nonrival* goods.

[8] Mas and Moretti (2009) report a similar finding for supermarket cashiers.

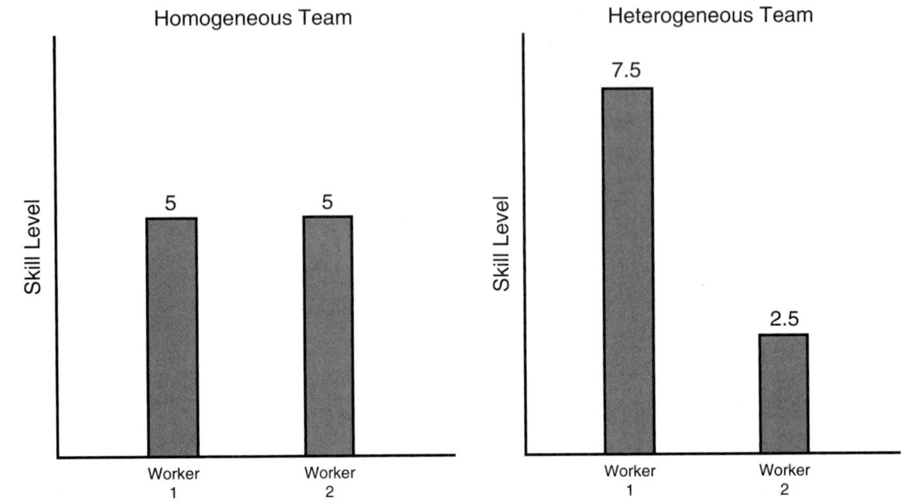

FIGURE 27.1. Homogeneous and Heterogeneous Teams when Workers Differ in Skill *Levels*

DEFINITION 27.2

If I own two iPads and I give you one of them, I will have one fewer iPad, and you will have one more. The same is true if I give you $50.

This same, simple fact is however *not* true if I give you my mother's to-die-for paprika schnitzel recipe, or if I show you a much simpler way to synchronize the contacts between your iPad and all your other devices. I can still use and enjoy those things even though I have "given" them to you.

When one person's consumption of a unit of a good does not preclude another's consumption of that same unit, economists call it a **nonrival good**. Important examples of nonrival goods include most types of knowledge and information, public goods like the temperature in a room and the air quality in a city, and many forms of art and entertainment. For example, your choice to watch the World Series does not diminish my viewing options, unless of course we are talking about the same seat at the live event.

The nonrival nature of knowledge and information is the key economic property that explains why heterogeneous teams have the potential to be more productive than homogeneous teams.[9] Put another way, the nonrival nature of information creates *complementarities* in production between workers *when workers possess different pieces of information.* As a result, the presence of an abler worker on your team can make you more productive because of the skills and information that worker can share with you.[10]

[9] Of course, some types of information *are* rival goods in the sense that they are more valuable when others don't have access to them. Examples might include a juicy piece of gossip, a patentable idea, or an insider stock tip. Most everyday job skills probably don't have this property, however.

[10] Let's also not forget that team-based pay *incentivizes* these abler workers to share their knowledge and information with their teammates.

Mandated Within-Team Heterogeneity at Harvard Economics: Assembling Study Groups

The entering class of Harvard Economics PhD students, although highly qualified as a group, has a surprisingly heterogeneous set of skills. Whereas many of these skills are important for eventually writing a dissertation and becoming an independent scholar, one skill that is particularly important for making it through the first year of the program is mathematics preparation. Entering students can range from having a master's degree or more in abstract mathematics to students who are accomplished in other areas (and have high math aptitudes) but have only a few college math courses.

At least when I was a student in the program, the department had a policy of *assigning* all the first-year students to study groups, which were explicitly designed to be heterogeneous in terms of math preparation. Students were not allowed to switch groups without the department's permission. In other words, the department enforced *negative assortative matching* (on math training) with the explicit goal of maximizing the amount of mathematical knowledge transfer that occurred within the groups. Letting students self-select into study groups, given the department's objective, could have led to an inferior outcome, with the "best teaming up with the best" and the rest falling behind.

The example in Figure 27.1 refers to a hierarchical type of knowledge where workers possess different *amounts* of the same skill type, and it is perhaps best suited to skills that tend to be acquired in a certain fixed order over the course of formal education and training, apprenticeship, or experience in a particular job or profession. In many cases, however, teams are composed of people with very different backgrounds doing a variety of tasks, with each worker bringing a different mix of skills and capabilities. Is the concept of skill heterogeneity still relevant in these contexts, and if so, how might we measure it?

Figure 27.2 addresses this question by imagining an entire *space* of skills, or pieces of information, that a worker can bring to a job. We represent this space by the the bold-outlined squares, with each point in the square standing for a skill or a fact that a worker might or might not possess. Now we draw a circle around all the skills that Agent 1 possesses, and similarly for Agent 2. In a two-worker team comprising these two agents, the area of overlap between the circles denotes the facts that both workers know; in some sense this is *redundant* information because (given that information is a nonrival good) once one worker knows it, the team has access to it. The areas inside the circles but outside the overlap (e.g., the two "crescent moons" facing each other in Part a of Figure 27.2) are *disjoint* information: these are things that the two *workers can learn from each other* if they join the same team.

In this more general setting, the *disjointness* between the agents' information sets is probably a more appropriate measure of within-team skill heterogeneity.

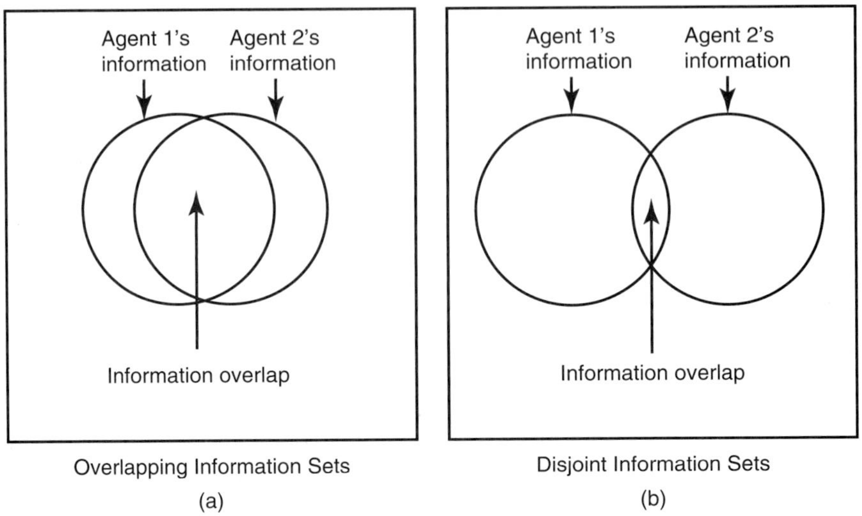

FIGURE 27.2. Teams with Overlapping versus Disjoint Information Sets

Disjointness can be measured by the *area* of the nonoverlapping parts of the circles, and is much greater in Part b (the two *gibbous* moons) than in Part a.

There are three noteworthy differences between Figures 27.2 and 27.1. First, Figure 27.2 allows us to think of skills in a much more general, multidimensional way than Figure 27.1. Second, the two figures use different measures of skill heterogeneity: the *difference* or dispersion in the agents' *level* of qualification in 27.1 versus the *disjointness* of their information in 27.2. Third is the *directionality* of information exchange and learning: In Figure 27.1 it was only the more qualified worker teaching the less-qualified; in Figure 27.2, both workers have things they can learn from each other. Despite these differences, both of these ways to think about skills and information lead to the same result: Heterogeneous teams are likely to have a productivity advantage over homogeneous teams because they offer greater opportunities to share information.

☑ **RESULT 27.6**

Predicted Effects of Skill Heterogeneity on Team Productivity

If all members of a team are doing a similar task but have different performance levels in that task, a reasonable measure of skill heterogeneity is given by the *dispersion in ability levels* within the team.

If team members bring different *types* of skills and knowledge to the group, the *disjointness* in the skills and knowledge they bring is a more appropriate measure of the team's skill heterogeneity.

In either case, the *nonrival* nature of information means that heterogeneous teams offer more opportunities for productivity-enhancing information transfers. For this reason, we should expect that, ceteris paribus, heterogeneous teams will be more productive than homogenous ones.

In sum, Result 27.6 formalizes a key reason—information sharing—why we might expect heterogeneous teams to be more productive than homogeneous teams. This source of heterogeneous teams' expected productivity advantages is distinct from their expected effects on workers' effort decisions, which we summarized in Result 26.14.

Teams versus Hierarchies

So far in this section, we've argued pretty forcefully that skill diversity and information sharing among team members is a good thing. Supporting this idea, many companies—especially start-ups navigating a rapidly changing environment and companies running complex processes— rely on skill-diverse teams that share information internally (i.e., "horizontally") to solve problems as they arise. Not all companies work this way, however. For example, some highly profitable firms are much more hierarchically organized. These firms encourage information to flow *up and down the hierarchy*, instead of within teams, and are more likely to require approval of decisions at higher levels of the hierarchy instead of delegating them to teams of experts. Under what circumstances might each of these two organizational modes—teams versus hierarchies—be optimal?

To shed light on this question, Lazear and Shaw (2007) ask us to imagine two fictitious teams, depicted in Figure 27.3. Part a of Figure 27.3 shows the skill mix of a three-person team: Person a is the "design expert," with two units of design skills and one unit of operations skills. Person b is the operations expert, with two units of operations skills and one of design skills. Person c has just one

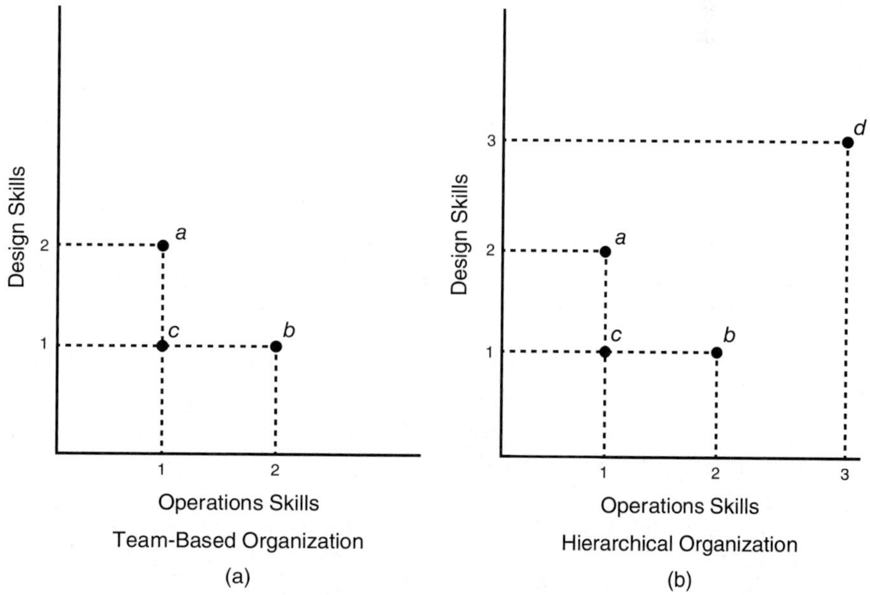

FIGURE 27.3. Team-Based versus Hierarchical Organizations

unit of either type of skill; that person is on the team either because extra manpower is needed to achieve a threshold output or because his wage is low enough to make this profitable. Notice that the team in Part a has disjoint skills (because *a* has some design information that *b* doesn't have, and *b* has some operations information that *a* doesn't have). For this team to function well, we would thus expect to see considerable communication and information exchange within the team, with *a* and *c* consulting *b* about operations issues, and *b* and *c* consulting *a* about design questions.

Now, let's add a fourth person to the mix. In Part b of Figure 27.3, we introduce person *d*, who has three units of design skills and three units of operations skills. If this person (who has an absolute advantage in both skills over all the other workers) was part of the operation, who would consult with whom? Now, if person *a* or *c* has a question about operations, person *d* is a better resource than person *b*. If *b* or *c* has a question about design, *d* is a better resource than *a*. Thus, person *d* in effect becomes an expert supervisor who is consulted by everyone. In this new organization, all information flows *vertically* (between the three original team members—*a, b,* and *c* at the "bottom"—and person *d* at the top) instead of *horizontally* among the three initial team members. Given *d*'s special expertise, *d* may even have to "sign off" on all major decisions made in the organization.

DEFINITION 27.3 In a **team-based** organization, information flows *horizontally* among a group of members, each of whom may have some expertise that is not available to the others. Decisions are made within the team, and there is not necessarily a formal team leader.

In a **hierarchical** organization, information flows *vertically* between a group of workers and a manager who has a high level of expertise in multiple aspects of the team's activities. Most important decisions are made, or at least checked, at higher levels of the hierarchy.

What are the advantages and disadvantages of these two alternative forms of organization? A first and obvious disadvantage of the hierarchical format is that it requires hiring an extra person, who—though very productive—might also be very expensive given that person's broad *and* deep skill mix. Another disadvantage may be speed: If the leader does not work in close proximity with the three team members, consultations with that person may be time consuming. Closely related, requiring all information to flow through person *d* could create information *bottlenecks,* as person *d* is not able to handle all requests in a timely manner. This is especially problematic if person *d* has many subordinates.[11] On the other

[11] In the HRM and organizational behavior literatures, the number of subordinates a manager has is known is the *span of control*. Theories about the optimal span of control have long history in these fields, and many are based on the problems of managing the flow of communication—which can quickly become overwhelming—in large, multilevel organizations. These questions are beyond the scope of our book. For a recent, interesting treatment of the subject (and a brief review of some of the literature) see Bandiera, Prat, Sadun, and Wulf (2013).

hand, the leader's high level of skill may result in better decisions and more output, which could more than make up for these disadvantages.

With these considerations in mind, under what conditions do we expect to see firms choosing teams versus hierarchies? One condition favoring the hierarchy is a *lower level of wage inequality* between skilled and unskilled workers because this makes it cheaper to hire person *d*, the "superstar" manager. Hierarchies also make more sense when *new problems arise infrequently*, and when *quick decisions are not essential*—in other words, in *mature industries and technologies*. Finally, hierarchies are especially valuable when *decision quality is very important*, that is, when the consequences of a bad decision are particularly severe. For example, because *Coca Cola* has invested so heavily in its brand value and in the shape of its traditional bottle, any change suggested by a product design team should be checked very carefully—by several layers of supervisors—before any change is implemented.

Conditions favoring teams are the opposite: high wage inequality and a frequent need for quick decisions with less severe consequences. These conditions are more prevalent in firms that use new and complex technologies; and in fact, this is where team-based work organization is most frequently used (Bartel, Ichniowski, & Shaw, 2007; Bloom & Van Reenen, 2007). Wage inequality may be high in these environments because the rapid evolution of information makes it difficult for any one person to have an absolute advantage in everything (like person *d* in Figure 27.3), whereas in more mature industries, knowledge doesn't obsolesce so quickly. Finally, new firms, with no brand value, can risk letting their teams of experts decide because the risk of making a poor decision is less costly.

☑ RESULT 27.7

Conditions Favoring Hierarchical versus Team-Based Organizations

A hierarchical mode of organization is more likely to be optimal when wage inequality between workers with different skill levels is low, when new problems arise infrequently, and when quick decisions are not essential, but decision quality is very important. These conditions tend to be more prevalent in mature industries and technologies, especially those with established brand names and reputations.

Team-based production is better suited to the opposite conditions: high wage inequality; frequent, complex problems requiring quick solutions; but relatively low stakes attached to each decision. These conditions tend to be more prevalent in firms that use new and complex technologies.

Crafting Teams that Work: Information Sharing and Collective Intelligence

By now, I hope I've convinced you that information sharing is essential to the functioning of teams. In doing so, however, I've (quietly and implicitly) assumed that this information sharing is in a sense *automatic*: Just put people on the same

Managers and Entrepreneurs as Jacks-of-All-Trades: The Revenge of Stanford's "B" Students

The model of hierarchical organization in Figure 27.3 Part b posited that leaders need to have both deep *and* broad skills. In many contexts, however, having deep skills in many different areas is simply not possible. In those situations, Lazear (2005) has argued that skill *breadth* is more important than depth for leaders. Specifically, Lazear argues that the most successful entrepreneurs, managers, and executives are not those with deep expertise in only one area, but are "jacks-of-all-trades" who know a little bit about everything. This broad knowledge helps them coordinate a large team of experts (each of whom has deep knowledge in one area) while not losing sight of the "overall picture" and direction of the company. Jacks-of-all-trades may even facilitate communication *between* specialists in different teams, who may speak different technical languages and belong to different organizational cultures.

To test this idea, Lazear (2005) turned to data on Stanford University's Graduate School of Business alumni, who were surveyed in the late 1990s about their careers—many of which had started decades earlier. In this sample of about 5,000 alumni, Lazear had information not only on the respondents' detailed job histories but also had access to each alumnus's academic transcripts, including information on courses taken and grades received. Lazear used this data to measure what sorts of academic and career records were most strongly associated with becoming an "entrepreneur" (defined as having founded a business), or with being a high-level manager of a business. For both of these measures of leadership, Lazear found that a having occupied a *wide variety of business roles* after graduating from Stanford, and having taken a *diverse mix of courses* while at Stanford, were strong predictors of leadership. Students who specialized deeply in one particular area (such as finance, marketing, or strategy) were much less likely to become leaders than those who "dabbled" widely. In fact, in a follow-up paper where he focused specifically on which Stanford Business graduates became C-level managers (CEO, CFO, COO, etc.), Lazear (2012) not only confirmed this pattern but found that—perhaps because they "dabbled"—these future CEOs had *lower* grades (GPAs) at Stanford than their less-successful peers. All told, Lazear's studies of Stanford Graduate School of Business graduates emphasize the important role of *skill diversity* in management and strongly support the hypothesis that being a *generalist* is a valuable asset in being an effective leader.

team and they'll be sure to share their knowledge, skills, and creative and critical ideas. Unfortunately (and not surprisingly), it's not always that simple: Not only do teams need *time* to share the information (making it important for the employer to provide paid time for that purpose), but creating the right *atmosphere* is also important. In this section, we discuss two empirical studies of communication in teams that make this point.

The first study, by Woolley, Chabris, Pentland, Hashmi, and Malone, was published in *Science* in 2010. Although many studies of factors affecting group performance had previously been done, these studies tended to focus one type of task and one set of explanatory factors at a time; in each case, some significant factors could be identified that improved performance. But there was little consistency in what mattered across tasks and studies.

Woolley et al.'s (2010) goal, however, was more ambitious. Inspired by a century of research on *individual* intelligence—which has established that one, easily measurable and stable factor (essentially IQ, or general intelligence, *g*) can explain individual human performance across a wide variety of cognitive tasks—Woolley et al. wondered if something similar could be true for *groups*. To address this question, they assembled 699 people over a period of time and allocated them into groups of two to five individuals. The groups were then asked to perform up to 10 different tasks, which were chosen to span a wide range of coordination problems that arise in work group situations. These included visual puzzles, brainstorming, moral judgments, an architectural design task, and negotiating over limited resources. In addition to measuring the groups' performance on these tasks, the authors also carefully monitored the groups to collect measures of their decision processes, such as who spoke when, for how long, and about what. The authors then used a statistical technique called *factor analysis* to assess whether there were any characteristics of the group's *members* (the "who" of the group) or of the group's *behavior* (the "how") that consistently predicted high group performance across all the tasks.

A first key result of Woolley et al.'s (2010) study is that a long list of factors you might expect to matter—like the average or maximum intelligence of a team's members, their personalities, or measures of the group's cohesion and motivation—did not have robust or statistically significant effects on team performance.[12] Three factors, however, emerged as strongly contributing to a *collective intelligence* (*c*) indicator that consistently predicted effective group performance across a wide variety of tasks. Two of these were "who" characteristics: the share of the members who were female and the average *social sensitivity* of the group's members. Social sensitivity was measured by a well-known instrument called the "Reading the Mind in the Eyes test" (Baron-Cohen, Wheelwright, Hill, Raste, & Plumb, 2001). This test shows a subject some photos of people's eyes and asks the subject describe what the people are thinking or feeling.[13] The "how" characteristic that mattered was the *variance in the number of speaking turns* across the group's members. In other words, "groups where a few people dominated the conversation were less collectively intelligent than those with a more equal distribution of turn-taking" (Woolley et al., 2010, p. 688). Interestingly, all three of these factors were positively correlated with each other: On average, women tend to score higher than men on the Reading the Mind in the Eyes test, and groups composed of women were more likely to ensure that all members were heard from in the discussion.

---

[12] The irrelevance of the members' intelligence is especially noteworthy because individual intelligence *does* predict performance on the same types of tasks when they are performed by a single person.

[13] Interestingly, the test was originally developed to diagnose autism; only later did the researchers realize that a modified version of the test could measure differences in social sensitivity among "normal" adults.

☑ RESULT 27.8

Determinants of Team Effectiveness in Woolley et al.'s (2010) Study of Collective Intelligence

Woolley et al.'s (2010) study of group performance revealed three characteristics that consistently predicted high levels of performance in a wide variety of team-based tasks. These were (i) the share of members who were female, (ii) the share of members who had high social sensitivity (as measured by the ability to detect emotions in others), and (iii) a form of group interaction in which all the members' speaking times were roughly equal.

Neither the average nor the maximum intelligence (*g*) of the group's individual members was a significant determinant of group's performance, even though *g* was a strong predictor of performance when the same people worked on similar tasks alone.

For personnel economists, two main lessons emerge from Woolley et al.'s (2010) study. The first, already alluded to, is that simply assigning people to the same group does not guarantee that they will share the disjoint pieces of information and complementary skills they bring with them. Instead, both the "who" and the "how" of group interactions affect the degree to which this happens. Second and more positively, in contrast to individual intelligence, which is extremely hard to change after a person has become an adult, the collective intelligence of groups may be something that can be improved. In addition to including qualified women on decision-making teams, Woolley et al.'s research suggests that encouraging group members to be more aware of emotional cues and creating "space" for every member to speak could lead to real productivity increases. In contrast, simply "hiring the smartest people," although helpful when people work independently, did not contribute to more effective teams in Woolley et al.'s experiment.

What Makes Teams Work? Google's Aristotle Project

In 2012, Google—probably the biggest and most effective data analytic organization in history, and a workplace where teams are ubiquitous—turned some of its attention inward and took a quantitative and analytical approach to the problem of "building the perfect team." Code-named *Project Aristotle*, the project collected reams of data on Google's own teams, including behavioral measures such as how often the members socialized outside of work and the members' backgrounds and personality types. Combining this data with Google's internal metrics of group performance, the researchers found in a first round of analysis that almost none of the "who" or "how" measures they collected had much association with group performance. Direct observations of groups, however, suggested that groups that looked very similar in the data often had very different informal rules or customs that governed their interactions. For example, some teams had a culture that encouraged vigorous debate, whereas others tended to avoid open disagreement. Some groups had a quasi-formal chairperson and were "strictly business" in their focus, while others were more loosely organized and encouraged the sharing of personal stories. Sociologists and psychologists refer to these informal rules and traditions as *norms*.

DEFINITION 27.4 **Norms** are the traditions, behavioral standards, and unwritten rules that govern how people interact when they gather. Norms are enforced both by verbal and nonverbal expressions of approval or disapproval, some of which can be very subtle. Because all human groups tend to develop their own norms, this can cause the same person to behave in very different ways, depending on the group he or she is interacting with.

When the Project Aristotle researchers delved more deeply into which types of norms were associated with better team performance, they encountered one type of environment was consistently effective. The researchers referred to this feature as "psychological safety," a term coined by Harvard Business School Professor Amy Edmondson in a 1999 article. According to Edmondson, psychological safety "is a sense of confidence that the group will not embarrass, reject or punish someone for speaking up," and "describes a team characterized by interpersonal trust and mutual respect." Essentially, Google engineers who had risky ideas for how to improve an existing project (or to create an entirely new, disruptive, paradigm-shifting one!) were reluctant to share those ideas if their group was one that quickly dismissed or even ridiculed unorthodox ideas.

RESULT 27.9

Determinants of Team Effectiveness from Google's Project Aristotle

Although very few measures of group membership and process were good statistical predictors of team effectiveness in Google's study, one feature of group interaction called *psychological safety* was predictive of team success. Psychological safety refers to an environment where ideas—however unorthodox or ill-formed—can be openly expressed by all members without fear of being ridiculed or dismissed.

Motivated by this finding (which echoes Woolley et al.'s, 2010, result on the importance of equal speaking time), some of the Aristotle researchers began to share them with groups of Google employees in late 2014. In part, their hope was that the employees themselves would suggest ways to improve social sensitivity in Google's teams and make them more "psychologically safe." Although Google hasn't publicly revealed any scalable ways to improve team performance that they may have discovered, the researchers at Project Aristotle have been encouraging Google's technical workers to have open and sometimes emotional discussions of the norms operating in their teams—especially any norms that might discourage the open sharing of ideas. For the Silicon Valley workforce—where the stereotypical employee is seen as being more comfortable interacting with computer code than people—Project Aristotle's data-driven discovery that social sensitivity matters for group productivity was perhaps a surprise. Of course, Woolley et al.'s and Google's intriguing discoveries about the role of social skills are far from the last word on the complex topic of *what makes teams work.* They are supported, however, by other recent evidence that interpersonal skills are becoming much more valuable in the U.S. labor market and deserve to be taken seriously by employers who wish to maximize the effectiveness of their workplace teams.[14]

Chapter Summary

- ☐ When team members are paid according to an equal-sharing rule, there are strong incentives for adverse selection into teams: It is mostly the workers with ability levels below a team's average level who will want to join that team. This is the Groucho Marx rule for joining teams.

- ☐ When team members are paid according to an equal-sharing rule, there are strong incentives for incumbent members to be overly restrictive about whom they will admit to their team. Financially, they will only gain from admitting members who are more productive than the average team member, even when admitting others would be economically efficient. This is the Groucho Marx rule for admitting team members.

- ☐ When a heterogeneous pool of workers is asked to self-organize into a set of output-sharing teams, economic theory predicts that positive assortative matching will result. Under positive assortative matching, the best workers match with the best (and the worst with the worst), generating a pattern where members of the same team have very similar abilities, but the teams are very different from each other. In other words, within-team heterogeneity is low, whereas between-team heterogeneity is high.

- ☐ Given the aforementioned consequences that arise when workers self-organize into teams, employers may prefer assigning workers to teams instead, especially when it's important to have ability heterogeneity within teams. Of course, involuntary assignment may also have a cost if workers have better information about their own capabilities and compatibilities than the firm does.

- ☐ Because of the nonrival nature of most forms of knowledge, teams with heterogeneous ability levels and disjoint information sets have important advantages over homogeneous teams, where there are fewer opportunities for information exchange.

- ☐ In team-based organizations, no single individual has an absolute advantage in all skill types. Thus, communication and information exchange are primarily horizontal, with workers consulting with and learning from each other. In hierarchical organizations, one individual with an absolute advantage in most skill types acts as leader. Thus, communication and information exchange are mostly vertical, with all the workers coming to the manager for consultation.

---

[14] See, for example, Deming (in press). Of particular relevance to IT workers like Google's, Weinberger (2014) shows that social skills have become especially important among workers with high levels of general intelligence.

- ☐ Team-based organizations are most effective when there is high wage inequality between skilled and unskilled workers and when there's a frequent need for quick decisions. Hierarchical organizations work best when there's less wage inequality between skilled and unskilled workers and when decision quality is more important than decision speed. The aforementioned conditions favoring team-based organizations are more prevalent in firms that use new and complex technologies, and this is in fact where team-based production is most prevalent.

- ☐ The sharing of disjoint information and skills within teams, although productive, is not automatic. Instead, recent empirical studies of group performance suggest that greater social sensitivity of team members, and a team culture that encourages equal speaking times and welcomes the expression of unorthodox ideas, can improve team performance. In Woolley et al.'s (2010) study, these factors were more important determinants of a team's effectiveness than the cognitive abilities of the team's members.

Discussion Questions

1. Results 27.2 and 27.3 characterize agents' incentives to join a team and incumbents' incentives to admit new members when all members are paid according to the equal sharing rule, $Y_i = Q/N$. Discuss how those results would change if the team used each of the following alternative pay schemes:

   a. Arbitrary, unequal shares: $Y_i = \alpha_i Q$, where $\sum_{i=1}^{N} \alpha_i = 1$ and the α's are randomly assigned to workers.
   b. Full pay for productivity: $Y_i = d_i$, that is, each worker is paid for full contribution to the team's output.
   c. Partial pay for productivity: $Y_i = \gamma d_i + (1 - \gamma)\bar{d}$, where $0 < \gamma < 1$. Here, every worker's pay is a weighted average of that individual's own ability and the group's average ability, where γ is the weight placed on individual ability.

   Which of the preceding schemes leads to adverse self-selection into teams? Which ones lead team members to prefer to admit only workers who are better than the team average?

2. When children "choose teams" for a competitive sport, a common tradition is for the two players considered the best to take turns selecting teammates from the group until nobody is left. What type of matching (positive, random, or negative) does this system produce? Why might such a custom be optimal when choosing two teams that are going to compete against each other?

3. Think of the last (or current) job you have worked on. Would you say that the organization was more hierarchical or team-based? Given Result 27.7 and the related discussion, would you say this was the appropriate form of organization given the conditions in that firm and industry?

4. At the end of Section 27.1, we argued that the recent increase in wage inequality might be one reason why marriage has become more positively assortative. What might be some other explanations for this change in marriage patterns?

5. Was your most recent boss a "jack-of-all-trades"? Based on your answer, do you think that being a jack-of-all-trades is an important characteristic of a boss, or are other qualities more important? In your answer, remember that—although the workers' happiness should be important to any profit-maximizing employer—making workers happy is not a manager's *only* responsibility.

6. Think of two different groups (not necessarily work related) you have recently participated in. Briefly describe the informal rules regarding how activities in the groups are managed. How do they differ? In which group would you feel more comfortable suggesting an innovative or "inconvenient" idea? If the groups differ, why do you think that is the case?

Suggestions for Further Reading

For a different theoretical approach to the question of self-selection into teams, see McAfee and McMillan (1991). In their model (in contrast to Section 27.1), all team members are equally productive when working alone, but abler workers have lower effort costs than other workers when working inside the team. Under these assumptions, it is the abler workers who disproportionately select into teams. This leads to a different set of issues in McAfee and McMillan's model, where the employers can't tell which workers are the ablest (because they can only see the output of the entire team).

For an experimental test of Result 27.6 (that heterogeneous teams are more productive than homogeneous ones) in the case of multiple skill types, see Huber, Sloof, and van Praag's (2014) large-scale study of schoolchildren who were assigned in different ways to teams in an entrepreneurship education program. Interestingly—at least for this entrepreneurship-related task—teams with a mix of verbal and math experts did not perform as well as teams composed entirely of children who *each* had a mix of these skills. This evidence suggests that multiskilled individuals (i.e. "jacks-of-all-trades") may be of special value not only as managers (as Lazear, 2005, argues) but as team members as well.

For additional analysis of the role of skill disjointness in team production, see Lazear (1999). Cremer (1993) provides a related, wide-ranging, and deep theoretical discussion of information sharing in firms, corporate culture, and organizational forms.

For an interesting recent look at gender and information sharing in teams, see Coffman (2014).

Charles DuHigg's (2016) *New York Times Magazine* article provides a very readable summary of Anita Woolley et al.'s (2010) study of collective intelligence and of Project Aristotle at Google (from the point of view of one of the team's members).

For additional theory on the productivity advantages of heterogeneous versus homogenous teams, see Prat (2002).

References

Bandiera, O., Barankay, I., & Rasul, I. (2013). Team incentives: Evidence from a firm level experiment. *Journal of the European Economic Association, 11,* 1079–1114. doi:10.1111/jeea.12028

Bandiera, O., Prat, A., Sadun, R., & Wulf, J. (2013, December). *Span of control and span of attention.* Unpublished manuscript, Harvard Business School, Boston, MA.

Baron-Cohen, S., Wheelwright, S., Hill, J., Raste, Y., & Plumb, I. (2001). The "Reading the Mind in the Eyes" test revised version: A study with normal adults, and adults with Asperger syndrome or high-functioning autism. *Journal of Child Psychology and Psychiatry, 42*(2), 241–251. doi:10.1111/1469-7610.00715

Bartel, A., Ichniowski, C., & Shaw, K. (2007). How does information technology affect productivity? Plant-level comparisons of product innovation, process improvement, and worker skills. *Quarterly Journal of Economics, 122,* 1721–1758. doi:10.1162/qjec.2007.122.4.1721

Bloom, N., & Van Reenen, J. (2007). Measuring and explaining management practices across firms and countries. *Quarterly Journal of Economics, 122,* 1351–1408. doi:10.1162/qjec.2007.122.4.1351

Burdett, K., & Coles, M. G. (1997). Marriage and class. *Quarterly Journal of Economics, 102,* 141–168.

Browning, M. J. (1987). Cooperatives, closures or wage cuts: The choices facing workers in an ailing firm. *Canadian Journal of Economics, 20,* 114–122.

Coffman, K. B. (2014). Evidence on self-stereotyping and the contribution of ideas. *Quarterly Journal of Economics, 129,* 1625–1660. doi:10.1093/qje/qju023

Cremer, J. (1993). Corporate culture and shared knowledge. *Industrial and Corporate Change, 2,* 351–386.

Deming, D. J. (in press). The growing importance of social skills in the labor market. *Quarterly Journal of Economics.*

DuHigg, C. (2016, February 25). What Google learned from its quest to build the perfect team. *New York Times Magazine*. Retrieved from https://www.nytimes.com/2016/02/28/magazine/what-google-learned-from-its-quest-to-build-the-perfect-team.html?smid=nytcore-ipad-share&smprod=nytcore-ipad

Edmondson, A. (1999). Psychological safety and learning behavior in work teams. *Administrative Science Quarterly, 44,* 350–383. Retrieved from http://www.jstor.org/stable/2666999

Greenwood, J., Guner, N., Kocharkov, G., & Santos, C. (2014). Marry your like: Assortative mating and income inequality. *American Economic Review, 104,* 348–353.

Greenwood, J., Guner, N., Kocharkov, G., & Santos, C. (2016). Technology and the changing family: A unified model of marriage, divorce, educational attainment and married female labor-force participation. *American Economic Journal: Macroeconomics, 8,* 1–41.

Hamilton, B. H., Nickerson, J. A., & Owan, H. (2003). Team incentives and worker heterogeneity: An empirical analysis of the impact of teams on productivity and participation. *Journal of Political Economy, 111*(3), 465–497.

Huber, L. R., Sloof, R., & van Praag, M. (2014). *Jacks-of-all-trades? The effect of balanced skills on team performance* (IZA Discussion paper No. 8237). Bonn, Germany: Institute for the Study of Labor.

Kuhn, P., & Villeval, M. C. (2015). Are women more attracted to cooperation than men? *Economic Journal, 125*(582), 115–140. doi:10.1111/ecoj.12122

Lazear, E. P. (1999, March). Globalization and the market for teammates. *Economic Journal, 109,* C15–C40.

Lazear, E. P. (2005). Entrepreneurship. *Journal of Labor Economics, 23,* 649–680. doi:10.1086/491605

Lazear, E. P. (2012). Leadership: A personnel economics approach. *Labour Economics, 19*(1), 92–101.

Lazear, E. P., & Shaw, K. L. (2007). Personnel economics: The economist's view of human resources. *Journal of Economic Perspectives, 21*(4), 91–114.

Niederle, M., & Vesterlund, L. (2007). Do women shy away from competition? Do men compete too much? *Quarterly Journal of Economics, 122,* 1067–1101.

Mas, A., & Moretti, E. (2009). Peers at work. *American Economic Review, 99,* 112–145.

McAfee, R. P., & McMillan, J. (1991). Optimal contracts for teams. *International Economic Review, 32,* 561–577.

Prat, A. (2002). Should a team be homogeneous? *European Economic Review, 46,* 1187–1207.

Ward, B. (1958). The firm in Illyria: Market syndicalism. *American Economic Review, 48,* 566–589. Retrieved from http://www.jstor.org/stable/1808268

Weinberger, C. J. (2014). The increasing complementarity between cognitive and social skills. *Review of Economics and Statistics, 96,* 849–861.

Woolley, A., Chabris, C., Pentland, A., Hashmi, N., & Malone, T. (2010). Evidence for a collective intelligence factor in the performance of human groups. *Science, 330*(6004): 686–688.

Wozniak, D., Harbaugh, W. T., & Mayr, U. (2014). The menstrual cycle and performance feedback alter gender differences in competitive choices. *Journal of Labor Economics, 32,* 161–198.

Index

Page references for figures are indicated by *f,* for tables by *t,* and for boxes by *b.*

D

E

F

L

M

N

O

T

U

V